The Country Life
International Dictionary of
CLOCKS

Consultant Editor Alan Smith

G. P. Putnam's Sons
New York

Frontispiece

Pendule Louis XV. Mantel clock of gilt
and bronze with Meissen figures of harlequin and
birds; signed 'Gille *l'aîné à Paris*', *c.* 1750.
National Trust, Waddesdon Manor.

First published 1979
This edition published 1979 by G. P. Putnam's Sons Inc.
Library of Congress Catalog Card Number: 78–65713

SBN: 399–12338–5

Printed in Great Britain by
Hazell, Watson & Viney Limited,
Aylesbury

Contents

Contributors

Consultant editor **Alan Smith** (AS) In 1954 entered the museum profession and is a Fellow of the Museums Association. From 1964 to 1970 was responsible for the horological collections at the Merseyside County Museum, Liverpool. Now Senior Lecturer in Art Gallery and Museum Studies, Department of Art History, University of Manchester. Author of *The Lancashire Watch Company, Prescot, 1889–1910* Fitzwilliam, New Hampshire, U.S.A. 1973; *The Connoisseur Guide to Clocks and Watches* London 1975; *A Catalogue of Tools for Watch and Clock Makers, by John Wyke* Charlottesville, Virginia, U.S.A. 1978.

*   *   *

Charles K. Aked (CKA) Prolific writer on horology; Chairman of the Antiquarian Horological Society Publications Committee; former Chairman of the A.H.S. Electrical Horology Group; Consultant to the British Horological Institute. Compiled the catalogue *Electrifying Times* for the exhibition of electrical timekeeping at the Science Museum, London, 1976/77. Has published *A Conspectus of Electrical Timekeeping* London 1976 and *Complete List of English Horological Patents up to 1853* Ashford 1975.

James Arnfield (JA) Trained as an electronics engineer, he is now working on the technical side of television broadcasting. Following his family tradition of interest in mechanical engineering, of which the movements of clocks and watches are an important aspect, he is a highly skilled horological restorer; he has made, to the last detail, one complete clock of outstanding quality.

José Luis Basanta (JLB) Now a technical manager in the chemical industry, he obtained his doctorate in chemical sciences in Compostela in 1951. Has published many papers on his two major interests, the history of paper-making and clocks. His books *Relojeros de España* and *Bibliografía relojera española* were published in Pontevedra in 1972 and 1975.

Dana J. Blackwell (DJB) Outstanding American horologist living in the heart of the 19th-century clockmaking area of Connecticut. A contributor to *Antiquarian Horology* and to the *NAWCC Bulletin*, he is also a Trustee of the American Clock Museum, Bristol, Connecticut and Chief Engineer for Howard Clock Products, Inc., Waltham, Massachusetts. He is an outstanding authority on marine chronometers and is also a highly skilled restorer of clocks and watches.

John H. Combridge (JHC) An authority on early Chinese water clocks, he has determined, by exhaustive research (including learning Chinese), the working principles of ancient Chinese timekeepers and astronomical devices. Has published articles on the subject in *Antiquarian Horology* and the *Horological Journal*.

Eric B. Gent (EBG) A practical craftsman with experience in the clock and watch trade for over 30 years, he is a specialist in the restoration of antique clocks and watches with a business in the Merseyside town of St Helens.

Donald R. Hill (DRH) A chartered engineer, with post-graduate qualifications in Arabic history, Dr Hill has published many articles on Arabic and Islamic engineering and clockwork devices. Was made co-recipient of the 1974 Dexter Prize awarded by the Society for the History of Technology, U.S.A. for his fully annotated translation of al-Jazari's *The Book of Knowledge of Ingenious Mechanical Devices* Dordrecht 1974.

F. Kats (FK) An antique dealer and clockmaker in Rotterdam, he collaborated with Dr J. L. Sellink in compiling the biographical entries on Dutch clockmakers.

Antonio Lenner (AL) Has a degree in electrical engineering and is a keen collector of, and an authority on, old Italian clocks. Living in Milan, his professional business is in the field of pasta manufacture.

Paul Lavoie (PL) Fellow of the National Association of Watch and Clock Collectors, he is also secretary-treasurer of Chapter 33, Ontario, Canada, and a Research Member of the American Branch of the Antiquarian Horological Society. Has done pioneer research in Canadian clockmaking, with several articles in the *NAWCC Bulletin* and Canadian antique journals.

John McDonald (JM) Curator of the Lady Lever Art Gallery, Port Sunlight, which has a distinguished collection of clocks. He is an acknowledged expert on period furniture and clocks, and is well-known as a lecturer and writer on these topics. He is also a member of the Liverpool Fine Arts Committee whom he has advised for a number of years.

P. Sarah K. Medlam (PSKM) A graduate of Oxford University, she entered the museum profession in 1973 and is an Associate of the Museums Association. Currently in charge of the fine collections of French furniture and clocks at the Bowes Museum, County Durham.

David F. Nettell (DFN) An authority on turret clocks, he is a founder member of the Turret Clock Group of the Antiquarian Horological Society and has been its honorary secretary since 1973. He is also a frequent contributor to *Antiquarian Horology* and is currently preparing a specialised book on turret clocks for future publication.

Kenneth D. Roberts (KDR) Private publisher of Fitzwilliam, New Hampshire and authority on Connecticut clockmaking in the 19th century, he is also a specialist on early American woodworking tools. Author of *Eli Terry and the Connecticut Shelf Clock* Bristol, Connecticut 1973 and *The Contributions of Joseph Ives to Connecticut Clock Technology* Bristol, Connecticut 1970. Formerly Director of the American Clock Museum, Bristol, Connecticut, U.S.A.

Mary C. Roehrich (MCR) Practised as an interior designer in Pittsburgh, Pennsylvania and is now working for a Master's degree in 19th-century American painting. A collector of Chinese and Japanese clocks for over fifteen years, she is one of the few Western scholars familiar with the intricacies of oriental timekeeping. A Director of the National Association of Watch and Clock Collectors, Inc., much of her research has been published in the *NAWCC Bulletin*.

Johan L. Sellink (JLS) A distinguished medical specialist in the field of radiology, in certain branches of which he is an international authority, his 'recreation' is the world of Dutch clocks. This led him to create one of the finest collections in Holland, and to write *Dutch Antique Domestic Clocks*, Leiden 1973.

E. J. Tyler (EJT) Member of the Antiquarian Horological Society Library Committee, he is an authority on Continental clocks and author of *European Clocks* London 1968, *The Craft of the Clockmaker* London 1973, *Clocks and Watches* London 1975 and *Black Forest Clocks* London 1977. Also interested in turret clocks and is adviser on church clocks in the Dioceses of Chichester and Southwark.

F. A. B. Ward (FABW) A Vice President of the Antiquarian Horological Society and retired Keeper of Physics, the Science Museum, London, he is a frequent contributor on many aspects of horology to *Antiquarian Horology*. He is also author of *Clocks and Watches: 1. Weight-driven clocks* 1973 and *2. Spring-driven* 1972. His catalogue *Time Measurement* 1966 is a standard reference work, and *Timekeepers – Clocks, Watches, Sundials, Sandglasses* appeared in 1963. All these works were published by H.M.S.O. for the Science Museum. London.

Introduction

Much has happened in the field of clock collecting and in horology generally, in the fourteen years since the late H. Alan Lloyd published his *Collector's Dictionary of Clocks*. The period has seen the widespread introduction of various types of electronic timekeepers, which must inevitably develop further in the coming years, and which probably herald the beginning of the end of mechanical timekeepers, though that end surely is yet a long way off. The price of old clocks and watches has escalated in proportion to the increased number of people whose interest has been aroused by the history of clockmaking; and, the traditional field of 'antique' clocks has widened to embrace areas not altogether accepted as 'legitimate' when Lloyd compiled his book. For example, investigation into the vast area of 19th-century American clockmaking, aimed as it was at producing a cheap and reliable clock for the masses, is now revealing the fascinating enterprise it was, with its imaginative new solutions to age-old technical problems of design and manufacture, and its entirely American style of case – albeit based on European prototypes. Likewise the contribution of the Black Forest area of Germany in the 19th century is now being taken seriously, with the first book in English on the subject having become available during 1977.

Electrical horology, whose early pioneers received some mention by Lloyd, is now developing a complete literature of its own as new investigations are made in this extremely important subject, and turret clocks of all periods are also coming in for detailed study on a scale unknown in the early 1960s. When H. Alan Lloyd was compiling his dictionary he made a special appeal through the pages of *Antiquarian Horology* for a suitable photograph of a French Comtoise clock movement; today as Europe seems to shrink in size these clocks are relatively well-known amongst collectors and dealers, and a new authoritative book on this humble but fascinating type appeared in French in 1976. Chronometers and regulators, not being domestic clocks, formerly received too little attention apart from the work of such horological giants as Harrison, Graham, Arnold and Earnshaw in England, Berthoud and Le Roy in France, but today specialist studies are appearing, in ever greater detail, on the 19th-century chronometer makers, and also providing new approaches to the work of the earlier 'masters'.

As the areas of investigation widen in both time and geographical location, and more people collect and study, practically everything is now grist for the horological mill. Coming to the end of many centuries of timekeeping invention in mechanical clockmaking perhaps it is right that this should be so. A nostalgic note is struck by the current upsurge of antique clock reproductions now commanding prices which, but a short time ago, would have been considered exorbitant for a genuine old clock, while there is also developing an interest amongst model engineers and horological enthusiasts to produce their own clocks, using traditional methods. In view of the foregoing and many other trends in horological interest today, it has been thought fit to produce yet another 'clock' book, but one which has been designed to embrace this more catholic view of the subject which has developed in recent years, in a format quite different from previous works of reference of this kind.

The book is divided primarily into five parts which are easily cross-referenced through the alphabetical arrangement of the entries in each part, the Index at the end of the book, and the occasional use of *See also*, which refers to entries in the Index (also, when the entry is in another section, the section number is given, for quick reference). Section I, therefore, is restricted to defining the *styles* of clock design, with limited reference to the technicalities of their movements, thinking of them primarily as either articles of domestic furniture, or types of clocks, e.g. *turret clocks*, which form specialised groups. The aim has been to produce a section in which collectors can obtain basic information on at least most of the clock types they are likely to meet, on an international basis.

Section II takes the reader into the complexities of the various types of movements which are most commonly found in clockwork. The illustrations for this section, specially prepared for this book, consist entirely of photographs of clock movements and their various details, for many people find diagrams alone difficult to interpret when confronted with an actual clock movement. As in Section I it has been necessary to restrict the range of this highly complex aspect of the subject to types most likely to be encountered, but the bibliography of currently available literature should help to take the student and collector further in his studies.

The contents of Section III are somewhat new to this type of book and seek to provide information in an area where more people than ever are seeking enlightenment. This desire for technical knowledge of manufacturing methods has come about in two ways. Firstly, collectors are learning more about traditional tools, materials and workshop methods in order to understand the ways in which clocks (and watches) were formerly made, and to appreciate the problems which our forebears had to face and often overcame so magnificently. Secondly, many people today are learning to carry out their own repairs, general maintenance and restoration. This is especially important at a time when the traditional clockmaker and repairer is becoming more difficult to find, and restoration and repair work is moving into the hands of a few specialised firms. How many times have those of us who are interested in old clocks been asked by owners where they could get their clocks repaired? Section III, therefore, with its explanatory text and illustrations of old and modern horological tools (often not very different) seeks to open up and offer good advice in this area of study, and has been written by a man with long practical experience in his craft.

In the biographical section (Section IV) an attempt has been made to chronicle the basic details of those clockmakers and clockmaking firms who have made important contributions to their art and science in the countries covered; a brief outline of the general history of clockmaking in each country is given. The difficulties of making the *best* selection of makers have been numerous, but overall the section has been designed to help the modern reader adjust to the wide field of study now developing in international horology, rather than to provide all the information available on a few selected 'great' makers. Thus many famous English and French makers are omitted, while included are, for example, many Spanish makers, whose names will be unfamiliar to most collectors, since Spanish horology is almost an unknown subject as far as most clock books are concerned. For similar reasons many 'famous' names are left out to make room for others, such as Joseph Finney or Henry Hindley who were, until recently, but little known, and for several chronometer makers who have long gone unappreciated in general horological literature. No claim is made for this section as a comprehensive reference source even for famous makers, let alone the countless thousands whose names appear on old clocks. Undoubtedly the whole section is something of a

compromise, but it will give the reader some indication of the horological histories of many of the major nations of the world, and within those histories some suggestions of the most important makers. Nothing, however, can replace detailed national reference works such as the English *Baillie*, the American *Drepperd* and *Brooks Palmer*, the Spanish *Basanta*, the Italian *Morpurgo* or the French *Tardy*, which are fully listed in the Bibliography.

Section V covers a range of instruments closely related to the history and science of timekeeping. Since astronomical instruments, sundials and astrolabes are not mechanical, wheel-driven devices it seemed rational to place them in a separate category, although they are intimately related to the basic theme. For similar reasons mechanical globes, orreries and the like, although they *are* often driven by clockwork, fall more naturally into this area.

The dividing line between clocks and watches can be a very fine one, and in the sense that watches are only small, portable clocks it is often difficult to define that line exactly. For the purposes of this book all horological devices normally carried about on the person have been omitted as 'watches', though portable timekeepers of all kinds have been included as clocks.

In conclusion I would like to record my sincere thanks to all those members of the team of contributors who have written either individual entries or complete sections for this work, always willingly and with enthusiasm for their respective specialisations. Together we have met the limiting restrictions of producing a book of finite length which attempts to cover an infinite field. The authorship of all entries is indicated by initials following each entry.

Many museums and private collectors have generously provided illustrations, and acknowledgement to them is made elsewhere.

Alan Smith

PLEASE NOTE

Picture references are in the form of
page number/picture number

SECTION I
The History and Styles of Clocks

1 Acorn clock Shelf clock with eight-day fusee brass movement; by J. C. Brown, Forestville Manufacturing Company, Bristol, Connecticut, U.S.A., *c.*1845. Old Sturbridge Village, Sturbridge, Massachusetts.

2 Adam style mantel clock of marble, porcelain, and ormolu; by Benjamin Vulliamy, *c.*1795. Lady Lever Art Gallery, Port Sunlight.

3 Act of Parliament clock with mahogany case; maker unknown, mid 18th century. Lady Lever Art Gallery, Port Sunlight.

2

1

3

Acorn clock An American clock, made in three styles: shelf, dwarf (smaller shelf case), and wall. All were exclusively manufactured by the Forestville Manufacturing Co. during 1847–50, and the design is attributed to Jonathan Clarke Brown, proprietor of that establishment. Many of the painted tablets within the shelf model illustrated his residence at Bristol, Connecticut. The acorn was a popular Connecticut motif, derived from the Constitutional Oak Tree at Hartford in which the colony's charter had been hidden in 1687. The cases, resembling an acorn in general shape, where moulded from laminated wood with a mahogany or rosewood veneer. Flanking the case were laminated wooden rods capped with acorn-shaped finials. Two different types of eight-day fusee movements were used in acorn shelf clocks. The larger case had wooden drums to contain the springs in a bracket below the movement, while the smaller case had the springs mounted integrally between the plates. Both were forms of reverse fusee. The wall case contained an eight-day timepiece movement without fusee. KDR

Act of Parliament clock A British act of parliament passed in 1797 levied a tax of five shillings per annum on all clocks and is said to have caused a decline in their manufacture. Rather than maintain a domestic clock which was liable to tax, people would consult clocks in public places, such as coaching inns. These were often wall clocks with wooden dials, sometimes more than 30 in. in diameter, with a short trunk below to protect the pendulum. Some, intended for halls and libraries in great houses, were produced in the decorative style of the times, but most were finished in black japanning with gilded, Chinoiserie ornament, the Roman numerals on the dial also painted in gold. The movements were either spring- or weight-driven. The name is misleading as this style of clock is known to have been in use many years before the act of 1797. 'Hall' or 'library' clocks would describe them better. JM

Adam style In Britain, the neoclassical style in architecture of the second half of the 18th century, named after its most notable exponent, Robert Adam (1728–92). It is said that the wonderfully preserved examples of domestic decorative art uncovered in the 18th century at the two Roman cities of Pompeii and Herculaneum (buried by the eruption of Mount Vesuvius in AD 79) fired the imagination of Adam and his contemporaries. The term 'Adam style' describes an aspect of neoclassical design popularised by the architect Robert Adam. Clock designs which are completely representative of the Adam style are fairly uncommon; longcase clocks, which are rare, are usually shorter and slimmer than earlier examples. Cases veneered in mahogany and satinwood are found with marquetry decoration and penwork designs based on the Adam repertoire of classical motifs such as the Grecian urn, Roman *paterae*, strings of husks and swags of leaves and flowers. Bracket and mantel clocks in the Adam style had broken-arch or rounded tops, dials that were usually circular and white-enamelled, and carrying handles at the sides in the shape of a ram's or lion's head. Mantel clocks are

4 Appointments clock by John Davidson, London, 1895–1900. Private collection.

5

6

5 Altar clock Walnut case, mounted with tortoiseshell and marble, and ebonised mouldings; Italian, 17th century. Museo d'Arte Antica, Milan.

6 Alarm clock An Italian monastic alarm with 24-hour rotating dial; 15th century. Science Museum, London.

found with the dial and movement mounted in bisque, or unglazed porcelain, in the form of circular miniature temples or figure groups derived from Greek funerary designs. JM

Alarm clock The earliest mechanical clocks were alarm clocks intended for the use of monks so that services could be held at the appointed ecclesiastical hours; all modern alarm clocks are descended from these monastic alarms. The word 'clock' is derived from the medieval Latin *clocca* meaning a bell, and the earliest alarm clocks did not possess dials but merely sounded a bell at an appointed time. Later forms [143/6] had dials, some fitted with touch knobs for ascertaining the time at night. Two weights were used, one to drive the timekeeping mechanism, the other to drive the alarm. In the clock illustrated [13/6] the hour dial turns once every 24 hours (on the Italian system: these clocks were first used in Italy) and the alarm can be set by inserting a peg into the hole nearest to the time required. At the appointed time a detent is released and the alarm bell rings.

Some horologists consider that the verge escapement, later universally used for timekeepers, was derived from the verge and crown-wheel mechanism originally devised for the ringing of bells before the mechanical clock was invented. CKA

Altar clock Clocks with wooden cases were rare before 1660, but as the pendulum became established wood was used in greater quantities. Clocks began to be made with wooden cases shaped like the altars of the time. They were most popular in Italy, although English examples are known, but the term 'altar clock' is German. The name relates to the shape and does not imply that the clocks were meant to stand on altars. The movements were much smaller than the cases, and the design was the inspiration of the Maltese clock. The altar clock usually had an ebony finish and stood about 24 in. high, but as fashions for other woods developed, the design passed away in the early 18th century. EJT

See also Maltese clock; Night clock; *Pendule religieuse.*

Appointments clock An aid for the professional or business man to help in keeping appointments – an aural equivalent of the desk diary. One of the best known early appointments, or memorandum clocks was devised by John Davidson of Wick, Caithness, about 1890 [13/4]. An ordinary spring-driven clock turns a drum with 48 slots into which small ivory tablets, on which messages and times may be written, are inserted. Each slot is marked with the time, and the tablet on which the appointment is written is placed in the appropriate slot. On reaching the required time, the slot in the drum lies directly over a slot in the top of the clock; the tablet drops through a duct into a small tray below the dial, causing it to fall. Electrical contacts are closed by this action and an electric bell in the base rings continuously until the tablet is removed. Modern appointments clocks generally move an index over a list of appointments written on a pad, but the principle is identical. CKA

Arch top A simple semicircular top to the cases of bracket and longcase clocks. The design appeared in the late 18th century and continued well into the 19th. It presented a satisfyingly simple shape to bracket and mantel clocks in the Adam and Sheraton styles, and occurred in both mahogany and painted-satinwood bracket clocks with simple brass lion-head or disc-ring handles at the sides. Longcase clocks with arch tops usually have engraved, silvered or painted dials with no separate chapter ring or spandrels. JM

Art nouveau The name given to a style in the decorative arts which flourished in Europe and North America during the 1890s. Influenced by Japanese art, it is characterised by whiplash lines and stylised natural forms. First introduced in architectural design by Victor Horta in Belgium, it was taken up by other artists in different media, such as the English illustrator Aubrey Beardsley and the American glass designer Louis Comfort Tiffany. In Germany the movement was called *Jugendstil* after the magazine *Jugend*, 'Youth'. The style had a brief effect on the case design of domestic clocks which otherwise contained standard movements. AS

Astronomical clock A number of public astronomical clocks were made in the late 14th and early 15th centuries. Most were inside cathedrals or churches, but some were outside and on public buildings. They represented a working model of a geocentric universe, and there were two types, the astrolabe and the armillary. Most of the medieval clocks have vanished, leaving only descriptions. Others have been rebuilt several times over the centuries. There appears to have been a resurgence of interest in these clocks in the 16th century, when they were often accompanied by automata or jacks – knights on horseback charging each

other, the Magi moving in procession past the Virgin and bowing to her, Jack Blandifer kicking and hammering his bells – who perform at the hour.

An astronomical clock of great size and complexity was constructed by Chang Ssu-hsun at K'ai-feng in China in the 11th century, driven by water and incorporating an escapement. DFN
See also Armillary sphere; Astrolabe, mariner's; Astrolabe, planispheric; Astronomical clocks (all Section V); Chinese clocks (Section IV).

Atmos clock The ancestor of the Atmos clock is the famous James Cox perpetual-motion clock *c.* 1760, now in the Victoria and Albert Museum, London. In 1913 J. E. Reutter, a student at Neuchâtel, considered by what means a perpetual clock based on the expansion of liquids or gases could be made, and in 1926 the first commercial Atmos clock appeared. It had a torsion pendulum driven from a train, powered by a spring wound by the driving mechanism. A sealed U-tube containing liquified gas in each limb, separated by mercury, has one side immersed in liquid of high specific heat insulated by a vacuum jacket; the other is exposed to the air in the glass dome protecting the clock. A slight rise in temperature expands the gas in the exposed limb, forcing mercury into the other limb insulated from the temperature change, unbalancing the mechanism on its axis. A ratchet wheel and click communicates the motion to the driving spring; reduction of temperature reverses the motion but still winds the spring. A variation of 1°C is sufficient to give 120 hours reserve of power to the clock.

Modern Atmos clocks use ethyl chloride (C_2H_5Cl) in a circular metal bellows, the internal pressure of which is sufficient to compress a strong spring fully at 27°C (81°F)

1 Arch top bracket clock in inlaid satinwood; by James Murray, Cornhill, London, *c.* 1800. Lady Lever Art Gallery, Port Sunlight.

2 Art nouveau mahogany case with applied repoussé silver decoration. French movement; Birmingham hall-mark 1910.

3 Astronomical clock dials from the City Hall, Prague, the upper being an astrolabe-type dial and the lower a calendar. Originally 1486, but restored 1864–5.

4 **Augsburg clock** with glazed, ebony base, and a reclining lion; the lion's eyes move with the balance and its mouth opens to show its tongue at the hour. The larger dial shows the hours and the smaller the quarters; by Johann Oth Halleicher, Augsburg, c. 1670. Gershom Parkington Collection of Time Keeping Instruments, Bury St Edmunds.

5 **Automata clock** with procession of the apostles and jacks striking the bell; wooden cased. From the Black Forest, 17th century. Historische Museum, Bamberg.

6 **Atmos clock** Self-winding clock with a torsion pendulum; by Jaeger-le-Coultre, Switzerland, c. 1935.

4   5   6

[15/6]. A small temperature fall allows the strong spring to expand, pulling a secondary spring which communicates power to the mainspring of the clock. A variation of 1°C gives 48 hours reserve of power, winding taking place on a fall in temperature only. The torsion pendulum has a massive balance and is suspended on torsion wire of elinvar, a special steel alloy, to reduce temperature errors in the timekeeping. The makers claim that the wear in the modern Atmos clock is so slight that it will run for 300 years before suffering the wear incurred by an ordinary watch in one year. CKA

Atomic clock Atomic and molecular vibrations constitute the most regular of motions in nature, but most are at such a high frequency as to be unusable as time standards with present knowledge. The earliest atomic clock was developed in the United States and made use of the ammonia molecule (NH_3) but other materials, such as caesium and rubidium, later proved far more suitable for time standards. Radio-frequency techniques are used to generate energy at the frequency of the atomic transition from a lower frequency generated by a quartz-crystal oscillator, while the atomic vibration controls the absolute frequency of oscillation, frequency division by electronic circuits being used to obtain the low frequency required to drive the clocks indicating absolute time. Accuracy to less than one second error in 100,000 years is now available with the caesium atomic clock. CKA
See also Caesium clock.

Augsburg clock The two cities of Nuremberg and Augsburg in Bavaria were both well-known centres of clockmaking during the 16th and 17th centuries but, while Nuremberg concentrated on the timekeeping function, Augsburg clockmakers specialised in automata which

performed as the clock went, or when it struck, or indicated the time by slowly revolving and pointing to the hours on a dial. The clocks from these cities were mostly spring-driven table clocks, but during the 17th century metal cases gave way to wooden ones with the figures themselves of metal, highly decorated.

An Augsburg clock in the British Museum, London, has a milkmaid milking a cow, and when a special receptacle is filled with milk it gradually fills the milkmaid's bucket; an aged peasant points to the time with his stick. Other Augsburg clocks have animals such as a lion or a bear which blink their eyes as the clock ticks. Clocks made in Augsburg were often identified by a pineapple stamped on the movement. EJT

Automata clock Automata clocks are those with moving figures of persons or animals which function while the clock is going or when it strikes. The earliest-known clock to carry automata is the original Strasbourg clock of 1352–4, of which only the crowing cock now remains.

The distinction between automata and jacks is that jacks are always employed in striking bells, while automata perform a variety of different actions. A common subject for automata in medieval times was a procession, such as apostles passing before Christ, the three kings passing before the Virgin and Child, or the electors passing before the emperor.

Automata, which were often an ingenious form of advertising, are usually associated with large clocks on buildings, but there are many examples on domestic clocks. The table clocks of Augsburg are well known for their automata, and even more humble clocks from the Black Forest have goats that butt each other, butchers who slay an ox, and so forth. EJT/DFN
See also Jacks.

1 **Basket top** Pierced and gilded brass top from a bracket clock by Daniel Quare, London, *c.* 1690. Merseyside County Museum, Liverpool.

2 **Battery clock** Transistorised 'lectric' clock with a T.S.M. movement; pendulum regulated by a disc above the bob. Made by Jahres-uhren Fabrik GmbH, Aug. Schatz & Söhne, Baden, Germany, *c.* 1966. Private collection.

Bain's clock Alexander Bain (1810–77) produced the first electromagnetically operated pendulum clock in 1842, a step leading to the awesome accuracy of the atomic clock. Bain was first interested in signalling time to distant clocks; he used an ordinary clock fitted with contacts operated by the pendulum to send pulses of current to subsidiary clocks. His first patent (no. 8783 of 1841) contains almost every idea applicable to electrical horology except the use of quartz crystals and atomic clocks. His first electric clock, of which little is known, was operated by batteries called Daniell cells, but these were expensive and insufficiently reliable. Bain therefore developed his 'earth battery' to give a constant voltage. But the current it could supply was limited, so Bain, undaunted, devised what became his standard electromagnetic drive for pendulums, a pendulum bob consisting of a solenoid swinging over a magnet; or the complementary design where solenoid and magnet were interchanged. The latter design had the advantage of not requiring connecting wires running down the pendulum. Very little current was required to drive this combination and the earth battery was found to be ideal, lasting for many years [19/4]. CKA

Balloon clock In the late 18th century a bracket clock appeared the case of which was circular in the upper part, descending to a waisted centre portion and then spreading out to a more stable, rectangular base. Dials were circular and usually enamelled or painted. Whether the name 'balloon clock' is Victorian in origin, or whether this type of case would have emerged anyway and received some other name but for the roughly contemporary invention of the aerial balloon is a matter for surmise [20/1]. JM

Banjo clock This term is believed to have been introduced early in the 20th century to describe American wall clocks of somewhat similar appearance to that originally developed by Simon Willard at Roxbury, Massachusetts. Willard's movement was patented in 1802 but may have been used slightly earlier. The patent specified a weight fall of 15 in. in eight days with the pendulum pivoted in front of the movement and weight from a cock or T-bridge. The three essential features of the case were a circular hood, a tapered waist accommodating a lead weight, and a rectangular box base. The dials were painted on iron and a

brass bezel held the dial glass. A gilded acorn finial was usually fitted above, and some models had cast-brass urns or spikes. The centre panel frame contained a painted glass tablet attached to the frame by screws. Brass curved arms flanked each side from base box to hood. The base compartment door also contained a painted or gilded glass panel. The sides of the case and frames for the panels were generally made of selected mahogany, frequently inlaid with crossbanding and satinwood. Many of Willard's apprentices and competitors followed this design, which remained popular in Massachusetts and New Hampshire throughout the 1830s [29/3]. KDR

Barograph clock A clock which continuously records changes in atmospheric pressure. Robert Hooke was the first to use a clock to drive a drum carrying a strip of paper on which a pen drew a continuous record of the air pressure, improving on Sir Christopher Wren's weather clock, which recorded temperature and wind direction. Alexander Cumming made what is commonly thought to be the first recording barograph clock [32/1] in 1765, for which George III paid £1,178. Two paper annuluses surround the clock dial; upon these a pencil moved by a column of mercury records the atmospheric pressure. The inner annulus turns once every six months, the outer once every twelve months, and both are removable.

Modern barographs utilise a clock to drive a drum on the surface of which is secured a strip of graduated paper, marked in days, with the pressure indicated in millibars or inches of mercury on a vertical scale. It is not usual to provide a clock dial to show the time. CKA

Baroque The dominant style in European painting and architecture during the 17th and early 18th centuries. The term is a 19th-century coinage derived from a Portuguese word meaning anything over-decorated or pompous and contrived to impress. Baroque marks the abandonment of Renaissance classicism for greater vigour and freer movement.

Domestic furnishings from the time of Charles II to the middle of the reign of George II are baroque in character, but English longcase clocks of the period remained largely unaffected, except for motifs like cherub-head spandrels, pairs of amorini bearing a crown, and the gilded basket tops

3

4

5

3 **Bell top** bracket clock in mahogany; by Thomas Green, Liverpool, *c.* 1780. Merseyside County Museum, Liverpool.

4 **Belfry clock** An example from the Black Forest, Karlsruhe, 1840–50. Badisches Landesmuseum, Karlsruhe.

5 **Bell top, inverted** Bracket clock in ebonised case; by Richard Fennel, Kensington, London, *c.* 1690. City Art Gallery, Manchester.

of bracket clocks. European clocks, particularly Dutch, with ornate finials and classical figures adorning the hoods, were distinctly baroque in feeling. JM

Basket top A shaped top to the cases of verge bracket clocks of the late 17th and early 18th centuries. In its simpler form it consisted of a rectangle of mitred ovolo mouldings veneered with ebony or ebonised wood, surmounted by a brass, bail-shaped carrying handle. In more elaborately decorated clocks this top section was made of fretted ormolu, and it was this open metalwork which suggested the name of basket top. Metal basket tops were not purely ornamental as their design permitted the sound of the striking and musical train of bells to be heard more clearly. JM

Battery clock Alexander Bain designed the first battery clock, operated by Daniell cells, shortly before 1838. Later he made use of his own 'earth battery', consisting of copper and zinc plates sunk in the ground. Today the term is more properly applied to a portable electric clock which depends on a dry cell or battery for its electrical power, normally a 1.5 volt Leclanché cell, or a 1.3 volt mercury cell in more modern types. Generally, the ability of the cell to withstand the destructive effects of low intermittent currents being drawn determines its useful life, normally approximately equal to its shelf life had it not been used. The older type of battery clock employing a large bell cell would run for long periods: the Eureka clock ran for 1,000 days, the Bulle clock for 800 days; whereas a modern battery clock using a small torch-type cell will run for approximately one year. The internal resistance increases rapidly towards the end of the cell life and this limits its usefulness. The cell may be used for rewinding at intervals, driving a small electric motor, periodic impulsing of a pendulum or balance or, more recently, driving a quartz-crystal oscillator and integrated electronic circuits. CKA
See also Bain's clock; Bulle clock; Eureka clock.

Beam-engine clock A clock in the form of an old-fashioned beam engine, with moving parts operated by the clock mechanism to give the appearance of a working model. If continuous motion is provided, the parts have to be very light; but most of these clocks set the engine parts in motion only at the hour and use a separate train to drive a substantial mechanism which gives a very realistic action. Many beam-engine clocks are of French manufacture; sometimes they are the work of an amateur engineer-horologist. The clock dial is usually insignificant and may be balanced by a small aneroid-barometer dial, together with a thermometer. Beam-engine clocks are rarely found for sale, nor are there many examples in museums. They are mid 19th century in origin. CKA
See also Steam-engine clock.

Belfry clock One of the earliest uses of clocks was in monasteries, to summon the monks to prayer at the proper time. Originally this was done by a water clock giving an aural indication of the hour, at which a monk rang a bell to summon the other brethren. Later, mechanical clocks performed that function. The idea was perpetuated in a type of clock made in France and Germany in the 19th century. As the name suggests, the clock is in the shape of a tower, and as the hour is due to strike doors open at the base of the tower to reveal the figure of a monk who pulls a cord and apparently causes the hour to sound from a bell at the top of the tower. EJT

Bell top The bracket clock, true bell-top pattern, with ovolo moulding surmounting the cavetto or concave shape, is usually associated with the introduction of mahogany. It was extensively used during the reign of George III, although the inverted-bell shape still appeared on important musical clocks. Mouldings used to build up both the true and inverted bell tops were originally glued together, and after 200 years or so the glued joints are not always strong. Old bracket clocks should therefore never be lifted by their carrying handles. JM
See also Bell top, inverted.

Bell top, inverted The inverted-bell top for wooden bracket-clock cases appeared *c.* 1715 and is associated with the general introduction of the arch dial. As its name suggests, the shape is that of a bell reversed and comprises a lower ovolo moulding upon which is stepped a cavetto or concave shape. This in its turn is surmounted by the brass carrying handle. A pleasing and popular design, it superseded the basket top. JM

1   2   3

Biedermeier A style of interior design of *c.* 1825–48, which takes its name from a comic character in German popular literature. It typifies homeliness, comfort and simplicity, with a tendency towards lightness of form and the use of light-coloured wood. The term is strictly applicable only to Germany and Austria, but contemporary furniture in England shows similar tendencies.

In the Black Forest the term 'Biedermeier' is applied to clocks of the period 1860–80, both wall and mantel types, which usually have engaged columns incorporated in the design. The style is loosely based on the earlier French Empire clocks. In spite of the original Biedermeier characteristic of light colours, many of these cases are finished in a shiny black. Some of the pillars are china or alabaster, while white inlay contrasts with the body-colour of the cases. EJT

Binnacle clock Morris Tobias of Liverpool and London took out a patent in 1812 for a marine clock to which this term is sometimes applied. It had what is now known as 'ship's bell' striking. The minute hand made a revolution every half hour and the hour hand every eight hours; a suitable but unconventional dial was provided. It was probably so called because it was supposed it might well be located near the binnacle on a ship. DJB

Birdcage clock An ornamental clock constructed in the form of a birdcage containing a mechanical singing bird. The clock movement is in the lower part of the cage and its dial is seen from below when it is hanging from the ceiling. Birdcage clocks were made in Switzerland towards the end of the 18th century, when mechanical singing birds in snuff boxes and similar luxury articles were popular, and when the mechanical musical box began to be made extensively.

The term 'birdcage' is also applied to a type of turret clock. AS
See also Turret clock, birdcage.

Black Forest clock The Black Forest in south-west Germany embraces the biggest centre of clockmaking in the world. The industry began because of the need for local farmers to adopt some indoor occupation during the hard winters. Many took up woodcarving and, according to tradition, a wooden-wheeled clock imported from Bohemia gave them the idea of producing wooden clocks. By the early 18th century certain men had found clock production more to their taste than farming [30/1], [31/2].

The earliest clocks had wooden wheels and frames, and were controlled by a wooden foliot balance. The driving weight was a stone, and the clocks only ran about twelve hours. The 18th century saw the addition of striking work, mechanism to operate a cuckoo, 'cowtail' pendulums, and, later, anchor escapements with longer pendulums. After brass casting had been introduced into the area *c.* 1780 brass wheels were used instead of wood, although wooden frames and arbors were retained. The making of organ clocks became a separate industry, and production was helped by various mechanical improvements in tools. Production increased until *c.* 1850, when American competition drove the old Black Forest wall clock off the market. The American clock was factory-produced with an all-metal movement and did not have exposed weights and chains. The only way the Black Foresters could fight the competition was to produce similar clocks themselves and, following such pioneers as Erhard Junghans (1823–70), the industry gradually went over to factory methods. By the end of the 19th century Britain was the best customer of the Black Forest. The old hang-up clock was still made to a limited extent, but provided with alarm only and sold under the name of 'postman's alarm'.

The two world wars had a serious effect on the Black Forest industry: many factories went over to military production, and overseas markets were lost. The area is now chiefly known for alarm and travelling clocks, but the cuckoo clock and the 400-day clock are still firm favourites.

1 Binnacle clock by Morris Tobias of Liverpool and London, early 19th-century. British Museum, London.

2 'Biedermeier' style in a Black Forest clock; white china pillars, black case; c. 1860. Historische Uhrensammlung, Furtwangen.

3 Birdcage clock with movement and dial in the base; the bird 'sings' by means of whistles and bellows, at the hour. Swiss, c. 1785. Musée de Horlogerie, Le Locle.

4 Bain's clock Electro-magnetically driven clock by Alexander Bain, c. 1850. National Maritime Museum, London.

4

1

1 Balloon clock Satinwood and painted case by T. W. Smith, Fenchurch Street, London, *c.*1810. Lady Lever Art Gallery, Port Sunlight.

2 Book clock showing the movement; signed 'Hans Kiening', Füssen, Bavaria, *c.*1580. Ashmolean Museum, Oxford.

3 Blinking-eye clock Shelf clock in cast iron case; by Bradley & Hubbard, West Meriden, Connecticut, U.S.A., *c.*1865. American Clock & Watch Museum, Bristol, Connecticut.

4 Bornholm clock with eight-day striking movement; carved case includes owner's initials and date 1848. Fretted gallery above hood missing. Købstadmuseet 'Den Gamle By', Århus.

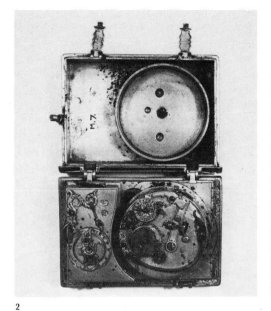

2 3 4

In the last few years a number of novelties have been produced, such as quartz clocks or battery clocks controlled by pendulums or balances. Some of today's models are reproductions of 19th-century styles. EJT

Blinking-eye clocks Soon after the iron-front case pendulum shelf clocks had been introduced in the United States, a series of one-day lever movement timepieces cased in cast-iron figures appeared. The earliest of these (*c.* 1856) was 'Sambo', a Negro figure 16 in. high holding a banjo, in which a printed-paper dial was enclosed under a glass with brass bezel. The eyes moved up and down, being attached to a swivel actuated by the alternate swings of the balance. By 1858 several other figures had been produced, comprising a line of timepieces known as 'winkers'. These included: 'Topsy', a black woman holding a watch which was the dial (16½ in.), 'David Crockett' (16 in.), 'organ grinder' (17½ in.), 'watchdog' (8 in.), 'dog' (10 in.), 'owl' (9 in.) and 'lion' (10 in.). 'David Crockett' was soon replaced by 'continental' (16 in.), which is now referred to as 'John Bull'. The iron cases were cast in two half-sections held together by screws; frequently the fronts of the castings were painted various bright colours. These were 'gadgets', sold principally in New York by such firms as the American Clock Co., Gilbert & Hubbard and the Waterbury Clock Co. They were discontinued *c.* 1875. The majority of castings were probably made by Bradley & Hubbard at Meriden, Connecticut, and the movements were made by various firms at New Haven, Waterbury and Bristol. KDR

Book clock In the late 16th and early 17th centuries, when elaborate designs were popular for both clocks and watches, a number of clocks were made in the form of a book, with the movement jointed to the case. The cases were of gilded brass, pierced and chased, and they may be regarded as 'form' watches. Like the watches of the time they contained striking work, alarms, and gave elaborate astronomical information as well as the time. The most famous maker of book clocks was Hans Kiening of Füssen, Bavaria. AS

Bornholm clock The Danish island of Bornholm is situated in the Baltic, south of Sweden. Clockmaking is said to have begun there *c.* 1750 when a cargo of English longcase clocks on its way to Russia was wrecked on the island. The inhabitants salvaged them and began making similar clocks of their own. By 1773 Copenhagen clockmakers were complaining about the number of Bornholm clocks on the market.

The Bornholm clock has much in common with the English longcase clock, though it may have a case painted white or some other light colour, with more panelling and rebates often gilded for extra decoration. Generally, the movements are based on those of the English longcase type, but are not so highly finished. Wooden barrels for the cords may be found rather than brass.

Bornholm clocks may be roughly divided into three groups: painted cases with floral decorations in imitation of Chinese lacquer (1750–1800); Empire style, with decoration of garlands, laurel wreaths, etc. (1800–30); round-topped cases. The industry had died out by *c.* 1890 as a result of Black Forest, French and American competition. Hand work was the rule and the makers never organised a factory system. Many Bornholm clocks are still in use in Denmark. EJT

1 Boulle work detail from a panel on a cartel clock case; *première partie* marquetry mounted in silver gilt; French, 1725–50. Case attributed to Charles Cressent; movement by Nicolas Gourdain. National Trust, Waddesdon Manor.

2 Briggs Rotary clock by John C. Briggs of Concord, New Hampshire, c. 1870. Private collection.

3 Bronze looking-glass shelf clock by Chauncey Jerome, Bristol, Connecticut, c. 1828. Private collection.

4 Bracket clock, Japanese, with adjustable rotating dial, stationary hand and flat bell; verge escapement and short pendulum. Science Museum, London.

2   3   4

Boulle work A form of marquetry of plain or engraved brass with tortoiseshell, taking its name from André Charles Boulle, *ébéniste du roi* to Louis XIV. Boulle developed its use greatly, though he has no claim to be its inventor. It was a technique well suited to the late 17th-century taste for rich colours, and the complex panel patterns of the designer Jean Berain were frequently carried out in this medium. To produce the veneers sheets of brass and tortoiseshell were glued lightly together and the design cut through both. When they were separated two versions could be made up: one with brass set into tortoiseshell (*première partie boulle*), the other reversed (*contre-partie boulle*). More elaborate versions involved the use of other materials such as pewter or mother-of-pearl, or the colouring of the tortoiseshell by foil or coloured mastic placed beneath.

Boulle marquetry never quite went out of fashion. Though it suffered a partial eclipse in the 18th century, its use on clock cases was quite usual in the middle years of the century. Fashionable pieces were made later in the century, and it regained popularity in the 19th century, usually in a fiery red version, and in reproductions of the 17th-century style. Its use was not confined to France. PSKM
See also Marquetry.

Bracket clock Many people regard the terms 'bracket' and 'mantel' clock as synonymous, but this is not correct. The bracket clock, as its name implies, was made to stand on a decorative, matching bracket fixed to the wall. Bracket clocks were introduced c. 1670, but the mantelshelf as a normal feature of a fireplace surround first appeared some

50 years later: with it came the mantel clock. Early Georgian conversation-piece paintings are invaluable for helping to place items of domestic art in their correct period, and, William Hogarth's *The Graham Family* of 1742 (Tate Gallery, London) shows to the left of the picture a large, arch-dial bracket clock in an ebonised case. It has a gilded figure of Father Time standing on the inverted-bell top instead of a carrying handle. The clock is on a large wall bracket, about waist height. Smaller bracket clocks were no doubt placed on mantel shelves, justifying the name mantel clock, and they were manufactured in increasing numbers as the 18th century progressed.

The design of bracket clocks changed with contemporary fashion. Between 1670 and 1690, square-dial clocks in ebonised pedimented cases were followed by basket-top clocks. Then came the arch dial, the inverted bell (c. 1720) and then the true bell top towards the middle of the century. Next came the break-arch case, the balloon clock, the lancet top, the arch top and, eventually, the chamfer top. The wood veneers for the cases were, consecutively, ebony, walnut, mahogany, satinwood and rosewood. Clocks complete with their original brackets are somewhat rare [17/3], [17/5], [41/5]. JM

Bracket clock, Japanese Japanese bracket clocks started to develop at the end of the 17th century but did not become widely available until the later period of Japanese clockmaking, after 1800. Spring-driven Japanese bracket clocks vary in size from c. 3½ to 16½ in. high, most commonly 5 to 9 in. They have all the characteristics of the

5 Bracket clock, Japanese, with adjustable rotating dial, calendar apertures and flat bell; balance controlled, with balance spring. Science Museum, London

6 Break-arch top of a painted satinwood mantel clock; by Arnold & Dent, Strand, London, *c.*1835. Lady Lever Art Gallery, Port Sunlight.

7 Bretteluhr Striking hours and half hours with one weight on the Huygens endless rope system, enamel dial; *c.*1830.

5

6

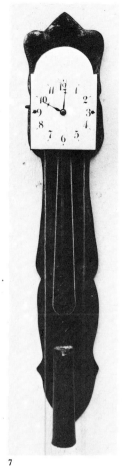

7

late period: brass cases and movements, flat bells, calendars, revolving chapter rings, fixed hands, balance wheels, and decorative, turned, corner pillars. Bracket clocks came in wooden cases and could be lifted in and out easily in the way that lantern clocks fitted into their hoods. Later examples are fastened to a small wooden base by two screws. The base contains a small drawer for the key, and the clock on its base slides smoothly into the case. MCR

Break arch A type of top for bracket clocks and longcase clocks which appeared *c.*1765 and is characteristic of the style of George Hepplewhite. The arch is incomplete, having a small ledge or step where it joins the sides of the case; it may be almost semicircular or alternatively quite flat in appearance. Break-arch clocks usually had circular dials with brass bezels, but a number are known with silvered all-over, enamelled or painted dials. Dials with a semi-circular top are also known as break arch. JM

Bretteluhren Literally, 'board clocks'; they date from the Biedermeier period in Austria, and were cheap clocks, popular with customers of limited incomes. *Bretteluhren* occur with both weight- and spring-driven movements. The movements are quite small, usually about 4 in. high, and the backboard is 20 to 30 in. long. The backboard appears to be purely decorative, but provides a contrasting surface so that the observer can see if the pendulum is still swinging. The type can be compared with the Dutch *staartklok*, although in those clocks the backboard is actually a box that houses the pendulum. EJT

Briggs rotary clock Invented by John C. Briggs of Concord, New Hampshire, and patented in 1855 (no. 13451). Many such clocks were made by the E. N. Welch Manufacturing Co. in the 1870s. The clock has a conical pendulum as the timekeeping element, a device first used by Robert Hooke in the 1660s for driving a telescope, although usually ascribed to the Dutch scientist Christiaan Huygens. Clocks using the conical pendulum have no escapement; the last wheel in the train carries an arm which rotates and turns the conical pendulum. Accuracy of timekeeping is less than with the conventional swinging pendulum because of the friction of the top support and the contact of the driving arm.

In the Briggs clock the wheel train is horizontally mounted on a wooden base, and the conical pendulum turns in front of the dial, the whole being covered with a glass dome for protection. Thirty-hour and eight-day models were made, and recently modern reproductions have been manufactured. The Briggs rotary clock's advantages are novelty appeal and complete silence of operation. CKA

Bronze looking-glass clock Said erroneously to have been invented in 1825 by Chauncey Jerome at Bristol, Connecticut, the distinctive features of the case consisted of a top slat on which was a stencilled design, applied with a bronze pigment, usually consisting of a bowl of fruit and cornucopia or a patriotic eagle, and, on the lower panel of the case door, a mirror or looking glass. This style of mahogany-veneer case contained a 30-hour weight-driven

wooden movement and a painted wooden dial. It was introduced in 1828 by the firm of Jerome & Darrow and almost instantly became the most popular case style made in Connecticut, causing the demise of the more graceful pillar and scroll by 1830. The original case was approximately 6 in. longer than the pillar and scroll and the movement was arranged for a $\frac{2}{3}$-second beat (a $17\frac{1}{2}$ in. pendulum instead of the 10 in. pendulum of the pillar and scroll). Half-round pillars were applied to the case each side of the full-length door; they were usually painted black and stencilled with bronze powder designs. After 1830 shorter cases were designed to accommodate the shorter-length pendulum movement of the outmoded pillar and scroll. Subsequent modifications incorporated carved half-columns, carved tops and claw feet, and gilded cases. Many enterprising sellers soon entered the Connecticut clock business by purchasing movements and cases from various sources, and this resulted in a price war which virtually excluded competition from other states. The design was manufactured in decreasing quantities until *c.* 1845. KDR
See also Pillar and scroll clock.

Bulle clock The basic operating principle of the Bulle clock, invented in 1920 by M. T. Favre-Bulle in collaboration with Professor Marcel Moulon, is identical to that of Alexander Bain's, invented some 80 years earlier. Bain's sliding-bar contact is replaced by a silver pin and a fork lever with a contact on one side only, to give an impulse at every other swing. A solenoid with a high-resistance winding swings over a magnet with consequent poles (south–north–south). When current flows through the solenoid, the magnetic field thus produced interacts with that of the permanent magnet to give impulse to the pendulum. An isochronal spring is fitted to the pendulum to reduce the circular error which would result with changing amplitude as the cell voltage varies with temperature and use. The single Leclanché cell used to provide motive power generally lasts two to three years. Two Bulle clocks are

shown [234/3] and [25/4]. Tens of thousands of these clocks were manufactured in France. Later models were housed in conventional clock cases as the novelty of the pendulum display wore off. CKA
See also Bain's clock.

Cadrature Another term for motion work, the mechanism lying immediately behind the dial outside the front plate, transmitting the rotation of the movement to the hands. The term may also include parts of the striking, calendar or alarm work, if these are external to the plates. PSKM

Caesium clock Dr Louis Essen and J. V. L. Parry of the National Physical Laboratory designed and constructed the first caesium atomic clock in 1955 (now in the Science Museum, London). Earlier work in the United States had resulted in the National Bureau of Standards building the first atomic clock based on the ammonia molecule. Its accuracy, although an improvement on that of the quartz-crystal clock, did not justify further development when the caesium clock appeared.

The caesium atom has an extremely accurate natural 'vibration' of 9,192,631,770 hertz which is used to control a radio frequency generated by a quartz-crystal oscillator and multiplier. The output may be fed through frequency-reducing circuits and used to drive a clock. The caesium clock shown [24/1] has an accuracy of about 1 part in 1,000,000,000, or 1 second in 30 years; later models are accurate to 1 part in 1,000,000,000,000 or even less. As the accuracy of the caesium clock is so high, it has led to the adoption of the caesium spectrum line as the time standard for defining the second, and the abandonment of the period of rotation of the earth as a primary time standard. With the caesium clock it is easy to detect the irregularities of rotation of the earth. CKA

Calendar clock Between 1860 and 1875 several U.S. patents were granted for mechanisms indicating the day of

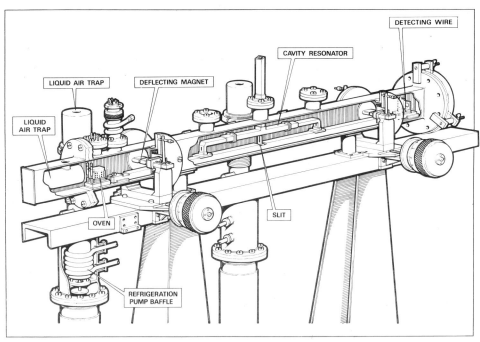

1 **Caesium clock** The atomic beam chamber for the caesium frequency standard. Science Museum, London.

2 **Capucine clock,** hour and half-hour striking, cylinder escapement, alarm; French, *c.* 1810.

3 **Calendar clock** Shelf version by Burwell & Carter, Bristol, Connecticut. Calendar mechanism by B. B. Lewis, *c.* 1860.

4 **Bulle clock** in a 'four glass' case, *c.* 1925. Private collection.

5 **Calendar aperture,** circular, from an English longcase clock, *c.* 1700. Lady Lever Art Gallery, Port Sunlight.

6 **Calendar aperture,** square, from an English longcase clock, 1680–1780. Lady Lever Art Gallery, Port Sunlight.

7 **Calendar aperture,** segmental, from an English longcase clock, 1760–1820. Lady Lever Art Gallery, Port Sunlight.

1

3

4

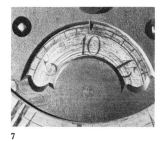

2

5

6

7

the week, the day of the month and the month of the year on a separate dial below the time dial, in the same case as the clock mechanism. The earliest patent was issued to J. H. H. Hawes of Ithaca, New York, on 17th May 1853, but this was not perpetual, as it did not compensate for leap-years, although adjusting for the varying lengths of the months. Atkins & Burritt of Ithaca, New York, were granted a patent (19th September 1854) for the first true perpetual-calendar mechanism, later improved by the Mix Brothers, (purchased by the Seth Thomas Clock Co. in 1864). Benjamin B. Lewis of Bristol, Connecticut, was granted a patent (4th February 1862) for a mechanism in which year, month and date gears turned on the same centre behind a dial indicating month and date, probably the simplest of all mechanisms for a perpetual calendar. This was used by several other Connecticut makers, while other inventors developed different ideas. During the period 1875–1900 many shelf clocks were made with a non-compensating hand on the single minute and hour dial, which was basically the same mechanism employed in English longcase clocks. KDR

Calendar aperture A slot in a dial which shows the day of the month (e.g. 1–31) engraved on a flat ring or annulus, toothed on the inner edge and moved every 24 hours by a pin in a 24-hour wheel geared to the hour wheel. Many early calendar apertures were circular in shape and were decoratively ringed to match the two winding holes; the aperture was most often situated just above the figure six inside the chapter ring. Subsequent calendar apertures were square in shape, but in the later 18th century a larger,

semicircular aperture was introduced so that several date figures were visible at the same time, with a small pointer to indicate the correct date. These semicircular apertures are usually found on 30-hour clocks, the date disc being moved every twelve hours in half-day intervals. JM

Calotte A modern travelling clock which folds into a leather case; also called a threefold or portfolio clock. *Calotte* (Fr. 'skull cap') properly refers only to the circular metal case of the clock. PSKM

Candle clock Tradition has it that King Alfred utilised the idea of marking a candle in divisions, each of which would take approximately one hour to burn. This is really not a clock but simply an interval timer, like a sand glass, and could be used for dividing the day or night into convenient parts. The principle is the same as that of an oil lamp clock; in both cases the flame has to be protected from draughts to avoid uneven burning. AS
See also Oil lamp clock.

Capucine A type of late 18th- and early 19th-century travelling clock, predecessor of the true *pendule de voyage*, also sometimes called a *foncine* or *lanterne d'écurie*. These rectangular brass clocks, surmounted by an open bell and stirrup handle, stand up to 12 in. high and were made with leather-covered travelling cases. Their tall thin shape suggests Gothic chamber clocks, which may be in their pedigree as they seem to have originated in the St Claude district of France where the Mayet family had worked as iron clockmakers in the early 17th century, encouraged first by repairing the clock in the Capucine convent. However, the name may derive simply from the hooded appearance of the clock. Capucines had eight- or 15-day movements, alarms, hour and half-hour striking and sometimes pull-repeat. Early examples had verge escapements and short pendulums; later they were fitted with cylinder escapements and balances. Capucines eventually replaced the *pendules d'officier*, another early form of *pendule de voyage*. PSKM

See also Pendule d'officier; Pendule de voyage.

Carriage clock Some horologists consider the coach watch [34/3], a very large watch usually of outstanding design and workmanship and often incorporating repeating work sounding on bells, to be the first carriage clock. Thomas Tompion made a few travelling clocks incorporating both pendulum and balance wheel control, the latter for use during the journey. The direct precursor of the carriage clock is the *pendule d'officier* of *c.* 1775, though the originator of the true carriage clock was the famous Abraham-Louis Breguet. Later, Paul Garnier founded the French carriage-clock industry. In its common form the carriage clock consists of a gilt-brass case with glass-panelled sides and top, hinged carrying handle and separate platform escapement; it often has alarm and repeating mechanisms, more rarely *grande-sonnerie* striking. It is the most popular of all clocks and is still manufactured today.

American carriage clocks had two distinguishing features: they were gaudy and cheap. The heyday of their mass production was 1880–1914. The majority were one-day only with pin-pallet escapements as timepieces or with alarm at slightly extra cost. Some were arranged for repeating strike, including half-hour, and a few were eight-day. Countless varieties were mass-produced by the Waterbury Clock Co., Ansonia Clock Co., Seth Thomas Clock Co. and E. N. Welch Manufacturing Co. The essential design was based on the French style of glass sides enclosed in a brass frame with a handle at the top. American models had practically no hand finishing, being mass-produced from stampings or pressings with gunmetal, gilded, or nickel-plate finishes. For the most part these were novelty clocks, to be thrown away rather than repaired. A few high-quality models were produced by the Boston Clock Co., Chelsea Clock Co. and the Vermont Clock Co. CKA/KDR

Cartel clock A decorative wall clock which had its origin in France during the 18th century. It was essentially a clock for the boudoir or salon and was frequently a timepiece without striking mechanism. French cartel clocks had circular drum movements, round dials with glazed bezels, and ornate ormolu cases. Earlier examples are rococo in style, while more balanced lyre shapes, adorned with bows and ribbons, appeared during the French neoclassical period of Louis XVI. English cartel clocks, while following the style of the French circular dial, were usually set in

1 Carriage clock American version called the 'Peep-o'-day' from the Ansonia Clock Company Catalogue, New York, 1886–7.

2 Ceramic clock case Wedgwood jasperware clock case without its movement; base missing; *c.* 1800. Merseyside County Museum, Liverpool.

3 Caryatid in cast and gilded brass from a German bracket clock; *c.* 1880. Private collection.

4 Ceramic clock case made by the Della Robbia Pottery Company Ltd, Birkenhead; French movement, *c.* 1900. Merseyside County Museum, Liverpool.

5 Carved column clock with eight-day wooden movement; by Atkins & Downs, Bristol, Connecticut, for G. Mitchell and R. Atkins, *c.* 1833.

6 Carriage clock eight-day quarter striking and repeating; by Charles Frodsham, London, *c.* 1845.

1

2

3

4   5   6

carved and gilded wooden mounts or cases. They often had asymmetrical rococo designs, some in the Chinese taste, and were frankly designed as wall ornaments as well as clocks [42/1]. JM

Carved column clock Clock cases with mahogany carved top splats, half-round side columns and paw feet were introduced at Bristol, Connecticut, *c.* 1828–30 and became most popular *c.* 1834. George Mitchell, an enterprising clock dealer, hired Elias Ingraham, a skilled cabinetmaker from Hartford, to design a new-style case to compete with the popular bronze looking-glass style made by Chauncey Jerome. Ingraham's style of case was compatible with the popular American Empire furniture designs used on bureaux and looking-glass frames, with heavy carving. In addition to wood-movement clock cases, Ingraham also made similar styles for triple-decker clocks for both George Mitchell and the firm of C. & L. C. Ives. Other firms soon copied these carved designs. The most common top splat was an eagle, then politically very popular, and another motif was a fruit basket, sometimes with carved pineapple finials. The carving was all done by German carvers who had immigrated to New York to work at the furniture trade, and then came to Bristol. KDR

Caryatid Architecturally, a carved or modelled half-length female figure, which serves as a pier or pilaster. According to legend, the Caryatids were the women of Caria who attempted to betray the Greeks to the Persians and for their treachery were condemned to be walled up alive. Similar figures, sometimes full or three-quarter length, were carved in wood on a smaller scale as decorative features in Renaissance wood panelling; in England, for instance, they are found on panelled oak chests and overmantels. Caryatids were occasionally used as orna-

ments on Louis XIV clock cases, and they occur as gilded, cast-metal decoration on the front corners of some large late 19th-century bracket clocks. JM

Case The protective and ornamental covering which supports and encloses a clock movement and dial. Clock cases are made of wood, metal, stone, ceramic, plastic, or a combination of these materials, and the wealth of case designs reflects current fashions and the financial means of the potential purchaser. The designer of clock cases is rarely concerned with the mechanical aspects of the movement, although he is necessarily conditioned in his approach to his art by those factors. The many different names and styles of clock cases are dealt with under separate entries. AS

Ceramic clock case The use of pottery and porcelain for clock cases goes back to about the middle of the 18th century. Many examples are simply metal cases with enamelled porcelain plaques set into mounts or perhaps porcelain flowers or figures as ornament. Enamelled porcelain introduces bright, clear colour into case design and the porcelain factories of Meissen in Germany and Sèvres in France supplied decorative details of this kind as well as vases to complete a *garniture de cheminée* with a clock.

The neoclassical period of the late 18th century produced many fine ceramic cases, sometimes using the new jasperware of Josiah Wedgwood from *c.* 1775. Parian porcelain, developed from biscuit (unglazed) porcelain, was a splendid material for decorative cases, somewhat resembling marble, and the 19th century saw fine ceramic cases from firms such as Minton, Doulton, or Charles Meigh of Stoke-on-Trent, as well as many cheap ones for standard mass-produced movements. AS
See also Porcelain case.

1

2

Chamber clock This term usually refers to small domestic clocks made in the 16th century for private use in a bedchamber. They were often hung on the wall, driven by weights and fitted with an alarm. They are generally smaller than the type of clock used in the hall and public rooms of the house, and small size distinguishes chamber clocks for private use well into the 17th century. AS
See also Lantern clock.

Chamfer top A chamfer is a woodworker's term for a sloping edge or bevel on a corner. The chamfer-top bracket clock was a product of the late neoclassical period and appeared during the first quarter of the 19th century. The tops of these clocks comprised one or two chamfered steps surmounted by a low, rectangular pyramidal shape. Chamfer-top clock cases were veneered in mahogany, rosewood or ebonised wood and decorated with inlaid ormolu stringing and frets. JM

Chandelier clock During the late 17th and early 18th centuries hanging objects such as chandeliers or birdcages sometimes contained clocks, the dials of which were visible from below. Such clocks contained balance-controlled movements rather than pendulums, which would have been difficult to fit under such circumstances. The design should not be confused with hanging ball clocks which are powered by their own weight and consequently hang at different levels at different times of the day. EJT
See also Birdcage clock; Hanging ball clock.

Chapters The hourly divisions on a clock dial, so named from the general sense of the word implying a division (as in a book) or a complete whole number. The division of the chapters into twelve, subdivided into quarters and minutes, is thought to have originated nearly 6,000 years ago in the mathematical calculations of the Sumerians, who also worked out the division of a circle into degrees and minutes. The Babylonians are said to have divided night and day into periods of twelve hours each, and the Romans

subsequently marked each third hour by an audible signal, a principle adopted by the Christian Church and called canonical hours. JM/AS

Chapter ring A flat silvered ring or annulus which bears the chapters, or numerals, and is attached to a clock dial by means of studs fitting through holes in the dial plate and held in place by pins. In the second half of the 18th century the separate chapter ring was gradually superseded by numerals and graduations engraved directly on the dial plate. The proportions of the numerals and their arrangement on the dial are of great assistance in calculating its approximate date. Early chapter rings are comparatively narrow and the hours engraved in Roman style. As the first longcase clocks had only one hand, no minute markings were necessary, and quarters only were shown round the inside edge of the annulus. Half-hour marks in the form of an arrow-head or fleur-de-lys were placed between each hour figure. One-handed clocks are not invariably an indication of early manufacture as they were still produced in isolated country towns until the end of the 18th century. Quarter markings were engraved on clock dials until about 1750. When Arabic minute numerals were first introduced, they were small and were placed within the graduations of the minute band, but just before 1700, possibly for greater visibility, the minute numerals were moved outside the minute band. As the 18th century progressed, these figures gradually increased in size until the Arabic minute numerals became almost as large as the Roman hours, particularly in northern provincial clocks. Half-quarter divisions of the chapter ring were sometimes engraved as an asterisk on the outer edge at $7\frac{1}{2}$, $22\frac{1}{2}$, $37\frac{1}{2}$ and $52\frac{1}{2}$ minutes past the hour. Towards the end of the 18th century, particularly on enamelled and painted dials, Roman hour numerals were replaced by Arabic figures. JM

Chess clock Early games of chess were often lengthy, for the rules did not set a time limit to a player's move (the slowest recorded move before modern rules was one of

3

1 Black Forest clock with wooden movement, painted wooden dial, single hand and alarm; *c.*1765. Quarter-hour dial below. Heimatmuseum, Triberg.

2 Black Forest clock with 'cowtail' pendulum hanging in front; verge escapement; mid 18th century. Heimatmuseum, Triberg.

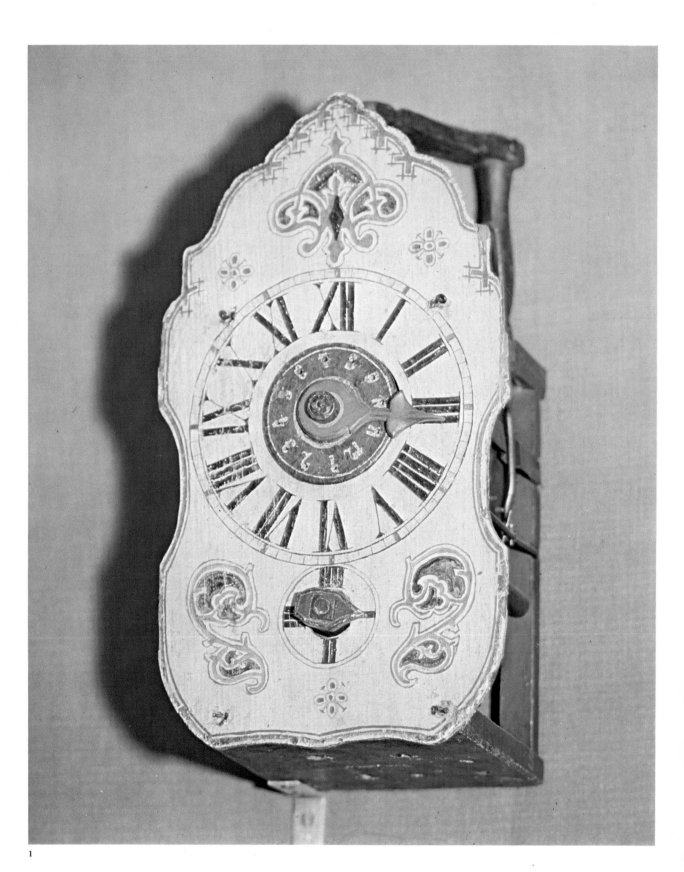

1

1 **Barograph clock** made by Alexander Cumming for King George III in 1765. Royal collection.

2 **Chronometer** in its original case, signed 'D. McGregor & Co. Glasgow & Greenock', c. 1865. Private collection.

3 **Chronometer** Movement of a large, eight-day version; No. 3592; by Charles Frodsham, London, with the Frodsham three-bar balance. Private collection.

4 **Chronometer** Movement of 33/2.

5 **Chronograph** from the instrument panel of a German aircraft; Junghans model (but not necessarily made by this firm), c. 1940. Private collection.

6 **Chinese bracket clock – Type II** in a gilt brass case with repeating work and automata; late 19th century.

eleven hours between Paul Morphy, the U.S. champion 1852–62, and Louis Paulsen). About 1860 time limits were adopted, and a special type of clock was developed to control the game. Two independent clocks are mounted side by side [28/2], recording the time taken by each player. When a player has made his move he presses a lever on his own clock, stopping it and starting that of his opponent. Similarly, his opponent presses a lever on completing his move to stop his clock and restart the other. Each dial indicates the total time taken as the game progresses. A little flag is operated at the hour. Commonly a player is allowed 20 moves per hour, and if the flag drops before his 20 moves are completed, he loses the game. CKA

Chinese bracket clocks There are two different types of 'Chinese' bracket clocks, distinguished here as types I and II.

Type I is the more common variety, measuring approximately 12 × 14 in. without the base, or 12¾ × 21 in. with the base. They were assembled in China by combining imported British workshop bracket-clock movements and enamel dials with rectangular Chinese teakwood cases and elaborately engraved and chased brass dial plates, to which the enamel dials were fixed. The clocks had fusee movements with various escapements and suspensions. Different models had varying degrees of complication, time and strike, alarm, repeater, calendar, and moon phases. The back plates were often engraved, sometimes with Chinese characters, often the name of the buyer or seller, and sometimes with nonsense ciphers made to imitate English signatures.

Type II 'Chinese' bracket clocks are smaller, more elaborate clocks in gilt cases. From side to side they measure approximately 9 in. and from the feet to the finial 17 in. They have highly finished bracket-type movements with short bob pendulums. They strike in elaborate patterns and automata perform. The cases resemble 18th-century English bracket-clock cases. These clocks are thought to have been produced in Europe for export to China in the late 19th century. The dials are European-style round enamel ones, fixed on brass plates with spandrels and automata in the arch. These clocks are quite rare. MCR

Chronograph Literally, a device for recording elapsed time in written form. Early devices had an inking arrangement to make a mark when an event was completed, hence the suffix 'graph'. Nowadays, the term is applied to a watch having a centre second hand, with or without minute and hour registers, which can be started, stopped, and returned to zero by means of the crown, or at the pendant or rim by a separate push piece. In more complicated forms – split-seconds chronographs – there are two concentric centre seconds hands which may be operated separately or together, one being stopped and the other continuing. The first one, after stopping, may be brought quickly to the other hand and additional readings taken. Such a device requires a complicated mechanism and employs the heart-shaped cam arrangements invented by Adolph Nicole in 1844 and 1862. The modern stopwatch used for sporting events is a form of chronograph. DJB

Chronometer Literally, a time measurer: the word could be applied to any timekeeper. However, in Britain and North America it means a marine instrument with a detent

1   2   3

escapement for longitude determination (box chronometer) or a precision pocket watch with a detent escapement (pocket chronometer). In Europe, especially Switzerland, the term is applied to wrist watches with lever escapements which have been adjusted so that the rates are within certain specified limits, those rates usually being stated in an observatory certificate.

In the quest for an accurate marine timepiece, tremendous effort was expended, resulting in the superb work of men like Harrison, the Arnolds, Mudge, Earnshaw, the Brockbanks, Pendleton, Pennington, Barraud, Dent, Frodsham, Kullberg and Jürgensen [32/2], [32/3], [32/4]. DJB *See also* Section IV for details of these makers.

Chronoscope A term which should strictly be applied only to what is today called a chronograph, as the latter implies a written record. Today, the name chronoscope, is sometimes used for a device that records events, astronomical or otherwise, by electromagnetically controlled marking. Though it seems to have no very precise meaning, the term is generally considered applicable to a device for measuring small increments of time with great accuracy. DJB

Clepsydra *See* Water clocks.

Clock watch A watch provided with a striking train which sounds the hours on a bell inside its case. They were popular during the 17th century but declined in the late 1680s after repeating work for watches had been introduced, making it possible to repeat the hours and quarters at will. AS

Comtoise clock A form of provincial, weight-driven clock made in the vicinity of St Claude in the Franche-Comté region of France, near the Swiss frontier, from the mid 18th century to the beginning of the 20th. They are sometimes called Morez clocks or Morbier clocks, from place names in the area. They represented the first move towards the popularising of clocks in France, and in the 19th century they were to be found far and wide across the country, virtually ousting other local clockmaking traditions. They were often marked with the name and town of the vendor rather than those of the maker.

Comtoise clocks were built on iron-strip frames in the manner of Gothic clocks. The clockmaking industry in the Morbier area had started with the Mayet family of ironworkers, who successfully repaired the clock at the Capucine convent in St Claude. In classic form the clocks had inverted verge escapements, later ones having anchor escapements, and hour and half-hour vertical rack striking. In common with many country clocks, they also re-struck the hour after a space of two minutes. The pendulum, usually but not invariably swinging between the movement and the dial, beat seconds or longer and operated with a cranked crutch. They also had a folding rod. Comtoise clocks might hang from a bracket or have a full long case, made from pine, with tapering or violin-shaped sides, frequently painted and grained in country fashion. Early dials were of pewter or brass with black-filled numerals and a single hand. Later, the hours might be shown on enamel cartouches, and by the 19th century dials were completely enamelled, or even of printed paper, and there was sometimes a third hand indicating the date. A pierced brass pediment surmounted early dials, showing a cock with the royal arms, or with motifs suitable to current political enthusiasms. Later pediments or *frontons* employed a wide variety of stamped brass devices, one of the most common incorporating a pair of cornucopias, classical anthemion ornaments, a basket of flowers and a sunburst. In the 19th century a fashion for over-large pendulums and bobs of stamped and painted brass or sheet iron developed.

After the Treaty of Frankfurt in 1871 German clocks were allowed into France without tax, which weakened the trade in the Franche-Comté despite diversification of output. The decline of these traditional clocks was completed by the First World War, after which the industry in the Morez–Morbier–Foncine area was reorganised for more modern productions. PSKM
See also Capucine; Morez clock; Revolutionary clock.

Congreve clock William Congreve (1772–1828), an inventive man notable for his development of the rocket, applied himself, while Comptroller of Woolwich Arsenal, to the design of accurate timekeepers. One of his clocks has a pendulum impulsed only once every minute, an early

1 Comtoise clock signed 'L. Faivre à Arnay le Duc', c.1870. Private collection.

2 Comtoise clock Movement of 34/1 showing the inverted verge escapement.

3 Clock watch, silver cased; signed 'Thomas Windmills, London', c.1700. Fitzwilliam Museum, Cambridge.

4 Chronoscope fitted in a 'field' case for use in taking astronomical observations; by Thomas Tompion, London, c.1690. Merseyside County Museum, Liverpool.

5 Crucifix clock, probably south German, late 16th – early 17th century. British Museum, London.

6 Cresting, illustrating this detail on the hood of a longcase clock by Joseph Knibb, London, c.1685. Fitzwilliam Museum, Cambridge.

7 Congreve clock A 19th-century example based on William Congreve's original design. British Museum, London.

6

4

5

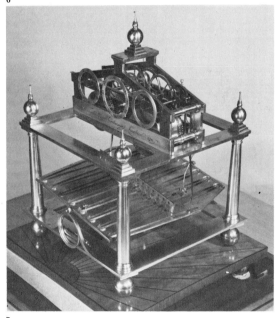

7

version of a free pendulum. The clock usually associated with his name was patented in 1808; the original is still at Woolwich Arsenal. In this clock the escapement is controlled by a steel ball rolling down a zigzag track on a tilted brass plate. Each complete journey takes almost 30 seconds, at the end of which the ball strikes a lever releasing the escapement and tilting the table in the opposite direction, causing the ball to retrace its path exactly 30 seconds after the start from the other end. A normal clock train tilts the table through a cranked arm; hours and minutes are shown on separate dials, seconds by marks on the track of the tilting table. Normally spring-driven, Congreve's original clock employed small cannonballs as driving weights. These clocks are poor timekeepers, yet many replicas have been made in recent years, for they have a hypnotic effect upon the viewer. CKA

Cresting English longcase clocks with square dials and flat tops to the hoods, produced during the reigns of Charles II and William and Mary, often had a decorative feature of carved wood fixed above the front cornice. The motif was almost invariably that of a cherub's head or putto with wings sprouting from the neck. Unfortunately, the method of attachment by wooden dowels fitted, but not glued, into holes meant that the cresting could easily be removed. It is a rare occurrence to find the original carved cresting on a late 17th-century clock hood, although small peg holes on the top may remain to indicate that it had once been present. JM

Crucifix clock A type of table clock in the form of a crucifix, popular in the 17th century. The movement was contained in the base and the time indicated by a small sphere at the top, which had the twelve hour figures on a band around its circumference. This band slowly turned past a fixed pointer, moved by a long arbor from the movement in the base. Crucifix clocks were usually fitted with striking work and more rarely with an alarm. The finish was generally of gilded metal, as in table clocks in

35

1 **Cuckoo clock** in a polished wooden case with enamel dial; retailed in England by Tritschler, Miller & Company, London, *c.*1855. Private collection.

2 **Cuckoo clock** in a carved wooden case; Black Forest, *c.*1900. Private collection.

3 **Cuckoo clock** with a wooden 'schild'-type, painted dial; Black Forest, early 19th century.

4 **Cushion top** from the hood of a marquetry longcase clock by Michael Knight, London, *c.*1690. Lady Lever Art Gallery, Port Sunlight.

5 **Dial, brass,** with engraved centre, from a 30-hour longcase clock by James Barfoot, Wimborne, Dorset, *c.*1785. Private collection.

6 **Dial, break-arch,** from a musical longcase clock with strike/silent, chime/silent and music indicator auxiliary dials; by John Ellicott, London, *c.*1750. Lady Lever Art Gallery, Port Sunlight.

7 **Dial, auxiliary** Tune selector and lunar indicator from a longcase clock by Joseph Finney, Liverpool, *c.*1770. Merseyside County Museum, Liverpool.

1   2

general, but some examples have a wooden base similar to other Augsburg clocks, a town where many crucifix clocks were made, and occasionally silver mounts embellish the gilded work. The position of the hour band was changed by inserting a pin in holes below it; winding and regulating were performed at the base. EJT

Cuckoo clock In spite of the jibe that Switzerland after centuries of peace had produced only the cuckoo clock, such clocks are not Swiss inventions at all, but hail from the Black Forest. Opinion is divided as to their inventor, but the most popular candidate for the honour is Franz Anton Ketterer of Schönwald. Probably Ketterer's first productions only imitated the call of the cuckoo and did not include a small model bird that emerged from a doorway. The invention is said to date from about 1730, when striking work was a novelty on Black Forest clocks, and to have been derived from the astronomical and performing clock in the minster of Villingen, which was a smaller edition of the famous Strasbourg clock.

Early cuckoo clocks followed the styles used in ordinary Black Forest clocks, with wooden dials covered by paper, then painted and varnished dials, and by the mid 19th century the picture-frame type of dial. About 1870 the popular design of today was introduced: a small house decorated with carved leaves, birds, stags, and so on, with white Gothic-style figures on a dark background and white carved hands.

Although the clocks were originally weight-driven, many spring-driven examples were made in the second half of the 19th century, and brass plates for the movement gradually succeeded the earlier wooden ones. Fusees were sometimes even applied to the spring-driven clocks. The carved-leaf design of case is still popular, but many examples with polished cases resembling mantel clocks were made prior to 1914. Well-known 19th-century makers were various members of the Kammerer family, who established a trading house in London, and Johann Baptist Beha of Eisenbach. EJT

Cushion top The name given to the shaped tops of hoods of longcase clocks towards the end of the 17th century, when carved cresting went out of fashion. Cushion tops appeared in a variety of shapes, such as a simple ovolo moulding surmounted by a small platform, or in the style of the wooden basket top to be found on the bracket clocks of the period. In more ornate clocks the cushion top might even appear as a double inverted bell. The cushion top was often ornamented with a pair of turned and gilded ball-shaped finials or similar ones in a spiral, flame-like form. It was usually veneered and decorated in the same way as the rest of the case and was a favourite hood top for taller, arch-dial longcase clocks, persisting until the introduction of the pagoda top about 1740. JM

Decimal clock In France in 1793 the Revolutionary government ordered decimalisation of the systems of measurement, including time. The new time, which divided the days into ten hours, the hours into 100 minutes and showed ten hours only on the dials of clocks, was paralleled by a new system of ten Revolutionary months, each named after a natural attribute of the season (September becoming Fructidor, the fruitful month), and divided into three 'decades', each of ten days. Twelve months of 30 days each gave a year of only 360 days; the five extra ones were to be used for national festivals and Leap-Year Day for a Festival of the Revolution. Clocks showing decimal time are rare and most clockmakers seem to have played safe by showing duodecimal time on the same or a subsidiary dial. The system lapsed with the rise of Napoleon and the establishment of the Empire [229/3]. PSKM

Dial, auxiliary A small dial either of flat ring, annulus shape, or engraved or painted, which is added to the main dial to indicate subsidiary movements such as calendar work, strike/silent mechanisms, alternative types of chimes, choice of tunes in musical clocks, moon phases, tidal readings, and so on. Auxiliary dials sometimes appear in pairs in the upper corners of square dials, and sometimes in all four corners in complicated clocks. JM

Dial, brass Although painted iron dials are sometimes found in early Gothic clocks, brass was the principal material in general use from the late 16th to the later years of the 18th century, when enamel or iron dials began to appear. Before the Industrial Revolution, when it became possible to produce sheet brass of even thickness in a rolling mill, brass dials were cut from sheet metal which had been cast and reduced to the required gauge by beating with trip hammers operated by water power. Faint, overlapping,

hammer marks on the back are characteristic of early brass dials. The front of the dial was stoned down to produce a flat, even surface prior to polishing. Later and cheaper forms of brass dials often had some of the area covered by the chapter ring cut away, to economise on the amount of brass used. The metal used for earlier brass dials was known as 'latten', an archaic name for brass. JM

Dial, break-arch An early form of arch dial: the top of the main, square dial is surmounted by a semicircular arch, slightly smaller in diameter than the width of the dial, leaving a small step or break at the base of the arch. Sometimes converted dials are found in which the arch is attached to the lower square section of the dial by riveted straps at the back. The first known example of a break-arch dial was that on a longcase clock made by Thomas Tompion for the Pump Room at Bath, c. 1709 [38/5]. The fashion for break-arch dials, however, did not become popular until c. 1720–1725. The extra area of dial in the break arch gave scope for the ingenuity of the clockmaker in developing auxiliary dials, lunar movements and a variety of automata actuated by the moving pendulum. JM

Dial, enamelled White enamelled dials were first introduced in England in the 1740s for watches, and for bracket clocks later in the 18th century. The use of enamel for decorating trinkets had already been adopted at Battersea in London and at Bilston in Staffordshire. Enamel dials were more legible than the engraved and silvered type, and were made by melting a vitreous enamel on a copper

3   4   5

 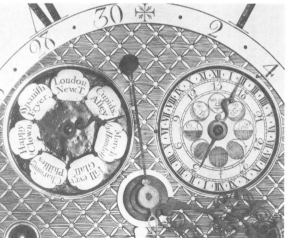

6   7

1 Dial, regulator, from the regulator which was formerly the standard of Yale Astronomical Observatory; by Henry Appleton, London, *c.* 1840. Collection of Historic Scientific Instruments, Peabody Museum, Yale University, New Haven, Connecticut.

2 Dial, enamelled, from a carriage clock by Arnold & Dent, London, *c.* 1830. Private collection.

3 Dial, lunar, from a longcase clock by John Wyke, Prescot, *c.* 1755. Private collection.

4 Dial, painted, from a country-style clock by Watkin Owen, Llanrwst, Wales, *c.* 1780.

5 Dial, equation, from the month equation clock presented to the Pump Room, Bath, by Thomas Tompion, 1709.

6 Dial, skeleton, from a regulator fitted with a four-legged gravity escapement; by Moore of Leeds, *c.* 1850. Private collection.

7 Dial, false plate Movement of a musical clock by Benjamin Willard, Grafton, Massachusetts, showing the false plate attachment between the movement and dial; the false plate is signed 'Osborne's Manufactory, Birmingham', 1773–5. Yale University Art Gallery, New Haven, Connecticut.

8 Dial, glass, from Pierre Le Roy's one-wheel clock, *c.* 1750. British Museum, London.

base. As the muffles used in the process were only suitable for small objects, it was difficult to produce the larger dials required for longcase clocks, which are therefore extremely rare, although the French succeeded in making large enamelled dials much earlier than the English. Another drawback was that the enamel surface was brittle and tended to crack or flake if subjected to even a small amount of shock or torsion, especially where the dial feet were riveted into position. JM

Dial, equation A rare form of auxiliary dial which indicates the difference between solar and mean or average time. Most early longcase clocks were sold together with a sundial which was an essential adjunct to the clock in order to set it to time. However, a simple conversion from solar time to mean time had to be first worked out. Solar time,

according to the season of the year, could be almost $16\frac{1}{2}$ minutes fast or slow of mean time. This difference was shown automatically by the equation dial, though a cheaper substitute was available in the form of a printed equation table, which could be stuck on the inside of the door of the clock for easy reference. JM
See also Equation of time; Mean time (both Section V).

Dial, false plate Towards the end of the 18th century the majority of longcase clock dials and movements were prefabricated in a number of regional centres, and painted iron dials became popular. The iron dial was supplied with a false plate already attached, leaving the 'maker' to drill holes in the front movement plate in a convenient position in relation to the working parts. The dial feet were fitted in the false plate instead of in the previously painted dial – a method which would clearly have been impossible without damaging it. Cast-iron false plates often carry the name of the manufacturer, most of them being made in Birmingham. False plates are mostly found on eight-day, not 30-hour clocks. AS

Dial, glass Glass dials are simply clock glasses on which the hour and minute numerals are marked instead of on a conventional dial. Such dials make it possible to see the movement of the clock in the same manner as in a skeleton clock. Although not common, glass dials are found on some early Connecticut shelf clocks, on a type of keyless rack clock made in the 1920s, and on a famous one-wheel clock invented by Pierre Le Roy in the 18th century. Another form of glass dial is used in a type of 'mystery' clock in which the hands are marked on revolving glass discs, driven from their edges, the clock thus appearing to have no movement. AS

Dial, lunar A subsidiary dial, usually situated in the arch but sometimes found as a segmental aperture in the main part of the dial, or as a circular aperture known as a 'halfpenny moon', or as the 'Halifax moon'. Early examples are known in German Gothic clocks, but lunar dials first appeared in England towards the end of the 17th century, when the first Astronomer Royal, John Flamsteed, was working out his tide tables with the phases of the moon. The complete lunar cycle takes almost 29½ days, and the purpose of the lunar dial was to record automatically the lunar phases. Although a lunar dial has often been regarded simply as an interesting addition to the dial, it was of great practical use in the days before street lighting. JM
See also Globular or rotating moon; Halfpenny moon or Halifax moon.

Dial, painted Painted dials were introduced shortly after the middle of the 18th century. The design of regional brass

clock dials had become so cluttered with decoration, auxiliary dials and sometimes as many as four separate hands from the dial centre (hour, minute, centre second sweep and calendar hand), that it was often difficult to tell the time at a distance. The solution was a white enamelled or painted dial. Large enamelled dials were difficult to manufacture, so the painted dial was adopted. It proved eminently functional, as well as being cheaper and easier to produce than the engraved brass dial with its separate chapter ring and spandrels. Early painted dials were designed in a restrained and elegant manner, in keeping with the other decorative arts of the Adam period. However, popular demand soon called for the production of more colourful dials with painted scenes in the corners and arch. JM

Dial, regulator In a regulator for astronomical purposes the dial is usually arranged with separate circles for hours, minutes and seconds, the outer circle being for minutes and large subsidiary dials below and above the centre indicating hours and seconds. In some such regulators the motion work is dispensed with to reduce friction, necessitating separate setting for hour and minute hands.

In England the seconds dial is usually above the centre and the hour dial below. In the United States, where E. Howard & Co. produced most of the clocks of this type, the location is often reversed and the seconds indicated at the six o'clock position. A special light form of Graham escapement, with the anchor moving in the opposite direction to the pendulum, makes this feasible. Watchmakers' regulators were also made with this type of dial. DJB

Dial, skeleton A dial cut away to reveal the action of the clock movement behind. Always used in skeleton clocks, it is sometimes also found in high-quality regulators. Turret-

7

8

1   3   4

clock dials made of cast iron with glazed apertures for back lighting are a form of skeleton dial [38/6], [114/1], [118/2]. As See also Skeleton clocks.

Dial, strike/silent Usually found in the arch of bracket clocks but also in some longcase clocks. Bracket clocks with verge movements were portable, and the owner, on retiring to bed, could take his bracket clock with him and turn the hand of the strike/silent dial to 'silent' so that he would not be disturbed by the clock striking while he was asleep. The strike/silent mechanism was only made possible by the introduction of rack striking at the end of the 17th century. Longcase clocks were not, of course, portable but silencing the striking mechanism at night is sometimes no less desirable. JM

Dial, thirteen-piece A form of enamel dial fashionable in France c. 1750, composed of twelve wedge-shaped cartouches bearing the hour numerals, fitting closely around a circular domed centrepiece painted with the maker's name. Enamelled hour plaques, set in a gilt-bronze frame and having a gilt-bronze centrepiece, had been popular since the late 17th century. The enamelling was done in specialist workshops, the white ground being produced by an enamel with pewter oxide, the black, or more rarely blue, numbers being added as a final firing. About 1715 a white enamelled centre to the dial became fashionable, but the bronze frame persisted, and it was not until 1740 that reference is made to

a clock with a dial entirely of enamel. The 13-piece construction was necessary because of the technical difficulties in producing large enamelled dials, difficulties which were not overcome until later in the century. PSKM See also Dial, painted; Enamelling (Section III).

Dial, tidal A fine example of the clockmaker's ingenuity. Two sets of Roman numerals, from one to twelve, were engraved, usually in the dial arch alongside the 29½ days of the moon's phase. By adjusting an indicator it was possible to forecast the approximate time of high tide at any given port. This was of particular value to mariners when ship departures depended on the tide. John Flamsteed, the first Astronomer Royal, is said to have drawn up tidal tables for use in the Port of London, the calculations being worked out in conjunction with the changes in the moon's phases. Clocks produced in seaports like London, Bristol, Liverpool, Hull and others during the 18th century were often equipped with tidal dials. Around the outer edge of the graduations was often engraved the legend 'High Water at...' with the name of a particular port. JM

Dial, turret-clock See Turret-clock dials.

Dial, universal-time For some time clockmakers have attempted to show the comparative time in different parts of the world; this became really important after the invention of the electric telegraph. A clock by Thomas

1 Dial, universal time A clock with several dials showing the time in various cities of the world. Made for the International Exhibition, London, 1862, by William Davis & Son, London. Museum of London.

2 Dial, tidal, combined with a painted lunar dial; from a longcase clock by James Condliff, Liverpool, 1820. Merseyside County Museum, Liverpool.

3 Dial, strike/silent, from a longcase clock by Thomas Pace, London, *c.*1790. Lady Lever Art Gallery, Port Sunlight.

4 Dial, thirteen-piece, from a *vernis Martin* bracket clock of the period Louis XV, *c.*1750. Bowes Museum, Barnard Castle.

5 Bracket clock by Daniel Quare, London, *c.*1690. Merseyside County Museum, Liverpool.

5

1

1 **Cartel clock** in carved and gilded wood illustrating Aesop's fable of the Fox and the Grapes; movement by James Gibbs, London, c. 1760. Lady Lever Art Gallery, Port Sunlight.

2 **Dial, up and down** An auxiliary dial on a two-day chronometer, indicating the position at which it should be wound daily. Private collection.

3 **Dial, velvet** Black velvet ground forming the dial plate of a clock by Salomon Coster, The Hague, 1657. Museum Boerhaave, Leiden.

4 **Dial, wandering hour,** from a night clock by Joseph Knibb, London, c. 1670. National Museum of Antiquities of Scotland, Edinburgh.

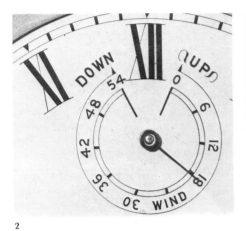

2   3   4

Lister of Halifax, Yorkshire, c. 1780, has a special dial from which the time in 24 places in the world can be calculated with reference to the main dial. Some chapter rings on 18th-century longcase clocks have the names of various foreign towns engraved on their outer edge: when the hour hand of the clock is opposite these names it is noon in the respective places. In the 19th century large universal-time clocks, or world-time clocks as they are sometimes known, were installed in the offices of commercial organisations with worldwide interests. These had multiple dials to show time in the principal cities of the world, the dials being set in phase with the main movement of the clock. AS

Dial, up and down A subsidiary dial, usually in the twelve o'clock position on a marine chronometer or precision pocket watch, which indicates the degree to which the mainspring is wound at the time of observation. It was usually fitted when failure to wind the timekeeper would have serious consequences, as on a chronometer used for longitude determination. On a fusee timepiece it consists of a pinion placed on the fusee arbor which moves a high-numbered wheel with an arbor carrying a hand, so arranged that a full run of the spring will carry the hand somewhat less than 360°. On going-barrel pieces it is much more complicated and sometimes employs planetary gearing. DJB

Dial, velvet Although rarely used on English clocks, velvet-covered dials with separately attached engraved and silvered chapter rings are not infrequently found in certain European bracket clocks produced towards the end of the 17th century. These clocks had somewhat plain, architectural or rectangular cases and were known as *religieuse* clocks in France and *Haagse klokje* in Holland. Also mounted on the deep blue or wine-coloured velvet, just below the chapter ring, was a cartouche bearing the

maker's name. A more elaborate bas-relief mount is also found in which a gilded or silvered figure of Father Time with his scythe supports the cartouche. JM

Dial, wandering hour Normally associated with certain watches of the late 17th and early 18th centuries, though a few such dials were made for both longcase and bracket clocks. These were night clocks, the figures occurring as slits behind which the light from a lamp shines through to show the time. In this type of dial the hour appears in a disc which advances from left to right across a segmental slot marked along the edge in minutes and quarters. As one hour completes its journey along the slot the next hour appears on the left, marking the divisions of the following hour.

There were two basic methods by which this action was achieved. In one, the hour discs were formed into a twelve-piece chain carried around a ten-sided wheel, bringing the correctly numbered disc into place at each succeeding hour. The other system employed a large revolving disc with two small revolving discs mounted on it opposite each other, one bearing the odd numbers I to XI and the other the even ones II to XII. Each smaller disc rotated one figure at each half-revolution of the main disc, bringing the respective hours into view as they moved along the aperture in the dial. AS

Dial, wooden Wood as a material for turret-clock dials has been universally used, but for domestic clocks the wooden dial seems to have been limited to clocks made in the Black Forest, other European peasant communities and North America, up to the early 19th century. The Black Forest dials were mostly made of fir, which tends to split after a time. The dials were made by cutting boards to shape and gluing a second layer to the first in the shape of a circle, to form the figured part of the dial. The whole was then turned on a primitive lathe so that the figured portion formed a

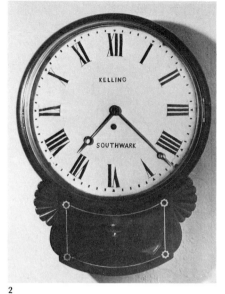

1   2   3

4   5

slightly convex shape, its surface gently merging with the base of the dial. The pores of the wood were filled with size and lime-water and the figures and decoration painted on, after which the whole was given one or more coats of varnish. Dials were packed in paper and were not fixed to movements until the whole consignment of movements, dials, chains, bells, etc. had reached its destination. The dials were made and painted by different craftsmen and fitted to movements by many makers in the same area. EJT

Dial clock During the latter half of the 18th century the English dial clock appeared, a descendant of the so-called 'Act of Parliament' or 'tavern' clock. Originally time-keepers only, consisting of a large circular dial about twelve inches in diameter with a spring-driven fusee movement, the early examples had a verge escapement and often a convex silvered dial. The dial was secured to a circular wooden surround, the rear of which had two wooden strips attached to locate its position on a rectangular wooden box, then pegged into position to hold the clock. A hook on the box allowed the clock to be hung on a wall. Later, dial clocks became more ornate and often incorporated striking trains and sometimes an alarm, the anchor escapement being universally used, with a door in the box to allow the pendulum to be seen or started. Modern dial clocks may have balance-controlled escape-ments, synchronous electric movements or, increasingly,

battery electric movements, including quartz-crystal types. CKA
See also Drop dial clock.

Dial feet Clock dials are attached to the front plate of the movement by means of short cylindrical pillars, which are riveted to the dial so that they cannot be seen from the front. They are usually sited so that the riveted ends are concealed beneath the chapter ring. The ends of these dial feet pass through holes in the front plate of the movement and are secured with tapered steel pins. There are usually four dial feet on an English longcase dial but country-made 30-hour clocks are often found to have only three. JM

Digital clock Any clock which indicates the time by a display of figures rather than by a dial. Occasional examples may be found at all stages of mechanical timekeeping; many early astronomical clocks in Italy have digital presentation in addition to normal dial work. The 'ticket' or 'flick' clock was the first produced in commercial quantities. It was invented and made in the United States and consists of a clock with the movement housed in a circular base, above which is a glass cylinder containing two sets of celluloid tickets bearing numbers moved by the motion work of the clock movement. The tickets are arranged to read hours above and minutes below, flicking over one by one to indicate the time. The action is so swift that it is difficult to follow. The modern form is all-electronic in action and uses neon indicators, light-emitting diodes, or liquid crystal displays for the digital presentation. Much controversy centres around whether analogue or digital presentation of time is the best [111/2]. CKA

Dolphin fret The figure of a grotesquely shaped, scaly fish with a large head and curved tail standing high above it, was a favourite motif in baroque decoration. Legs of tables and arms of chairs were frequently carved in this form, known as a dolphin and resembling the ocean fish, not the mammal, of that name. Dolphin frets may be seen masking the bell on lantern clocks, and more often as supports on either side of the boss in arch-dial clocks. Like spandrel mounts, they are cast, chased and gilded, and attached to the dial with small screws. JM

Drop dial clock Similar to the dial clock but with the addition of a trunk below the dial, allowing a longer pendulum, for better timekeeping, and additional carved decoration. A glass panel is usually fitted to allow the pendulum bob to be seen; often these clocks also strike on a bell. The original drop dial clock is a typical English design dating from the mid 18th century, later produced in vast quantities in the United States, where they are known as 'school' or 'regulator' clocks. The quality of these is not to be compared with the English drop dial fitted with spring-driven fusee movements. A fine example by Thomas Grignion, dated 1760, may be seen in the lecture theatre of the Royal Society of Arts in London. CKA
See also Dial clock.

Drop octagon wall clock The octagon wall clock with a lever movement and an 8 in. dial with brass bezel became popular c. 1850 as a timepiece for travelling by sea or rail.

The drop octagon, with pendulum movements, striking and silent, installed, is believed to have been introduced by Chauncey Jerome for the London Great Exhibition of 1851. The case design was a modified, abbreviated English Act of Parliament type. The usual dial size was 12 in. The earliest models had a veneered octagon top with a projecting compartment at the base and a glass-panelled door revealing the pendulum. Frequently, carved pieces were mounted flanking the door and extending on each side of the base octagon section. This style of timepiece was available as an eight-day striker and was occasionally furnished with an alarm. It was the forerunner of what became known in North America as the 'schoolhouse' clock, manufactured in millions until c. 1930. The usual height was 24 in.; later a smaller 17 in. size with 8 in. dial was made. A simple calendar mechanism was also available. Movements made by the New Haven Clock Co. were exported to England, where a model of this style was made by the Anglo-American Clock Co. KDR

Drum clock Table clocks of the 16th century can be divided roughly into two groups, tower clocks and drum clocks. On the former the dial was vertical and on the latter it was horizontal, occupying most of the top surface of the clock. Some drum clocks were small and plain, and this design eventually developed into the watch and, much later, the marine chronometer. Some drum clocks, however, were quite large, with richly decorated cases and even additional dials. In some instances the clock was arranged to stand on three feet.

In the last quarter of the 19th century the shape came into vogue again but now standing upright, in the still-popular style of the alarm clock. It is believed that the first clocks of this type were made by the Seth Thomas Co. in the United States in 1876, but Junghans in Germany was also in

1 Dial clock with alarm; signed 'Bunyan & Gardner, Manchester', c. 1840. Private collection.

2 Drop dial clock with white painted dial, carved mahogany and inlaid brass case; eight-day movement. Sometimes known as 'trunk dials'. Signed 'Kelling, Southwark', c. 1845.

3 Drop octagon wall clock with 30-day movement using J. Ives's lever spring (wagon spring); by Atkins, Whiting & Co., Bristol, Connecticut, c. 1855.

4 Digital clock An LED digital clock radio, with alarm. Metamec Ltd, Dereham.

5 Drum clock with gilded case. Door allows one to observe fusee when winding necessary; by Nicholas Plantart, Abbeville, c. 1530. Uhrensammlung Kellenberger, Winterthur.

6 Dolphin fret on a lantern clock signed 'Nicholas Coxeter at ye 3 Chaires in Lothbury, Londini fecit', c. 1650. G. S. Applebee.

7 Dolphin fret dial mount on a longcase clock dial signed 'Windmills, London', c. 1730.

6

7

1   2   3

4

the market early. A good selling point was that the clocks were portable and did not have to be set in beat like a pendulum clock. Millions of the type must have been manufactured before 1900. A finer version came from France, with the drum of sheet brass, the spring contained in a barrel, and the escapement mounted on a separate platform screwed to the movement. More rarely a tiny pendulum with tic-tac escapement was fitted. EJT

Drum clock, Chinese Truly Chinese, such clocks are in the form of an oriental drum, designed to be supported vertically on a stand. The cases are pierced engraved chased brass cylinders of varying diameters, all about 3 in. deep. The movements vary, but all are copies of European timepieces and similar in workmanship. Since the Chinese hour system closely matched the western diurnal system there was no need to adapt the mechanism in any major way. Chinese clocks have twelve fixed equal hours, with no way of altering either the dial or the rate of escapement for a system of varying hour lengths. Most have alarms, consisting of a brass setting disc, with six small knobs and a window, placed over another disc with the Twelve Terrestrial Branches, representing the twelve fixed hours, each marked with a Chinese character, closely associated with the twelve animals of Chinese folklore, engraved on it, fastened directly to the dial plate. Not many of these clocks were

made and, although they can be found, they are not common. MCR

Drum table clock, Japanese Adaptations of European table clocks, they were not modelled after an oriental drum on a stand nor displayed vertically, and are therefore called table clocks. Almost all such clocks are from a late period, after the 18th century, and feature revolving, adjustable chapter rings and a fixed hand. The engraved decoration tends to be of the common variety found on Japanese clocks. The cases are cylindrical brass drums with simple verge balance-wheel movements and horizontal dials. MCR

Dwarf tall clock This anomalous title describes a miniature American tall, or longcase, clock, more popularly known as a grandmother clock. Although made in small numbers by comparison with tall clocks, they were popular between 1800 and 1825. Examples vary in height between 2 ft and 5 ft. The earliest were probably made c. 1770–80 in Grafton, Massachusetts by Simon Willard, but the most prolific maker appears to have been Joshua Wilder of Hingham, Massachusetts, c. 1820. A few were made in New Hampshire, Maine and Pennsylvania. The movements were usually eight-day brass; some were timepieces; most had striking trains and a few also had alarms. While the more sophisticated cases were scaled-down replicas of hooded scroll tall cases in mahogany with inlays, several provincial cases had plain flat tops of unique country style, in pine and maple. Most dials were iron, painted and decorated in the United States. KDR

Eight-day clock Longcase and bracket clocks with a going duration of eight days first appeared c. 1670 and have been popular ever since. Although the interval for winding is seven days, an extra day's going is added to allow for delay in carrying out the weekly procedure. Eight-day longcase clocks may usually be recognised by the winding squares on the clock dial. These, however, can be misleading, as it was fairly common in the later Georgian period to fit the dials of 30-hour clocks, either brass or painted, with dummy winding squares and holes. Month-going clocks have

1 Drum clock, Chinese, on a stand decorated with floral motifs; late 18th – early 19th century.

2 Drum clock, Chinese, with dial of twelve equal hours, alarm setting in arabic numerals; the Chinese signs of the Zodiac serve as hour numerals. Case pierced with Buddhist emblems. Science Museum, London.

3 Equation clock Dial from a longcase equation clock by William Barker of Wigan, *c.*1765. Merseyside County Museum, Liverpool.

4 Drum clock, Chinese Movement of 46/1, illustrating its watchlike form, fusee and spring barrel, and cylinder escapement.

5 Drum clock, Chinese Back plate of 46/1 showing English-type balance, balance cock and engraving.

6, 7 Empire clock American style, mahogany veneered eight-day clock with movement by the Forestville Manufacturing Company, Connecticut, *c.*1840.

8 Dwarf-tall clock Mahogany clock by Joshua Wilder of Hingham, Massachusetts, 1815–25. Henry Francis du Pont Winterthur Museum, Winterthur, Delaware.

5

6   7   8

winding squares similar to eight-day clocks, but they wind anticlockwise. JM

Empire clock The term 'American empire' applied to furnishings describes the style of *c.*1825–40, which followed the Federal and preceded the Victorian. In clocks, this includes such types as bronze looking-glass, triple-decker carved, gilded and veneered, and some plain rectilinear cases. Among collectors the term 'Empire' case usually refers specifically to the two-door type of Connecticut shelf clock, having full rounded pillars flanking the larger two-section top door. The top section of this door enclosed the dial, and the lower section generally had a painted tablet. The bottom door usually had a mirror and was flanked by mahogany-veneered corbel sections. The base of the clock was supported by turned feet dowelled into the bottom and the top splat was generally carved. Such cases were most frequently used with eight-day weight-driven brass movements, though a few are known containing wooden movements. KDR
See also Pendule empire.

Equation clock The challenge of devising a clock which recorded solar as well as Greenwich mean time occupied the great makers of the golden age of English clockmaking, men like Thomas Tompion and Daniel Quare. Their less famous contemporary, Joseph Williamson, designed a number of equation clocks and also constructed several movements which Quare used. The problem was to compare mechanically solar time, derived from a sundial, with mean time. Tompion worked out an equation table, which he had printed, to show the number of minutes and seconds solar time was fast or slow of mean time on any day of the year. An equation clock constructed by Daniel Quare had an auxiliary dial in the front of the case, below and separate from the main dial. It had two hands, a long one revolving once in 365 days and a shorter one with a sun to show the difference in minutes, fast or slow, between solar and mean time. Another of Quare's equation clocks had a double movement with two pendulums and, although it was not capable of recording accurately the equation of time, it was a reasonably acceptable solution [270/1]. JM
See also Dial, equation.

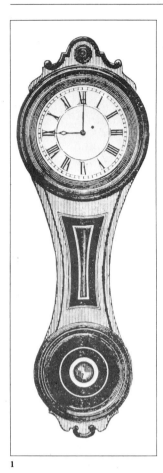

1 Figure-8 clock Howard Watch & Clock Company, Boston, Massachusetts, 1874 catalogue.

2 Flying pendulum clock made by the New Haven Clock Company. New Haven, Connecticut, and sold under the name of Jerome & Company, Connecticut, U.S.A., 1884–5. Sheffield City Museum.

3 Figure clock Drum clock with automata figure; made by Hans Gutbub, Strasbourg, c.1590. British Museum, London.

4 Figure clock Madonna and child table clock; hour dial at the foot and quarter dial on revolving coronet; signed 'Jeremias Paff, Augspurg, 1643'. Gershom Parkington Collection of Time Keeping Instruments, Bury St Edmunds.

5 Eureka clock in inlaid mahogany case with open dial to show the movement; Eureka Clock Company, London, c.1912. Private collection.

6 Four glass clock with standard drum movement and mercury compensated pendulum; French, 1890–1900. Private collection.

1   2   3

Eureka clock Invented in 1906 by T. B. Powers, an electrical engineer in the United States, the Eureka clock was the first electrically maintained balance-wheel clock. Convinced that he had devised a perfect timekeeper, Powers called it 'Eureka' (in Greek 'I have found it'). Manufacture did not commence until 1909 at Clerkenwell, London. The earliest models were enclosed under a glass dome where the large compensated balance could be seen swinging. Later models were fitted in a variety of cases, many of which have only 'Eureka Electric Clock – 1000 days' on the dial to indicate that the clock is electric. Timekeeping did not prove as good as Powers had hoped, though the clock made with the balance and mechanism visible had a powerful novelty appeal. The arm of the balance is a soft iron core with two soft iron arms which form a U-shaped magnet when current passes through its solenoid winding. A silver pin on the balance arm touches a fixed silver contact at the correct point for impulsing the balance, the balance arm being attracted to a fixed soft iron armature; the resulting swing operates a cam on the balance arbor to move the clock train through a pawl and ratchet wheel. About 10,000 of these clocks were made before manufacture ceased in 1914. CKA

Fiddle-cased clock The term 'fiddle-cased clock' was applied to any clock narrow in the centre and swelling out at the base, to give roughly the shape of a violin. French longcases of this type often housed movements of the Comtoise type, and smaller wall versions were developed in Switzerland and Austria from the end of the 18th century. The longcase version appears in Sweden and Finland in the early 19th century. Other hanging versions were the Girandole clock and the banjo clock by the Howard Co. of Boston. Further variations are encountered from some of the Connecticut factories, such as the Seth Thomas Clock Co., which marketed, c.1890, an eight-day spring-wound time and strike movement in a violin shaped case, supported upright on a frame. A single door panel contained a glass exposing the dial and pendulum. Apparently this model was made in limited numbers for a very short period, then discontinued. The expense of making such an exotic case for a relatively cheap movement probably resulted in a non-competitive product. Originals are rare. EJT/KDR

Figure clock Any clock with moving figures and more specifically with a human figure or figures, either forming part of the decoration of the case or partially involved in the movement. Examples are a clock with a revolving dial and a figure holding a pointer to indicate the hour, or French 'mystery' clocks of the late 19th century with the pendulum held by a female figure apparently stationary but actually moving slightly from side to side to impulse the pendulum. There are also French clocks in which the pendulum consists of a child on a swing which moves to and fro (requiring a special escapement) and many splendid French designs with decorative figure sculpture as part of the case. EJT

Figure-8 clock The American Howard Watch and Clock Co. (E. Howard & Co.) introduced, c.1870, their weight-operated timepieces, Nos. 6–10. The cases were made of polished black walnut, and the configuration of case design has led collectors to refer to these as 'figure-8' models. The sizes were as follows:

model no.	diameter of dial	length of case	pendulum beats per second
6	14 in.	4 ft 10 in.	1.00
7	12 in.	4 ft 2 in.	1.10
8	11 in.	3 ft 8 in.	1.17
9	9 in.	3 ft 1 in.	1.20
10	8 in.	2 ft 9 in.	1.33

No. 6 was advertised as the 'Watchmakers', Bank and Public Office Clock'. It had dead-beat escapement and maintaining power, and showed seconds separately from minutes and hours. Nos. 7–10 were advertised as 'School, Office, Bank, House and Counting-room Clocks'. These were all timepieces with recoil escapements. They were superior to the general run of contemporary Connecticut clocks, and much more accurate timekeepers. KDR

Floral clock Extremely popular, the floral clock originally used mechanical clock movements driving the hands through a long shaft. Today it is general to use a synchronous motor placed in a space below the centre of the hands. The dial is set out with hundreds of plants, the figures being flowering plants, usually in troughs for ease of maintenance. The hands may be of metal only or contain troughs with plants, in which case they are very heavy and the drive requirements difficult to meet. Dials are generally twelve or more feet in diameter and are inclined on a sloping bank for viewing, unless the dial can be viewed from above [59/4]. CKA

Flying pendulum clock This is not so much a clock as a horological entertainment, invented in 1883 by Alder Christian Clausen, the clock being sold by Jerome & Co.,

Connecticut, U.S.A. A clock train carries an arm on an extension of the arbor of what would normally be the escape wheel, and on this arm is hung a length of thread carrying a light metal ball. Two vertical metal rods are mounted on the top of the clock at diametral points, a short distance from the radius of action of the turning arm. As the arm turns, centrifugal force causes the metal ball to fly outwards and the thread touches one of the vertical rods, upon which the inertia of the ball causes it to wind round the rod until it comes to rest. Its weight, however, causes it to unwind until the thread leaves the rod and returns to the vertical, the arm remaining stationary during this sequence. Immediately the thread leaves the post the arm is released and accelerates, while the ball is thrown outwards once more and the sequence repeated. The time is shown on a dial but it is reputed that these clocks are the most inaccurate timekeepers ever invented. Replicas have been made in recent years. CKA

Four-glass clock A modern term for mantel clocks of the late 18th and 19th centuries, especially popular in France, with rectangular cases panelled on all sides with glass held in narrow frames of gilt metal, brass or wood. Brass was generally used after the first quarter of the 19th century. Such cases were first used for high-quality regulator movements by clockmakers such as Berthoud, Breguet and Janvier, the movement thus having its own decorative value. Later in the 19th century they were produced with standardised drum movements. The case style has some affinities with those developed for the smaller carriage clock or *pendule de voyage*. PSKM

Four-hundred day clock The first year-going clock with a torsion pendulum was devised by Aaron D. Crane in the United States, probably patented 18th March 1829. Fifty years later Anton Harder in Germany devised a similar type which later became known as the '400-day clock' to

4

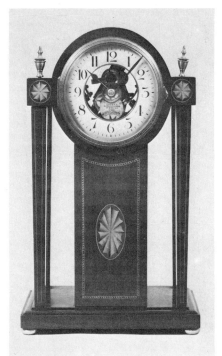

5

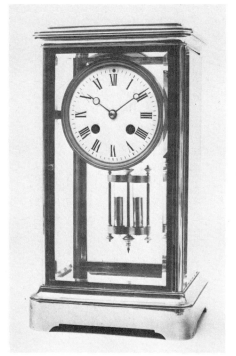

6

1 Franklin clock fitted with the Franklin spiral dial; signed 'Vulliamy, London', *c.* 1800. Time Museum, Rockford, Illinois.

2 Friesland clock (**staartklok**) Movement of 51/6 showing the twisted pillars, anchor escapement and shell motif on the hands.

3 Four-hundred day clock, sometimes known as an 'anniversary clock', with torsion pendulum; glass dome removed. German, early 1900s. Private collection.

4 Friesland clock (**staartklok**) A high case clock, sometimes called 'double hood', containing a perpetual calendar, *c.* 1875.

5 Friesland clock (**staartklok**) Carved wooden clock, possibly from Groningen, *c.* 1800.

6 Friesland clock (**staartklok**) A short version, by Rinse Durks, Grouw, *c.* 1775.

7 Friesland notary clock Like an ordinary Friesland clock, but smaller; the 'season' spandrel mounts and 'bridal wreath' round the chapter ring indicate that it was a wedding present; *c.* 1775.

1

2

3

Europeans, and 'anniversary clock' to Americans, since they were given as presents and required winding one year after the gift. A torsion pendulum with a period of oscillation of 15 seconds is used, with a dead-beat escapement, the torsion wire being a thin strip of nickel steel in modern types for temperature compensation; the original type had phosphor bronze suspension strips which resulted in bad timekeeping. The 'bob' was a lead-loaded brass disc in early clocks; later, ornamental arrangements such as four balls were used, including temperature-compensated arrangements to counter the change of elasticity of the phosphor bronze suspension. Clocks of this type are still made today, and the Atmos clock is a development of the original '400-day clock'. There are modern types with battery movements indicating the time which retain the rotating bob for appearance. CKA
See also Atmos clock.

Franklin clock During visits to London in the late 18th century, Benjamin Franklin became friendly with James Ferguson, the famous astronomer and designer of orreries and astronomical clocks. Few of Ferguson's designs were built, but his ideas led Franklin to devise a clock with as few parts as possible. His clock has a dial divided into four segments marked 0–60 minutes for each segment, and three hour figures on the centre line of each segment, the whole series of twelve hour figures lying between four concentric rings. A single hand indicates the minutes and hours simultaneously, but not unambiguously as three hour figures are indicated. A later version employed a spiral groove with a steel ball to overcome the difficulty. The ball rested in the spiral to show the hours, being gradually moved to a hole in the centre from which it fell by gravity through a tube behind the dial to the outer end of the spiral every twelve hours. Some of Franklin's clocks also indicated seconds on a dial in the arch of the clock. Ferguson made a number of variations based on Franklin's design, some going for one day and one going for a week, but without seconds indication. These clocks are described in Ferguson's *Select Mechanical Exercises* (1773). CKA

Friesland clocks (staartklokken) During the third quarter of the 18th century a type of domestic clock was produced in Friesland which was entirely new to the province. The case was a simple hanging version of an Amsterdam longcase clock with the movement of the Friesland bracketed *stoelklok* modified to an anchor escapement. The case of the common Friesland *staartklok* consists of an upper part which contains the movement and dial, and a lower part housing the pendulum. The total height of the case is about 2 ft 3 in.; as this is about half the height of a longcase clock, the Friesland clock is sometimes referred to as a half-case clock. Mostly, the case is made of oak, French-polished to a reddish hue. Other examples occur in elm and, from the third quarter of the 19th century, mahogany. In the east Netherlands some Friesland clocks are found with whitewood cases, most, though perhaps not all, originating in the neighbouring part of Germany. At the level of the pendulum bob there are so-called 'cheeks' on either side of the case, in the front part of which is a sliding

wooden panel with an oval 'window' instead of the usual pendulum aperture. Around this oval window an ornamented plate is mounted, lead in older models, moulded brass in later ones and thin brass plate in cheaper examples. The pendulum bob in the normal Friesland clock has a diameter of almost 2¾ in., although in office clocks and certain others it may be larger. On the clock hood are three little wooden plinths bearing wooden figures, or vases with gilded glass balls, or ornaments in thin brass plate. The painting of the dial is exceptionally beautiful in some cases, but in general it is very simple. Around the chapter ring, spandrel mounts of thin brass representing the four seasons are usually added. There are a number of variations on the standard Friesland clock, listed below.

Variations of the movement. (1) Moon phases with or without indication of date. (2) Automata movement attached to the anchor arbor and therefore in continuous motion, or linked to the striking work and therefore intermittent. The display is usually above the chapter ring, but may sometimes be found beneath it. Since all mechanical additions clearly hinder the functioning of the escapement and therefore the proper running of the clock, they were often totally or partly removed during later repairs. (3) Fitted with repeating rack striking instead of locking plate striking. (4) An organ or musical cylinder fitted (rare).

Variations in the size of the clock. (1) Abnormally large size, the so-called 'burgomaster's' clock (rare). (2) The hood has its normally flat top decorated with carved leaf cresting or with a carved or painted broken pediment. The dial arch is usually filled with fine engraving or painting. (3) A luxuriously executed clock case, in which case the clock is

4   5   6   7

1 **Friesland stoelklok** of the most common type; only the ornamentation on either side of the dial is unusual; mid 19th century.

2 **Friesland stoelklok** Movement of 52/1 showing the verge escapement and striking mechanism.

3 **Friesland 'little skipper' clock** with 'Turkish knot' decoration in the back panel; second half of the 19th century.

4 **Leeuwarden stoelklok** with matching mermaids on the dial plate and back panel; second half of the 18th century.

5 **Friesland and Groningen clocks (stoelklokken)** An elaborate Groningen *stoelklok* by Daniel van Barkel, 1728.

6 **Friesland and Groningen clocks (stoelklokken)** Movement of 53/5 showing the verge escapement.

7 **'Little skipper' Friesland clock**, *c.* 1850.

1

2

often larger than usual. The case may be completely covered with carving, or finely painted, or inlaid with other kinds of wood, or made with a more valuable kind of wood. The finest examples have a separate silvered chapter ring, while the spandrels may be painted instead of being of brass. (4) The so-called 'short' Friesland clock or 'big head' of which there are two types. In later examples the width of the dial is the same as in a normal Friesland clock, but in older models it is narrower, about 10 in. instead of 12 in. The length of the pendulum of the short Friesland clock is about 26 in., while that of the normal model is about 3 ft. (seconds

3

4

pendulum). Although short Friesland clocks were manufactured until well into the 19th century, older examples of the shorter type should still be considered as forerunners of the standard Friesland clock. (5) Smaller examples, such as the office clock or notary's clock which only differ from the standard Friesland clock in having a smaller movement and case; they are relatively rare. They measure about $4\frac{1}{4} \times 3\frac{3}{4}$ in., and $4\frac{3}{4}$ in. in height. As with the short Friesland clocks, the late 19th-century notary clocks are slightly larger. (6) Very small examples, the so-called 'skipper' clocks. As with the bracketed *stoelklok*, the Friesland clock has a small version for use in inland navigation, although there is some doubt whether they were specifically manufactured for that purpose. The back panel of these clocks does not contain a pendulum, and it is pierced with a Turkish knot motif or star design. They are only classified among Friesland clocks because of their external appearance, since their movement does not differ in principle from that of the 'little skipper' *stoelklok*. JLS
See also Friesland and Groningen clocks.

Friesland and Groningen clocks (stoelklokken) The most common Dutch bracketed clock is the Friesland *stoelklok*; it is still produced according to a design which has hardly changed for over 200 years. Its development took place as much outside Friesland as in it, and was almost certainly introduced from the richer province of Groningen to the east. A small number from the early period clearly show both Groningen and Friesland characteristics, and it is difficult, sometimes impossible, to determine their origin. Some authorities hold that the Groningen *stoelklok* differs from the Friesland both in external design and in the movement. The case of the Groningen clock is generally stronger and more elaborately finished, greater attention

5   6   7

being paid to the cast lead ornaments. The extra-thick back panel is often decorated with eels, mermaids or other fine carving [53/1]. Examples from Friesland have mermaids simply in flat outline. Eels and mermaids, incidentally, were supposed to symbolise time because of their elusiveness.

The construction of the verge movements of Groningen clocks was also more robust than Friesland examples; the pillars are usually plain or with a single decorative ring and a round or square plinth. The hands of Groningen clocks also differ slightly from those of Friesland models

During the second and third quarters of the 18th century the fast-developing clock industry of Friesland gradually ousted the more solidly constructed Groningen clocks from their leading position.

As with *stoelklokken* made in other provinces of the Netherlands, the decoration of the dial in Friesland clocks displays considerable conservatism. There is often a little landscape within the hour circle, but frequently there is either no decoration at all or only a simple tree branch motif [52/1]. Until 1850 it was customary to paint the figures of two women above the hour circle; thereafter a small landscape was often depicted instead. Not unexpectedly, dials of older clocks have often been repainted one or more times. In 18th-century examples the decoration on either side of the dial is usually of putti in cast lead. Flower vase or parrot motifs usually indicate that the clock dates from the second half of the 19th or beginning of the 20th century. Considering that the Friesland clock was in production for so long, the development in its movement is far from spectacular. Later movements are generally smaller than the older ones, the wheels are slimmer and the pillars less robust. The typical profile of a Friesland movement pillar, from which there was little deviation, displays two ornamental rings before 1780, and afterwards three.

A special place in the history of the Friesland clock is occupied by the beautiful and relatively large *stoelklokken* produced in the second half of the 18th century in the provincial capital, Leeuwarden. These clocks can easily be recognised, as the back panel is flanked by large mermaids in relief, strongly carved in openwork fashion [52/4]. The movement has a double top plate and measures $7\frac{3}{4} \times 6\frac{1}{4} \times 7\frac{3}{4}$ in., larger than that of the usual Friesland clock ($6\frac{3}{4} \times 5\frac{1}{4} \times 6$ in.).

During the second half of the 19th and early 20th centuries, possibly because of competition from cheap German regulator and Black Forest clocks, simple bracket alarm clocks of a slightly smaller format were produced. They have no striking mechanism and the eel motif has been restored to the back panel.

In addition to the normal Friesland *stoelklok*, the slightly larger Leeuwarden clock, and the smaller alarm clock, there is another, much smaller Friesland clock which is about half the size of the normal models. It is sometimes called *schippertje*, 'little skipper', as it was made specifically for inland navigation [53/7]. The verge escape wheel of the little skipper is placed, as in a lantern clock, horizontally above the top plate, while in the case of the ordinary *stoelklok* it is vertically beneath it. The short pendulum, almost always behind the movement, though once in a while it may be at the side, is joined directly to the verge pallet arbor so that it does not strike the movement or the brackets. The later skippers are usually larger than earlier examples, and the mermaids are sometimes carved in wood. The movement of older examples is usually about 4 in. in height; later movements vary between $4\frac{1}{4}$ and $5\frac{1}{2}$ in.

Among unusual *stoelklokken*, it is possible to find examples which indicate the moon's phases and the date. Such clocks were usually made by 19th-century master clockmakers. Although calendar mechanism is much less frequently found in *stoelklokken* than in *staartklokken* or Dutch longcase clocks, it is not a rarity. *Stoelklokken* which were originally equipped with a simple going train, and did not have this accessory added later, are undoubtedly rare. As in Groningen, a number of Friesland *stoelklokken* with music cylinders were produced, but these are rare and now valuable. Examples where particular attention has been paid to the finish of the case are also extremely rare. Some

1 **Gothic clock** with wheel balance, decorated canopy and moonphase; hour and quarter strike and alarm. Erhard Liechti, Winterthur 1572, Uhrensammlung Kellenberger, Winterthur.

2 **Girandole clock** with pine case grained to simulate mahogany, and gilding; eight-day movement; by Lemuel Curtis, Concord, Massachusetts, c. 1818. Old Sturbridge Village, Sturbridge, Massachusetts.

3 **Gallery clock** in a gilded case surmounted by an eagle; eight-day weight-driven movement; by Simon Willard, Roxbury, Massachusetts, c. 1800. Museum of Fine Arts, Boston, Massachusetts. Gift of S. Richard Fuller in memory of his wife, Lucy Derby Fuller.

4 **Globe clock** known as 'The Empire Clock' and retailed by S. Smith & Son, London; French movement, c. 1910. Science Museum, London.

5 **Globular or rotating moon** on the dial of an English longcase clock, signed 'John Seddon, Frodsham'; the clock was made c. 1750, but the moon in the break arch may be a later addition. Private collection.

6 **Gothic clock** Round Gothic, or 'beehive', shelf clock in a mahogany veneered case with eight-day movement, iron dial and cut-glass tablet; by Elias Ingraham, Bristol, Connecticut for E. C. Brewster, c. 1841. Kenneth D. Roberts.

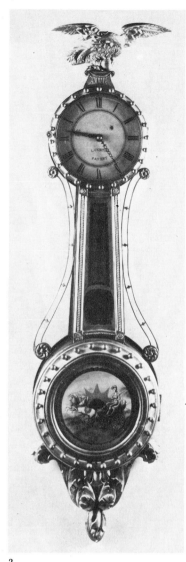

1   2

are decorated with rich wood carving; in others the top may be missing. Such oddities are rarer in Friesland than in Groningen. About 1800, when Friesland *staartklok* production was beginning, the *stoelklok* industry reached its peak. Although *stoelklokken* were manufactured in countless small towns in Friesland, the most important centre of production was Joure, where members of the Aleva family were the most important makers. JLS

Gallery clock Gallery clocks, in the American sense, were used in banks, halls, public buildings, railway stations and churches. Perhaps the most famous was made and installed by Simon Willard in the Supreme Court, Washington, D.C. on 21st October 1837. More ornate examples with gilded cases and carved eagles with brackets made by the Willards are known. A line of marble dial clocks, listed 'For Halls', were manufactured by E. Howard & Co., Boston, the dial sizes varying from 14 in. to 36 in. and the cases from 2 ft 4 in. to 4 ft 9 in. The earliest spring-driven Connecticut types were made by Brewster & Ingrahams, c. 1850. Atkins, Whiting & Co. of Bristol brought out, c. 1852, a 30-day model with double wind arbors, driven by a lever spring and roller pinion movement designed by Joseph Ives. The E. Ingraham Co. of Bristol offered a line of corrugated

walnut, chestnut and gilt eight-day spring movement styles with 10 in. – 24 in. dials, also available in plain round cases in the same three finishes.

In the United Kingdom, however, the name 'gallery clock' refers specifically to the clocks frequently found on church galleries. KDR

Girandole clock A distinctively American clock which derives its name from the similarly shaped mirror with convex glass and gilded balls surrounding the frame. Somewhat similar to the banjo clock, though larger, the bottom frame is circular rather than rectangular and the base piece below (bracket) has carved acanthus leaves rather than the scrolled pediment of the presentation banjo form. The girandole is attributed solely to Lemuel Curtis who worked in Concord, Massachusetts, from 1814 to 1829 and then in Burlington, Vermont, in partnership with Joseph Dunning, until 1832. They were made as eight-day timepieces having a pendulum 2 in. longer than the Willard patent. The case is somewhat larger and gold leafed, usually with an ornately carved eagle. By many this is regarded as the most handsome clock case ever designed in America. Exceedingly rare, there are believed to have been only 50 originals produced. KDR

Globe clock The earliest globe clocks were mechanically turned globes with clock dials made in 16th-century Europe. Another type has a globe with an inscribed revolving hour band and a fixed indicator to show the time, usually made to stand on a table. The more modern globe clock, early 20th century, takes the form shown [55/4], giving the time at any point on earth in addition to local mean time.

In the United States two types were made, the Timby and the Juvet. About 600 Timby globe timepieces were made, based on four patents of 1863–5 granted to T. R. Timby of Saratoga Springs and Baldwinsville, New York, but manufactured by L. E. Whitings of Saratoga Springs. The movement was an eight-day timepiece with jewelled balance. The case supported a rotating globe, showing the time of sunset on any part of the globe. A separate dial indicated the time, which could be adjusted for a specific meridian. Apparently the manufacturer was never able to produce this mechanism to the inventor's patent, and it remained merely a novelty. A 30-hour solar timepiece, consisting of a 12 in. diameter globe mounted on a stand, turning every 24 hours, was manufactured at Canajoharie, New York, 1879–86. This was the result of two patents issued in 1867 to Louis Paul Juvet of Glen Falls, New York. A large floor model had an 18 in. diameter globe. Manufacture ceased when a fire destroyed the factory on 18th October 1886. Both Timby and Juvet timepieces have become rare collectors' items [315/3]. CKA/KDR

Globular or rotating moon This is probably the most realistic reproduction of the changes in the moon's phases which has ever been contrived for use with clockwork. It consists of a sphere, half white and half black, rotating vertically in a circular opening in the arch of a dial, driven from the main movement by a bevel gear. As the 29½ days of the lunar month pass, the moon turns imperceptibly, showing an approximately true visual image of the moon at any given time. One of the earliest clockmakers, Ahasuerus Fromanteel, who worked in London during the reign of Charles II, knew of the principle of the rotating moon. JM
See also Dial, lunar.

Gothic clock The earliest mechanical clocks are believed to have been turret clocks, probably introduced

c. 1280–1320. By the beginning of the 15th century smaller versions of the turret clock were being produced for domestic use. As turret clocks were located in towers, the frame of the domestic version was also made to resemble a tower. The clocks were controlled by a wheel balance or foliot, and usually needed winding twice a day. They were produced in most countries of western Europe, but Germany and Switzerland had a particular reputation for the type. Later examples had elaborately painted dials of sheet iron, and it is probable that the iron parts of the movement were originally given a protective coating of tin, which accounts for the numbers of these clocks that survive. The Liechti family of Winterthur had a particular reputation for making Gothic clocks. The type virtually died with the introduction of the pendulum in the mid 17th century, though the Gothic clock has descendants in the shape of the English lantern clock and 30-hour longcase clock, the typical Black Forest movement, the Dutch *stoelklok*, and various types of country-made clock in other parts of Europe.

In the United States, when spring-driven clocks were introduced *c.* 1840 at Bristol, Connecticut, new case designs appeared. Elias Ingraham, Bristol's foremost cabinet-maker, first conceived the round Gothic case, followed by the sharp Gothic, respectively termed by collectors 'beehive' and 'steeple'. Actually Ingraham's designs were copies of Gothic cases that had appeared in England *c.* 1820 as an aspect of the Gothic revival. Both of Ingraham's concepts were marketed before 1842, the date at which a design patent could first be acquired, and consequently both styles were widely copied by his competitors. The round Gothic continued popular until *c.* 1890, and the sharp Gothic is still popular for reproduction and electrically operated clocks. EJT/KDR

Gothic-on-frame clocks As small spring-driven shelf clocks became popular, Birge & Fuller of Bristol, Connecticut, introduced *c.* 1844 an eight-day movement powered by Joseph Ives's patented 'accelerating lever spring' (wagon spring), housed in a modified sharp-Gothic-on-frame case. This style is often referred to as 'steeple-on-steeple' or 'double-decker steeple'. There are two distinct styles, each produced in two sizes. The earlier, offered only by the Birge firm, had long candle-style finials on each side

3   4   5   6

1 Gravity clock The silent 'Kee-Less' clock marketed by the Watson Clock Company (later the Kee-Less Clock Company), London, c.1925. Private collection.

2 Hague clock (Haags klokje) of the simpler, old style, wall-hanging type; signed 'Paulus van Loon', c.1675.

3 Gothic-on-frame clock Sharp Gothic-on-frame shelf clock with twin candle finial; by Birge & Fuller, Bristol, Connecticut, with J. Ives's lever spring (wagon spring) movement, c.1846. Kenneth D. Roberts.

4 Hague clock (Haags klokje) A later example showing French stylistic influence; signed 'Johannes van Ceulen, Haghe', late 17th century.

1

2

3

4

5

of the case, mounted on top of the lower frame. The large case for eight-day movements had double finials, and the smaller 30-hour movement case had single finials. The other style had the conventional finials found on the regular sharp Gothic case, with two mounted each side on top of the lower frame and two on top of the upper frame. Such cases were used by Terry & Andrews, Elisha Manross, M. W. Atkins, as well as Birge & Fuller, but the style was only popular for a short period, 1844–8. A few firms in New York purchased such clocks and pasted in their own labels, but all were probably manufactured in Bristol. KDR

Grandfather clock *See* Longcase clock; Tall clock.

Gravity clock Any clock which is driven by its own weight. The earliest appeared in the mid 17th century. They had a bracket in the form of an arm attached to the wall, the hand holding a chain on which the clock, in the form of a globe, hung. To wind the clock it was lifted, a spring retracted the chain inside the clock and, when released, the clock descended. Maurice Wheeler described one of his devising in 1684, the clock descending an inclined plane. A pivoted weight inside the clock provided the power to the train as it tried to assume a vertical position, though the actual power came from the clock descending the inclined plane. Hours and minutes were indicated on the clock, the days of the week on the plane.

Nowadays the term more often refers to the silent keyless clock made in the early 1900s. This has a base carrying two columns with a toothed rack in one which engages a wheel in the clock movement. The clock is raised to the top of the columns by hand, thereupon its own weight drives it; the escapement is visible and impulses a short pendulum. These clocks, also called rack clocks, were popular for a limited period only. CKA

See also Hanging-ball clock; Inclined plane clock; Rack clock.

5 Hague clock (Haags klokje)
Movement of 56/4 showing the
cycloidal cheeks and engraving of
the back plate.

6 Hanging clock A simple
version with time and alarm only;
wheel balance iron movement.
Germany, second half of 16th
century. Württembergisches
Landesmuseum, Stuttgart.

7 Hanging-ball clock with 30-
hour movement; by Jacobus
Mayr, Augsburg, c.1700. British
Museum, London.

8 Halfpenny moon on the dial
of a longcase clock; signed
Anthony Batty, perhaps of
Halifax, Yorkshire, c.1750.

6

7

8

Hague clocks (Haags klokje) The older Hague clocks of the 17th century, of which only a few examples are known, contain a small rectangular movement, controlled by a short pendulum and verge escapement. The movement is attached to the brass-hinged dial front panel in a simple, rectangular case which could be hung on the wall from two hooks. On the dial panel, the front of which is covered with velvet, is mounted a pierced chapter ring. Beneath the chapter ring, suspended from two hooks, is a little signature plate covering an aperture through which it is possible to reach the pendulum. Both the chapter ring and the signature shield are in silver. In later examples the hour numerals are engraved, while the hinged shield disappears; the clock is also equipped with a striking mechanism. The case has little bun feet, and a domed top to hide the bell. The back panel of the Hague clock, unlike that of the French *religieuse* cannot be opened, and often has a star figure in rosewood inlaid inside. The movement and the striking mechanism were originally driven from the same spring barrel, but separate barrels were introduced c.1685. Sometimes there is also an alarm, which was originally situated in the upper part of the case against the back panel, though in later examples it is next to the movement on the front plate [56/2]. After 1685 the restrained, sober quality of the Hague clock began to change under the influence of French clockmakers who had emigrated to Holland. There was a clear development of styles towards those of the *religieuses* and all kinds of moulded decoration were added when possible. Pieter Visbach was the leading clockmaker of The Hague until c.1685, when the honour passed to Johannes van Ceulen, Sr [56/4].

Not all Hague clocks were made in The Hague. Identical examples were made in other towns: Amsterdam, Leyden, Utrecht, Leeuwarden and Middelburg. Hague clocks are now extremely rare and therefore valuable. JLS
See also Pendule religieuse.

Halfpenny moon or Halifax moon A form of auxiliary lunar dial of circular shape which was adapted for use on square-dial clocks. Although halfpenny moons were occasionally used by London makers as early as 1735, the vast majority of examples are to be found on the clocks of Lancashire and Yorkshire makers later in the 18th century. An alternative to the halfpenny moon on a square-dial clock was the segmented moon opening, like the usual moon movement in an arch dial but here inverted, the moon's disc descending to full moon then ascending, instead of the climbing and descending path followed in an arch dial. Many such clocks were made in Halifax, Yorkshire. JM

Hanging-ball clock A clock devised in the mid 17th century which enclosed a balance-controlled mechanism in a metal sphere to indicate the time by means of a band rotating on its circumference past a fixed pointer. The weight of the clock itself was the driving force, and it was suspended from a cord wound round a barrel inside the clock, the clock gradually descending as the hours passed. Winding was accomplished by raising the clock to the top of the cord, and a spring inside the barrel caused the latter to rotate and wind it up. The fusee of conventional clocks was eliminated but a barrel and spring still had to be provided. Reproductions made in London in the early 1970s. EJT

1 **Hood, slide-up** Longcase clock with its trunk door open and the hood in the 'slide-up' position; by Thomas Tompion, *c*.1675. National Trust, Trerice House, St Newlyn East.

2 **Hollow column clock** A shelf clock with 30-hour wooden movement; by E. & G. W. Bartholomew, Bristol, Connecticut, *c*.1830.

3 **Hood, slide-off** Removing the hood from a longcase clock by Peter King, Long Acre, London, *c*.1710. Lady Lever Art Gallery, Port Sunlight.

1

2

3

Hanging clock Gothic weight-driven clocks needed to be positioned so that the weights had room to fall. This was usually done by standing the clock on a bracket or hollow pillar. A simplification was to provide a hanging loop at the back of the clock and spurs to grip the wall and keep the clock in position. This idea was often used on English lantern clocks, but the method is less practical and even dangerous the heavier the clock becomes. The hanging clock therefore is usually limited to the lighter type such as the South German or Austrian *Telleruhr* [111/1]. (A hooded clock is not a hanging clock, which implies that the clock movement itself hangs, not its case.) Sometimes small spring-driven clocks in the shape of Gothic clocks or table clocks of tower form were hung from a small chain fastened above the cupola. Such a clock, *c*.1460, is shown in the portrait of Jehan Lafever by Rogier van der Weyden in the Museum of Fine Arts, Antwerp. EJT

Hollow column clock E. & G. Bartholomew, casemakers at Bristol, Connecticut, introduced the hollow column Connecticut shelf clock for 30-hour wooden movements *c*.1830. This Empire-style case had a moulded cornice with 3 in. diameter hollow columns on each side at the front, about two-thirds the length of the case, to accommodate the cast-iron weights. The bottom section of the case had veneered side panels and a framed door, containing a painted glass tablet or looking glass. A double panelled door was mounted in the upper section with the dial glass and either a painted tablet or mirror. While not common, this style of case was made for other firms who marketed and manufactured clocks both at Bristol and other Connecticut locations, and even as far west as Ohio. The veneer on the columns was applied as strips about 3 in. wide, wound helically. Modifications of this style were made with carved top splats and carved feet. The case was in vogue until *c*.1840 and a few examples are known containing 30-hour brass movements. KDR

Hood, slide-off The most common method of removing the hood of a longcase clock to gain access to the movement. An overlapping strip of wood runs in a groove on either side of the case itself so that the hood does not tip forward when sliding off. The slide-off hood was introduced shortly before the end of the 17th century. It is normally fitted with a glazed, hinged door. JM

Hood, slide-up The first longcase clocks had hoods which were lifted vertically to gain access to the hands or movement. The slide-up hood moved in wooden grooves on the upper part of the backboard of the case and was locked in position by a spring catch known as a spoon, which had to be depressed to allow the hood to be raised. This was a satisfactory method of fitting the hood when longcase clocks were little more than 6 ft in height, but as the design of clock cases developed their height increased, and towards the end of the 17th century slide-up hoods became inconvenient. The slide-up hood was glazed but had no door, and because the hood had to be slid upwards to wind the clock hinged doors came to be fitted in most instances. JM
See also Spoon fitting.

Hooded clock A type of wall clock [61/4] in which only the movement and dial are enclosed by a hood and the weights and pendulum hang down below. This is a considerable disadvantage as the pendulum may easily be disturbed and stop the clock. Sometimes a lantern clock designed to hang on a hook was provided with a wooden bracket and a wooden hood to act as a dust cover, but most hooded clocks were designed as such. By 1700 they were often made with elaborate marquetry hoods. Most were of the single-hand variety, with simple country-made fruitwood cases, but clocks with minute hands are also known. Hooded clocks continued to be made throughout the 18th century but were eventually replaced by the English dial clock with its eight-day spring-driven fusee movement. JM

Horologium The term was used in medieval manuscripts to denote any sort of timekeeper, were it a weight-driven clock or a water clock or a sundial. Consequently the

4 **Floral clock** near the Sir Adam
Beck Power Plants at Niagara
Falls, Ontario, Canada. This clock
is forty feet in diameter; about
25,000 plants comprise its dial.
The hour and minute hands each
weigh 500 pounds, the seconds
hand 250 pounds.

4

1

1 Hydrogen clock Skeleton movement frame seen through the open enamel dial, zinc ball magazine above and red glass acid container below; designed by Pasquale Andervalt, *c.* 1835. Clockmakers' Company Museum, London.

2 Hour glass clock by Joseph Ives, Plainville, Farmington, Connecticut, *c.* 1840.

3 Impulse clock Movement of an impulse dial showing the electro-magnet coil, armature, pawl and ratchet wheel, and motion train to the hands, *c.* 1930. Private collection.

4 Hooded clock The hood and bracket are later than this lantern-type clock; by William Ball, Bicester, *c.* 1745. Private collection.

2

3

4

researcher has to be wary of the term. The word was also used by the Dutch scientist, Christiaan Huygens, in the title of his work, written in 1658, describing the use of a pendulum to control a clock. EJT

Hour-glass clock A very rare American 30-hour clock movement designed by Joseph Ives, *c.* 1840, mounted in a figure-of-eight shaped laminated wood case of late Empire design. The case was mounted on a base board, flanked on each side by turned columns with finials. A full-length door contained the dial glass and a painted tablet. The brass movement was powered by a horseshoe-shaped thin steel strip, secured inside at the top. Fusee barrels attached to the great wheel arbors of the time, and striking trains had cords to each end of the spring; this may have been the earliest spring-driven Connecticut clock. It is among the few known direct fusee-operated mechanisms, and although the label within the case stated 'patent brass clocks manufactured by Joseph Ives', the specific patent covering features of this movement is unknown. KDR

Hydrogen clock A version of the hydrogen clock, also known as the gas-operated clock, is in the Clockmakers' Company Museum in London; it was designed by Pasquale Andervalt in Italy *c.* 1835. It consists of an open-centred dial exposing the mechanism, with a pin-pallet escapement and ornate gilt pendulum bob, the clock movement being mounted on supports fixed to a large red glass cylinder. Above the movement is a coiled spiral brass tube holding balls of zinc which, as the driving weight nears its lower position, are released one by one to fall into a solution of dilute sulphuric acid in the red glass jar. Hydrogen gas is

generated and the resulting pressure lifts the entire mechanism behind the dial, winding the going weight, the larger of the two visible. The smaller weight is used to maintain the clock in motion whilst the larger is wound, the winding process being quite slow. On completion of the winding the hydrogen gas is released in preparation for the next cycle. These clocks are rare; hydrogen is a most inflammable gas and perhaps the majority have exploded in use. CKA

Impulse clock First invented in the 19th century by Carl August Steinheil of Munich University as a means of indicating time on a number of clocks simultaneously from a central master clock fitted with electrical contacts which allowed pulses of current to flow in a circuit. The impulse clock does not itself keep time but uses the pulses to drive an escapement in reverse, which turns the hands of the clock through a normal train, used as a reduction train only. Steinheil used a pin-wheel escapement rocked by an electromagnet; Daniell cells from England provided the power. About the same time Alexander Bain independently devised several forms of impulse dial; he called his impulse dials 'companion' clocks or 'affiliated' clocks. Victor Reclus of Paris patented the first impulse dial which was locked at all times by two clicks; earlier impulse dials had the disadvantage of being inaccurate in operation by responding to intermittent pulses, or by the minute hand running on two or more spaces for one impulse only. W. E. Palmer, in 1902, and Frank Hope-Jones, later, improved impulse dials so they became completely reliable. George Bennet Bowell invented the first silent type, using a rotary iron armature moved by an electromagnet and locked by a

1 Inclined plane clock Brass, drum-shaped case engraved; ebonised and gilt inclined stand of a later date. Single hand movement with a circular silvered metal chapter ring. Probably French, *c.* 1685. British Museum, London.

2 Incense clock, Japanese koban dokei, top and base with utensils, cover, ash receptacle, grid, rake, turn-table and tamper. Silvio A. Bedini, Washington, D.C.

3 Inro clock showing the open *inro* case and key compartment in the lid. The scaphe sundial on the left is the *netsuki* for this *inro*.

2

3

permanent magnet system, first marketed *c.* 1906. Modern impulse dials differ only in the style of dial and case; the mechanism is virtually unchanged from the earlier ones. CKA

See also Master clock.

Incense clock, Chinese The most primitive incense clock is a graded incense (joss) stick; the time elapsed is registered by the speed at which the trail of incense is consumed. Powdered incense was formed into a stick of hardened paste and graded for hour intervals. In the T'ang dynasty (618–907) references to an 'incense seal' refer either to a block of incense imprinted with hour characters in the seal style of calligraphy, burned in an incense basin, or to a method of forming a seal character with powdered incense that was burned in an incense basin.

There are three common types of post-16th century incense seals. All consist of a metal base, tray for the ash bed and powdered incense, perforated grid pattern (the seal), and perforated cover. The utensils include a tamper and a small shovel, stored in the base which insulates the burner. A bed of wood ash is put into the tray and tamped. The grid is placed on the ash and the sharp end of the shovel traces the path of the grid. Powdered incense is placed in the groove and smoothed. The grid is removed and small bamboo pegs, each stamped with an hour character, are placed at regular intervals along the incense track. The seal is then covered with the perforated lid to protect the incense from draughts, and the incense is ignited. The types are: the single seal, round, square or rectangular; the double square seal having two trays and two different seal grids stacked one on top of the other; and the Ju'i sceptre, in the shape of the ancient sacred mushroom.

A rarer type is the dragon vessel, of bronze or lacquered wood, lined with pewter and fitted with V-shaped wire

racks to hold an incense stick. Strings with metal weights at each end were suspended perpendicular to the body at regular intervals, or at one place only, depending on the specific use; when the heat from the burning incense ignited the string, the balls fell into a metal platter over which the dragon was suspended. The resulting clatter served as an alarm for a light sleeper. MCR

Incense clock, Japanese The Japanese, like the Chinese, used graded joss sticks as the basic method of incense timekeeping; the charge for a geisha's time was in terms of half-hour incense sticks. Incense seals in Japan were solid cubes of hardwood with the seal character carved into the top in a square groove to a depth and width of $\frac{1}{4}$ in. Powdered incense was placed in the groove and burned along it.

The *Ji koban* was essentially a large free-standing incense trail in a wooden container with time plates of various materials inserted at regular intervals to mark the hours. The *koban dokei*, in principle, was the same as the Chinese seals or the *Ji koban*. A trail of incense was laid out on a bed of ash in a container; in this case the grid was a simple one that rotated a quarter turn, four times, so the seal formed was that for the 'heart of Buddha'. Small hour markers were laid out at intervals and timekeeping proceeded with the burning of the incense. MCR

Inclined plane clock These clocks were mostly made in the 17th century. The movement was housed in a drum-shaped canister that rolled down a slope; rewinding was effected by placing the clock at the top of the slope again. Sometimes the edges of the slope were marked off in seven-day intervals so the position of the clock could also indicate the day of the week. The clock mechanism contained a heavy weight which, in association with wheel train and escapement, controlled the tendency of the clock to roll down the slope. The time was indicated by a fixed single hand, kept in equilibrium by the weight of the mechanism and the heavy weight working against each other. The idea appears to have been revived by a Dutchman named Isaac Jones Drielsma, working in Liverpool *c.* 1835, but his plans for producing the clocks in quantity were not fulfilled. EJT *See also* Gravity clock.

Inro clock *Inro* were small, rectangular lacquered wood or metal cases in which Japanese gentlemen carried their necessities, attached to the *obi* (sash) by a silken rope. Usually they had four compartments, but when a clock movement was put into one, the case was unsegmented. *Inro* clocks are small and might be classed as watches, but the design of the movement is similar to that of small Japanese clocks. The clock was usually the simple verge variety with a balance wheel and a revolving chapter ring. It was a self-contained unit that slipped in and out of the *inro* case, which usually had a compartment in the lid for the key. MCR

Interval timer There are two main forms of interval timers. The earlier was devised by Matthäus Hipp, Charles Wheatstone and others for measuring small intervals of time. A clockwork mechanism, controlled by a reed, is started and stopped electrically to measure a particular interval. Bashforth's chronograph of 1865 was used to measure the time of flight of projectiles; modern versions are electronically operated. The other form is a clockwork mechanism which, after a set period of time, sounds a bell or buzzer. It is popular for kitchen operations, telephone calls, car parking and so on. These timers may be incorporated in other equipment, e.g. in an electric oven for starting and stopping a period of cooking, and are also much used in industry for timing processes automatically. CKA

Iron clock The mechanism of the earliest clocks was of iron, forged in the case of turret clocks, cut cold with a file in the case of smaller clocks. Iron used in early days was wrought, produced by smelting ore and flux in a furnace,

then hammering the slag out of the soft, but not molten mass that resulted. Such iron contained many impurities and could only be improved by repeated heating and hammering. About 1500 the blast furnace was invented, the higher temperature of which melted the ore and flux; the product could then be cast. Although hard it was brittle, but with the addition of a little carbon it became steel. In earlier days steel was produced by continually hammering wrought iron which had been brought into contact with carbon at a high temperature. The difficulties of preparing brass were overcome in the second half of the 16th century, when brass began to be used extensively in horology.

Lord Grimthorpe considered cast iron suitable for turret-clock wheels, and during the 19th century the material was used for clock cases, particularly in the United States. EJT

Iron-front clock The earliest American cast-iron clock case was a round Gothic which appeared in 1852, painted black and inlaid with mother-of-pearl. This was a less expensive imitation of the then popular papier-mâché. Increasing numbers of designs for mantel clock front cases of cast iron or bronze appeared after 1856. These remained popular until 1875, but were almost entirely discontinued thereafter. Nicholas Muller of New York was granted several design patents for such case fronts. During this period of approximately 20 years, trade catalogues illustrated over 125 styles of bronze and 65 designs of cast-iron clock fronts. Most were a hideous form of rococo art of the period, with trade names like Lattice, Wide Awake, Vine Gothic, Alhambra, Bird's Nest, Ceres, and Renaissance. KDR

Jacks In early times cities employed a watchman who struck the hours of day and night upon a bell; sometimes he wore armour. With the introduction of clocks and a more peaceful regime the watchman's job was mechanised. He was represented as a model, often in armour. Through the striking mechanism of the clock his arms moved to raise a club or axe to strike the bell. Sometimes jacks appeared in pairs and struck the quarters.

4 Interval timer Modern English timer for recording up to two hours; the time of interval required is set by pressing the top right lever, which starts the clock and winds the alarm.

5 Iron-front clock Eight-day, spring-driven mantel clock with a painted and gilded cast-iron front; made by the American Clock Company, *c.* 1865. American Clock & Watch Museum, Bristol, Connecticut.

4

5

The name is supposed to have been derived from 'jaccomachiardus', a man in armour, or 'jacquemart' – the name 'jacques' plus 'marteau' (hammer). It may even have been derived from the simple word 'jack', meaning a piece of apparatus such as a bootjack or roasting jack.

Jacks can be seen in Britain at St Mary Steps church in Exeter, Wells Cathedral, Wimborne Minster, Rye Church in Sussex, All Saints Church in Leicester, York Minster and many other churches. Among the most celebrated European jacks are those at Dijon. The Dijon clock was traditionally captured from Kortrijk in Flanders in 1382, and some extra jacks have been added to the original one. Another famous pair of jacks are the Moors on the campanile of St Mark's in Venice.

Domestic clocks have sometimes been provided with jacks; examples are known in both the Gothic type of clock and the Renaissance clock with gilded outer case. Some Black Forest clocks in the early 19th century had a little stage above the dial where two small contemporary figures sounded the quarters and a larger one the hours. DFN/EJT *See also* Automata clock.

Jackwork, carousel Jackwork comprising one or more horizontally rotating wheels or platforms carrying puppets which circulate around a vertical axis. They are used for displaying written time announcements in medieval Chinese astronomical clock towers and decoratively in later western public clocks. JHC

Japanese bell clock Japanese bell clocks are spring-driven lantern movements in a temple-bell case. Balance wheels and fully developed rotating dials indicate that these clocks are of the late period, after the middle of the 18th century. The mechanism is inside the bell and the dial in its mouth. Such clocks were hard to read, as they sat on legs going through the dial. It may be, however, that the striking of the temple bell was the over-riding purpose of these clocks and that the dial only served to activate the strike and adjust the length of the hours for the season. MCR

Japanning A pseudo-oriental form of decoration simulating Chinese or Japanese lacquer work. Because of the demand for oriental lacquer cabinets all over Europe in the late 17th century, a process was devised, using paint and varnish, to imitate the much harder, more durable, oriental lacquer. In 1688 two London craftsmen, John Stalker and George Parker, published *A Treatise of Japaning and Varnishing, Being a compleat Discovery of those Arts...*, which described a method for imitating lacquer and decorating woodwork with gilded scenes of oriental life and landscape in relief. Japanning was extensively employed for decorating longcase clocks throughout much of the 18th century. Black with low-relief gilded decoration was the most popular form, but other colours like red and blue were often used. The drawback of japanned work was that in time the surface became covered with fine cracks, like an old painting. JM

Jockele clock The usual size for the movement of a Black Forest clock is about $6\frac{1}{4}$ in. high, $4\frac{1}{4}$ in. broad and $5\frac{1}{2}$ in. deep. About 1760 a smaller version was made nicknamed

1

Schottenuhr, and about 1790 Jakob Herbstreith of Hinterzarten near Neustadt produced the *Jockele* which is even smaller, measuring about $3\frac{1}{4}$ in. high, $2\frac{3}{8}$ in. broad and $1\frac{1}{4}$ in. deep. EJT

Keyless rack clock *See* Rack clock.

Kitchen clock From *c.*1890 several models of kitchen mantel clocks were mass-produced in the United States. They had cases of oak, embossed with various decorative designs and highly varnished. Properly finished wood was withdrawn from a kiln and placed under a press where metal dies imparted various configurative impressions to the surface. The sash material for the doors was similarly embossed by running the wood through metal rollers. The usual dial size was 6 in. diameter. A door frame enclosed the dial, movement, wire strike gong and pendulum, and contained a single glass. The part of this glass, below the dial was decorated with various designs applied by a special printing technique in bronze or silver gilt. These kitchen clocks were produced by the million and sold for between four and six dollars. Most homes throughout the United States had at least one, usually kept in the kitchen. The inexpensive movements could readily be cleaned and many of them ran satisfactorily for 50 years or more. KDR

Label The practice of inserting a printed paper label within a clock by the maker or retailer may have developed from a similar, earlier usage among American cabinetmakers. Early labels were printed from engraved plates, after 1800 from type. Printed labels were used by the Willards at Boston and Eli Terry and others in Connecticut before 1812, but increasing competition among clock manufacturers led to the almost universal introduction of labels, 12 in. by 10 in., pasted inside the backboard of cases. Originally it may have been the intention of Terry to protect his patent clock by the label, but it soon became an important advertising technique. Between 1825 and 1835 almost a standard format was available from several Connecticut printers. The centre panel denoted the type of clock, the maker or seller and his location, and almost always added 'warranted, if well used'. Although many labels denoted

1 **Label** A manufacturer's paper label from a looking-glass clock; by Williams, Orton, Preston's & Co., Farmington, Connecticut, 1840.

2 **Jacks** on a table clock, the movement of which is seen out of its case; the jacks strike the bell; English or German, *c.* 1540. British Museum, London.

3 **Jack** at Southwold, Suffolk. This wooden jack has been cleaned to reveal its original colours; 15th century.

4 **Jack** which kicks two bells and strikes a third bell at the hours and quarters. Said to be the oldest jack in England and known as 'Jack Blandifer'; north transept, Wells Cathedral, Somerset.

5 **Jockele clock** with enamelled dial set in a porcelain front, decorated in coloured enamels; fitted with alarm. Black Forest, *c.* 1870.

6 **Lancet clock** Mantel clock of lancet shape, mahogany with inlaid decoration; French movement. An early 20th-century English 'reproduction' style case. Private collection.

7 **Japanning** A red lacquer, or 'japanned' longcase clock; by John Vyse, Wisbech, Cambridgeshire, *c.* 1745. Wisbech Museum.

2

3

4

5

6

7

makers of clocks, the majority were inserted by business entrepreneurs who purchased movements and cases in the wholesale market and had the labels printed to assist sales. The use of smaller printed paper labels continued throughout the 19th century. KDR

Lacquer A decorative process used by oriental craftsmen from ancient times. The material used was a resinous gum obtained from the lac tree, which was coloured and applied to the object to be decorated in numerous layers. Each layer was allowed to dry and was then rubbed down before the next was applied. A variety of colours were used, black and red being the most popular, but also blue, green and yellow. The surface of the lacquer was usually decorated with gilded oriental motifs in low relief. During the 18th century, when Chinese art was exported to Europe, lacquer cabinets

were much sought after, and the process was imitated by the European technique of japanning. Panels, screens and doors of European manufactured cabinets were sometimes sent east to be lacquered by Chinese craftsmen, and occasionally the long narrow doors of the trunks of longcase clocks were treated in this way. JM
See also Japanning.

Lancet clock A type of longcase or bracket clock with a case shaped at the top in the form of a pointed Gothic arch. This design is encountered during the early 19th century in England and continued into the reign of Queen Victoria. It is typical of other domestic furnishing of the late Gothic Revival and often included the decoration of the mahogany or rosewood veneered case with inlaid classical ornament and stringing in brass. JM

1 **Lantern clock, Japanese,** with double foliots, one adjusted for the six night hours and the other for the six day hours, the change-over taking place automatically from the striking train; the varying lengths of hours are adjusted by the foliot weights; an alarm is also incorporated. Science Museum, London.

2 **Light clock,** which is powered by light falling on the photo-electric cell on the top of the clock to keep the battery charged. Modern, by Kienzle of Germany. Science Museum, London. Private collection.

3 **Lighthouse clock** fitted with alarm; by Simon Willard, Roxbury, Massachusetts, 1819–30. Henry Francis du Pont Winterthur Museum, Winterthur, Delaware.

4 **Longcase clock** in a kingwood or cocuswood case; three-train movement; the only recorded longcase clock by Samuel Knibb, c.1670.

5 **Longcase clock** veneered in mulberry wood, standing 8ft 2in. high, month movement with calendar; by Thomas Tompion, London, c.1700. British Museum, London.

6 **Longcase clock** in mahogany, English north-country style; by Robert Lawson, Leigh, c.1775. Private collection.

7 **Longcase clock** in mahogany with painted dial and musical movement; by James Condliff, Liverpool, 1820. Merseyside County Museum, Liverpool.

Lantern clock So called because of its frame's resemblance to a lantern. Other names have been used, including Cromwellian and bedpost clock, the former because the bell at the top suggested a Cromwellian helmet and the latter because of the four turned columns at each corner of the frame. The lantern clock was developed in England with similar versions in other countries, during the 17th century, and superseded the wrought-iron wall clock. Originally it was designed to hang from a hook on the wall, and early specimens still retain their iron hook rings and distance spurs. The spurs were fitted into the rear pendant 'feet' to permit the clock to hang vertically and to allow space for the pendulum, which was adapted to lantern clocks by Ahasuerus Fromanteel I just before 1660. Previously, a large wrought-iron balance was the only form of escapement employed, and it was notoriously inaccurate. Verge escapements with short bob pendulums were used for lantern-clock movements until well into the 18th century, but with the introduction of the long 'royal' pendulum with a one-second beat, many conversions were carried out. About the time of these conversions lantern clocks were

often arranged to stand on wooden wall brackets. With only a few exceptions, the lantern clock was fitted with one hand, but sometimes there was also an alarm mechanism [69/4]. JM

Lantern clock, Japanese Lantern clocks were the first type produced by the Japanese to imitate European clocks. Other styles of clocks were developed, but the lantern remained the standard for large clocks until 1873. The Japanese usually substituted two ropes and weights, one for each train, for the single rope and weight for both trains commonly found on contemporary European lantern clocks. Notched, weighted foliots or balance wheels with verge escapements were the common method of governing the rate. Seasonal adjustments for varying hour lengths were made by moving the weights on the notched foliots (single or double), or, on balance-wheel clocks, by moving the adjustable hour indicators. Single and double window calendars appear in the 18th century, and late clocks have turned corner pillars. The construction of Japanese houses usually prevented lantern clocks from being hung on the

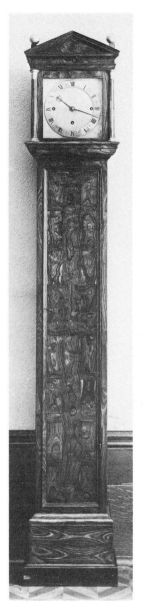

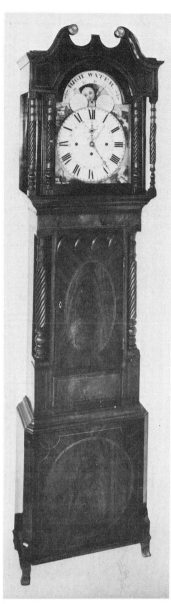

4   5   6   7

walls, so they were frequently placed in a wood and glass hood on top of a pyramidal or table stand which enclosed the weights. Some lantern clocks, usually small ones, were put into wall bracket cases suspended from a support column. MCR

Light clock In 1960 Patek Philippe, a Geneva-based firm, marketed a clock to rival the Atmos clock for perpetuance of motion. Housed in a variety of case styles, the clock has a transparent panel on the top of the case which allows light to fall upon a photocell, this generating electrical power when the light intensity is sufficiently high. A delicate electric motor transforms this power into mechanical motion, which is used to wind up the mainspring of a conventional mechanical movement fitted with a lever escapement, the clock being of the highest quality. Four hours of illumination with natural or artificial light is sufficient to give 24 hours of spring reserve of going, and higher levels of illumination give a more rapid rate of winding. When fully wound, the mainspring can power the clock for three days without further exposure to light. CKA

Lighthouse clock A form of American case, modelled on the famous Eddystone lighthouse at Plymouth, one of the earliest in England. It was introduced by Simon Willard *c.* 1822, and contained an eight-day, weight-operated, alarm-timepiece movement under a glass dome. The movement was a development from a patent granted to Willard in 1819 for an alarm attachment. A few lighthouse clocks had provision for striking once each hour. The case was generally of mahogany, frequently embellished with decorative cast-brass trimmings and feet. The design was not, apparently, successful and it was only manufactured in small numbers. There are less than 25 known examples in existence. KDR

Longcase clock This domestic clock first appeared in England shortly after the Restoration of 1660, about the same time as longcases appeared in Europe. At first it was less than 7 ft high, with ebonised case, architectural hood, gilded ormolu mounts and a narrow trunk. Early brass dials were about 9 in. square; later, the case was made wider to accommodate the long 'royal' pendulum which superseded

1 Longcase clock, Dutch (staande klok), with three-day 'staartklok' movement; by A. van Oostrom, Amsterdam, c.1725.

2 Longcase clock, Dutch, with marquetry decoration and square dial; by J. van Brussel, Amsterdam, early 18th century.

3 Longcase clock, Dutch, from the East Netherlands, showing neighbouring German influence; enamelled dial; by I. Rathmer, Wenterswik, 1800. Stedilijk Museum, Zutphen.

4 Lantern clock converted from verge to anchor escapement; signed 'John Peacock and Henry Stevens', dated 1680. Merseyside County Museum, Liverpool.

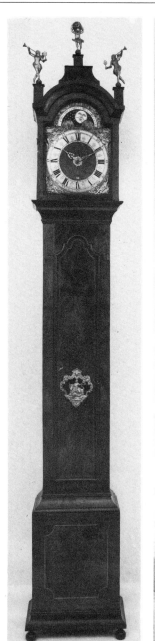
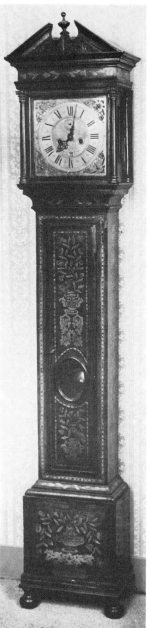
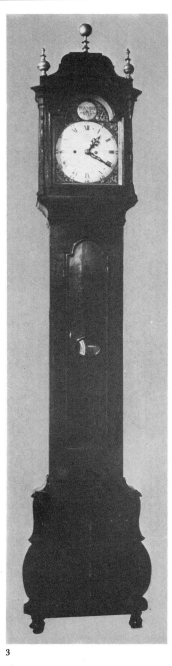

1   2   3

the short bob pendulum, c. 1675. Cases then became taller and wider until the appearance of the elephantine cases of provincial clocks of the early 19th century. All longcase clocks had brass dials until the introduction of the painted dial, c. 1770. Casework, in keeping with other furniture fashions, made use of marquetry and walnut veneer until the introduction of mahogany, c. 1735. Satinwood was used in the Adam period and rosewood during the Regency, though oak was retained for the cheaper type of clock throughout the era.

Certain characteristics are useful in estimating a date of manufacture. Convex mouldings under the hood were fashionable until c. 1700, when they were replaced by hollow mouldings; a lenticle dates a clock to c. 1675–1725; the arch dial and arched door appeared c. 1725. In early longcase clocks, architectural columns were attached to the hood doors, but shortly before 1750 the columns became free-standing. The first longcase clocks had pedimented

hoods which, after 1680, gradually gave way to flat-top hoods ornamented with carved wood cherub-head crestings. These were of short duration and a cushion top was in favour from the late 17th century until the advent of the hollow pediment, c. 1730, and the swan-neck or broken pediment later in the century. The so-called pagoda top, in keeping with furniture in Chinese style, was introduced in the 1740s. JM

Longcase clock, Dutch (staande klok) Amsterdam was the most important centre for the making of longcase clocks in Holland, principally because it had become an important commercial centre by the second quarter of the 18th century. The first longcase clocks made in the Netherlands, c. 1680, were probably in imitation of English examples. The older types of Dutch longcase clock have square dials, while their plinths are flat on all surfaces [68/1], [68/2].

4

1 Longcase clock, Italian, of
English/Dutch influence; made in
Venice by Casparo Astori, *c.* 1720.
Private collection.

1

2 Lyre clock, wall-hanging, with painted tablets; eight-day, weight-driven movement; early 19th century.

2

1

1 Marquetry detail of decoration from a walnut longcase clock by Michael Knight, London, *c.*1700. Lady Lever Art Gallery, Port Sunlight.

2, 3 Longcase clock, Dutch, illustrating French influence; by Frans van Leeuwen, Haarlem, *c.*1780. Gemeentemuseum, The Hague.

4 Longcase clock, Dutch, from the South Netherlands, showing Liégeois influence; by Jacobus Schoufs, Thorn, *c.*1750.

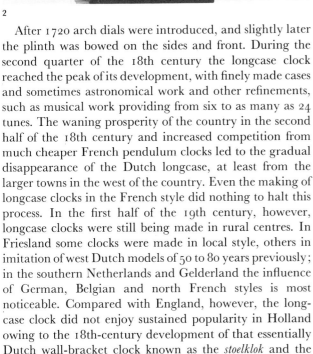

2

3

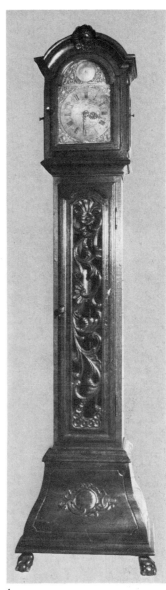

4

After 1720 arch dials were introduced, and slightly later the plinth was bowed on the sides and front. During the second quarter of the 18th century the longcase clock reached the peak of its development, with finely made cases and sometimes astronomical work and other refinements, such as musical work providing from six to as many as 24 tunes. The waning prosperity of the country in the second half of the 18th century and increased competition from much cheaper French pendulum clocks led to the gradual disappearance of the Dutch longcase, at least from the larger towns in the west of the country. Even the making of longcase clocks in the French style did nothing to halt this process. In the first half of the 19th century, however, longcase clocks were still being made in rural centres. In Friesland some clocks were made in local style, others in imitation of west Dutch models of 50 to 80 years previously; in the southern Netherlands and Gelderland the influence of German, Belgian and north French styles is most noticeable. Compared with England, however, the longcase clock did not enjoy sustained popularity in Holland owing to the 18th-century development of that essentially Dutch wall-bracket clock known as the *stoelklok* and the equally Dutch 19th-century *staartklok*, with anchor escapement and long pendulum. JLS

See also Friesland clocks; Friesland and Groningen clocks.

Longcase clock, Italian Between the 17th and 19th centuries in Italy, as in other countries, domestic clocks were made to be placed either on brackets or shelves, or to stand on the floor. Many craftsmen made clocks of the latter kind, with movements much like those of English lantern clocks but generally in much simpler cases. The finest examples were made in Emilio and Bologna during the 18th century, with Carlo Maria Fiorini, Binaldo Gandolfi, and Guiseppe and Filippo Bellei in Modena, the most prominent makers [70/1].

Although the clocks were more functional than decorative, they were noticeable for their elegance of form. Fine brass dials, generally with delicate engraving, brass feet and mouldings, finely made movements and sometimes an almost eccentric brilliance in the solution of problems of striking, were all characteristic. Movements usually consisted of two main horizontal plates of iron, four pillars in iron or brass at the corners and vertical brass strips to

1 Mains clock Synchronous electric clock; made by Everett, Edgcumbe & Co. Ltd. under the trade name 'SYNCLOCK', *c.* 1931. Science Museum, London.

2 Looking-glass clock in a reeded-column, scroll-top case; by Merriman, Birge & Co., Bristol, Connecticut, *c.* 1822.

3 Maltese clock in a painted, carved and gilded wooden case, with alarm. Weight-driven with pendulum aperture; 19th century.

1   2   3

support the trains. In the upper part were one or more bells, with generally a decorative moulding on the upper one. AL

Looking-glass clock Joseph Ives received letters patent in March 1822 for incorporating a looking glass as a major part of the design of a clock case. But a letter written in 1830 to Samuel Terry of Bristol, Connecticut, by Aaron Willard Jr, indicated that Willard had used looking glasses in clock cases during the previous 25 years, and others had used them earlier than that.

Perhaps more famous than the looking-glass clocks of Joseph Ives were the bronze looking-glass cases introduced by Chauncey Jerome after 1827. Following the Ives wall clocks, several Bristol firms used looking glasses in a modified reeded-column, scroll-top, shelf-clock case between 1820 and 1824. In triple-decker clocks looking glasses were often used for either the middle or the lower frame rather than a decorative tablet. Many cases of bevel and ogee styles with 30-hour wood or brass weight movements were furnished with looking glasses in the lower door panel. KDR
See also Bronze looking-glass clock.

Lyre clock An American wall timepiece, somewhat similar in appearance to the banjo, but with its centre portion lyre-shaped, generally made of mahogany. It frequently has acanthus leaves coarsely carved on the centre panel, a base piece below the framed or panelled door and ornamental figure or finial on top. This design, attributed to Aaron Willard Jr (nephew of Simon), was introduced soon after 1823. The most prolific maker was John Sawin of the firm of Sawin & Dyer, Boston, in 1822–8. Some cases were

entirely gilded and some had solid wood panels rather than painted or gilded glasses. On rare occasions both lyre and banjo wall clocks were made as strikers, with two weights running within the centre portion. A few were made outside the Boston area, in New Hampshire [71/2]. KDR
See also Banjo clock.

Mains clock At one time this term would have been applied to one kind of clock only, the synchronous electric clock. The synchronous electric clock is not strictly a true clock; it has an electric motor synchronised to the frequency of the public power supply with a reduction train to give a time indication. Today there are electric clocks driven from the main power supply which count the number of electrical oscillations and display a time indication based on the total elapsed. Again, these are not clocks as there is no self-contained time measuring device, and they are connected to the mains principally to use the frequency as a time source. The greatest disadvantage of the mains clock is that it must be connected to the mains supply by an electric lead from a suitable power point. Alternating current supplies with strict frequency control are necessary for accurate time indication. CKA

Maltese clock The Italian altar clock died out in the early 18th century, but the general design was revived in the early 19th century in the island of Malta. The pioneer is believed to have been Kalcidoniju Pisani in the village of Siggiewi; he was followed by others in the same village and in the village of Zebbug. The design differs from its prototype in that the Maltese clock hangs on the wall instead of standing on a table, but the size and shape are

4 Marble clock Heavy French 'marble' mantel clock with gilded mounts; late 19th century. Private collection.

5 Lyre clock in mahogany case with eight-day movement; by Curtis & Dunning, Concord, Massachusetts, c. 1820. Old Sturbridge Village, Sturbridge, Massachusetts.

6 Marblised clock Ansonia shelf clock with black enamelled case; brass, eight-day spring-driven movement with strike, c. 1884. Fond du Lac Historical Society, Wisconsin.

5

4

6

similar, though the case has been simplified and the decoration is of painting and gilding, the dial being decorated with flower designs. A small aperture allows the pendulum to be seen. The clocks are weight-driven with the lines carried over a pulley; some have a double pulley with a heavier weight for a longer going period. The escapement is at the bottom of the movement as in the altar clocks. Early examples possessed an hour hand only; late ones had minute hands also. Alarm work is known but striking clocks are rare. EJT
See also Altar clock.

Mantel clock A clock designed to stand on a mantel shelf, above a fireplace. Whereas bracket clocks were portable, mantel clocks were designed to remain in one place; consequently, carrying handles were not included and many mantel clocks are extremely heavy. Their introduction reflected the availability and popularisation of clocks as permanent room furnishings in the 19th century. In North America the term 'shelf clock' is normally used to describe the type; French ones are known as *pendules de cheminée*. AS
See also Shelf clock.

Marble clock A generic term applied to a type of clock first manufactured in France towards the end of the 19th century. While true marble has long been used for clock cases, the so-called 'marble' clock has a case made mainly from slate with a high surface polish. These cases are very heavy and provide great stability to pendulum clocks; this, combined with their excellent movements, gives long and satisfactory timekeeping. Ornamentation with true marble

may be found in elaborate cases, combined with gilt metal pillars and medallions. One disadvantage of slate is its tendency to chip. It is dangerous to lift marble clocks except by the base, for the case may break apart under its own weight. The surface polish is easily damaged by water and is very difficult to restore. Recently despised, these clocks are now rapidly appreciating in value. CKA

Marblised clocks A decline in solid walnut, popular in the United States between 1870 and 1885, resulted in the introduction of many styles of black marble and onyx clocks, inlaid and engraved, frequently with gilded bronze ornaments. Some of these case materials were imported from France and Brazil. The black marble was soon imitated in enamelled cast iron. In 1880 the Seth Thomas Clock Co. patented a process of impregnating and baking a finish on wood, simulating marble, which was called 'adamantine'. Other clockmakers developed similar processes, and imitation marble clocks, today known as 'blacks', followed; they were popular mantel clocks until c. 1914. The E. Ingraham Co. noted in their 1897 trade catalogue: 'Our Imitation French Marble Clocks are a reproduction of the French designs in wood, HIGHLY POLISHED, nicely engraved and gilted. We guarantee the finish on these cases to stand equal to any iron case on the market...' This period of degeneration of American art as applied to clock cases was only equalled by the oak kitchen clocks of 1890–1920. KDR

Marine clock A clock designed for use on board ship. Usually such clocks are of good quality, have a jewelled and adjusted lever escapement of platform type, and run for

1 Marine clock, brass-cased with eight-day lever movement; centre seconds hand missing; *c*.1900. Private collection.

2 False, or mock pendulum Detail from a bracket clock by William Tomlinson, London, *c*.1710. University of Liverpool.

3 Master clock A conventional weight-driven clock which controls the sending of an electric pulse every minute to impulse clock dials; patented by Fischer of Zurich in 1900 and known in the U.K. as the magneta clock. Science Museum, London.

4 Master clock in which the pendulum rotates a count wheel, making electrical contact every minute, providing pulses for subsidiary impulse dials, and also impulse to maintain pendulum through a flat spring; patented by M. A. and H. Campiche, 1893–9. Science Museum, London.

5 Massachusetts shelf clock (case-on-case) Lower case accommodates the weights; made by Elnethan Taber, Roxbury, Massachusetts, *c*.1810. Old Sturbridge Village, Sturbridge, Massachusetts.

6 Mirror clock, eight-day movement; by A. Chandler, Concord, New Hampshire, U.S.A., *c*.1835.

7 Mirror clock A unique New Hampshire example showing normal time and strike, seconds, day of the week, month and alarm; the only one known with these indications, the movement partially shown through a skeletonised dial. Made by David French, New Ipswich, New Hampshire, *c*.1825. New Hampshire Historical Society, Concord, New Hampshire.

1

2

3

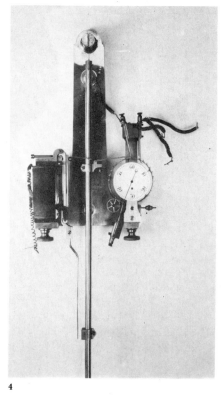

4

eight days. Though the great majority are timepieces only, many are equipped with striking trains which sound ship's bells, i.e., one at 12.30, two at 1.00, etc., thus striking eight bells at 12, 4, and 8 o'clock. Being exposed to the corrosive influence of sea air, the cases are generally of solid construction in cast bronze or marine brass, with the bezel threaded on or a gasket seal to keep out moisture. They are equipped with second hands, are good timekeepers but are not to be confused with marine chronometers. Having lever movements, they are not affected to any great degree by ship motion. DJB
See also Chronometer.

Marquetry A form of surface decoration used in cabinetwork in England from *c*. 1675 to *c*. 1725, and revived in the Adam period, *c*. 1770. Used much earlier on the Continent. A number of sheets of different coloured veneers were pinned together and a pattern was pricked through paper on to the top veneer. The pattern was then cut out with a type of fretsaw known as a 'markatree cutter's

donkey'. The various pieces were rearranged like a jigsaw puzzle to give as many designs of contrasting coloured woods as there were sheets of veneer. A sheet of paper was then pasted over each arrangement to hold the pieces together and the whole was glued on to the cabinet front, clock case or wherever the marquetry was required. In England there were three types of marquetry: the bird and flower patterns contained in panels of boxwood stringing, all-over flowered patterns, and the all-over patterns of finely worked scrolls and arabesques known as 'seaweed' marquetry [72/1]. JM
See also Boulle work.

Massachusetts shelf clock (case-on-case) Both Simon and Aaron Willard made 30-hour wall clocks cased in two sections in Grafton, Massachusetts. The upper portion with dial rested on feet on a separate lower section which contained the pendulum. A similar design, introduced by the Willards before 1802, developed into the case-on-case style. Basically, this was an English bracket case above and

5   6   7

a large supporting base to contain the pendulum and weights below. This style became popular during the 1820s; examples display both Sheraton and Hepplewhite influence, many with inlaid lower panels and kidney-shaped dial doors. Decorative glass panels, both gilded and painted, were popular later, often with dished (concave) dials. Pendulum lengths for these timepieces ranged from $7\frac{1}{2}$ to 24 in. Besides being popular with Boston and other Massachusetts makers, such styles were produced by several New Hampshire clockmakers. KDR

Master clock All time distribution systems must have an accurate controlling clock. Carl August Steinheil, who first applied electricity to time distribution, used the term 'central' clock; Alexander Bain later referred to the 'parent' clock, where in England the term 'master' clock would be used for the central clock which supplies accurately controlled current pulses to the circuit of controlled or impulse dial clocks. The first master clock capable of combining both functions was devised by Steinheil in 1839, Bain's following a little later. It was not until 1895 when Frank Hope-Jones and George Bennet Bowell invented the synchronome clock, or remontoire, that electric master clocks became absolutely reliable, their clock sending out current pulses at half-minute intervals. Many other makers devised similar clocks later, but the synchronome was the most successful. Modern master clocks are of the quartz-crystal type and have electronic circuits generating the current pulses to drive the impulse dials. CKA
See also Impulse clock; Slave clock.

Mirror clock A term used almost exclusively in connection with New Hampshire wall clocks cased in frames with split columns on all four sides, usually with corner blocks mounted with brass rosettes, and containing a looking-glass front and decorated dial glass. The period of their popularity was 1825–38. They were eight-day, both strikers and timepieces, all weight-operated. While a few were made in adjacent Massachusetts and Maine, the majority were confined to New Hampshire. Benjamin Morril of Boscawen may have been the earliest to use this form of case, *c.* 1825. Perhaps no other place in America developed such unconventional styles of clock movements, some of which have become known as 'wheelbarrow', 'rat-trap striker' and 'fly-wheel striker'. KDR

Mock pendulum A small secondary pendulum bob attached to the real pendulum arbor, which appears in a segmental aperture on the dials of some 18th-century verge bracket clocks. It showed that the clock was going and enabled it to be started or stopped without opening the door; it also gave the clock a lively appearance. Mock or false pendulum bobs are usually small, about $\frac{1}{2}$ in. in diameter. JM

Monastery clock Monasteries in the Middle Ages, required to hold services at certain hours of the day and night, originally used water clocks to indicate the time. Later, simple verge escapement mechanical clocks with alarm work were made, and although these are now rare illustrations of them have been preserved in tarsia panels from Italy, one of which is in the Victoria and Albert Museum, London [78/1]. This shows the clock in a cupboard with a square hole cut below it for the weight cords to descend, and casts light on an item in the records of Battle Abbey, Sussex, in 1512, 'For repairing the clock in the Cubiculo of the Sacristy XXd'. EJT

1   2   3

Monastic alarm clocks, Italian In the late 15th and early 16th centuries, the art of pictorial marquetry or inlay work was widespread in Italy as a decoration for studies, other rooms and monastic choir stalls; a fair number of these marquetry pictures show clocks, almost always of the type known as monastic alarm clocks. The oldest of these panels is from the *studiolo* of Duke Federigo da Montefeltro at Urbino and was made *c.* 1475. It is a particularly clear picture, and shows nearly all the main characteristics of this type of clock. The simple structural framework is kept at a distance from the wall against which it is standing. The train has three wheels, of which the main one has four crossings and carries the winding drum, there being two cords, one for winding and the other for the weight. The escape wheel has a lantern pinion, and the arrangement for striking the alarm consists of a simple winding drum which, when released, vibrates a vertical verge-type arbor to shake a platform which holds a bell. The clock dial is of the rotating, 24-hour type with Roman figures, and has a series of holes in its edge in which a pin is placed to free the alarm as required. The foliot is S-shaped and has two small weights to regulate the period of oscillation.

Later marquetry pictures show clocks which are not unlike this. The structure is of iron or brass and always very simple; occasionally, wood is used in parts of the structure. The train has two or three wheels, and the dial always rotates through 24 hours; the time controller is of the foliot or balance type. Few clocks of this kind have survived. Two in private collections in Italy [78/3] are comparatively well known. The first, completely in brass, is in the High Gothic style with three wheels, a circular balance and a catherine-wheel alarm. It also has a mechanism, now almost entirely missing, with which it could strike a single blow at regular intervals, presumably every hour. It can be dated about the middle of the 15th century. The second, of iron and brass, is late 15th century, and has an alarm of the oscillating type and a foliot regulator [81/3]. AL

Monstrance clock A monstrance is a vessel used in the Roman Catholic Church to display the consecrated bread; clocks are known made in a shape similar to that of this receptacle. The movement is placed in a drum supported

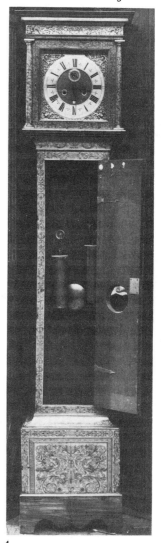

4   5

by a stand and is of the type usually found as a horizontal table clock. Astronomical work is normally provided and the quality of these clocks altogether is high. The period of manufacture was from the mid 16th to the mid 17th century, and Augsburg was probably the origin of the type. EJT

1 Monastic alarm clock, Italian A marquetry panel made in 1475 shows an early Italian monastic alarm; from the study of Duke Federigo da Montefeltro. Victoria & Albert Museum, London.

2 Monastic clock A marquetry panel showing an early Italian clock of the 16th century. Church of S. Domenico, Bologna.

3 Monastic clock Brass-framed early Italian alarum, with steel pinions and balance control; 15th century.

4 Month clock Longcase clock with door open to show the large weights; by Peter King, Long Acre, London, c.1710. Lady Lever Art Gallery, Port Sunlight.

5 Musical clock Longcase clock with automata and musical movement; signed 'P. J. van Bockstael, Rexpoede', late 18th century. Bowes Museum, Barnard Castle.

6 Monstrance clock of square form, gilded brass with silver ornament and silver and enamel dial; Augsburg, south Germany, early 17th century. Uhrensammlung Kellenberger, Winterthur.

7 Mystery clock A French model, with a bronze figure supporting and impulsing the pendulum, on a marble case containing the movement; c.1880.

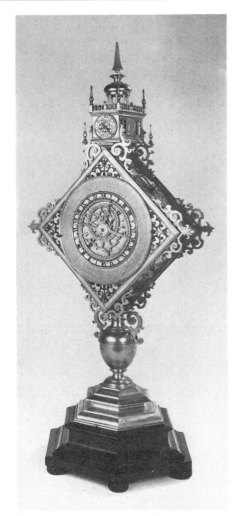

6

7

Month clock The late 17th and 18th centuries witnessed many innovations for improving methods of timekeeping. It was but a short step to convert the principle of an eight-day clock into one going for a month, three months, or even a year. All that was required was the addition of a fifth wheel to the existing train of four wheels. While this extended the going duration, the extra wheel reduced the power to the escapement because of the higher gearing, and accordingly a heavier weight had to be used to drive it. The addition of the fifth wheel also meant that instead of turning the winding key in a clockwise direction as for an eight-day clock, the key of a month clock was turned anticlockwise. This was so that the second hand, on the escape-wheel arbor, would rotate clockwise. JM

Morez clock Another term for Comtoise clock. Morez is a small village in the Morbier district of the Franche-Comté region of France, near the Swiss border, and both Morez and Morbier are descriptive terms for clocks produced in the region between c.1750 and 1900. During the 19th century Morbier and Morez seem to have been the centre for the production of the decorative stamped-iron pendulums used with certain forms of cased Comtoise clocks. PSKM
See also Comtoise clock.

Musical clock A clock which plays a tune at the hours or

at certain specific hours, (e.g. 3, 6, 9 and 12 o'clock). The name is also sometimes given to clocks with musical chimes only. The musical movements of clocks fall into three categories, in all of which the tune is played by a revolving barrel, occasionally a wheel, set with metal pins. In the first type pins activate hammers to play a carillon on bells, in the second the pins play a tune directly on a steel comb, and in the third (organ clocks) pins or metal bridges control the supply of air from bellows to pipes. Nicholas Vallin in 1598 made a clock with a musical movement playing on 13 bells, now in the British Museum, London, and organ clocks were known at the same time. Musical-box movements and organ clocks were both popular in the 18th century when certain composers of note wrote tunes for such toys. Nor did the greatest clockmakers despise such frivolity: the Dansk Folkemuseum at Aarhus has a musical clock in a gilt-bronze case with a movement by the famous French maker, Julien Le Roy. In the 19th century the trade in automata and musical boxes, including those incorporated in clocks, passed almost wholly to the Swiss. PSKM
See also Carillon (Section II); Organ clock.

Mystery clock A clock in which the mechanism is not immediately apparent or explicable. The idea originated very early, probably in Germany or France, but most mystery clocks date from the 19th century when the French particularly were keen on such devices. In the later 17th

1 **Mystery clock** of marble and gilt bronze; by A. M. Guilmet, Paris, c.1872. Victoria & Albert Museum, London.

2 **Night clock** The Tele-Time, a modern Japanese clock radio which announces the time when the top is touched or a button pressed on an extension lead. Private collection.

3 **Monastic alarm clock,** with 24-hour rotating brass dial; iron movement with foliot control; Italian, 15th century. Private collection.

1

2

the other in one week. A clock by Abraham-Louis Breguet in the same collection has its movement and dial forming the bob of a freely suspended seconds pendulum, to which it gives impulse by resonance. In 1808 John Schmidt of London produced a clock with a single hand in the middle of an open chapter ring and no base to conceal a movement. The hand is counterpoised and a small movement in the counterpoise revolves a small weight which alters the balance of the hand and causes it to rotate. A small auxiliary weight, suspended from the centre keeps the centre of gravity of the whole below the centre of revolution. A popular version of the mystery clock [80/1], produced in France c.1872, had a figure above the clock mechanism and dial, seemingly unconnected with it, holding aloft in one hand a swinging pendulum. The secret lies in an almost imperceptible oscillation of the base of the figure which is connected with the escapement and which impulses the pendulum.

The commonest form of mystery clock, produced cheaply in great numbers from c.1880, is in the form of a figure with outstretched arm holding a timepiece; an elephant holding a timepiece in his trunk was also popular. The clock movement and dial form an upper weight on a rod with a pendulum bob at the lower end. This compound pendulum is supported just above its centre of gravity so that it swings slowly from side to side. The pendulum movement releases the escapement, which causes a small weight to move in the opposite direction to that of the pendulum, thus keeping it swinging [167/5]. PSKM

Night clock It is perhaps difficult today to realise how poor the lighting of house interiors was in the days before gas and electricity, and the need for a clock which could be seen in the dark, or in a dimly lit room, was a consideration of which we are hardly aware. Clocks with dials which could be illuminated from behind were designed in Italy in the 17th century, and some similar models were made in England. Other ideas such as the oil lamp clock and the projection clock were tried, but the necessity for renewing the oil and attending to the wick prevented them becoming common. For nocturnal purposes, therefore, repeat-striking mechanisms were far more convenient and universal. Silent escapements were also devised for clocks intended for the bedroom, and today many electric clocks have their dials dimly illuminated at all times, or have luminous hands and dials. A Japanese clock which speaks the time as well as having a conventional dial was marketed in the 1970s. Perhaps the most recent version of a night clock, it provides its audible message at the touch of a disc on top of its case. AS

See also Campani (Section IV); Dial, wandering hour; Oil lamp clock; Projection clock; Repeating work (Section II); Escapement, silent, (Section II).

century Grollier de Servière produced the amusing 'tortoise clock', a horizontal table clock on which the centre of the dial within the chapter ring was dished and filled with water. On this floated a small turtle which crept round the edge of the chapter ring pointing to the hours. The secret of the movement of the tortoise lay in a magnetic hour hand fixed under the chapter ring, which attracted to it the turtle body which was primed with a small amount of soft iron. Versions of this principle with, for example, a mouse inching along a flat arch marked with the hours, have been described. Later horological enigmas took several forms, one of the most popular having hands which appear to revolve of their own accord. The dial, in fact, is three layers of glass, the centre one, to which the hand is attached, having a toothed edge which is rotated by a movement concealed in the base.

In the Conservatoire des Arts et Métiers in Paris is a mystery clock of Louis XV date showing Father Time with his scythe supporting on his wings an annular dial with a single hand, revolving by itself, and bearing as dumb-bell weights two small dials showing the hours again and the days of the week. The movement is hidden in an eccentric drum placed behind the axis of the hand, which it turns. Each of the small drums attached to the hand contains a weighted wheel which remains constantly vertical and which turns the dial hands, in one case in twelve hours, in

Night clocks, Italian The three Campani brothers, Giuseppe, Matteo and Pietro Tommaso, were, during the 17th century, inventors and first makers of Italian night clocks. It is hard to determine who was the first – both Giuseppe and Pietro Tommaso claimed the honour. The first night clocks were made for Pope Alexander VII, who wanted clocks which made no noise and were softly illuminated at night. The prototypes had rotating drums,

3

1

run on mercury, like the clock of Alfonso of Castile, but they were soon superseded by conventional 30-hour movements, those of Pietro Tommaso Campani having a particular type of silent escapement in which the pendulum controlled a continuously revolving escape wheel, resulting in a completely silent action. This was an original idea (which may be seen in action in the British Museum, London) but it was unsatisfactory as far as timekeeping was concerned. Other forms of silent verge escapements were more generally applied.

As a rule cases were in ebonised pearwood in the shape of a baroque altar. The most remarkable characteristic of these clocks was the dial, which was painted copper and looked like an altar piece. The subject of the painting was usually mythological or religious, or of landscapes and flowers. The hours were indicated by means of pierced discs, lit by an internal lamp, which moved along a segmental slit cut into the painting itself. The minutes were shown by the position of the hour disc along the divisions, also pierced, made along the slit. The movements were always well made, some with striking, nearly always spring-driven but sometimes with weights and a system of pulleys to prolong their descent. These night clocks were first made in Rome, and later in other Italian cities. Besides the Campani brothers, makers included Giovan Carlo Caerugi in Rome, Stefano Santuel and Giovan Battista Gonnon in Milan, Giovan Battista Callin in Genoa with Enrico Capello, Francesco Papillon and Filippo Treffler in Florence, Ludovico Manelli in Bologna, Marco Santucci in Naples, and Alfonso Vaccari in Ferrara. AL

Normande clock A French provincial longcase clock, from Normandy. The clock industry in this area was established in the 17th century. Centres such as Pontfarcy were making 30-hour clocks with short pendulums, but in the course of the 18th century they began to be superseded by Comtoise clock movements, and the individuality of Normande clocks was expressed only in the diversity of case styles. Woods used for Normande cases were oak, chestnut, pine, cherry and occasionally walnut. Shapes were multifarious: some had trunks the same width as the hood, others had swelling enlargements to allow for the swing of the pendulum; there were curved forms, lyre shapes and waisted models. Dials maintained a regional character; some were made in Rouen faience (of which the whole hood might be made in rare instances). Pediments of stamped and pierced brass followed the Comtoise models. Areas within Normandy had their specialities. In Caen and Bayeux waisted cases known as *demoiselles* were popular. These occurred too in Avranches and Bressey, where violin-shaped cases were also favoured.

In St Nicolas-d'Aliermont the clock trade seems to have been started *c.*1680 by men from Dieppe. After the Revolution it became a centre for the manufacture of *pendules de voyage*, and the factory system has flourished there since. PSKM
See also Comtoise clock.

Observatory clock A clock of great precision used for the study of astronomical phenomena, also for rating other precision timekeepers such as marine chronometers and

1 **Night clock, Italian,** by Pietro Tommaso Campani, Rome, 1681.

2 **Normande clock** Three examples of provincial French longcase clocks, those on the left and on the right being known as 'demoiselles'; made in the *Départements* of Calvados or Manche in Normandy.

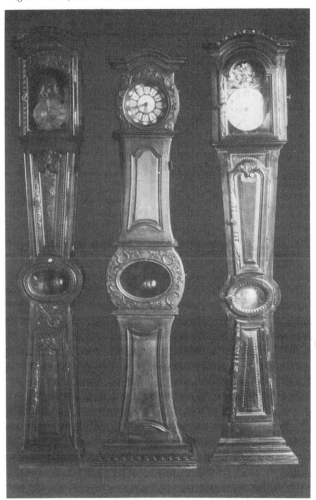

2

deck watches. For many years pendulum clocks reigned supreme. With George Graham's mercury pendulum (1721) and John Harrison's gridiron pendulum (1725), the problems of temperature error were greatly reduced and resulted in accuracy undreamed of in the 17th century. From the 1720s regulators improved through refinements such as better finish, higher-numbered trains, and jewelled escapements. The better makers devoted much study and care to the tooth and leaf forms, to proportioning of the train and to keeping all parts as light as was consistent with strength to reduce inertia. The discovery of nickel steels such as invar and elinvar by Charles Edouard Guillaume revolutionised design of compensated pendulums and resulted in the amazing accuracy of Riefler, Shortt, and Leroy clocks, which were usually mounted in pneumatic cases under constant pressure to eliminate barometric error. These have now been largely superseded by atomic (or molecular) clocks devised in 1947 as a refinement of the quartz clock. DJB
See also Regulator.

Oil lamp clock Known also simply as a lamp clock, this fulfilled the dual purpose of providing light, like an ordinary oil lamp, and telling the time. The principle is simple: a conventional clock movement revolves a lampshade marked with the hours and quarters and read against a fixed pointer. Another version has a conventional dial and hands on one side of the opal or frosted-glass shade, illuminated by the flame of the lamp behind. The idea never seems to have been exploited widely; the form originated in the 19th century and several designs were produced in France.

Another, earlier type of oil lamp clock, datable to the 18th century, consisted of a pewter stand, not unlike a candlestick, at the top of which a glass container of oil fed a wick supported by a holder projecting at right angles to the stand. The glass container was marked with hour divisions which corresponded to the time it took for the oil level to drop in the container as it burned at the wick. AS

O.G. clock A term derived from the ogee or cyma curve of architecture and cabinetmaking, much used in American Empire and Victorian furniture, especially for looking-glass frames. About 1840 this design was applied to clock cases, perhaps developed by William Carpenter of Bristol, Connecticut, for both 30-hour brass and wood movement, weight-driven shelf clocks. Its use spread rapidly and it was the most frequently used case style of the cheap 30-hour brass weight clocks by Chauncey Jerome, also of Bristol, Connecticut, who claimed to have first exported them to England in 1842. By mass-production methods the pine cases veneered with mahogany on front and sides cost in labour less than 20 cents apiece and, with the stock, less than 50 cents. The bottom door glass was either a mirror or a painted tablet, frequently of a stencilled, mass-produced design. A slightly larger case, sometimes having double doors, was soon produced for an eight-day weight movement. A smaller case, about half the size of the 30-hour weight clock, was popular after 1850 for a 30-hour spring movement. These O.G. cases remained in demand in all three sizes until *c.* 1890. KDR

1 Oil lamp clock with revolving glass dial driven by clockwork in the base; French, *c.* 1860. Time Museum, Rockford, Illinois.

2 Oil lamp clock As this oil lamp burns the passage of time is measured by the fall of the oil in the glass container; probably German, *c.* 1800. Merseyside County Museum, Liverpool.

3 Organ clock A Black Forest example with moving figures and large weight for driving the organ, *c.* 1830. Heimatmuseum, Triberg.

4 Organ clock in an 'architectural' case, the organ playing on the hour with a choice of six tunes; by Alan Walker, London, *c.* 1760 (though the case may be later). Lady Lever Art Gallery, Port Sunlight.

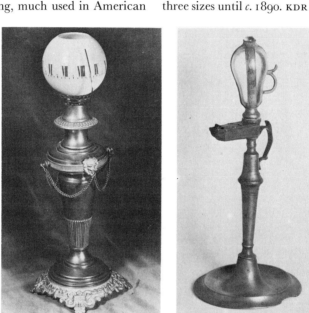

1   2   3

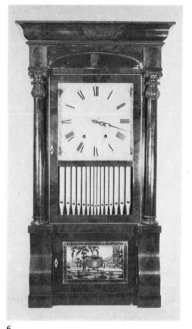

4   5   6

5 Ogee clock in mahogany case with 30-hour movement; glass tablet printed with the British Royal Arms; by the E. M. Welch Manufacturing Company, Forestville, Connecticut, *c.* 1870. Private collection.

6 Organ clock American version with bellows and real pipes inside, but simulated pipes on the case front; by Kirk and Todd, Wolcott, Connecticut, *c.* 1848.

7 Organ clock An elaborate eight-day clock with organ inside and automata dial; by George Pyke, London, *c.* 1755. Temple Newsam House, Leeds.

8 Organ clock An elaborate eight-day clock with organ inside; by J. George Gruning, Amsterdam, *c.* 1750. For dial see 99/5. Lady Lever Art Gallery, Port Sunlight.

7

8

Ogee moulding The name given to the cyma recta moulding, used architecturally and in furniture; the reversed ogee (or O.G., O-gee, etc.) is known as the cyma reversa. The section of the moulding is simply a double, concave–convex curve, or shallow S. It gives its name to a popular type of American clock. AS
See also O.G. clock.

Organ clock An unusual form of clock in which the chiming of the hour is preceded or replaced by a short tune played on a miniature pipe organ. The sound made by these clocks is comparable to that of the hurdy-gurdy, a portable organ formerly carried by itinerant street musicians. Sometimes the organ clock only plays every third hour, probably to conserve power.

The Dutch have always been fond of miniature organs and are thought to have been among the first to adapt this form of mechanism to a clock. Dutch organ clocks are more common than British, but one London clockmaker who favoured this type of musical clock was Alan Walker. In 1760 he made the journey to Amsterdam to study the manufacture of organ clocks, and there is a large specimen from his workshop in the Lady Lever Art Gallery, Port Sunlight [84/4]. Two other important 18th-century English organ clocks were those of Henry Bridges (1734), the movement of which is now in the British Museum, London, and Jacob Lovelace of Exeter (unfinished 1755) which was almost totally destroyed in Liverpool during the Second World War.

The organ clock appears to have had its origin in the 16th century. About 1580 Hans Schlottheim made a nef for the Emperor Rudolph II which among other things played an organ, and in 1599 Thomas Dallam, an Englishman, was sent to Turkey with an organ he had made for the Sultan as a present from Queen Elizabeth I. This organ was combined with a clock by Randolph Bull. It was in the Black Forest, however, that the organ clock was manufactured in earnest, being introduced *c.* 1770. Furtwangen was always the centre of production. The clocks needed a heavy weight to drive them, not only for operating the mechanism to open the pipes but also for providing the bellows with air. An organ clock was, therefore, a large instrument, often housed in a case like that of an English longcase clock, but much deeper.

The only known American organ clock extant has a label 'Patent Eight Day Repeating MUSICAL BRASS CLOCKS manufactured and sold by KIRK AND TODD, Wolcott, Conn.', *c.* 1848. An eight-day brass spring movement, patented by Kirk, actuated the time and strike while a separate direct fusee mechanism ran a type of hurdy-gurdy organ, set off at noon each day from the clock mechanism. Unfortunately Kirk did not apparently have good business judgement. The Wolcott business failed when only a small number of these clocks had been made. JM/EJT/KDR

Ormolu Ornamental metalwork made from cast bronze, worked and chased before being gilded. It originated in France in the 17th century for decorating cabinetwork and the cases of clocks. By *c.* 1725 almost the entire casework of some French clocks was of ormolu, often further embellished with Boulle work. Introduced into England in the late 17th century, ormolu gained in popularity and by the 1760s and '70s a number of outstanding makers, notably Matthew Boulton of Birmingham, were producing fine

1 2 3

examples of ormolu. During the Regency and early Victorian periods clock sets consisting of a clock in an ormolu case flanked by matching candelabras or vases were placed on the market. These were known by the French name of *garniture de cheminée*. Eventually, inferior reproductions were made from a soft white metal known as 'spelter' which was gilded over. JM

See also Chasing; Gilding (both Section III).

Orpheus clock A group of nine mid 16th-century table clocks bear decoration in the form of Orpheus charming the beasts with music, and Eurydice and Cerberus at the entrance to Hades. The cases are believed to be the work of a Nuremberg goldsmith, and the association between the Orpheus scene and the clocks is that the scene is an allegorical presentation of musical harmony, closely linked with the theories of cosmic harmony and the music of the spheres propounded by Pythagoras. Some of the clocks have round cases and others square ones, but while the decoration has the same theme the movements differ widely. Except that the clocks are believed to be south German, made 1560–80, no definite conclusions about them can be reached until more is known [100/1]. EJT

Orrery clock A clock mounted with a mechanism of rotating spheres designed to show the relative sizes, positions and motions (but not distances) of the heavenly bodies. In the late 18th and early 19th centuries the scientific clockmakers of France experimented with such devices. Antide Janvier produced several, and those made a few years later by his pupil Z. Raingo were so successful that the term 'Raingo clock' became synonymous with a type of orrery clock. PSKM

See also Orrery (Section V); Raingo clock.

Oyster-shell veneer A type of veneer used on the cabinetwork of longcase clocks, which was produced by cutting the smaller boughs of walnut and laburnum trees in thin slices across the grain. When these are arranged in a pattern, sometimes edged with boxwood stringing, the

4

effect is like that of the irregular layers on an oyster shell; hence the name. The style reached its greatest popularity during the last quarter of the 17th century. JM

Pagoda top A term occasionally applied to the curved, oriental tops of some 18th-century bracket clocks, based on the Europeanised version of the Chinese pagoda roof. The form was an element of rococo Chinoiserie in Chippendale furniture designs. AS

See also Rococo.

Paperweight clock, Japanese Paperweight or doctor's clocks are small spring-driven timepieces (average length about 4¼ in.). They resemble pillar clocks, being long and thin with a linear dial that shows the time on a graduated scale. The mechanism is of the pillar-clock variety with the spring and balance in a compartment at one end of the case. The spring is wound by drawing the hand to one end of the dial; as it unwinds the hand passes along the slot showing the time on the adjustable scale. Most such clocks are from the late period, after the 18th century, and have a balance cock in European style. MCR

Papier mâché Originally, 'mashed paper', mixed with glue and other materials, which could be moulded. In the early Victorian period there was a vogue for small items of

1 **Ormolu** A pierced and gilded ormolu fret on the case of a Dutch organ clock, *c.*1750 (85/8). Lady Lever Art Gallery, Port Sunlight.

2 **Orrery clock** of a type made by Raingo *frères* of Paris; fitted with a drum movement, gridiron compensated pendulum, day of the week dial indicator and orrery work above, powered by its own spring, but governed by the clock movement, *c.*1825.

3 **Papier mâché** forming the case of a shelf clock, with mother-of-pearl inlay and painted decoration; movement by Chauncey Jerome, New Haven, Connecticut; case by the Litchfield Manufacturing Company, 1851–4. American Clock & Watch Museum, Bristol, Connecticut.

4 **Oyster shell veneer** surrounding a panel of floral marquetry, *c.*1690. Lady Lever Art Gallery, Port Sunlight.

5 **Paperweight clock, Japanese** A small clock similar to a pillar clock, powered by a spring; sometimes known as a 'doctor's clock'. British Museum, London.

6 **Parquetry case** veneered with maple wood and decorated with parquetry; movement by Thomas Wheeler, London *c.*1680.

7 **Pedestal clock** in boulle marquetry with gilt-bronze mounts; signed 'Julien Le Roy, Paris'; case attributed to André Charles Boulle, *c.*1715. J. Paul Getty Museum, Malibu, California.

5   6   7

furniture made from layers of tough paper which were glued on to a wood or metal framework and also known as papier mâché. Each layer of paper was rubbed down before the next was applied, producing a strong, hard surface. When finished, the object was coated with black lacquer, decorated with painted flowers in gilded panels and sometimes further adorned with inlaid mother-of-pearl.

About a dozen different styles of American clock cases of papier mâché were made during the period 1850–5. The Litchfield Manufacturing Co. of Litchfield, Connecticut, was the principal maker, the cases being gilded by English immigrant japanners. Frequently, mother-of-pearl from the Connecticut seashore and imitations of it were added as decoration. The only other firm known to have made cases of this type was the Otis & Upson Co. of Marion (Southington), Connecticut. Some other firms purchased cases and installed their own movements; many, apparently, were exported to England. Those made by the Litchfield Manufacturing Co. had 30-hour and eight-day balance-wheel movements of unique design. Papier mâché was soon imitated by making cases with cast-iron fronts, similarly painted and gilded. These were at first referred to as 'iron mâché'. JM/KDR

Parquetry A form of marquetry, produced by the same process, in which the pattern, instead of a free arrangement of bird and flower designs or scrolled arabesques, is a geometric layout of different coloured veneers. It is a form of decoration more rarely encountered than ordinary marquetry, but it is occasionally found on the long trunk doors of early walnut-veneered longcase clocks. JM
See also Marquetry.

Pedestal clock A clock designed with its own pedestal, to stand in the centre of a room or against a wall; also sometimes called 'column' clock or 'term' clock. Certain Renaissance clocks were made in this form, with dials on all four faces, as objects of prestige and curiosity. With the revival of clockmaking in France in the late 17th century, ensembles of large bracket clocks with matching pedestals became extremely popular. Long-pendulum clocks (*pendules longue ligne*) were never as popular in France as in England, and the pedestal clocks were a reasonable compromise which did not diminish the importance of the clock. Pedestal clocks might be spring-driven but pedestals could also serve to hide weights. Decoration was lavish, frequently in Boulle marquetry. After the middle of the 18th century the relegation of most clocks to the chimneypiece killed the idea of pedestals except in rare cases. PSKM

Pediment An architectural term to describe a low-pitched triangular gable on the façade of a classical building, usually surmounting a portico in Greek and Roman times, but later employed for doorways, windows, etc. Used on longcase clock hoods the pediment was an important feature which gave height and dignity to the overall design. There are five basic types of pediment used on clocks; the triangular pediment, of strictly classical derivation; the broken pediment, in which the centre portion of the two sloping sides is left open to contain an ornamental urn or other decorative feature; the hollow pediment, in which the sides are shaped as concave curves, emphasising the central apex; the swan-neck pediment, in which the sides are scrolled in an S shape, terminating in two central bosses; the segmental pediment, in which the normally straight sides of the broken pediment are formed from two segmental curves, or the upper edge consists of one segment of a circle. There are many variations, popular at various periods both in humble country-made cases and in the highest-quality clocks of London, Philadelphia and other centres of fashion. AS

Pendulum aperture A feature of the design of bracket-

clock dials during the first half of the 18th century. A curved hole was cut in the dial above the centre to show the small engraved brass disc attached to the verge escapement arbor which moved from side to side as the clock was going. JM
See also Mock pendulum.

Pendule directoire A clock made during the period of the Directory in France (1795–1800). The Revolution had caused a break in the clockmaking tradition but, encouraged by the government, it resumed after the re-establishment of stable rule. Gilt-metal cases, especially with decorative figures incorporated, continued to have the greatest popularity, the style becoming heavier and neoclassical elements displaying a worthy correctness of detail. Clocks with Negro figures clearly derived from the debate over slavery, and from confused idealisation of the 'noble savage', while clocks showing figures in Roman attire often pointed to the republican ideal. At the same time small astronomical regulators like four-glass clocks and skeleton clocks of similar visual austerity were being developed. PSKM

1

2

3

4

5

6

1 Pediment, broken, on a longcase clock, by J. van Brussel, Amsterdam, early 18th century.

2 Pediment, swan's neck, on a longcase clock, by John Wyke, Prescot, c. 1755. Private collection.

3 Pediment, hollow, on a longcase clock, by John Ellicott, London, c. 1750. Lady Lever Art Gallery, Port Sunlight.

4 Pediment, segmental, on a longcase clock, by Thomas Tompion, London, 1709. The Pump Room, Bath.

5 Pendule empire Mantel clock of patinated and gilded bronze, designed by Antoine Ravrio, c. 1810. Bowes Museum, Barnard Castle.

6 Pendule longue ligne Longcase clock with floral marquetry on a kingwood ground; gilt bronze mounts. Movement by Jean Charost, Paris; case by Jean Pierre Latz; 1745–8. National Trust, Waddesdon Manor.

7 Pediment, triangular, on a bracket clock; by Henry Higginson, London, c. 1662.

8 Pendule directoire Mantel clock of patinated and gilded bronze; unsigned, c. 1795. Bowes Museum, Barnard Castle.

9 Pendule Louis XIII Table clock of pierced and gilded bronze originally belonging to the Duc d'Orléans, c. 1635. Musée du Petit Palais, Paris.

10 Tooled leather carrying case for 89/9.

7

8

9

10

Pendule empire A clock made during the period 1802–14, when Napoleon ruled as emperor of the French. Gilt-bronze cases with figures developed the Directoire themes, but these became subtly influenced by the symbolism of the Empire, as well as by the taste for Egyptian, Roman and Greek antiquities encouraged by the excavations ordered by Napoleon during his Egyptian campaigns. On the case of the clock illustrated [88/5] a robed woman sits reading classical texts beneath a bust of Homer, watched over by an eagle holding a lamp. This gilt-metal form of mantel clock, with figures dominating the case, was to remain popular in France in various forms until after c. 1830. PSKM

Pendule longue ligne The French term for longcase clocks. They were never as popular in France as in England, but some magnificent examples were made, the cases often by distinguished *ébénistes*. *Pendules longue ligne* were cased in wood long after smaller clocks had abandoned wood in favour of gilt bronze, marble or porcelain. The earliest

varieties, c. 1670, take the form of a *religieuse* above a shaped body. Gradually the suggestion of separation between hood and trunk died out and by the 1740s they had developed into the full rococo form of the clock by Jean Charost, cased by Jean Pierre Latz [88/6]. From the mid 18th century the longcase form was used for *régulateurs* by such makers as Ferdinand Berthoud and Pierre Le Roy, the form and decoration of the cases becoming more severe but no less handsome, to match the dignity of their movements with gridiron pendulums, specialist escapements and other refinements. Comtoise clocks and Normande clocks were provincial versions of the *pendule longue ligne*. PSKM

Pendule Louis XIII The reign of Louis XIII (1610–43) spanned the last period of Renaissance clockmaking in France before the mid 17th-century fashion for watches apparently caused the almost complete cessation of clockmaking (a largely unexplained phenomenon). Survivals from this period are rare but tend to be of very high quality, like the clock made for the brother of Louis

XIII [89/9]. The style was international; cases were of gilded metal for the small square, cylindrical or octagonal table clocks, and for the larger versions with horizontal dials. Surfaces were elaborately engraved, the subjects often taken from engravings of allegories or myths. PSKM
See also Renaissance clock.

Pendule Louis XIV The early part of Louis XIV's reign (1643–1715) was a bad time for clockmaking, though watches were fashionable. The development of the pendulum caused renewed interest in clocks, leading to the introduction of the *religieuse*. Early influences on both the science and art of clock-making came from Holland, but the French soon outstripped their masters in both fields. Louis XIV was lavish in his patronage of all the arts and under his influence the decoration of the *religieuse* developed and

other styles grew up. Designers like Daniel Marot and André-Charles Boulle produced sketches for clock cases, while members of the Martinot family produced equally fine clocks. Forms became somewhat stereotyped; the *tête de poupeé* form and the arch-topped, scroll-footed clock, now seen as typical of the period, succeeded the *religieuse* and continued into the Regency. Pedestal clocks were popular, both clock and pedestal heavy with ebonised mouldings and gilt-bronze mounts. PSKM
See also: Pendule religieuse; Tête de poupée.

Pendule Louis XV Louis XV's long reign (1723–74) was a period of great development and diversification in clock casework. At the beginning of the period clocks still retained some of the prestige value of the preceding century. As the century progressed clocks were produced in

1

2

3

4

5

6

1 Pendule Louis XIV Bracket clock of Boulle marquetry with gilt bronze mounts; by Pierre Gaudron, Paris. The medallion of Louis XIV's head is dated 1677, but the clock is somewhat later. Victoria & Albert Museum, London.

2 Pendule Louis XV Bracket clock in boulle marquetry of green backed tortoiseshell and gilt bronze mounts; movement by F. Lournay; case stamped 'F. Goyer J.M.E.'. Victoria & Albert Museum, London.

3 Pendule Louis XVI Cartel clock of gilt bronze, the dial signed 'Buzot à Paris'; the movement signed Bourgeois, Paris; 1770–5. Bowes Museum, Barnard Castle.

4 Pendule Louis XVI Mantel clock in lyre form, gilt bronze and white marble, signed 'Gille à Paris', c.1780. National Trust, Waddesdon Manor.

5 Pendule Louis XVI Mantel clock of white marble with gilt bronze mounts, signed 'Harel à Paris'; dial signed by the enameller Coteau, c.1790. Bowes Museum, Barnard Castle.

6 Pendule Régence Mantel clock of *tête de poupée* form; movement by Jacques Gudin, Paris; case attributed to André Charles Boulle; c.1720. J. Paul Getty Museum, Malibu, California.

7 Pendule d'officier, signed 'Cugnier, Leschot', c.1780. Musée International d'Horlogerie, La Chaux-de-Fonds.

8 Pendule portative by Robert Robin, Paris, c.1780. Victoria & Albert Museum, London.

7   8

far greater numbers, and their casing records their assimilation into decorative schemes.

Pedestal clocks and *pendules longue ligne* had their place, but increasingly clocks were relegated to the wall, standing on brackets or, as cartel clocks, being hung directly on panelling, or even on an overmantel mirror. The classic Louis XV clock, if such a thing can exist amid such diversity, was the wooden-cased, waisted clock standing on its own bracket, the dial perhaps of thirteen pieces, the case veneered with horn or tortoiseshell, or coloured with vernis Martin, and set with gilt-bronze mounts. This was to be the last use of wood for casing small clocks in the 18th century. Gilt bronze came into favour once more, particularly for cartel clocks, which incorporated all the extravagances of the new rococo style – ragged shells, asymmetric scrolling, animals and fanciful Chinese figures.

About the middle of the century clocks found their way to the chimneypiece. Highly decorative clocks were produced, some of the most fanciful with the clock in the branches of a gilt-bronze tree amid porcelain flowers or birds from Vincennes or Germany (*see* Frontispiece). *Garnitures de cheminée* came into favour, the form of the clock echoed by flanking vases or candelabra, together forming a major element in the decoration of a room. Clock movements, apart from the horologically more sophisticated *régulateur*

movements, began to be standardised in drum form. Early gilt-metal dials with enamel hour cartouches were superseded in turn by the large thirteen-piece dials, and with the advent of smaller movements by one-piece enamel dials. Gilt-metal hands were cast and pierced with very delicate patterns. PSKM
See also Cartel clock.

Pendule Louis XVI Louis XVI's reported interest in horology is often cited to explain the horological sophistication attained during his reign (1774–92). It may explain the encouragement given to precision timepieces, but it was the atmosphere of luxury which furthered the development of exquisite casework. The two traditions sometimes met, as in the *pendules régulateurs* made by men such as Ferdinand Berthoud [101/2].

For small clocks gilt bronze continued predominant. The use of porcelain developed, for plaques and for whole cases, and marble was used above all. Cartel clocks, of gilt metal only, were produced with fashionable neoclassical motifs – rams' heads, urns and swags of flowers – superseding the rococo motifs of Louis XV. But mantel clocks were more fashionable. Vase clocks and lyre clocks traded on the popularity of neoclassicism, and clocks set with mythical or allegorical gilt-bronze figures were common. *Pendules montgolfières* paid light-hearted tribute to the ballooning craze, incorporating the balloon outline in a most elegant case form. Marble was used in conjunction with gilt bronze on clock bases or in portico clocks [90/5], which were popular at the end of the reign. PSKM
See also Balloon clock; Porcelain case.

Pendule d'officier A gilt-metal or brass travelling clock made in France, Germany or Switzerland from c.1780 until c.1820. Of several types, they preceded the classic *pendules de voyage* of the later 19th century, and often had complicated repeating work as well as alarms. Their popularity during the Napoleonic wars probably earned them their name, and many of the cases were decorated in high relief with laurel wreaths or trophies of arms. Leather cases were originally supplied with these clocks. PSKM

Pendule portative A small clock, usually fitted with a handle, designed to be moved from place to place in the house, like an English bracket clock. *Pendule portative* is in no way synonymous with *pendule de voyage*. The example by Paul Garnier [230/1] has no alarm, which would be almost indispensable to a travelling clock, and its plinth suggests a stable home. The clock made by Robert Robin, which is believed to have belonged to Marie Antoinette [91/8], may be considered a *pendule portative*, but its leather case clearly marks it as a travelling clock. But an astronomer's clock made in 1795 by Ferdinand Berthoud, in the National Maritime Museum at Greenwich, shows a brass carrying handle for what is essentially a working, and normally static, clock. PSKM

Pendule Régence The short period of the Regency in France (1715–23) was truly a transition period, the massive grandeur of Louis XIV designs softening, but not yet forming the new, lighter curves of Louis XV clocks. Forms

1 Pendule religieuse by François Thuret, Paris, c. 1680. Victoria & Albert Museum, London.

2 Pendule de voyage (Carriage clock) in a case of gilt bronze with tourbillon escapement; signed 'Breguet, Paris', c. 1810. Ashmolean Museum, Oxford.

3 Pendule sympathique by Breguet *et neveu*, Paris, for Philip, Duc d'Orléans, pretender to the throne of France; dated 1835. Time Museum, Rockford, Illinois.

4 Pigeon-racing clock A German example of a clock for recording the flight times of racing pigeons. Private collection.

5 Photographer's clock A type of interval timer, designed for use in a photographic darkroom.

6 Picture clock painted on wood with two dials; wound by pulling cords; Swiss, c. 1800. Musée International d'Horlogerie, La Chaux-de-Fonds.

7 Pillar clock Renaissance clock mounted on a pillar. Quarter and hour striking with dials on front and rear and glass side doors to see the movement; possibly Augsburg, c. 1590. Uhrensammlung Kellenberger, Winterthur.

1   2   3

such as the *tête de poupée* persisted as did the large pedestal clocks. Boulle marquetry and combinations of ebonised wood with gilt-bronze mounts continued popular. PSKM

Pendule religieuse The French bracket clock of the late 17th century, of plain architectural form. The name probably derived from their simplicity or by analogy with the architectural form of churches. These clocks are sometimes called Louis XIII clocks, but this is misleading for clocks not popular until 20 years after his death in 1643. Such late 17th-century bracket clocks, whether French, English or Dutch, developed as a result of the invention of the pendulum. The plainer type of casing takes the form of a portico with flanking pillars or pilasters, with pediment above. It is derived from Italian cabinets of the 16th century and Dutch cabinets of the mid 17th century. Decoration tended to greater flamboyance as the 17th century progressed. Early examples were of ebonised wood with simple pierced brass mounts in place of pillars, and a pierced brass pediment. More elaborate forms had pilasters and segmental pediments, sometimes inlaid with Boulle marquetry or decorated with black or red lacquer with brass or gilt-bronze mounts. From c. 1675 the segmental pediment gave way to a domed top in imitation of the architecture of Mansart, supported by Corinthian pillars, the whole richly mounted in gilt bronze, including flambeau finials or small figures in the Renaissance manner. The dial, covered with black or dark-coloured velvet, occupied the whole of the front. The chapter ring was marked for each minute and the hands were of delicately pierced gilt metal. Below the chapter ring the dial might be mounted with a gilt-bronze lambrequin carrying the maker's name, or with a fanciful mount such as Father Time [228/1]. PSKM

Pendule sympathique One of the most intriguing inventions of Abraham-Louis Breguet, first made c. 1805–10. The *pendule sympathique* consisted of a table or mantel clock with a special clip above to hold a watch during the night hours, in the manner of a watch stand. At a fixed hour the clock not only set the watch to time but also regulated any error. The clock was capable of regulating an error of up to $7\frac{1}{2}$ minutes and, as it was used daily, greater error was unlikely. Few of these clocks were made. Some were designed to wind the watch as well as to regulate it and set it to time. They appear to have been designed by Breguet to satisfy a challenge and to promote his business interests, for Breguet was more than capable of making watches which did not require this kind of attention. There is a *pendule sympathique* in the Rockford Time Museum, Illinois [92/3], and one in the English Royal Collection, made for the Prince Regent in 1814. During the period of Breguet *neveu et Cie* (1830–60) a simpler version was made, which merely set the watch to time. PSKM

Pendule de voyage A travelling clock, normally with a cylinder or form of lever escapement mounted on a separate platform, developed in France in the early 19th century and made in great numbers in that country in the later 19th and early 20th centuries. The form began to evolve at the end of the 18th century, the fashion led by Abraham-Louis Breguet who produced small square clocks with glass sides owing something to the shape of *pendules d'officier* or Capucines, but most perhaps to the four-glass clocks or small *régulateurs*. The general form remained constant, though thousands of variations were made in details of panels and frames – or in size, which might vary in height from 2 or 3 in. to 12 in.

By the 1830s the production of *pendules de voyage* was a major industry, centred chiefly on the area of St Nicolas-d'Aliermont, near Dieppe, and in the Montbéliard area of the Jura. A few high-quality clocks were made in Paris. Famous names included Japy, Délépine, Couaillet *frères*, Martin, Duverdrey, Drocourt, Le Roy and Leroy. The largest market for the standard clocks, known as carriage clocks, was in England, although English makers also produced clocks in the style, concentrating on high-quality pieces. Names associated with English clocks are Vulliamy, Dent, Frodsham, James McCabe, and several others. The Swiss also had a version, as did some other European countries and the United States. PSKM
See also Carriage clock; Travelling clock.

Photographer's clock A clock with a large dial and centre sweep seconds hand moving over a 0–60 graduated scale, with a subsidiary hand to indicate elapsed time on a second scale graduated 0–60 or 0–100 minutes; expressly designed for photographic darkroom use. Generally, the hands are coated with luminescent paint to allow them to be seen in total darkness. A simple clock movement with a balance wheel is used, often fitted with pull winding but sometimes wound from the rear, which can be set to zero,

started and stopped by other cords, pushbuttons or levers. An alarm bell may be fitted to remind the user that the required period has elapsed. These clocks are mounted in circular drums, often of tin plate or plastic; synchronous electric clock movements are also used. CKA

Picture clock In the early 19th century it became the fashion to own an oil painting of a town or village scene incorporating the tower of a church or similar building bearing a clock dial. The dial was not part of the painting but an actual clock dial, the mechanism of which was concealed in a space behind the picture. Some of these clocks also had music and mechanism to make the sails of a windmill rotate, fishermen mend nets, and so on. They usually have good French or Swiss mechanisms, and the musical and automata work is also of high quality, though the paintings as works of art may leave something to be desired. EJT

Pigeon-racing clock For recording the arrival time of racing pigeons, developed originally in the 19th century by W. H. Turner. The birds are taken to the point of departure and released at a given time, their homing instinct compelling them to return to their home loft as rapidly as possible. On arrival the identification ring each pigeon carries is detached and placed in a small thimble for insertion into a slot in the pigeon clock, and a lever is pressed which causes the time of insertion to be recorded on a paper tape. The

4

5

6

7

1   2

rings are stored in a container in the order in which they are inserted into the clock. Various devices are fitted to prevent tampering and the clocks are sealed. After the race the records are removed to determine the exact time of arrival of the birds. Early pigeon clocks were made in Britain, others in Belgium where the sport is also popular. CKA

Pillar clock Early Gothic clocks usually stood on brackets fastened to the wall, or were hooked to the wall, but such clocks were made to stand on hollow pillars, which contained the weights. As clocks on pillars generally stood lower than wall clocks, more frequent winding was necessary [93/7]. After the Renaissance, table clocks with astronomical dials began to be made with the dials on both sides, and similar weight-driven clocks were also produced; they needed to stand on a pillar so that the dials at the rear could be easily seen. EJT

Pillar clock, Japanese Pillar clocks, often referred to as 'stick' clocks, were made to hang on the supporting column of a Japanese house, since the screen walls were not designed to support heavy objects. Pillar clocks were usually long and narrow, hence their nickname. They had simple four-wheel weight-driven movements at the top. Very early ones have a foliot; most have balance wheels; occasionally, later ones have short-bob pendulums. The single hand was attached to the weight and as the weight descended the hand passed a graduated scale, or dial, indicating the time. More elaborate pillar clocks have a striking mechanism in the weight, activated by pins projecting inwards from the hour plates on the vertical dial. The striking pattern of Japanese clocks is unique; it proceeds backwards from nine to four starting at sunset (6): 6–5–4–9–8–7–6–5–4–9–8–7. MCR

Pillar and scroll clock This exclusively American design of clock was probably introduced by Eli Terry in 1818 as a more graceful case for the 30-hour wooden movement

patented by him (1816) and previously marketed in the so-called 'box case'. The handsome scroll top, usually with three brass (sometimes wood) finials mounted on side and centre blocks, was constructed with crotch mahogany veneer. Two gracefully turned pillars flanked each side between top and base. The door contained a dial glass, below which was a reverse-painted glass tablet. There were several important varieties of movement: outside escapement; inside-outside escapement; off-centre (Seth Thomas); eight-day brass (attributed to Heman Clark); Torrington horizontal train; etc. This style of case was produced in hundreds of thousands between 1818 and 1828, when it was suddenly almost wholly superseded by Chauncey Jerome's bronze looking-glass clock. The common movement was the five-train 30-hour time and strike, of which several variants were made to circumvent a series of Eli Terry's patents. This style of case was referred to as 'the patent clock'. The scroll design, copied from the hoods on English longcase clocks, was also used by Joseph Ives, c. 1819, for his looking-glass wall clock, as well as others in Bristol, Connecticut, making a longer-cased reeded-column shelf clock. KDR

Planetary clock It has been suggested that such clocks were originally devised to provide a driving mechanism for models showing the planetary system, and that telling the hours of the day was a secondary consideration. Many monumental clocks in Europe showed the movements of the planets, among them that of Giovanni Dondi at Padua in 1364 and the famous clock at Strasbourg, dating from 1352. Most of these early clocks indicated planetary movement by dials, but in the 16th century armillary spheres appeared, driven by clockwork and containing bands to represent the movements of planets. The earth was still shown at the centre of the solar system.

The earliest-known model to represent the solar system in the modern sense was that by Thomas Tompion and George Graham in 1710, but this only showed the relative

1 Pillar clock, Japanese, shown with its complete set of seven *sekki* (fortnight) scales.

2 Postman's alarm with the side doors removed to show the movement; enamel dial with wooden surround; Black Forest, *c.* 1900. Private collection.

3 Portico clock with alabaster pillars and gilded capitals; hours and half hours striking on a gong; probably Viennese, *c.* 1840.

4 Pillar and scroll clock fitted with the rare 'outside escapement' and front hanging pendulum; by Eli Terry, Plymouth, Connecticut. *c.* 1819. American Clock & Watch Museum, Bristol, Connecticut.

3

4

movements of the earth and moon and did not show the correct scale of the planets or their orbits. During the 18th century further instruments of this type were made, but driven by clockwork, among them those of Dauthiau in France and Philipp Matthäus Hahn in Germany. Antide Janvier of Paris produced a number of planetary clocks at the end of the century, and Z. Raingo is another maker associated with this type of clock. EJT
See also Astronomical clock; Orrery clock; Raingo clock.

Plate clock The *Telleruhr* or dish clock was popular in south Germany and Austria in the late 17th century, and the idea was revived in the 20th using a china plate instead of a metal one. The movements were similar to the going part of an alarm clock with an open mainspring and were controlled by a balance, but the mainspring arbor had a winding square allowing the clock to be wound through a hole in the dial. These clocks were mass-produced by the Black Forest factories in the 1920s, and were, in effect, a development of the china dials found on Black Forest wall clocks of the mid 19th century. Their fragility has greatly reduced their numbers and they are now seldom seen. EJT
See also: *Telleruhr.*

Porcelain case Porcelain is a hard translucent material of which an important ingredient is china clay (kaolin), with various other materials added according to type, and fired to a high temperature in a potter's kiln. Most porcelain clock cases are of hard-paste porcelain and are of French or German manufacture. The material is adaptable to the making of ornamental cases combining modelled figures, flowers or other decorative features, and it can be coloured by painting and firing enamels on its surface. Individual decorative figures, or sometimes complete cases, are made in biscuit (unglazed) porcelain, and such cases are normally protected from dirt by glass domes or shades. Porcelain, like all ceramic materials, shrinks and is inclined to distort during firing, and for this reason clock movements are fitted

to porcelain cases with screws from loosely fitting rings at the back [102/1]. AS
See also Ceramic clock case.

Portico clock A portico is a classical porch with a decorated entablature supported on columns, and often completed by a triangular pediment. On modern buildings in classical style, the pediment sometimes contains a clock dial. The term 'portico clock' is also applied to the style of French clock usually known by the name 'Empire'. Here the entablature is supported by four columns on a base, and the movement is suspended below it with the pendulum exposed. This design can also be seen in earlier examples from Austria, the essential feature being the entablature supported by columns. Other Austrian designs, especially in the Biedermeier period, include columns, but do not necessarily qualify as portico clocks. EJT

Postman's alarm The Black Forest industry was hard hit by American competition in the years 1842–60 and in the 1860s began to make clocks on the American pattern in factories. The old type of wall striking clock, with the striking train behind the going train, had sometimes included a small alarm mechanism placed at the side of the movement. When striking clocks began to be replaced by the new American type, the manufacturers of the 'hang-up' clocks remodelled the design to place alarm work where the striking train had been, providing it with a long chain to give a protracted ring. The mechanism was more solid than before, and the clocks competed successfully with the American clocks with alarm work because of their greater accuracy. No one knows how the name 'postman's alarm' came to be applied to these clocks, but as late as 1948 a faded inscription could be seen on a shop wall in Islington, London, 'The original Postmens' Alarms'. Sometimes these clocks were made without a separate glass, the dial itself being glass with the figures behind it. Various sizes were made, and the type did not die out until *c.* 1914. EJT

Projection clock A form of night clock incorporating an internal light and projection lenses to throw an image of the dial and hands on a wall or other convenient surface. The idea dates back to the 18th century, and some models with oil lamps were made early in the 19th century. Even with the introduction of electric lighting, however, the idea was never exploited to any large extent, since any form of artificial illumination can be adapted to reading a clock at night without the complication of projection apparatus. AS *See also* Night clock.

Quartz-crystal clock Shortly after the excellent stability of frequency control by quartz crystal when applied to valve oscillator circuits was discovered, efforts were directed to producing a clock using this principle for time measurement. Warren A. Marrison of New York was pre-eminent in the application of quartz-crystal clocks to timekeeping, producing his first design *c*. 1929. Progress in the understanding of the quartz-crystal oscillator and the associated circuits needed to divide the high frequency down to a suitable value for operating small synchronous motors led to the quartz-crystal clock being adopted as a time-measurement standard in place of the pendulum clock in astronomical observatories from *c*. 1943. A frequency of 100,000 hertz was adopted in all the early clocks, the quartz crystal being kept at a constant temperature by an electrically heated oven. Dr Louis Essen of the National Physical Laboratory developed the quartz-crystal ring, greatly improving the stability of frequency to about one part in one hundred million, and these were adopted as NPL standards for frequency and time measurement; this represents about 0.001 second in 24 hours. Modern quartz-

crystal oscillators for clocks often operate at 32,768 hertz, which is divided down by binary circuits to 1 hertz for the direct operation of the seconds hand of the clock in the case of analogue display. CKA

Rack clock A clock which uses its own weight as motive power and gradually descends a toothed rack which meshes with the first wheel of the train. Winding is effected by pushing the clock to the top of the rack again. The type was popular in south Germany and Austria in the 18th century, especially in a miniature version with a cow tail pendulum which is now being reproduced in quantity. These clocks have the advantage that they rarely run down, because the unbalanced appearance of the movement when it has descended the rack a little way induces one to push it to the top again. A version of this clock was produced in 1919 with a double pendulum beating seconds and a special escapement based on the cylinder escapement used in watches. These clocks were manufactured in Kentish Town, London, and the idea was revived about 1948. The advantage of this design was that the clock only fell a short distance and could be used for a mantelpiece or desk. EJT

Raingo clock A type of orrery clock made by the firm of Raingo *frères* of Paris. The firm made the usual range of domestic clocks but in the decade 1820–30 became particularly well known for orrery clocks. These take the form of circular, four-pillared clocks of gilt or patinated bronze, the drum movement hanging between the front two pillars, the orrery surmounting the entablature. The case [97/5] includes four figures representing the seasons. The orrery mechanism, which has its own spring, can be

1   2   3   4

1 Quartz-crystal clock Equipment formerly used by the British Post Office Research Station, indicating the position of the quartz crystal oscillators (below), frequency dividers, clock error calculators and an analogue dial. Science Museum, London.

2 Rack clock with lead case, verge escapement, short pendulum and enamel dial on a gilded wall bracket; probably Viennese, *c.* 1780. Uhrensammlung Kellenberger, Winterthur.

3 Regulator, American, wall hanging in a walnut case; partially jewelled movement and deadbeat escapement. By the E. Howard Watch & Clock Company, Boston, Massachusetts; made to order in 1872 for the Charter Oak Insurance Company Office, Hartford, Connecticut. American Clock & Watch Museum, Bristol, Connecticut.

4 Regulator Vienna type of wall regulator in walnut case with three-train *grande sonnerie* striking; by Martin Bock, Vienna, *c.* 1850. Private collection.

5 Raingo clock Orrery clock in a case of gilt bronze with figures representing the seasons, signed 'Raingo Frères à Paris', *c.* 1825. Sheffield City Museum.

6 Projection clock, Italian; by Ludovico Lanzcron, Bologna, second half of the 17th century.

5

6

disengaged from that of the clock and rotated by a small handle to show the movements of the planets more quickly. The founder of the Raingo firm had been making orrery clocks from *c.* 1810, some of the earliest bearing the name of Antide Janvier; he patented his own version in 1815. George IV bought a Raingo clock in 1824 for 300 guineas; it is now at Windsor Castle. PSKM
See also Orrery clock.

Regulator A standard clock used for the regulation of other timekeepers. It is usually a clock with seconds pendulum compensated for temperature changes, deadbeat or gravity escapement, weight-driven, with everything reduced to the greatest simplicity and having fine finishes on the acting parts, its prime purpose being accuracy. European makers often used the pin or pinwheel escapement invented by Louis Amant in 1741 but later modified by Jean André Le Paute. English and American makers preferred the Graham escapement, often in conjunction with the Graham mercury pendulum, instead of John Harrison's gridiron, used on the Continent. Early regulators were cased as longcase clocks with large glass doors. Later, it was realised that floor clocks are more prone to errors from vibration than clocks mounted on solid walls, and many were then designed in wall cases.

Both full-size and smaller wall clocks of fine quality with 80-beat or other length pendulums were made in Vienna in the late 18th and during the 19th centuries. German makers copied the style, but usually in less refined cases and with factory-produced movements lacking the fine finish.

Both the mercury and gridiron pendulums had shortcomings that were difficult to overcome completely. Air in large clock cases tends to stratify in layers at different temperatures, the upper portion of the case being warmer than the lower section. This means that the expansion or contraction of the mercury may not correspond exactly to the change in length of the rod. The gridiron, having rods extending more nearly the full length of the case, reacts more uniformly but often in a jerky or erratic manner because of the friction of the rods running through supporting cross-members. The mercury pendulum has usually been preferred, however, because it can be more readily corrected if over- or under-compensated by adding or subtracting mercury [119/6]

For well over 200 years the regulator, basically as designed by George Graham, was the time standard for most of the world. It was superseded only in recent years by quartz clocks.

The term is used to describe the lever which allows alterations to be made in a clock's rate. DJB
See also Index.

Regulator, American The term 'regulator' was commonly misused by American clock manufacturers during the period 1860–1930 as only a small number of timepieces described as regulators were sufficiently accurate to deserve the name. Simon Willard, and later his disciples in the Boston, Massachusetts, area, produced an extremely accurate regulator *c.* 1828, which was continued in several styles by E. Howard & Co. throughout the 19th century. Silas B. Terry, son of Eli, produced a regulator movement during the 1850s that was later acquired and redesigned as several wall types by Seth Thomas & Co. About 1870 the term 'regulator' was employed by American clock manufacturers advertising spring-driven (without fusees) recoil escapement, non-temperature-compensating pendulum wall clocks. Frequently these had striking trains and supplementary dials for calendar mechanisms. KDR

97

1 Renaissance clock Gilt metal table clock in the 'International Renaissance' style; by Gilbert Martinot, Paris, 1572–80. Musée Paul Dupuy, Toulouse.

2 Revolving-band clock in the form of a celestial globe of blue enamel, with gilt bronze mounts, on a bronze and ebony base with boulle-work panels; movement signed 'Martin, Paris', c.1780. Bowes Museum, Barnard Castle.

3 Riefler clock mounted in an evacuated cylinder, with glass cover, c.1895. National Maritime Museum, London.

4 Riefler clock Movement of 98/3 with an electrical remontoire. National Maritime Museum, London.

5 Organ clock Dial of 85/8 painted by Jacobus Buys. Lady Lever Art Gallery, Port Sunlight.

1   2   3   4

Renaissance clock The name now normally given to clocks made from c.1500 to c.1650, when regional styles of clockmaking began to evolve in Europe. The style was international in character, most of the clocks of the period being made to similar designs in Italy, south Germany and France, with some English examples later in the period. It has also been called 'the age of decoration', for in general the gilded-brass cases of either spring- or weight-driven clocks were lavishly decorated with engraved, cast and chased ornament, in a style derived from classical prototypes. The introduction of the pendulum c.1657 suggests a suitable date to mark the end of this period of clockmaking, the date at which accuracy of timekeeping gradually began to assume more importance than splendour of casework. The first portable clocks and pocket watches also began to appear during the period. AS

Revolutionary clock In 1793 the introduction in France of what revolutionaries regarded as rational time measurement, on a decimal base, prompted the production of decimal clocks. Revolutionary fervour was otherwise shown on casework by studied use of revolutionary symbols such as the Phrygian bonnet or the tricolour in place of such royalist motifs as the fleur-de-lys, or by including figures emblematic of liberty, plenty or equality. The rise of Napoleon soon brought a quite different range of motifs and symbols into fashion. PSKM
See also Decimal clocks.

Revolving-band clock A clock on which time is shown by numbered bands revolving past a fixed marker. The idea possibly developed from early Gothic moving-dial clocks which similarly had a fixed pointer, and was first used on globe clocks of the 16th century. In the 18th century, the revolving-band idea became popular, particularly in France where opportunities for elaborate casework were fully exploited. Double bands appeared, giving minute readings as well as hours, and pointers in the form of snakes or lizards, or encrusted with stones, were popular. The revolving bands were ideal in conjunction with vase clocks, but other forms also appeared. The bands might run around the top of a classical ruined pillar, and a clock in the Wallace Collection, London, incorporates hour and minute bands around the edge of a circular table in a sculptural composition of the Toilet of Venus. The band system of showing time continued during the 19th century. In its concentration on numbering and disregard for the traditional visual indication of time on the dial, it was a predecessor of ticket and later digital clocks [120/1]. PSKM
See also Vase clocks.

Riefler clock Sigmund Riefler of Munich became the most famous maker of regulator clocks for observatory use, continually striving for perfection of timekeeping. He invented a mercury-in-steel pendulum with mercury almost filling a hollow pendulum rod to avoid temperature differential effects, patented in 1891 but surpassed when Charles Edouard Guillaume invented the alloy invar in 1895. In 1889 Riefler improved his regulators by an escapement which impulsed the pendulum through its suspension spring, making the pendulum virtually 'free' and giving a performance with a daily variation of less than 0.01 second under good conditions. Riefler's final development was to adopt electrical rewinding and place the pendulum and mechanism in an evacuated cylinder to isolate the clock from atmospheric disturbances, making his regulator the standard timekeeper for most of the world's observatories. Riefler's clock represents the final phase of the development of the purely mechanical regulator. CKA
See also Regulator.

5

1

Orpheus clock Square table clock, with alarm, the gilded brass case decoration based on the Orpheus legend; probably south German for the Italian market, c. 1585. British Museum, London.

2 Pendule Louis XIV Regulator by Robert Robin in kingwood and tulipwood case; gilt bronze mounts; case by Balthazar Lieutaud; c. 1770. Victoria & Albert Museum, London.

2

1 Porcelain case Clock by Gavelle *l'aîné*, Paris, in biscuit porcelain case, *c.* 1780. Bowes Museum, Barnard Castle.

2 Rolling-ball clock in ebony case; silvered dial with gilt brass mounts, showing hours, quarters, day of month, moon's age and phases. Mirror in the lid allows the rolling ball to be seen; by Johann Sayller, Ulm, 1626. Württembergisches Landesmuseum, Stuttgart.

3 Roman bracket clock A type of Italian pendulum clock known by this name; by Carlo Antonio Duretti, Naples, 1718. Private collection.

4 Round Gothic clock showing an eight-day fusee, spring-driven movement; by Elias Ingraham, Bristol (55/6). Kenneth D. Roberts.

5 Rocking ship in the arch of the dial of a longcase clock; by John Simpson of Wigton, *c.* 1775. Private collection.

1

2

3

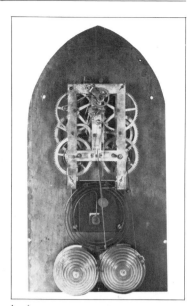

4

Rocking ship One of several variations of simple automata used to fill the arch space on the dials of some late 18th-century longcase clocks. The painted cut-out shape of a sailing ship is attached to the arbor of the anchor escapement, and as the pendulum vibrates the ship rocks from side to side. JM

Rococo The decorative style which succeeded baroque during the first half of the 18th century. Compared with the monumental symmetry of baroque ornament, the asymmetrical shapes of rococo are lighter, more feminine and often entertaining. The term 'rococo' is said to be a corruption of the French words *rocaille* and *cocaille* which refer to the picturesque formations of rocks and shell patterns frequently forming part of rococo ornament. This style was most popular during the reign of Louis XV. Its arrival in Britain coincided and merged with the Gothic Revival and the often whimsical patterns of Chinoiserie. The rococo style had only a marginal effect on clock decoration. It revealed itself mostly in the flower and shell designs and C scrolls of 18th-century brass spandrel mounts on clock dials, and in the engraving of little landscapes on dial centres and on the backplates of bracket clocks [42/1]. JM

Rolling-ball clock The principle of the rolling-ball clock was defined by Galileo: a ball rolling down a constant slope takes the same time to cover the same distance at any part of the slope. This principle was first put to practical use by Christof Margraf of Vienna in 1597, and in the early 17th century other makers such as Hans Schlotheim and Johann Sayller followed suit. John Evelyn described such a clock, which had been presented to Charles I and was later in the possession of Cromwell. This clock had a crystal ball, but the usual practice was to use a steel one. The idea was superseded by the invention of the pendulum clock, but it was revived in the early 19th century by William Congreve. EJT
See also Congreve clock.

Roman pendulum clock An 18th-century bracket or shelf clock, made almost throughout the century, recog-

5

nised from the shape of its case and the bronze ornament. The case usually incorporated mirrors, or else was made of ebonised wood, lavishly decorated with fine carving, pilasters, cornices, etc., and adorned with gilded-bronze finials, fillets and borders. The movement generally included striking for the hours (six) and for the quarters, and often an alarm was fitted. The most famous makers of this type of clock were Angelo Passeri, Domenico Crudeli, Agostino Amonier, Gio Batta Villacroce, Pellegrino Amorotti, Giobatta Vesperiani and Agostino Ajmunier. AL
See also Bracket clock.

Round Gothic clocks The earliest form of American Gothic case design was conceived by Elias Ingraham at Bristol, Connecticut, c. 1840. Subsequently copied and made in large quantities by other firms, it was usually constructed with a mahogany veneer applied to a glued pine frame. J. C. Brown at his Forestville Manufacturing Co. made a limited number, c. 1848–52, in artistically cut fronts, known today as 'rippled fronts'. About 1880 a design patent was issued for an ogee-moulded base, and at this date the E. N. Welch Manufacturing Co. offered this with a single glass door through which a simulated mercury pendulum was visible. This style in both a full rounded top and Gothic form was continued until c. 1890. The earlier form of Gothic rounded arch is referred to among present-day collectors as 'beehive' because of its similarity to the old straw beehives. KDR

1

2

TWO-DIAL STREET CLOCK.

Movement to be placed in building, and connection made under sidewalk.

IRON COLUMN.

15 feet to center of Dial. Dial 40 inches.

1 Rudd's clock Movement of Rudd's slave clock which imparts impulse to the free pendulum above, each minute, and is in turn regulated by the free pendulum, 1899. Science Museum, London.

2 Sidewalk clock illustrated in the Seth Thomas Clock Company catalogue for 1874, Thomaston, Connecticut.

3 Sedan clock with a watch-type movement set in a turned wooden frame; by R. Haworth, Liverpool, possibly using an old dial, c. 1800. Merseyside County Museum, Liverpool.

4 Slave clock made by Gents of Leicester, c. 1930. This slave clock, controlled by a master electric clock elsewhere, is of conventional dial clock design. Private collection.

5 Sharp Gothic clock An American shelf clock; by Smith and Goodrich, Bristol, Connecticut, c. 1850.

6 Sheep's-head clock Lantern clock with balance control; by William Bacon, Colchester, c. 1650.

7 Skeleton clock with its plates cut in the Gothic style; timepiece only; glass dome removed, c. 1860. Private collection.

Rudd's clock A free-pendulum clock made by R. J. Rudd of Croydon, now in the Science Museum, London. A large heavy bob is suspended freely above a fusee clock movement having a small pendulum, used as a slave clock. Every two minutes a constant-force impulse is given to the free pendulum at the centre point of its swing by an arm driven by the slave-clock movement, and as the arm leaves the free pendulum it synchronises the slave clock and simultaneously adjusts the rate of the slave pendulum, if necessary. Rudd described his invention in the *Horological Journal* of August 1898 and July 1899, but it was ignored by the rest of the horological world. Rudd's clock did not incorporate the first free pendulum, as is commonly stated; this was achieved by Sir William Thompson in the 1860s with his centrifugal regulator clock. CKA

Sand glass A mechanical instrument for measuring time, depending on the uniform flow of sand or other fine-grained material through a narrow aperture between two glass bulbs. In the simplest and commonest form the two bulbs are of equal volume, and the unit of time measured is that taken for the whole of the sand content to flow from one bulb to the other. Occasionally, the assembly consists of one large bulb and four smaller bulbs, the time unit being thus divided into four. The earliest-known records of sand glasses date from the 14th century, and one is shown in a fresco of 1338 by Ambrogio Lorenzetti in the Palazzo Pubblico in Siena [121/2]. There are records of sand glasses in ships' inventories from about this date, and it seems that their principal early use was for dead reckoning at sea, for

measuring the progress of a ship requires a timekeeper. Slow-running glasses, emptying in two or four hours, were also used at sea for timing the duty watches.

Sand glasses were sometimes assembled and mounted in groups of four timed for $\frac{1}{4}$-hour, $\frac{1}{2}$-hour, $\frac{3}{4}$-hour and one-hour periods [121/3]. All early sand glasses were made with two glass bulbs separated by a thin metal plate with a central hole, the assembly being waxed together and covered with thread. From the mid 18th century, however, they were blown in one piece, the central constriction being of glass and the opening sealed by a cork. From c. 1800 the opening was sealed after filling by the glass blower, making the whole airtight. FABW

Sedan clock The name given to small clocks which are traditionally associated with the 18th-century sedan chair, though there is no direct evidence that they were used exclusively for this type of conveyance, if at all. They have dials 3 to 4 in. in diameter, mounted in a circular wooden frame turned with mouldings on the front and polished; a pendant bow is fitted at the top for hanging. Their movements are normally those of 30-hour pocket watches, and it is possible that they are derived from the large coach or travelling watches of the late 17th century. AS

Sharp Gothic clock An American case style, designed by Elias Ingraham c. 1843 for use with spring-driven movements, and first produced by Brewster & Ingrahams, probably for the English export market. The design was soon copied by many other firms, including Birge & Fuller

3

4   5   6   7

who made a modified case-on-frame for wagon-spring and later fusee movements. Probably the greatest variety of fusee and spring-wound movements, *c.* 1843–52, appeared in this case. About 1852 a smaller version 16in. high was introduced for casing 30-hour time and strike-and-alarm spring movements. These are known among collectors as 'baby or miniature steeple' clocks. The case was made of pine veneered with mahogany, rosewood, and other exotic woods. About 1888 the E. N. Welch Manufacturing Co. introduced a form with a single glass door exposing the dial and pendulum. The sharp Gothic case was probably the most popular design ever made during the century of Connecticut clockmaking. KDR

Sheep's-head clock A type of lantern clock in which the chapter ring protrudes a considerable distance beyond the normal lantern-clock frame. Although the sheep's-head clock first appeared *c.* 1700, it only became popular towards the middle of the 18th century. The larger chapter ring made it easier to tell the time. The distended appearance of this clock, with the exaggerated curves of the chapter ring on either side, perhaps suggested the coiled horns of a ram, though the term 'sheep's head' seems somewhat strange. JM
See also Lantern clock.

Shelf clock A case-on-case Massachusetts clock made by the Willard school and others in New Hampshire *c.* 1800–40 is often called a shelf clock, but the largest varieties so classified are the Connecticut wood and brass weight movement clocks made 1818–45 in various designs: pillar and scroll, bronze looking-glass, carved column, Empire, ogee, Gothic-on-frame (spring movement), etc. Similar shelf clocks were made in New York, New Hampshire, Massachusetts, Pennsylvania and other states, though the majority were manufactured in Connecticut, the major clock-producing centre in the world by 1840. KDR
See also Mantel clock.

Sidewalk clock Post or sidewalk clocks were first commercially produced in the United States *c.* 1870. The leading firms were the E. Howard Clock Co. of Boston and

A. S. Hotchkiss of New York. The clocks were available in two- or four-dial models from 30in. to 40in. in diameter, supported on decorative cast-iron frames, usually measuring 12 to 15ft from base to dial centres. The clocks made by Howard had the pendulum movement mounted in a compartment about street level. These were eight-day, weight-operated timepieces, with a locked door at the base opened weekly for winding. The Hotchkiss models had the movement placed in an adjoining building and connection was made under the sidewalk. Illuminated plate-glass dials were available. Those made by Hotchkiss were marketed by the American Clock Co., a New York sales combine of prominent Connecticut clockmakers. Probably between 1865 and 1868 the Seth Thomas Co. of Plymouth, Connecticut, acquired A. S. Hotchkiss; it continued to manufacture tower and sidewalk clocks during the first quarter of the 20th century. Many sidewalk clocks were later electrified. KDR

Skeleton clock Most of the craftmanship and decorative features of the mechanism of a clock are seen only by the repairer and restorer, but the skeleton clock is arranged to reveal as much of the mechanism as possible. While the earliest skeleton clocks are mostly French, it is considered to be mainly an English type, mostly of mid Victorian origin: great numbers were produced at the time of the Great Exhibition of 1851. Most have single striking on a bell at the hour, the striking hammer being lifted by a pin on the minute wheel; more complicated examples have full striking, chiming and other features. Escapements are usually recoil anchor, with chronometer, *coup perdu,* pinwheel, dead-beat and gravity examples as variations. Ordinary skeleton clocks have movements on a wooden plinth, but those of better quality have a marble plinth; a glass dome keeps the clock free from dust. A clockmaker usually wound these clocks in Victorian times because of the fragility of the glass domes. CKA

Slave clock Any clock which indicates time without possessing its own internal means of measuring time, depending on an external control, may be called a slave

clock. The term is usually applied to the controlled clocks in a system operated by an electric master clock which sends out pulses at either 1-second, 30-second, or 1-minute intervals to advance the hands of the controlled clocks. Carl August Steinheil of Munich was the first to use slave clocks, these being driven by Daniell cells switched by contacts on the master-clock pendulum. Reliable slave clocks were not produced until the beginning of the 20th century, although one installed at the gate of the Old Observatory at Greenwich by Charles Shepherd in 1852 has been operating almost continuously since then. Slave clocks may be operated in series or parallel, by pulses in one direction, or by pulses reversing for each step; generally today slave clocks work from single-direction pulse circuits and are connected in series, large systems having groups of series clocks further connected in parallel and energised by a relay circuit to handle the large current required. CKA
See also Master clock.

Speaking clock In his journal for 27th April 1762, John Wesley gives a description of a speaking clock made by a Mr Miller of Lurgan, Ireland. The Paris Exposition of 1900 featured a clock 6ft high which announced the hours in a human voice by means of a phonograph. The first true speaking clock was the invention of Bernhaard Hiller of Berlin. An endless celluloid band carried 48 tracks upon which was recorded, 'It is one o'clock, it is quarter past one o'clock' and so on, for a 12-hour clock; or the half-hours for the 24-hour clock. A gramophone motor turned the band and a gramophone soundbox converted the recording on the track into sound, amplified by a small trumpet. The best-known speaking clocks today are those which give the exact time via the telephone system, of which the earliest was installed in Paris in the early 1930s. The British system commenced on 24th July 1936 with a voice recorded on glass record discs. A Hipp-Toggle maintained pendulum was used for the time control with master-clock control correction, an error of one-tenth of a second being maximum allowed. An electric, domestic speaking clock was introduced by the Japanese in the 1970s. CKA
See also Night clock.

Spoon fitting An early hood-locking device found on some late 17th-century longcase clocks in which the hood was raised vertically on runners for access to the movement. The spoon fitting consisted of a small pivoted metal plate rather like a spoon handle, which locked the hood in position. Access to the spoon was obtained by unlocking the trunk door; the device could then be depressed to unlock the hood. The spoon fitting served a dual purpose. It prevented access to the winding holes in the dial without first opening the trunk door, rendering any chance of overwinding the weights (with the consequent risk of snapping the gut lines) unlikely. It also prevented any unauthorised person from tampering with the clock hands. JM
See also Hood, slide-up.

Staande klok The Dutch name for a longcase clock.

Staartklok A type of Dutch clock which derives its name from the resemblance of its long swinging pendulum to an animal's tail (*staart*). AS
See also Friesland clock.

Steam-engine clock During the late 19th and early 20th centuries a number of French novelty clocks were made incorporating a clock movement and dial in models of steam engines, railway locomotives, warships and other such machinery. In these clocks the engines are periodically released by the clock movement and their subsequent motion is derived from a separate spring. Thus the beam-engine flywheel or the wheels of the railway locomotive begin to turn, or the guns of the warships revolve.

One type was made in the form of James Nasmyth's steam hammer, the hammer of which moves up and down at each oscillation of the clock pendulum [107/3]. In this case the pendulum is of U shape, swinging inside the hollow legs of the case and controlling, through a system of levers, a conventional brocot escapement. The clock is of patinated black iron and polished brass fittings, and the clock shown was retailed by a London dealer about 1900. A fine collection of novelty clocks of this type may be seen in the Time Museum at Rockford, Illinois. AS

Steeple clock A steeple is usually thought of as the spire surmounting a tower, but the term was often loosely applied

1

2

1 Speaking clock Automatic equipment to provide the time for telephone subscribers. Installed by the British Post Office in 1936.

2 Stockuhr by Franz Xavier Gegenreiner, Augsburg, *c.* 1770. Maximilianmuseum, Augsburg.

3 Steam-engine clock in the form of a steam hammer; French, *c.* 1900. Said to have belonged to King Edward VII in 1901. Museum and Art Gallery, Salford.

4 Steam-engine clock in the form of an American locomotive; the wheels turn and the bell rings when the brake is released; French, *c.* 1890. Time Museum, Rockford, Illinois.

5 Sweep second hand as applied to an eight-day dial clock fitted with a ½-seconds pendulum and detent escapement; signed 'J. Hanny, Shrewsbury', *c.* 1840. Private collection.

6 Strut clock with rectangular frame in cast brass; made by the British United Clock Company, Birmingham, *c.* 1890. Private collection.

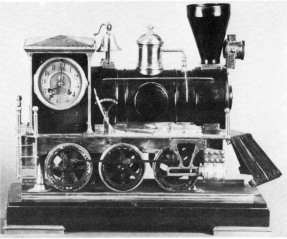

3

4

5

6

in the past. 'The clock in the steeple' can mean one high in the tower or nearer ground level. The placing of a turret clock actually in the spire is met with in Europe but is rare in Britain. When the dial is extremely high it becomes difficult to see the time.

The term 'steeple clock' is used in the United States for the sharp Gothic design introduced by Elias Ingraham in the early 1840s. EJT

Stockuhr The German name for what is usually known in English as a bracket clock. EJT

Stoelklok A type of Dutch clock deriving its name from the suspended, chair-shaped bracket or seat (*stoel*) on which the clock is supported. AS
See also Friesland and Groningen clocks; Twente and Achterhoek clocks.

Strut clock A small portable or carriage clock, designed to stand either in a leaning position supported by a pivoted strut at the rear in the manner of a photograph frame, or vertically supported by a swivel foot mounted on the lower edge. The idea for such a clock was first conceived by Thomas Cole, an eminent Victorian clockmaker, *c.* 1845. The clocks were made to be as thin as possible when folded and were frequently fitted with standard 30-hour Swiss watch movements. Although many minor variations of shape occur they were generally of rectangular, oval or diamond form. A manually adjustable calendar was sometimes a feature of the dial. These clocks can be regarded as a type of *calotte*, a travelling clock which has become very popular in the 20th century. AS
See also Travelling clock.

Stutzuhr The German verb *stutzen* means to cut down in size, and as applied to a clock it implies one not made to stand independently, like a longcase clock, but needing a pillar, piece of furniture or mantelpiece to support it. EJT

Sweep second The introduction of the dead-beat escapement enabled the seconds hand of a longcase clock to advance without the slight recoil which is evident with the anchor escapement. This permitted a much longer second hand, known as a sweep or centre second, which had a 'tail' or counterbalance and extended in length as far as the minute band near the outer edge of the chapter ring. The minute divisions then represented seconds as well, the sweep second completing its full revolution in one minute. Sweep centre seconds were occasionally used for clocks fitted with chronometer-type detent escapements, and they are now common on synchronous electric clocks, on which they move in a steady progression. JM

Sympathetic clock A term first applied to Abraham-Louis Breguet's clock, which had a receptacle into which a pocket watch designed for the purpose could be placed in the evening. The clock would then wind and reset the watch to time, besides regulating it. However, the term now means a clock controlled by a central master clock. Alexander Bain was the first to produce this kind of sympathetic clock, using a pendulum with two solenoids, one for driving the pendulum, the other swinging over a separate magnet, the electrical current thus generated being passed via connecting wires to the solenoid of a second clock, the pendulum of which then swung in sympathetic vibrations. Bain demonstrated two such clocks in 1846, the master clock in Edinburgh, the sympathetic clock in Glasgow, 46 miles away. Frederick James Ritchie of Edinburgh adopted Bain's system with some improvements, the sympathetic pendulums driving the dials of the sympathetic clocks. But none of the sympathetic clocks devised proved successful over a long period. The best of such systems was invented by Professor Charles Féry of France and used in the Paris Observatory for many years in the modified form due to the firm of L. Hatot of Paris. CKA
See also : Pendule sympathique.

Synchronome clock Frank Hope-Jones, in collaboration with George B. Bowell, devised the synchronome remontoire in 1895 after a visit to an exhibition to see an installation of a system of electric clocks devised by Van der Plancke of La Precision Cie., Brussels. The remontoire was first used to rewind the train of a pendulum clock; later, it was arranged to act directly on the pendulum to give an impulse through a roller and pallet. The roller falling off the pallet caused two electrical contacts to close, and an electromagnet replaced a gravity arm in preparation for the next impulse. A count wheel was used to measure out periods of half-minutes from one impulse to the next, the closing of the contacts also transmitting pulses of current to slave clocks in a system. The synchronome clock [266/1] became a standard pattern which varied little over a long period of manufacture. It is probably the best known of its type for use as a master clock, and it was sold in greater numbers than any other thanks to the publicity measures of Hope-Jones. In 1921 it was used by William Hamilton Shortt as the slave clock for his 'free-pendulum clock', installed in Edinburgh Observatory. An accuracy of less than one-tenth of a second a day error was achieved, ousting the Riefler regulator clocks from observatories all over the world. CKA
See also Riefler clock.

Synchronous clock Synchronous clocks were developed in the United States by Henry E. Warren, who obtained his first patent in 1918. There was no general application for this type of clock until alternating-current power supplies were available to large numbers of consumers and the frequency could be maintained at a fixed and accurately maintained value. A rotor is kept synchronously in step with the generator at the electricity generating station, and gearing is used to drive the clock hands; often worm drives are employed to achieve great reduction with the minimum number of wheels, immersed in oil baths to achieve silent running, as the early rotors ran at high speeds. Later models

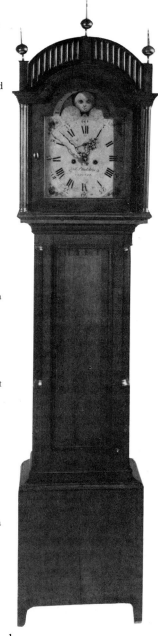

1 Tall clock by Abel Hutchins, Concord, New Hampshire, *c.* 1810. New Hampshire Historical Society, Concord.

2 Sympathetic clock Movement of a clock which is driven by means of an electrically maintained pendulum; each gravity arm is lifted in turn by the pendulum (not illustrated) imparting forward motion to the ratchet wheel of the movement; patented by F. J. Ritchie in 1872. Science Museum, London.

3 Synchronome clock A synchronome remontoire mechanism used to re-wind a converted, but otherwise conventional skeleton clock once each hour; 1897. Science Museum, London.

4 Table clock Gilt bronze pierced case with feet formed as turtles and dolphins at the corners. Outer dial for minutes. Moon phase shown by a globe; Augsburg or Nuremberg, dated 1548. Württembergisches Landesmuseum, Stuttgart.

5 Synchronous clock The movement of an electric mains synchronous clock; it is also fitted with a balance controlled movement which comes into action if the current fails. The balance escapement is 'exercised' every 12½ hours to prevent the oil from congealing through inactivity. Science Museum, London.

6 Tabernacle clock with side removed to show the movement; German, *c.* 1600. British Museum, London.

7 Tablets Painted glass tablets on a banjo clock; the lower one commemorates the action between the *Enterprise* (American) and the *Boxer* (British) during the war of 1812. Henry Francis du Pont Winterthur Museum, Winterthur, Delaware.

1

used a greater number of poles in the field magnet to reduce the rotor speed and, together with the use of plastic gears, minimised the noise levels without the need for lubrication. Strictly speaking these are not clocks but time indicators, for there is no means of measuring time within the synchronous clock mechanism. CKA

Tabernacle clock A table clock with a gallery and, usually, a small cupola above it. The type was made in various European towns from the mid 16th to the early 17th centuries. EJT

Table clock The earliest domestic clock was the hanging iron Gothic clock, but the application of the mainspring led to its being redesigned to make it portable. The earliest spring clock movements resembled those of Gothic clocks; the most important changes in the design were the provision of a case to protect the wheels, the provision of a *horizontal* dial, and the introduction of the fusee connected to the spring barrel with a gut line. The movements of early table clocks were of iron; the cases were richly decorated with engraving, decorative castings, repoussé work and gilding. Some examples were provided with cases of precious metal, and for that reason many have been destroyed. EJT

Tablet The painted glasses decorating the fronts of American clocks have become known as 'tablets'. During the Sheraton period, 1790–1820, looking glasses had reverse-painted upper panels. Massachusetts shelf clocks of 1800–20 frequently had decorated glasses around the dial opening in the upper door and decorative scenes painted on the lower glass panel. The banjo timepiece introduced in 1801 had painted waist glasses, the word 'patent' often appearing in gold leaf. The bottom tablets usually had gold-leaf borders and painted patriotic, allegorical, architectural or landscape scenes. These églomisé paintings were done by professional dial artists in Boston and Philadelphia and, as demand increased, young ladies were trained in this technique. The design was drawn, then painted in reverse on the glass, and coated with a thin layer of white varnish. After Eli Terry had introduced the pillar

and scroll clock, c. 1818, the bottom-door glass consisted of painted tablets combined with gold-leaf or stencilled borders. Such primitive painting, often composed as reverse paintings from landscape scenes, were produced by the thousands, becoming an important aspect of American folk art. After 1830 the quality degenerated with mass production. Although a number of attractive geometric designs were introduced, the former art was almost lost. By the 1860s decal transfers had replaced hand painting. KDR

Tall clock Before 1775 the styles of the American longcase clock closely followed those current in England. Mahogany predominated from c. 1730 to c. 1840, with walnut used earlier and up to c. 1770. Cherry and maple became increasingly popular after 1775, particularly in provincial areas. The scroll top was fashionable in the United States c. 1770, the form and ornamentation being influenced by the progression of Chippendale, Hepplewhite and Sheraton styles of furniture designs. While many native-born craftsmen developed into successful clockmakers, the majority of brass movements with dials, hands, pendulums and weights were imported from England in the period up to 1820. Most were of the eight-day type, arranged for rack

2   3   4

5   6   7

striking. Brass dials decreased in popularity from *c.* 1780 as the imported, Birmingham-enamelled, arched 'white dial' superseded them. Often these imported dials were signed on the face by local dealers. Although case designs closely followed English styles, ornamentation with carvings and inlaid decoration was uniquely American. The 30-hour tall-clock wooden movement which developed in Connecticut achieved importance in rural communities after *c.* 1790 and became common by 1810. This shorter case, usually 6 ft 6 in. high, from less expensive pine or white wood and frequently grained to simulate mahogany, was made in thousands annually by local cabinetmakers in the period 1810–20. The numerous primitive styles reflect the country furniture of New Hampshire, Pennsylvania, Ohio, etc., where they were widely used until replaced by the Connecticut shelf clock during the early 1820s. The more sophisticated eight-day brass tall clock continued to be made in Boston, Massachusetts, and in areas of Portsmouth and Concord, New Hampshire, until *c.* 1840. The term 'grandfather clock' did not become general until after Henry C. Work's song 'My Grandfather's Clock', published in 1875, popularised the name. KDR

Tavern clock Another name for the large-dialled wall clock known as an Act of Parliament clock. JM
See also Act of Parliament clock.

Telleruhr In the 17th century the pewter dish was a familiar household object. The shape must have suggested a clock dial, for in the 17th century clocks began to be made for hanging on the wall with dials in the shape of the normal domestic dish. The movements were light and usually provided with a cowtail pendulum that swung in front of the dial, allowing the clock to hang close against the wall. The movement was usually a timepiece only, without striking mechanism, and contained in a case of thin sheet-iron. The dish itself was of iron, covered with decoration in brass or copper relief. Sometimes the type was adapted to stand on a table and had small feet at the back, and later examples departed from the true dish shape. The German name for this type of clock is *Telleruhr* ('dish clock'). The type is found in south Germany and Austria but does not seem to have been popular in other countries. EJT

Tête de poupée A French clock case of 'doll's-head' shape which evolved during the third quarter of the 17th century. The overall appearance of the clock is, in fact, of an oval head standing on a spreading moulded base, the top of the case being of segmental form and the sides deeply scrolled. In an elaborately decorated finish of Boulle work and applied gilded mounts, and often with an oval aperture embracing the dial, it survived until the Regency (1715–23). AS
See also: Pendule Louis XIV.

Thirty-hour clock A clock which requires to be wound daily, with a margin of generally something over six hours to allow for a delay in rewinding. In particular, the name is associated with longcase clocks of 30-hour duration as opposed to eight-day clocks. Such 30-hour clocks are fitted with an endless rope or chain, the single weight driving both the going and striking trains; consequently, their dials have no winding holes. If they do show winding squares, they are dummy squares intended to suggest that the clock is an eight-day type. It should not, however, be thought that the eight-day type is necessarily superior to the 30-hour, for 18th-century examples of the latter occur in high-quality finish with fine brass dials. There are advantages in daily winding: the clock will probably be checked more frequently, and the endless chain system provides its own maintaining power. AS
See also Endless chain or rope; Maintaining power (both Section II).

Ticket clock An American invention of 1903 utilising the spring-like properties of thin celluloid sheet. Two small circular drums bear a large number of small celluloid tickets free to pivot at the point of attachment on the periphery of the drums, and marked with numbers to indicate hours and minutes. Each ticket in turn is flexed against a pointer until released at the precise moment, upon which the ticket flicks over to display the opposite side, passing over a fixed index which then holds it in place to show the time. The drums holding the tickets are rotated by extended arbors from normal motion work powered by a small, spring-driven balance-wheel clock in the circular base; a glass tube surmounts this and is sealed by a metal circular top with a carrying handle. The visible metal parts are usually nickel plated, occasionally silver plated, and rarely gold plated. The clock was very popular in the United States and was later made in huge quantities in France and Germany. Alternative names for the ticket clock are Plato, digital, flick, flick-leaf and figure clock. In a different form the ticket display is used for the digital display of time in some modern electric clocks, for instance, the Caslon electrical digital clock made by the Copal Co. CKA

Time measurement The presumed-unvarying flow of time is measurable differentially by observing a constant-rate process such as the movement of the sun's shadow on an equatorial sundial, or integratively by counting a series of evenly repeated events such as meridian transits of the sun (solar time) or of a star (sidereal time). For multiples of whole days, time has always been measured integratively, and the necessary counting of days and their multiples of weeks, months and years has been assisted by the use of tallies, diaries, calendars and historical records.

Precision in differential time measurement of fractions of days was dependent first upon the development of accurate means of measuring the constant-rate apparent angular displacement of the sun and stars. The availability of alternative differential methods followed the discovery of such other constant-rate processes as flows of liquids under constant pressure. Precision in the use of these methods depended in the first instance on accurate measurements of length.

The first use of an integrative method for measuring periods of time less than a whole day was probably the mental counting, or tallying, of the constant periods required for the repeated slow filling or emptying of a vessel full of water, or later sand. More general use of integrative methods was, however, dependent upon the eventual discovery of unvarying repetitive processes such as the vibrations of a foliot, spring-controlled balance, pendulum, tuning fork, quartz crystal, or atomic particle, and the development of mechanically or electrically operated apparatus for maintaining such processes.

Time-measuring mechanisms. All time measurements, whether by differential or integrative methods, originally required the attention of a watchman. The need for such attention only ceased when, besides automatic means of maintaining any artificial process involved in the measurement itself, automatic means of differentiation and/or integration had been developed.

Automatic time measurement by a method combining differentiation and integration of time in a single mechanism was employed in early Chinese waterwheel clocks. Other methods of automatic differentiation were those of the Chinese and Arab water clocks in which an anaphoric-dial mechanism of the Greek type was made, by an axle-and-string arrangement, periodically to operate visible time signals and to release metal balls to operate audible signals. Automatic integration followed in some Chinese examples in which the metal balls also operated carousel jackwork.

The Chinese waterwheel clocks also provided continuous integration of time over intervals longer than that required for a single rotation of the water wheel, by toothed wheelwork. With the development of weight-driven mechanical clocks, such wheelwork gradually came into general European use, but it is now being superseded by digital electronic integration in electronic clocks.

Time annunciation. For the results of time measurements to be useful they had formerly to be announced by voice or other audible or visible signal. Parallel with the development of automatic time-measuring apparatus, there was thus a need for the development of automatic time annunciators.

Audible signals have included bells, drums, gongs, rattles, musical wind instruments, guns and, latterly, electronically produced sounds, including voice recordings, for use in telephone and radio systems. Audible signals were at first sounded personally by watchmen, and later by puppets called jacks, operated mechanically.

For literate audiences such as those in early Chinese cities, watchmen also displayed written time announcements on banners or signboards. When jacks replaced the watchmen in the first Chinese astronomical clock towers, it was natural that by the horizontally rotating wheels of carousel jackwork the jacks should have been made to move horizontally across elevated stages like those previously used by the watchmen. The formerly widespread use of carousel jackwork for decorative purposes in European public clocks may owe its origin to this former practical function.

Visible time announcements to the non-literate European public were at first possible only by the use of analogies such as a rotating statue whose hand pointed in the general direction of the sun, or an anaphoric dial carrying the sun's image behind a planispheric astrolabe rete. The European use of fixed dials with circumferential digit markings and rotating pointers, which were originally shaped like human hands, was a late development from the

1 Telleruhr of the late 17th century; by Marcus Bohm, Augsburg.
2 Ticket clock American model, brass-cased with movement inside the base, *c.* 1910. Private collection.

3 Tête de poupée Louis XIV clock known sometimes by this name; signed 'P. Duchesne, à Paris', *c.* 1700. Musée de Dijon.
4 Thirty-hour clock Dial from a longcase 30-hour clock with 'dummy' winding squares to suggest an eight-day movement; signed 'Brown, Liverpool', *c.* 1735. Merseyside County Museum, Liverpool.

1

2

3

4

use of toothed wheelwork for time integration. Recently it has increasingly been replaced by written time announcements in digital displays operated mechanically, electrically or electronically. JHC

Time-switch clock Originally developed for switching shop-window display or street lighting on an automatic programme. Similar clocks had earlier been used for controlling gas lamps by turning a gas cock instead of opening and closing electrical contacts. The use of time-switch clocks was greatly extended during the Second World War, when they were used for time-delay bombs, mines, etc. Nowadays they are incorporated in many devices for control of domestic heating, cooking ovens, lighting for intruder deterrence, process control, etc. An English firm, Horstmann of Bath, have pioneered much of the work in this field. Later developments include the programme clock which will carry out switching duties on a

1 Time-switch clock Control panel and setting dial for a central heating system.

2 Travelling clock, silver cased, in the art nouveau style; hall-marked for 1906.

3 Touch pieces on the outer edge of the dial of a south German drum clock, mid 16th century. Merseyside County Museum, Liverpool.

4 Triple-decker shelf clock by C. and L. C. Ives, Bristol, Connecticut, c. 1830. Kenneth D. Roberts.

5 Torsion clock Skeletonised brass shelf clock with eight-day movement; by Aaron Dodd

Crane, Belleville, New Jersey, c. 1842. New Jersey State Museum Collection, Trenton, New Jersey. Gift of James R. Seibert.

6 Trumpeter clock Black Forest *trompetenuhr,* by Emilian Verde, Furtwangen, c. 1865. Wuppertaler Uhrenmuseum.

7 Türmchenuhren case of gilt copper; the movement rebuilt about 1700. Unconventional quarter chimes moon phase and age. A subsidiary dial on each side shows respectively the last hour and quarter struck; south German, c. 1550. Württembergisches Landesmuseum, Stuttgart.

2

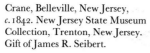

1

3

4

weekly basis, suppressing operations at weekends if required. Many millions of these clocks are in daily use throughout the world; the majority are electrically driven, spring reserve being fitted where a break in supply might result in disastrous disruption to the programme. CKA

Torsion clock The name is derived from the use of a torsion pendulum, which consists of a heavy bob suspended by a thin strip of metal or wire, having the property of combining a long period of vibration with a low energy requirement for maintenance of oscillation when the bob is rotated about the axis of the supporting wire. Robert Leslie of London patented a torsional pendulum in 1793 (patent

no. 1970, dated 13 December). However, the torsion clock is generally attributed to the American Aaron D. Crane, who in 1829 and 1841 received patents for a single-ball torsion-pendulum weight-operated timepiece. This was made for eight-day, 30-day and one-year durations from a single winding and was produced in relatively small quantities, c. 1845, by the J. R. Mills Co., whose New York office was known as The Year Clock Co. In 1855 Crane was granted another patent for a torsion pendulum having 'two or more weights or balls', which was said to be temperature-compensated. After 1857 Crane move to Boston where the one-year clock may have been made in limited quantities until his death in 1860. Silas Burnham Terry received a patent for a torsion balance in 1852, probably for a marine clock. This was adapted to a cheap 30-hour spring movement in either a miniature sharp Gothic or marine wall octagon case. The escapement was a conventional recoil attached to a thin ribbon placed in torsion through a cross-bar connecting rod, but the movement was only manufactured for a short period.

Anton Harder in Germany appears to have devised his torsion pendulum clock independently c. 1879. It went for 400 days, but some models are only of one month duration. The final development of the torsion pendulum clock is the Atmos clock, deriving its power from temperature changes and therefore of unlimited duration. The earliest torsion pendulum clocks are very rare, but modern ones have been manufactured in hundreds of thousands. CKA/KDR
See also Atmos clock; Four-hundred day clock.

Touch pieces Small knobs or points found on medieval and early Renaissance single-handed clocks, for feeling the time in the dark. They were used for weight-driven clock dials and on spring-driven horizontal-dial drum clocks, both of which often had the Italian 24-hour notation. To distinguish the knobs that for XII was usually larger than the others. Their use declined after c. 1600, but the earliest watches of the 16th century were also fitted with touch pieces. AS
See also Hours, Italian (Section V).

Travelling clock A broad term for any clock made to be used when travelling. In the 17th century it usually took the form of an extremely large watch, but bracket clocks and even lantern clocks were made during the 17th and 18th centuries to accompany travellers. They were provided with stout wooden carrying cases, but if pendulum-controlled could not, of course, keep time during an actual journey. Thomas Tompion made at least two clocks which could be converted from pendulum to balance control for travelling; early domestic clocks were very expensive and it was often convenient to be able to carry one's own clock. The Capucine and *pendule de voyage* were the French ancestors of what is now known as the carriage clock which, with balance control, were made in enormous numbers in France during the 19th and early 20th centuries. They were fitted with carrying handles and protective outer cases in a style which was often copied in England and North America. The modern travelling clock, which is known as a *calotte,* unfolds from its case to stand on the hotel bedside table. Among early clocks it is important to distinguish

5   6   7

between those which are travelling clocks (*pendules de voyage*) and those which have handles merely for moving about the house (*pendules portatives*). AS
See also Capucine; Carriage clock; *Pendule de voyage*.

Triple-decker shelf clock A late 20th-century name given to a series of different Empire designs of American shelf case. They were introduced at Bristol, Connecticut, *c.* 1830 to market the eight-day weight strap brass movement with roller pinions developed by Joseph Ives, the original design having been conceived by Elias Ingraham. The features common to all designs consisted of an upper dial door with plain glass; a smaller lower door with a tablet or looking glass in front of the pendulum; and a glass panel between these two doors which extended the width of the case and contained either a looking glass or a painted tablet. Both doors were flanked by half-columns, veneered, stencilled, gilded, grained or carved. Each side of the middle glass was inset with a short whole column, generally turned and decorated to match the door half-columns. On top a splat was set between two short pilasters. Two types of feet were early additions: carved lion paws with the carved column and top cases; turned-ball types, frequently gilded, with the other cases. There were numerous modifications. This style of case continued until *c.* 1850. KDR
See also Empire clock; Shelf clock.

Trumpeter clock The cuckoo clock was well established in the Black Forest by the mid 19th century, but a new product was needed to capture new markets. Jakob Bäuerle in Furtwangen had the idea of using a current of air to sound a trumpet instead of the normal organ pipe of the cuckoo clock, and built the first trumpeter clock in 1857. The figure 'blowing' the trumpet was of a lookout man on the railway who blew his horn to warn men working on the track of an approaching train. The following year a model was produced that played a tune, with the figure in the form of a postilion, a soldier or a Tyrolese. The clocks were expensive, and not many were made; they never challenged the popularity of the cuckoo clock, which is still with us

today. The centre of manufacture was Furtwangen, and the clocks were made in decreasing numbers into the present century. EJT

Turkish market During the 18th century a large trade was built up between Turkey and England. Turkish-market watches are more common than clocks; both had dials with Turkish numerals and often Turkish signatures on their movements. Turkish-market clocks were generally expensive articles, decorated with inlay, tortoiseshell and lacquer, with silver or gilded mounts and frequently incorporating musical work. The type is almost entirely confined to bracket clocks, their decoration being in the European taste except for the exclusion of human representations. A few makers specialised in this trade, notably Markwick Markham of London. The trade declined early in the 19th century [122/1]. AS

Türmchenuhren A German expression meaning 'little tower clocks', applied to the form of table clock that has a vertical dial, in contrast to the horizontal dial of drum clocks. Tabernacle clocks come under this heading and also those clocks whose shape more directly suggests a tower, particularly the hexagonal type favoured in 16th-century France. EJT

Turret clock Turret clocks are large, normally public clocks, housed in church towers, town halls, stable buildings and similar structures. A complete history of European turret-clock development over the centuries would be far too lengthy to attempt here, but eight notable clocks have been selected for detailed review.
Vor Frelsers Kirche, Copenhagen. This clock of monumental proportions, standing about 7 ft from floor to top rail, bears the inscription, 'Johann Mercki Koppenhagen – Anno 1699'. It is of birdcage construction but like so many European clocks it has an additional pair of feet midway between the corner posts to support its great weight, and the corner posts continue downwards to form legs. Each leg has an outward set in it, forming a knee, and at the end the legs

turn over to form feet. The frame bars are fastened by wedges.

The striking and chiming trains are arranged end to end in the outer compartments of the clock, enabling the fly and count wheel of each to hang outside the frame at each end. The going train in the central compartment is at right angles to the other two. Lantern pinions engaging contrate wheels on the striking and chiming trains, and with a spur wheel on the going train, permit winding from the front.

The escapement is of the pinwheel type but this is evidently a later modification. The original recoil escape wheel, together with its anchor, are mounted on the wall of the tower. Many of the train arbors are mounted on anti-friction rollers.

There is extensive decoration. Every lever and supporting bracket is accompanied by a wealth of scroll-work; there is extensive moulding on the horizontal bars, and the end pivot bars terminate with large volutes. The whole front top bar is surmounted by elaborate ironwork decoration, of branches, leaves and flowers. There is a central cartouche containing initials above which is a crown, and elaborate leaf and flower decorations above the front corner posts. The clock itself is painted red throughout, while the decorative ironwork is picked out in green and grey, pink and gold.

Around the walls of the tower is kept a whole range of spare parts. The clock is hand-wound daily, but in spite of its immense size it drives a single dial of very modest proportions.

Cotehele House, Cornwall. The Cotehele House clock is an iron-framed clock of the door-frame variety and dates from the 15th century. The clock is unusual in that it still retains its foliot, which is underslung, a not uncommon arrangement in the door-frame variety. The clock is situated in an alcove of the chapel attached to a late medieval manor house. Above the alcove is a structure resembling a chimney in which the weights are hung. The clock itself is fastened to a stout wooden post which in turn is secured to the wall. The clock owes its survival to the remoteness of the house and the innate conservatism of the noble family that lived there for generations. It must be noted, too, that conversion to pendulum control would have been difficult with the escape wheel so near the ground.

The going train comprises two arbors only. The great wheel drives the escape-wheel arbor below it and is wound by capstan handles on the barrel. The foliot is suspended by means of a metal swivel and link instead of the usual cord.

The striking train above the going train has a count wheel with inside notches and an elementary type of warning control. The wheel teeth are almost triangular in form, and the crown or escape wheel has long slender teeth which engage smoothly with the pallets. There is no dial, as was customary at the time.

The clock has recently been overhauled with great understanding and is in going order.

Cuernaváca, Mexico. This clock, now in the Cortez Museum, Mexico City, came from the nearby cathedral. It is of the birdcage type with end-to-end trains; it has a crown wheel and verge escapement and was probably converted from a foliot. There is a rectangular hole in the top crossbar to which the foliot bracket was originally fastened. Further

1

signs of the conversion are a set in the pendulum to miss the crossbar and a notch in the top bar to allow an even greater swing.

The framework terminates in outward curving feet, and the wheelwork is finely cut. These features, together with the retention of the crown wheel after conversion, suggest Dutch influence. The conversion also indicates that the clock was originally made before 1658 and was converted after that date. It is perhaps surprising that a clock in a Roman Catholic cathedral in Mexico, which was then part of the Spanish Empire, should have come from a Protestant country like Holland, but the contemporary Spanish social structure lacked an artisan class and hired skilled men from other industrious nations – the Dutch, the Swiss and the Germans. Whether the clock was made in Spain or Holland it is impossible to say. Nor is it certain whether the conversion was made in Europe or in Mexico.

St Jacobstoren, The Hague. This large movement with its carillon barrel is preserved in a museum in Utrecht. It measures 8 ft 6 in. × 7 ft 9 in. × 5 ft 3 in. It is constructed of massive iron bars and elaborately decorated with applied iron scroll-work in Gothic arcading, cusping and finials along the upper horizontals, and the frame has 'buttress' posts.

The framework forms three compartments, those housing the going and striking trains on the outside, with the central compartment containing the carillon drum. The latter is made of iron and is 5 ft in diameter. The going train terminates in a verge-and-foliot escapement. The wheel teeth have a square profile and lantern pinions are used throughout; the wheel crossings are divided and splayed.

The striking train is of similar construction. An interesting feature is the two-toothed gathering pallet which drives the count wheel, the corresponding teeth on the count wheel being shaped to engage properly. The arbor carrying the gathering pallet also carries a double lifting cam which lifts the locking piece out of the count-wheel notches. The striking train also drives the carillon, and a very heavy weight was required. To wind this weight a huge wheel has been provided which acts as a fly wheel through reduction gearing. A handle large enough for two

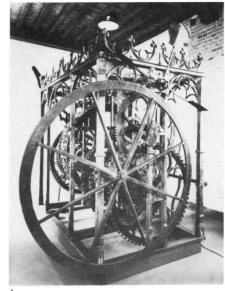

2   3   4

5   6

men to grasp protrudes axially from one spoke at about a third of the radius from the centre. The clock is said to date from 1542, but this probably applies only to the carillon.

The Grand Master's Palace, Valletta, Malta. Manoel Pinto de Fonseta, former grand master of the Knights of St John, rulers of Malta, presented this clock about the middle of the 18th century. It has a three-train movement, the trains arranged end to end, of bar-framed birdcage construction partly assembled with wedges, some of which are split, and partly with nuts. The nuts are either square, decorated with grooves on the flats, or wing nuts formed by winding thin round extensions to the body of the nut into spirals. The frame has crescent finials at each corner; it appears that the crescent originated in Pinto's coat of arms.

The going train has a dead-beat escapement and there is a surprisingly long arm attaching the pallet anchor to the pallet arbor. Lantern pinions are used extensively and the wheel teeth are roughly triangular. The arbors are forged square and have buttress mouldings at the shoulders where the wheels are fitted. The striking control is by means of a count wheel and cam plate – a variety of hoop wheel. The locking of this train, however, takes place on the fly arbor.

Winding arbors are provided at right angles to the main arbors and carry hanging lantern pinions, engaging with contrate wheels on the barrels.

The clock drives a single hand over the dial but there are in addition three other open dials on the stone tower. One is a calendar dial showing the month of the year, another shows the day of the month, while the third is a moon dial similar to that found on longcase clocks.

On top of the tower are three jacks striking the hour bell and the ting-tang quarters. The jacks are dressed as Moors, the traditional enemies of the Knights of St John. The bells are of an unusual shape, resembling large versions of a domestic-clock bell rather than the usual waisted type. The whole clock is in excellent condition.

St Stephan's Church, Vienna. This interesting clock is preserved in the Vienna Clock Museum. It was made by Jakob Oberkinche of Vienna in 1699–1700. The clock is of birdcage construction with flat bars. The corner posts and an additional pair of central verticals are extended downwards to form legs. These have typical knees and feet; the frame bars are held together with nuts [117/5].

There are two trains arranged end to end; the count

1 **Turret clock** from Wells Cathedral, Somerset. Dial inside the south transept with platform for the jousting knights.

2 **Turret clock** at the Palace of Westminster, London. Exterior of the clock, familiarly known as 'Big Ben'.

3 **Turret clock** Wells Cathedral. Original movement of 1392 and 19th-century bells. Lent to the Science Museum, London by the Dean and Chapter of Wells Cathedral.

4 **Turret clock** Flat-bed movement of 1116/2.

5 **Turret clock** from St Stephan's Church, Vienna, now in the Uhrenmuseum der Stadt Wien.

6 **Turret clock, birdcage** Movement from Aynho, Northamptonshire, by Edward Hemins of Bicester, 1740.

1

2

3

4

wheel lies outside the main frame and has square-edged notches. A light cam wheel inside the frame acts as a hoop wheel for strike control. A single locking lever parallel with the arbors and passing through the pivot bar engages the cam wheel and the count wheel. The going train is of interest. The great wheel engages a lantern pinion on the second arbor and this arbor carries a contrate wheel. The contrate wheel drives a short arbor in a horizontal plane on which is mounted a rather coarse recoil escape wheel. The escape wheel, therefore, lies at right angles to the other train wheels. Brackets from each top horizontal support a crossbar which extends beyond the width of the clock. A potence hangs down from the crossbar to carry the pallet-arbor outer pivot. From this arbor there falls a long crutch, while farther out the bar carries the pendulum suspension.

A great deal of decoration has been applied. The brackets supporting the striking-control levers are formed of scroll-work, and the arms of the count wheel are formed into scrolls. The arms of the train wheels are divided at the end. The corner posts and pivot bars terminate in elaborate leaf-like volutes. Heavy scroll-work has been applied to the

lower-end horizontals, some of it actually inside the framework.

Wells Cathedral, Somerset. The movement of this ancient clock is preserved in the Science Museum in London. It is a three-train movement of unusual design. The going and chiming trains lie end to end in a conventional birdcage frame of substantial construction. The striking train is at right angles on a separate frame attached to the other two. In this respect the arrangement is similar to the old clock of Rouen and another at Sammière in France.

The corner posts are set at 45° and have very pronounced buttress mouldings at the bottom. The bottom frame is all of one piece and comprises a flat bar frame (widest side vertical) fastened to the inside of the corner posts by pegs on the corner posts and wedges. The top frame is also all of one piece (widest side horizontal). Holes at each corner have received vertical pegs in the corner post and the whole is secured by wedges. The crossbar is secured by a wedge bearing against a castellated and crosshatched plate similar to that found on the Salisbury Cathedral clock. There is some trefoil iron work on the supporting brackets for the outside pivot post of the striking train. The lighter wheels of the going train and leading-off work are modern. The clock has been converted to anchor escapement with a pendulum beating seconds. The motion work is supported in the museum on a modern wooden stand. The bells are of cast steel, made in the 19th century. The movement was taken to London in 1871 and replaced by a modern one.

When in its original position the clock drove two dials, one of them an armillary astronomical dial, with automata. The mechanism and dial probably date from *c.* 1390.

The Great Clock of Westminster ('Big Ben'). This clock represents the culmination of development of mechanical turret clocks. Its designer, E. B. Denison, later Lord Grimthorpe, incorporated a number of novel features including the flat-bed arrangement, the gravity escapement and precision letting-off of the striking train, and yet Denison was an amateur called in to assist the Astronomer Royal, Sir George Airy, to adjudicate the plans already submitted. These included designs by Whitehurst of Derby, Vulliamy and E. J. Dent. Denison condemned them all as unsatisfactory, but conceded that Dent had been misled about the weight of the bells. He set to work to design the clock himself, and Dent built it. The subsequent history was of acrimony and litigation: Denison met with opposition at every stage, and a less forceful personality would have been deterred. Dent received the order for the clock in 1852 and work started, but he died shortly afterwards and was succeeded by his stepson, F. Dent, who was an unenthusiastic clockmaker but continued the business. A prototype of the gravity escapement was made and tried out successfully in a clock now in the church at Cranbrook, Kent. The Westminster clock was completed in 1854 and ran satisfactorily in Dent's workshop until 1859, when it was installed in the tower at Westminster.

In the meantime there had been trouble with the hands, designed in cast iron by the Westminster Palace architect, Sir Charles Barry. They were far too heavy, so Denison redesigned them using thin copper tube. There were also difficulties with the bells. The first hour bell, which weighed 16 tons – two tons heavier than expected – cracked after being rung occasionally for a few weeks, and after recasting

it cracked again. It was turned so that the crack appeared at the node of vibration, and it has been used ever since without further mishap.

The clock completely vindicated the designer's ideas. It has proved an excellent timekeeper and ran reliably for well over a century. In 1976, however, the clock suffered a serious accident when part of the quarter-chiming train gave way and the energy thereby released from the $1\frac{1}{2}$-ton weight caused extensive damage. The failure was due to cracks caused by metal fatigue in the fly and other parts. Subsequent repairs incorporated safety devices to prevent a recurrence.

The clock is 15 ft 6 in. long and 4 ft 7 in. wide. It is of cast-iron construction, the bed having a deep box section to give rigidity. The four dials are 22 ft 6 in. in diameter; the bells weigh $13\frac{1}{2}$ tons, 4 tons, $33\frac{1}{2}$ cwt, 26 cwt and 21 cwt respectively.

The clock derives its name 'Big Ben' from the hour bell, which was named after Sir Benjamin Hall, Chief Commissioner of Works. DFN

Turret clock, birdcage Early turret clocks were made of wrought iron, which was available in flat bars, easily worked by the blacksmith. The bars were fashioned into a rectangular framework with four corner posts connected by upper and lower horizontals all round. Other vertical bars were fixed to the horizontals, and in these the train wheels were pivoted. Until the 17th century the frames were held together by morticing the horizontals through the uprights and securing them with wedges or rivets.

Most clocks had two trains; some even had a third for chiming. The verge and foliot was the only escapement known, and an end-to-end construction was found convenient. The foliot hung on a central crossbar. After the invention of the pendulum, a few birdcage movements were built with verge and short bob pendulums, and many more were converted from foliot. With the anchor escapement and long pendulum, *c.* 1670, the side-by-side form of construction proved more suitable. When cast iron came into use, the birdcage turret clock gave way to the four-poster turret clock. DFN

5

6

1 Turret-clock dial, 18th century, diamond-shaped.

2 Turret clock Interior of 118/4 with leading-off work.

3 Turret clock dial in early 19th-century dished copper.

4 Turret-clock dial in 19th-century cast iron from Derby Guildhall. Exterior view.

5 Turret clock, cast-iron four-poster, from Wittersham, Kent; by Moore of Clerkenwell. Anne of Cleves Museum, Lewes.

1

2

3

4

5

Turret clock, cast-iron four-poster About 1750 Abraham Darby at Coalbrookdale, Shropshire, discovered how to use coal to smelt iron in a blast furnace, and to run the metal into a mould to form complex shapes. In clockmaking cast iron replaced the wrought iron of the birdcage movement by the end of the 18th century; initially the parts were just cast-iron replacements, some clocks being made with a mixture of cast and wrought iron. The rectangular shape of the birdcage was retained until the mid 19th century, when it was succeeded by the flat-bed design. In the intervening period more and more parts of the frame were cast as one piece.

Unlike wrought iron, cast iron is not strong in tension, and care must be taken to ensure that the members are not weakened by casting defects. Clocks of this type, therefore, tend to be massive, heavy and rigid. The casting of intricate shapes in cast iron led to several decorative features. Clocks by Moore of Clerkenwell, for example, have an arch-like formation at the upper side horizontals and a pineapple finial on the corner posts. These clocks nearly always have two or three train movements with side-by-side trains. Brass train wheels and dead-beat escapements were common. DFN

Turret clock, chair-frame The peculiarity of this type of clock is that the barrels project outside the main frame, which means that the train wheels are on short arbors, avoiding distortion. There are three types of chair-frame, or armchair clock, distinguished by the method of supporting the barrels. In the first type a pair of rods passing through the main frame extend beyond it and are screwed to an end plate, which carries one end of each barrel, the main frame carrying the other. In the second type a complete framework (often cast iron) carries the barrels and is attached to the main frame. The third type is similar, except that the frame carrying the barrels also supports the clock.

Chair-frame clocks are found mainly in the Midlands and north of England. They date from the late 18th and early 19th centuries [131/4]. DFN

Turret-clock dials Apart from astronomical clocks, early turret clocks had no dials and told the time by striking a bell. Dials arrived in the 17th century and at first were one-handed. They were marked in small Roman numerals, mounted on the square and made from wood, stone and occasionally iron. The spandrels were filled with decoration as in contemporary bracket clocks. Very few of the early wooden dials survive. In the late 17th and 18th centuries dials were set on the diamond and the points filled with decoration or the date of installation. Octagonal dials also became common about this time. In the late 18th and early 19th centuries copper dials were often used, circular in shape and dished to present a convex surface. By the mid 19th century cast-iron dials were common. They were made as skeleton dials, and sometimes the interstices were filled with suitable material and painted. At the same time the use of translucent opal glass, which could be back-lit,

6 Regulator, mahogany-cased in 'Egyptian' style, with mercury pendulum; signed on the dial 'Jones, Gray & Co., Liverpool', and on the movement 'James Condliff, Liverpool', *c.* 1830. Private collection.

6

1 Revolving-band clock A large French globe clock with supporting bronze figures symbolising fire and water; signed 'Romilly à Paris'; mid 18th century. Lady Lever Art Gallery, Port Sunlight.

2 Sand glass The earliest existing illustration of a sand glass in a fresco by Ambrogio Lorenzetti, 1337–9. Palazzo Publico, Siena.

3 Sand glasses in a set of four to measure intervals of $\frac{1}{4}$, $\frac{1}{2}$, $\frac{3}{4}$ and 1 hour; mounted in ebony and ivory; probably Italian, dated 1720. Science Museum, London.

1

2

3

1 Turkish market Clock-watch by George Prior, London, c. 1800, in a triple silver case. Fitzwilliam Museum, Cambridge.

2 Turret-clock dial, 20th century, marked with batons on the Shell Mex Building, London.

3 Turret clock, flatbed Movement of a three-train turret clock by E. Dent, now in the Science Museum, London.

4 Turret clock, electric Detail of the 'waiting train' mechanism; the gathering pawl is in the action of being lifted clear of the ratchet wheel by the cam, to re-start at the next half minute in response to a signal from an accurate master clock. Science Museum, London.

GEORGE PRIOR

LONDON

1

2   3

became widespread. A 20th-century tendency has been to omit the dial as such and fix batons to the tower to mark the hours. DFN

Turret clock, electric The most common electric turret clock is driven by a synchronous motor, which runs in synchronism with the alternator at the power station. There is no protection against power failure. Special multipole low-speed motors have been developed for turret clocks. Since the power is applied to the fastest-running arbor in the train, the gearing may often be a single worm reduction running in an oil bath. Impulse dials controlled from a master clock have been used for small turret clocks, but the high load on the mechanism for a short period does not make for satisfactory operation. Rather more successful are electrically driven clocks which are corrected at half-minute or one-minute intervals from a master clock. In the 'waiting train' movement a heavy pendulum is kept in motion by an electromagnet under the control of a Hipp contact. A pawl and ratchet on the pendulum moves the hands forward at each forward swing of the pendulum through a worm reduction gear. The ratchet wheel makes one revolution in 28 seconds, and at the end of a revolution a cam on the ratchet wheel lifts the pawl out of engagement and latches it. An electromagnet receiving a pulse at exactly the half-minute from the master clock releases the pawl, and the hands move steadily forward for another half-minute. In another system an automatically wound, weight-driven train terminates in a fly or eddy current brake. The fly controls the speed of one arbor so that it makes a half-revolution in c. 28 seconds. At the end of a half-revolution it engages a detent which is released by an electromagnet on receipt of a pulse from the master clock. This mechanism is known as the 'half-minute release'. In all cases a range of electric motor driven units are available for hour striking, quarter chiming, angelus ringing or carillon driving. DFN

Turret clock, flat-bed The characteristic of the cast-iron flat-bed clock is the main frame, a shallow rectangular

4

casting with a web around the top and feet integral with the frame. The web was machined generally by planing, and the arbor pivots, like small plummer blocks, screwed into holes tapped in the web. The cast-iron frame provided great rigidity without excessive weight, and its great advantage was that individual arbors could be removed without disturbing the others. Sometimes this was not fully exploited and in some designs it is only possible to remove sub-assemblies as individual units. In many designs provision was made to bolt the pivot blocks beneath the frame, while in others demountable bearings were located in the frame walls. A separate cast-iron block was provided

1 Turret clock – Remontoire
The remontoire train is mounted in a frame, pivoted above and carrying a weight (left). The locking arm and fly are released every half minute causing the main train to carry the remontoire frame to the left, thus gradually imparting power to the escapement as the frame returns to its upright position. The escapement is of Grimthorpe's gravity design. Made by T. Cooke & Sons, York, 1876. Winwick Parish Church, near Warrington. *See* Remontoire, turret clock (Section II)

1

for the pendulum suspension, often combined with the pallet arbors and escapement.

The style probably originated in France, but it was promoted in England by Lord Grimthorpe, who adopted it for the Great Clock at Westminster. Many thousands of flat-bed clocks were made in factories and found their way to all parts of the world. No other design has superseded the flat bed for mechanically driven turret clocks. DFN
See also Turret clock.

Turret-clock, iron marks Occasionally turret clocks of the birdcage type are found with marks stamped in the iron. These are often attributed to the maker of the clock, but in fact often belong to the maker of the iron. From early times Sweden was a large producer of iron and shipped much of it abroad. In 1600 the Swedish government issued an ordinance that all bars must be stamped with a mark to indicate the originating forge. Over 400 forges existed and more than 2,300 stamp marks have been collected. Most of the Swedish iron imported into England was converted into steel in Sheffield. A few bars were used for making clocks and some of these carry the stamp marks. The mark often bore the initials of the owner of the forge, beneath a crown if he were a nobleman. Other marks were symbols, or the initial of the town in which the forge was situated, or

connected with the iron-making process. Not all marks originated in Sweden; some may have been the mark of the clockmaker. DFN

Turret clock, iron two-post The economic design of the wooden door-frame clock was occasionally realised in an all-iron construction. These appear as one-above-the-other or end-to-end layouts. A particularly fine example came to light in 1955 at Cotehele House in Cornwall, complete with its original verge-and-foliot escapement. This was dated to the 15th century and since careful restoration is in working order [115/2]. Like other clocks of this type, the verge and its weights are underslung. A clock of end-to-end construction, probably of the late 18th century, comes from Bere Regis in Dorset. This clock has a great deal of decorative scroll ironwork for a clock of English origin. DFN

Turret clock, medieval The earliest mechanical turret clocks, of which very few now remain, were large iron structures of the birdcage variety. The verge and foliot was universally used and this type of escapement is most easily accomplished with end-to-end trains. Winding was often by capstan, although cranks with withdrawable step-down pinions sometimes appeared as later conversions.

The earliest-known clock still in service is said to have been built in 1389 at Rouen. In England the Salisbury Cathedral clock of 1382 and the Wells Cathedral clock of c. 1390 are good examples. There are records of other early clocks which have unfortunately vanished. Before the invention of the pendulum put an end to the medieval type of turret clock, a number of smaller turret clocks appeared, of which the Dover Castle clock is typical. DFN
See also Turret clock, birdcage.

Turret clock, plate-and-spacer The introduction of cast iron made it possible to produce large areas of metal of comparatively thin section as well as intricate shape. From about the mid 19th century turret clocks were constructed of cast iron as large versions of a domestic clock. These clocks comprise a pair of plates front and back held by spacers, which generally have threaded studs at each end passing through the plates and secured by nuts and washers. The large area of metal, and hence the weight of the plates, made it impossible to assemble the clock like a domestic clock. The arbors were therefore pivoted in demountable bushes which allowed them to be inserted or removed one by one, though it was sometimes necessary to remove some of the other arbors first. The side plates were frequently cast in one piece with the equivalent of pivot bars and stiffeners. Sometimes an open frame was cast to which pivot bars were fixed. The technique of casting allowed the inclusion of some attractive decorative moulding and often the maker's name. DFN

Turret clock, wooden door-frame Iron was expensive until the late 18th century, but wood provided a good substitute for turret-clock structures. Oak beams of about 6in. square section were often used. The great majority were shaped like door frames and are known by this name. There are, however, often two or even three vertical posts inside the main frame, making separate compartments for

2 Turret clock, iron marks
Details of Swedish iron marks from
the frames of English turret clocks:
(a) On a clock by A. & E. Bradley
from the Finnåker forge in the
province of Orebro, Sweden;
(b) On a clock at Lechlade,
Gloucestershire, from the
Lögdö forge.

3 Turret clock, mediaeval
Salisbury cathedral clock (c. 1382)
as found in the tower, but altered
later, as shown here, to an anchor
escapement. In recent years it has
been restored to verge and foliot
and is exhibited in the cathedral.

**4 Turret clock, plate-and-
spacer** at Presteigne, Powys, Wales,
early 19th century.

**5 Turret clock, wooden door-
frame,** with original anchor
escapement and a modified 'kick
starting' for the striking; from
Martley, Worcestershire, c. 1680.
Science Museum, London.

**6 Turret clock, wooden four-
poster,** with original anchor
escapement and pendulum
hanging in the central
compartment of the frame; from
Croxton, Cambridgeshire, dated
1682.

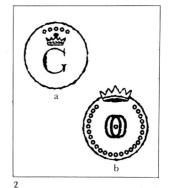
2

3

4

5

6

the barrels and train wheels, thus keeping the arbors for the latter relatively short. Often an incomplete post or strut hung from the lintel of the frame to support an arbor pivot. More rarely the door post sits on a wooden base of similarly sized timbers, strutted with diagonal timbers on one or both sides. The trains are sometimes one above the other, the striking train often being the upper of the two as this suited the striking control, though some clocks have been inverted

during the course of their lives. End-to-end arrangements are less commonly found.

Wooden-framed clocks are common in the central counties of England, especially around Bedford. They date from the 17th century. Early ones have verge-and-foliot escapements, and although most were later converted to anchor escapement, a few are still in use. A feature of wooden-framed clocks is the striking control, which is

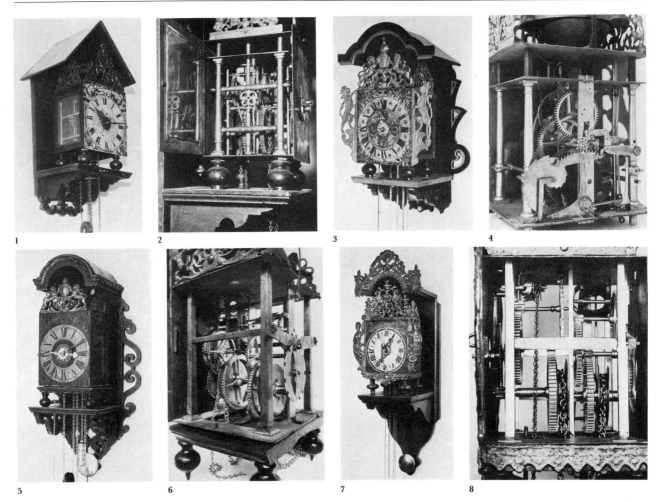

1 2 3 4

5 6 7 8

nearly always of the flail, kick-starting or flirt type. DFN

Turret clock, wooden four-poster Although wooden door-frame clocks are common, the use of timber for clocks having a birdcage or four-poster layout is rare. Edith Weston Church (Leics.) and Coddenham Church (Suffolk) contain examples, both having side-by-side trains. Although timber was used for the main frame, the arbors were pivoted in iron bars as in a birdcage design.

An interesting but unusual group of clocks in this category exists in the churches around St Neots (Cambs.). They are at Croxton, Great Staughton, Buckden and Abbotsley. All four are of similar design and undoubtedly by the same hand. Additional wooden posts and crossbars form separate compartments for the trains at either end. At Croxton, which has end-to-end trains, the pendulum hangs in the central space between the two compartments. At Great Staughton, also with end-to-end trains, the 14-ft pendulum hangs from a separate support on the wall six feet away. The other two have side-by-side trains [125/6]. DFN

Twente and Achterhoek clocks (stoelklokken) The *stoelklokken* made in Twente (the eastern part of the Dutch province of Overijssel) and in Achterhoek (the eastern part of Gelderland province) about the mid 18th century differed considerably from the conventional Friesland type. Among the numerous regional characteristics, apart from those of individual clockmakers, two are easily recognisable. The first is the alarm mechanism. In the centre of the

dial is a large aperture behind which is situated the alarm release lever, which is operated by a long peg perpendicular to the plane of the dial. This peg is screwed into one of 12 or 24 numbered holes in a disc secured to the back of the hour hand. Later clocks lack this disc and the twelve alarm holes are located in the much broadened centre of the hour hand [126/3]. The second characteristic is the relatively precise nature of the cast-lead ornaments above and below and especially on either side of the dial [126/7].

Other types of clock from the east Netherlands which should be mentioned include Laren and Ruempol clocks. During the first half of the 18th century the Gelderland village of Laren was the home of a clockmaker of considerable repute, Gosselik Ruempol. The clocks by this master can be recognised immediately: the top of the bracket is pointed, a lily motif is carved at the bottom of the back panel, and in the bracket support a round hole about 4 in. in diameter allows the cords for both going and striking trains to pass [126/1, 2]. The rectangular dial protrudes on all sides beyond the movement, and the minute hand is curved to accommodate the thumb screw of the alarm peg. The weights are always cylindrical and heavy, the alarm weight 10½ oz., the going and striking trains 11–12 lb. The pulleys are made of wood, while the pendulum bob is usually more or less pear-shaped, with ornamental grooves. Only the oldest specimens have a round or oval disc bob. The pendulum rod is always in two parts, but this is a characteristic found in many other clocks from Twente and Westphalia until well into the 19th century. The move-

1 Twente and Achterhoek clock (stoelklok) by Gosselik Ruempol, Laren, Gelderland, c.1725. Stedelijk Museum, Zutphen.

2 Twente and Achterhoek clock (stoelklok) Movement of 126/1.

3 Twente and Achterhoek clock (stoelklok) by Hendrik Ruempol, Laren, Gelderland, 1751. Frets flanking the dial are unusual in Hendrik's clocks.

4 Twente and Achterhoek clock (stoelklok) Back view of movement of 126/3, showing rack striking work, and wire to link the verge escapement with the pendulum.

5 Twente and Achterhoek clock (stoelklok) An example from Goor ascribed to Jan B. Spraekel, mid 18th century.

6 Twente and Achterhoek clock (stoelklok) Movement of 126/5, showing the anchor escapement.

7 Twente and Achterhoek clock (stoelklok) Gelderland example ascribed to a member of the Rikkert family; typical lead ornaments.

8 Twente and Achterhoek clock (stoelklok) Side view of movement of 126/7.

9 Twente and Achterhoek clock (stoelklok) in a white wooden case, c.1770.

10 Twente and Achterhoek clock (stoelklok) Movement of 127/9, showing verge escapement and alarm.

9   10

ments of the Gosselik Ruempol clocks were not solidly made; they were, however, made with great precision. Gosselik Ruempol's oldest-known clock dates from c.1715, and from 1751 to 1754 he worked with his son Hendrik. There are few Dutch clockmakers about whom so much is known as the Ruempols, thanks to years of research by the collector-clergyman J. H. Kluiver. These researches have been published by J. Zeeman in *De Nederlandse Stoelklok* (see Bibliography). In the clocks made by Hendrik the pointed gable top has a wider angle, and in front it is finished by a triple-arched decorative border. The carved motif at the foot of the back panel is also different; only in Hendrik's earliest work can the modified lily motif be found. There are a number of clocks by Hendrik which do not have carved back panels, possibly to save expense.

A dozen miles east of Laren, in the village of Goor, another clockmaker, Anthony ter Swaek, settled. He undoubtedly competed with the Ruempols, and his competitiveness seems to have been based on cheaper construction and the application of new ideas. In his *stoelklokken*, for instance, ter Swaek did not use the customary verge but the anchor escapement and long pendulum. To prevent the back panel being unduly long, he directed the crutch upwards instead of down, so the pendulum could be suspended high inside the rounded top of the case. The wheels used in ter Swaek's movements are only about half as thick as those in Ruempol clocks; the square pillars and crosspieces are made of iron, and there is no double top plate. However, the alarm operation is similar and follows the east Netherlands pattern. The iron minute hand is also curved to accommodate the thumb screw of the alarm peg, but the hour hand is completely different from those on Ruempol clocks. It is worth noting also that the fly is not situated between the middle and back pillars but between two added side pieces [126/6]. If the total of surviving Ruempol clocks is estimated at 80–100, then the number of surviving Goor clocks is certainly less. Ter Swaek probably sold fewer clocks, and they probably withstood wear and tear less well.

In addition to the Goor centre of manufacture, clocks

with anchor escapements were also made around the little town of Zutphen on the Yssel by members of the Rikkert family. In some cases the back panels of Rikkert clocks are rectilinear [126/7], while other examples resemble the Goor clocks. The pillars and crosspieces of the movement are of thick square iron, but can also be of twisted brass.

A third type of clock among east Netherlands variations is the little stove clock. The simplified movement of this clock is usually contained in a cheap case of white wood [127/9], [127/10]. The function of these little clocks was as an alarm and a rough timekeeper in this country of poor farmers. The minute hand is usually missing and not all the alarm holes have a time indication. JLS
See also Friesland clocks.

Universal clock A clock with multiple dials, which indicates the time in various parts of the world, all the dials being driven in synchronisation from one master-clock movement. The universal clock is also known as a world-time clock, and many were made for the offices of commercial firms, steamship companies, etc., in the 19th century. An outstanding example by Christian Gebhard, begun in 1865 in Marseilles and finished in Germany in 1895, may be seen at the Time Museum, Rockford, Illinois. Since this clock, however, also incorporates mean time, solar time, sidereal time, decimal time, a 24-hour revolving globe, a star and constellation indicator, planetary indicator, perpetual calendar, lunar cycle, Dominical letter indicator, sunrise and sunset indicator, automata figures, a crowing cock and numerous other indications, as well as showing the time in nine of the world's principal cities, it is known as an astronomical and world-time clock [133/2]. AS
See also Dial, universal time.

Vase clock A clock with case in the form of an urn or classical vase. These clocks first appeared in the mid 18th century, when the fashion for classicism was at its height. They are found in great numbers among French clocks, forming a distinct group, but were also fashionable in England and elsewhere. The urns may be of marble,

porcelain, crystal or patinated bronze, usually set with gilt-bronze mounts and often made with a paired calendar in the same form. Most vase clocks are revolving-band clocks, but they may also be fitted with a conventional dial like the Sèvres porcelain clock [128/1]. They were usually of the highest quality and are often found in a dazzling *garniture de cheminée*, the urn clock flanked by candelabra of similar form. The 19th-century makers continued to produce vase clocks but never attained the quality of the first 50 years. PSKM
See also Revolving-band clock.

Veneer A thin sheet of wood cut from timber of fine quality and glued on to a ground of cheaper wood such as pine or oak. Before *c*. 1825 veneers were hand-sawn and were comparatively thick, often more than $\frac{1}{16}$ in., but as industrial mechanisation progressed veneers were cut almost paper-thin by machine. The craft of veneering reached England from Europe after 1660, when the most popular wood was walnut. For good-quality veneering a deal or pinewood ground was used as, once seasoned, it was not liable to shrink or swell with changes of temperature and humidity. The same is unfortunately not true of oak, however well seasoned, as may sometimes be seen on the veneering of the door of a longcase clock where the cross-battens have contracted and torn the veneer in a ragged crack about two inches from the top or bottom of the door. JM
See also Marquetry; Parquetry.

Vernis Martin A general term for all varnishes and lacquers used in the decoration of interiors, furniture, boxes and clocks in 18th-century France. The name is taken from the four brothers of the Martin family who perfected the varnish. In 1730 two of them obtained a monoply for 20 years to make 'all sorts of relief decoration in the manner of China and Japan'. As well as copying oriental lacquer, the Martins also developed a varnish called chipolin which was applied in several coats and rubbed down, like coach varnish. Green and red were the favourite colours but yellow, grey, lilac and other colours were made. In 1749 the Martins' Parisian establishments were created *manufactures royales*, and in the same year they decorated the Dauphine's apartments at Versailles. At the height of their fame they had three workshops in Paris. Louis XV clock cases were frequently decorated with this varnish, but though the technique was inspired by the Orient, the motifs of flowers and leaves painted on the coloured ground were indisputably French [134/1]. PSKM

Vienna Empire clock A term loosely applied to clocks made in Vienna in the early 19th century which were influenced by the French style. While the Austrian clocks were delicately made and were often more complicated than French ones, they usually ran only for one or two days at each winding in contrast to the eight or 14 days of the prototype. Arabic figures were often used on clocks of this type. EJT
See also Portico clock.

Vienna regulator The Vienna regulator resulted from attempts to produce a smaller precision clock than the longcase clocks existing at the end of the 18th century, while retaining the advantages of a long pendulum and weight drive. The earliest examples had the pronounced hood, base and trunk of the longcase clock, but later models had the familiar straight-sided case. The case had glass on three sides, allowing the pendulum and weights to be seen, and although a true regulator has no striking or chiming mechanism, the Vienna clocks were often so provided, and displayed up to three weights. The cylindrical weights had brass cases which, together with the polished pendulum

1

2

3

1 **Vase clock** in green Sèvres porcelain with gilt bronze mounts; movement by L. Montjoye, Paris, *c.* 1770. Wallace Collection, London.

2 **Vienna Empire Clock** in patinated bronze and gilding, *c.* 1800. Uhrenmuseum der Stadt Wien.

3 **Wagon-spring clock** showing J. Ives's patent lever spring mechanism on an American twin-candle finial, sharp Gothic-on-frame clock. Private collection.

4 **Watchman's clock** in an oak case with hood removed; eight-day movement; by Peter Clare of Manchester. Helmshore Textile Museum, Lancashire County Museum Service.

5 **Watchman's clock** Movement and dial of 129/4.

4

5

bob and veneered case back, made a pleasing and dignified effect. The pendulum rod was nearly always of wood, varnished black, but examples with a gridiron pendulum are known. Early dials were plain and had slender hands. The usual length of the case was something over three feet, but some tiny ones were made. Some clocks ran longer than the usual eight days, for a month or three months, and some were provided with subsidiary dials [96/4].

The Viennese clocks were all hand-made, but factory production was started in Germany, where most of the clocks found in Britain were made. The firm of Gustav Becker in Freiburg, Silesia, is well known for this type of clock, and the various Black Forest factories such as Junghans and Kienzle also made them. A German development was the smaller, spring-driven clock, with a gridiron pendulum bearing the letters R A on the bob; but these were not true regulators as they lacked the dead-beat escapement and weight drive. In the absence of a name, the Austrian clocks have certain distinguishing features: the movement is on a wooden seat board; the gong is fixed to the movement rather than to the case. EJT

See also Regulator.

Wagon-spring clock A 20th-century term used by American collectors to describe a clock driven by an arrangement of flat iron strips bolted together at the centre, with each end deflected elastically to function as a spring. These were used only by Joseph Ives or by his permission. The name is derived from their similarity to carriage or wagon springs; Ives referred to them as 'patent elliptical springs', while labels within some clocks call them 'patent accelerating lever springs'. They were first used in eight-day brass and 30-hour wood movements in Empire cases, *c.* 1825, at Long Island, New York, and at Bristol, Connecticut, a few years later. The arrangement appeared again, 1844–7, in 30-hour and eight-day brass movements cased in sharp-Gothic-on-frame clocks with the label of Birge & Fuller, Bristol, Connecticut. Many were exported to England. Ives designed the curved lever arm to

provide for constant tension, thus eliminating the necessity of a fusee, but coiled springs became available which, with fusees, were apparently less expensive than lever springs. The final arrangement of this mechanism was used by Atkins, Whiting & Co., Bristol (1850–6) as a 30-day timepiece with both ends of the levers connected to two barrels, each driving great wheels geared to the time train. These powerful springs were held in a cast-iron frame to which the movement was attached, and were put in both octagon wall and shelf cases. KDR

Watchman's clock This type of clock was introduced for use in factories in the 18th century, when it was known as a recording clock. Controlled by a conventional weight-driven movement, the clock had a series of small pegs mounted round the perimeter of the revolving twelve hour dial, and when one of these pegs was depressed it recorded the time that the action took place. The clocks were mounted in locked cases to prevent any tampering with the time recording, and the peg-depressing lever was operated by pulling a cord, perhaps even located in another room. In this way a watchman responsible for factory premises at night could record for his employer's inspection the timed evidence of his attention to his duties. The pins on the dial were automatically reset every twelve hours by a fixed cam. Several clocks of this type made by Whitehurst of Derby for the pottery firm of Josiah Wedgwood are still preserved by that company. AS

Water clocks Although water wheels were used in Byzantium and Islam to drive machines which displayed automata, there is no evidence that they were used anywhere to drive water clocks. In Europe and western Asia almost all medieval water clocks were operated by the rise or fall of a float in a clepsydra – a vessel into or from which water pours. In its earliest form in ancient Egypt, the clepsydra was of the simple outflow variety – a container with a small hole in the bottom from which the water discharged. Because the rate of flow varies inversely with

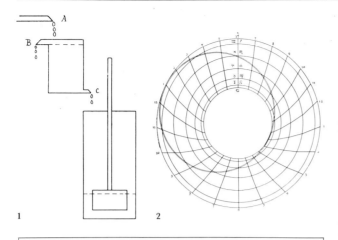

1   2

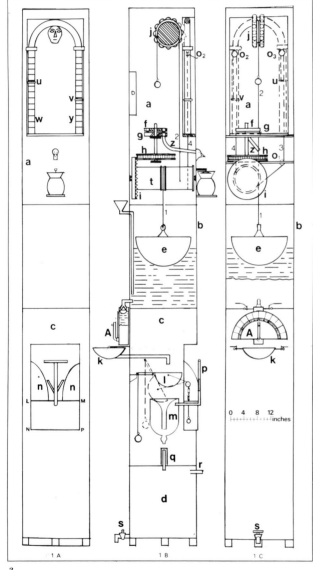

3

the static head of liquid, it was necessary to calibrate the clepsydra by observation: a vertical line was drawn on the inside of the vessel and a mark was made on this line at water-level as each hour passed.

The first true water clock was introduced by the Greeks [130/1]. This used an inflow clepsydra of uniform cross-section, and the water was conducted first into a balance tank with an overflow, so that a constant static head of liquid was maintained, ensuring a constant rate of flow into the clepsydra. The vertical rod soldered to the top of the float in the clepsydra was set against a graduated scale, from which the passage of the hours could be read. With a few exceptions, water clocks recorded temporal hours, and in order to vary the length of the hours from one day to another, a rotatable cylinder was probably used instead of a linear scale. Hour lines were inscribed around the cylinder, to give twelve divisions whose length could be varied by rotating the cylinder by slightly less than one degree a day.

The anaphoric clock described by Vitruvius in 24 BC was driven by a float in a clepsydra constructed on the constant-flow principle. The water flowing into the lower container lifted a float to which was fastened a bronze chain going round an axle and carrying on its other end a sandbag as a counterweight; the axle made a full turn in 24 hours. The axle carried a disc on which was engraved a map of the stars of the northern hemisphere, with the North Pole in the centre of the disc. The ecliptic was shown as a circle eccentric in relation to the pole; along this circle 365 small holes were drilled to take a small image of the sun, which served as a pointer. The scale consisted of a grating of thin bronze wires placed in front of the disc, divided into seven circles concentric with the rotating disc, to represent the zodiacal months – one circle each for Cancer and Capricorn and one for each pair of the other signs. The hours were marked by another system of wires. The construction of disc and grating is fairly complex, and was probably done by methods similar to those used in the marking-out of astrolabes [130/2].

Throughout the Middle Ages there was no real break in the development of the water clock. The transmission seems to have followed the route from Byzantium into Islam and thence into western Europe. It is known that monumental water clocks were constructed in Syria in Byzantine times and that this tradition was continued in Damascus after the Islamic conquests. Thereafter, the construction of these machines was improved and elaborated in Islam. It is not certain when the tradition became established in western Europe, perhaps in Spain early in the 12th century. Ibn Mu'adh, writing in Cordoba in the 11th century, describes complex water clocks that include gear trains and automata. They were probably similar to the water clocks mentioned by Dante, and it seems likely that all the large water clocks of medieval Islam and Europe were of a similar pattern, as exemplified in the clocks described by Ridwan (1203) and al-Jazari (1206). As al-Jazari acknowledges, the basic water machinery of these clocks was derived from a treatise attributed to Archimedes, although al-Jazari made significant improvements to the control systems. In the 'Archimedes' clock the clepsydra is of uniform cross-section and the outflow is kept constant by a sophisticated feed-back control system comprising a float chamber and a conical valve. The rate of discharge was varied for the temporal hours by moving the orifice from day to day around a graduated semicircular disc. (In al-Jazari's clock this was a full circle, accurately calibrated by empirical means.) A string tied to the top of the heavy float in the clepsydra drove the gears and other mechanisms that actuated automata – birds that dropped balls from their beaks on to cymbals, moving human and animal figures

1 Water clock Diagram of the first water clock; more water comes into the clepsydra from A than comes out at C; B is the overflow.

2 Water clock Diagram of the grating of the anaphoric clock described by Vitruvius; the eccentric double circle shows the circle of the Zodiac.

3 Water clock Reconstruction showing three views of the complete Archimedes clock, including clepsydra with control system, drive, transmission and automata.

4 Turret clock, chair-frame Movement of a clock by Henry Hindley of York, National Trust, Wallington Hall, Cambo.

4

1

1 Turret clock, Copenhagen
View of clock and steeple of St
Saviour's Church, Copenhagen,
Denmark (114/1).

2 Universal clock The Gebhard
astronomical and world clock
begun in Marseilles in 1865,
finished in Germany in 1895.
Time Museum, Rockford, Illinois.

2

1

1 **Vernis Martin,** red, on a
French bracket clock with gilt
bronze mounts, *c.* 1750. The dial is
possibly a later replacement.
Bowes Museum, Barnard Castle.

2 **Water clock** Outside view of
al-Jazari's first clock showing the
falcons which discharge balls from
their beaks, jackwork musicians, a
semi-circle of glass discs, one of
which is illuminated every hour,
and a Zodiac circle at the top
which rotates at constant speed.
Museum of Fine Arts, Boston,
Massachusetts. Goloubew
collection.

3 **Water clock** Various types of
cylinders (A, B, C, D) and
partitions (E) for water clocks; A
for swift motion, B for slow
motion, C and D for compound
(irregular) motion. Adapted from
Domenico Martinelli, *Horologi
Elementari*, Venice 1669.

4 **Year clock** This fine example
has a barometer in the door, but
the original movement has been
removed; by Thomas Aynsworth,
Westminster, *c.* 1690. Chetham's
Hospital, School and Library,
Manchester.

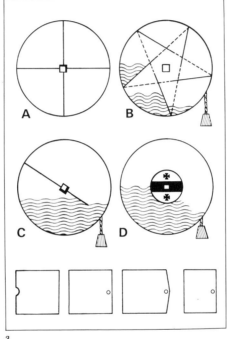

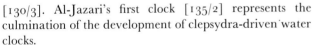

2   3   4

[130/3]. Al-Jazari's first clock [135/2] represents the culmination of the development of clepsydra-driven water clocks.

Another type of water clock is first described in the Alfonsine *Libros del Saber* (1276–7), but it was known in the Arab world at least two centuries before this. It consisted of a drum divided into two or more compartments, the divisions between the compartments being pierced by small holes. The drum was partially filled with liquid – mercury or water – and was mounted on a horizontal axle. The drive was provided by a falling weight whose rope was wound around the axle or around a large pulley wheel fixed to the axle. The torque of the weight was partially counteracted by the torque due to the liquid steadily seeping through the holes, and the drum therefore rotated slowly. The greater the number of compartments, the steadier was the rotation of the drum [135/3]. The displays were of various kinds, but the essential mechanism consisted of a plate attached to the axle, which rotated behind a fixed plate. The moving plate carried astronomical representations or the hour numbers, and the symbols

came into view as each hour passed through apertures cut out of the face of the fixed plate. There is no evidence for the construction of this type of clock between the 13th and 16th centuries, but at the beginning of the 17th century it was described in two treatises, one Italian and one German. It enjoyed a vogue among the rich in western Europe in the 17th and 18th centuries. Some clocks of this type incorporated ingenious striking trains.

Apart from their intrinsic interest, the various ideas deployed in water clocks – gears, automata, etc. – exerted an influence upon the development of the mechanical clock. DRH

Waterwheel, timekeeping An early Chinese timekeeping mechanism dependent upon division of a constant flow of liquid into equal portions by automatic weighing in buckets carried on a vertical wheel. JHC
See also Clockmaking in China: Early History (Section IV).

Year clock Clocks with a going duration of a year were produced as early as the second half of the 17th century, but

135

1 Zaandam clock A simple *stoelklok* with painted wooden dial, *c.* 1730.

2 Zaandam clock Movement of 136/1 showing the striking train behind the going train.

3 Zaandam clock An old type of *stoelklok* with hour hand and separate quarter hour dial; signed 'W. D. Visser tot Wessane ao 1688 – 6/9'.

4 Zaandam clock Movement of 136/3 within a wooden frame; the alarm mechanism is on the left.

5 Zappler clock with its miniature glass dome, signed 'J. Rettich, in Wien', *c.* 1850. Uhrenmuseum der Stadt Wien.

1   2   3   4

they are very uncommon. They were generally timepieces only, as striking mechanisms to go for 365 days at a winding could not easily be accommodated as well as the going train. As it was, the going train of six wheels required a weight of massive proportions. Longcase year clocks look much the same as eight-day clocks from the outside. Only the very robust construction of the movement, the single central winding hole and the size of the weight indicate a year clock. JM

See also Four-hundred day clock; Torsion clock; Train, year (Section II).

Zaandam clock A clock made between *c.* 1680 and 1730 in the area around the town of Zaandam in north Holland. The case of the Zaandam clock has an oak back panel, which is almost always outlined in multiple curves, though it may occasionally be rectangular. This panel is usually veneered in rosewood, or in less elaborate models painted. At the rear is an opening to accommodate the pendulum; at the front, on either side of the pendulum aperture, are brackets that carry the wooden case containing the movement. The case has four twisted or plain pillars and is usually surmounted by moulded frets with tiny glass doors at the sides. The dial is either of painted wood or of velvet-covered brass on which the chapter ring is mounted. In exceptional examples, the case of the clock is made of brass or gilded iron rather than wood.

The striking train in the Zaandam clock is placed behind the motion train. The vertical strip pillars carrying the trains are not, however, connected by a top and bottom plate but by a horizontal bottom and top strip, thus forming a simple frame. The rigidity is obviously inferior to that of the Friesland clock. Nevertheless, the oldest Zaandam clocks take their cage construction from bracketed and Friesland clocks, although in most cases the pillars and the top and bottom plates are of wood. Old Zaandam clocks often have a quarter-hour hand beneath the hour hand.

The alarm system, when fitted, is usually mounted behind the dial as in the ordinary *stoelklok*. The crossings of the wheels are often forked to form heart-shaped apertures. As a rule the pear-shaped weights are suspended on cords rather than chains, and the pulleys are made of wood.

These stylish clocks are early and were produced for only about one-third the time the conventional Dutch bracket clock was made; they are therefore much rarer. JLS

See also Friesland clock; Stoelklok.

Zappler clock A miniaturisation of the standing *Telleruhr* made in Austria. They are only about 2 in. high. The name is derived from the rapidly moving pendulum suggesting the German 'fidget'. EJT

See also: *Telleruhr*.

5

The Mechanical Parts
of Clocks

1 **Arbor** with lantern pinion; the escape-wheel arbor from a regulator (38/6).

2 **Barrel arbor,** with mainspring set-up square on the left, from a fusee clock movement.

3 **Balance,** plain, from a French carriage clock with cylinder escapement; 19th century.

4 **Balance** from a mid 19th-century chronometer.

5 **Balance spring,** of flat spiral form.

6 **Balance, floating,** from a modern kitchen clock.

7 **Barrel, going,** showing the protruding winding square.

8 **Barrel** with Harrison's maintaining ratchet, from a regulator.

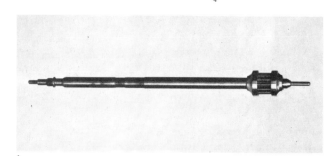

1

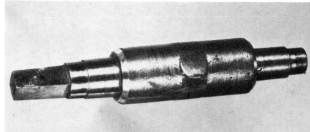

2

3

4

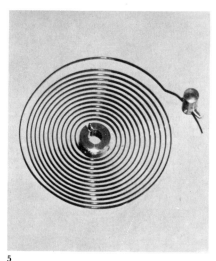

5

Alarm That part of a clock which may be set to give audible warning at a predetermined time. The mechanism is usually triggered by a lever which moves into a slot in a cam driven by the hour wheel, allowing a hammer to strike the bell. JA

Arbor The axle upon which a clock's pinions and wheels are mounted. The arbor carrying the balance or pallets is often called a 'staff'. Before the introduction of economic steel-making methods in the 19th century, clock arbors were usually made from case-hardened wrought iron and subsequently from hardened and tempered steel; but because of the difficulties involved in obtaining and working good-quality steel, early American and Black Forest clocks were often fitted with wooden arbors, steel pins forming the pivots. JA

Balance The oscillating wheel which controls the speed of an escapement, generally used in a portable timekeeper. The time taken for an oscillation of a balance depends upon (*a*) its mass, (*b*) the radius of gyration from its centre of rotation (its diameter), and (*c*) the magnitude of the restoring force, usually the balance spring.

The most important cause of a change in rate in clocks controlled by a steel balance spring is an alteration in the elasticity of the balance spring as a result of temperature

variations. This error was almost eliminated by compensation, the principle which was first applied by John Harrison in the mid 18th century and eventually developed into the bimetallic split balance used until the early part of this century in watches and clocks and still used in marine chronometers. JA

Balance, chronometer The chronometer balance has a split laminated rim made by fusing brass on to a steel ring. This is usually fitted with two large compensation adjusting weights with, at the ends of the arms of the balance, two timing nuts which are used to alter the rate of the chronometer. Many variations of this principle were designed. JA

Balance, floating An interesting pin-pallet lever variant which appeared in the 1960s, the floating balance was designed to reduce balance-pivot friction. This was achieved by supporting the weight of the balance assembly by a balance spring of double helical form, half right-handed and half left-handed, which maintains a constant distance between the pinning points while the spring winds and unwinds. The balance staff and pivots are of unusual construction: the staff is tubular with a jewel hole in each end, and the balance assembly rotates on a vertical fine taut wire. The clock train is laid out between the usual vertical plates, and the lever is arranged to work at right angles in conjunction with the horizontal balance.

The advantages of the floating-balance clock are that errors in poise of the balance have very little effect on timekeeping, and the low balance-pivot friction reduces the energy required at the escape wheel, thereby reducing manufacturing costs and improving life and accuracy. JA

Balance spring Introduced in the last quarter of the 17th century, this device improved the accuracy of balance-control timekeepers from e.g. 15 minutes per day to within two minutes per day.

Early balance springs had few turns and some were even made from straight wire; then Abraham-Louis Breguet discovered that by raising the outer turn of the spring and bending it towards the centre to form an over-coil, the centre of gravity of the spring retains greater concentricity to the axis of rotation of the balance, thereby improving the clock's accuracy.

During the early part of this century it was discovered that a nickel-iron alloy retains an almost uniform elasticity when subjected to changes in temperature. Improved self-compensating alloys have now practically replaced steel balance springs in modern balance-controlled escapements, except in marine chronometers, which still use steel or palladium-alloy helical balance springs and compensation balances. JA

Barrel The cylindrical brass box containing a mainspring. JA

Barrel arbor The mainspring barrel generally rotates on the barrel arbor, and the centre of the mainspring is attached to it by a hook. In going-barrel clocks it is squared at one end to take the winding key. JA

Barrel, going A barrel driving the train directly via a toothed ring on its periphery. In fusee clocks, the barrel drives the train through a gut or wire line, or chain. JA

6

7

8

Barrel, hanging The hanging barrel differs from the going barrel in that it is attached to the clock plates, and drives the clock through the barrel arbor, which turns the great wheel through a ratchet and click. JA

Battery When a number of electrical cells are connected together in a series or parallel arrangement, they are collectively known as a battery. This term is also frequently applied to a single cell. JA

Beat The tick of a clock, or the time taken for a pendulum or balance to swing from its centre, or dead point, to one extreme and return to centre again. Most clock escapements beat twice per cycle. The beats should be equally disposed about the centre or dead point of the pendulum or balance. Single-beat escapements, such as the chronometer and duplex, have one beat on each alternate swing of the balance. JA

Bell The sonorous metal dome on which clocks and alarms strike. Antique clocks have bells cast in bell metal, which is a copper-tin alloy containing approximately four parts copper to one part tin. Modern alarm-clock bells are often pressed from sheet steel, and bells have been made of glass, though rarely. JA

Bells, nest of A number of bells mounted together in chiming or musical clocks. JA

Bob The weight fitted to the lower end of the pendulum. The commonly found lenticular bob [141/4] has the advantage of low air resistance. Regulators and electric impulse clocks are often fitted with cylindrical bobs. JA *See also* Pendulum.

Bob, false The introduction of the pendulum in clockmaking so revolutionised the timekeeping of clocks that makers found it desirable to show that their clocks were fitted with pendulums. Therefore a small additional bob was attached to the verge staff so as to be visible through an aperture in the dial [144/1]. JA

Bolt and shutter *See* Maintaining power.

Bridge A bracket with two feet commonly used to support the pivot of an arbor outside the plates of a clock. JA

Brocot suspension A device fitted to a clock's pendulum suspension cock to allow rate adjustment from the dial. The pendulum spring is embraced by sliding brass chops or jaws threaded to receive a vertical screw which can be rotated

1

2

3

4

5   6

by bevel wheels from a small square, usually fitted to the dial at 12 o'clock. This alters the effective length of the pendulum. JA

Calendar work The function of calendar work is to indicate the date, and in some clocks the day and month also. In simple calendar-work clocks, the calendar has to be reset manually when a month has fewer than 31 days. In this system, a wheel rotating once in 24 hours carries a pin which engages with ratchet teeth on the calendar wheel or ring.

Perpetual-calendar clocks have the advantage of automatic adjustment at the end of short months, and even during leap years, when February has 29 days. This mechanism has a lever operating once daily and banking on a disc which is slotted for the short months, and carries one double-depth slot for 29th February in leap years, thus allowing the lever to gather two teeth of the date wheel in short months, and three on 29th February in leap years. The dial which indicates months on clocks having this mechanism is often divided into four parts, each showing the twelve calendar months and numbered one to three, the fourth carrying the legend 'Leap Year'. JA

Cam Usually a disc or cylinder of irregular profile, contacted by a lever which follows the contour of the disc. JA
See also Kidney piece.

Carillon A set of bells, musically tuned and hung in a tower, played by a pin barrel or by hand. The carillon is

occasionally associated with domestic clocks, and in both types two hammers are sometimes provided for each bell, lifted by separate pins, to increase the striking rate of one note. Domestic carillon barrels were mostly of brass, but tower carillon barrels were of wood with pins driven in like nails, though some later barrels were of iron. To change tunes the barrels could be moved axially to engage a different set of pins. In Europe tower bells are hung dead for tune playing, but in England they are hung for change ringing with wheels and ropes, the mechanical carillon playing the bells in the 'down' position. JA/DFN

Centre seconds A long slender hand indicating seconds, rotating about the centre of a clock's main dial; also called 'sweep seconds', especially in the United States. The centre seconds hand should be very light and counterpoised, as the inertia of an over-heavy hand inevitably results in a loss of energy reaching the escapement [161/5]. JA

Chime, bells Mechanical clocks first indicated the passing of time by striking on bells; dials were not fitted until some time later. Chiming clocks usually have three trains, the chiming train rotating a pinned barrel which lifts hammers to play a short musical phrase on bells or gongs at each quarter-hour. A well-known chime is that of the Great Clock of Westminster called 'Big Ben'. This chime is said to have been taken from part of a phrase in the fifth bar of G. F. Handel's 'I Know that my Redeemer Liveth' (*Messiah*), formerly known as the 'Cambridge Chimes' because they were first heard in 1793 from Great St Mary's Church, Cambridge. JA

1

2

4

3

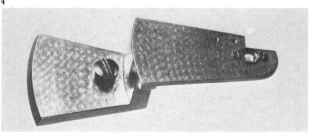

5

1 **Chimes tubes** Longcase clock chiming on tubes.

2 **Click** and ratchet wheel from a skeleton clock.

3 **Chime, gongs** Chiming ting-tang on gongs.

4 **Chime, rods** Synchronous electric clock, chiming on rods.

5 **Cock** for a chronometer balance.

6 **Alarm** A domestic alarm clock, weight-driven, iron-framed, verge and foliot escapement; revolving dial with holes for fitting alarm peg; 15th century. British Museum, London.

Chime, gongs Early clocks and watches all chimed on bells, but this made striking watches very thick. In the last quarter of the 18th century, when the fashion changed to thinner watches, a steel-wire open ring was fitted around the band of the movement and fixed to it at one end. When struck near the fixed end, a good bell-like sound resulted. Wire gongs were later made with many turns in spiral form, to give a low-pitched sound. With their advantage of occupying only a small volume, they have been extensively used in clocks of many kinds since the early 19th century. JA

Chime, rods Modern clocks often strike on metal rods which, like gongs, must be fitted to a substantial metal block attached to a sounding board to give their best effect. JA

Chime tubes Late in the 19th century, musical and chiming longcase clocks were made fitted with tubes from 1 to 1½ in. in diameter and of varying lengths, which were suspended at one end in the back of the case. Tubular bells in this form – the best are marked 'Harrington Patent' – give a mellow, bell-like sound and make a decorative feature at the back of the case when finished in nickel plate. JA

Click The pivoted bar which allows movement in one direction only of a ratchet wheel. In engineering, the term 'pawl' is generally used for the part which horologists call a 'click'. JA

Cock A bracket with one foot, often used for pivoting clock arbors outside the plates, as in the case of a balance or escape cock. JA

1

1 **Bob, false** From a bracket clock with false pendulum bob; by Richard Fennell, Kensington, end of 17th-century. Private collection.

2 **Count wheel** or plate, from a French lantern clock.

3 **Cock,** pendulum suspension, from a longcase clock.

4 **Cycloidal cheeks,** on clock by van Ceulen [56/5]. Hessisches Landesmuseum, Kassel.

5 **Collet,** wheel, from a French 19th-century clock.

6 **Crossings** A crossed-out wheel.

7 **Crutch,** pendulum, the lower end showing engagement with the pendulum of a longcase clock.

2

3

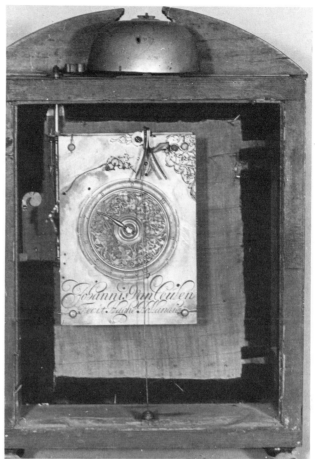

4

5

6

7

Cock, suspension The bracket from which the clock pendulum hangs. In regulator clocks, the suspension cock is attached to a bracket fixed to the backboard of the clock. This in turn should be screwed to a solid wall, gaining greater rigidity than the usual arrangement in which the suspension cock is fixed to the backplate of the movement. JA

Collet The brass ring by means of which a wheel is attached to its arbor. A collet is soft-soldered or driven on to its arbor, then the wheel seat is turned and the wheel riveted on. JA

Count wheel or plate A wheel carrying notches or pins which determine the number of blows struck at each hour or quarter – often termed 'locking plate'. The count-wheel striking mechanism has the disadvantage of striking the hours in progression, easily losing its relationship to the position of the hands. JA
See also Striking.

Crossings The clockmaker's name for the spokes of a wheel. Good-quality clocks generally have five or more crossings in their wheels. JA

Crutch The lever which communicates the movement of the pallet staff to the pendulum of a clock. Two forms of pendulum crutch are commonly encountered: one has a single pin at its lower end, working in a slot in the pendulum rod; the other has a small plate slit to embrace the pendulum rod. Both forms should fit with very little shake. JA

Cycloidal cheeks Poor timekeeping in pendulum clocks results when the pendulum follows a circular path for, when the amplitude of swing changes, the clock loses or gains. Circular error is most apparent in clocks fitted with escapements requiring a large pendulum arc, such as the verge. The error may be corrected by making the pendulum follow a cycloidal path. This was first attempted

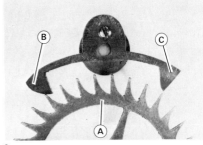

1   2   3

by Christiaan Huygens when he fitted cycloidal checks to the pendulum suspension cock. Other errors in the verge escapement made any improvement gained by fitting cycloidal cheeks very small, so the idea was soon abandoned for general purposes, but was successfully applied in some precision clocks such as John Harrison's regulators. JA

Detent A catch which is moved into the path of a wheel. In the Harrison maintaining power, the detent is the pawl which is pivoted to the plates and engages the maintaining-power ratchet; in the detent escapement, the detent is the steel piece carrying the locking stone, which detains the escape wheel until it is released by the discharge pallet [148/3]. JA

Endless chain or rope *See* Maintaining power.

Escapement The mechanism which releases energy stored in the mainspring or driving weight of a clock at regular intervals of time, maintaining a balance or pendulum in oscillation. The evolution of clock escapements results from the search for a reduction in the influence which a clock's mechanism has on its pendulum or balance. Clock escapements fall into three main classes:

    (*a*) Recoil (verge, anchor).
    (*b*) Frictional rest (dead-beat, cylinder, pinwheel).
    (*c*) Detached (chronometer, gravity, lever). JA

4

Escapement, anchor, inverted-anchor, recoil The recoil escapement most commonly found in pendulum clocks, first used in the last quarter of the 17th century. In an anchor escapement from a 19th-century bracket clock [146/2], the escape wheel A rotates clockwise and gives impulse to the entry pallet B. The pendulum is moving to the left. The tooth will leave the end of the entry pallet, and a tooth will drop on to the exit pallet C. The pendulum will still be moving to the left and the exit pallet will drive the escape wheel backwards. This constitutes the recoil. When the pendulum's swing to the left is complete, the exit pallet will receive impulse from the escape wheel until the tooth leaves the end of this pallet; then the next tooth will drop on to the entry pallet while the pendulum is still swinging to the right. This will again reverse the motion of the escape wheel until the pendulum's swing to the right is completed. The cycle is then repeated.

    The inverted-anchor escapement is a form found in American and German clocks; its action is as described above. The anchor is bent up from strip steel and is often mounted on an adjustable pillar on the dial plate of the clock. The pendulum crutch is riveted directly on the anchor. JA

Escapement, Brocot A form of pin-pallet escapement invented by Louis-Gabriel Brocot, which, when fitted visibly in front of the dial of 19th-century French or American clocks, forms an interesting feature. The pallets are made from cylindrical pins of cornelian or steel. The diameter is slightly less than the distance apart of two escape-wheel teeth, the non-acting half of each pallet being cut away to give clearance. The locking is against the highest point of each semicircular pallet face. Impulse is given on the quarter-circular face from the highest point to the lower lip of the pallet. The escapement can be made dead-beat by cutting the locking faces of the escape wheel tangential to a circle drawn about the axis of the pallet staff, or the escapement may be made with slight recoil by cutting the escape-wheel teeth radial to its axis. The operation of the Brocot escapement is similar to the dead-beat. JA
See also Escapement, dead-beat.

Escapement, constant-force Also known as 'remontoire escapement', and having many differing designs. These escapements achieve a uniform impulse by the use of the driving force to wind an auxiliary spring or weight during a detached part of the escapement's action; the energy stored in the auxiliary spring or weight is used to give impulse to the balance or pendulum while the clock train is locked, thereby providing a constant driving force to the escape-

1 **Detent** from a chronometer escapement.

2 **Escapement, anchor,** from an English 19th-century bracket clock.

3 **Escapement, Brocot,** with escape wheel rotating anti-clockwise, from a French centre-seconds clock.

4 **Escapement, coup-perdu,** from a skeleton clock.

5 **Escapement,** Secticon constant-force.

6 **Escapement, cross-beat,** from an early 17th-century clock. British Museum, London.

5

ment. The Secticon clock constant-force escapement [147/5] was introduced in the 1960s. The driving motor roller A winds the remontoire spring B via the intermediate roller C and the impulse arm D, which is latched by the permanent magnet E. On the anticlockwise vibration of balance F, the impulse pin enters the fork of the impulse arm, which unlatches from the permanent magnet and gives impulse to the balance. At the end of the impulse arm's travel, the roller C's locking nib G is advanced by pallet H, enabling the action to continue. Constant-force escapements can give the highest performance, but cost of manufacture and difficulty in adjustment make this complicated escapement rather rare. JA
See also Remontoire.

Escapement, coup-perdu This escapement is sometimes found in high-quality French clocks; it enables a seconds hand to jump full seconds with a pendulum which beats half-seconds. This is usually achieved by a form of pin-wheel escapement, having one pallet hinged to the anchor on to which the pins of the pinwheel drop. When the pendulum swings to the left, the weight at the outer end of the pivoted pallet lifts the *coup-perdu* pallet clear of the exit pallet, enabling the pendulum to receive impulse on its swing to the right. The next pin drops on to the *coup-perdu* pallet, closing it on to the impulse pallet, thus continuing the cycle of operation. JA

Escapement, cross-beat This 16th-century escapement was an early attempt to improve on the verge. The friction caused by the necessity of coupling the two pallet staffs by gearing or cranks must reduce the performance relative to the verge. In the illustration [147/6], escape wheel A is giving impulse to pallet B. Arm F moves anticlockwise, its motion being communicated to arm G through pinions D and E. When the escape-wheel tooth leaves pallet B, a tooth

drops on to pallet C, receiving recoil, and when the energy stored in arms F and G is expended, the arms reverse, pallet C now receiving impulse until the tooth escapes. Pallet B then gives recoil, thus completing one cycle. This escapement is very interesting to see in action. JA

Escapement, cylinder Sometimes called the 'horizontal escapement', a form of which was patented by Thomas Tompion in 1695 and subsequently perfected by George Graham. It will be found in many platform escapements fitted to 19th-century, and later, carriage clocks, etc. This escapement, the earliest dead-beat escapement for watches, has a steel cylinder A with resting surfaces inside and

6

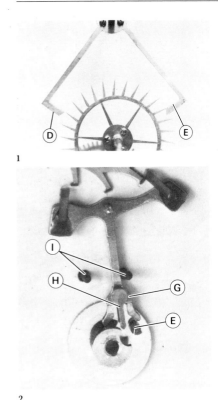

1

2

3

outside for the escape-wheel teeth [149/4]. The lifting face of tooth B is giving impulse to exit lip E, the balance rotating anticlockwise until tooth B is released by lip E, allowing tooth C to drop on to the outside of the cylinder. The escapement remains under frictional lock until the balance, on its return swing, allows tooth C to move on to its impulse face against entry lip D, the balance thereby receiving impulse and tooth C eventually dropping into the frictional rest position inside the cylinder, until the balance again reverses and releases this tooth to continue the cycle. The apparent advantages of this simple dead-beat escapement are offset by the difficulty of retaining oil in its proper place, and by the large radius of the frictional rest from the centre of rotation of the balance, which causes variations, the result of friction and rapid wear. JA

Escapement, dead-beat, half dead-beat, Vulliamy

The dead-beat escapement is attributed to George Graham and was introduced *c.* 1730. This escapement gives excellent results over long periods when fitted to well-made clocks. The locking faces D and E [148/1] form arcs of a circle centred on the axis of the pallet staff. The impulsing is similar in action to the anchor escapement, but between impulses the escape wheel remains stationary, locked on the faces D or E on the pallet. This escapement is admirably suited to weight-driven longcase regulators. For spring-driven clocks, the half dead-beat escapement is more suited. In this escapement, the locking faces are formed to give an amount of recoil judged by the maker to counteract any changes in motive power which must occur in a spring-driven clock, as the resistance offered by the recoil counteracts the increase in pendulum arc which occurs when more motive power is available, and vice versa. Towards the end of the 18th century Benjamin Vulliamy introduced a variant of the dead-beat escapement in which

the angle between the arms of the pallets is adjustable by a screw. JA

See also Escapement, anchor.

Escapement, detached-lever, straight-line lever, right-angle lever

This escapement, which has finally ousted all others in mechanical balance-controlled time-keepers, was first invented in the mid 18th century, although its merits were not fully appreciated until the second quarter of the 19th century, when it began to be produced in large quantities.

The lever escapement may be classified in three main types, the action being identical in each case. The first type, made mostly by the English, has all the lift or impulse on the pallets, and the escape wheel has ratchet-type teeth. The second type has what is known as 'divided lift', i.e. some of the impulse is on the escape-wheel teeth, which are of club shape, and the remainder of the lift is on the pallet stones. This form is fitted to most good-quality balance-control clocks today. The third type is the pin pallet, which has all the lift in the escape-wheel teeth. It is found in low-quality clocks and, although cheap to make, suffers from the disadvantage of rapid wear, mainly because of poor oil retention.

The disposition of the parts allows further classification: English makers usually mounted the lever arm tangentially to the escape wheel, the balance, pivot and escape-wheel pivot holes making a right angle, while the Swiss planted the pivot holes of the balance, pallets and escape wheel along a straight line [148/2].

The escape wheel to pallets action is similar to the dead-beat escapement with one major exception, which is that the pallet stones are angled on their locking faces to give a small amount of recoil, used to draw the lever on to the banking pins I. The forked end of the lever G is about to receive the impulse pin E. The balance is rotating anticlockwise, the impulse pin entering the lever fork, moving the lever to the left, and unlocking the escape wheel and receiving impulse. The escapement then re-locks on to the opposite pallet, and the balance continues its anticlockwise swing. The draw on the pallet stone moves the lever to contact the banking pin, making contact between the guard pin H and the guard roller unlikely.

Frictional-rest escapements, such as the cylinder or duplex, suffer from the interference caused during the locking. In the lever escapement, interference is isolated from the balance during most of its swing, thus detaching the balance from its driving force, except during unlocking and impulse, and gaining the name 'detached-lever escapement'. JA
See also Escapement, dead-beat.

Escapement, pivoted-detent, spring-detent

During the 18th century, great efforts were made to develop a practical marine chronometer. John Arnold and Thomas Earnshaw, working on entirely different lines, developed the detent escapement, commonly called the 'chronometer escapement', Earnshaw's design being adopted by most makers since.

In the modern form of spring-detent chronometer escapement [148/3[the discharge pallet A is just beginning to move the detent C to the left. The locking stone B will release the tooth of the escape wheel G, allowing an escape-wheel tooth to fall on impulse pallet D. As the balance's clockwise swing continues, the discharge pallet releases the gold spring E, allowing the detent to be returned by detent spring F in readiness to receive the next escape-wheel tooth on completion of the impulse. On the return swing of the balance, the discharge pallet is allowed past the detent by the gold spring. This is the only escapement action in the anticlockwise half of its cycle. The action is known as 'single-beat' [189/5].

The chronometer escapement is even more detached than the lever; another great advantage is that the escape-wheel teeth and discharge pallet require no oil. Originally most makers mounted the detent on pivots, with a separate adjustable return spring. This system was used extensively by European makers during the 19th century, but the necessity of oiling the pivot holes was a disadvantage, and the detent and spring formed from one piece of steel is usually found in marine chronometers. JA

Escapement, duplex

A type of frictional rest escapement, utilising an escape wheel with two sets of teeth, one for locking and the other for impulsing. It is normally used only in watches, though occasionally occurring in 19th-century clocks for the Chinese market. AS

Escapement, Galileo's

The story of the discovery of the isochronism of a pendulum by Galileo Galilei's observation of a swinging lamp in Pisa Cathedral is well known. Galileo believed that the pendulum took the same time to swing both wide arcs and small arcs, i.e. that it was isochronous, whereas, in fact, the shorter arcs take slightly less time than the wide swings. Vicenzio, Galileo's son, in 1641, drew a design of a form of duplex clock escapement, given to him by his father [149/5]. The ratchet-shaped locking teeth,

1 Escapement, dead-beat, from an English regulator.

2 Escapement, straight-line lever, from the platform escapement of a carriage clock.

3 Escapement, spring-detent, from a 20th-century chronometer.

4 Escapement, cylinder, from a model illustrating this type of escapement. E. Vanner, Manchester.

5 Escapement, Galileo's, illustrated in Vincenzo Viviani's letter of 20th August 1659 to Prince Leopold [279/5]. Biblioteca Nazionale Centrale, Florence.

4

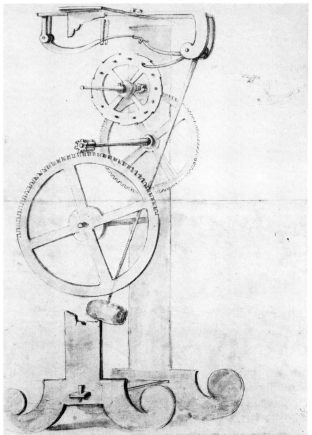

5

formed on the periphery of the escape wheel, are locked by the detent which is shown in the lifted position. The pendulum staff carries two arms; the lower arm is shown receiving impulse, while the upper is lifting the detent. No original examples of this escapement are known to exist. JA

Escapement, grasshopper The very poor quality of oil led the brothers James and John Harrison to develop a clock escapement which would run without oil [151/6]. The brass frame A carrying the pallet arms B and B— is attached to the pendulum crutch D. The pendulum is shown at the start of its swing to the right, and is receiving impulse from escape-wheel tooth F on to pallet C. During the pendulum's swing to the right, frame A brings pallet C— to intercept escape-wheel tooth G, which receives a small amount of recoil, freeing pallet C from tooth F and allowing spring K to move pallet C clear of the escape wheel. The pendulum then moves to the left, receiving impulse from the escape wheel via pallet C— and tooth G, until pallet C is again brought into contact with the next escape-wheel tooth, which under recoil releases tooth G from pallet C—, enabling the cycle to continue.

Only recently have the merits of this interesting escapement begun to be appreciated. This early work by the Harrison brothers eventually led to John Harrison being awarded almost £20,000 for the discovery of a method of finding a ship's longitude at sea to an accuracy of within half a degree of longitude, although the timekeeper which achieved this success was not fitted with the grasshopper escapement. JA

Escapement, gravity *See* Escapement, turret-clock.

Escapement, Lepaute's This escapement is a variant of the pinwheel escapement. In the usual French pinwheel escapement, the two pallet arms are of unequal length. Jean André Lepaute reasoned that the friction and impulse at the pallets must differ, and constructed an escape wheel with two sets of pins. The pallet arms are of equal length, one arm engaging pins on the front of the escape wheel, the other engaging pins on the back. This arrangement made impulse and frictional losses equal on both pallets. JA

Escapement, magnetic Various arrangements have been tried to silence the tick of a clock, but none so successful as the magnetic escapement, in which energy is transferred from the movement to the pendulum by magnetic attraction. In a magnetic escapement [150/1] invented by C. F. Clifford of Horstmann Clifford Magnetics Ltd, and similar to one marketed a few years ago, the escape wheel has a sine wave shaped rim, which runs between the poles of a magnet mounted in the upper part of the pendulum. The spokes and teeth on the escape wheel allow for the pendulum's free swing, impulse being given to the pendulum by the half-sine wave sections of the escape wheel rim.

The escapement has been used in an electrically maintained, transistor-switched, tuning-fork clock to drive the wheelwork from the vibrations of the tuning fork. JA

Escapement, pin-pallet In this escapement the pallets are made from small-diameter pins which engage the club-shaped teeth of the escape wheel, all the lift and draw being formed in the escape-wheel teeth. This escapement is only fitted to low-quality clocks; it is often poorly made,

1   2   3

4   5

and retention of oil on the working surfaces is another problem. JA

Escapement, pinwheel In this escapement, the escape wheel carries pins inserted into one or both sides of the rim and is usually made with the pallets dead-beat. The pallet arms are of different lengths when made to work with pins in only one side of the escape wheel. Although the layout is very different from the dead-beat escapement, the action is similar. The pinwheel escapement has the advantage that the pallets are always in tension, therefore wear in the pivot holes has less effect on timekeeping but, like the pin-pallet escapement, retention of oil on the pallets is poor, causing wear and inferior performance.

This escapement is commonly found in good-quality French clocks made in the second half of the 18th century, and sometimes in English turret clocks. JA

Escapement, Riefler The development of escapements has aimed at reducing interference to the pendulum by the movement. Earlier this century, Sigmund Riefler produced a clock [151/7] the pendulum of which is maintained by flexing the suspension spring. The upper chops of the suspension spring are carried by block A which is free to move on agate blocks BB along the line of flexure of the suspension springs CC. Block A carries the anchor D. The pallet pins E engage two escape wheels FG (F for impulse and G for locking). This type of escapement provides outstandingly accurate timekeeping in mechanical clocks. JA

Escapement, Savage two-pin An early form of lever

1 **Escapement, magnetic,** from a demonstration model.

2 **Escapement,** pin-pallet, from a cheap modern alarm clock.

3 **Escapement, pinwheel,** from a turret clock.

4 **Escapement, Savage two-pin,** illustrated from a watch movement.

5 **Escapement, silent,** with verge gut pallets, from an English 18th-century bracket clock.

6 **Escapement, grasshopper.**

7 **Escapement, Riefler** Movement of electrically wound Riefler regulator, c. 1905. Royal Scottish Museum, Edinburgh.

8 **Escapement, tic-tac,** from a bracket clock.

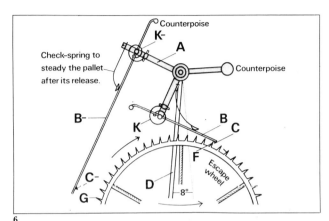

6

8

escapement, designed by George Savage of Huddersfield, Yorks. (d. 1855), in which the impulse pin is replaced by two pins engaging a wide lever notch. This allows the pins, which only perform an unlocking function, to roll in the lever notch, thus reducing friction. Impulse is given to the balance through the guard pin working in a square notch in the roller. JA

Escapement, silent Clocks for use in bedrooms are required to produce as little noise as possible. To this end various escapements fitted with resilient pallets have been made. In a verge bracket clock fitted with gut pallets [150/5], the escape wheel has triangular-shaped teeth which engage short pieces of gut stretched between spring pallet arms carried by the pallet staff. The escapement action is identical to the verge. JA
See also Escapement, verge.

Escapement, tic-tac or drum A form of anchor escapement in which the anchor only spans one to three teeth of the escape wheel. It is fitted to French drum clocks with short pendulums swinging through a large arc. Sometimes one pallet is formed to give frictional rest only, all the lift being on the other pallet. JA

7

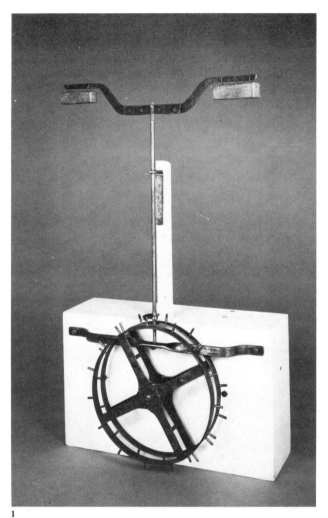

1

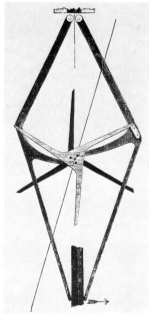

1 Escapement, turret-clock
Richard of Wallingford's
escapement; model by Thwaites
and Reed. British Museum,
London.

**2 Action of gravity
escapement** Diagram to show
the action of the double three-
legged gravity escapement [153/7].

3 Escapement, verge, from a
French bracket clock.

4 Fly from an English 18th-
century bracket clock.

5 Flirt striking work on a carriage
clock (part dismantled).

6 Escapement, turret-clock
Pinwheel type, from a clock by
Gillett & Johnston Ltd, Croydon.

**7 Escapement, turret-clock,
gravity** Double three-legged type,
from a clock by Gillett & Johnston
Ltd, Croydon.

2

3

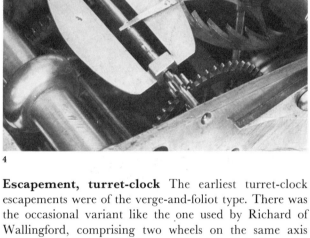

4

5

Escapement, turret-clock The earliest turret-clock escapements were of the verge-and-foliot type. There was the occasional variant like the one used by Richard of Wallingford, comprising two wheels on the same axis between which the balance was pivoted [152/1]. A curved bar at the bottom of the balance engaged alternately the spokes of the two wheels. After Christiaan Huygens developed the pendulum in 1650 a number of clocks were built with crown wheel and large-arc bob.

The improved timekeeping of the recoil anchor escape-ment in 1671 brought a demand for conversion from verge-and-foliot, and the dead-beat escapement also found wide application in turret clocks for many years. It appears in various forms apart from the normal anchor type. In some the pallets are adjustable, either by sliding through the bow of the anchor or by a two-part bow, the relative positions of which can be adjusted by a screw. In one variant the teeth protrude axially from a disc rather than radially from the wheel's periphery.

The pinwheel [153/6] was also widely used. Evidently it

6

7

had a good reputation, as a few recoil escapements were converted to pinwheel by the expedient of inserting pins in the rim of the wheel, leaving the teeth in position. Some very large pinwheels were made, and sometimes the pins fell on pallets fixed directly to the pendulum and not through a crutch.

A major improvement was the gravity escapement [152/2], [153/7], perfected by Lord Grimthorpe (E. B. Denison) and used in the Great Clock of Westminster. The commonest version is the double three-legged. As the pendulum swings, it engages the beat pin on one of the gravity arms, moving it outwards. This unlocks the arbor which rotates $\frac{1}{6}$ turn, locking on the other gravity arm. During the $\frac{1}{6}$ turn, one of the three lifting pins has lifted the gravity arm a little as the pendulum moves. On the return stroke, therefore, the gravity arm moves under its own weight a greater distance than it moved out. The difference of the two movements represents the energy delivered to the pendulum, i.e. the impulse. The importance of the gravity escapement is that the impulse delivered to the pendulum is constant and quite independent of the load on the clock resulting from wind and weather. The fly on the 'scape arbor is essential to provide enough damping to prevent tripping. Other versions of this escapement have appeared – double four-legged and single three-legged. In one version developed by Thwaites & Reed, the impulse takes place on one side only. Commonly 15 legs are used. DFN

Escapement, verge The first escapement known, used in most clocks until the introduction of the recoil anchor escapement in the third quarter of the 17th century. By the end of the 18th century the verge was rarely made, and many earlier verge-escapement clocks were modernised by fitting an anchor escapement. The photograph [152/3] shows a tooth of escape wheel A giving impulse to pallet flag

B. On completion of impulse, a tooth drops on to pallet C, receiving recoil as the pendulum forward swing continues. When the motion of the pendulum is reversed, pallet C receives impulse until the tooth escapes, and the next tooth drops on to pallet B, which receives recoil until the pendulum reverse swing is complete, the cycle then continuing.

The verge escapement has an undeservedly bad name for timekeeping. A clock in good condition, well maintained, will average one or two minutes of error per week over long periods. JA

False plate After 1750 most common longcase clocks were made by batch production methods. When large quantities of engraved or painted dials were required it became impractical to specify pillar positions individually, so shorter standard pillars, which were also less likely to work loose and ruin a painted dial, were provided by the dial maker, to mate with an intermediate or 'false' plate between the dial and movement. This false plate was originally made from sheet iron, later cast iron. It often carried its maker's name, and it could easily be provided with holes and pillars to unite the dial and movement. JA

Flirt A weighted or spring-loaded lever which is wound by the going train and released to let off strike work, etc. with a hammer-like blow. JA

Fly The last element in chiming and striking trains, the fly is a fan brake used to control by air resistance the interval between hammer blows. JA

Foliot The first form of controller used in verge-escapement clocks. The foliot is made from a metal bar, usually with saw cuts in its upper edge which are used to locate two equal

1 Foliot control on a reproduction iron Gothic clock.

2 Fusee from a marine chronometer.

3 Great wheel from a regulator.

4 Fusee, reverse, from a marine chronometer.

5 Fusee stopwork from a marine chronometer.

6 Gears, helical, as used in a month-going skeleton clock by Charles McDowell, Wakefield.

7 Gears, wolf tooth, from a travelling clock.

8 Gears, worm, from an 18th-century bracket clock with platform escapement, for regulation from the dial.

9 Gimbals for a boxed chronometer.

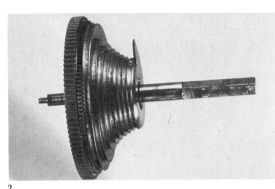

1   2   3

4   5

weights, one on each arm, enabling the clock's rate to be adjusted. JA

Frame The bars, plates and pillars which together carry the mechanism of a clock, most commonly of brass but sometimes of iron or wood. JA

Fusee A mainspring directly driving the great wheel provides maximum power at the escapement when fully wound; the power decreases as it unwinds. This may cause clocks, through escapement error, to gain during the first half of their going period and lose during the second half or vice versa, according to the type and condition of the escapement. The fusee provides a method by which this error is practically eliminated. A grooved cone-shaped brass drum, mounted on the great-wheel arbor and carrying a ratchet wheel at its larger end, is engaged by a click on the great wheel, now running free on its arbor. The mainspring is connected to the fusee by a chain or gut line, which is attached to the fusee at its larger end. As the clock is wound, the line or chain winds from the mainspring barrel on to the fusee until the smaller end is reached, when fully wound. The greatest power of the fully wound mainspring is reduced by the small leverage it has at the small end of the fusee. As the mainspring unwinds, the line winds on the mainspring barrel, and the increasing radius of the fusee matches the reducing power of the mainspring, keeping the torque available at the great wheel almost constant. JA

Fusee, reverse The reaction of engagement of the great wheel with its pinion is transmitted to its pivot and, in the usual layout, the pull of the fusee line adds to this load. In the alternative layout [154/4], the chain unwinds from the opposite side of the fusee, and the mainspring's pull is in opposition to the load imposed by the great wheel's pivot reaction, thus reducing the pivot load. JA

Fusee stopwork A mechanism used to prevent the line or chain being torn from the mainspring barrel in fusee clocks. The stopwork acts when a hinged arm is moved by the line or chain into the path of the hook formed as part of the fusee cap. JA

Gears Gearing is the basis of clockmaking and the ability to calculate the necessary ratios is a fundamental clockmaking skill. To reduce pivot frictional losses, high gear ratios are necessary, leading in turn to losses in the gearing. Ratios above 10 to 1 require very high-numbered wheels to achieve a smooth gear action. The shape of gear teeth is carefully selected so that one tooth rolls on another – ideally, eliminating sliding friction. In clocks this is normally achieved by making the acting parts of wheel or pinion teeth of epicycloidal form (the curve generated by a point on the circumference of one circle rolling around another).

In general engineering, the involute tooth shape is more generally used (the curve traced by a point on the diameter of a circle rolling on a plane). This tooth shape is used because of its strength and because it is possible to generate pinions or wheels of any number, using only one cutting hob. Involute pinions of less than 20 leaves cut with normal cutters have seriously weakened tooth roots, making involute gearing unsuitable for most clockmaking applications. Epicycloidal pinions have teeth with radial sides, giving stronger roots, and can be made with as few as five leaves. The best clocks have high-numbered pinions, with more than eleven leaves, but to obtain the necessary ratios they are more expensive to manufacture. JA

Gears, helical Charles McDowell, a Yorkshireman, pioneered the use of helical gearing in clocks early in the 19th century. Helical gearing allows more uniform transmission of power, even using high ratios, allowing pinions to be made with only one long spiral leaf. JA

Gears, wolf-tooth A buttress-shaped gear profile, sometimes used in the winding work of high-class clocks. It is stronger than the normal symmetrical tooth shape, which allows power transmission in both directions. JA

Gears, worm Large ratios may be obtained using a form of helical gearing in which the driving wheel is in the form of a cylindrical screw, cut with a single or multistart thread and meshing at right angles with the plane of the worm wheel. Worm gearing is occasionally found in the calendar work of clocks, and commonly encountered in the reduction train of synchronous electric clocks. JA

Gimbals The device used in marine chronometer boxes to hold the movement horizontal however the ship may roll or pitch. JA

Great wheel The first and usually largest wheel in a clock train. The wheel mounted on the line or spring barrel in going-barrel clocks, or on the fusee arbor in fusee clocks. JA

6

7

8

9

1 **Hammer** from an English 18th-century bracket clock.

2 **Hour wheel** from an English 18th-century bracket clock.

3 **Impulse face** of a jewel pallet from a platform lever escapement.

4 **Impulse pallet** from a chronometer escapement.

5 **Impulse pin,** from a lever escapement.

6 **Impulse roller** from a chronometer escapement.

7 **Index,** for regulating, from modern Swiss platform escapement.

8 **Index pins,** for regulating, from a modern Swiss platform escapement.

9 **Hipp-toggle** from a modified Bain clock. Royal Scottish Museum, Edinburgh.

10 **Hammer tail** from an English 18th-century bracket clock.

11 **Hog's bristle** regulation on a late 16th-century clock. Hessisches Landesmuseum, Kassel.

1 2 3 4 5 6 7 8

Hammer An arm carrying a weight which moves to strike the bell or gong in the striking part of a clock. JA

Hammer tail The part of the hammer arm which extends below its pivot and is moved by the lifting pins in the pinwheel. JA

Hipp-toggle A mechanism developed by Matthäus Hipp to maintain a pendulum in oscillation electrically (also called 'Hipp's butterfly switch'). The pendulum rod carries a free-swinging vein or trailer which passes over a notched block mounted on the upper pair of contacts. When the pendulum amplitude falls sufficiently, the lower edge of the vein enters the notch, and on the return swing of the pendulum, the contacts close. Mounted on the lower end of the pendulum is an iron bar, which passes close to an electromagnet, which is energised on closure of the contacts in a phase relationship to the pendulum, so as to maintain the

pendulum's amplitude. Alternatively, the same system may be used to energise, whenever the amplitude of the pendulum falls, a coil mounted on the lower end of the pendulum, swinging over a fixed magnet. JA

Hog's bristle Prebalance-spring clocks sometimes had an adjustable arm carrying two hog's bristles positioned to bank the foliot or balance arms. They allowed finer adjustments of rate than were possible by altering the mainspring set-up. JA

Hoop wheel *See* Striking.

Hour wheel The wheel in a clock which carries the hour hand and forms the last member of the motion train, usually rotating twice in 24 hours. JA

Impulse That part of an escapement's cycle during which

energy is transferred to the pendulum or balance from the escapement; also called 'lift'. JA

Impulse face The face on an escape-wheel tooth or pallet nib, shaped to give or receive impulse. JA

Impulse pallet In clocks with escapements such as the chronometer escapement, where locking and impulse are separated, the pallet receiving impulse is called the 'impulse pallet'. The radially mounted stone in a chronometer escapement's impulse roller is termed the impulse pallet. JA

Impulse pin The ruby pin cemented in the impulse roller mounted on the balance staff in a lever escapement. JA

Impulse roller The steel disc mounted on the balance staff of a lever or chronometer escapement clock and carrying the impulse pin or impulse pallet. JA

Index The lever, also termed 'regulator', which alters the effective length of the balance spring in a clock, allowing alterations in the rate to be made by the clock's owner. The best clocks are free sprung, no index being used, as the effectiveness of costly escapement adjustments is reduced by altering the effective length of the balance spring. Rate adjustments in free-sprung clocks may be made by alterations to the balance, using movable weights or screws. JA

Index pins The curb pins, carried by the shorter end of the index, which embrace the outer turn of the balance spring, for making adjustments to its effective length. JA

9

10

11

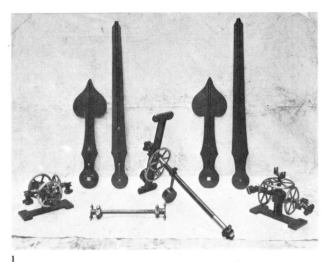

1 **Leading-off work** showing two sets of bevel gears, one motion work plate and two pairs of hands for turret clocks; made by Gillett & Johnston Ltd, Croydon.

2 **Jumper** from an English 18th-century bracket clock.

3 **Lifting piece** from an English 18th-century bracket clock.

4 **Maintaining power,** Harrison's, from an English regulator.

5 **Lunar motion work** of simple form, from a longcase clock. Norman Harvey.

6 **Kidney piece** from a French calendar clock; late 19th century.

7 **Kidney piece** Dial of equation clock, with equation dial (above) sidereal time (left) and mean time (right); the clock has two pendulums and a kidney piece for the equation work; by Daniel Quare, London, c.1710. Royal Naval College, Greenwich.

2   3   4

Invar At the beginning of this century, Charles Edouard Guillaume, in the course of research into alloys suitable for standards of length, discovered that a steel alloy containing 36 per cent of nickel possessed a practically zero coefficient of expansion, some samples even having a negative coefficient. Guillaume suggested the use of this alloy, which he called 'invar', for pendulum rods in clocks. JA

Jewelling One of the early improvements in clockmaking, pioneered by English makers, was the replacement of brass pivot holes with pierced jewels. This was first accomplished early in the 18th century, remaining a closely guarded secret until nearly the end of the century when Abraham-Louis Breguet, among other European makers, started to use pierced jewels in his work. Precision timekeepers were jewelled with natural ruby or sapphire; in work of lower quality, garnet was used.

The pallets of regulators are often jewelled with agate, but synthetic ruby is now used for most horological jewelling. Manufactured by automatic machines, it permits jewelling of movements for a fraction of the cost of former times. The high-speed escapement parts should receive attention from the jeweller before the slower-moving train wheels, and in the lever escapement, the impulse pin, the pallet stones, the end stones and pivot holes of the balance are the seven most important jewels. JA

Jumper A spring-loaded arm, a type of click, shaped to hold the teeth of a star wheel stationary between movements, although allowing the wheel to rotate in either direction. JA

Kidney piece A cam with a profile resembling a kidney commonly used for indicating solar time. Mean time and solar time coincide four times a year and differ by as much as 16 minutes at other times. A kidney-shaped cam rotated by the clock's mechanism may be used to drive an additional hand, indicating solar time, and a sundial may then be used to regulate the clock to mean time, without reference to equation tables. Clocks having a hand indicating solar time are known as 'equation clocks'. JA
See also Equation clocks (Section I).

Leading-off work Early turret clocks seldom had dials, and indicated the passage of time by striking the hours on a bell. When dials were fitted, the hands were connected to the clock by rods; the gears and rods to the dial (or dials) are known as leading-off work.

In the 18th century the leading-off work was fitted with a friction clutch and a setting dial. These features made it possible to set the clock to time without having to 'pump' the escapement or stop it. DFN

Lift *See* Impulse.

Lifting piece The two-armed lever used in striking clocks to release the striking work. JA

Line, gut The strong thin cord used to hang a clock weight or to connect the mainspring to the fusee in lower-quality fusee clocks, good fusee clocks having chains. The best gut clock lines were made from sheep's intestines, but monofilament nylon is now used as a safer alternative. JA

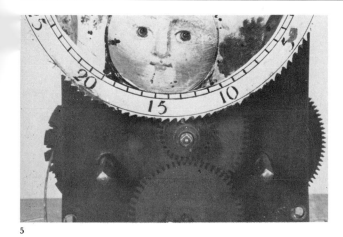

5

Line, rope Rope is often used to drive early lantern-frame clocks and has a special open weave which is not easily damaged by the spiked pulley. Clock rope is still available in various thicknesses.

Several methods are used to make the necessary joint in the Christiaan Huygens endless-rope winding system. Splicing or sewing are satisfactory, but perhaps the simplest way is to bind the rope ends, cut cleanly across, then join the severed ends with epoxy resin adhesive and allow to set before removing the binding. The aim should be to keep the rope flexible and the same thickness throughout. JA

Line, wire Clocks with a longer going time than eight days require heavy weights or strong springs to drive them, and stranded steel-wire lines are often used. Steel lines, however, disfigure the barrel and fusee and should only be used on clocks requiring them. JA

Locking plate *See* Count wheel.

Mainspring *See* Spring, main-.

Lunar motion work The mechanism driving the lunar dial or hand of a clock. The period between one full moon and the next is stated by the British *Nautical Almanac* to be 29·530589 days. Few clocks achieve anything like this accuracy; most show 29½ days as the lunar period. A double lunar dial cut with 59 teeth and advanced by a pin in the 24-hour calendar wheel is a common arrangement. Many clocks have 118 ratchet teeth on the lunar disc, and are advanced by a pin in the hour wheel twice per day.

An error of only 57·1 seconds per lunation is achieved with this train: a pinion of four, revolving once in twelve hours, driving a wheel of 45, has on its arbor a pinion of twelve driving the moon disc, cut with 126 teeth. Clocks with this lunar motion train require resetting much less frequently than those made to show a lunation of 29½ days. JA

Maintaining power A mechanism to maintain a clock's drive during the operation of winding. The poor accuracy of pre-pendulum clocks meant that there was little need to keep them going during winding.

The Christiaan Huygens endless rope or chain provides the simplest maintaining power. A continuous band of rope is run over two pulleys, forming two loops. The driving

weight hangs in one loop with a smaller weight or lead ring hanging in the other to tension the system. In a striking clock, one of the top pulleys drives the striking train through a ratchet and click, the other pulley being fixed to the great wheel of the going train. The clock is wound by pulling down the length of rope between the smaller weight and the striking-train pulley. This raises the larger weight without removing its effect from the going train, and one weight drives both trains. The problem with this system is that it is difficult to arrange for the clock to run for longer than 30 hours, whereas in timepieces the top pulley with its ratchet is attached to the case or movement, allowing the timepiece to run for up to eight days.

In a domestic or turret clock fitted with bolt and shutter maintaining power, the shutter(s) normally covering the winding square(s) can be raised by moving a lever or pulling a cord, which at the same time raises a small weight, coupled with a train wheel by the bolt or a click, to drive the clock during winding [179/5].

6

7

1 **Movement**, brass, eight-day, from an English bracket clock; front plate with striking action.

2 **Movement** Back plate of 160/1 with maker's signature; by Ollivants, Manchester, c. 1800. Private collection.

3 **Movement**, brass, eight-day, three-train, from an elaborate longcase clock by Joseph Finney, Liverpool, 37/7. Merseyside County Museum, Liverpool.

4 **Motion work** from an 18th-century bracket clock, including the calendar work (lower wheel on right).

5 **Centre-seconds** skeleton clock with gravity escapement and mercurial pendulum.

The most common type of maintaining power was invented by John Harrison for use in his clocks and chronometers. In this form, the driving weight is attached to the barrel in the normal way, transmitting its power through the barrel ratchet to a click mounted on a thin wheel cut with fine ratchet teeth. The teeth of this wheel, which runs free on the barrel arbor, are engaged by a detent pivoted to the plates. The power then passes through springs to the great wheel, also running free on the barrel arbor. The springs between the great wheel and the thin ratchet wheel are loaded by the mainspring or driving weight. During winding, the loading is removed and the springs are prevented from expanding by the detent pivoted to the plates, thereby giving their power to the great wheel and maintaining the action of the clock for a number of minutes until winding is complete. This method is also used on some turret clocks [158/4].

In the 'sun and planet' maintaining-power mechanism, an epicyclic wheel train is mounted between the barrel and great wheel. The winding arbor rotates the planet wheels around the axis of the barrel, winding the weights by differential action, without stopping the clock.

Lord Grimthorpe devised a special winder for the Westminster clock. This is not unlike an epicyclic except that the planet carrier engages the annulus by a click and ratchet arrangement, thus limiting the movement of the arm to about 60°. A stop prevents further movement, but the winder can run the device back and take another bite. In this case the barrel is attached to the sun wheel and the winding square is on the planet wheel. JA/DFN

Motion work The train of wheels in a clock giving the usual 12 to 1 reduction between the minute and hour hands. JA

Motor The term used in the United States for the mainspring and barrel. It also applies to the driving unit of electric clocks. JA

Movement The whole mechanism of a clock, excluding the dial and case. Until the end of the 16th century in Europe, clock plates and wheels were usually made of wrought iron, but this was followed in the 17th century by cast brass, hammer-hardened and finished by scraping and

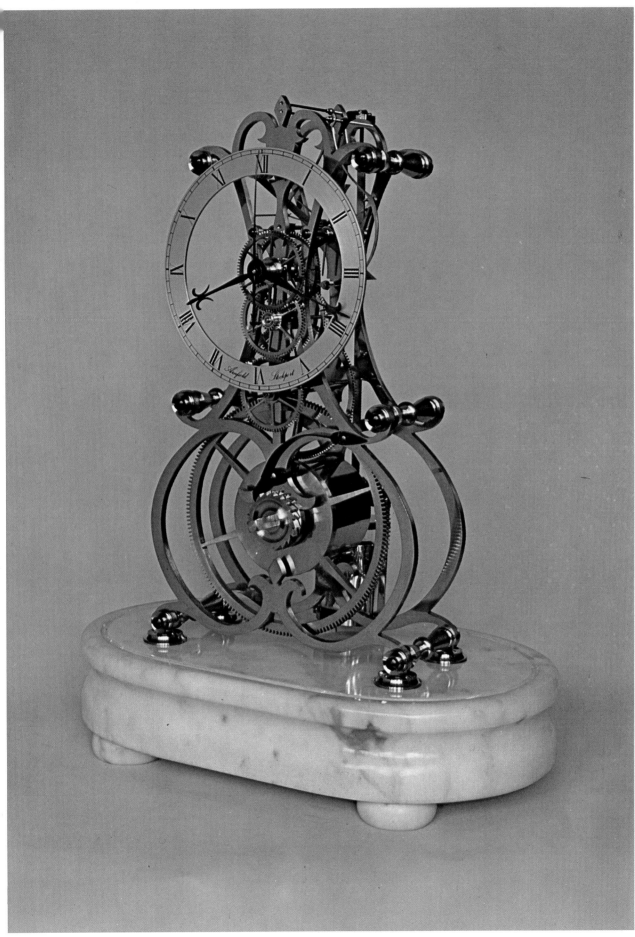

1

1 French urn clock fitted with a tic-tac escapement, early 19th century.

2 Movement, brass, eight-day, from an American longcase clock, showing the striking action and the way in which the brass plates have been cut away to save metal; by James C. Cole, Rochester, New Hampshire, early 19th century. Private collection.

3 Movement, wooden, 30-hour, from an American longcase clock, showing wooden wheels, pinions and arbors; signed 'Thomas & Hoadley, Plymouth', Connecticut, *c.* 1813.

4 Movement, brass, French drum type, alarm/timepiece only. Seen from back plate showing the external lever escapement; by Victor-Athanase Pierret, *c.* 1890. Private collection.

5 Movement, wooden, 30-hour, from an American shelf clock, showing striking train and wooden count plate; the escape wheel is brass. Eli Terry's 1823 five-wheeled time train patent.

6 Movement, brass strap frame, eight-day, from an American 'triple decker' shelf clock; by Joseph Ives, Bristol, Connecticut, *c.* 1835.

7 Movement, tinplate, eight-day, from an American mantel clock; made by Joseph Ives, Bristol, Connecticut, for a clock with the label 'E. Ingraham & Co.', 1861.

2   3   4

5   6   7

polishing, a method followed well into the 19th century. However, rolled brass replaced cast brass in the United States, where it was introduced by Joseph Ives *c.* 1825–32, when he first made clock frames from wrought-brass strips. Owing to the difficulty of obtaining brass, wooden movements were extensively made for tall clocks in the United States, perhaps as early as 1750. There is no direct evidence that the idea came from Europe, even though wood continued to be a traditional material for movements in Austria and Switzerland until the 19th century. Again for economic reasons, wooden movements became standard for American shelf clocks, being produced in hundreds of thousands *c.* 1830–40. In 1859 a tin-plate movement was designed by Joseph Ives in which the plates and wheel blanks were made from tinned cold-rolled iron, though the method was discontinued a few years later. JA/KDR

1
2
3
4
5
6

Musical work The parts of a clock which play a tune, by means of a pin barrel, on bells, organ pipes or reeds; similar in action to a music box [180/1]. JA

Nut The threaded metal block used to secure components with the aid of a screw. By the middle of the 16th century screws had begun to be used by clockmakers, and they have been used increasingly since. However, the old wedges or pins continued well into the 20th century. JA

Nut, wing Nuts with flattened 'ears', allowing easy adjustment by the fingers. They are sometimes found in place of a knurled rating nut at the lower end of a pendulum. JA

Oil To lubricate clocks effectively is one of the horologist's greatest problems. In the past, mixtures of animal and vegetable oils were used. Great care is necessary in refining oils, to prevent their decomposition into a corrosive varnish-like substance after a few months of running. Only the best-quality oil, which must be of the correct grade for the size of the parts to be lubricated, should be used. The mainspring and escapement require different grades. Many beginners make the mistake of over-oiling clocks, even to the extent of lubricating the wheel and pinion teeth, which are designed to run dry. Only sufficient oil to form a small meniscus in the bottom of the oil sink should be applied to the pivot holes.

Frictional rest and recoil escapements should have the pallet faces lightly oiled, although some clock repairers maintain that clocks fitted with the verge escapement suffer less wear if the pallets run dry. The chronometer escapement should never be oiled, except in the pivots of the balance and escape wheel. The mainspring should be lubricated with a suitable heavy oil or grease, and the levers of the striking work should be lightly oiled where they come into contact, as should the crutch's contact points with the pendulum. JA

Oil sink The depression surrounding a pivot hole. Early in the 18th century, Henry Sully discovered that a small basin around the pivot hole reduced the tendency for oil to spread across the plate and dry up. The idea was eventually perfected by Julien Le Roy, and was generally adopted by the mid 18th century. Most clocks made before that time, without oil sinks, have subsequently been modified. Narrow deep oil sinks are more effective than wide shallow ones. JA

Pallet The nib at the end of the anchor or lever arms acted upon by the escape wheel. The illustration [164/4] shows a lever and pallets from a lever escapement; the unit is usually known as 'pallets complete', abbreviated to 'pallets'. JA

Pallet arbor Or pallet staff: the axis of the pallets. JA

Pallet, entry and exit The entry pallet is the first encountered by an escape-wheel tooth. The exit pallet is that encountered as a tooth leaves engagement with the pallets. JA

Pallet, gathering In striking work, the arm sometimes called a 'tumbler' which restores the rack to its resting position, gathering one tooth for each blow struck during the striking action. JA
See also Striking.

Pallet stones In better-quality lever escapements the pallets are made from rectangular jewels known as 'stones'. Regulator clocks with dead-beat escapements have the acting faces of the pallets jewelled. These are then referred to as 'jewelled pallets'. JA

Pawl A click mounted on an oscillating arm used to advance a ratchet wheel. The term is generally used by engineers to denote a click. JA

1 **Nut,** wing type, used as a pendulum rating nut, from a turret clock.

2 **Oil sink**

3 **Pallet stones,** lever, from a platform escapement.

4 **Pallets,** lever, from a platform escapement.

5 **Pallet arbor** from an 18th-century longcase clock.

6 **Pawl** and ratchet wheel from the tune change mechanism of a fusee, seconds pendulum wall clock.

7 **Pallets, lever, entry and exit,** the escape wheel giving impulse to the exit pallet.

8 **Pendulum, bob,** from an English 18th-century bracket clock.

9 **Pallet, gathering,** in the locked position, from an 18th-century bracket clock.

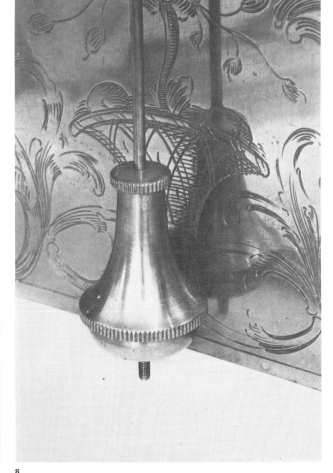

7

Pendulum The pendulum was first used as a clock controller in the mid 17th century by Christiaan Huygens. The introduction of the pendulum revolutionised clockmaking, and by the end of the century it was possible to make clocks of sufficient accuracy to be of use in astronomical observations. As the time taken for a vibration of a pendulum is directly related to the earth's gravity, the only factor governing the time taken for one vibration is the distance between the point of suspension and the centre of oscillation of the pendulum for a particular location on earth. A pendulum vibrating once per second at the equator will need to be lengthened by 0·2059838 in. if moved to the pole, because of differences in the earth's gravitational field at the two points. JA

Pendulum bob The adjustable weight at the lower end of a pendulum. The lenticular-shaped pendulum bob, often in cast iron for turret clocks, is probably the most common; it has the advantage of offering the lowest air resistance and therefore requires less energy from the train to maintain it in oscillation. The cylindrical pendulum bob found in many high-quality regulators and electrical impulse master clocks gives excellent results. The cylindrical shape has more air resistance, but this may be used to counteract changes in rate due to circular error.

By the 19th century many turret-clock pendulums had become cast-iron cylinders with domed tops to prevent dust settling. Weights of several hundred pounds were not uncommon, as this was found to overcome the action of

wind and weather on the hands. The bob of the Great Clock of Westminster ('Big Ben'), for example, weighs 700lb. Some 18th-century and earlier clocks have the major axis of a bun-shaped bob at right angles to the pendulum rod. JA/DFN

See also Pendulum, turret-clock.

Pendulum, compound Generally, a pendulum having part of its weight above the point of suspension. The greater the proportion of weight above the suspension, the longer the period of vibration of the compound pendulum. A theoretically perfect pendulum has all the matter composing it at its centre of oscillation. This is, of course, impossible in practice. The pendulum rod, for example, however thin,

9

1

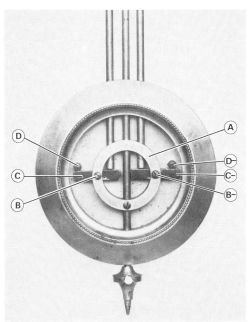

2

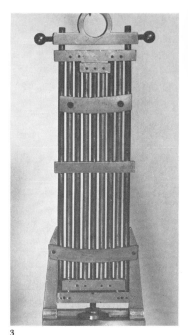

3

must have some weight which is not concentrated at the pendulum bob's centre of oscillation. All practical pendulums are partially compound, because the weight of the components cannot be concentrated at the centre of oscillation [167/5]. JA

Pendulum, conical A pendulum with a bob describing a horizontal circle, used in some Victorian novelty clocks and also to control the driving mechanism of equatorially mounted telescopes. The pendulum is normally driven at its lower end by a slotted arm which allows the pendulum to move away from the central position which it occupies when the clock is stopped. The time taken for one circle to be completed is the same as that required for one complete cycle of a normally oscillating pendulum of equivalent length. JA

Pendulum, Ellicott Temperature errors, caused by expansion of the pendulum rod in heat slowing the clock's rate, led John Ellicott, probably after seeing John Harrison's gridiron compensation, to the idea of using levers to magnify the differential-expansion effect of brass and steel rods, so as to reduce the number required in a pendulum to two brass and one steel. In the illustration [166/2] the brass ring A is secured to the central steel rod by a screw, and it carries the pivots B, B—. The levers C, C—, are free to move on the pivots B, B—, and carry the pendulum bob supported by the screws D and D—. All three rods are fixed in the block at the pendulum's upper end. As the temperature rises, the brass rods expand more than the steel rod, moving the inner ends of the levers downwards and raising the pendulum bob, maintaining the pendulum's effective centre of oscillation in its original position. The action is reversed on a fall in temperature. Owing to friction this system was not entirely satisfactory. JA
See also Pendulum, gridiron.

Pendulum, free It has been known for a long time that a 'free' pendulum clock will achieve perfect timekeeping. A

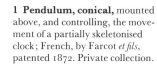

4

1 **Pendulum, conical,** mounted above, and controlling, the movement of a partially skeletonised clock; French, by Farcot *et fils*, patented 1872. Private collection.

2 **Pendulum, Ellicott**-type compensation, from a French clock.

3 **Pendulum, gridiron** compensation, from a French clock.

4 **Pendulum, mercurial** compensation, from a skeleton clock.

5 **Pendulum, compound** Movement mounted above the suspension and swinging with the pendulum; Junghans factory, late 19th century. Norman Harvey.

6 **Pendulum, rhomboid** View of pendulum from a longcase clock. A barometer is mounted on the trunk door to the right; by Joseph Finney, Liverpool. Merseyside County Museum, Liverpool.

pendulum, to achieve this, would maintain its arc and do no work, without ever receiving impulse – perpetual motion, clearly impossible! Early this century, William Hamilton Shortt, in collaboration with Frank Hope-Jones, produced an almost free pendulum clock system which was used as the time standard in observatories throughout the world until superseded by the quartz-crystal clock in the late 1930s.

Briefly, in the Shortt clock system, a synchronome master clock is used as a slave. The master free pendulum receives impulse released by the slave clock and in turn controls the slave clock's rate by a hit and miss governor. The master pendulum operates in a steel cylinder at a constant temperature and reduced atmospheric pressure; small changes in operating pressure are used to make minute adjustments to rate by air-friction loss and circular error. JA

Pendulum, gridiron It was apparent to John Harrison that the greatest error to be counteracted in pendulum clocks fitted with a good escapement was that due to expansion or contraction of the pendulum rod in heat or cold. The Harrison brothers measured the coefficients of expansion of most metals and alloys available then and discovered that brass expanded relative to steel in the ratio approximately of 10 to 6. They made pendulums working on this principle, incorporating four brass rods acting upwards, and five steel rods acting downwards. The upwards expansion of the brass rods compensated for the downwards expansion of the steel rods and maintained the centre of oscillation of the pendulum at a constant distance from the suspension point. This principle was used in their early marine chronometers to alter the effective working length of the balance spring, thus compensating for their temperature errors. JA

Pendulum, mercurial George Graham, with his mercurial compensation pendulum, preceded John Harrison by a few years in solving the problem of temperature error caused by the expansion or contraction of the pendulum rod in heat or cold. Graham discovered that the upward expansion of mercury in a cylindrical jar, used as the pendulum bob, approximately 2 in. in diameter and $7\frac{1}{4}$ in. high, will compensate for the downward expansion of a one-second steel pendulum rod.

Pendulums are sometimes made with two or more jars containing mercury. The increased surface area exposed to the air speeds the transfer of heat on change of temperature. Glass jars, usually adopted for appearance's sake, are not the best substance to contain the mercury. Steel or iron jars allow quicker heat transference because of their higher conductivity. JA

Pendulum, rhomboid A form of pendulum sometimes seen on turret clocks, though rarely on domestic clocks, in which the rod takes the form of a diamond-shaped frame composed of four steel strips connected horizontally across the centre by a strip of brass. Any increase in length of the steel due to heat is compensated for by an outward expansion of the central brass strip. JA

Pendulum, royal The verge escapement, being virtually the only one known when the pendulum was introduced, calls for a large pendulum arc, unless gearing is introduced between the escapement and pendulum, or the escapement is very much modified, as in 18th-century Comtoise clocks. Verge-pendulum clocks usually have short pendulums swinging through a large arc. When the anchor escapement was introduced, the smaller pendulum arc enabled much longer pendulums to be used, and led to better timekeeping because of the reduction in circular and escapement errors. This led to the title of 'royal' pendulum being given to the pendulum beating seconds with an effective length of 39·139921 in. JA

Pendulum, simple Scientifically, a theoretical pendulum, the mass of which is all concentrated at its centre of oscillation. The term is also often used to describe a pendulum without any form of temperature compensation. JA

5

6

1 Pinion, ten leaf, for an eight-day carriage clock.

2 Pinion leaf, enlarged details from 168/1.

3 Pinion, lantern, detail from 138/1.

4 Pipe and bridge, hour wheel, from an English 18th-century bracket clock.

5 Pivot from a wheel train arbor.

6 Pivot, conical, from a balance staff.

7 Pendulum, torsion, controlling a 400-day clock.

8 Pendulum, turret-clock, by Gillett & Johnston Ltd, Croydon.

9 Plates, latched Pillar latch on late 17th-century clock.

10 Plates, pinned, on an 18th-century bracket clock.

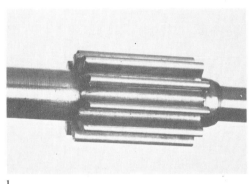

1

2

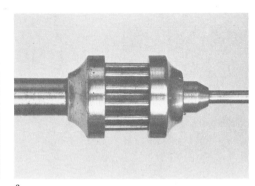

3

4

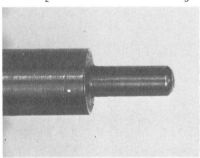

5

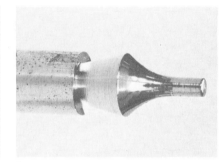

6

7

8

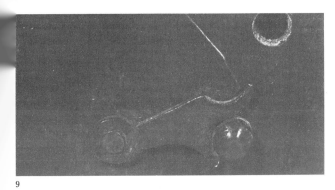

9

10

Pendulum, torsion A form of balance suspended by a thin narrow metal strip. As the balance rotates, the suspension strip is twisted, moving an arm situated near the upper end of the suspension. The arm communicates its movement to a form of anchor escapement which, on release, causes the impulse to twist the suspension a little more, thus maintaining the balance in oscillation. Torsional pendulums are commonly found in 400-day or anniversary clocks. Because of escapement error and poor temperature compensation, timekeeping is usually poor. JA

Pendulum, turret-clock Early turret clocks used wrought-iron pendulum rods, which were forged bars of rectangular section. The rating nuts were wing nuts formed from a long thin rod wound into spirals. Wooden rods were in frequent use, as wood has a very small coefficient of thermal expansion and, provided it is properly sealed, suffers little from humidity. Pitch pine and hickory were often used, in more recent years mahogany.

Compensated pendulum rods on turret clocks were introduced in the 19th century. They are nearly always a combination of zinc and steel and are tubular in construction. A steel rod hangs from the suspension; at its lower end a collar supports a zinc tube running upwards the appropriate length. From the top of this tube a further steel tube descends and, fitting snugly over the bottom collar, carries the pendulum bob. This system was first devised by Edward Troughton.

Although turret-clock pendulums beating seconds are the most common, the location of turret clocks provides scope for longer rods. Rods beating $1\frac{1}{4}$ or $1\frac{1}{2}$ seconds are common and at one time rods of astonishing length were introduced. Many beat 2 seconds and thus have a theoretical length of over 13 ft, while there are a few recorded beating $2\frac{1}{4}$, $2\frac{1}{2}$ and even 3 seconds. It was thought that these long pendulums exercised 'dominion over the clock', evening out irregularities caused by friction and other imperfections in the train. Recent studies have shown that this view was erroneous, for the performance of a clock depends on the drain of energy in the pendulum due to windage and friction in comparison with the total energy in the system. DFN

Pinion In clock gear trains a pinion is usually the smaller driven member, and normally has less than 20 teeth, which are termed 'leaves'. The hypocycloidal form is mostly used for pinion leaves. A hypocycloidal curve is that traced by a point on the circumference of a circle rolling inside another circle. JA

Pinion leaf *See* Pinion.

Pinion, lantern A form of pinion construction in which the pinion leaves are made from round steel pins, held by brass discs. In some cheap clocks the steel pins are held at one end only, by a die-casting technique which also forms the wheel collet. Lantern pinions are also found in high-quality clocks, and they are often used in turret clocks. The gear action between a lantern pinion driven by a correctly formed wheel, is excellent, but a lantern pinion is unsatisfactory as the driver. JA

Pinion, rolling-leaf To reduce friction, lantern pinions are sometimes made with the leaves pivoted to allow them to rotate. JA

Pipe Any extended hollow boss, as in a key. The key-pipe is the hollow squared part which fits the winding arbor. JA

Pivot The reduced-diameter arbor end which turns in the hole made in the clock plate (or jewel) to receive it. JA

Pivot, conical Cheap alarm-clock balance staffs often utilise a cone-shaped pivot. In higher-grade work the term also applies to pivots designed to run in capped jewel holes. The acting part is parallel; the conical section is used to blend the small-diameter pivot into the larger staff and reduce the chance of pivot breakage. JA

Pivot hole The bearing in which a pivot runs. JA

Plates The two shaped metal or wooden plates, or strips of wood or metal which together with the pillars form the clock frame and carry the various moving parts. JA
See also Movement.

Plates, latched To make dismantling and assembly easier, some late 17th-century makers used small latches to secure their pillars and plates. The idea is still occasionally used and during the 1960s the makers of the Section clock used latches to secure the sub-assemblies. JA

Plates, pinned Taper wedging pins have been used from the earliest times to secure mechanical assemblies. In the usual pillar and plate assembly the pillars are riveted to the backplate and are reduced in diameter, forming a shoulder to support the front plate, which is secured by a tapered pin passing through a small hole pierced in the protruding pillar end. JA

1 **Plate, split,** with one section removed, from a 17th-century English clock. Fitzwilliam Museum, Cambridge.

2 **Plate, split,** showing one section detached, from an early 18th-century French clock.

3 **Plates, screwed,** on a mantel chronometer.

4 **Potence** supporting lower end of verge crown-wheel arbor, from a French bracket clock.

5 **Quartz crystal** mounted in an evacuated glass tube.

6 **Rack,** hour, from an English 18th-century bracket clock.

7 **Rack tail,** as 171/6.

8 **Pulley** for a regulator weight.

9 **Rack hook,** as 171/6.

10 **Ratchet** mechanism in Holden electric clock.

11 **Rating nut,** on the pendulum of an English regulator.

1

2

Plates, screwed Occasionally clocks are found in which the pillars are screwed into the clock backplate, rather than riveted. This makes cleaning the clock much easier. Modern clocks usually have the pillars threaded at both ends and secured to the plates by washers and nuts. JA

Plates, split Assembling a large three- or four-train clock often presents great difficulty. High-quality clocks sometimes have the front or backplate divided, so that each train may be assembled independently. JA

Platform A plate carrying a sub-assembly which may be removed for attention without disturbing the main frame of the clock. The platform escapement of a carriage clock is an example. JA

3
4
5
6
7
8
9
10
11

Potence A bracket or cock mounted between the clock plates. In a verge clock the potence is the bracket carrying the lower escape-wheel pivot. JA

Pulley A wheel grooved on its circumference to retain a rope or line. The weight of an eight-day clock is usually hung from a pulley. The line passes from the barrel round the pulley and is attached to the seat board. This arrangement halves the weight's fall, but demands a weight twice as heavy to drive the clock as one hung directly from the line without using a pulley. JA

Quartz crystal A crystal of quartz suitably cut and mounted will produce an electrical effect when mechanically deformed; conversely, it mechanically deforms when subjected to an electrical field. This is known as the 'piezo-electric effect'. When a suitably cut quartz crystal is connected in an electrical circuit, it can be made to vibrate at its natural frequency, and may be used to control the frequency of an electronic oscillator which, after suitable frequency division, will indicate time on a digital or analogue display. JA

Rack A number of gear teeth cut along a bar enabling rotary motion to be converted to linear motion. Also, in

striking clocks, the arm cut with ratchet-shaped teeth which count the number of blows to be struck at the hour or quarter. JA

Rack hook The arm acting as a click for the rack in rack striking clocks. JA

Rack tail The lower extension of the rack which contacts the snail and determines the number of hours or quarters to be struck next. JA

Ratchet A mechanism allowing rotation in one direction only. A ratchet wheel having teeth of saw-tooth shape engaged by a click is used to prevent a mainspring unwinding. JA

Rating nut The knurled nut supporting the pendulum bob. To bring a losing clock to time, the pendulum bob is raised by rotating the rating nut clockwise. Conversely, to bring a gaining clock to time, the pendulum bob is lowered.

Compound pendulums, such as those with the clock movement mounted above the suspension point and forming part of the oscillating structure, require the reverse procedure to bring them to time. JA

1 **Repeating work** on Swiss bracket clock, late 18th century.

2 **Stackfreed** Clock watch, late 16th century, showing use of the stackfreed; possibly by Christopher Pleig of Ulm. Gershom Parkington Collection of Time Keeping Instruments, Bury St Edmunds.

3 **Roller,** double, from a platform lever escapement.

4 **Roller, anti-friction** Roller bearing on barrel arbor of early 19th-century regulator.

5 **Snail,** hour, from an English 18th-century bracket clock.

6 **Spring, suspension,** on a regulator pendulum.

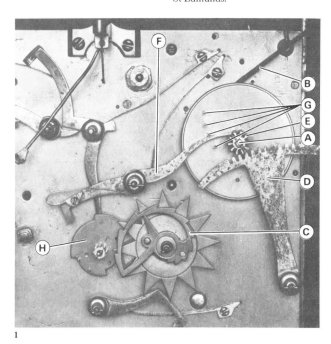

1

2

Remontoire A device found in high-quality clocks [124/1], which winds an auxiliary spring or weight at regular short intervals to provide a more constant driving force for the escapement. JA
See also Escapement, constant-force.

Remontoire, turret-clock In most mechanical clocks the source of energy, the weight, drives the escapement through a large step-up gear ratio; thus the impulse the escapement gives to the pendulum at each swing is small. Any changes in friction in the pivots caused by the viscosity of the oil varying with temperature have an appreciable effect on impulse. An even greater effect in turret clocks comes from the action of wind and weather on the exposed hands. Variations in impulse cause changes in the pendulum arc and lead to erratic timekeeping. To overcome this, a device known as a 'remontoire' is sometimes adopted for providing a constant force at the escape wheel arbor. Essentially, it comprises a differential gear. The train proper is connected to the input of the gear through a detent, and the output of the gear drives the escape wheel arbor. The differential cage carries a weight on the end of an arm, and when the train input is locked the weighted arm provides the torque for driving the escape wheel. When it has dropped through a small arc it unlatches the train detent, the train runs and lifts the arm to its upper position and relocks the train. In this way the torque at the escape wheel and the impulse to the pendulum stay constant. The weighted arm continues to provide the same driving torque during the rewind.

Other types of remontoire exist. Christiaan Huygens developed one using his endless-chain principle. In some, two local energy stores are provided so that one is rewinding while the other drives the escapement; they change from

rewind to drive at regular intervals. Most turret clocks use weight-driven remontoires, although spring types are known. Taken to its logical conclusion, the remontoire can be fitted to provide a constant store of energy for impulsing the pendulum directly. This arrangement manifests itself in the gravity escapement. Some clocks have a remontoire *and* a gravity escapement, which is clearly absurd; one or the other is adequate. DFN

Repeating work Before the introduction of the match, the difficulty in obtaining a light at night to see the time made it desirable to have clocks capable of striking the time at will by the operation of a lever or by pulling a cord. In the simplest form of trip repeat mechanism, a lever is arranged to lift the rack hook, allowing the clock to strike the previous hour. In clocks with full repeating action, an additional train of wheels is used to control the speed of the hammer blows. It is similar to an ordinary striking train, and is driven by an additional spring wound by operating the repeating action, which allows the clock to be repeated as often as desired.

In the illustration [172/1], the repeat mainspring, not visible, is mounted on the inner end of the arbor A. On pulling cord B, the arbor A rotates, winding the mainspring and moving the segment D via the pinion E until the segment D contacts snail C and prevents further winding. The arbor A carries a wheel between the plates fitted with twelve lifting pins on one side for the hours; the number of pins which pass the hour hammer tail on pulling the repeating cord is controlled by the snail C. When the repeating cord B is released, the mainspring drives the repeating train, delivering a blow for each pin which passes the hammer tail. Arm F controls the final resting position of the repeating train. The right-hand end of arm F passes between one pair of pins G. The position of arm F is controlled by quarter-snail H. The hammer-lifting wheel carries, in addition to the hour-lifting pins, three longer lifting pins which lift both the hour hammer and an additional hammer striking on a higher-toned bell.

If the clock is repeated during the first quarter after an hour, the previous hour is struck and the mechanism is stopped by arm F before any of the quarter-lifting pins can act. When the mechanism is operated during the second quarter, the tip of arm F passes between the innermost pair of pins, allowing arbor A to rotate a little more than in the first quarter, which in turn allows one of the quarter-lifting pins to operate both hammers, thereby indicating the time by a *ting-tang* double blow. The action for the remaining two quarters is similar, with an additional *ting-tang* for each.

Clock repeating mechanisms have never achieved the standardisation found in striking and going trains. Many repeating clocks have additional bells and play a short musical phrase for each quarter. Repeating clocks were first made towards the end of the 17th century. By the 19th century, clocks were rarely fitted with full repeating mechanism. J A

Roller In the lever escapement, the cylindrical metal piece mounted on the balance staff and carrying the impulse pin; it also performs the safety action. In English work, the single table roller with passing crescent formed in the rim is the most common type, whereas in European and American work a double roller is most often used. J A

Roller, anti-friction A type of bearing in which two or more rollers are used to carry a pivot. Anti-friction rollers used in clocks take the form of pivoted wheels without teeth, arranged in different planes with the circumferences intersecting to leave an aperture of the pivot's diameter. The pivot friction is reduced by the leverage which the roller radius provides over the roller pivot friction. The provision of anti-friction roller bearings indicates work of the highest quality. J A

Screw By the mid 16th century screws had begun to be used in clockmaking, and they have increasingly replaced pins and wedges, although pins are still used to secure certain parts. Standardisation of screw threads has been attempted at various times, but a huge variety of sizes, pitches and thread angles remains. J A

Seat board The wooden board to which the movement of a longcase clock is attached by two screws through the lower movement pillars in London-made and other good-quality clocks, and by J-bolts in provincial clocks. Seat boards should be secured to the clock case to prevent accidental overbalancing of the movement during dismantling. J A

Set-up When a fusee clock is being assembled and the line or chain is wound on the barrel, the mainspring is pre-tensioned by winding the mainspring arbor, usually one half to one and a half turns, enabling the fusee to deliver an even amount of power until the end of its run. This is known as the mainspring set-up. J A

Snail A cam, the spiral profile resembling a snail's shell, commonly used to determine the number of blows struck in rack striking work at the hour or quarter. J A

Spring A spring may take many forms, and the perfect spring, when deflected within its elastic limit, always returns to the same shape. The most common material for all clock springs is hardened and tempered steel although, particularly in longcase clocks, certain click and return springs are made from hammer-hardened brass. J A

Spring, balance *See* Balance spring.

Spring, main- The coiled metal ribbon used to drive a clock's mechanism. Originally clocks were all weight-driven, and it is thought that a spiral spring was first used to drive a portable clock early in the 16th century. Mainsprings are usually made from hardened and tempered steel strip, although recently special alloy steel springs have become available, and these offer advantages such as greater resistance to breakage and more power for a given size over standard steel springs. J A

Spring, suspension The spring steel strip from which the pendulum is hung. Kinking of the suspension spring through careless handling is the most common cause of a pendulum rolling as it swings. J A

Stackfreed A device used until the early 17th century to equalise the force of the mainspring over its period of run. The mechanism usually takes the form of a cam geared to the mainspring arbor, and a roller following the cam profile, impelled by a powerful spring. The cam profile is designed to resist the force of the mainspring over the first half of the clock's period of run, and to assist it over the remaining part of the run. J A

Staff *See* Arbor.

3   4   5   6

1

2

3   4

Star wheel A wheel with pointed teeth, used in conjunction with a snail in rack striking work. JA

Steady pin The dowel pins commonly used in pairs to ensure the accurate location of a balance cock, etc. JA

Stopwork The mechanism used to limit the number of turns, up or down, of a mainspring. The usual fusee stopwork consists of an arm pivoted to a stud fixed to the clock plate. The arm is moved from the path of the fusee snail nose by a weak spring, until the clock is nearly wound, when the chain or line moves the stop arm into the path of the snail nose, thus preventing further winding.

Maltese Cross stopwork is commonly used for going-barrel clocks. A disc with a projecting finger is fixed to the barrel arbor and advances the Maltese Cross wheel one notch per revolution of the barrel arbor, until the shoulder contacts the raised contour of the Maltese Cross wheel at the end of the wind. This stopwork also limits the unwinding of the mainspring, reducing the poor perfor-

mance of non-detached escapements, such as the cylinder, when operating with insufficient driving force. JA

Striking It is thought that originally clocks indicated the passing of time by striking a bell once each hour, a dial probably being added to allow the clock keeper to see when the next hour was to be struck. The earliest form of automatic striking work is the count-wheel mechanism, also termed 'locking plate' or 'count plate'. Count-wheel striking work has the disadvantage of sounding the hours in succession; thus, if the mechanism is tripped accidentally, the hands and striking get out of synchronism.

In the illustration [175/5], approaching the hour, arm A is lifted by the pin B, warning detent C attached to the same arbor as arm A, which raises detent D clear of pin E, allowing the striking train to run until pin F comes to rest on the end of warning detent C, thus stopping the striking train. Count-wheel detent G on the same arbor as detent D is raised until it clears the slots in count wheel H. At the hour, release arm A drops clear of pin B. Pin F is released

1 **Star wheel,** hour, from an English 18th-century bracket clock.

2 **Steady pins** on a balance cock, platform escapement.

3 **Stopwork,** Maltese Cross, from a carriage clock.

4 **Striking work,** rack, from an English 18th-century bracket clock. (Photographed using a transparent perspex sheet instead of the front plate.)

5 **Striking work,** count wheel, from a French lantern clock.

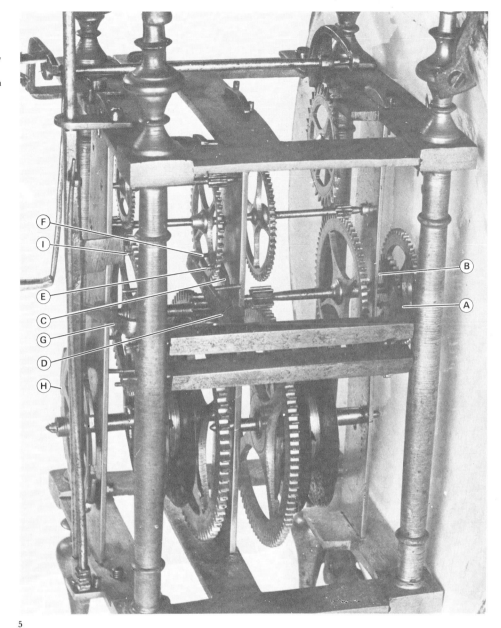

5

and the train continues to run, the lifting pin I moving the hammer until the hammer flag is released and the bell struck. The mechanism continues to act until detent G can fall into one of the slots in count wheel H, allowing detent D on the same arbor as detent G to arrest the train by moving into the path of pin E.

Rack striking work was developed towards the end of the 17th century. It has the advantage that the relationship between the hands and striking cannot readily be lost.

In the illustration [174/4], approaching the hour, lifting piece A is moved by pin B, raising rack hook C which releases rack D, the pin in the tail of rack E coming to rest on snail F. Until the release of the rack the striking train was held by the tail of the gathering pallet H resting on pin G, and the striking train is now free to run until pin I comes to rest against the warning piece carried by lifting arm A. At the hour, lifting piece A falls clear of pin B, thus releasing pin I which in turn releases the striking train. Lifting pins J raise the hammer, which strikes one blow for each revolution of gathering pallet H, the number of blows being determined by the number of teeth on rack D which have been allowed to pass rack hook C by snail F on the release of the rack preceding the hour. The action continues until pin G arrests the tail of the gathering pallet when all the rack teeth are gathered in.

In quarter-striking work, many different layouts are used, but the action may be understood by careful examination related to the above examples. JA

Striking, Dutch Early Dutch clocks sometimes use a striking system in which the hour is struck on a large low-pitched bell and at the half-hour the succeeding hour is struck on a small high-pitched bell. The Dutch striking system is found occasionally in clocks from other countries. JA

Striking, grande sonnerie In clocks with quarter striking the first, second and third quarters are indicated by striking from one to three strokes on a bell differing in tone from the hour bell. In clocks with four-quarter striking,

1

1 **Striking, turret-clock,** count wheel, pin-type, on an early 19th-century chair-frame turret-clock; restored by Smith's of Derby. Worsley Parish Church, near Manchester.

2 **Striking, turret-clock** Grimthorpe's cams for striking work, mounted on the quarter-striking barrel of the Great Clock of Westminster.

3 **Surprise piece,** shown removed from quarter-snail beneath, from a quarter-repeating carriage clock.

4 **Synchronous motor** from a modern domestic striking clock.

5 **Striking, turret-clock** Diagram showing the action of the cams and levers, from Lord Grimthorpe's *Treatise on Clocks, Watches, and Bells,* 7th edition, London 1883 [177/2].

each quarter, including the hour, is struck on bells differing in tone from the hour bell. In clocks with full *grande sonnerie* striking, the quarter and the preceding hour are struck at each quarter in passing. JA

Striking, hour and half-hour Sometimes referred to as 'French striking'. Besides striking the hour, the clock strikes once at the half-hour, usually on the hour bell. JA

Striking, Roman Joseph Knibb designed clocks of long-running duration, and to reduce the power requirements of the striking train, he devised a system of striking which utilised one bell for the Roman numeral I and another of differing pitch for the Roman V. Thus the maximum number of blows necessary to indicate any hour is four. Knibb used the true Roman IV instead of the conventional IIII, saving a further two hammer blows. He thus used only 30 blows instead of the usual 78 in twelve hours. JA

Striking, Sürrerwerk The striking system known by the German term *Sürrerwerk* ('whizzing work') has been recorded in Italian and German clocks during the 18th and 19th centuries, and variants of the device are known from the 17th century. The system is based on the use of pins of graduated length mounted on opposite sides of a single pinwheel. These pins lift the two hammers to strike the hours and quarters, six on one side operating the hour hammer, the arbor of which is axially changed in position by a stepped-face cam to engage each of the pins progressively as the hours go by. The three pins on the other side of the pinwheel operate in a similar way to strike the quarters progressively by one, two and three strokes, the pinwheel making one complete revolution each quarter of an hour. In a full day the system thus strikes 228 blows in the following way: hours, $1+2+3+4+5+6 \times 4 = 84$ (a six-hour system of striking); quarters, $1+2+3 \times 24 = 144$.

Grande sonnerie striking by this system is known; it strikes 864 strokes per day. AS

Striking, ting-tang A clock striking the quarters on two differently pitched bells or gongs, the sound for the first quarter being similar to the name, with each successive quarter indicated by an additional *ting-tang.* Sometimes, before the hour is struck in the usual way, four *ting-tang* hammer blows indicate the final quarter. JA

Striking, turret-clock The great majority of turret clocks use count-wheel control in one form or another. Count wheels appear with notches on either the inner or outer side of the ring. Many of the older clocks had internally cut teeth, and were supported by four arms offset from the disc to allow the driving pinion space to turn.

Another type of tooth has pins set axially in the periphery of the wheel, rather than notches. The pins are set either into a wheel driven directly by a pinion, or into a wheel having ratchet-shaped teeth collected tooth by tooth by a rotating gathering pallet.

Rack striking appears on a few later clocks. In clocks made by the E. Howard Clock Co. of Boston, Massachusetts, the rack slides linearly against the snail rather than rotating as is more common.

Many turret clocks of the wooden door-frame variety have a long lever on the second arbor which has become known as the flail [125/5], the end of which is turned at right angles and locks against a similar lip on the locking lever, which in turn normally rests in a notch in the count wheel. The hour wheel carries an arm which lifts the locking lever but prevents the flail rotating by engaging with the lip. When the hour wheel rotates far enough the hour lever disengages the train, which runs until the next notch in the count wheel allows the locking lever to drop and lock the flail.

Another type of control, frequently found on wooden-framed clocks, is the percussive type. The locking takes place against a protruding stud on the second wheel, and a second locking lever falls into a notch in the count wheel. A small arm on the hour wheel raises a pivoted weight and lets it go on the hour. A thin rod or wire communicates the impact of the weight falling to the locking levers and knocks them out of engagement. Before the levers fall again under the action of gravity the train starts to run, and continues to do so until the next notch in the count wheel causes it to relock. Percussive letting-off work is occasionally found on iron clocks.

Pins for lifting the hammers were in use until the mid 19th century. Normally six or eight in number, they were on either the great wheel or second wheel, depending on the number of wheels in the train. Lord Grimthorpe introduced a specially shaped cam [177/2] for the purpose which gave a rolling rather than rubbing action, with less wear. As many as 60 were cast integrally with the great wheel. DFN

Sun and planet gearing *See* Maintaining power.

Surprise piece A plate attached to the quarter-snail and free to move forward as the star wheel is advanced. It prevents the wrong quarter being struck by a repeating clock, close to the hour. JA

Synchronous motor The number of revolutions per minute of the driving motor of an electric clock driven from the public electricity supply is directly related to the frequency of the supply. A motor controlled in this way is said to be 'synchronised', and the addition of a simple train of gears to drive the hands makes a cheap, reliable, time indicator possible. A synchronous clock of this type is not a timekeeper, but merely a slave controlled by the frequency of the electricity supply, which is regulated within close limits. In periods of heavy electricity demand, load shedding causes synchronous clocks to lose, but this loss is regained automatically during the following night. JA

Timepiece A clock, strictly speaking, is a timekeeper which strikes the hours in passing, while a timepiece indicates the time by means of dial and hand(s) only. JA

Tooth The shaped projections on a gear wheel which intermesh and transmit power are termed 'teeth' [178/2]. JA *See also* Gears.

Train The collective term for the wheels and pinions of a clock. JA

2

Train, eight-day The timekeeping trains of clocks are designed to go for a little longer than the period required between windings. A clock designed to be wound weekly will go for eight days before stopping. The usual eight-day longcase clock train consists of four wheels and three pinions. The great wheel carried by the barrel arbor drives the centre pinion. The centre arbor rotates once per hour and drives the minute hand and motion work through a friction spring, to allow adjustment of the hands. The centre wheel drives the third-wheel pinion, and the third wheel drives the escape-wheel pinion, which rotates once per minute. The 30-tooth escape wheel is mounted on this arbor, and an extension through the frontplate carries the seconds hand. JA

Train, going The timekeeping train of a clock. JA

Train, month Month-going clocks are usually arranged with an extra arbor carrying a wheel and pinion to give an additional 4 to 1 ratio between the great wheel and the centre arbor. JA

Train, seconds A clock train suitable for a seconds-beating pendulum or, alternatively, for driving a hand indicating seconds. JA

Train, striking The gear train controlled by the striking mechanism of a clock. JA

3

4

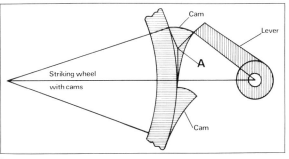

5

1

Train, 30-hour The 30-hour train has one wheel and pinion fewer than the eight-day clock. In the common 30-hour longcase train, the motion wheels are driven directly from the great-wheel arbor. Many 30-hour spring-driven trains are arranged to have the great wheel driving the centre pinion, whereas in an eight-day going-barrel clock an intermediate wheel and pinion are used. JA

Train, year The problem of providing sufficient power to drive the escapement with the very high gear ratios necessary to make a clock go for a whole year has been successfully overcome by only a few makers. The wheel work must be proportioned with due regard to its work in the train; the faster-moving wheels (and particularly the escapement) must be made very light so that inertial losses will be minimal; and the tooth profiles and pivots must be designed to reduce frictional losses to a minimum.

Weight-driven year clocks may be arranged by providing two extra wheels and pinions between the great wheel and the centre pinion, which gives an additional ratio of 52 to 1 over that found in eight-day clocks.

Spring-driven year clocks are usually found to contain a number of standard mainsprings, connected end to end, driving the great wheel; though a magnificent year clock driven by single springs and fusees was made by Thomas Tompion for King William III, between 1695 and 1700. The gear frictional losses are reduced by this layout, at the cost of a large number of turns being necessary to wind the clock annually. JA

Tumbler *See* Pallet, gathering.

Warning piece A projection on the lifting piece of a striking clock which intercepts a pin in the warning wheel and holds the striking train ready until the exact hour of striking. JA
See also Striking.

Warning wheel Usually the penultimate wheel in a striking train, carrying a pin which locks the striking train after release, until the lifting piece falls at the hour and the clock strikes. JA
See also Striking.

Weights, brass The best clocks have brass-cased driving weights. Clock weight design may be used as a guide to the date of manufacture of a clock. However, dealers and repairers frequently interchanged weights between clocks, brass weights being used to improve a clock, or a heavier weight being substituted for the original to make the clock go. JA

Weights, iron Cast iron was first available commercially towards the end of the 18th century, and it soon became cheaper than lead. Its use for clock weights became almost universal in the 19th century. The original lead or brass-

2

3

4

1 Train year Year-going, spring-driven French clock utilising five barrels.

2 Tooth, wheel, 19th century.

3 Warning piece about to intercept the pin in the warning wheel, seen through a slot in a transparent perspex front plate, (mounted in this way to demonstrate the action).

4 Warning wheel, as 178/3.

5 Maintaining power Dial of Tompion & Banger longcase clock with bolt and shutter maintaining power. The lever raises the shutter visible to the right of II on the dial.

5

1

1 **Musical work** Movement of a musical clock which plays four tunes on 14 bells; by Reid & Son of Newcastle-on-Tyne, c. 1835.

2 **Weights, turret-clock,** of cast iron, cheese-shaped sections, to adjust the total weight required, driving the going and striking work of a flat-bed turret-clock with automatic winding.

3 **Wheel, contrate,** from a conical pendulum clock (166/1).

4 **Wheels, bevel,** as used to drive four dials for a turrent clock.

5 **Wheel, crown verge,** from a French clock (152/3).

2

3

4

5

cased weights on early clocks have often been lost and replaced by cast-iron weights. JA

Weights, lead The earliest weight-driven clocks probably had stones as weights. Lead is perhaps the best material. It is easily worked, is reasonably cheap, and has a high density, which permits smaller driving weights occupying less space in the clock case. JA

Weights, turret-clock The weights of early turret clocks were of stone, pear-shaped with rough edges smoothed off. A bolt was let into the top, sometimes run in with lead. Many stone weights are still in use, often supplemented by miscellaneous cast-iron pieces of a later era.

Until the 18th century lead, being a great deal cheaper than iron, was commonly used, beaten or cast into a roughly cylindrical form around an eye bolt. When iron castings became available, weights were made like flat cylindrical cheeses, with a hole in the middle and a slot so that they could be slipped over an eye bolt, and as many as required could be added. Box-shaped weights were also used, with an aperture for adding extra weights.

In the early days turret-clock lines were of rope, half an inch or more in diameter. Later, steel wire was introduced;

owing to its greater strength and smaller diameter, far more turns could be accommodated on the barrel. Recently, very strong plastic line has become available. This is much softer, and kinder to elderly barrels. DFN

Wheel, anti-friction A method, found only in very high-quality work, of supporting clock pivots on smooth wheels to reduce friction. JA
See also Roller, anti-friction.

Wheel, bevel A gear wheel with teeth cut at an angle and meshing with a similar wheel to drive an arbor at any angle up to 90°. Bevel gearing is seldom found in ordinary clockwork, the main horological application being in the leading-off work in turret clocks. JA

Wheel, contrate A wheel cut with teeth on one face which mesh with a pinion at 90°, used in verge clocks to drive the vertical escape pinion. The contrate wheel is also found in platform-escapement carriage clocks, again driving the escape pinion. JA

Wheel, crown The verge escape wheel, so named because of its resemblance to a crown. JA

1 **Wheel, escape,** anchor-type, from an English 19th-century bracket clock.

2 **Wheel, ratchet,** from a skeleton clock.

3 **Winding, automatic,** turret-clock winder, on the endless chain principle; by Gillett & Johnston Ltd, Croydon.

4 **Winding keys** A selection: A Skeleton clock. B. Modern French clock, key of steel. C. French clock. D. Early longcase clock (without the wood). E. Double-ended for a carriage clock. F. Chronometer. G. Double-ended for a carriage clock. H. English bracket clock, 19th century. I. Regulator. J. French clock.

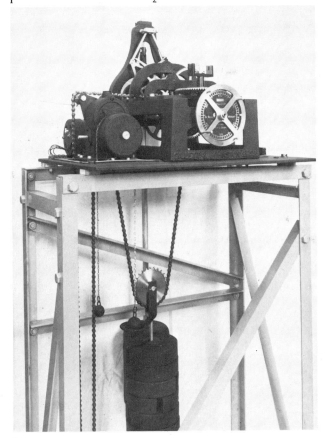

3

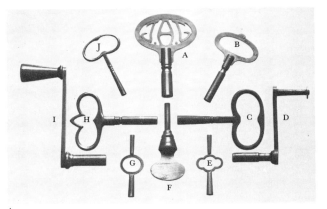

4

Wheel, escape The final wheel in the going train of a clock. The escape wheel interacts directly with the clock escapement. JA

Wheel, ratchet A wheel cut with teeth like a saw and used in conjunction with a click or pawl to make rotation possible in one direction only. JA

Winding, automatic A mechanism for winding a clock automatically at regular intervals. Large turret clocks require a great deal of effort to wind manually, and are increasingly being converted to automatic winding. In one common type, a continuous loop of bicycle chain passes round a sprocket on the clock barrel or other convenient arbor, thence round a pulley carrying the driving weight, and then over a sprocket driven by the electric motor. The remainder of the loop is carried out of the way by pulleys and kept taut by a counterweight. The clock is driven by the gradually falling weight which, when it reaches a lower limit, actuates a switch starting the electric motor, which hauls in the chain on the other side of the main weight. The

switch cuts out when the weight reaches the upper limit. This system closely resembles Christiaan Huygens's winding mechanism so often seen on 30-hour clocks, and is called by that name.

In another system, a mechanical epicyclic differential is used. In this case, one connection to the differential drives the clock through a roller chain, and the other two connect with a weight drum and the electric motor respectively. A third type incorporates the electric motor with the weight. It climbs the chain, which passes as a loop over the barrel or other arbor of the clock. The motor may be a synchronous type, which climbs the chain at the same rate as the clock lets it out. Some clockmakers couple electric motors directly to the striking and chiming trains, disconnect the escapement, and use a synchronous motor to drive the hands. Much damage has been done in this way. Turret clocks rewound by hydraulic power are also known.

Mechanical domestic clocks, with their more modest power requirements, are rarely wound automatically, although some 30-hour clocks have been converted to automatic winding to avoid this daily chore. The Atmos clock, which utilises atmospheric changes in pressure and temperature to provide winding energy, is a novel domestic automatic-winding clock. JA/DFN
See also Atmos clock.

Winding key The tool for winding a clock. Crank keys are best suited for weight clocks and eight-day fusee clocks, while the plate key is best suited to going-barrel spring clocks and clocks requiring a high winding torque. JA

Winding, pull Thirty-hour longcase clocks are usually arranged for pull winding on Christiaan Huygens's system. The length of rope or chain between the smaller weight and the ratchet wheel is pulled down, thus raising the driving weight without stopping the clock. JA

SECTION III
Tools, Materials and Workshop Methods

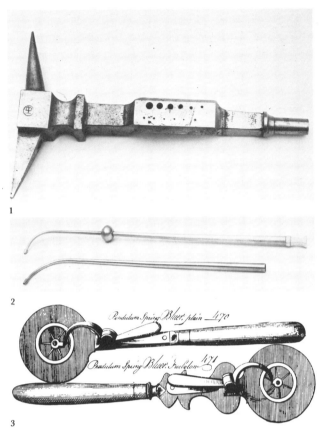

1 **Beak iron or beck iron** combined with stake, vice held. Private collection.

2 **Blowpipes,** one with bulb and ivory mouthpiece.

3 **Bluing** pans for balance spring bluing. John Wyke, *Tool Catalogue,* Liverpool, *c.*1770.

4 **Bench** Hirst Bros, *Catalogue of Tools, c.*1900.

1

2

3

4

Adjusting Adjustments made to the balance, balance spring or pendulum of a clock to compensate for the effects of variations of temperature are known as compensating. Adjusting refers specifically to minor alterations made to a fusee to ensure constant power output, especially for chronometers and other precision clocks. EBG
See also Fusee; Spring, main- (both Section II).

Annealing A process of heat treatment for reducing the degree of hardness of metal to give it maximum malleability or ductility. The purpose of annealing is to remove the effects of previous hardening, thus making the metal suitable for further work such as bending, cutting or drawing into wire. The factors affecting the process are the temperature to which the metal is raised, the time it remains at this temperature, the rate at which it is cooled and the atmosphere in which the work is done. These factors are varied according to the type of metal or alloy being used, and its ultimate purpose. Steel is annealed by heating it to redness and allowing it to cool gradually, while non-ferrous metals can also be cooled gradually or quenched in cold water. EBG

Anvil *See* Beak iron.

Arkansas stone A hard fine-grained whitish stone quarried in Arkansas and used to sharpen or hone tools to a fine edge. Arkansas pencil slips are lengths of various sections – flat, square, triangular, round, half-round, etc. – used to grind or hone steel clock parts and sometimes pivots. Slips of the stone can be rubbed down to suitable shapes on emery or other abrasive paper. Arkansas grinding wheels are also made. EBG

Ayr stone Water of Ayr stone is of Scottish origin. It is a fine bluish-grey stone used with water worked up into a paste to impart a finish to brass or other soft metals. Filing or scraper marks are removed in this way, and the dull grained or 'grey' finish obtained on brass is a preliminary to gilding, spotting or polishing. The stone is easily shaped with a file or abrasive paper to suit the contours of the work. EBG

Beak iron, or beck iron A somewhat archaic term for a steel anvil or stake on which hot or cold metal is hammered or bent to shape. For clockmaking, anvils may be quite small and formed for holding in a bench vice, larger ones being screwed or driven into the bench top or a large wooden block, and very large ones having an integral base to stand free. The flat table of the anvil is used when planishing or flattening sheet or strip metal for general forging and riveting. The beak is particularly useful for curving strips of metal in making rings, hoops and hooks. EBG

Bench A clockmaker's bench is the basic support for manufacturing or repairing, and carries tools and other equipment. The bench is normally made of timber, but for brazing, soldering or other heat treatments an insulated surface is provided. The bench illustrated [184/4] is suitable for repair, assembly and adjustment of small clocks. In contrast to heavy workshop benches it is an attractive piece of furniture, perhaps intended for a retailer's front shop. EBG

Blowpipe A long tapered metal tube through which air is blown by mouth or bellows to increase the heat of a flame and to direct it on to the point where it is needed when brazing or soldering. The blast from the blowpipe through the flame of a spirit or gas burner throws forward a bluish

5 **Breast plate** with hole above for neck cord. Merseyside County Museum, Liverpool.

6 **Brace, hand,** with countersink bit fitted, and loose broach. Antoine Thiout, *Traité de l'horlogerie*, 1741.

7 **Brace, wheel,** with self-centring chuck.

5

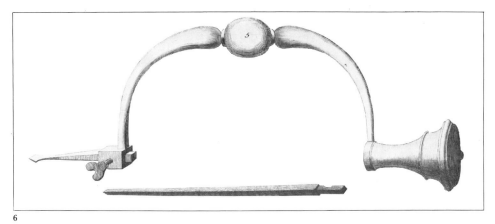

6

7

flame which is hottest at its tip, and this is particularly useful where fine controlled heat is required. Some blowpipes have a bone mouthpiece, and a swelling or bulb is sometimes incorporated to collect moisture. Sometimes blowpipes are available in two sections with a removable extension tube, and some simple types combining gas and air take the air from a tank or compressor. EBG

Bluing The process of changing the colour of polished steel by heating to give a protective film of oxidation which also has a pleasing colour, e.g. brown, purple and blue. The bluing of clock components is normally carried out in a flat thick-bottomed copper bluing pan, the parts to be blued being first polished and cleaned. Care must be taken to heat the parts evenly, keeping them free from cold draughts. Heating is stopped immediately the desired colour is obtained. Parts which will not lie flat on the bottom of the pan are blued on a deep bed of brass filings placed in the pan. Screws are blued in holes in a metal block placed in the bluing pan, and a special pan with a clamp is used when bluing or tempering flat, spiral balance springs [184/3]. EBG

Boiling-out pan A small pan used for boiling out parts in methylated spirits, to remove shellac from clock parts after they have been cemented with shellac to a chuck; it is also used for tempering small clock parts in oil. EBG

Brace, hand Clockmakers' hand braces are used primarily for broaching large clock pivot holes. They are made of steel, with a cranked handle and square socket for accommodating the squared shank of a broach. EBG
See also Broach.

Brace, wheel This is primarily a drilling tool and is driven by a hand wheel which is geared directly to the chuck, rotating it – and thus the drill – at increased speed. It is a comparatively modern tool and is not entirely satisfactory for accurate work since the tool is hand-held throughout the drilling operation. Twist drills and countersink drills are used with this tool. EBG

Brazing A method of bonding metallic surfaces with a more fusible metal or alloy. Unlike welding, in which the metals being joined are themselves most often melted together, brazing makes use of a bonding or filler metal of different composition and lower melting point than the metal being joined. This is the same as soldering, but as soldering is a term applied to many related processes it is normal to distinguish brazing from soldering. A common form of brazing brass or spelter consists of 50 per cent zinc, 44 per cent copper, 4 per cent tin and 2 per cent lead, although it sometimes contains nickel, manganese or silicon. Strength in a brazed joint is achieved by building up a fillet of brazing metal around the joint. Other forms of brazing use bonding metals in ascending order of melting points, starting with aluminium. Silver or silver-alloy brazing uses a metal based mostly on silver and copper, a process known as silver soldering and hard soldering, and in this type of brazing the main aim is to fill the gap in a joint. Brazing metals are obtained as wire, rod, sheet, foils and powder-paste preparations, and as they consist of various metals or alloys they require various types of fluxes to help the metal to flow and prevent oxidation. EBG

Breast plate A curved plate or disc which is held against the body to support the pivoted end of a drill. Steady

185

pressure can thus be applied to the drill while the breast plate is held on a cord hung around the neck. EBG

Broach A long hardened steel tool, mostly tapered but also available in parallel form, usually with five cutting edges and used for enlarging pivot holes to size after drilling. Burnishing broaches, for finishing or burnishing holes, have smooth sides and no cutting edges. Broaches usually have a squared tapered tang for fitting to a drillbrace, tapwrench, wooden handle or pintongs; while some small ones have long knurled integral steel handles. In diameter, clock-makers' broaches range from a few thousandths of an inch to about three-quarters of an inch, for very large clocks. Half-round broaches are good for opening holes, and at one time broaches could be obtained with a wide range of cutting edges for coarse or fine work. Paper wrapped around a broach helps to obtain roundness of the hole. EBG *See also* Reamer.

Buff A tool for grinding or polishing, mounted on a machine as a cone, disc or other suitably shaped piece of felt or leather, or of wood covered with felt or leather, or as a mop made of layers of cloth, string or other material to be charged with an abrasive or polishing compound. This is rotated in the machine at the appropriate speed for buffing. Emery buffs can be covered with various grades of emery paper. Hand buffs, or buffing sticks, are made in various sections of wood, covered like machine buffs but used by hand. Hand emery buffs or emery sticks are of assorted shapes and sizes, covered with various grades of emery paper. EBG

Buffing, or mopping To grind or polish various surfaces by machine or hand using a buff charged with abrasive or polishing compound, in clockwork normally metal surfaces, but latterly including plastics. In machine buffing the part to be polished or ground is held against the edge of the rotating buff or mop, fast-cutting buffs being used first, then finer, softer buffs to obtain the desired degree of finish. Machine buffing requires great care to prevent rounding off square corners of the work, or overheating, or 'snatching'. A face guard is advisable to prevent injury by particles of buffing compounds and mop fibres. Awkwardly shaped pieces not suitable for machine buffing and areas such as the inside surfaces of shaped holes in clock plates are worked with hand buffs. Hard or soft, ferrous or non-ferrous metals can be buffed, as well as other materials such as plastics or glass. EBG

Burnisher A hand tool, generally a length of hardened steel, shaped and sized according to need, with a highly polished surface to burnish or polish metal to a smooth bright finish. Burnishers may be straight or curved, flat, oval or round, or formed with a burnishing foot and provided with a tang to fit in a wooden handle. A pivot burnisher or pivot file is double-ended or sided, one surface being finished as a very fine cross-grained file, the other being of the same shape but finished for burnishing. Good burnishers can be made by grinding smooth an old file and polishing it, while retaining its hardness. EBG

Burnishing Bringing the surface of metal to a brilliant finish by friction, the action slightly compressing and

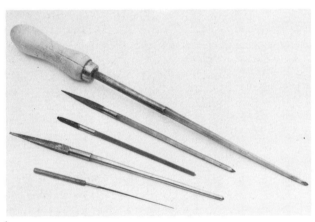

1

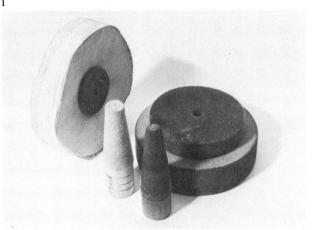

2

3

4

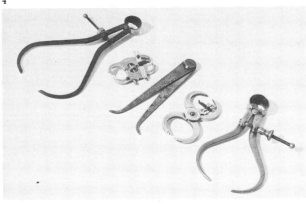

5

1 **Broaches,** an assortment, one with wooden handle, smallest with knurled handle.

2 **Buff** An assortment of polishing buffs and mops.

3 **Buff** Treadle-operated buffing head. Hirst Bros, *Catalogue of Tools,* c. 1900.

4 **Carborundum wheels** of various shapes and sizes.

5 **Calipers** A selection, two bow-jointed, one inside/outside and two poising.

6 **Burnishers** An assortment, two being combined with files.

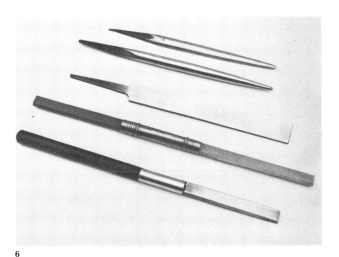

6

hardening the metal surface but removing no metal. The metal surface to be burnished is first cleared of all file marks or scratches. The surface of the appropriately shaped burnisher must always be kept absolutely clean and highly polished, for the burnished surface will never be finer than the surface of the burnisher. In burnishing pivots with the pivot burnisher, the file surface is first used to remove any turning marks or burrs, then finishing is done with the burnishing surface. Wheel crossings, arbors, winding squares, etc. are burnished to provide a good finish. EBG

Bushing The remedy for a worn pivot hole, bushing provides it with a new bearing surface. The worn hole is opened further to round it up and to bring it to its original centre. The new brass bush has a fine hole drilled in its centre and is then turned to fit tightly the new hole in the clock plate, and adjusted for length. Finally the bush is hammered or pressed into the hole and the new pivot hole in its centre is broached out and burnished to suit its pivot. An oil sink or reservoir is cut on the outside of the new bush. Rebushing of a worn hole previously bushed is more simple, for the worn bush can easily be replaced with a new one, and some clocks have removable bushes fitted at the time of manufacture. Bushing wire is obtainable in lengths of brass tube of various dimensions, which can be cut off for bushing, and manufactured bouchons can also be purchased in different sizes. EBG

Calipers Pivoted calipers are brass or steel instruments with two pivoted legs adapted to point inwards or outwards according to type or need. They are used for taking external or internal comparative measurements, particularly of curved surfaces or bores. Sometimes they have a locking screw and means of making fine adjustments, as when fitted

with a geared quadrant. Figure-eight calipers have two pairs of legs at opposite sides of the joint, thus forming a figure 8; proportional calipers have shorter legs at one side than the other and give comparative proportional measurements between each pair of legs in the ratios of $\frac{1}{2}$, $\frac{1}{3}$, $\frac{1}{4}$ etc. Poising calipers superficially appear to be similar tools, but they have male and/or female centres at the tips of the legs and a pivoted toucher bar. Between these centres wheels are mounted to test them for roundness or buckle using the toucher bar, and the wheel can also be tested for poise or balance using the same tool. Some figure-eight poising calipers have their joint at one end so that they can be opened and closed with one hand, and plier-pattern calipers with two pairs of centres in the jaws are also available. EBG

Carborundum wheel An abrasive disc or wheel of artificial stone mounted on a machine spindle and rotated at speed for grinding. Carborundum wheels are obtainable in many diameters, widths, spindle sizes, shapes and grades. The material is quick-cutting and useful for shaping steel clock parts and tools, though care must be taken not to overheat the work. As with buffs and mops, when using a carborundum wheel the eyes and body should be protected. A tool rest is also necessary. EBG
See also Emery wheel.

Casting Metal castings for clock movements, dials and case parts have been produced since the earliest days of clockmaking, and founding is probably the oldest branch of engineering. Brass is cast to produce clock plates, dial plates, pillars, bridges, cocks, wheel blanks, fusee blanks, skeleton clock plates, ornamental dial spandrels, clock cases, handles, feet, decorative case mounts and many other parts.

187

1 Chucks, step Left: contracting; right: expanding.

2 Chuck, box, with eight work-holding screws.

3 Chucks, collet

4 Chucks, self-centring, with tightening keys.

1

2

3

4

Patterns for these are first made and used to form sand moulds, into which the molten brass is poured. The castings are then filed, turned, cut into wheels and otherwise cleaned up to produce the finished parts. Brass cast into sheets is hammered or planished to flatten and harden it for clock plates, but in recent times sheet is obtained as rolled brass, and lengths of brass in many sections are produced by extrusion, forcing the metal through an opening of the desired shape, in a variety of grades and composition. EBG

Chasing Chasing can be a method of decoration, or a means of forming or finishing a thread on material rotated in a lathe. As a decorative technique in metal, chasing is done with a hammer and various punches to obtain an embossed or incised effect, being punched from behind to produce embossing. The chasing punch is blunt, and no metal is removed in chasing. The other method, to form a screw thread on metal rotated in the lathe, employs hand tools obtained in pairs for internal or external threading of required pitch and form. The rod to be threaded is first turned to size on the lathe; the chaser is then held firmly against it and allowed to move along at its own pitch, to produce the thread. This method was mostly used on soft metals such as brass, and the main purpose for hand chasing today is to correct the form of threads produced in a screw-cutting lathe. EBG
See also Engraving.

Chops Jaws of wood, fibre or soft metal placed in a vice to protect work being held there from being marked by the vice. EBG

Chuck, box Accessories to lathes; they are used for holding work during turning. The box chuck consists of a hollow cylinder fitted with radial screws which grip the work to be turned. This type of chuck is particularly useful for mounting work eccentrically. EBG

Chuck, collet This type of chuck is often called a split chuck. It consists of a hollow spindle, usually threaded at one end, the forward end being accurately drilled or broached and split, and able to close on and grip the work being turned as it is tightened into the hollow driving spindle of the lathe headstock, using the draw bar or draw screw. It is mostly used for comparatively small work and sets of variously sized split chucks are available for a given lathe. Being hollow it has the advantage that it can accommodate long lengths of wire, and for this reason it is often called a 'wire chuck'. EBG

Chuck, lantern This is a specialised chuck for holding parts such as screws, and is used with the screwhead or screwpoint polishing tool. EBG

Chuck, self-centring A useful chuck adaptable to many sizes of work. It has three or more radial jaws which close together on the work held by means of a screw or scroll inside the chuck, in such a way as to centre the work automatically as they close. This chuck is widely used on engineers' lathes as well as for clockmaking. EBG

Chuck, step The step chuck is similar in operation to the split chuck or collet chuck except that it has a stepped face, with concentric steps or rings which are suitable for holding small clock wheels or similar parts. Like split chucks they are available in a range of sizes, with different diameters of steps. EBG

Chuck, wax A wax chuck can be simply a flat plate, suitable for attachment to the driving spindle of a lathe, on which small or delicate clock parts can be cemented to hold them for turning. Shellac is used for this purpose when the parts are not suitable for holding in an ordinary chuck. Some wax chucks are drilled or hollowed out to accommodate an arbor, pinion, staff, verge, etc. These often take

5 Platform escapement on a
modern mantel chronometer.
Private collection.

5

1 Engine, wheel-cutting Brass-framed, hand-driven; signed 'Wyke and Green, Liverpool', *c.* 1770. Merseyside County Museum, Liverpool.

1

2 Lathe A small, modern
engineering lathe fitted with
dividing attachments, vertical
slide and fly cutter, for wheel
cutting.

2

1 Mandril, fitted with a hand wheel for driving; English, first half of the 19th century. Private collection.

2 Clams Peter Stubs, *Tool Catalogue*, Warrington, *c.*1801.

3 Compasses of various kinds and sizes. John Wyke, *Tool Catalogue*, Liverpool, *c.*1770.

1

the form of a brass rod partly drilled or recessed. The rod holding the required part is then held to be rotated in a split chuck, etc. EBG

Clams Soft linings for the jaws of a vice, spring-, bow- or pivot-jointed and used to hold work in the vice jaws. EBG *See also* Chops.

Cleaning Periodic maintenance and cleaning of a clock is advisable for continuous satisfactory timekeeping and to preserve the life of the mechanism. To be cleaned properly a clock should be completely dismantled and all parts cleaned and examined before reassembly and lubrication. Methods of cleaning depend on the type of clock and its condition. Turret clocks and longcase clock movements do not present the same problems as fine small carriage clocks with balance escapements, which have a good deal in common with watches. A seriously corroded and worn clock requires restoration rather than simple cleaning. Generally clock parts are soaked in a cleaning fluid and worked on with brushes and pegwood to remove congealed

oil and dirt. Some repolishing may be carried out before the parts are finally rinsed in a cleaning or degreasing solution and dried in sawdust for assembly. Cleaning was formerly carried out entirely by hand, but today it is often done in machines, in prepared solutions which are mechanically or ultrasonically agitated. EBG

Compasses An instrument for describing circles, with two pointed legs pivoted together in a joint at one end and set to distance by hand. Various forms and sizes of compasses are available. Clockmakers' compasses often have a conical point fitted to one leg to enable exact location to be made in a previously drilled hole when scribing out a clock plate. Compasses may have a pivoted slotted bar with a knurled set screw or a quadrant plate (wing) with a locking screw, and they may also have interchangeable points. Bowed leg compasses have pivoted joints in the legs, and bowed compasses have a spring bow instead of a pivoted joint. EBG

Compasses, beam Beam compasses, more recently called 'trammels', consist of a length of rod, usually square or rectangular in section, having a combined pivoted handle with a pivot or conical point set squarely to the axis of the rod at one end, and a sliding block fitted with a scriber and a locking screw to slide along the rod. They are used for describing large circles. On some both the pivot block and scriber block can be moved along the beam or rod; some are also provided with a micrometer adjusting screw. Trammels may be fitted with interchangeable points as scriber, caliper, needle, pen, pencil, or with cone or ball points to locate in a previously drilled hole [194/1]. EBG

2

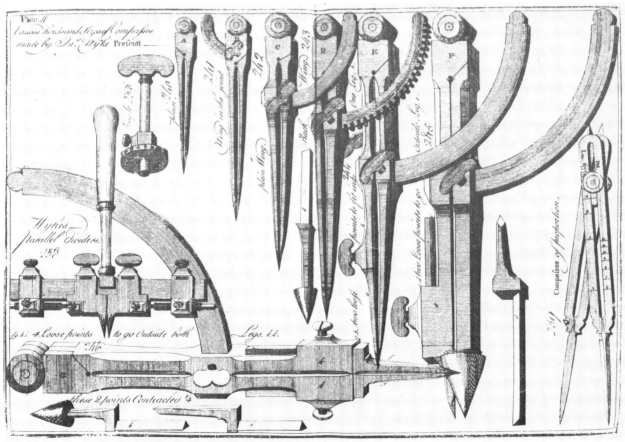

3

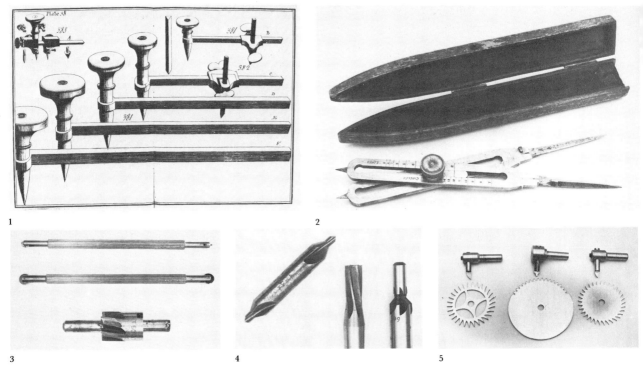

1

2

3

4

5

Compasses of proportion, or proportional dividers. This instrument has two brass or steel legs with longitudinal slots and steel points at the ends. The legs are pivoted together through a block which can slide and be set in the slots of the legs. A mark on the block can be set against a scale numbered from one to ten on one or both legs. According to this setting the distance between the opened points at each end will be proportional in the ratios given on the scale. This useful dividing tool is also valuable for increasing or reducing a given measurement to a desired proportion. Some are proportioned for dividing the circumference of a circle based on the length of the radius. EBG

Cutter, countersink A countersink cutter is designed to form a conical recess to accommodate the head of a countersunk screw in a clock plate or part. They are variously shaped and used either by machine or by hand when fitted with a handle. This kind of cutter is used to form the oil sink for a pivot hole or to chamfer hole edges. A chamfering tool with wheels has a cutting wheel at one end and a burnishing wheel at the other, and performs a similar function. A counterbore is used to cut the recess in a hole to fit the head of a cheesehead or squarehead screw, and a combination centre drill is used for centre-boring in the lathe, drilling, chamfering and counterboring in one operation. EBG

Cutter, fly A single-bladed cutting tool, clamped in a holder and rotated in a machine for facing work, cutting slots and flutes, or cutting gears. It is easier and cheaper to produce for cutting any desired profile than a multi-toothed milling cutter, though the milling cutter is more suitable for many operations. The fly cutter is made from heat-treated high-speed steel or from a tool steel to be hardened and tempered. To form a cutter for gashing (cutting teeth) or cutting a pinion, the required profile is shaped at the end of the cutter and given cutting and clearance edges. In use the

cutter revolves at suitable speed and is fed slowly into the work; excellent gears can be produced by fly cutting, especially in brass. EBG

Cutter, milling Produced in a variety of shapes, with a number of cutting teeth round their edges, which in profile constitute a counterpart of the sectional form to be reproduced, milling cutters can be used in a lathe, or in a milling or gear-cutting machine, etc., for cutting flutes, shaped sinks, recesses, or wheels and pinions. Milling cutters are made in a wide variety of forms by commercial manufacturers and are much more suitable for cutting steel than fly cutters as they cause less vibration, give a cleaner cut and last longer. EBG

Cutter, rose A circular rod with cutting teeth at the end, available in various shapes and sizes; used in a lathe, drill, or in the hand when fitted with a handle. One type with a cone-shaped cutting end is used to chamfer a hole. For reducing the diameter of lengths of wire when making screws, the cutter has a hole of the required shank size in its centre, usually called a hollow mill; when fitted with a pilot to guide it into a hole it is called a 'counterbore', and used for counterboring for cheeseheaded screws. It can also be used to give clearance or endshake to an arbor. EBG

Depthing tool A tool to determine the correct distance apart and depth of engagement of wheel teeth and pinions. It has a pair of parallel runners between the centres of which two wheels, or wheel and pinion, or escape wheel and pallets, may be adjusted to work properly together. The distance apart of the runners is transferred, as with dividers, to the plate where the arbors of the wheels are to be planted. Some old catalogues show a triple depthing tool which has an additional pair of runners in a frame at 90° to the other runners, for adjusting the interaction of a contrate wheel, escape wheel and pallets for a verge escapement. EBG

1 Compasses, beam John Wyke, *Tool Catalogue*, Liverpool, c.1770.

2 Compasses of proportion and leather-covered case. Private collection.

3 Cutters, countersink, two with knurled handles, double-ended, wheel chamfering and burnishing; one hollow mill with pilot.

4 Cutters, countersink Left: for centring, drilling and chamfering; middle: for sinking; right: for chamfering.

5 Cutters, fly Left and right: with escape wheels; middle: for gear wheel.

6 Cutters, milling A selection of various designs.

7 Cutters, rose A further type of chamfering tool.

8 Cutters, rose, in tools for hand use.

9 Depthing tool Denis Diderot, '*Horlogerie*', *Encyclopédie*, Paris, 1751.

10 Die in a holder and one hexagonal die nut.

6   7   8

Diamantine A white powder prepared from boron, processed to obtain the utmost purity. It is normally obtainable in three grades and used with a little oil for finishing and polishing steel. The coarsest grade, No. 1, is for grinding and smoothing, while grade No. 2 is commonly used to obtain the final polished finish. Grade No. 3 is exceedingly fine and little used by clockmakers. EBG

Die One kind of die is a tool used for cutting a thread on a rod. It usually takes the form of a disc of tool steel, with a centre hole and two or more radially disposed holes which break into the central hole to form cutting edges. The central hole is first tapped with the required screw thread. The outer edge of the disc has flats or shallow holes which allow it to be gripped in a die holder or die stock when in use. The finished die is hardened and tempered, and some dies have a slit from one edge to the centre hole to enable this cutting hole to be opened or closed slightly when fixed into the stock. Split dies are made in two halves which are put together in the screw stock; they normally have one size of thread only, but are sometimes made with a number of differently sized holes in the split. A die nut is similar to an ordinary die but of hexagonal or square outer shape for cleaning up threads and useful for threads which cannot be reached with dies held in stocks.

Another, entirely different tool called a die is a shaped metal block used to produce a form or shape by metal stamping or pressing; these are called 'metal-forming' or 'punching' dies. Die casting is a process in which molten metal is forced under pressure into a die or mould to produce a casting. EBG

Dividers Dividers, or measuring compasses, differ little from compasses except that they are spring-hinged and are adjusted by a knurled nut and screw for fine measurement. They are used for taking comparative measurements, as a drawing instrument, or for scribing out a clock plate. EBG

Dividing This term refers to dividing the length, diameter or circumference of circles as required, by means of dividers or dividing plate, or by other means. Clockmakers use dividing plates to produce wheels, pinions, count wheels or locking plates, and other clock parts such as dials. EBG

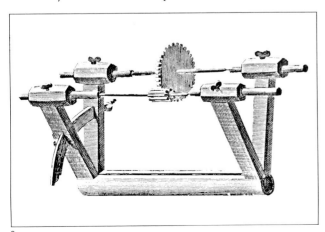

9   10

III TOOLS, MATERIALS, METHODS

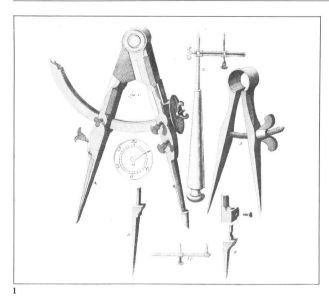

1 Dividers Antoine Thiout, *Traité de l'horlogerie*, 1741

2 Dividing plate from an 18th-century wheel-cutting engine. Private collection.

3 Drawbench from a Clerkenwell workshop, now in the Merseyside County Museum, Liverpool.

4 Drawplate, well worn, showing tapering holes. Merseyside County Museum, Liverpool.

5 Drill arbors Verreles are the same as modern ferrules. John Wyke, *Tool Catalogue*, Liverpool, c. 1770.

6 Drills, Archimedean, of various sizes.

7 Drill bows, one of steel with tensioning device, the other of whalebone. Merseyside County Museum, Liverpool.

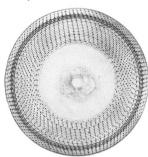

Dividing plate A flat circular plate fitted to a wheel- or pinion-cutting machine, or to a lathe spindle or dividing accessory for a lathe or other machine. On the plate a number of concentric circles are marked, each divided into a different number of equal divisions. Work held on the arbor of the dividing plate can therefore be rotated and divided according to the number of divisions, using a detent located on a selected circle. Alternatively the dividing plate may have teeth on its edge, driven forward by a worm or endless screw, and advanced to the required position by a previously calculated number of rotations of the worm. A useful method of marking out a dividing plate, used by

Henry Hindley of York early in the 18th century, is to cut a series of small, equally spaced holes in a long strip of metal, equal in number to the largest number of divisions required on the plate, plus an extra one. The strip is bent to form a complete loop and the two end holes joined by a rivet or peg. A disc of wood is then turned on the lathe until the loop fits tightly around its circumference, which is thus divided into the required number of equal divisions. These divisions can be transferred to a circle on a blank dividing plate and the same strip of metal reduced in stages to produce decreasing numbers of divisions on smaller circles on the dividing plate by the same basic method. The position of

196

the first division of each circle on the dividing plate is usually placed on a radial line, with the numbers of divisions clearly marked for each circle. EBG

Drawbench A long, strongly built bench used for drawing lengths of wire to a desired section. One end of the bench is fitted with a large capstan or wheel, and the other has supports to hold the drawplate. The wire to be drawn is threaded through the drawplate and clasped in the jaws of special draw pliers which are hooked to a strong leather belt. The other end of the belt is wrapped around the arbor of the wheel. As the wheel is turned the belt tightens and pulls the wire slowly, with great force, through the drawplate. EBG

Drawplate A hardened steel plate in which a number of graduated, tapering, round or suitably shaped holes have been formed to enable wire to be drawn successively through diminishing sizes of holes, to be reduced in diameter. Plates may be obtained for drawing round, square, half-round, triangular or other sections of wire. When a wire of a certain section is needed, a wire of slightly larger diameter is prepared with a long taper at one end which is passed through the larger side of the largest hole in the plate. The wire is then steadily pulled through the hole by means of the drawbench, which squeezes the wire into shape and reduces its size. Repeated drawings through diminishing sizes of holes bring the wire to the required size and section, but after a number of drawings it should be annealed, otherwise it will become too hard and may break. Pinion wire for making small clock pinions is produced by drawing wire through plates with holes gradually shaped to the pinion section. EBG
See also Annealing; Pinion wire.

Drill, Archimedean A hand tool which gives reciprocating motion to a drill. It consists of a rod with a spiral 'quick' thread, having a handle pivoted at one end and a drill holder or chuck at the other. A sliding nut on the threaded rod imparts motion to the drill. Some drills of this type have the nut formed in the base of the handle, the rod passing into the handle as pressure is applied and returning by means of a spring when pressure is released, thus giving reciprocating drill action. Another type of drill often referred to as archimedean is the drill with cords and inertia wheel. This is also called a 'bob' drill or 'upright' drill, the weighted bob causing the cords to wrap around the stock on the overrun, motion being imparted as the handle is pressed down. This type is normally used only by jewellers and casemakers. EBG

Drill arbor A spear-shaped tool or flat drill having cutting edges on the flattened end, a male centre at the other end and a pulley, or ferrule, on its elongated shank. It is rotated for drilling by the use of a drill bow, which produces reciprocating motion. In use the drill arbor is supported at the cutting end by the drill point and at the other in a centre hole of a breast plate, or in a hole in the end of a vice jaw or vice block. This type of drill, depending on the exact shape of the cutting edges, when used with plenty of oil will penetrate hard brass or even tempered steel. The name is also given to pintongs which are intended to hold a drill and be rotated in a large chuck or collet. EBG

Drill bow The bow is used to impart reciprocating motion to work in the turns, to the spindle mandril of a lathe, to a drill or drill stock, or to an arbor, by coiling the line of the bow once around a pulley or ferrule. As the bow is moved to and fro the work rotates in alternate directions. Bows are made of thin strips of whalebone or cane, drill bows usually being of flexible steel with a tensioning device at one end. Various sizes of bow are available and, according to the size and nature of the work, gut, horsehair or human hair is used for the line. EBG

Drill box A drill holder with a square box-shaped aperture at the end of a drill stock or drilling tool. A screw-nosed drill box has a nut on a tapered slotted nose box by which the

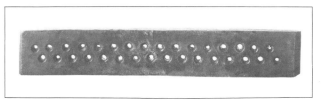

4

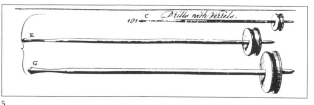

5

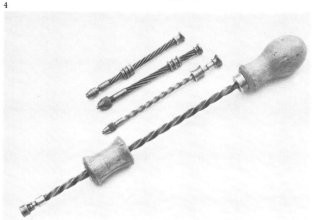

6

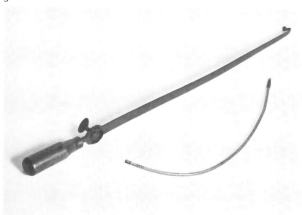

7

nose is squeezed or closed to secure the drill. Drills for use in a drill box have a square shank. EBG

Drilling There are drills for numerous different purposes. Two basic methods are employed when drilling: rotating the drill with the work stationary, or rotating the work with the drill stationary. When drilling holes in clock plates or other parts it is convenient to hold the work still on a drilling table, but when drilling down the axis of arbors or pinions greatest accuracy is achieved by rotating the work in a lathe. Drills are rotated by a bow, drill or wheel brace, archimedean drill or drilling machine, while work is rotated in a mandril or lathe for making a hole with the use of a boring tool. EBG

Drill stock A steel arbor fitted with a ferrule, a male centre at one end and a drill holder at the other. Available in various sizes, it is rotated for drilling by a bow. Some drill stocks have a simple tapered box or screw-nose drill box or chuck; others have a plain round hole for the drill with a hole in the side of the stock and screw-set collar to clamp the drill in position. In use a drill stock is supported in a frame, or operated like a drill arbor. EBG

Emery wheel A disc or wheel of artificial stone for grinding by machine. It is composed of emery grit bonded together, of even texture in various grades of fineness, and in various shapes and sizes. Rapidly rotated to grind many different metals the wheel can be run in water to keep it cool. A worn wheel may be cleaned or trued with a diamond truing tool.

1 Drill stocks fitted with ferrules and drills.
2 Drill box fitted with a drill. John Wyke, *Tool Catalogue*, Liverpool, *c*.1770.

3 Engine, clock-barrel and fusee shown with a grooved clock barrel in place and accessory for use in an ordinary pair of turns. John Wyke, *Tool Catalogue*, Liverpool, *c*.1770.

4 Engine, clock-barrel and fusee of more complicated design than the previous example. John Wyke, *Tool Catalogue*, Liverpool, *c*.1770.

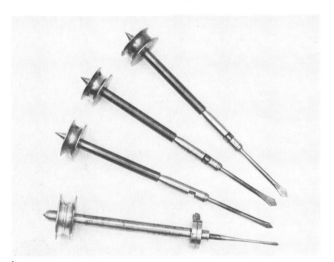

1

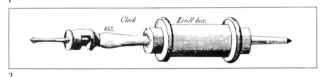

2

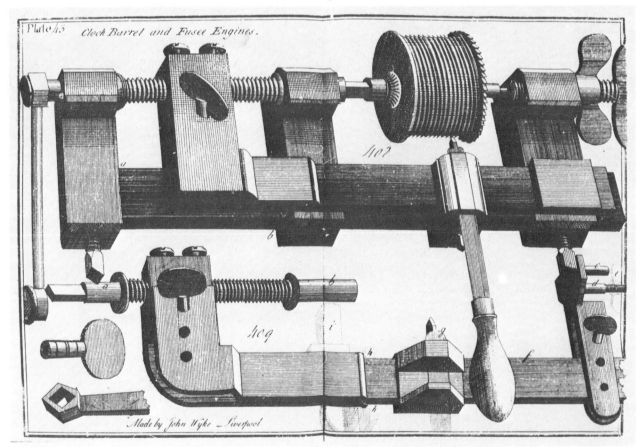

3

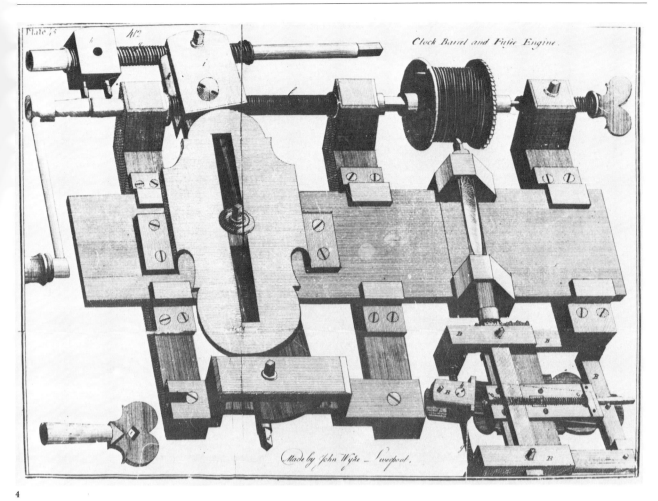

Clock Barrel and Fusee Engine.

Made by John Wyke — Liverpool.

4

Enamelling The process used to give a hard vitreous finish to clock dials and sometimes ornamental parts of clock cases. It should not be confused with painting. Enamel is a fusible vitreous silica-based compound which is mixed with water and applied to a sheet of copper or other metal and fused in an enamelling kiln, in which it melts to form a hard glossy surface. Obtaining the right thickness of enamel often calls for several coats, each applied and fired in turn after the previous coating has been rubbed down. Although normally opaque white, enamel can be coloured with different metallic oxides; decoration such as numerals, signatures and other decoration on dials, can be added in other colours and fused. The technique was extensively used for French clock dials, earlier ones being built up from individual enamelled plaques for each hour numeral.

In cloisonné enamelling, the area to be decorated is divided up by a design made in fine wire soldered to the ground metal and forming a series of compartments or *cloisons*, which are then filled with different colours of enamel and fired. EBG

Engine, clock-barrel In the past complex tools were often known as engines. Clock-barrel engines were used for cutting the spiral groove to take the gut lines of an eight-day longcase clock barrel. The tool was made rather like a pair of turns in which the barrel to be cut was centred, on its winding arbor, between a runner and a rotating or driving arbor. This arbor, which held the barrel winding square, was threaded along its length on which a block or carrier

would travel axially as the work was turned. An arm extending from this block carried the hand cutter, and as the barrel was turned towards the operator pressure was applied to the cutter to form the spiral groove in the barrel. The illustration [198/3] shows an accessory by means of which an ordinary pair of turns could be converted into a barrel engine. Today such work would be carried out on a screw-cutting lathe. EBG

Engine, fusee The clock-barrel engine could also be used for cutting the groove in fusees for bracket clocks, except that the cutter would follow the conical profile of a fusee instead of the straight cylinder of a barrel. Because variation was often needed in the pitch of fusee or barrel grooves, a more elaborate form of engine was devised in which the pitch of the groove could be altered. See 199/4: it has a barrel in place but could also be used for fusees. In general terms it follows the same principle as the earlier engine, but in this case the cutter carrier, which is a flat rectangular bed free to travel axially, is moved by a lever from the guiding block on the driving arbor thread, this lever having a pivot which engages a slot in the carrier. By adjusting this pivot the amount of travel of the carrier can be varied; when the pivot is nearer the front of the machine the tool carrier will travel less for a given number of turns of the work than when it is at the rear. By this means, and by having differently threaded driving arbors and blocks, considerable variety of pitch of fusee or barrel groove could be cut. Many modern Swiss fusee cutting tools use the same principle. EBG

1

Engine, wheel-cutting A wide variety of wheel-cutting engines have been made over the past three centuries, but all follow more or less the same general principle. It is generally agreed that the wheel-cutting engine evolved from manual methods of dividing a wheel in the 17th century, when revolving cutters to cut the separate wheel teeth spaces replaced hand filing, and when the blank to be cut was divided mechanically into the required number of teeth. For this purpose a dividing plate was used, on the arbor of which the blank wheel to be cut was mounted. The dividing plate was supported in a frame of various designs according to country and date, and a detent on the frame allowed the dividing plate, and thus the work, to be rotated at the chosen number of intervals required for cutting the

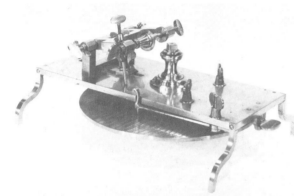

2

3

4

1 Engine, wheel-cutting, wooden-framed, pulley-driven; American, 18th century. New Hampshire Historical Society, Concord, New Hampshire.

2 Engine, wheel-cutting, brass-framed, pulley-driven; signed 'Hulot *et Fils*', Paris, mid 18th-century. Musée du Conservatoire National des Arts et Métiers, Paris.

3 Engine, wheel-cutting, iron-framed, hand-driven; signed and dated 'William Terry fecit 1774'. Tolson Memorial Museum, Huddersfield.

4 Engine, wheel-cutting, shown in the foreground of a clockmaker's workshop; signed 'Sam'l Nelson, Liverpool fecit No. 63' and dated 1785. This machine formerly belonged to Benjamin Louis Vulliamy. Laurence Harvey.

5 Rounding-up tool used for small clock or watch wheels; Continental, second half of 19th century. Private collection.

5

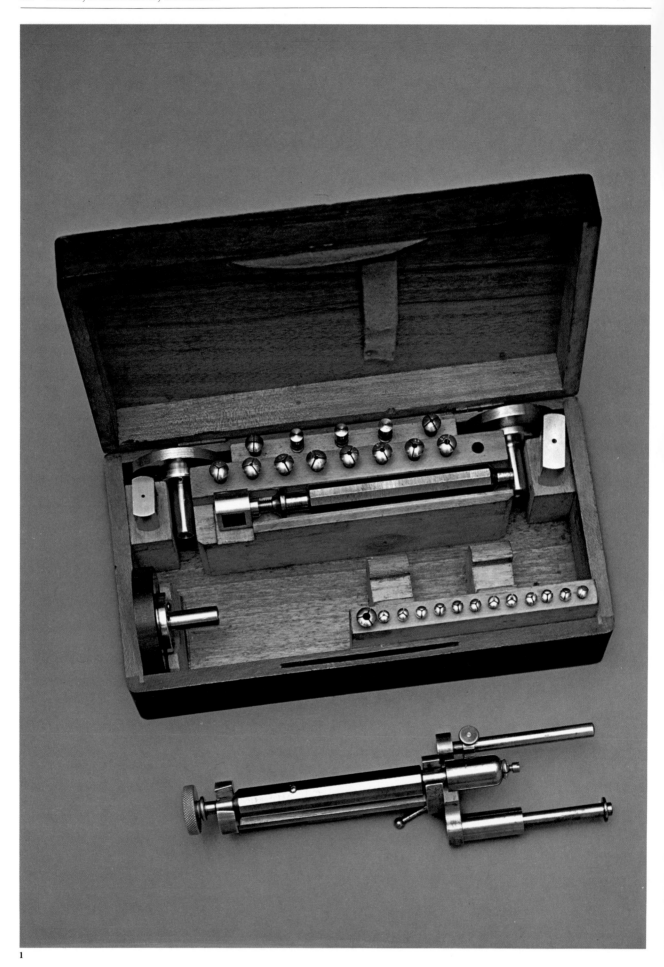

1

1 Screwhead tool A boxed set of screwhead tools, runners, collets and polishers. Continental, probably *c.* 1900. Private collection.

2 Engine turning Dial from an early 19th-century English mantel clock decorated with machine engraving.

3 Ferrules A selection of various sizes, and four drivers.

4 Eyeglass on a bench stand, shown in a portrait of A. L. Perrelet, *c.* 1775.

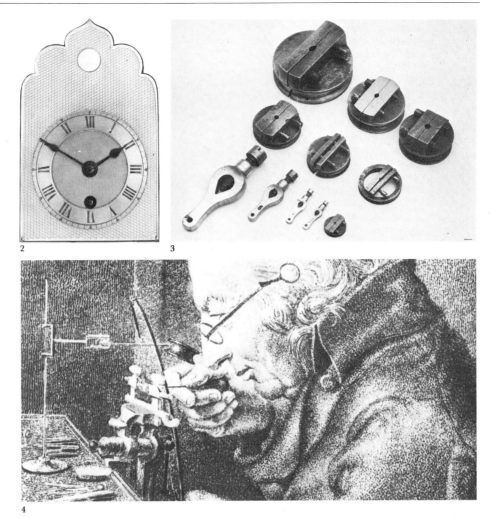

2

3

4

chosen number of wheel teeth, according to the divisions of the circles on the dividing plate. As the blank was indexed round, therefore, a tooth space was cut by the rotating cutter, which was driven by an endless cord from a foot wheel or other power source. In some cases the cutter was advanced into and retracted from the edge of the blank, while in others the blank was advanced to the cutter. Early engines produced work which still required the teeth to be formed to their correct shape later with a rounding-up tool, but later machines were more advanced and had cutters which were shaped to produce the final tooth form, sometimes using three or more cutters mounted in a multiple cutting head for progressive work. Modern wheel cutting is normally done on a lathe with specially designed dividing heads, while in clock factories a cutter traverses a large number of wheel blanks mounted on a common arbor, cutting wheels in stacks. EBG

Engine turning Engraving produced by a machine. Beautiful decorative engraving in many designs can be done with the work in a specialised lathe or rose engine, in which the eccentric movement of the work, or cutting tool, or both, results in a repetitive pattern or moulding on the surface of the work. Such engraving is used to decorate clock dial centres and clock cases. EBG

Engraving Engraving was used extensively in the decoration of clocks, for dial centres, backplates, cases,

hour, minute and second numerals, and the maker's name. Numerals when engraved were usually filled with black wax to give them visual clarity. The usual method of engraving is to gouge or chisel out the surface design by hand using a sharpened tool called a 'graver' or 'burin', or a chisel and hammer. Engraving can also be performed by machine using a form of milling cutter and an engraving machine fitted with a pantograph, which can accurately copy a design. EBG

Eyeglass An eyeglass is an optical instrument required by the clockmaker to magnify the image of an object and bring it closer to the eye. Eyeglasses may consist of a round, tapered tube fitted with a lens, usually single but occasionally multiple, and shaped to be held in the eye socket; or they may be held to the eye by a band worn round the head. Eyeglasses are also made in hinged frames which can be fitted to spectacles as required, and old illustrations show eyeglasses held in bench stands over the work [203/4]. Lenses of different powers of focal length are available, and two-, three-, or four-in. eyeglasses are used when the work is to be viewed at those distances. A double eye glass will allow the object to be seen *c.* $\frac{1}{4}$ in. from the lens. Eyeglasses with a tube are internally finished in matt black to prevent disturbing reflections, and have a ventilation hole in the side to prevent condensation on the lens. EBG

Ferrule A form of pulley attached to a tool or part to

enable it to be rotated by the cord of a bow or wheel. Ferrules are produced in many forms and sizes, simple ones being small brass pulleys of different diameters and centre-hole sizes held on the work either by friction grip or shellac. Split ferrules are made in two halves and screw-tightened on to arbors of different sizes. A loose ferrule or pulley may be used with a 'driver', i.e. a small split bridle, to rotate very small arbors between dead centres of pairs of turns. EBG

File A most important tool for clockmaking, having a serrated surface for removing metal by cutting and abrasion. Files are made in innumerable shapes and sizes and cuts, for many purposes. At one time almost all parts of a clock, including wheel teeth and pinions were shaped with files, and some files are named from the parts for which they were used, such as verge, pallet-wheel, endless-screw, pivot, etc. Common files are classified as flat, round, half-round, three-cornered, rat-tail, crossing and slitting, etc., while types of cut are known as rough, bastard, smooth and dead-smooth. Clock sizes of files are made with a tang and should always be fitted in handles. A new file should preferably be used with brass until its keenness has worn off, when it becomes more suitable for iron and steel. The most common method of cleaning files is to brush them with a wire brush. EBG

Flux A substance applied to metals which are being brazed or soldered. The flux is designed to help the liquid brazing and soldering metal properly to 'wet' the parent metal or metals being joined by reducing the risk of an oxide film forming on the work. EBG
See also Brazing; Soldering.

Fly press The fly press is one of the simplest forms of press, providing an economical method of rapidly producing parts. In principle, it utilises the energy of hand-moved weights to operate a ram for stamping, pressing, blanking, piercing and forming, some of these being possibly combined in one operation. EBG

Frosting The granular or matted finish given to the surface of brass clock parts prior to gilding. It is produced by dipping the parts briefly into a concentrated mixture of nitric and hydrochloric acid, after which they are rinsed

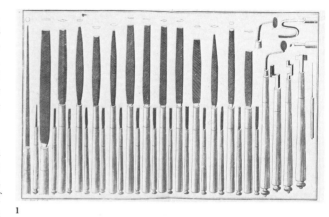

1

and brushed in a circular direction with a scratch brush. A 'grey' surface on steel or brass is produced by rubbing the parts on the surface of a glass plate smeared with a paste of oilstone dust and oil. EBG

Gauge, mainspring A fine gauge similar to a pivot gauge, used for measuring the thickness of mainsprings. Another mainspring gauge is used to measure the height of the spring, and is known as a 'width' or 'height' gauge. It consists of a flat plate with graduated slots on its edges, each slot being marked with numbers or measurements to check the height of a given spring. These gauges are used for small clocks only. EBG

Gauge, micrometer A type of gauge for accurate measurement of small parts to thousandths of an inch, obtained by turning a precision, fine-pitched, threaded screw a known number of revolutions, or parts thereof, from a fixed datum position. This movement is indicated by a rotating scale against a fixed scale. Micrometers are made in many shapes and sizes, adapted to many different measuring needs. EBG

Gauge, pinion A gauge similar to a slide gauge, used to measure the distance between the plates of a clock or the length of a pinion from shoulder to shoulder, showing both measurements at the same time. The name is also applied to a caliper-type of instrument with legs adjusted by a nut on a screw to take pinion measurements. A further type is like a wire gauge and measures the diameter of a pinion; it is

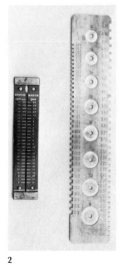

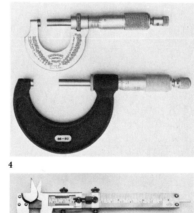

1 **Files** Antoine Thiout, *Traité de l'horlogerie*, 1741.

2 **Gauge, mainspring** Left: for mainspring strength; right: for height, barrel diameter and strength.

3 **Gauge, pivot**

4 **Gauge, micrometer** Top: 0–1 inch; bottom: 25–50 mm. Private collection.

5 **Gauge, sliding,** with vernier scale; imperial and metric.

6 **Gauge, vernier,** detail of 204/5.

2   3   5   6

particularly useful when measuring a pinion with an odd number of leaves. EBG

Gauge, pivot A gauge for measuring the diameter of clock pivots. It consists of two flat steel plates fastened together by strips of metal at their ends to form a tapered slot between the inner plate edges. The size of the gap between the edges at any point is given on scales marked out on the plates. By inserting the pivot at the wide end of the slot and moving it along, its diameter can be determined. EBG

Gauge, sliding A name applied to numerous measuring tools which have a jaw, or jaws, adapted to slide along a bar or beam, and set in position on it. It is also an old name for sliding calipers. The beam is usually provided with a scale and, in vernier instruments, with a secondary scale on the jaw sliding box. Sliding height gauges are designed with a heavy base for placing on a flat surface, and the sliding jaw is moved up the vertical column to check the height of work, also on the flat surface. Sliding calipers have many uses and may be fitted with two pairs of jaws and a depth probe for taking external, internal and depth measurements in one operation. Dial calipers have a dial and pointer and are rapidly read, without a vernier. EBG

Gauge, vernier Many measuring instruments are fitted with a vernier, a subsidiary scale for making subdivisions of the main measuring scale. For subdividing a main scale in units of ten the vernier has ten equal divisions totalling the length of nine of the main scale, and the reading is taken from the vernier where alignment takes place on the divisions of both scales. Some vernier gauges are made which can be read to 0·01 mm; a vernier protractor divides degrees of a circle into minutes. EBG

Gauge, wire A steel plate with a range of graduated round holes or slots, accurately gauged to a standard legalised in 1883. Each hole is marked with the standard wire-gauge number, and the equivalent imperial or metric size may be added; some firms retained their own gauge sizes for many years. The tool is used to measure the diameter of wire or sheet metal. EBG

Gilding The process of coating a base metal such as brass with a very fine layer of gold, much used in watch-movement finishing. For clocks it is largely confined to decorative external details such as spandrel mounts for dials. Because gold does not oxidise or tarnish it makes a good finish and gives an attractive appearance. The early gilding process was known as 'fire', or 'mercurial' gilding; in simple terms, the gold surface was obtained by rubbing it with a mercury–gold amalgam and heating until the mercury evaporated away, leaving a layer of pure gold behind. After this treatment the gilding was washed and finished by burnishing to bring up the bright quality of the metal. This method was highly injurious to workers because of the toxic effects of mercury, and in the 19th century it was replaced by electrogilding. EBG

Gilding, parcel Partly gilding. Normally, a term used in connection with partially gilded domestic objects made of silver, it also applies to parcel-gilt clock dials and in some instances decorative metal clock cases. EBG

Graver A cutting tool of hardened steel, square or lozenge-shaped in section and of varying thickness. One end has a tang for fitting in a handle and the other is ground off at an angle to obtain the cutting point or face. A graver may be used by hand for turning in the lathe or turns, or as a hand-engraving tool. The cutting face is sharpened on a fine oilstone and finished on an Arkansas stone. EBG

Hammer A hammer provides the means of using the energy of a moving mass. Hammers come in various shapes and sizes, and are usually made of steel, brass, aluminium, lead, or other metal, according to purpose. Types of hammers include round-face, flat-face, cross-pane, ball-pane, claw, ball-end, chisel-end, riveting, chasing and planishing. EBG

Hardening The term used to describe any of the hot or cold methods of hardening metal. It is frequently followed by tempering. Some metals, like brass, can only be hardened by a cold working operation, while a heat treatment is used for steel. Mild steel cannot be hardened, except in instances when it can be case-hardened, converting the metal skin into a harder steel. Carbon steel, containing various amounts of carbon, is affected by the

7 **Hammers,** one ball-pane and four cross-panes.
8 **Gravers** fitted in wooden handles.

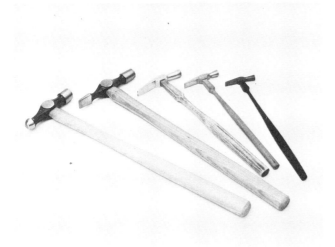

7

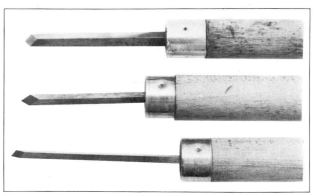

8

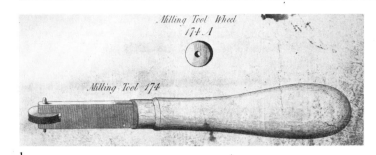

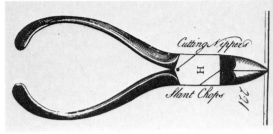

1

2

temperature to which it is raised, the time it remains at this temperature, the rate at which it is cooled, and the atmosphere in which the work is carried out. Specialist manufacturers of steel tools and parts use carefully controlled methods of heating and cooling the steel, while clockmakers in small workshops acquire considerable skill in judging the correct temperature of the steel before plunging it into water, or oil, or otherwise cooling it to ensure the correct hardness. EBG

Hardening, hammer Brass, copper, gold, silver and certain other metals or alloys are hardened and made more resilient or springy by hammering them in a cold state on an anvil or stake. Hammer hardening produces a change in the microstructure of the metal, making it more suitable for certain needs. The same effect can be produced by rolling the cold metal through pressure rollers. Clockmakers harden brass by these methods for clock plates, wheels (especially escape wheels), and for making springs. Surface hardening of metal can be achieved by burnishing. EBG

Hobbing *See* Milling.

Knurling Serrations or other indentations on a metal surface such as a clock hand-set button, designed to improve the grip of the fingers upon it. Knurling is produced by a knurling tool which carries a hardened steel wheel with the desired pattern upon it. This wheel turns on a hardened shaft lying across a slot cut in the holder. The part to be knurled is rotated in the lathe while the tool is pressed hard against it. In mass production, special machine-knurling tools are used. EBG

Lacquering Various lacquers are used to give metal or wood a protective or decorative covering. They are applied hot or cold, by brush, spray or by dipping. Shellac dissolved in methylated spirit, or cellulose solution, or other lacquers, are used for brass parts such as clock plates, cases, dials, etc. Clear lacquers are suitable on silver to protect it from tarnish. Lacquering on wood is a specialised decorative treatment. EBG

Lathe A machine in which metal, wood or other material is mounted horizontally, rotated, and cut or turned. Material to be revolved in a lathe is mounted either between the centres of the lathe or fixed to the headstock spindle. A lathe can be a small simple tool or a large complicated machine. An ordinary 'clockmaker's' or engineering lathe is seldom made for any special purpose, but when suitably equipped with accessories its versatility is such that an endless variety of work can be machined on it. It can be converted into a

drilling, milling, dividing or planing machine. The basic part of a lathe is the bed on which the headstock, which contains the rotating spindle, the tailstock, which has a detachable centre, and the toolrest, which supports the cutting tool, are mounted. The headstock spindle and the tailstock runner or barrel can be solid or hollow, and can also be provided with a loose centre, face plate, collet or chuck. The toolrest in its simple form supports the cutting tool for hand work, but a compound slide rest has a top slide on which the cutting tool is secured, and permits the tool to be moved axially along the work in the lathe. The top slide is mounted on a cross-slide which moves across the lathe axis, both slides being operated by screws. A compound slide is often fitted to a carriage which moves along the bed of the lathe by means of a rack and pinion, or by gearing to the headstock spindle. The latter is incorporated for automatic feeding or screw-cutting. A top slide can often be swivelled to an angle relative to the lathe axis for taper turning. EBG

Lathe, automatic A lathe specially designed and set up for the purpose of mass-producing specific parts by automatically performing several machining operations in succession, such as turning, threading, milling, counterboring and parting off. With some automatic lathes it is possible to feed the material in long lengths, which will be made into many parts without further attention from the operator. Sometimes blanks on a conveyor are fed into the lathe at great speed, and some automatic machines have a number of rotating spindles and cutting tools which are horizontally or vertically mounted. EBG

Lathe, capstan A type of lathe fitted with accessories set up for rapid production of identical parts. The distinguishing feature is the self-indexing capstan or tool head which holds several previously positioned tools that perform in succession various cutting operations, such as turning, drilling, counterboring and threading. The capstan is mounted on a slide, the base of which is clamped to the lathe bed at a convenient distance from the headstock. Movement of the slide carries the capstan to the work, the reverse movement removing the slide and indexing the capstan by rotating it with the next tool in position before it is again brought back to the work. It is usual to have a cut-off slide fitted to a capstan lathe for parting-off work produced from a rod. To permit more rod to be quickly brought ready for cutting, a quick-change collet chuck is fitted to the lathe spindle. EBG

Mandril A lathe with a face plate fitted with dogs for gripping work such as flat plates and parts. It is equipped

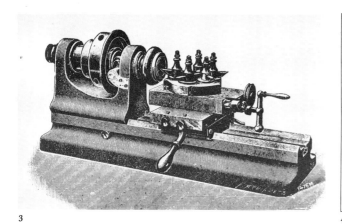

3

4

with a spring or pump centre with a conical point down the centre of the lathe spindle, used to centre the work on the mandril. The English mandril is driven by a gut line from a hand wheel or treadle, fitted around a pulley at the back of the lathe head, while Swiss mandrils are hand-driven through gears. The mandril has a slide or toolrest and sometimes a back or tail centre which is used to centre the work from the front. EBG

Matting The granular finish given to the centre of a brass clock dial, or a type of finish for clock parts. The effect is produced by punching the matted centre dial all over with a single or multipointed punch, or by rolling the dial between rollers, one of which has fine spikes. A matted effect can also be obtained by etching with acid. EBG

Milling A method for giving specific shape to metal parts with revolving cutting tools, mostly known as milling cutters. It is faster than other methods of shaping. Although milling cutters may be used in a lathe, they are more often employed in a milling machine. These machines are of two types, those with vertical spindles and those with horizontal ones. Milling cutters are made to produce clock wheels or pinions, and they cut or 'gash' one tooth space at a time in the wheel or pinion blank. When cutting a wheel with a milling cutter, the milling machine can be arranged so that the revolving cutter moves through the stationary blank; alternatively, the blank can be mounted in an attachment which moves it in the path of the revolving cutter. Hobbing is a quicker and more accurate way of cutting gears; hobs are cutters in the form of a worm, the cutting edges being formed by flutes across the worm thread. The work and the hob are revolved together, the two often being suitably geared by the hobbing machine. EBG

Nippers Cutting tools consisting of a pair of jointed steel levers with hardened cutting edges which close together. They are used for cutting wire, small clock pins, etc., and are shaped as end or side nippers. EBG

Oilstone An abrasive stone such as Arkansas, India or Turkey, used with a lubricant for sharpening tools to a fine edge. Fine oil is normally used. Oilstones can be obtained in grades such as fine, medium and coarse, and in different shapes and sizes. Dirty or clogged stones can be cleaned by soaking in paraffin or benzine. Oilstone dust is oilstone ground to powder and combined with oil for grinding or polishing steel. EBG

Pegwood The name given to sticks of wood, preferably dogwood, which are used for cleaning out pivot holes. They are usually about six inches long and up to $\frac{1}{4}$ in. in diameter. The wood is sharpened to enter a pivot hole and rotated to remove the dirt, a process which is repeated until the wood is clean when removed from the hole. Pegwood is also used for cleaning pinion flutes and other awkward places in clockwork. EBG

Pinion-facing tool A tool for finishing and polishing the end face of a pinion. A facing tool is made of soft steel or bell metal and used with coarse red stuff for squaring up the pinion face. For finishing or polishing it is made of bell metal and used with slightly moistened diamantine. In form the tool is a short tube with a slightly tapered hole to allow the pinion arbor just to pass through the small end, the end wall of the tube being the finishing face, having itself been finished dead square. When facing a pinion, the pinion arbor is supported at one end in the turns and at the other by the facing tool, the pinion being rotated by use of a ferrule and bow. To keep the facing tool true to the work, the tube itself may be pivoted in a hand frame. EBG

Pinion-milling machine Pinions for watches and sometimes also for small clocks were usually made from pinion wire, but for larger clocks pinions were milled from a cylinder of steel left standing when the clock arbor was turned on the lathe. Determination of the dividing of the pinion was done by using a dividing plate in a manner rather similar to that used on a wheel-cutting engine, though the dividing plate for pinions had a much smaller range of divisions marked on it. Early pinion-cutting machines employed a simple hand-operated file cutter running parallel with the pinion arbor, the cutter being guided by a frame which also held the pinion being cut between centres; later, machines were devised on the same principle but using revolving cutters, travelling longitudinally to form the pinion leaves. Factory methods employed milling machines in which the pinions to be cut were presented to the revolving cutter by automatic means, each slot between the leaves being milled out in turn. EBG

Pinion wire The basic material from which steel or brass pinions are made for small clocks, brass pinions sometimes being used in clock motion work. The pinion wire is produced by drawing wire through drawplates. When making a pinion, a length of pinion wire of the desired diameter, having the required number of leaves, is mounted in a lathe or turns and cut to form the pinion and arbor in one piece. To do this a cut is first made at each end of the pinion and the surplus leaves broken off before the final turning. Pinions made from wire require to have their leaves finished to shape by filing along the flutes, and steel pinions are finally finished by hardening and polishing. EBG

Pintongs or pinvice or pinchuck. Pintongs are used to hold wire, drills, broaches and for other purposes. Sliding and screw-nose pintongs or pinvices have a small loose or fixed split chuck at the end of a hollow handle through which wire can be passed and gripped true in the centre of the tool. The chuck is closed either by a ring which slides on the tapered body of the chuck, or by a knurled nut which has part of its hole tapered and screws over the chuck jaws. The tool is made in a range of sizes, either for hand use or for

fitting into the jaws of a large machine chuck. When made with a back centre point it can be fitted with a ferrule, driven by a bow, and used for turning. EBG

Planishing The operation of working a metal surface to a smooth, evenly rounded or flat shape, usually in soft metal such as copper, silver or brass. The metal is hammered with a planishing hammer on an anvil, the anvil and hammer having specially shaped and polished working surfaces. For clock plates the work can be finished with a wide-edged chisel-shaped tool with the edge squared off to act as a scraper, but rounded forms in casework are completed with the hammer when hand-produced. EBG

Planting Positioning and marking out the parts of a clock between or on the clock plates, so that they will function correctly. It includes the correct positioning of the hands and winding squares on the dial. EBG

Pliers Hand tools for gripping or holding material which is to be bent, twisted, pulled, pushed, etc. There are many different types of plier jaws for different purposes, and the two levers are pivoted or 'boxed' to ensure that the jaws meet accurately. Sometimes the jaws are lined with brass to prevent damage to parts held in them. EBG

Polishing There are several methods of producing a smooth or glossy surface on clock parts made from metal, glass, stone, plastic, wood, etc. Almost all the metal parts in a clock movement can be polished; parts such as pallets, pinions and pivots are polished to reduce friction on their working surfaces, allowing the parts to slide easily together and reduce the possibility of injurious material clinging to them. Other clock parts such as brass weights, pendulum

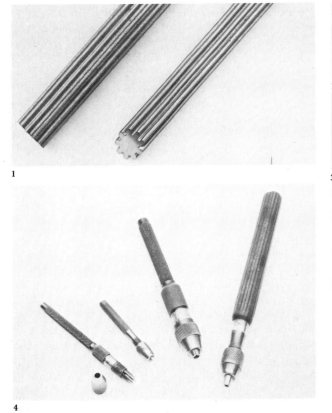

1

4

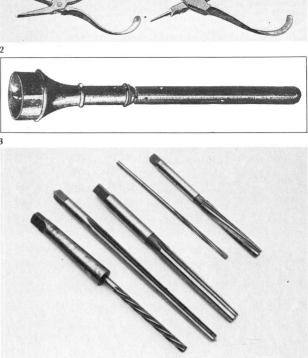

2

3

5

bobs, bezels, frets and finials are polished for the sake of appearance. Metal surfaces are polished with a polisher of soft steel, iron, bell metal, tin, zinc, lead or wood according to circumstances. In all cases the polisher is softer than the surface being polished, and is charged with compounds ranging from carborundum and oilstone dust to rouge and diamantine. EBG

Polishing, pinion The flutes and leaves of a pinion are polished in a pinion polishing tool; it consists of a frame in which the pinion is mounted between centres and free to rotate. The frame is fitted to slide on a base which has a wooden disc pivoted to a block, adjusted so that the edge of the disc is slightly askew to the pinion axis. As the disc is rotated the pinion revolves, cutting a screw thread in the edge of the disc, which is charged with polishing material. During the operation the pinion is made to slide back and forth so that its whole length is polished. EBG

Polishing mills, or laps Tools with a revolving disc charged with a polishing compound. These are of various designs, some being made for the specific purpose of polishing one type of component. Depending on the work, the mill or lap disc can be made of wood, copper, nickel, bell metal, iron or steel. EBG

Polishing muller, or stake A block of steel with a flat polished surface on which a polishing medium such as rouge is mixed with oil. It is usually contained in a wooden box to keep out dust and grit. EBG

Punch A steel or brass rod, used to transmit pressure or a sharp blow to a required point. Punches are made for many purposes, e.g. making centres before drilling, and for riveting, chasing, matting, blanking and stamping out shaped holes or parts. Serial letters and numbers are marked on clock parts with punches. Punches may be solid, hollow, flat, round or otherwise shaped at the working end. Many of them are designed to be used in a staking tool in which the punch is held in a guide for accurate positioning in relation to an anvil or stake. EBG

Punch, bell A self-centring punch, with a centre punch point at one end, designed to slide down a tube or sleeve which has a cone- or bell-shaped mouth. With the bell mouth placed directly over the end of a rod, the centre of the rod can be accurately marked with the punch, provided that the end of the rod is itself square to the rod's axis and the axis of the bell punch is correctly in line with the axis of the rod. Bell punches are available in various sizes and are used to centre-punch a rod prior to turning it between male centres in a lathe. Some bell punches have the centre punch fitted with a return spring. EBG

Quill A device by which a spindle may be rotated and at the same time moved axially, as in the driving spindle of a bench drill in which the drill can travel to and from the work while spinning. It may take the form of a sleeve which does not itself rotate, but may be moved axially, usually having its outer surface machined with rack teeth to engage with the teeth of the feeding mechanism. The spindle is

1 Pinion wire, lengths of, showing section.

2 Pliers, flat-nosed and round-nosed. Denis Diderot, '*Horlogerie*', *Encyclopédie*, Paris, 1751.

3 Punch, bell Hirst Bros, *Catalogue of Tools, c.*1900.

4 Pintongs A selection of various sizes.

5 Reamers of various sizes.

6 Planishing hammers and stake. John Wyke, *Tool Catalogue*, Liverpool *c.*1770.

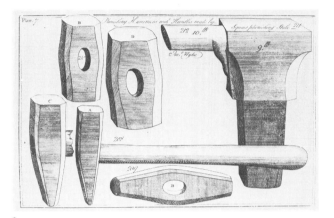

6

carried in bearings fixed inside the quill, and its driving end is provided with a long groove or keyway which engages with a corresponding key inside the bore of the pulley which rotates it. EBG

Reamer Reamers are similar tools to broaches though not made in such small sizes. They have a number of spiral or straight longitudinal flutes to form the cutting edges, and are made for either hand or machine use. The purpose of the reamer is to bring to exact size a hole purposely drilled under-size, or to taper a parallel hole to receive a tapered pin. Some reamers are partly split lengthwise and have an adjusting screw fitted down the centre which is used to increase slightly, or decrease, the diameter of the reamer. Expanding reamers are also available, which have a number of cutting blades adjustable for size. EBG

Red stuff, or rouge A refined red oxide of iron which is used for polishing gold, silver, brass and steel work. It is sold in various grades of fineness; the coarse, hard type, bluish-purple in colour, is known as 'crocus'; the finest grade is scarlet and known as 'rouge'. A white preparation known as 'white rouge' can also be obtained. EBG

Restoring To restore a clock is to make it as nearly as possible as it was when it was first made, bearing in mind that its case, movement and dial will inevitably carry evidence of use which it is not necessarily desirable to remove or disguise. There is considerable difference of opinion on this matter, which involves both ethics and aesthetics; for example, in the restoration of an engraved brass dial. Some people prefer to see the dial looking dull and old, probably scratched and with the silvering gone. Others wish to have the dial filled with new wax in the engraving and the chapter ring resilvered as new, as the

1 Riveting stakes, hexagonal for bench, the others for vice use. Private collection.

2 Screwplates of various sizes. Private collection.

3 Saw, piercing Top: 18th-century pattern; bottom: modern. Private collection.

4 Screwdrivers John Wyke, *Tool Catalogue,* Liverpool, *c.* 1770.

5 Saw, clockmaker's Lancashire pattern, early 19th century. Private collection.

6 Sector formerly belonging to R. T. Jump and engraved with his name. Jump was apprenticed to Vulliamy in 1825. Laurence Harvey.

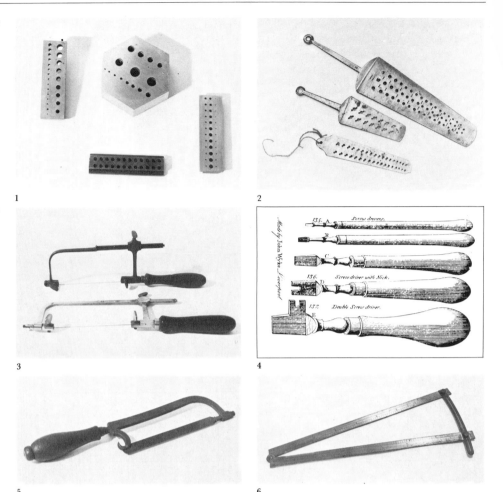

maker originally intended. It is a matter of taste when restoring a clock to ensure that it does not look *too* new yet regains its original dignity and quality. AS

Riveting In clockmaking certain parts such as metal plates are sometimes fastened together with rivets, which are pins or pegs generally of the same metal as the parts being joined, with a head of suitable shape. The rivet is passed through corresponding holes in the parts to be joined and hammered or punched to spread the metal out, or to 'rivet' it. By the same method pillars are often riveted to the pillar plate of a clock and finished in such a way that the riveted area hardly shows. Riveting is frequently used for securing arbors, pinions and collets to wheels and for joining levers to arbors, all these operations depending on the burring over of one part to secure the other. To rivet a wheel directly to an arbor the arbor is formed with three diameters. This provides a seat or shoulder to support the wheel and a flange which can be spread at the other side of the wheel. EBG

Riveting stake A block of hardened steel with a polished surface, pierced with a number of different-sized holes to receive arbors, in order that a pinion or staff can be supported while it is being riveted to a wheel. Alternatively, in the form known as riveting tongs, the stake is jointed and can be opened to admit the part required and closed to grip it, supporting the part to be riveted. Riveting stakes are made to be used in a bench vice, or on a block or solid part of a bench. EBG

Rotten stone A natural friable stone, resulting from the decomposition of a siliceous limestone, which is a powerful abrasive. It is obtained either in crushed form, when it is mixed with oil to form a polishing paste, or in composition blocks, which may be wiped over with oil to obtain a cleaning medium for metal parts. Rotten stone imparts a dull polish to brass and steel and can be mixed with rouge and oil to give a bright polish. EBG

Rounding-up tool An ingenious tool or engine for re-cutting or re-shaping wheel teeth. It is also sometimes called a 'topping tool', and with it a wheel can be reduced in diameter or corrected if not perfectly round, or have its teeth re-formed. The wheel which is to be 'topped' is mounted in the tool between centres where it is free to revolve, the cutters being formed in such a way that as each tooth is topped the wheel is automatically turned to bring the next tooth into position. The cutters are discs with cutting serrations on about half the circumference, and the disc is radially split so that its edge forms a shallow screw. The leading edge of the cutter thus picks up a new wheel tooth to be topped at each revolution. A topping tool is used on wheels which have been cut in the wheel-cutting engine, to cut the correct profiles to the teeth. EBG

Saw, clockmaker's A frame saw, now called a hacksaw, consisting of a frame and handle and detachable metal-cutting saw blade. Sometimes the blade is held in the frame by the tension of the frame itself, while other frames have blade hooks with threaded extensions and wing nuts to tension the blade. With this kind of fitting the blade can be turned in the frame to permit long cuts to be made. The blade is intended to cut in one direction only, and should be fitted so that it saws in the direction away from the handle. Another type of metal-cutting saw is known as the 'backed saw'. It has a wide blade with a stiff, ridged backing and a handle. EBG

Saw, piercing A saw consisting of an adjustable frame with jaws for clamping the ends of a fine, wire-like blade. The frame is adjustable so that blades of different lengths can be fitted, normally with the cutting teeth pointing towards the handle, so that the saw cuts as it is pulled. Piercing saws are used to cut decorative work in sheet metal, clock hands, and internal holes and shaped slots. The blade is threaded through a previously drilled hole before it is fixed into its frame. EBG

Screwdriver Usually, a steel blade and handle with a thin flat driving element which engages in the slot or other recess of the screw. Recently, specially shaped recesses in screws to fit special screwdrivers have come into use, available in many sizes. EBG

Screwhead, or screwpoint polishing tool This tool is held in a bench vice and has support bearings for a spindle which is rotated by rolling the hand over its knurled or octagonal body. It is furnished with a range of large and small brass and steel chucks, lanterns and polishing laps. The thread of a screw is first polished by screwing it into and out of a piece of soft wood, charged with oilstone dust and oil. The screwhead is then stoned with Arkansas, and its slit is cleaned with pegwood cut to a chisel shape and charged with oilstone dust and oil. After all traces of the polishing mixture have been removed with soft bread, the screw is mounted in the polishing tool and polished with an iron or bell-metal lap charged with red stuff or diamantine at its

head and point. An earlier tool for polishing screws was rotated with the bow. EBG

Screwplate A flat piece of hardened tool steel with various-sized drilled and tapped holes for producing screw threads on metal rods, up to about $\frac{1}{4}$ in. in diameter. The holes are often in pairs or sets of three, one row finished normal size while the others are over-size, which enables this somewhat primitive tool to be used partly to form a thread using an over-size hole, and to finish the thread with the normal size of hole. This is necessary because the tool does not actually cut the thread, but squeezes it into shape, which requires considerable force except for the smallest sizes of rod. To attempt to make a full thread in one operation would risk a fracture of the rod. To cut threads more easily some screwplates have extra holes drilled at the side of, and breaking into the threaded hole to give cutting edges and clearance for swarf. EBG

Screw stocks A tool in the form of nutcracker pliers, with jaws adjusted by means of a set screw and nut, and a number of screw-forming holes between the jaws. The number of screw-forming holes between the jaws. Also means a tool in which split-screw dies are held. EBG

Sector A simple proportional measuring gauge consisting of two straight brass or steel arms, pivot-jointed at one end to form an adjustable gap gauge which is set to the required size (or gap) by a slotted quadrant plate secured to one arm at the opposite end from the joint, and locked with a screw. The two arms and quadrant plate are marked with numbered scales and are used primarily to ascertain the correct proportions between a clock wheel and the pinion to be geared with it. As a wheel and pinion gauge it is limited in its accuracy above and below certain dimensions, for it cannot take into account the various forms of pinion-leaf addenda curves. The gauge, however, is invaluable to the clockmaker for obtaining other measurements. EBG

7 Rounding-up tool of horizontal reciprocating motion to the cutter; signed 'Saml. Gautier 1766 Paris'. Musée du Conservatoire National des Arts et Métiers, Paris.

8 Screw stocks An actual tool and loose dies. Private collection.

9 Screw stocks John Wyke, *Tool Catalogue*, Liverpool, c.1770.

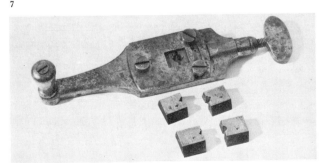

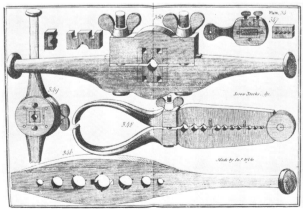

7

8

9

1 **Shears,** two pairs.

2 **Spotting** as applied to the plate, bridge, cock and barrel on a chronometer; by John R. Arnold.

3 **Taps** and holders or wrenches. Private collection.

4 **Spring winder** stamped 'Walker' 18th-century, English. Merseyside County Museum, Liverpool.

5 **Stake** or staking tool, modern.

6 **Throw, clockmaker's,** shown with accessories. John Wyke, *Tool Catalogue,* Liverpool, c. 1770.

2

1

3

4

5

Shears Hand shears or snips are used for cutting thin sheet metal. They may be curved or straight, curved ones for cutting small inside curves and straight ones for making straight or curved cuts. Some shears are designed to allow one handle to be held in a vice, while others have one handle mounted on the bench. Besides the normal cutting jaws these are often provided with a means of shearing wire or rod. EBG

Shellac A resinous substance produced as a protective coating by the lac insect of India. It is available as small orange flakes which are dissolved in methylated spirit to form a varnish or lacquer, and in sticks. It can be melted and used as a cement for holding delicate or awkwardly shaped parts on the face plate or wax chuck of a lathe, or in clockwork for cementing lever pallets and roller jewels in position. EBG

Silvering A process for forming a slightly matt or frosted finish of chemically deposited silver on brass or copper clock dials, chapter rings, etc. To silver a dial with the engraved numerals already filled with black wax, the surface is first cleaned and given a matt or grained finish. A silvering paste made from silver nitrate, cream of tartar and common salt, mixed with water, is applied to the dial and rubbed on until the surface is whitened with a deposit of silver. The dial is then washed, dried and lacquered to prevent the silvered surface from tarnishing. EBG

Snailing A process which imparts a decorative finish to metal clock parts. This finish takes the form of a series of curved lines radiating from a common centre. Snailing on steel is produced by a copper mill with a hollow face and a thin projecting rim, charged with abrasive. In operation, the work being snailed is free to rotate between centres while the rotating mill acts upon it, producing the continuous snailed effect when the mill is charged first with emery and finished with coarse red stuff. For brass or other soft metals, a bone or ivory mill is used. EBG

Soldering The term used to describe the uniting of chemically clean surfaces of suitable metals or alloys, which are not themselves melted, by using heat and a fusible alloy or solder. There are two distinct forms of solder – soft and hard. The more fusible one is usually called 'soft' or 'lead' solder; lead has a relatively low melting point. Ordinary soft solder consists of two parts tin and one part lead, but a range of soft solders is available which contains silver with tin, lead, copper, cadmium or zinc added. Depending on purpose, soft solder is suitable for use on copper, nickel, tin, iron, zinc, lead and numerous alloys. Hard or silver soldering, or 'silver alloy brazing' as it is called to distinguish it from soft soldering, is used for most nonferrous metals and alloys as well as for steel and iron. Hall-marked silver is soldered with silver solder of high silver content, and various hardnesses and melting ranges of solders of this type are available. Hall-marked gold is soldered with a gold solder of high quality in various carats, hardnesses and colours. Solders may be purchased in various forms of wire, rod, sheet or powder-paste.

Different fluxes are necessary for different types of work. Soldering fluxes help the metal to flow and prevent oxidation under heat. Although many fluxes are available, soft-solder flux generally consists of resin, or killed sulphuric or hydrochloric acid, or one of a series of patent preparations. Hard-soldering flux is traditionally boracic acid (or borax), made up into a paste with water. EBG

Spotting A finish or form of decoration given to chronometer plates or clock parts, consisting of equidistant circular spots or rings which sometimes overlap each other. The rings are produced by a rotating bone or ivory tool charged with an abrasive, and the rings can be arranged in many different patterns – straight rows, wavy rows, concentric circles, etc. EBG

Spring winder A tool for safely winding a clock mainspring and inserting it into its barrel. There are various types, older ones consisting of a frame with a hooked projecting arbor on which the spring is wound by a handle. The handle has a ratchet and reversible click pawl to control winding or unwinding, and the tool is vice-held. A pivoted bar holds the outer spring hook during winding. Some mainspring winders have a range of false-bottomed barrels with a slit in the side wall; the spring is wound into the false barrel and a pusher used to force it into its clock barrel. EBG

Stake A support for work of various kinds. A stake is usually, but not invariably, made of steel. There are many designs, from a simple steel block placed on the bench, to complex tools with a wide variety of specialised parts for such purposes as riveting wheels to their collets or setting jewel stones. In the complex form, in which punches, pushers, sinkers or chamfering cutters and numerous anvils or small stump stakes are essential parts, the tool is usually called a staking tool. EBG
See also Anvil; Riveting stake.

Tap A tool for making a screw thread in a hole which has previously been drilled under-size by an amount equal to approximately twice the thread depth. It is made by cutting a thread on the outside of a rod of annealed tool steel, forming grooves or flutes longitudinally to form cutting edges, and finally hardening and tempering. These tools are available in sets of three of various sizes, taper, intermediate and plug, and are used in this order. Taps have a squared shank which can be gripped with a tap wrench or other holder, and sometimes they simply have flats on the side of the threaded part instead of flutes. EBG
See also Die; Screwplate; Screwstocks.

Tempering The term used to describe several heat treatments for reducing the hardness of previously hardened steel to the degree required for its purpose. These processes are used by tool makers, following the advice of the steel makers. Clockmakers, when making such things as cutting tools, pinions, pallets and springs, learn to judge the

6

temperature to which the steel must be heated and tempered for its particular purpose, and this is sometimes done by observing the colour change as the metal is heated. It is sometimes important that the surface of the steel should not become oxidised by exposure to a flame, and to avoid this it can be coated with fire clay, lime, ash or other substances. A hardened part may be tempered by boiling it in oil or by heating it to the required temperature and immersing it in water or oil. A small part can be bound with iron binding wire when it is hardened or tempered to avoid distortion. The colours indicating the degree of tempering or reduced hardness of hardened and polished steel are:

colour	temperature	purpose
pale straw	420°F	tools for cutting iron
straw	450°F	clockmakers' tools
yellow-brown	500°F	small pinions and arbors
purple	530°F	large pinions and arbors
bright blue	580°F	clock springs
deep blue	590°F	small balance springs
blue-black	640°F	chronometer balance springs

EBG

Throw, clockmaker's A clockmaker's 'dead-centre' lathe, a form of turns operated through a cord from a large grooved wheel or pulley which has a handle attached. The hand wheel is fixed to a bracket fastened on the back of the lathe. EBG

1 Tongs, riveting, for use in a vice. Private collection.

2 Tongs, sliding, of various forms.

3 Turning arbors with ferrules.

4 Tweezers, showing a variety of points.

5 Turns or turnbench, early pattern, vice-held. Private collection.

6 Vice, bench, with bench clamping screw, stake and drilling centres on jaw ends; 18th century. Merseyside County Museum, Liverpool.

7 Vice, hand, with wooden and steel integral handles, parallel and bow jointed.

1

2

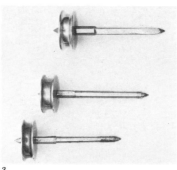

3

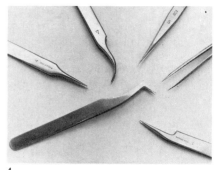

4

5

6

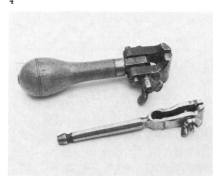

7

Tongs, riveting An old-fashioned bow-jointed tool which has jaws in which an arbor or similar part is gripped when the tool is clamped in a bench vice to enable the part to be riveted in some particular way. EBG
See also Riveting stake.

Tongs, sliding Various forms of pliers which have a sliding loop, link or thimble embracing the handles or levers, so that work can be held securely in the jaws without continuous pressure on the levers. EBG

Turning The process of shaping work by cutting while it is rotating between centres, as in a lathe or throw. In the most accurate method of turning the work is rotated on its own centres mounted between male or female centres, as in dead-centre lathes, turns or throws; but for speed and convenience a lathe with a live spindle fitted with a chuck, collet or face plate is used. Various tools are used in turning; they may be hand-held or mounted in the tool holder of the lathe. EBG

Turning arbor A small steel shaft of tapered, round or square section on which a part can be mounted, having centres, usually at each end, and fitted with a ferrule so that it can be turned in a dead-centre lathe or turns. There are various turning arbors for specific purposes, some with a box or split chuck at one end. A screw arbor has part of its shaft threaded and has a disc or face plate and nut so that a flat wheel can be firmly gripped against the plate. An eccentric arbor is made in two parts so that the shaft can be adjusted to allow the part being turned to be properly centred; it has a box chuck and is chiefly used for turning a fusee or barrel arbor. EBG

Turns, or turnbench A pair of turns is a small dead-centre lathe consisting of a frame held in a bench vice and provided with a pair of runners or centres between which an arbor or part is rotated and cut by a cutting tool, hand-held and supported on a T-rest. The work between the centres is rotated either by a bow or by an endless cord from a wheel driven by hand or foot. Turns have specialised runners which fit into the poppets for turning and polishing arbors and pivots as well as general pivoting work. EBG

Tweezers Small spring tongs for taking up and holding small objects, sometimes designed for bending, cutting or extracting small parts; there are many designs for specialised purposes. They are made from such materials as hardened and tempered steel, stainless steel, nickel, brass or plastics. EBG

Uprighting tool A tool by means of which the vertically true position of a pivot hole in a clock plate or part, in relation to a corresponding hole in the opposite plate or part, may be correctly marked or drilled. It has an accurately machined table or platform with a pump centre on which the work is centred and clamped. A column secured to the edge of the table carries an arm through which a centre runner or drilling attachment is inserted in precise alignment with the axis of the pump centre. When required it is sometimes possible to centre the work from the centre runner above, and drill through the table in place of the pump centre. Uprighting can also be carried out using the mandril lathe. EBG

Vice, bench All vices are designed either to hold work which is to be worked on, or to hold specialised tools such as turns, mandrils, stakes, etc. A bench vice is one which is either clamped or screwed to the top surface or edge of the bench. Most vices today have jaws which, by means of a screw, open in such a way as to keep them always parallel, the jaws being part of cast- or wrought-iron members, one of which slides through the other. Many older bench vices had pivoted jaws which necessarily opened at an angle and were therefore limited in their gripping action. A bench vice is sometimes fitted with a stand secured to the bench, enabling the vice to be swivelled to a desired angle, and some large vices have a leg or pole extending to the floor for extra stability when doing heavy work. EBG

Vice, hand Hand vices can have pivoted, bowed or sliding jaws, closed with a wing nut and screw; they are used for holding work, or sometimes tools, in the hand. EBG
See also Pintongs.

8 Uprighting tool Denis Diderot, '*Horlogerie*', *Encyclopédie*, Paris, 1751.

9 Turns illustrated in Antoine Thiout, *Traité de l'horlogerie*, 1741.

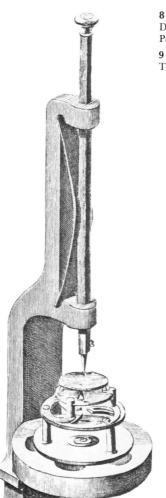

8

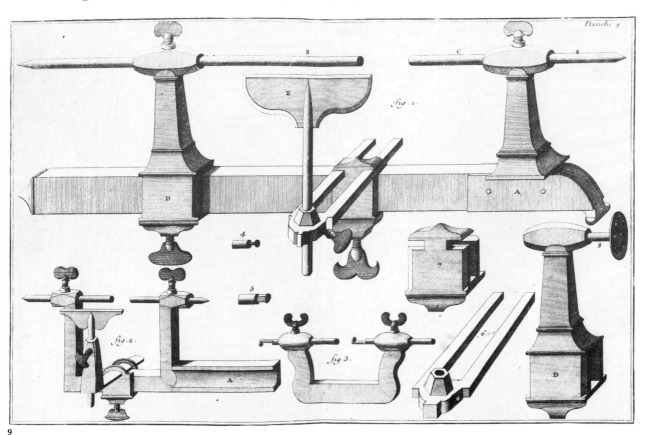

9

215

1

2

1 **Wheel, bench,** 19th century. Private collection.

2 **Wheel, hand,** with bracket, attached to vice-held turns. Private collection.

3 **Wheel, foot,** and treadle. Hirst Bros, *Catalogue of Tools, c.*1900.

4 **Wig-wag tool** from F. J. Britten, *Watch and Clockmaker's Handbook, Dictionary and Guide,* 11th edition, 1915.

3

4

Wheel, bench A large grooved wheel fitted with a handle and mounted on a bracket or stand, fixed to the workbench in a suitable position for driving turning tools or lathes by means of an endless cord. The bench wheel remains fixed in one place while the turning tools are vice-held. The bench-wheel bracket usually has a sliding adjustment for tensioning the cord. EBG

Wheel, foot The foot wheel, like the bench wheel, is used to drive a lathe or other machine, but it is much larger. It is mounted below the bench and rotated by means of a foot-operated, pivoted treadle. A stepped foot wheel has two or more diameters of cord groove so that the speed ratio between the wheel and the machine it is driving can be changed, and some foot wheels are made sufficiently out of balance for the wheel always to come to rest in a suitable position for starting again by downward pressure on the treadle. An intermediate pulley, jockey pulley or countershaft can be used between the foot wheel and the machine. EBG

Wheel, hand The hand wheel is like a bench wheel except that its bracket is fixed directly to the frame of the lathe or machine it is driving instead of to the bench. The Swiss mandril and some other tools have the hand wheel geared directly to the spindle of the machine, and for many purposes the hand wheel has an advantage over the bow in that it imparts continuous motion in one direction. EBG

Wig-wag tool A tool which imparts a reciprocating or backwards and forwards motion to a pinion, or a tool for polishing a pivot or pinion leaves. In the pivot-polishing version of this tool the polisher, which is either a burnisher or soft-metal polisher charged with a polishing compound, is worked to and fro, while at the same time a rotary motion is imparted to the pivot. For polishing pinion leaves the pinion is moved axially back and forth over a charged polisher which can be a rotating disc. EBG

International Clockmaking

with a selection of important makers

Clockmaking in Austria

The first difficulty in writing about Austrian clocks is to define the term 'Austria'. The present republic comprises only a small portion of the former Austro–Hungarian Empire, parts of which are now included in Czechoslovakia, Hungary, Poland, Jugoslavia and Italy. During past centuries the frequent wars that beset the country resulted in changes to its territory, and the frontier was never stable. At one time Belgium was Austrian territory, and so were small parts of Germany. For the present purpose Austria will be considered as that portion of the present republic which includes Vienna, Salzburg and Styria, as well as the Tyrol, part of which is now Italian territory, and Bohemia, which is now part of Czechoslovakia.

The early records of clockmaking in Austria go back to the 14th century; a clock keeper in Olmütz, Bohemia, is mentioned in 1392. At this time, national styles in horology had scarcely developed, and one can infer the contemporary large iron frame with going and striking trains and possibly no exterior dial. As time went on, quarter-striking would have been added together with automata and astronomical dials. The famous clock at Prague City Hall is traditionally believed to date from the late 15th century. It includes a procession of Christ and the Apostles, astronomical indications, a perpetual calendar and various other automata. Being a Czech clock it is arranged to show the day beginning at sunset.

On the other side of Austria there are early clockmaking records from Graz, Styria. A number of public clocks are mentioned in the archives, and the clock on the hill outside the town is well known; its very large dial can be seen from a great distance. Turret clocks are frequently met with in Austria and south Germany, but many of them have a peculiarity also seen on some domestic clocks. Originally, clocks had a dial indicating hours only, but later a small dial below indicated quarter-hours, and performed virtually the same function as a minute hand. Later, this small dial was combined with the larger one and the Roman figures I to IIII were painted inside the hour figures. The hand for the quarter-hour dial was made concentric with the hour hand and the transformation to a modern type of dial was complete, except that the quarter-hour hand was shorter than the hour hand. Many turret clocks in Austria still possess this feature, and care must be taken when reading the time.

As far as domestic clocks are concerned, early Austrian examples do not differ greatly from others produced in the period, when the usual domestic clock was the iron Gothic clock supported by a bracket. South European clocks tend to be more decorative than those made farther north, but those of Austria, south Germany and Switzerland are similar. An example in the museum at Innsbruck has both a wheel balance and a foliot, trying to make the best of both worlds.

After the Gothic clock came the spring-driven table clock. Not many of these were made in Austria, but the famous example by Geremias Metzger of Augsburg appears to have had Austrian predecessors, since clocks of this type

1 Baroque bracket clock generally based on the British prototype, but with Dutch-style arcaded minutes, c.1750.

2 Metal wall clock with single hand, 'cowtail' pendulum and painted dial, c.1700–25. Uhrenmuseum der Stadt Wien.

1

are known by Nikolaus Lanz of Innsbruck, c.1550, and Andreas Illmer of the same town, c.1559. The Lanz clock is rather plain, but the other maker's work more nearly approaches the traditional Augsburg type.

Clocks with wooden cases were rare before the mid 17th century, although 16th-century examples from Austria are known. There is the famous 'Bohemian' clock from the Kunsthistorisches Museum, which belonged to Archduke Ferdinand of the Tyrol. This clock is believed to have been made c.1550–60 and its dials suggest those of the clock on the City Hall of Prague.

The introduction of the pendulum in the mid 17th century had a profound effect on clockmaking everywhere; in southern Europe it led to a type known as the *Kuhschwanz* ('cowtail'), which had a short pendulum swinging in front of the dial and controlling a verge escapement with horizontal escapewheel [219/2]. It is difficult to tell which examples are Austrian in origin, but the dials may be broadly divided into two groups, the painted dial and the *Telleruhr*, literally 'dish clock'.

The early 18th century saw the long pendulum increasing in popularity, and the wall clock of the period in Austria had a birdcage movement with a painted iron dial, but instead of having the trains one behind the other (as in the older Gothic clocks or English 30-hour clocks), they were placed side by side. This was also the arrangement in clocks that sounded the quarters, which were country productions and rather rough.

The type of clock made in the larger towns in the 18th century was a bracket clock based on the English model [218/1] with arch dial and ebonised case, but usually having more elaborate decoration that its English counterpart. 'Repoussé' dials were known but where they followed more closely the English pattern they often had a number of subsidiary dials, or an arcaded minute circle, as was popular in Holland. Some examples were more simply constructed than those mentioned, with a cowtail pendulum in front of the dial, and therefore no glass.

After the mid 18th century Austrian makers tended to take their inspiration from France, which might have been due to the marriage of Marie Antoinette to the future Louis XVI in 1770. Dials became smaller, Arabic figures replaced Roman, and movements took on a new delicacy.

At the end of the 18th century the Vienna regulator

2

1

2   3   4

began to be made, based on the typical longcase clock but with the refinements of a dead-beat escapement and very fine wheelwork. Its austere lines formed a striking contrast to the decoration applied to the French styles then in vogue. Other plainer clocks appeared, still with French inspiration, but French styles themselves became more sober after the Revolution.

During this period a popular Austrian style was a mantel clock with the dial and movement supported by several pillars forming a small colonnade. The movements of these clocks were comparatively small but often included quarter-chimes and/or provision for repeating. Arabic figures were frequently used on the dials. Another popular design was a clock resembling a picture frame, with a small dial surrounded by decorative metalwork and a gilded frame [221/2].

The cheaper market was provided with the *Bretteluhr*, a simple type of wall clock with exposed weight and pendulum but of a design in keeping with the tendency to make everything smaller. The extreme example of miniaturisation was the *Zappler*, a tiny version of the standing *Telleruhr* with a very short pendulum and a form of tic-tac escapement.

By the 1880s designs had become large and heavy once more, under the influence of the factories in the Black Forest and Silesia. An advertisement by Otto Steiner in the Austro–Hungarian watchmakers' journal, 1882–6, describes his establishment as the only clock factory in Vienna, but it is not certain whether he made complete clocks or only the cases, obtaining the movements elsewhere; the cases are extremely heavy in appearance.

A factory at Ebensee, established by Resch Brothers,

made Vienna regulators, but was acquired by the German firm of Junghans in 1901. Otherwise, apart from a works producing clock movements in Karlstein, there was little factory production in Austria, although many handmade clocks were still produced in Vienna. By the 1880s, however, the advertisements in the trade journals suggest that much of the Austrian clock market was being supplied by Germany or France. EJT

Aureliano, Father, à San Daniele An 18th-century Augustinian friar in the Imperial Court monastery in Vienna, Aureliano was also a teacher of mathematics. He is remembered today for an elaborate astronomical clock preserved in the Bayerisches Museum in Munich. The case of this clock is extremely ornate and detracts somewhat from the seriousness of an astronomical clock, but it is not known whether it was made by Aureliano. In the centre of the clock is a 24-hour dial and surrounding this another dial showing the signs of the zodiac. The remainder of the dial plate is occupied by various subsidiary dials with the spaces between decorated in matting and engraving. The moon's phases are shown by a sphere. The clock was made *c.* 1770 and is contemporary with that of David à San Cajetano, but Aureliano's clock appears to be intended more for domestic use in view of its decoration. Both mechanisms are extremely complicated, Aureliano's including a pinion with twisted leaves for showing the difference between solar and mean time. EJT

Cajetano, David à San David à San Cajetano was a friar in Vienna who lived *c.* 1730–1800. An able mathematician, he completed a clock in 1769 which is now in the Clock

Museum at Vienna. The central dial is surrounded by a number of smaller ones giving various astronomical indications, and the wheelwork is complicated in the extreme. As well as showing the various movements of the planets, Cajetano's clock shows the length of daylight and darkness, Italian hours, times of sunrise and sunset and has a perpetual calendar. It is interesting to compare the clock with that of Father Aureliano, which dates from the same period. Cajetano later wrote a very complex book on epicyclic gearing. EJT

Zech, Jacob Long credited with the invention of the fusee, Zech was working in Prague in the early 16th century and died *c*. 1540. But illustrations of the fusee occur in the works of Leonardo da Vinci, Paulus Almanus and a manuscript of 1450–60 in the Royal Library, Brussels, proving that it must have been known in the previous century.

There is a clock by Jacob Zech in the possession of the British Society of Antiquaries made in Prague and dated 1525. For a long time this was regarded as the oldest surviving clock with a fusee, but there are two drum clocks by Peter Henlein containing fusees which are dated 1510, besides the remains of a table clock dated 1509 in the

Bayerisches Museum in Munich which includes a rough iron fusee. EJT
See also Almanus manuscript.

Clockmaking in Canada

By the time Canadians began to make their own clocks, England and the Continent had already passed their years of clockmaking perfection. The early 18th-century settlers in Canada brought over or had shipped to them standard English bracket and shelf clocks, and Canadian clockmakers prior to 1800 were mainly dealers and repairers. They imported English clocks and often had their names engraved on the dials and backplates, although occasionally one comes across a clock, parts of which may be attributed to a Canadian maker. Since it was not practical to import long cases, the merchants would order only the movements, and have the cases made by local cabinetmakers. Many of these early cases were of pine and painted to add colour to the home, like the provincial clocks of Germany and France.

1

2

3

4

5

1 Cajetano, David à San
Astronomical clock completed
1769. Uhrenmuseum der Stadt
Wien.

2 Cajetano, David à San
Astronomical dial of 222/1, of
great complexity, indicating mean
astronomical time, civil time,
Italian hours, day of the week,
motions of the moon and planets,
and many other indications.
Uhrenmuseum der Stadt Wien.

3 Zech, Jacob Drum clock
belonging to the Society of
Antiquaries of London. Made in
Prague, it is dated 1525.

4 Painted dial of a tall clock by
J. B. Twiss, Montreal; early 19th
century. Private collection.

5 Empire style shelf clock made
for W. H. Vantassel, Brockville,
Canada West, Ontario, with
movement by Seth Thomas,
c.1850. Private collection.

6 Tall clock in a plain, country-
made case by J. B. and R. Twiss,
Montreal; early 19th century.
Private collection.

7 O.G. shelf clock made for
T. L. Abel, Leeds County, Canada
West, Ontario, c. 1850. Private
collection.

8 Shelf clock with half-pillars
made for H. & C. Burr, Dundas,
Upper Canada, c. 1834.

9 O.G. shelf clock Printed label
inside 223/7. Private collection.

10 Shelf clock Printed label
inside 223/8.

6

7

8

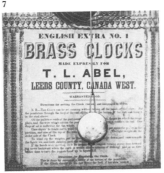

9

10

Little research has been done on Canada's early clockmakers, and the names we have were culled mainly from city directories, which do not distinguish between a true manufacturer of clocks and an importer or dealer.

In the early years of the 19th century some enterprising Canadians imported movements from the United States and inserted them into locally made cases, or in some instances ordered the complete clocks from U.S. distributors, including printed labels showing the importer's name and town, as well as tablets and carvings depicting the Canadian coat of arms [222/5], [223/7], [223/9], [223/8], [223/10].

Probably the most famous of the early 19th-century Canadian makers were the Twiss brothers of Montreal. Five brothers (Austin, Benjamin, Joseph, Ira and Russell) and their father Hiram had a clock factory in Connecticut, and made wooden movements for longcase and shelf clocks

[222/3], [223/6]. The brothers came to Canada at intervals from 1821 to 1834 and established their own businesses, which included lumber, saw mills and taverns as well as the making of clocks.

George Savage, born in England in 1767, is listed by G. H. Baillie in *Watchmakers and Clockmakers of the World* (1947) as 'a very able watchmaker'. He patented a remontoire in 1808 and while in London invented a lever escapement known as the 'Savage two-pin'. He came to Montreal in 1818 and was in partnership with J. A. Dwight. In 1826 the shop was taken over by his son Joseph; George died in 1855. Another Savage from England, David, had a shop in Guelph, Ontario from c. 1848 to 1863, continued by his descendants until 1927.

Many Canadian cities had tower or turret clocks erected during the 19th century, the movements of which were mainly imported from England or the United States. One Canadian maker of tower clocks, however, was George Hess, who was born in Germany and learned his trade in Switzerland. In 1866 he settled in Zurich, Ontario, and during the following 25 years built several tower clocks, including those in Zurich, Sebastopol, and Exeter, Ontario. He obtained a patent in 1888 for improvements in the striking mechanisms of tower clocks and another in 1889 for an electrical apparatus for slave clocks. George Hess died in 1891.

Regulators used in clock shops were usually imported from Germany and the United States, but one notable exception was a fine example made by George Lacey Darling of Hamilton, Ontario. The pendulum is compensated by a glass tube holding 26 lbs of mercury. Darling is recorded as a watchmaker from 1851 to 1874. He died in 1899. PL

Canada Clock Co. In June 1872 John F. Collins started the Canada Clock Co. in Whitby, Ontario. John and his brother Edward were the first Canadians to undertake the manufacturing of complete clocks, and their modest building (100 × 50 ft) of two storeys contained all the necessary machinery for producing movements comparable to those made in the United States for similar mantel and shelf clocks, and workshops for making and veneering the wooden cases. The approximate value of the plant was 20,000 dollars and it employed about 15 workers at the beginning. In 1875 the company was selected to make 500 time clocks for bank vaults; they were designed by a lock and safe maker in Hamilton. By this time the company was selling clocks across Ontario and Quebec and even received orders from Britain. On 2nd December 1875 the clock factory caught fire and was nearly destroyed. The following spring the stock which escaped the fire was being offered for sale at greatly reduced prices. The company was then relocated in Hamilton by John Collins, with James Simpson and George Lee, in a shop on the corner of Cathcart and Kelly Streets, from 1877 to 1884. During this time the name was changed to the Hamilton Clock Co., but in 1882 it reverted to the Canada Clock Co. Adam Rutherford was the manager. The company ceased to operate in 1887. PL

Péquegnat, Arthur, Clock Co. Arthur U. Péquegnat was born at La Chaux-de-Fonds, Switzerland, in 1851. In 1874 he left Switzerland with his parents, brothers and sisters, numbering 16 in all, for Canada. In Switzerland the family had worked at assembling watch movements in their home for a large watchmaking firm in La Chaux-de-Fonds. The family settled in the community of Berlin, Ontario, which changed its name to Kitchener in 1916. Father and sons returned to the old family trade of watchmaking and repairing. Arthur first opened a jewellery-repair shop in Mildmay, Ontario, but soon returned to Berlin to open a shop with his brother Paul. Later, Paul opened his own shop. The other brothers also opened shops in Ontario: James in Stratford, Léon in New Hamburg, George in Neustadt, Philemon in Paris, Albert in Brantford, and Joseph in Guelph. The last is the only shop still in existence.

In his spare time Arthur repaired and assembled bicycles at a shop behind his store, and the bicycle trade flourished until 1904 when a slump in the market forced Arthur to seek a different product. This resulted in converting part of the building into a clock factory. The manufacturing of bicycles was slowly phased out, and the clock company was firmly established. In the company's first catalogue 33 clocks were listed ranging from a four-dollar mantel clock to a 36 in. weight-driven regulator, which sold for 30 dollars. The Péquegnat movements were made in Berlin of fine, robust brass and the plates were occasionally nickel-plated. Many of the clocks were modelled after styles popular in the United States. Cases were mainly of solid oak (walnut and mahogany cases were made on request) and were manufactured at a small factory also owned by Arthur in Breslau, an adjacent village. The Berlin factory employed between eight and twelve clockmakers. Most of the original building was demolished in 1964. Arthur Péquegnat died in 1927. After his death the company was continued by his sons, Edmond and Marcel but production ended c. 1941. PL

1   2   3

Clockmaking in China:
Early History

In ancient China time was measured by means of equatorial sundials, incense clocks and clepsydras. Some Chinese clepsydras had complex arrangements for ensuring a constant flow of water or mercury. In others, showing the possible influence of Arabic anaphoric clocks (clocks with a rotating dial showing the successive rising of constellations at night), the rise of a float was made to rotate a dial and/or to release metal balls for operating sound signals and time-announcing jackwork.

There was also a long history of the use at the imperial court of the more accurate hydromechanical timekeeping method traditionally said to have been originated by Chang Heng for astronomical purposes in the 2nd century. This history was little known before the studies by Joseph Needham and others (*Science and Civilisation in China*) of a compilation printed in 1172 under the title *Hsin I Hsiang Fa Yao* ('New Armillary-sphere and Celestial-globe System Essentials') and ascribed to Su Sung. This work ostensibly deals with a waterwheel-driven 40-ft astronomical clock tower designed by Han Kung-Lien under Su Sung's sponsorship and built at Kai-feng, Honan province, in 1088, but it has been shown actually to comprise an extensively illustrated description of the mercury-driven astronomical clock tower [225/4] of Chang Ssu-Hsun, 979, with subsequent alterations relating to a water-driven revised design by Chou Jih-Yen and others, 1078, as well as to Han Kung-Lien's further-revised design of 1088.

Each clock tower had an armillary sphere on its flat roof for astronomical observations, a clock-driven celestial globe inside for astronomical demonstrations and predictions, and a five-stage, pagoda-like, external, time annunciator [225/5] containing horizontally rotating wheels operating stationary jacks on two stages for sounding audible time signals on bells, drums and gongs, and carrying carousel jackwork (horizontally rotating) on three stages for the display of written time announcements.

In the 979 clock tower, calendar work, thought to have included wheels with 487 and 586 teeth, coupled by layshaft pinions of 10 and 12 giving a gear ratio of $365\frac{1}{4}/366\frac{1}{4}$ to suit a Chinese 1st-century quasi-Julian calendar, was used to provide both solar-time and sidereal-time drives to the celestial globe, which had an orrery system of circulating sun and moon models. Calendar work was also provided in the time annunciator for regulating automatic sound signals and written time announcements for sunrise, sunset, and variable night watches. In the clock tower design of *c.* 1078 there was apparently no calendar work, but a solar-time chain drive to the sidereal-reference subassembly of the armillary sphere was added in an attempt to improve the accuracy of astronomical observations. In the clock tower of 1088 Han Kung-Lien perfected this attempt by substituting a sidereal-time shaft drive via calendar-work gearing of the 979 pattern, and reintroduced similar gearing into the celestial-globe drive.

The time-measuring element of each clock tower [225/6] was a large timekeeping waterwheel (11 ft diameter in

1 Péquegnat, Arthur, Clock Co. Wall clock, 'Canadian Time' model, *c.* 1910. Private collection.

2 Péquegnat, Arthur, Clock Co. Wall clock, Beaver model, *c.* 1910. Private collection.

3 Péquegnat, Arthur, Clock Co. Wall clock, King Edward model, *c.* 1910. Private collection.

4 Chang Ssu-Hsun's mercury-driven astronomical clocktower, AD 979, from a contemporary drawing slightly altered *c.* AD 1078 and printed AD 1172.

5 Chang Ssu-Hsun's time annunciator in his astronomical clocktower, AD 979. Its carousel jackwork may have provided the pattern for that later used decoratively in many western public clocks.

6 Timekeeping waterwheel, Chinese, reconstructed from the illustrated description in Su Sung's *Hsin I Hsiang Fa Yao,* AD 1172.

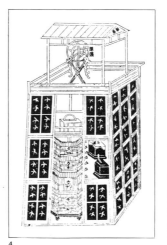

4

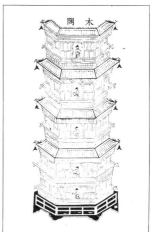

5

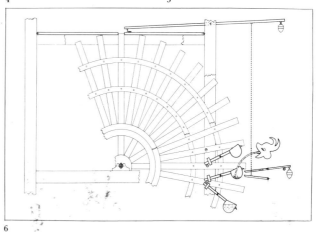

6

1088) equipped with 36 buckets (48 in 979 and 1078) for receiving a flow of water (mercury in 979) from the dragon's-head spout of a constant-level tank fed by a manually refilled cistern. The buckets (each $12 \times 6 \times 5$ in. in 1088) were so arranged that the weight of liquid entering each in succession was compared with that of a single control weight on an adjacent checking lever. When correctly weighted, the bucket was allowed by the checking lever to fall and engage the lower of a pair of chain-coupled levers, the upper of which during a short resulting swing acquired sufficient kinetic energy to jerk a loosely linked locking lever from engagement with the uppermost wheel spoke. The single time-unit step then taken by the waterwheel represented in 1088 a fraction of $\frac{1}{3600}$ of a whole day, equal to 24 of our seconds of time, and caused a 0·1° rotation of the armillary-sphere sidereal-reference scale. Modern reconstructions [226/1] have shown that the

1 Timekeeping waterwheel, Chinese, a half-scale working reconstruction, 9 ft high. An electrical contact operates the modern wall dial. Merseyside County Museum, Liverpool.

1

mechanism was capable, if well maintained, of keeping time with an accuracy unequalled before the 17th century pendulum clock.

Chinese sand-driven wheel clocks of doubtful time-keeping accuracy were briefly reported by 16th-century Jesuit missionaries, who introduced European spring-driven and weight-driven verge-escapement clocks, including a turret clock with a single-handed public dial and bell. Early in the 17th century some short-lived attempts appear to have been made to use European-style clock movements to operate Chinese-style visible and audible time annunciators based on those formerly used with anaphoric-dial and ball-release clepsydras. European-style clock dials, with or without Chinese-style markings, were, however, soon accepted. JHC

Chang Heng A Chinese astronomer and mathematician who lived from AD 78 to 139, Chang is historically recorded as the first to employ water-operated wheelwork for the accurately time-controlled rotation of demonstrational armillary spheres or celestial globes. This probably implies the invention by him of the timekeeping waterwheel, the later use of which included that by I-Hsing and Liang Ling-Tsan (7th–8th centuries) for driving a celestial globe with an orrery mechanism and time-announcing jackwork, and by Chang Ssu-Hsun and his successors (10th–11th centuries) in their astronomical clock towers. JHC

Chang Ssu-Hsun A Chinese clockmaker of the late 10th century, Chang was the builder of the first recorded (mercury-driven) astronomical clock tower, detailed descriptions and illustrations of which have been preserved in the *Hsin I Hsiang Fa Yao* ascribed to Su Sung. JHC

Su Sung A Chinese scholar-statesman who lived from 1020 to 1101, Su Sung was the author of an imperial report on astronomical timekeeping, written in 1092 and printed in 1172 as an introduction to *Hsin I Hsiang Fa Yao*. This work

has been shown to have originated as an illustrated description of Chang Ssu-Hsun's astronomical clock tower (979), with successive revisions relating to those built by Chou Jih-Yen and others *c.* 1078, and by Han Kung-Lien under Su Sung's sponsorship in 1088. JHC

Later Styles

Calendars and time measurement have been important in China since ancient times. The right to promulgate the calendar was reserved to the emperor along with the minting of money and collection of taxes. Since he was the 'Son of Heaven' and was considered the point of connection between Heaven and Earth, the time at which he celebrated various rites and ceremonies was of the utmost importance, and those who affected such decisions, i.e. astronomers and astrologers, were very important. Techniques were developed to help in carrying out this important function.

CHINESE TIMEKEEPING SYSTEMS

Chinese astronomy was based on an equatorial and polar system. It therefore dealt in time divisions of equal duration. There were three different systems of time measurement. Two marked off the day in equal fixed intervals, one in hundredths of a day, *k'o*, equal to 14 minutes 24 seconds of our day, and one in twelve fixed equal hours (themselves each divided into halves) centred on midnight. The third, the night watches, was usually measured by candles, incense sticks, etc. Time-measuring devices indigenous to China show the division of the day into equal parts even after the arrival of Europeans. The dials of indigenously made Chinese clocks or sundials have Chinese characters at the centre of each hour division. These traditional Chinese characters are the Twelve Terrestrial Branches, each standing for a different double-hour. Since ancient times they have been associated with the twelve animals of Chinese folklore, but their connection, though strong, is unclear. Because of this association, the dial symbols have been erroneously referred to as zodiac characters.

TYPES OF CHINESE CLOCK

There are two common types of mechanical clock generally referred to as 'Chinese'. The first category is of genuinely indigenous models which were copied from European examples, and the second is of clocks made in Europe for the Chinese market. During the 18th and early 19th centuries great effort was expended to find exports to China to ease an imbalance of trade. Timepieces were pressed into service as part of that effort.

The early clocks brought to China by Marco Ricci and his Jesuit brothers were probably Italian or Dutch chamber clocks, similar in design to those we now refer to as 'lantern' clocks. Clocks were called 'self-ringing bells' by the Chinese, and became a status symbol after the emperor had one installed in the imperial household. The imperial household began to assemble a large collection of fine European clocks.

In 1680, when the Emperor K'ang H'si established the imperial workshops to stimulate technological development in China, he included among them a horological workshop under the direction of François Louis Stadlin, a Swiss lay brother. The products of this workshop are very rare and infrequently referred to in horological literature. During the late 18th century, James Cox made a career out of producing very elaborate clocks with an astonishing variety of automata for sale to wealthy Chinese. In the 19th century, other workshops produced to more modest specifications large numbers of bracket-type movements and round enamel dials for shipment to China, where they were assembled and cased according to the Chinese style. These were typically bracket-type spring-wound fusee movements with various escapements: verge, anchor, with crutch or knife-edge suspensions, balances with spiral or helical balance springs, and even duplex escapements. There were repeaters, time and strike, timepiece only, or very elaborate striking clocks with automata. The mechanisms were generally adequate but not refined. The round enamel dials were typical European dials with Roman numerals; no gesture was made towards Chinese forms. Such clocks are referred to here as Type I Chinese bracket clocks.

The Chinese themselves made clocks derived from other types of European timekeepers. The most common are called 'drum' clocks. These were cylindrical and were displayed in a stand that held them in a vertical position with midnight and noon on the vertical axis. This method of support derived from Chinese drums on stands, hence the appellation. They are similar to European table clocks and seem to have combined early table-clock features (specifically the alarm system) and characteristics of imported watches. They have spring-wound fusee movements, usually with verge or cylinder escapements with balances and balance springs. The movements seem relatively crude in comparison with their European counterparts of the same period. In style of workmanship they may be compared with portable clocks of the 16th and 17th centuries.

There are other forms of clock ascribed to China. One of the rarest is the Type II Chinese bracket clock, generally smaller than Type I and more elaborate. They have cases of gilt brass with beading and chasing and European bracket-type movements with automata. These cases are more like 18th-century English bracket-clock cases than any Chinese wood or brass case. The dial plates have applied spandrels and the white enamel dials resemble those imported for the Type I bracket clocks. In the arch, automata of various descriptions perform. These clocks have been ascribed to various sources, both Chinese and European, but the European attribution seems most probable: there are no distinctly Chinese aspects to these clocks, and even when copying from European models the Chinese workman seems to have endowed his work with a Chinese character. The dials and decorative features can all be found on European clocks, and the movements are finished and complicated. They resemble each other sufficiently to suggest workshop production and they have European striking patterns. The only Chinese aspects that they do possess are the oriental figures that sometimes appear as automata. Most of them, however, have come to light in the Far East. The physical evidence suggests that they are properly put into the 'Chinese-market' category. Their possible date is also open to question, but the latter half of the 19th century seems logical.

The clocks produced in China were not great in number. In 1851 D. J. MacGowan, a medical missionary, estimated the yearly production of clocks by Chinese craftsmen in China to be approximately 1,500. He listed the clock shops: Nanking had 40, Süchow 30, Hangchow 17 and Ningpo 7. These shops were mainly engaged in repairs, although they did make some clocks and a few watches by hand.

There are two types of Chinese timekeepers that antedate the European mechanical clock and continued to be produced during the period from the 16th to the 19th century. They are sundials and incense clocks, and are discussed in detail in individual entries.

20th-CENTURY CHINESE CLOCK MANUFACTURE

During the 19th century China was, in general, a captive market for European and American goods. As she became more industrialised the clock industry got under way. In 1915 the first mechanised clock factory, Teh Shun Hsing, was started in Shantung province; others started in Shanghai and elsewhere. Most of them assembled imported parts and were eventually bankrupted by inflation and foreign imports during the 1930s. After the Communist Revolution the clock industry was revived to time the industrial and agricultural production of Mao's China. Designs are standardised and specific clocks are created for specific purposes, e.g. sporting-event chronographs. Now, for the first time in her history, China is producing timepieces for her own mass market. MCR

Clockmaking in France

Though the origins of clockmaking in France are obscure, it seems likely that France, with Italy, was an important pioneer in the art. Early turret clocks were made by alliances of blacksmiths and locksmiths, and it is from these that the clockmaking trade developed. In 1292 a 'Jehan l'Aulogier' was recorded in Paris, which from that time onwards was the centre of the trade in France, though cities such as Blois, Rouen, Besançon and Strasbourg also boasted their own clockmakers from the 16th century. By the 15th century Gothic chamber clocks were being produced – miniature versions of turret clocks with the same uncompromisingly structural open cage and the dial perfunctorily added to one side; few such early clocks survive.

During the 16th century the French clockmaking trade came under the control of the guild system. Bronze workers had been protected by a guild since the 13th century, but it was only in 1544 that the clockmakers' guild was incorporated in Paris (in Blois, the centre of court life, by 1597). The statues of the Paris guild were modified several times, but its control was maintained until the Revolution.

Guild regulations also covered the conduct of shops, and were intended to give quality control as well as defending the rights and privileges of its members. Guilds of the different trades closely controlled the division of labour. The clockmakers' guild obtained for its members the right to work in gold and silver without recourse to goldsmiths, but when other materials were involved in casework other craftsmen had to be called in. By the 18th century so great was the sophistication in case design that several workers might be involved: an *ébéniste* for wooden cases, a stoneworker for marble, and two men to cast, finish and gild the metal mounts. It is not known how the trades worked together to produce the elegantly unified cases of the late 17th and 18th centuries, but it seems likely that the clockmakers (a more educated class than *ébénistes* or metalworkers) sent out their own commissions.

Before the reign of Louis XIV such complications did not arise, for clocks were made wholly of metal. The internationalism of early clock design continued into the 17th century, both Louis XII and François I favouring the style of the Italian Renaissance. Small spring-driven chamber clocks were made in varieties of a common form, cylindrical or hexagonal, proportionately tall, the trains arranged in a double tier within, with horizontal wheels and pinions and vertical arbors. The dials of such clocks were fixed directly to the movement, the whole fitting within a case with elaborately engraved surface ornament (often taken from published engravings) and topped with urn or figure finials surrounding a pierced bell-cage. Another standard form was the drum clock or the square table clock, also of engraved metal, with dial uppermost. This form, reduced in scale, was the basis of the watch. At first rare, by the mid 17th century watches had become such an adjunct of fashion that all clockmaking attention was turned to them, to the detriment of the clock trade.

Clockmaking did not revive until the introduction of the pendulum so dramatically improved the accuracy of clocks that interest in them was rekindled. Louis XIV was as

1 **Pendule religieuse** in ebonised wood with brass mounts; I. Thuret, Paris, *c.*1670. Science Museum, London.

2 **Bracket clock** of Boulle marquetry with gilt-bronze mounts, signed 'Gourdain à Paris', the case ascribed to Cressent, *c.*1735. National Trust, Waddesdon Manor.

3 **Decimal dial clock** mounted in a Doric 'portico'-style case, with gridiron pendulum; by Pierre Daniel Destigny, Rouen, *c.*1825. Fitzwilliam Museum, Cambridge.

1   2

assiduous in encouraging clockmaking as the other arts, and while clockmakers worked for the court in the Louvre, others worked for lesser patrons in Paris workshops. The early clocks of Louis XIV's reign, the *religieuses*, were influenced by the sober Protestantism of Dutch taste [228/1]. Later, as artistic life blossomed, clocks rapidly became more splendid and more colourful, with lavish use of ebonised wood, gilt bronze and Boulle work. All styles of the *pendule Louis XIV* began to develop the rounded top and scrolled feet. Clocks were beginning to lose their status as curiosities and to be assimilated into the furnishings of a room. This domestication of clocks continued through the Regency and was fully achieved in the reign of Louis XV. New forms (the cartel clock, the bracket clock) and new materials (horn, tortoiseshell, *vernis Martin*) began to appear in the 18th century providing for the gayer forms of rococo interiors [230/2].

A break begins to be noticeable at this time between the decorative and scientific aspects of clockmaking. For decorative domestic clocks, neat unobtrusive movements began to be favoured, the predecessors of the *pendule de Paris* movement. But at the same time *pendules longue ligne* or *regulateurs* were catering for a growing interest in fine movements with elaborate calendar work and other refinements. Julien Le Roy's equation clock of 1736 set the style, and his son, Pierre Le Roy's work on marine chronometers carried on the tradition.

The mid 18th century marked a great expansion in clockmaking, in small towns as well as in Paris. It was at this time that the Comtoise clock began to be made, a country clock which proved so popular that by the end of the century it was distributed all over France. In Paris the tradition of scientific clockmaking was continued by such

1

1 Garnier, Jean Paul *Pendule portative* in a gilded Rococo-style case with hour and half-hour striking; *c.*1840. Private Collection.

2 Le Roy, Pierre French cartel clock with enamel dial and gilded case, *c.*1750.

2

231

1 Robin, Robert Clock in a gilt-bronze case; the mounts are emblematic of the continents; signed 'Robin à Paris' c.1780. National Trust, Waddesdon Manor.

2 Gilt-bronze mantel clock on a base of marbled iron, by Jean André Lepaute, c.1780. Wallace Collection, London.

3 Mantel clock in a cast, gilded metal case with porcelain plaques enamelled in the style of the painter Antoine Watteau; c.1890.

4 Berthoud, Ferdinand Skeleton clock, year duration, c.1800. British Museum, London.

1

  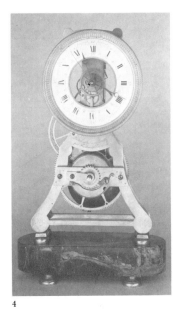

2   3   4

men as Ferdinand Berthoud and the Le Pautes, while
decorative clockmaking came to its apogee, with neoclassicism prevailing [233/2]. Marble portico clocks and
pillar clocks, urn clocks and lyre clocks were all fashionable,
and above all figure clocks [235/4], which in the hands of
such men as the sculptor Etienne Falconet and the *bronzier*
Pierre Gouthière, became an excuse for pure sculpture.

The French Revolution did not seriously undermine the
clockmaking trade, suggesting that it had sunk strong roots
in the mercantile and bourgeois classes. After the terror
years of 1792–5, during which some of the court clockmakers fell into disfavour, successive Revolutionary
governments actively encouraged the establishment or reac-
tivation of trade in several areas. Abraham-Louis Breguet
[234/1] declined to take on such a task in Besançon, but he
fought for his own re-establishment in Paris, and while
others were working on the industrialisation of French
clockmaking, he, with Antide Janvier and others, was
building its reputation with clocks of extreme complexity
and sophistication and a surpassing series of high-quality
watches.

In terms of case styles the period 1800–30 was one of
surprising conservatism. Figure clocks in patinated and gilt
bronze had been dominant since the 1790s and continued in
popularity into the 1820s, when the subjects and figures
subtly lapsed into a more romantic vein, with heroines and
chivalric heroes echoing the Gothic and rococo revivals.

Energy in the early 19th century had been directed
towards the development of the old trade as a new industry.
In the Franche-Comté Frédéric Japy worked quietly
through the Directory and Consulate years building up, by
1801, a factory producing 100,000 movements a year. And
in the region around Dieppe a similar development on
factory lines took place a little later to produce the *pendule de
voyage* (carriage clock) industry. This industrial production
of movements did not reflect a standardisation of case styles.
In the 19th century the French, like others, were afflicted
with a romantic yearning for historical styles and a keen
desire for expense and ostentation. The elaboration of cases
was encouraged by the growth of a middle-class market and
by a spate of international exhibitions [233/3]. A similarly

based taste was for novelty clocks, either mystery clocks or
skeleton clocks, clocks with steam-engine cases or other
fancies, and automaton clocks. During the century the
export trade grew steadily, and French clocks of all
qualities, above all carriage clocks, were especially popular
in England.

French taste for ornate clocks and for reproductions
continued into the 20th century, side by side with *art
nouveau* and even *art déco*. At the same time it was the
French who first produced an electric clock for large-scale
distribution, the Bulle clock, working with a Leclanché cell
and having a pendulum bob in the form of a coil of wire
swinging around a curved magnet. The Swiss and the
Americans soon followed this idea and improved upon it,
but France had shown the way to a more clinical and
accurate method of timekeeping.

After the Franco–Prussian war of 1870–1 the Treaty of
Frankfurt almost ruined the French industry by allowing
German clocks to be imported without duty. After the First
World War the industry in the traditional areas was
reorganised to supply the new demand for alarm clocks and
common timekeepers. PSKM

Berthoud, Ferdinand One of the most famous clock- and
watchmakers of the 18th century, Berthoud (1727–1807)
was born at Plancemont, Switzerland, and went to Paris in
1747 where he was apprenticed to Julien Le Roy, attaining
his mastership in 1754. In 1767 he acquired a property at
Groslay where he spent much of his time, but from 1789 to
1806 he was registered in Paris at the rue de Harlay. From
1786 he was *horloger pensionnaire* to the king and *Inspecteur-
général des machines* for the navy. These appointments, in
fact, were intended as a form of subsidy for Berthoud's work
on precision clockmaking, particularly in the field of
marine chronometers – he had completed his first marine
timekeeper in 1761.

Other notable inventions included bimetallic compensating balances and a detent escapement. In 1792 he
was stripped of all his offices and income, but after
complaints to the authorities in 1792 and 1793, a pension
was restored to him. PSKM

Boulle, André-Charles Architect, painter and *ébéniste*, working as an influential designer of clock cases, amongst other furniture, Boulle (1642–1732) gave his name to a particular form of marquetry, Boulle work. In 1673 he was appointed *ébéniste du roi* and given apartments in the Galeries du Louvre. The royal appointment gave holders freedom from guild regulations and allowed them to oversee work which would normally be done in separate workshops. Thus Boulle was certainly free to cast and gild his own mounts and may also have commissioned clock movements. PSKM
See also Boulle work (Section I).

Breguet, Abraham-Louis Breguet (1747–1823) was the most famous French clock- and watchmaker of all time. He was born at Neuchâtel, probably of French Huguenot stock. He went to Paris when he was 18 and served his apprenticeship under several masters, first at Versailles, possibly under Ferdinand Berthoud, later under Étienne Gide. In 1775 he established himself as clockmaker in Paris in partnership with his master's son, Xavier Gide. They gathered a brilliant clientèle in England as well as France. At the beginning of the Revolution they were very prosperous under the trade name Breguet *et cie* but by 1791 they had split up the partnership. In 1790 Breguet was a member of the new municipal assembly of the Commune, but by 1793 he was a suspected person and had to flee to Neuchâtel with his son, Antoine-Louis. By 1795 Breguet was back in Paris with the support of the Commission for Arts and Manufactures. They tried to induce him to build up the clock industry at Besançon, but he felt it beneath his capabilities and pleaded instead for the Versailles works. In support of his request he marshalled a formidable list of his inventions; the workshops were re-established, refitted and given to him free for 15 years. He turned again to the luxury trade in clocks and watches, and by the Empire period was employing 100 workers.

Most of Breguet's work was luxurious, expensive and of superlative quality, but in watches he produced one 'subscription watch', a slightly cheaper piece, still of high quality. His great virtuoso performance was the production of the *pendule sympathique*. Chronometers and small regulators were also made. Breguet's case style was usually severe, his metal and glass cases for small clocks giving rise to the form of the later *pendule de voyage*. The simple frames might be engraved and gilded but the more elaborate cases of other clockmakers of the period were not favoured. PSKM
See also: *Pendule sympathique*; *Pendule de voyage* (both Section I).

Breguet et fils Abraham-Louis Breguet's son, Antoine-Louis, born 1776, followed in his father's footsteps as a maker of high-quality clocks and watches. He joined him in partnership in 1807 and after his father's death in 1823 continued the firm, later taking into partnership his own son, Louis-Clément-François, born 1804, to whom he sold the business in 1833, retiring to Buisson where he died in 1853. The 13-year period when the firm bore the name of Breguet *et fils* was one of great achievement.

The firm outlived its first two generations. After 1840 Antoine-Louis, a nephew, joined and the name of the firm was then changed to Breguet *neveu et cie*, and in 1853 to L. Breguet *et fils*. PSKM

Brocot, Achille Brocot (1817–74), eldest son of Louis-Gabriel Brocot, carried on his business in Paris in the mid 19th century. He patented several improvements in escapements and rack striking and also invented an adjustable pendulum spring suspension which bears his name. PSKM

Brocot, Louis-Gabriel A Parisian clockmaker, working from 1820 until after 1850. His name is chiefly associated with a visible pin-pallet escapement which he invented. It was widely used in contemporary clocks and as an improvement on older movements. PSKM

Bulle, M. T. Favre- A well-known 20th-century horologist in Paris, best remembered for his invention of the Bulle electric clock. In 1920 his work in collaboration with B. M. M. Moulin, resulted in a patent being taken out in both their names during 1920. In 1921 a further patent was taken out in respect of the Bulle clock in Bulle's name only. Basically it is a reinvention of Alexander Bain's original system with an improved fork contact; one of the most interesting features is the isochronous spring used to overcome the circular error which affects all electric battery clocks as the terminal voltage changes. It is one of the few isochronous devices applied to a pendulum, and its use made the Bulle electric clock successful. CKA
See also Bulle clock (Section I).

1   2   3

1 Breguet, Abraham-Louis
Portrait by Langlumé after a
painting by A. Chazal.

2 Breguet & fils 'Humpbacked'
silver-cased *pendule de voyage*, signed
'Breguet & fils, No.3629', 1822.
British Museum, London.

3 Bulle, M. T. Favre- A mantel
clock with the Bulle electric mechanism concealed, unlike many
of the earlier versions, *c*.1930.

4 Boulle, André-Charles Clock
case from a design by A-C Boulle,
with gilt-bronze mounts showing
'Love conquering Time';
Martinot family, early 18th century, Wallace Collection, London.

5 Janvier, Antide *Regulateur*
showing equation of time, mean
time, sunrise and sunset, signs of
the zodiac and date, *c*.1800.
Musée des Beaux Arts, Besançon.

4   5

Garnier, Jean Paul Garnier (1801–69) became the pupil
of Antide Janvier, commencing business in Paris in 1825. In
1830 he took out a patent for a frictional rest escapement
applicable to clocks and watches. Another patent, taken out
by him in 1847, covers the distribution from a master clock
to an unlimited number of slave clocks by electrical means.
He was awarded a gold medal for an electric clock exhibited
in 1849; in 1851 he was at the Great Exhibition in London
to show his carriage clocks [230/1]. CKA

Hautefeuille, L'Abbé Jean An Orléans clockmaker who
anticipated several important inventions in clockmaking,
Hautefeuille (1647–1724) published in the *Journal des
Savants* in 1674 a 'Note on the method of equalising the
oscillations in the balance of a portable clock' using a thin
spring, closely paralleling Christiaan Huygens's work. In
1675 he published *Factum de M. l'Abbé de H., touchant les
pendules de poche, contre M. Huygens*, and he later opposed the
granting of privilege to Huygens, claiming himself to be the
inventor of the balance spring, but without success. His
best-known invention (1722) was a type of rack-lever
escapement, which might also be described as a rack-
anchor. The rack-lever escapement for watches was reinvented in England in a different form by Peter
Lintherland in 1791. Hautefeuille also had ideas for a
marine timekeeper, which involved a pendulum suspended in a jar of sea water; it could have had no practical
use. PSKM

Janvier, Antide Janvier (1751–1835) was a Parisian
clockmaker, scientifically one of the most famous, who
contributed many inventions to the development of
accurate timekeeping and mechanical astronomical instruments. He was born at Lavans-lez-St-Claude in the Jura,
the son of a peasant. At a very early age he made a complex

astronomical clock which was shown at the Besançon
Académie, and in 1771 he went to Paris. He presented an
orrery to Louis XV in 1773. The following year he had to
return to the Jura, then set up shop in Verdun, where he
married, and continued to make astronomical clocks. In
1784 he returned to Paris, bringing with him an astronomical sphere clock which was presented to Louis XVI by
Lalande. He became *horloger breveté du roi* (official
clockmaker to the king) and was given a workshop and
lodgings in the Louvre.

During the Revolution Janvier was imprisoned for a
while at Ste Pélagie with Robert Robin and afterwards was
sent to Morez as Commissioner for Public Safety charged
with the establishment of an armaments factory and
installing telegraph signals. He advised the Revolutionary
government on the question of decimal time and by 1800
was established with lodgings in the Cour du Muséum,
then, in 1804, in the Palais des Beaux Arts aux Quatre
Nations, and elsewhere in subsequent years, retaining his
official position through changes of government. He used
his status to establish a school of horology in Paris. PSKM

Japy, Frédéric Father of the French horological industry
of the 19th century, Japy (1749–1812) was born in
Beaucourt in the Franche-Comté, the son of a blacksmith.
In 1773 he set up a workshop in Montbéliard, moving again
to Beaucourt in 1777 where, by 1779, his new workshop, or
factory [236/1], was in full production of *ébauches* (unfinished
movements) and employing more than 50 workers. By 1801
he was employing 300 and producing 100,000 *ébauches*
annually, using machines in the production of certain parts.
Japy's inventiveness was enormous, and patents for new
refinements in clock parts and for the machinery to make
them were produced regularly.

In 1807 Japy took his sons into partnership and began to

1

expand the number of his factories, which they managed. Japy *frères* continued active in all branches of the clock- and watchmaking industry. PSKM

Le Roy, Julien One of the most famous of a long dynasty of clockmakers in Paris, Le Roy (1686–1759) was born in Tours and went to Paris in 1699. He was apprenticed to Alexandre Le Bon, and gained his mastership in 1713.

His inventions were many. He devised a horizontal layout for turret clocks and became known for this type of clock. Much of his output was in watches: he devised a repeating mechanism suitable for the thinnest cases. He introduced George Graham's cylinder escapement to France and generally drew to France, from England, the status of the leading clockmakers of Europe. One of his most useful and individual suggestions was the oil sink, the result of some years' work on the question of oils and on pivoting. In Geneva poor-quality watches bearing his name were made by the gross; the majority of these were sent to America. PSKM

Le Roy, Pierre Parisian clockmaker, eldest son of Julien Le Roy and probably surpassing him in importance, Pierre (1717–85) became a master clockmaker in 1737 and was patronised by the court, being given lodgings in the Louvre which he shared with his brother Jean-Baptiste [231/2].

His specialisation was precision clockmaking, in particular marine chronometers. One which he presented to Louis XV in 1766 established him, in the opinion of R. T. Gould, as 'one of the very greatest masters of horology who ever lived'. He submitted two chronometers in a competition initiated by the Académie Royale des Sciences, one of which had an error of only $5\frac{1}{2}$ seconds computed over three months. It was tested in the yacht *Aurore*, which had been specially built for the purpose.

Le Roy's inventions included detached-detent escapements and compensated balances, and his publications were numerous. PSKM

Raingo frères A Parisian clockmaking firm of the 19th century, founded by Z. Raingo who worked in Ghent and Paris. He started to make orrery clocks *c.* 1810, the earlier ones carrying the name of Antide Janvier, who made the movements. In 1815 Raingo patented his designs for an orrery and published them in 1823: *Description of a clock with moving spheres*. The firm of Raingo *frères* was trading in the rue Vielle du Temple in 1829, and continued until after 1900. PSKM

See also Orrery clock (Section I).

Robert, Henri A Parisian clockmaker, pupil of Abraham-Louis Perrelet, Robert (1795–1874) became clockmaker to the navy in 1847 and published several works on clockmaking. In 1832 he set up in the Palais Royal, rue de Valois, and in 1834 moved to the rue du Coq, in the Faubourg St Honoré. His inventions included a half-second compensated pendulum, a bimetallic strip for chronometer balances, and a marine chronometer fitted with a pivoted detent escapement and a going barrel instead of a fusee, which he advocated for chronometers though not for watches. The going barrel was used by several French chronometer makers, including Ferdinand Berthoud, Breguet and Julien Le Roy, and was preferred by the French while the English continued to use the fusee. It has several advantages, particularly ease of manufacture. PSKM

Robin, Robert Robin (1742–99), clockmaker to Louis XV, Louis XVI, Marie Antoinette and the Republic, was one of the leading French horologists of the 18th century. His mechanical inventions were many, but he is also known for highly decorative clocks. Little is known of his early life. He became a master clockmaker in 1767, and later set up his workshop in the Faubourg St Honoré. In 1785 he obtained a lodging in the Galeries du Louvre, where he lived until his death [232/1].

He frequently presented papers to the Académie Royale des Sciences, such as a memoir on the properties of remontoires and one on perpetual calendar mechanisms. After the Revolution he worked as happily for his new masters, making a present of a decimal clock to the National Convention in 1793 and in 1798 converting the so-called 'Louis XIV' clock to a 'Clock of Liberty'. PSKM

Sully, Henry Born in London, Sully (1680–1728) was a celebrated early 18th-century horologist of remarkable talents who was apprenticed in 1697 to Charles Gretton. He went to Holland and Austria, and later to France, where he was befriended by Julien Le Roy, *horloger du roi*. Though Sully did not succeed in establishing the watch factories he was commissioned to undertake for John Law and the Maréchal de Noailles, he left his mark on French watchmaking and raised its standards. He made great efforts to perfect a marine timekeeper, using a modified Debaufre escapement (a modified form of verge escapement utilising two coaxially mounted escape wheels). Preliminary tests looked encouraging, but in tests on the open sea it failed. Discouragement and misfortune brought on lung disease and an untimely death in 1728. He published several important works: *Règle artificielle du temps* (Vienna, 1714; Paris, 1717), *Méthode pour régler les montres et les pendules* (Paris, 1717), and a work on marine timekeepers, as he conceived them, in 1726. DJB

Thiout, Antoine Born at Joinville, Haute-Marne, Thiout (*c.* 1694–1761) became master clockmaker in 1724. He is recorded in the Quai Pelletier, Paris, between 1741 and 1748; became clockmaker to the Duc d'Orléans in 1751.

In 1724 Thiout presented to the Académie Royale des Sciences two designs for equation clocks to show solar time and mean time. Two years later he exhibited a clock showing solar time, a marine timepiece and a striking

1 Japy, Frédéric Factory at Beaucourt in the Franche-Comté district, France; mid 19th century.

2 Le Roy, Julien Cartel clock in gilt-bronze case. Movement by Julien le Roy; case by Jacques Caffieri; 1745–9. J. Paul Getty Museum, Malibu, California.

3 Robert, Henri Marine chronometer, with pivoted detent escapement and without a fusee; 1845. Musée National des Arts et Métiers, Paris.

4 Raingo frères Orrery clock in Empire style and decorated with mother-of-pearl; c. 1820. Private collection.

5 Sully, Henry Movement and case of the marine clock sent by Sully to Graham in 1724, with his description and notes. Clockmakers' Company Museum, London.

6 Thiout, Antoine Illustration of a wheel-cutting engine by Henry Sully from Antoine Thiout, *Traité de l'Horlogerie*, Vol. I, pl. 19. An example of the elaborate design of many French horological tools; 1741.

7 Verité, August-Lucien Monumental clock in Beauvais Cathdral; 1870.

2

4

3

5

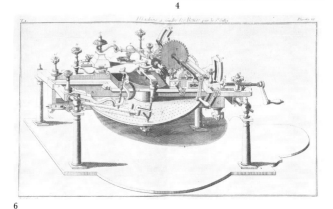

6

mechanism based on solar time. In 1737 he demonstrated his repeating work, and in 1741–2 he published his *Treatise on Mechanical and Practical Horology*, which was reissued in 1767 and has remained a significant work ever since. The book is in two volumes and contains 85 plates showing clock- and watchmaking tools, wheel-cutting engines, measuring instruments, clock and watch escapements and a wide range of clock and watch designs. PSKM

Vérité, August-Lucien A clockmaker in Beauvais and Beaudoin, Vérité (1806–87) made many public clocks and

7

1

2

explored the use of electricity for synchronous timekeeping. As early as 1824 he published a modified form of George Graham's escapement with reversed anchor.

During the 1840s and 1850s he patented a free pendulum with constant-force escapement, and in 1853 he read to the Académie Royale des Sciences a paper describing a large regulator with constant-force electric escapement which he patented and exhibited three years later. He made clocks for the northern railway company in France and astronomical clocks of outstanding interest for the cathedrals of Beauvais and Besançon. These cathedral clocks are of phenomenal complexity; that at Beauvais is also of monumental proportions. Both clocks rival Jean-Baptiste Schwilgué's third Strasbourg clock, which shortly preceded them. The Besançon clock was built between 1856 and 1860, the Beauvais clock between 1865 and 1868. PSKM

Wagner, Jean An outstanding Parisian clockmaker, born in Pfalzel, now in West Germany, Wagner (1800–75) came to Paris when he was twelve and devoted himself to the scientific aspect of clockmaking, working on large public clocks and precision instruments. Between 1830 and 1850 he produced a constant stream of inventions, which included his perfecting of a pinwheel escapement, several forms of free escapements, compensated pendulums, improvement to turret-clock mechanisms, the addition of double levers for striking work to even the succession of blows, various kinds of musical carillons, and numerous other devices, some electrical and some of particular importance to engineers. PSKM

Clockmaking in Germany

It is not certain where the mechanical clock was invented, but it seems probable that it was in the area where Germany, Switzerland, Italy and France come together. While Italy has a good claim to the actual invention of the mechanical clock, the aptitude of the Germans for fine mechanical work suggests that its origin could well have been in one of the south German states. It is noteworthy that the leading horological museums in Germany are all in the south, in the Black Forest, Stuttgart, Nuremberg, Augsburg and Munich.

Old drawings of German towns sometimes show towers embellished by dials. A painting by Lucas Cranach dated 1565 in the museum at Hamburg shows a clock dial on a tower, and in the realm of early turret clocks Germany was certainly not behind the rest of Europe. During the Renaissance the fame of Germany was largely based on the products of Nuremberg and Augsburg. Nuremberg in particular was celebrated because of Peter Henlein and his small portable clocks while Augsburg specialised in decoration and in the creation of automata clocks in which mechanical figures, human and animal, performed.

Growing interest in astronomy resulted in the production of clocks with astronomical dials, and many German towns boasted very large clocks which showed astronomical features and also, to a greater or lesser extent, provided automata which performed when the clock struck. They include the *Mannleinlaufen* at Nuremberg, the town-hall clocks at Heilbronn and Ulm, the battling oxen at Ochsenfurt and the drinking burgomaster at Rothenburg-ob-der-Tauber.

Towards the Austrian frontier, baroque church-clock dials are similar to those of Austria, with the quarter-hour figures inside those for the hour and indicated by a shorter hand, which virtually performs the function of a minute hand. It is a feature of some German church clocks that they strike the hour on a bell of one tone and immediately repeat it on a bell of a different tone. The old movement of the clock from the Stiftkirche in Stuttgart is of this pattern (it is preserved in the Altes Schloss museum close to the church). The present clock repeats the hour in the same way.

In domestic clockmaking, the outstanding feature of German work during the Renaissance is the stackfreed, which seems to have been used almost exclusively in

German clocks and watches (the derivation of the name is not clear). Many writers have criticised the stackfreed, but without seeing the performance of one that was new; in view of the low standard of timekeeping in the 16th century, it was perhaps not so bad a device as has been suggested. It would appear that the stackfreed and the fusee were used contemporaneously, and that the stackfreed did not necessarily pre-date the fusee, as has often been stated.

After the mid 17th century the dominance of Augsburg and Nuremberg declined, as they did not readily adapt themselves to change. During the 17th century clockmaking was introduced into the Black Forest and in other parts of Germany; simpler clocks began to be made, mostly with a 'cowtail' pendulum (as in Austria), to provide the time for people with more modest incomes than the customers of Augsburg and Nuremberg [239/3]. In the larger towns clocks were made which were loosely based on English models such as the longcase clock and the bracket clock, but the German examples seem to be less graceful in outline than their prototypes and more heavily covered in decoration [238/1].

In the north of Germany, particularly in the industrial area of Westphalia, the longcase clock was popular, but the case was straighter than that of its English prototype and the division into hood, trunk and base was less pronounced. Dials were often circular and enamelled, in contrast to the dials of brass or painted iron used in England. The circular dial enjoyed a short period of popularity in Britain, notably in Scotland c. 1830, but it was soon abandoned for the traditional type.

The Black Forest clock penetrated the whole of Europe and even reached the United States. It was based on a cottage industry with agents supplying the salesmen at the overseas points, but there is a consistency about movements and dials which allows the clock to be easily recognised. The Black Forest clocks were in great demand in the early 19th century. The Black Forest felt a decline, however, between 1840 and 1860 because of competition from American factories producing more sophisticated clocks. Eventually the industry adopted American methods and by 1900 was beating the Americans at their own game. In Silesia the firm founded by Gustav Becker produced clocks similar to those from the newly established factories in the Black Forest working on American principles. By the turn of the century the Becker factory and others in the area which had amalgamated with it accounted for one-seventh of the total German production.

Factory production in Germany began with direct copies of American models, but this was soon abandoned and more typical German styles took their place. The Vienna regulator was a firm favourite and was made with both weight and spring drive. The latter clocks usually had a mock gridiron pendulum with the letters R/A (*retard* and *avance*) on the bob and were made in two sizes which were smaller than the normal weight-driven clock, as well as in the same size.

Some German clocks in the late 19th century had very heavy cases with sombre decoration, fitting the late Victorian mood. After being criticised in various exhibitions, the designs were lightened and much superfluous decoration omitted.

3   4

While German factories were mostly making clocks on the American system and constructing them as cheaply as possible, there were some firms which were endeavouring to turn out a high-quality product. Among these were Carl Werner of Villingen; L. Furtwangler & Söhne; Lenzkirch; and Winterhalder & Hofmeier. The latter firm specialised in imitating English designs, and in the early 20th century their clocks were being sold in Britain at about half the price of an equivalent British clock. Lenzkirch specialised in Vienna regulators, which have a very high reputation in Germany to this day although the factory closed in 1932.

Since 1945 German production has concentrated on cuckoo clocks, 400-day clocks, and chiming clocks of the traditional type, but a great deal has been done in producing new designs to suit modern tastes. Some factories have made reproductions of the clocks of the late 19th century, albeit driven by batteries. Various firms have produced kits for constructing the old type of Black Forest foliot clock, and other Black Forest designs have also been made in kit form. EJT

Becker, Gustav Becker (1819–85) was born at Oels, Silesia, and learned clockmaking in Silesia but later travelled to Frankfurt, La Chaux-de-Fonds, Dresden, Munich, Berlin and Vienna. In 1845 he returned home and in 1847 began a clock business in Freiburg. Two years later he was able to start a small factory in two rooms with one assistant and six boys for the manufacture of wall and standing clocks.

After placing his work in an exhibition in 1852 he obtained contracts to manufacture clocks for post and telegraph administrations, and c. 1860 was able to branch out with more elaborate cases. His success encouraged others to open clock factories, but in 1899 all the clock factories in Freiburg were amalgamated under the Becker name. In 1926 the group merged with Junghans. EJT

Bodeker, Jost Bodeker (late 16th–early 17th centuries) is known to us from a manuscript at Osnabrück describing an elaborate astronomical clock he made for the cathedral there in 1587. The importance of the clock lies not in its complexity but in the two methods of control provided, a foliot and a conical pendulum. A brake could be applied to stop the mechanism and the control changed at will, but it is not clear why this should be needed or who would decide to

1 Burgi, Jost Clock with cross-beat escapement in an elaborate pierced, gilded and rock-crystal case, *c*.1615. Kunsthistorisches Museum, Vienna.

2 Burgi, Jost Observatory clock with cross-beat escapement, made before 1600. Hessisches Landesmuseum, Kassel.

3 Burgi, Jost View underneath the movement of 240/2 showing the cross-beat escapement.

4 Haas, Philipp 'Dumpling Eater' clock; when the clock strikes the man appears to eat a succession of dumplings; by Philipp Haas & Söhne, St Georgen, *c*.1880. Heimatmuseum, Triberg.

5 Habrecht, Isaac and Josias Isaac's miniature reproduction of the famous Strasbourg clock, signed and dated 1594. De danske Kongers Kronologiske Samling pa Rosenborg, Copenhagen.

6 Sorg, Josef Black Forest *Sorguhr* clock. Hour strike on bell and alarm. Enamel dial with decorated brass surround; *c*.1850. Ekkehard Blender, Titisee-Neustadt.

1

2

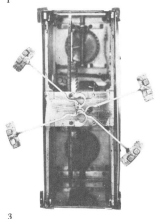

3

4

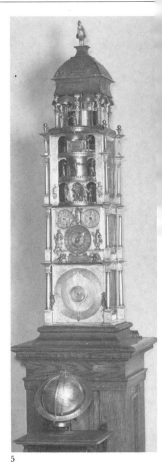

5

make the change. Attempts have been made to prove that Bodeker was the pioneer of the pendulum, preceding Galileo and Christiaan Huygens, but the conical pendulum is an inferior timekeeper to the swinging pendulum. Bodeker died probably after 1626. EJT

Burgi, Jost Burgi (1552–1632) was among the earliest makers who sought to make a precision clock. His greatest achievement was the cross-beat escapement. In this escapement two light arms with weights at each end replace the single foliot. There is a slight springiness in the arms which may make up for the absence of a balance spring, to a very slight degree, but the results obtained were greatly superior to those of the verge escapement without a balance spring. In 1604 Burgi was appointed clockmaker to the Emperor Rudolf II in Prague. EJT

Dilger, Friedrich Simon Dilger (b. 1677) from Schollach was one of the founders of the Black Forest clock industry in the 18th century. He taught his son Friedrich, who went on the road to sell clocks and found his way to Paris *c*.1720. Though not speaking French, he managed to visit a number of clockmaker's workshops, and studied the tools they used. Returning home after a year, he used the knowledge he had gained to turn out clocks superior to those then being made by other Black Forest makers. Dilger also introduced the wheel-cutting engine into the Black Forest as a result of his visit to Paris. EJT

Haas, Philipp Haas (19th century) was among the pioneers of the American system of clockmaking in the Black Forest. He established a London office in 1871, before any of the American factories, and was putting labels into his clocks in German and English before 1875. In 1876 he registered a trademark entirely in English and adopted the name 'Teutonia Clock Manufactory' (previously in German, *Uhrenfabrik Teutonia*).

A Haas movement, although on the American system, is well made. He even used a dead-beat escapement, and rather unusually gave the movement a serial number, something generally found only on clocks of better quality. As well as the American type of striking and alarm clocks, and small timepieces, the firm produced clocks in the traditional Black Forest style.

The factory was located at St Georgen, and the firm traded under the name 'Philipp Haas und Söhne', the letters P. H. and S. intertwined being sometimes found on clocks manufactured by Haas. EJT

Habrecht, Isaac and Josias The brothers Isaac (1544–1620) and Josias (1552–75) Habrecht will be best remembered for their work on the great clock at Strasbourg Cathedral. The Habrecht brothers had been introduced to Dasypodius, who made the calculations for the second Strasbourg clock and generally supervised the work, which was completed by 1574. Isaac made two smaller reproductions of the clock, not exactly alike, one of which is in the British Museum, London, and the other at Rosenborg Castle, Copenhagen. Isaac also made astronomical clocks for the towns of Heilbronn and Ulm in Germany.

He left a clock for the château of Kaiserswerth incomplete at his death. EJT

1

1 Winterhalder & Hofmeier
Black Forest bracket clock in
carved oak case; brass movement
with fuses. Dial of steel plate with
brass decoration; *c.*1890.
Ekkehard Blender, Titisee-
Neustadt.

2 Herbstreith, Jacob (d. 1801)
who gave his nickname to the
Black Forest 'Jockele' clock.
Historisches Uhrensammlung,
Furtwangen.

3 Hoys, Leopold An ebony
bracket clock with gilded bronze
mounts and three-train movement, known as a *Standuhr*. Signed
'Leop Hoys-Bamberg'; *c.*1750.
Bayerisches Nationalmuseum,
Munich.

**4 H.A.C. (Hamburg American
Clock Co.)** Two clocks by H.A.C.,
c. 1882, showing how different
models can be produced with very
slight alterations in the design of
the cases.

2

3

H.A.C. (Hamburg American Clock Co.) Paul
Landenberger was the son-in-law of Erhard Junghans who
founded the clock factory which is still active at
Schramberg in the Black Forest. Landenberger worked for
the Junghans factory until 1876, when his brothers-in-law
took control, and then, with a partner, founded a firm of his
own known as Landenberger & Lang. In 1883 it was made
into a company called the *Hamburg Amerikanische
Uhrenfabrik (H.A.U.)*, or Hamburg American Clock Co.
(H.A.C.).

For about 40 years H.A.C. and Junghans carried on
intensive competition, but in 1926 H.A.C. came into the
Junghans group. There appear to be more clocks by H.A.C.
dating from the late 19th century still in circulation in
Britain than Junghans clocks of the same period.

H.A.C. began with the trademark of Landenberger &
Lang, a steamship with the words 'In God we Trust', but in
1892 the firm registered the trademark of crossed arrows
which has become known all over the world. EJT

Herbstreith, Jakob Herbstreith (d. 1801) lived in
Hinterzarten near Neustadt in the southern Black Forest,
and *c.*1780 produced a very small example of a Black
Forest clock, $3\frac{1}{4} \times 2\frac{1}{4} \times 1\frac{1}{4}$ in. His nickname was 'Jockele',
the diminutive of Jakob, and the clocks were also known
by this name. The type was subsequently made by other
makers. EJT

Hoys, Leopold Born in Vienna, Hoys (1713–97) studied
at Klagenfurt under Christoffer Prunner until 1732 and was
a journeyman in Augsburg in 1739. He made his
horological masterpiece in 1741 and was admitted to the
Guild in 1742. From 1757 to his death he was official
clockmaker to the Prince Bishop of Bamberg, in spite of
protests by Bamberg clockmakers.

Hoys is best remembered for two things: bracket clocks
loosely based on English models, but standing on curved

4

legs; and the use of double pendulums. His bracket clocks
nearly always have ebony cases and are decorated with
applied bronze mounts in a style reminiscent of France; a
number of them have three trains and subsidiary dials. EJT

Junghans, Erhard (Gebr. Junghans Uhrenfabrik)
Erhard Junghans (1823–70) was the son of a designer in a
porcelain factory at Schramberg in the Black Forest. He
worked with his father and after he had accumulated a little
capital he decided in 1861 to make accessories for clocks, then
to make complete clocks. He sent for his brother Xaver, a
cabinetmaker who had emigrated to the United States, and
asked him to order machinery in America for producing
clock parts. When this was installed, Xaver took charge of
the case shop, Erhard the business activities, and a
professional clockmaker was called in to superintend the
movement shop.

Erhard Junghans died in 1870 and the business then
passed to his sons Erhard Jr and Arthur. Various other
members of the family were involved in the firm's

243

management as time passed, and other firms were amalgamated with Junghans, including H.A.C., Lenzkirch, Thomas Haller and Gustav Becker. The factory, now owned by Diehl, is the largest in Germany.

The importance of the Junghans undertaking was its adoption of American methods of manufacturing, which paved the way for other factories to do the same. EJT

Ketterer, Franz Anton One of the earliest Black Forest clockmakers, Ketterer (1676–1750) lived in the village of Schönwald between Triberg and Furtwangen. His main claim to fame is as the alleged inventor of the cuckoo clock, *c.* 1730, which formed an important article of commerce for the Black Forest. EJT
See also Cuckoo clock (Section I).

Kintzing, Christian and Peter Christian Kintzing (1707–1804) was a miller who became a clockmaker at Neuwied on the Rhine. The elaborate longcase clock in the Goethehaus at Frankfurt was built by him in collaboration with his brother Peter (d. 1763), who was an organ builder.

Christian continued as a clockmaker until 1782, when he handed over to his son, another Peter (1745–1816). Several of his early clocks possess an escapement which is probably his invention; it combines the pinwheel of Louis Amant with the type of pallets used by George Graham. The pins are not inserted in the wheel but are cut from the solid and are oval in section. This escapement appears to be an attempt to replace the verge with something more accurate.

Peter, the son, who altered the spelling of the name to Kinzing, came more under French influence. He collaborated with David Roentgen and made the piano-playing automaton now in the Conservatoire des Arts et Métiers, Paris. EJT

Knauss, Johann Louis J. L. Knauss of Darmstadt was active *c.* 1730–70 and is best remembered for a silver-mounted clock with automata in the Hofburg, Vienna, made *c.* 1750 and presented to the Empress Maria Theresa and her husband Franz. The action takes place on a stage below the clock dial. The Empress and her husband move from left to right, and pages deliver the imperial crown of the Holy Roman Empire to Franz while Maria Theresa receives the crowns of the kingdoms of Hungary and Bohemia. A black demon (Frederick the Great?) appears in the sky but is driven away by the Archangel Michael. EJT

Lenzkirch Eduard Hauser (1825–1900) at the age of 15 went to work for Johann Georg Schöpperle, a builder of mechanical musical instruments in the village of Lenzkirch in the Black Forest. He improved his knowledge in Switzerland and began to make clockmakers' tools in Lenzkirch. In 1850 he began a factory for producing rough movements which were easy for clockmakers to finish. He had 18 employees but the machinery was all hand-driven.

He founded the 'Company for making clocks in Lenzkirch' in August 1851, and in 1852 the factory was completed. Production was first concerned with finishing rough movements from France; later, rough movements were produced, and finished clocks, especially Vienna regulators. The company's trade mark was registered in the 1870s and consists of a branch of a tree with 'Lenzkirch A.G.U.' in an oval. The factory always had a reputation for high-quality work, and Lenzkirch products are highly esteemed in Germany today. The firm amalgamated with Junghans in 1928 but the factory was closed in 1932. EJT

Leupold, Jakob Leupold (1674–1727) published in Leipzig a book entitled *Theatrum Machinarum Generale* (1724), in which he described a wheel-cutting engine incorporating a dividing plate. This was probably the machine that Friedrich Dilger saw in Paris; Dilger tried to make the dividing plate of wood, without success. EJT
See also Dilger, Friedrich.

1, 2 Junghans, Erhard Two small Junghans timepieces in the American style, *c.* 1870. Private collection.

3 Lenzkirch, Vienna regulator with striking work, signed behind the eagle, *c.* 1890. Private collection.

4 Knauss, Johann Louis The 'Maria Theresa' automata and musical clock with silver mounts, dated 1745. Präsident-schaftskanzlei, Vienna.

5 Mayr, Johann Hans Georg Table clock with *grande sonnerie* striking, general view, *c.* 1660. Bayerisches Nationalmuseum, Munich.

6 Mayr, Johann Hans Georg Engraved rear dial of the Mayr clock showing the original cross-beat arms, the later crutch, dials indicating the striking sequence and dial for elapsed minutes each hour. Bayerisches National-museum, Munich.

1 and 2

3

7 Kintzing, Christian and Peter Writing desk in the French style by David Roentgen fitted with a clock by Peter Kintzing, *c.* 1790. Kunstindustrimuseet, Copenhagen.

8 Riefler, Sigmund Riefler regulator mounted in an evacuated cylinder with glass cover, wound by an electrical remontoire; *c.* 1900. Royal Scottish Museum, Edinburgh.

4

5

6

7

8

Mayr, Johann Hans Georg Mayr (active 1650 – d. 1684) was court clockmaker in Munich from 1663 to 1671. His most important clock is in the Bayerisches National Museum in Munich. This is a table clock in an architectural case with a gallery on top and above it a small tower surmounted by an armillary sphere. The main dial contains various subsidiary dials.

The clock is an early example of a *grande sonnerie* in which the previous hour is repeated when the quarters are struck, a system seldom found before the introduction of rack striking work. This clock required a very large count wheel for controlling the number of blows, which had to be accurately made. The clock has subsequently been altered from cross-beat to pendulum control. This may have been done when the clock was fairly new, in view of its date. The alteration included cutting a piece out of the top plate, which slightly interferes with the engraving. EJT

Riefler, Sigmund The firm of Clemens Riefler of Nesselwang and Munich was founded in 1841, and has a long history of making precision mathematical instruments and clocks. Sigmund Riefler, born in the Bavarian village of Mariarein, improved the performance of astronomical regulators by removing the escapement from acting directly on the pendulum, impulsing the pendulum via the suspension spring by a rocking support controlled by two escape wheels, one for impulsing, the other for locking. In 1899 Riefler adopted invar for the pendulum, with a short

245

1

2

1 **Sayller, Johann** Table clock of gilded bronze with unusual striking train and dials indicating day, date and month; *c.*1650. Württembergisches Landesmuseum, Stuttgart.

2 **Sayller, Johann** Movement of 246/1 showing the large striking train fusee and the small remontoire spring barrel, re-wound every six hours; also Sayller's name plate. Württembergisches Landesmuseum, Stuttgart.

3 **Schwilgué, Jean-Baptiste Sosime** General view of the third Strasbourg clock, completed in 1842. Strasbourg Cathedral.

3

length of aluminium for the final compensation, and later adopted the electrical remontoire of Frank Hope-Jones, enabling him to enclose the regulator in an airtight case at reduced pressure and obtain rates of 0·01 second a day, thus making it the standard for precision timekeeping.

The University of Munich gave Sigmund Riefler an honorary doctor's degree in 1897, and his book on precision pendulum clocks was published in Munich in 1907. When

246

he died in 1912 he was the owner of the Nesselwang factory for making precision clocks. CKA/EJT

Rinderle, Thaddäus (Matthias) Matthias Rinderle (1748–1824) was born in Staufen, and showed his inclination for mechanics and mathematics while still a boy. At 19 he entered a Benedictine monastery in St Peter and was given the name 'Thaddäus'. He was sent to study at the University of Salzburg, and in 1772 he was ordained.

Rinderle's talent for solving astronomical and mathematical problems was widely known, and in 1781 he was asked to establish a mathematical museum and an observatory in another monastery. He built an astronomical clock in 1787, and the following year was appointed professor of mathematics at Freiburg.

Apart from his astronomical clock, Rinderle's main claim to fame is his hole-boring tool for inserting the wires in lantern pinions. It could also be used for drilling the rims of wheels in striking clocks for inserting the pins that acted on the hammer tail.

Rinderle's clock of 1787 is now in the museum at Furtwangen. The movement was made by Rinderle himself, but the carved dial was the work of Matthias Faller. The part of the movement that provides for normal timekeeping is typical of Black Forest clocks with wooden arbors and lantern pinions, but the astronomical work has solid pinions.

Rinderle's epitaph on his memorial in the cemetery at Freiburg states 'He has defined many things mathematically with figure and letter but the hour of death remains more unknown than x.' EJT

Sayller, Johann Born in Angelburg, Lower Bavaria, Sayller (1597–1668) moved to Ulm where he was master in 1646. His careful workmanship and original ideas made him famous in his own time, and many of his watches and clocks are now in European museums.

The Württembergisches Landesmuseum, Stuttgart,

possesses a rolling-ball clock by him which shows the day of the month and the age and phases of the moon. This clock has quarter-hour marks outside the hour figures and what is virtually a concentric minute hand – a very early application of this feature. Sayller made another attempt to achieve constant force in a clock in the same museum in which there is an enormous fusee on the striking side, its wheel meshing with a pinion which winds a small spring to keep the going train in motion. In this primitive type of remontoire the greatest power is exerted after the clock has struck twelve, and the least after six o'clock, but the cycle repeats itself every six hours and thus evens matters out. EJT

Schuster, Paulus There were several makers named Schuster in Nuremberg in the 16th century, but Paulus Schuster, who died in 1634, is particularly remembered for his masterpiece, an elaborate clock now in the Mathematische Physikalische Salon, Dresden. It has eleven dials with a wide range of astronomical indications and automata. It is thought to have been completed in 1591. EJT

Schwilgué, Jean Baptiste Sosime The second Strasbourg clock made by the Habrecht brothers in 1574 was worn out by the late 18th century, and Schwilgué (1776–1856), who saw it at the age of ten, was determined to make it go again. He moved from Strasbourg to Silestat, where he had to study on his own, made some horological productions, and invented a calendar for showing automatically the movable feasts of the Church. This resulted in a commission from the mayor of Strasbourg to repair the cathedral clock. It was decided to replace the Habrecht mechanism with one of Schwilgué's, which would be more accurate, and he began work in 1838. The clock was going for the first time in 1842.

Schwilgué's calculations for the astronomical indications are of a high degree of accuracy. The movement of the clock is much smaller than the Habrecht movement and is controlled by a gridiron pendulum. The automata of the previous clock all perform, and a cock crows at 12 o'clock. The Habrecht movement is now in the local museum together with the cock from the original clock of 1352.

Schwilgué worked on the Strasbourg clock with his pupils Albert and Théodore Ungerer. After his death in 1856 his son took over its maintenance for two years. EJT

Sorg, Josef Sorg (1807–72) was born in Neustadt. His father, also called Josef, was also a clockmaker, and they both produced various types of Black Forest clock [241/6].

Josef Jr is best known for the *Sorguhr* which became a speciality of Neustadt. It was a Black Forest clock scaled down to an even smaller size than the *Jockele*. The wheels were not much larger than those of a pocket watch. By 1845 at least three other Neustadt makers were producing them but the Sorgs were the most important clockmakers in the town. Though *Sorguhren* are often placed *c.* 1800 the dates of Sorg's birth and death show that they originated much later than this. EJT

See also: Jockele (Section I).

Treffler, Johann Philipp One of many craftsmen who hailed from Augsburg, Treffler (1625–97) probably left the

4 Rinderle, Thaddäus
Rinderle's astronomical clock with traditional wooden parts of Black Forest style, in a case carved by Matthias Faller, 1787. Historische Uhrensammlung, Furtwangen.

4

5 Treffler, Johann Philipp
Night clock in the Italian style with fixed light slits for the quarter-hours and rotating hour slit, *c.*1675. Museo della Scienza e della Tecnica, Milan.

5

city before completing his training, as he did not become a master and in consequence was continually in trouble with the authorities after his return in 1664.

He went to Florence and worked for the Grand Duke Ferdinand of Tuscany. He first appears in the records as clockmaker to His Highness in 1656, his work being to produce scientific instruments. The evidence is not clear, but it seems that the idea of a pendulum clock came to him about that time, and a drawing of it was sent to Christiaan Huygens in Holland. In the clock Treffler made for the Medici Palace in Florence the escapement was placed at the bottom. The only other signed clocks by Treffler also include this arrangement.

In 1664 Treffler returned to Augsburg, and worked as a maker of mathematical instruments incorporating clockwork.

Two night clocks by Treffler are known, one in the Museum of Science at Milan and the other in the Hessisches Landesmuseum at Kassel. The arrangement of movement and pendulum suggests Maltese clocks. EJT

Winterhalder & Hofmeier The Winterhalder family came from Friedenweiler, and Anton Winterhalder, born 1838, married the daughter of Johann Hofmeier. He established himself in Neustadt in 1895 and the business was continued by his four sons, each running his own factory while one of the four handled all the marketing. The firm of Winterhalder & Hofmeier began by making simple clocks which were a mixture of Black Forest and American styles. Their early models had wooden plates, although spring-driven, but later movements were constructed entirely of metal. Towards the end of the 19th century the firm exported a great many clocks to Britain, and special emphasis was given to the reproductions of British styles. A 12-in. dial movement incorporating a fusee was made which is virtually indistinguishable from the prototype except for the firm's initials W & H SCH on the backplate. The firm came to an end during the depression of the 1930s [242/1]. EJT

Clockmaking in Great Britain

The early history of clockmaking in Britain, as in other European countries, is shrouded in some mystery. Undoubtedly, however, turret clocks were known in the country by the late 13th century, examples being recorded at Westminster Palace in 1288 and at Canterbury and old St Paul's, London, in 1292 and 1286 respectively; others are known. Several church clocks are recorded for the 14th century including, among others, Exeter, Norwich, Wells and Salisbury, while stories of Peter Lightfoot and the more firmly based knowledge of Richard of Wallingford suggest the close connection between the Church, the spread of learning in medieval times, international cultural connections within Europe and the development of clockmaking expertise [152/1].

By the 15th century the construction of public clocks in church towers was well established, although they did not have dials, and it is likely, too, that by this period smaller clocks for use within the monasteries were well known in England, though not necessarily made there. It was not until the 16th century that clocks began to appear in England as domestic articles. Records show that chamber clocks were purchased for the household of Henry VIII, and the iron-framed weight-driven hanging clock, which was the precursor of the lantern clock, was well known among Elizabeth I's possessions. Whether these clocks were of foreign make, or made by foreigners working in England, is not altogether clear, but it is most likely that they were imported, since the craft of fine clockmaking was well established at this period in south Germany, Italy and France, while it had not become identified as a separate craft in England.

It was not until the incorporation of the Clockmakers' Company in 1631 that there is evidence of the craft being firmly established and widely organised among Englishmen in London, and the period, therefore, of the late 16th and early 17th centuries can be said to be transitional, with the English clockmaking trade emerging from the European tradition.

Following the establishment of the Clockmakers' Company, and especially after 1660, clockmaking blossomed with an intensity which made London the clockmaking centre of the world. Several factors combined in the second half of the 17th century to produce the scientific pre-eminence manifest in scholars of the stature of Robert Hooke and the founding of the Royal Society, which obtained its charter in 1660. In clockmaking the new search for scientific progress saw the introduction of the pendulum in the mid 1650s, for which England as well as Holland can be given credit. The period also saw the introduction of the balance spring, for which invention Robert Hooke claimed the honour in 1660, and it is also clear from Hooke's diaries that the wheel-cutting engine, which was to make such an important contribution to clockmaking accuracy, was being used in London at this time. This was the period of Thomas Tompion, Daniel Quare, the Knibbs, Edward East and many others who not only raised the art and science of mechanical clockmaking to the highest point it had ever reached but also established

1 **Turret clock,** four-post, iron-framed, with its original foliot and verge escapement, formerly at Cassiobury Park, Hertfordshire; c.1620. British Museum, London.

2 **Turret clock,** chair-frame type, pinwheel escapement, pendulum 29 ft 6 in. long; designed and built by the engineer John Buchanan, Ramsbottom, 1834. St Andrew's Church, Ramsbottom.

3 **Lantern clock,** 30-hour, with alarm, signed 'William Bowyer – fecit', London, c.1640. British Museum, London.

4 **Table clock,** eight-day, spring-driven, signed 'Edwardus East, Londini', London, 1665–70. British Museum, London.

5 **Bracket clock** in a 'chinoiserie' painted case with side carrying handles, by Francis Atkins, London, c.1765. Fitzwilliam Museum, Cambridge.

6 **Mantel clock** in the 'Gothick' style, signed 'Widenham, 13 Lombard Street, London'; with eight-day, three-train movement, quarter-striking on eight bells, the hour on a gong; c.1835. Private collection.

1

a purely English style for longcase, bracket and lantern clocks [249/3], [249/4].

Two further factors which carried English clockmaking forward in the second half of the 17th century were the interest and patronage of the royal court and the establishment of the Royal Observatory at Greenwich (1675), which was primarily intended to produce accurate astronomical charts for mariners. The use of astronomical observations for navigation, especially in the determination of longitude, led to the passing of an act in 1714 establishing the Board of Longitude and offering a scale of awards for any 'generally practicable and useful' method of finding longitude at sea. It is impossible to overestimate the importance of this legislation (whatever its ultimate shortcomings might have been) in forwarding the endeavours of several horologists of the finest calibre, whose work during the 18th century was built on the technical and theoretical achievements of the late 17th-century clockmakers. The work of George Graham, who did not attempt to solve the longitude problem but was a most exacting horologist, of John Harrison, Thomas Mudge and, in the later 18th century, Thomas Earnshaw and John Arnold can hardly be over-valued [259/5].

While the precision makers of the 18th century were furthering their ideas in London, the trade of domestic clockmaking continued to flourish there and in many other regions of the country [250/3], [258/1]. Lantern, longcase and bracket clocks (although fewer in number, started to be made in the provinces during the 17th century, but their manufacture increased enormously during the 18th, in a wide variety of qualities and styles. Regional variations developed so that it is possible to distinguish the clocks of one area from another. Research in the clockmaking of specialised areas is now being promoted to explore the characteristics of different makers and 'schools' of clockmaking, and far more credit is now given to country makers than was previously the case. The regional variations within the basic 18th-century style are too complex to itemise in detail here.

The gradual onset of industrialisation, the growth of regional populations and the marked improvements in transport heralded the national decline of the craft of fine clockmaking in the early decades of the 19th century. Mass-produced standard movements and parts started to be made for the regional clockmakers, though more remote areas such as Scotland and Wales maintained their regional characteristics longer than others. In spite of the decline of the craft in the provinces, however, London maintained its position as the centre for fine-quality clock production until well into the 19th century [249/6].

Besides the Industrial Revolution, other factors caused the breakdown of the English tradition of clockmaking in the 19th century, the most important being the importation of vast numbers of extremely cheap yet reliable clocks from Connecticut. Also important was the development of cheap German and Austrian clocks, which undercut the English product. Although England lost its pre-eminence in domestic clockmaking in the 19th century, chronometer makers retained their worldwide prestige, supplying the international merchant fleets and navies.

There are other British clockmakers of the 19th century whose work has recently been re-evaluated, such as James Ferguson Cole and Thomas Cole. The field of electrical horology is another area which has only recently begun to receive its share of attention, and in this sphere, too, British horologists of the 19th century made extremely valuable

2

contributions, although they were digging the grave of traditional English clockmaking. The pioneers were Alexander Bain, C. O. Bartrum, Percival A. Bentley, Robert Mann Lowne, Thomas J. Murday, James Ritchie, Francis Ronalds, R. J. Rudd, Herbert Scott and Charles Wheatstone.

In the present century the work of Frank Hope-Jones and William Hamilton Shortt must go down to posterity for their production of the electrical-mechanical free-pendulum clock which was the ultimate in precision timekeeping until the advent of the quartz-crystal clock. Its electrical remontoire was one of the finest horological devices ever conceived.

Great Britain also maintained its prestige in the 19th and early 20th centuries in turret-clock engineering [249/2], [256/2], in which firms such as Gillett & Johnston, Gent & Co., J. B. Joyce & Co., John Smith & Sons and Thwaites & Reed, made outstanding contributions. Many of their clocks are still giving good service on the national and international scene, and those firms remaining in business still supply mechanical turret clocks to countries where electrical supplies are unreliable. AS

Arnold, John Born in Bodmin, Cornwall, Arnold (1736–99) followed his father's (also John Arnold) trade of clockmaker. He went to Holland where he is

3

4

5

6

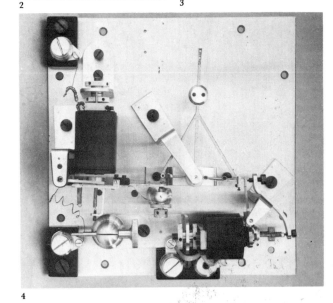

said to have received additional watchmaking experience. Returning to England *c.* 1755, he obtained financial assistance to open a London shop at Devereux Court, off the Strand.

Arnold produced a number of fine chronometers, employing outworkers rather than constructing everything himself. He was one of the first to popularise the use of the chronometer at sea as he was able to produce timekeepers at considerably lower prices than his contemporaries.

There is no space here to review Arnold's pivoted-detent escapement, various balances, his later employment of the spring detent usually ascribed to Thomas Earnshaw, and the bitter controversies that took place between Earnshaw and Arnold. His son carried on his business, which in 1843 was purchased by Charles Frodsham. Arnold's invention of the helical hairspring with terminal curves was a most important contribution to the development of the art of chronometer making. DJB

Bain, Alexander Born at Houstry Dunn near Watten in Caithness, Scotland, Bain (1810–77) went to Edinburgh in 1831. By 1837 he had travelled to London and was working in Clerkenwell as a journeyman clockmaker. He attended lectures on electricity at the Adelaide Gallery, these turning his mind to the application of electricity to clocks. By June 1840 he had made models of a printing telegraph and an electric clock, which he showed to Charles Wheatstone in August 1840, the cause of a deep and lasting dispute between the two men. Later, in 1844, Bain returned to Edinburgh and practised as an 'Electric Clock and Telegraph Maker'. In 1846 he demonstrated the synchronisation of clocks between Edinburgh and Glasgow over a telegraph line erected by himself. In 1851 he exhibited his electric clocks at the Great Exhibition in London and had a manufactory in Old Bond St. His wife died in 1856 leaving Bain broken-hearted; his career declined and he lost all his money in litigation. He died a disappointed man at the newly opened Home for Incurables at Kirkintilloch in January 1877. CKA

Barker, William Barker (d. 1786) was one of the outstanding northern English clockmakers. Having been admitted a freeman of Wigan as 'gunsmith and clockmaker' in 1754, he appears to have resisted the efforts of rival clockmakers to trade in the town, and from the number of high-quality clocks which survive he clearly ran a good business.

His masterpiece of *c.* 1775–80 is now in the Merseyside County Museum at Liverpool. This complicated clock, with hour- and quarter-striking on seven bells, in a northern-style mahogany case some nine feet high, has a rising and setting sun indicator giving amplitude and declination, a globular moon showing its phases and the times of high water at Bristol, Hull, London and Dover, an equation of time indicator, a zodiac scale and a daily calendar, Old Style and New Style (the latter came into use in 1752), with important ecclesiastical dates marked on a scale which has to be manually adjusted annually, the dominical letter appearing at the bottom edge of the dial [46/3]. AS

Barlow (Booth), Edward Booth (1636–1716) was born

1

2

3

4

1 **Bain, Alexander** Portrait. Science Museum, London.

2 **Bain, Alexander** His patent electric clock, with case removed to show pendulum and sliding electrical contacts; *c.*1850. Royal Scottish Museum, Edinburgh.

3 **Barker, William** Mahogany longcase clock; by William Barker of Wigan, Lancashire, *c.*1780. Victoria & Albert Museum, London.

4 **Bartrum, C. O.** Mechanism from Bartrum's clock for impulsing the master pendulum at one-minute intervals, signalled by the slave clock. Science Museum, London.

5 **Bentley, Percival A.** Earth-battery-driven clock, showing the pendulum with sliding contacts, moving solenoid and fixed magnet; *c.*1912. Leicester Museum and Art Gallery.

6 **Arnold, John** Marine chronometer signed 'John Arnold. London, No 3, Invt. & fecit', which accompanied Captain Cook during his second voyage in 1772. This chronometer is not mounted in gimbals. Royal Society, London.

7 **Bentley P. A.,** (left) greeting Sir Oliver Lodge when he visited Bentley's works at Leicester.

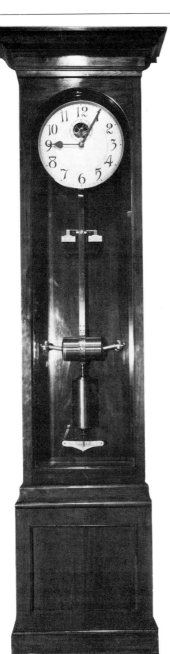

5

6

7

near Warrington, Lancashire. He was ordained priest at the English church in Lisbon and through a condition in his godfather Ambrose Barlow's will took the name of Barlow. He devised a number of improvements, for example in rack striking and repeating work for clocks, first used by Thomas Tompion in 1676. In 1686 he applied for a patent for his repeating work for watches; Daniel Quare heard of this and also produced a repeating watch. An invention of Barlow's which was to become significant long after he was dead is the cylinder escapement, which he patented in conjunction with William Houghton and Thomas Tompion (no. 344 of 1695), the only patent in which Tompion's name occurs. The patent describes the invention as 'ballance wheele either flatt or hollow, to works within and crosse the centre of the verge or axis with a new sort of teeth made like tinterhooks to move the balance and the pallets of the axis or verge ...'. CKA

Bartrum, C. O. Bartrum was a British physicist who, during the First World War, developed an electro-magnetically driven free pendulum. The free pendulum receives an impulse below its bob from an arm released by an electromagnet operated by the slave clock. After the impulse a pair of contacts close to reset the arm and also transmit a synchronising signal to the slave clock to correct both the rate and the phase of the slave pendulum. If the slave pendulum is early, the jewelled roller on the gravity arm falls on the top of the free pendulum pallet and does not give impulse until the correct part of the impulse face is reached; if late, the impulse is shortened slightly. The impulse is given every minute and lasts for only a fraction of a second. Had Bartrum's free pendulum been mounted in an evacuated cylinder and its construction been of higher quality, he would have surpassed the free pendulum of W. H. Shortt made in 1921, since in Bartrum's clock the pendulum is interfered with less. CKA

Bentley, Percival A. Bentley was apprenticed to A. E. Slater & Oakes, who produced electrical equipment for the Great Western Railway, and secured a scholarship to the Liverpool Technical School. In 1902 he made a self-winding electric skeleton clock for which he was awarded a

1

1 **Clement, William** Turret clock originally at King's College, Cambridge until 1817, then in St Giles' Church, Cambridge; signed 'Gulielmus Clement, Londini fecit 1671', with anchor escapement (possibly not original). Science Museum, London.

2 **Brockbank, John and Myles** Engraving showing the basic layout of a Brockbank chronometer; from Pl. XV of Abraham Rees, *Clocks, Watches and Chronometers*, 1819–20.

3 **Dent, Edward John** Arnold & Dent rosewood-cased travelling clock, with folding brass carrying handle and enamel dial, *c.*1835. Private collection.

4, 5 **Dent, Edward John** Original model of Grimthorpe's gravity escapement, made by E. J. Dent. The rear view, 253/4, shows the train remontoire, with its small driving weight and its fly mounted horizontally above. The escapement is six-legged with a single gravity arm. The view from the winding side, 253/5, shows Harrison's maintaining power on the great wheel. It is said that this was the design preferred by Dent for the Great Clock of Westminster. R. A. Stephens, Lake Forest, Illinois.

medal by Lord Derby. Bentley decided to start his own business as a watchmaker and jeweller in Burton-on-Trent, and began to think of making electric clocks. He took out his first patent in 1910. He had not studied the history of electrical horology and independently reinvented Alexander Bain's clock almost 70 years later, even using the earth battery. A factory was opened in 1912 to produce Bentley's earth-driven electrical clocks. These clocks were sold all over the world. On an earth battery they had excellent performances; the example in Leicestershire Museum ran for 40 years without attention. He remained Chairman of the Bentley Engineering Company until some time after 1954. CKA

Brockbank, John & Myles John Brockbank, apprenticed in London in 1761, took in his brother Myles (d. 1821) as an apprentice in 1769 when he himself became a Liveryman of the Clockmakers' Company, which he remained until 1806. The firm continued as Brockbanks until 1806 and under other names for many years. John Brockbank was much involved in making chronometers and employed Thomas Earnshaw for finishing. It was while working on pivoted detent escapements, *c.*1780, that Earnshaw conceived his idea of using a spring detent. The result of his showing this to John and Myles Brockbank was, he claimed, John Arnold's application for a patent on this concept.

The firm of Brockbanks produced chronometers for a number of years. The early ones contain Peto's 'cross detent' in which the passing spring and detent are 180° apart. Peto, about whom little is known, worked for the Brockbanks and created this system to avoid patent infringement. John Brockbank devised a banking system of delicate construction using the outer turn of the hairspring. DJB

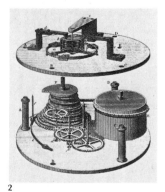

2

Clement, William Clement (1638–1704), a leading London clockmaker of the late 17th century, was born at Rotherhithe, and was brought up by his brother, who had a seagoing background. William became an anchorsmith for a few years, but on moving to Southwark he turned to clockmaking and in 1671 he made a clock (now in the Science Museum, London) for King's College, Cambridge, which incorporated a recoil escapement. As a result of this work and his previous trade, Clement was credited with the invention of this type of escapement. The King's College clock, with its side-by-side trains, has a strangely up-to-date look about it, although the escapement may not be original.

Clement made many domestic clocks and became Master of the Clockmakers' Company in 1694. DFN

Clockmakers' Company Early in the 17th century London's clockmakers were beginning to feel the competition from immigrant craftsmen who had begun to follow their trade in England, most of them being French Huguenots. The London clockmakers at that time were members of the Blacksmiths' Company, but being eager to establish themselves as an independent craft they petitioned

3   4   5

the Crown to form their own company. This petition, though opposed by the blacksmiths, was granted by Charles I on 22nd August 1631, and it gave the London clockmakers control of the conditions of their trade up to a distance of ten miles from the centre of the city. The first master of the Company was David Ramsay. Since the charter was first granted the governing body of the Clockmakers' Company has consisted of the master, three wardens and ten or more assistants.

The motto of the Clockmakers' Company is *Tempus rerum imperator* ('Time is the ruler of all things'). AS

Cole, James Ferguson One of the most highly regarded horologists of the 19th century, Cole (1798–1880) has long been known as 'the English Breguet'. Although best known for his watches, Cole made several clocks in the style of Breguet [234/2], as well as producing the first datable English carriage clock in 1823.

Cole became a vice-president of the British Horological Institute soon after its foundation in 1858, but refused renomination in 1863 because of his dissatisfaction with the way that the Institute was administered. DJB

Cole, Thomas Thomas Cole (1800–64) was all but forgotten until 1975, when John B. Hawkins's *Thomas Cole and Victorian Clockmaking* appeared, since he was eclipsed by the fame of his brilliant brother, James Ferguson Cole. Thomas was born at Nether Stowey in Somerset and was taught the craft of clockmaking by his father, James Cole. James Ferguson Cole was at 3 Old Bond St, London, in 1823, where Thomas joined him in partnership until 1829. Thereafter he worked as a watchmaker until 1845, when he removed to Clerkenwell describing himself as a 'designer and maker of ornamental clocks'. Charles Frodsham reported on Thomas Cole's clocks in the International Exhibition of 1862: 'nothing could exceed the beauty of design and good taste of the varied models and general excellence of workmanship.' Thomas Cole's clocks were sold to retailers and generally bore their names on the dial, which contributed to the gradual decline in his fame. CKA

Congreve, Sir William Congreve (1772–1828), the son of a British general, studied law, but by 1795 had developed the rockets for which he is best remembered. In 1811 he became equerry to the Prince Regent and a fellow of the Royal Society, in 1812 a member of parliament. He succeeded to the baronetcy on the death of his father and became Comptroller of the Royal Laboratory at Woolwich Arsenal. He died in Toulouse.

In 1808 Congreve took out a patent for his rolling-ball clock. The original was presented to the Prince Regent and is now in the Rotunda at Woolwich; it bears the inscription, 'The first experiment of a new Principle for the Measurement of Time, invented by Wm. Congreve Esq.; is humbly presented to His Highness the Prince of Wales, 1808'. It is driven by what appears to be a cannon ball, though further models were driven by springs [35/7]. CKA

Dent, Edward John Dent (1790–1853) was apprenticed to a London tallow chandler, which he found distasteful. Fortunately he was housed with Richard Rippon, who made repeating mechanisms for London-made watches. At Dent's request Rippon trained him in this branch and Dent continued in it until 1830, when John Roger Arnold, John Arnold's son, took him in to run his business at 84 The Strand. For ten years (1830–40) Dent and J. R. Arnold were associated and the firm was known as Arnold & Dent. During his years with Arnold a number of chronometers were issued with interesting and unusual features resulting from Dent's intensive experiments with balances and hairsprings to eliminate middle-temperature error and hairspring aging.

Dent made a number of fine astronomical clocks, some of which incorporated the ideas of Sir George Biddell Airy, the Astronomer Royal. It was this connection that led to Dent receiving the contract for the clock for the new Houses of Parliament. DJB

Earnshaw, Thomas Born in Ashton-under-Lyne, Earnshaw (1749–1829) was apprenticed at 14 to a watchmaker. He appears to have gone to London as a

1 2 3

4 5

watch finisher soon after his apprenticeship. Having limited means, he taught himself the art of watch jewelling, but also developed other specialised skills in order to do finishing work, as the term was then used. In his famous *Longitude, An Appeal to the Public* (1808), he set forth his claim to be the inventor of the spring-detent escapement, which soon revolutionised the manufacture of marine timekeepers.

Earnshaw was without doubt an extremely gifted horologist and might have accomplished even more had he not been so obsessed with the idea that he was being persecuted by everyone. His form of detent escapement came to be the accepted form and is still manufactured.

Earnshaw worked by fine finishing only the acting portions of his timekeepers and he was able to produce superior chronometers at reasonable prices. Time has proved his escapement design to be above reproach. DJB

Eiffe, James Sweetman Eiffe (1800–80) for many years operated a successful chronometer business in Lombard St, in the City of London. He devoted considerable attention to the middle-temperature error of chronometers and developed auxiliary compensations both by using a curb acting on the hairspring and by a discontinuous auxiliary on the balance. Eiffe's auxiliary might have received more

general acceptance had not Robert Molyneaux, another well-known maker, simultaneously developed a similar – and in early trials more successful – auxiliary. In addition to chronometers, Eiffe made some outstanding regulators.

Eiffe is now chiefly remembered for his auxiliary compensation which, to his death, he felt was insufficiently appreciated, and for the odd names he gave some of his chronometers instead of numbers. Though the Admiralty apparently did not object to the 'Off-She-Goes' or the 'Arctic Circle' they refused to accept the 'Fool of the Strand' (a reference to Edward Dent) without a change of name. Upon Eiffe's retirement his business was taken over by John Fletcher, a Lancashire pinion maker turned chronometer maker. DJB

Ellicott, John Ellicott (1706–72) was the son of a London clockmaker of the same name at Austin Friars. One of the most distinguished of 18th-century London clockmakers, he produced clocks and watches of superb workmanship.

He is best known for his compensation pendulum, described in a paper presented to the Royal Society in June 1752, wherein a brass rod, fixed at the top to the iron supporting member, slides within and raises the bob through adjustable levers in heat, and lowers it in cold, to compensate for the variations in the iron. Though highly regarded at the time, it could not compete with George Graham's mercury pendulum owing to its jerky action. A simplified version was used in fine-quality French mantel clocks in the mid 19th century with some success. DJB

Eureka Clock Co. Founded by the Kutnow brothers, manufacturing chemists, to exploit the invention of the Eureka electric clock by the American T. B. Powers (English patent no. 14614 of 1906). A large terraced house at 361 City Rd, London, was used as a manufactory, and a large number of the clocks were being made when the new clock was announced in *Electrical Engineering* of 17th June 1909. Each Eureka clock was individually hand-made and therefore expensive, making sales lower than expected. The venture was a financial failure, and the Kutnows eventually gave the clocks to customers who purchased more than a certain amount of their chemical products. Production came to an end in 1914, and the remaining parts were sold in the nearby Caledonian street market. About 10,000 Eureka clocks were made. CKA

Facio de Duillier, or Fatio, Nicholas Facio (1664–1753) is primarily known in the clockmaking world because of his invention of the means for working precious and semi-precious stones for watch jewels, also crystal and glass, for which he took out a patent (no. 371) in 1704 with Peter Debaufre. He was a Swiss optical worker residing in London, following periods of working in Paris and The Hague. He was a fellow of the Royal Society and a member of the Académie des Sciences. AS

Finney, Joseph Finney (c. 1708–72) stands with a few other north-country clockmakers, e.g. William Barker of Wigan, Thomas Lister of Halifax, John Whitehurst of Derby, as a maker who strove for higher things. He was born near Wilmslow, Cheshire, and became a freeman of Liverpool in 1733. A few longcase clocks signed by him are known before 1760. During the 1760s he made two complex astronomical musical clocks of the highest quality, and in 1769 a year regulator of great originality in a tapering pedestal case.

Links with the high-quality London trade have been established for Finney: he was making clocks and scientific instruments, notably a barometer and pyrometers, for George III in the 1760s. When he died, his obituary described him as 'an eminent Clockmaker . . . his excellence procured him the notice and encouragement of the first Personage of the Kingdom.' AS

Frodsham, Charles The father of Charles Frodsham (1810–71), William J. Frodsham, was active in the London firm of Parkinson & Frodsham and there, from 1824, trained his son Charles. At that time chronometer manufacture was the main concern of the firm, and Charles took a great interest in this art. At 20 he submitted two chronometers, Nos 1 and 2, to the Admiralty premium trials. He was awarded the second prize of £170 for his No. 2 in 1831.

Upon his marriage to Elizabeth Mill in 1834, Charles Frodsham began to issue chronometers from his new home at Barossa Place. In 1837 he opened a shop at 12 Finsbury

1 **Ellicott, John** Detail of the bob of Ellicott's compensated pendulum, in which can be seen the pivoted levers that raise the bob as temperature increases, together with lateral lever adjusting screws and spring below to assist the compensation effect. Time Museum, Rockford, Illinois.

2 **Eureka Clock Company** 'Eureka' electrically driven clock (side view) with glass dome removed; c. 1910. Science Museum, London.

3 **Frodsham, Charles** Boxed chronometer with auxiliary compensation balance used by the Astronomer Royal in Egypt, to survey the transit of Venus in 1874. Private collection.

4 **Earnshaw, Thomas** Earnshaw's large model of his escapement made for the Board of Longitude in 1804. National Maritime Museum, London.

5 **Frodsham, Charles** An eight-day chronometer movement. Private collection.

6 **Fromanteel, Ahasuerus, I** Longcase clock made in London, c. 1670. British Museum, London.

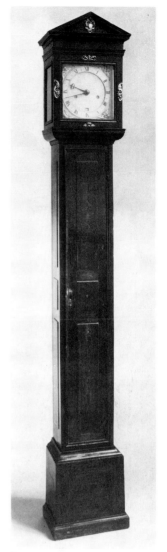

6

Pavement but finding this too small he moved to No. 7 the following year. Superb two- and eight-day chronometers were sold from Finsbury Pavement. One eight-day chronometer, No. 1477, was giving a creditable performance 135 years later.

In 1843 Frodsham purchased J. R. Arnold's business at 84 The Strand, where he greatly expanded his business, experimenting extensively with watch design. He wrote a number of papers and in 1849 published *On the Laws of the Isochronism of the Balance Spring*, which won him the Telford Medal. The pocket chronometers and lever watches he produced are distinguished by their elegant simplicity of appearance and excellent performance.

The business was carried on after his death by Harrison Mill Frodsham and his brother-in-law George Moore as Charles Frodsham & Co., a firm that over a century later, maintained a reputation second to none. DJB

Fromanteel, Ahasuerus, I Generally considered a Dutchman, though Brian Loomes has shown (*Antiquarian Horology*, Vol. 9, No. 2) that the origins of the family, who came to England as religious refugees, were probably Flemish, Ahasuerus Fromanteel I (1607–92) was a second-generation Englishman. He went to London from Norwich

1

1 Grimthorpe, Edmund Beckett Denison, Lord The great bell of Westminster, the manufacture of which was superintended by E. B. Denison and which was cast by Warner & Sons, Norton, near Stockton-on-Tees. It was called 'Big Ben' after Sir Benjamin Hall, the corpulent Commissioner of the Office of Works. The *Illustrated London News* of 1st November 1856 shows it being drawn to the Palace of Westminster by a team of sixteen horses.

2 Gillett & Johnston Ltd Turret clock movement and hands for the Shell Mex Building, Thames Embankment, London. Note the counterpoise weights on the hand driving arbors.

3 Fromanteel, Ahasuerus, II Hague-type, with the moon's phases and calendar; signed 'Ah. Fromanteel, Amsterdam', *c.*1695.

in 1629, and worked as a clockmaker in East Smithfield, applying to join the Blacksmiths' Company in 1631. He was accepted on showing proof of his apprenticeship. In 1631 the Clockmakers' Company was granted a charter and Fromanteel applied late in 1632 to join. In 1658 Fromanteel's advertisement for the new pendulum clocks he was making appeared in *Mercurius Politicus*. John Fromanteel, his eldest son, had been studying the making of pendulum clocks with Salomon Coster from September 1657 to May 1658, and Christiaan Huygens's *Horologium* appeared in September 1658 also. Fromanteel survived until just before his 86th birthday. CKA

Fromanteel, Ahasuerus, II Ahasuerus II (1640–1703) was the son of the famous English clockmaker Ahasuerus Fromanteel I, who produced the first pendulum clocks in England after his eldest son John (brother of Ahasuerus II) had learned the new techniques in The Hague from Salomon Coster. Ahasuerus II married Anne Brown in London in 1672 and settled with his brother John in the Vijgendam in Amsterdam *c.*1680. In an advertisement of 1695 he called himself the 'English clockmaker on the Dam'.

Fromanteel made some exceptionally beautiful longcase clocks, which had both velvet-covered as well as brass-covered dials. FK/JLS

Gent & Co. John Thomas Gent (b. *c.*1840) formed a company in Leicester in 1872 trading under his name. Its business was principally in light electrical engineering and very early it developed and exploited the electric bell.

Electric clocks of the master and slave variety were compatible with Gent's manufacturing ability. The company developed the 'Pul-syn-etic' system, which became very popular and is still in production. A natural development was a suitable movement for a turret clock and Gent's produced their 'waiting train'. This had all the power necessary for large and exposed clock hands, but adjusted its demands of power to suit the circumstances.

2

Many waiting-train systems were made and they found their way to all parts of the world.

Shortly after its formation the company changed its name to Gent & Co. It naturally diversified considerably; nevertheless, it still retains an important section dealing with public time-distribution systems. DFN

Gillett & Johnston Ltd William Gillett started as a clockmaker in Hadlow, Kent. He moved to Clerkenwell, London, and in 1844 to Croydon, Surrey, where he was later joined by Charles Bland. The firm traded as Gillett & Bland, manufacturing turret clocks. In 1877 Arthur Johnston became a partner and the name was changed to

Gillett & Johnston. The activities were extended to include bell founding and the supply of carillons and carillon machines.

Cyril Johnston, son of Arthur, joined the firm on the death of his father in 1916. He died in 1950, and seven years later the bell foundry was closed. The business was transferred to the Portland group of companies for a few years, but became independent again in 1965. The company still makes turret clocks if required, and undertakes overhaul and maintenance. DFN

Graham, George Born in Cumberland, probably in the Kirklington district, Graham (1673–1751) is considered one of England's greatest horologists. The inventions for which he will always be remembered are his improvements to the cylinder escapement, if he did not actually invent it, the dead-beat escapement, and the mercury-compensated pendulum. The latter two were of particular importance in precision timekeepers. Graham was the first London clockmaker to encourage John Harrison. He was a member of the Clockmakers' Company from 1695, and its master in 1722, a fellow of the Royal Society, to which he read many papers, from 1720, and a member of its council in 1722.

George Graham came from an excellent horological background in that he entered into the service of Thomas Tompion and married his niece. The lifelong friendship between the two men caused Tompion to leave his business to Graham when he died in 1713. When Graham died he was buried in Tompion's tomb in Westminster Abbey. AS
See also Clockmaker's Company; Escapement, cylinder (Section II); Escapement, dead-beat (Section II); Pendulum, mercury-compensated (Section II).

Grimthorpe, Edmund Beckett Denison, Lord Denison was born in 1816, became Baron Grimthorpe in 1886, and died in 1905. A lawyer by profession, he specialised in the litigation that surrounded the purchase of land for the first railways, from which he amassed a considerable fortune. He was also a first-rate horologist and took a particular interest in turret clocks. He promoted in England the flat-bed type of construction and developed the gravity escapement, the common variety of which bears his name.

He will always be associated with the Great Clock of Westminster, popularly known as 'Big Ben'. The horologists of the day thought that the accuracy he specified would be unobtainable, but he stubbornly persisted and carried through the work in spite of quarrelling with almost everyone concerned. In the event the clock completely vindicated Denison's design and proved highly reliable [116/2], [116/4]. DFN

Harrison, John and James One of the brightest lights in the horological firmament, John Harrison (1693–1776) was the son of a carpenter, born at Foulby, near Wakefield, Yorkshire. Though trained as a carpenter, he showed an early interest in natural philosophy and music, and a borrowed copy of the lectures of the mathematician Nicholas Saunderson kindled his interest. He and his younger brother James (1704–66) appear when very young to have repaired clocks in Barrow-on-Humber, to which their family had moved. They made clocks of wood of

4 Harrison, John and James
Longcase clock movement, the earliest recorded by John Harrison, made when he was twenty. The clock has a wooden movement and dial, anchor escapement, and silvered brass chapter ring. The bottom left spandrel is removed to reveal the winding hole. Signed and dated 1713. Clockmakers' Company Museum, London.

5 Graham, George Equation regulator of month duration; dead-beat escapement and mercury-compensated pendulum; *c.*1740. British Museum, London.

3

4   5

remarkably good design and sound construction, ordering the grain and laminating the wheels to provide maximum strength. John Harrison's achievement in making, by *c.*1736, a successful marine timekeeper resulted in fame so great that James was, until recently, largely overshadowed.

The familiar story of John Harrison's long struggle to solve the longitude problem by an accurate and seaworthy timekeeper is described at length in the studies by William Laycock (1976) and Humphrey Quill (1966). Harrison's determination, dedication and ultimate success have inspired others for over 200 years. His successful timekeeper, No. 4 (in the National Maritime Museum, Greenwich) is the most famous ever made. With its

1

2

3

4

complicated remontoire it is clearly described in Gould's historical, technical and rhetorical masterpiece, *The Marine Chronometer*, 1923. It achieved the goal, and proved the possibility of accurate longitude determination, though it was soon made obsolete by simpler devices. DJB

Hindley, Henry Henry Hindley of York (1701–71) was for many years neglected, but through recent research by R. J. Law and J. R. M. Setchell, his contribution to English clockmaking has been recognised. He was probably born in Manchester and served his apprenticeship to the Manchester firm of Scholfield before moving to York where in 1731 he was granted the freedom of the city.

A contemporary described Hindley as 'one of the greatest mechanical geniuses and most accurate artists of the age'. About 1734 he made a year clock incorporating a globe moon and having a dead-beat escapement, and in 1750 he built a turret clock for York Minster which is still in use, though it has had later alterations. It originally had a temperature-compensated pendulum of four-seconds beat, i.e. 52 ft 2 in. long, extremely long pendulums of this kind being found in several later turret clocks in Yorkshire.

Hindley appears to have used John Harrison's grasshopper escapement in one of his clocks. In his spring-driven bracket clocks he used his own form of fusee with the winding square at the wide end.

Perhaps Hindley's most significant work was his contribution to the art of dividing. He became friendly with the mechanical engineer John Smeaton (1724–92), builder of Eddystone lighthouse, who read a paper to the Royal Society in 1785 in which he described a dividing engine constructed by Hindley which was cut with 360 teeth at its edge, advanced by an endless worm screw. This idea was not original to Hindley, but his carefully designed form of it was of previously unparalleled accuracy. Hindley also devised other tools including a form of inclined-plane fusee engine. It has been suggested that Hindley was the first to adopt triangular bars for lathes. AS

Hooke, Robert Born in the Isle of Wight, Hooke (1635–1703) was educated at Westminster School and Oxford University, and became assistant to Robert Boyle, the famous chemist. He accepted the post of 'Curator of Experiments' to the newly formed Royal Society in 1662. His

Hindley, Henry Eight-day
clock in a lacquered case; by
Henry Hindley, York, c. 1750.
Castle Museum, York.

Harrison, John *Left*: Harrison's
No. 4 Timekeeper, first officially
tested in 1761, then again in 1764
after which he received an instal-
ment on his reward of £20,000.
Right: Timekeeper No. 5, completed by John Harrison and his
son William in 1770. National
Maritime Museum, London, on
loan from the Ministry of Defence
(Navy).

Hindley, Henry Fusee engine
devised by Hindley in which the
pitch of the cutter carrier is determined by means of an adjustable
inclined plane. From Abraham
Rees, *Clocks, Watches and
Chronometers*, 1819–20.

4 Hooke, Robert Watch movement and bob of a 12-ft pendulum
in a reconstruction of Hooke's experiment with a pendulum kept
going by the balance of a watch.
Science Museum, London.

5 Regulator with enamel dial
and equation-of-time work; by
William Dutton, c. 1780.
Fitzwilliam Museum, Cambridge.

5

1

many contributions to horology include the wheel-cutting engine, the use of the long pendulum with a heavy bob (1669), the balance spring for watches and the conical pendulum drive for telescopes.

Hooke had many disputes with other scientists, including Christiaan Huygens, Isaac Newton, Henry Oldenburg, and others; in all of these he appears to have had a genuine case for grievance. For example, in the dispute about the origination of the balance spring for watches, Huygens claimed priority in 1674, and Hooke disputed it. This can easily be resolved, since the paper written by Hooke on the subject is dated 1660 (it is now at Trinity College, Cambridge). CKA

Hope-Jones, Frank The youngest of nine children, Hope-Jones (1868 – 1950) was born at Hooton Grange. He was apprenticed to an insurance company, but when his brother Robert, eight years older, founded the Hope-Jones Organ Co., he took Frank to assist him. George Bennet Bowell was an apprentice in the firm and had ideas of applying electricity to winding clocks, and in 1894 they produced a self-winding electrical clock, covered by a patent in 1895. They moved into a workshop at Furnival's Inn for a short time, then to Victoria St, forming the Synchronome Syndicate Co. Following a difference of opinion, Bowell left in 1899, but Hope-Jones continued alone, improved his Synchronome electric clock, and became the most successful maker of such clocks. He raised the electric clock from an object of derision to become the world's standard timekeeper. CKA

Joyce, J. B., & Co. The English firm of Joyce of Whitchurch was founded in the 1690s and remained in family control until 1963. Its turret clocks were of superlative quality. In the 19th century, the company was associated with E. B. Denison (Lord Grimthorpe) and took up his gravity escapement and flat-bed design. In conjunction with George Bennet Bowell, Joyce produced an electrically driven turret clock, but it was not widely adopted. The last member of the family to run the business was Norman Joyce, who had no son or close relative anxious to take over and, following a serious fire in 1963, sold the company to John Smith & Sons of Derby. DFN

Kendall, Larcum Born at Charlbury, Oxford, Kendall (1721–95) was apprenticed as a watchmaker to John Jeffreys in Holborn, London. His reputation must have been high, as he was one of those appointed to examine and pass judgement on John Harrison's timekeeper No. 4.

After some reduction of his original price, he agreed to make a duplicate of Harrison's No. 4 for £450, to see if reproduction by other makers was possible. In two years, with Harrison's advice, he completed the piece, an almost exact copy apart from minor exterior details. Though it was exquisitely finished, Kendall omitted the regulator dial and other superfluities, the use of which Harrison had himself dispensed with [260/1].

Kendall's piece, known as 'KI', underwent satisfactory testing at Greenwich and was carried by Captain Cook in the *Resolution* on his second voyage of exploration, from 1772 to 1775. Its performance was remarkable and Cook,

1 Kendall, Larcum Chronometer No. 1, made as a duplicate of Harrison's No. 4, finally adjusted and completed in 1770. National Maritime Museum, London. On loan from the Ministry of Defence (Navy).

2 Knibb, Joseph Mantel clock in an ebony case with gilt metal mounts, pierced top and eagle feet; by Joseph Knibb, London, c. 1672. Leicester Museum and Art Gallery.

3 Knibb, Joseph Longcase clock in veneered, ebonised pearwood case; by Joseph Knibb, London, c.1670. British Museum, London.

2   3

not given to superlatives, praised it as 'our never failing guide'. DJB

Knibb, Joseph Knibb (1640–1711), one of the finest English clockmakers of the 17th century, was apprenticed to his cousin Samuel Knibb in Newport Pagnell, Buckinghamshire, and moved to Oxford about 1662, establishing his own business there. In Oxford he experimented with a type of cross-beat escapement as applied to a seconds (royal) pendulum which, like the 16th-century version, employs separate arbors for the two pallets.

The death of his cousin Samuel, who had moved to London some years earlier, may have induced Joseph to take his business to London in 1670. He obtained the freedom of the Clockmakers' Company and began to make all types of clocks – longcase, lantern, bracket, hooded wall clocks – of individual design incorporating such features as skeleton chapter rings and Roman striking, which economised on the number of strokes used for striking. Joseph made night

1 Mercer, Thomas Modern carriage clock with chronometer-type escapement and leather carrying case.

2 Mercer, Thomas Movement of 262/1 showing 'spotted' plates, fusee with Harrison-type maintaining power and chronometer-type platform escapement.

3 Mudge, Thomas Perhaps Mudge's first attempt to produce a longitude timekeeper, this clock is known as the 'Ilbert Mudge lever clock'. It has an exceptionally accurate lunar train, and is controlled by a large balance employing a lever escapement; 1777. British Museum, London.

4 Mudge, Thomas Rear view of 262/3 showing the two large, antifriction rolls, the large balance beating seconds, the temperature compensation device acting on the two balance springs and the remontoire 'let-off' and fly at the bottom. British Museum, London.

5 Lowne, Robert Mann Photograph taken when he was in his sixties. Private collection.

6 Murday, Thomas John A Murday electrically driven wheel-balance clock, shown without its glass dome; c.1910.

clocks and was possibly the first to use the tic-tac escapement.

Besides Joseph and Samuel, there were other clockmaking members of the Knibb family, including Joseph's younger brother John (1650–1722) and his cousin Peter (born 1651). Joseph made a clock for Wadham College, Oxford (now in the Museum of the History of Science, Oxford), which incorporates what is perhaps the earliest example of an anchor escapement, and the invention of the anchor escapement is now usually attributed to him rather than to William Clement, though the controversy has by no means been settled. AS/DFN

Kullberg, Victor Born in Visby, Sweden, and apprenticed to a chronometer maker in 1840, Kullberg (1824–90) was thoroughly trained in all aspects of the art since there was no source for semifinished materials in Scandinavia. However, standards were high, and this accounts for the fact that many Swedish-trained workmen did superb work in other countries. Kullberg was employed in the famous house of Jürgensen in Copenhagen, whence he visited

London to see the Great Exhibition in 1851. Moved by the magnificent work displayed by eminent London makers, especially the extensive exhibit of Charles Frodsham, he found employment without difficulty in London as an escapement maker, and by the late 1850s he had established his own business as a chronometer maker. His work was soon recognised as outstanding. In 1882 the Astronomer Royal pronounced Kullberg's chronometer No. 4066 the finest ever on trial.

After his death the business was carried on by his son and nephew, and later by others. Many fine watches of both lever and chronometer construction were sold by Kullberg, some to other retailers, such as Moore of Dublin and Belfast, and Russell of Liverpool. DJB

Lightfoot, Peter A legendary figure of the English west country in the early 14th century. He was a monk at Glastonbury Abbey and was reputed to be a skilful craftsman. Under the direction of the abbot, Adam of Sodbury, it is said he made an elaborate astronomical clock for the abbey.

At the time of the Dissolution of the Monasteries, the story continues, the clock was transferred to Wells Cathedral. There is a similarity between the dials of the clocks at Wells, Exeter, Wimborne and Ottery St Mary, and this led to the association of Peter Lightfoot with all of them. The legend has persisted, particularly at Wimborne. In reality, only a few mechanical clocks existed in England in Peter Lightfoot's time, and no local records associate them with his name. The four clocks mentioned were probably made in the late 14th or early 15th centuries, after his time.

The legend was strengthened by a comment from Leland's record of Wells in the 16th century, which implies that the Wells clock was by Lightfoot. DFN

Lister, Thomas Lister (1745–1814), an English north-country clockmaker, produced fine and complicated clocks, often incorporating musical work and containing complex astronomical information. His father, also called Thomas (1717–79), was a clockmaker of repute and himself the son of a clockmaker of Keighley, Yorkshire.

Among several outstanding clocks which survive from Lister's hand perhaps the most elaborate is an eight-day longcase clock which shows on its dial a yearly calendar with fixed and movable feast days; subsidiary dials for the dominical letter, the golden number and epact; moon indications, including a small revolving globe for the phases and rising and setting tabs; rising and setting of the sun; a star plate, with Halifax as the centre of rotation, showing the principal stars and constellations; local time in various cities and countries, with London showing G.M.T.; and the other normal day and date indications. AS

Lowne, Robert Mann Son of a doctor, Lowne (1840–1924) was born at Holborn, London. He became interested in instruments and in 1885 he produced his first horological invention, to make watches dust-proof. By 1901 Lowne was living in Catford and was well known as a scientific-instrument manufacturer. He turned his attention to applying electricity to clocks and took out a series of patents for master electric clocks and impulse dials, forming the Lowne Electric Clock Co. which supplied a master clock and 46 impulse dials to the Royal Arsenal, Woolwich in 1903. Lowne's master clock is one of the most complicated and difficult to understand, but it gave excellent service over many years. He died with over 24 patents to his name. CKA

Mercer, Thomas, & Son Thomas Mercer (1822–1900) was born at St Helens in Lancashire. He went to London where he learned chronometer springing from John Fletcher, who later took over James Eiffe's business. For some years he was at 45 Spencer St, and later at 161 Goswell Rd, Clerkenwell, where he made fine marine and pocket chronometers. He devised a modification of Robert Molyneaux's balance that was effective in reducing middle-temperature error. His name survives in the firm still making chronometers at St Albans. DJB

Mudge, Thomas One of the world's most celebrated horologists, Mudge (1715–94) was born at Exeter. His

5   6

father, a clergyman and schoolmaster, apprenticed him to George Graham.

It is the invention of the lever escapement that will ever keep Mudge's name famous. While he appreciated the fitness of this escapement for pocket watches he did not pursue it, but as a result of his examination of Harrison's timekeeper No. 4 turned all his attention to the perfection of a marine timekeeper. Leaving the running of the business, which he had taken over on Graham's death in 1751, to his partner William Dutton, he went to Plymouth. There, his work on the marine timekeeper culminated in a piece of superlative workmanship which, however, contained a highly complex and delicate constant-force escapement. Though very effective in Mudge's hands, this device could not be considered practical because of the skill and expense involved in making it [269/4].

Mudge made two other famous marine timekeepers known as 'Blue' and 'Green', based on the same principles. These all demonstrated their maker's exquisite craftsmanship but had little effect on the course of development of the chronometer. After his death, his son, a lawyer, ventured to have such timekeepers produced, but encountered financial problems as they were simply too expensive to make. DJB

Murday, Thomas John Little is known of the personal affairs of Murday (19th–20th centuries) beyond the fact that he was basically an electrical engineer who turned his attention to the application of electricity to timekeeping, and took out a series of patents from 1897 to 1921. All had some connection with improvements in electric clocks, but none of them affected the development of electrical timekeeping in any significant way.

The most interesting of his ideas is the Murday electrically driven wheel-balance clock of 1910, in which he applied the principle of the Hipp-toggle to a large horizontal balance having a period of oscillation of four seconds. Such clocks were manufactured by the Reason Manufacturing Co. of Brighton: about 300 were produced. CKA

Parkinson & Frodsham The London firm of Parkinson & Frodsham was established c. 1800 by William Parkinson and William James Frodsham. W. J. Frodsham, born in 1778, was considered an expert on the work of John

1 Pearson, Page & Jewsbury
Water clock activated by means of a chain attached to a float which descends as water is slowly released from the cylinder. Early 20th century; the clock bears the spurious date of 1672. Burnley Borough Council, Towneley Hall Art Gallery and Museum, Burnley.

2 Ritchie, James, & Son
Ritchie's sympathetic pendulum mechanism shown removed from its case. The pendulum is electrically driven 'in sympathy' with a master clock. Royal Scottish Museum, Edinburgh.

3 Shelton, John Shelton regulator, probably used by Captain James Cook on his second and third voyages to the Pacific in 1772 and 1776. The tripod was made in 1968 at the National Maritime Museum, London, to fit existing case holes and based on an old engraving. National Maritime Museum, London, on loan from the Royal Society.

4 Scott, Herbert Front view of the Scott electric clock, with outer glass case removed, c.1910. Science Museum, London.

5 Shelton, John The Radcliffe Observatory, Oxford, showing the Shelton clock at the bottom of the staircase. From Ackermann, *History of Oxford, its Colleges, Halls and Public Buildings*, Vol. II, 1814.

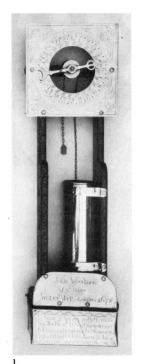

Harrison and Thomas Earnshaw. Parkinson & Frodsham continued making and selling chronometers and fine watches for nearly a century.

Their early chronometers are often small and housed in spring-loaded inner cases for shock resistance. Parkinson & Frodsham's aim seems to have been to produce what the marine market required at a reasonable price. They did, however, make many splendid pieces and some of their eight-day examples are particularly elegant. DJB

Pearson, Page & Jewsbury In the early part of the 20th century the firm of Pearson Page made ornamental brass products at their Ileene Works, Sherlock St, Birmingham. Among these products was a series of waterclocks made in an antiquated style. These waterclocks were never intended to deceive; nevertheless, even experienced horologists have been deceived including F. J. Britten who included one in the sixth edition of his *Old Clocks and Watches* as a genuine example. These waterclocks all bear fictitious names and are dated in the 17th century; none of them functions as a timekeeper, and no genuine waterclock of English make of this date exists. CKA

Quare, Daniel A contemporary of Thomas Tompion, Daniel Quare (1647–1724) was a London clock- and

watchmaker of equal repute who made fine lantern, longcase and bracket clocks and watches for the fashionable market of his day.

Although Quare will always be associated with London clockmaking of the highest quality, his main scientific claim to horological fame rests upon his invention of a type of quarter-repeating work for watches. It operated by pushing a single push-piece, and was preferred to that of Edward Barlow. Quare has also been associated with the introduction of the equation of time indication in clocks, but it would seem that all the equation work used by English makers of the period was produced by Joseph Williamson who had worked for Quare at one time and used the principle of the equation kidney. Current opinion, however, credits Christiaan Huygens with this invention [270/1].

Quare was admitted to the Clockmakers' Company in 1671, and was its master in 1708. About 1718 he took his former apprentice Stephen Horseman into partnership, and after Quare's death, Horseman continued to manage its affairs. AS

Richard of Wallingford The son of a blacksmith, Richard (1292–1336) was a brilliant mathematician. He lived from the age of ten in the Priory of Wallingford, a subsidiary of St Alban's Abbey. In 1326 he was elected abbot of St Albans.

While abbot of St Albans he devised a large astronomical clock which was constructed for him by Roger of Stoke. Unfortunately, nothing remains of the clock, which was said by Leland to have no parallel in Europe. In the 1970s a number of manuscripts describing it came to light (they are discussed by John North in *Antiquarian Horology*, September 1975). More important to the designer than ordinary daily timekeeping was the accuracy of the representation of the movement of the heavenly bodies. The clock had a striking train that struck the hours 1–24. The escapement was not a crown wheel and verge, but a special form utilising a pair of coaxial wheels, the spokes of which extended beyond their rims and acted as pallets on a pair of detents attached to a vertical spindle surmounted by a heavy arm. Locking and unlocking took place as this spindle oscillated in the manner of a verge and foliot. A model of the escapement [152/1] is in the British Museum, London. DFN

Ritchie, James, & Son Little is known about the elder Ritchie. When Joseph Durward, clockmaker at 2 Leith Street, Edinburgh, retired in 1819, he advised his customers to patronise James Ritchie 'whose professional abilities and attention to business will give every satisfaction to his employers'.

From 1836 the firm was known as James Ritchie & Son, the son being awarded many prizes for his work in connection with electricity applied to horology, for example a paper on electro-sympathetic clocks and time signals, and another on a method of correcting clocks by hourly currents of electricity. A brass inlaid mahogany bracket clock dated 1841 and signed 'Ritchie & Son' is illustrated in John Smith, *Old Scottish Clockmakers* (1921). James Ritchie retired in 1842, by which time the firm had a world-wide reputation. Frederick James Ritchie carried on the business, concentrating mainly on applications of electricity to horology. CKA

Rudd, R. J. Born of a farming family in Norfolk, Rudd (1844–1930) was apprenticed to Maudsley, Sons & Fields, engineers at Thameside. From 1872 until 1893 he worked for the turret-clock manufacturers Gillett & Bland at Croydon, retiring early but continuing to develop his ideas in horology in retirement. His main achievement was the synchronising of a slave clock by a free pendulum in 1898, which he patented. Professional horologists did not understand his ideas which were only rescued from oblivion when Frank Hope-Jones and Sir Henry Cunynghame visited Rudd in 1908 to see the models.

Rudd retired to Norfolk in 1930 and died in the same year. Though Rudd's ideas were not adopted, they inspired Hope-Jones to conceive the principle of the free pendulum, later realised by William Hamilton Shortt. CKA
See also Rudd's clock (Section I).

Scott, Herbert Born in Bradford, Yorkshire, Scott (1865–1943) interested himself in the improvement of electric clocks, his first patent being taken out in 1893. Further work enabled Scott to take out a new patent in 1902 and another in 1903.

Scott's electric clock used the well-known Hipp-toggle principle invented by Matthäus Hipp in 1834, but improved by a special count wheel having notches cut in the tips of the count-wheel teeth turned by a gathering pallet from the pendulum. As long as the arc of the pendulum's swing was sufficient to gather the teeth of the count wheel (and thus drive the hands) the gathering pallet passed over the notches in the count-wheel teeth, but when the amplitude fell the gathering pallet dropped into a notch and then closed a contact to give impulse to the pendulum. Unlike almost all other clocks, the pendulum swung in a plane at right angles to the dial. The clocks were manufactured by the American Electrical Novelty and Manufacturing Co., 102 Charing Cross Rd, London. Scott's principles did not advance the science of electrical horology. CKA

Shelton, John A famous London maker of regulators and precision clocks, Shelton (18th century) was apprenticed in 1711, was made a freeman of the Clockmakers' Company in 1720, and was active as a maker for many years in Shoe Lane. He was a fine workman producing clocks used in a number of 18th-century observatories, including one at Göttingen supplied as a gift from the king. Rudolph Ackermann's *History of Oxford* (1814) has a coloured plate of the Radcliffe Observatory there with its Shelton clock at the foot of the staircase. His clocks are usually fitted to small cases with curved sides to the waist giving them a delicate but pleasing appearance. DJB

Shortt, William Hamilton Shortt (1882–1971) spent all his working life in the employment of the London and South Western Railway and its successors. In 1908 one of the main problems with trains was to establish their safe speed on curved tracks. An accurate time standard was required which Shortt devised. In 1910 he met Frank Hope-Jones who offered him facilities for making experimental models. Many designs were produced before Shortt invented his 'hit-and-miss' synchroniser for a slave clock and his 'free' pendulum. He personally fitted the first Shortt free-pendulum clock in the Edinburgh Observatory in 1921 [266/1]; its performance astounded the whole astronomical fraternity, and it was adopted as the time standard for the world, revealing the earth's irregularities of motion for the first time. For his work Shortt was awarded the gold medal of the British Horological Institute in 1928, and made a fellow in 1932. The Clockmakers' Company awarded him the first Tompion Medal in 1954. CKA

5

Smith, John, & Sons One of the leading turret-clock makers in the world, Smith's had its origins in the company founded in Derby in 1736 by John Whitehurst. Smith's of Derby took over William Potts of Leeds in 1937 and Joyce of Whitchurch in 1965.

Traditionally the company has been famous for its flat-bed movements made in all sizes and supplied throughout the world. Most use pinwheel or gravity escapements. The firm pioneered the synchronous movement for turret-clock purposes and have developed electrically operated striking and chiming trains to go with them. DFN

Thwaites & Reed Turret-clock makers of Bowling Green Lane, London. One of the early members of the firm, Aynsworth Thwaites, was made a freeman of the Clockmakers' Company in 1751. He had already (1740) made a clock for the Horse Guards.

Over the years the company has made over 300 turret clocks. They have been responsible for the automata of Fortnum & Mason, the well-known grocer of Piccadilly; for overhauling the astronomical clock at Hampton Court; and for providing an astronomical dial for the Smithsonian Institution in Washington. The company is now largely concerned with overhaul and maintenance of turret clocks, including the Great Clock of Westminster ('Big Ben'), and have developed an automatic winder.

Thwaites' have always engaged in horological activities other than turret clocks, and have been concerned with making longcase clocks, bracket clocks and chronometers. After reorganisation in 1974, the company left its old-established London works and moved to Hastings in Sussex. DFN

Tompion, Thomas One of England's greatest horologists, and certainly the most famous, Tompion (1639–1713) has been referred to as the 'father of English clockmaking'. He was born at Ickwell Green Northill, Bedfordshire, the son of a blacksmith. He possibly followed that trade himself, but the early years of his life remain a mystery. In 1671 he was elected as a 'Brother by Redemption' in the Clockmakers' Company of London (meaning that he had followed an apprenticeship of some other company). His business was established in Water Lane in 1674, and at this time he made the acquaintance of Robert Hooke who entrusted to him the application of the spiral balance spring to a watch, according to Hooke's design, and Tompion thus became the first English maker to do so. In 1674 Tompion was commissioned to make two accurate clocks for the Astronomer Royal, John Flamstead, at the Greenwich Observatory, which he made using pendulums of two-seconds beat (14 ft long) suspended above the clock movements and impulsed below their bobs. Another milestone in Tompion's career was his collaboration with two Lancashire men, Edward Barlow and William Houghton, in patenting, in 1695, a type of cylinder escapement, while a little earlier, in 1688, he had made Barlow's repeating mechanism for a watch which competed against that of Daniel Quare. In 1695 Tompion devised a clock with equation work which was made for William III, though for this development Joseph Williamson claimed priority. From 1701 Tompion was in partnership with Edward Banger. He became Master of the Clockmakers' Company in 1703, but the Banger partnership came to an end in 1708. Three years later he formed a new partnership with his nephew George Graham, who was a more gifted horologist.

As well as making some 650 clocks, most of very high quality, the business was responsible for about 6,000 numbered watches, and in these, as in Tompion's clocks, precision of manufacture and quality of design and craftsmanship were always of the highest order. AS

Vulliamy The Vulliamy family of London clockmakers consisted of Justin (1712–97), Benjamin (1747–1811) and Benjamin Louis (1780–1854).

Justin Vulliamy came from Switzerland to London c. 1730, and one of his most remarkable pieces is his 'Timer', a weight-driven movement (now lacking its case) fitted with a cylinder escapement controlled by a quarter-second pendulum suspended on anti-friction wheels and having nine dials which show minutes, second, third and fourth minutes, seconds, eighth-seconds, second, third and fourth seconds. Magnificently made, it would appear to have had some astronomical timing purpose, and it is thought to have

1

2

3

1 Shortt free-pendulum clock
Right: synchroniser; *left:* controlling
free pendulum.

2 Tompion, Thomas
Movement of the Tompion
chronoscope (35/4), *c.*1690.

3 Tompion, Thomas Miniature
bracket clock (timepiece only)
signed 'Tho. Tompion Londini
fecit', with alarm and pull repeat
work on two bells; *c.*1695.
Fitzwilliam Museum, Cambridge.

4 Vulliamy, Benjamin
Regulator by Benjamin Vulliamy
made for King George III and
used in his observatory at Richmond;
fitted with the grasshopper escapement and gridiron pendulum.
Science Museum, London.

5 Vulliamy, Benjamin Back of
movement of 267/4 showing extensive use of anti-friction wheels to
support the pivots of the wheel train.

6 Wheatstone, Charles Master
clock, constructed by Wheatstone's company, The British
Telegraph Manufacturing
Company. The clock is entirely
mechanical and the current generated in the coil on its pendulum,
swinging over a fixed magnet, is
used to drive subsidiary dials.

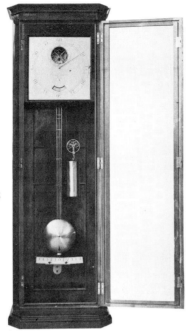

4

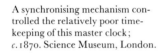

A synchronising mechanism controlled the relatively poor timekeeping of this master clock;
*c.*1870. Science Museum, London.

5

been made for George III's observatory at Richmond.

His son Benjamin was also a producer of high-quality
clocks, but as many Vulliamy clocks are simply signed
'Vulliamy', it is not always easy to tell which member of the
family was basically responsible. Perhaps Benjamin's most
famous clock is the regulator made for George III for his
observatory, now in the British Museum, London.

Benjamin Louis Vulliamy, son of Benjamin, continued
the tradition of fine-quality clocks; he was also a man of
great learning and a fellow of the Royal Society. He made
several turret clocks and submitted proposals for the Great
Clock of Westminster ('Big Ben') which were rejected. He
appears to have supplied new movements to replace those of
several old clocks and to have altered the dial signatures,
but if this practice seems rather dubious today it must be remembered that attitudes to such matters have changed. AS

Wheatstone, Charles Wheatstone (1802–75) was born in
Gloucester. In 1816 he was sent to learn the musical-
instrument trade with his uncle in the Strand, London:
however, he spent most of his time devising and carrying
out experiments. In 1834 Wheatstone was appointed
professor of experimental philosophy at King's College,
London, and attempted to measure the velocity of light,
obtaining too high a value at about 280,000 miles per
second. Co-operating with William Fothergill Cooke, he
devised many telegraph instruments. He came into conflict
with Alexander Bain over the priority of invention of the
electric clock in 1840 and the printing telegraph, but up to
the time of his death he had never succeeded in making an
electric clock which operated properly. CKA

Whitehurst, John A geologist and skilled mechanic,
Whitehurst (1713–88), born at Congleton, Cheshire, moved
to Derby in 1736. He made a clock for Clumber Park,
Nottinghamshire, and another for Derby Cathedral. He
became a burgess of Derby and presented a clock to the
town hall.

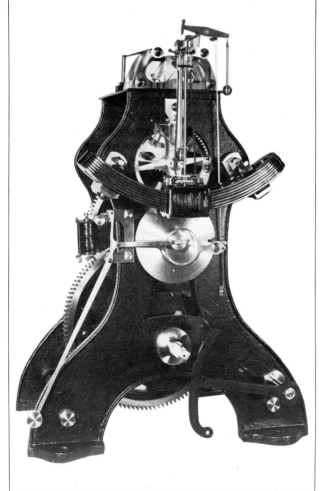

6

1

Whitehurst was a member of the Lunar Society, which included such notable figures as Josiah Wedgwood, James Watt and Joseph Priestley. In association with Matthew Boulton, and advised by James Ferguson, Whitehurst made several ambitious astronomical clocks. Latterly he moved to London where he became involved in standardisation of the coinage. He was appointed 'Stamper of the Money Weights' in 1775 and became a fellow of the Royal Society in 1779.

He was succeeded by his nephew, also John Whitehurst. A third of that name continued the business well into the 19th century. The firm made a number of chair-frame clocks. In 1856 the business became John Smith & Sons. AS/DFN

Williamson, Joseph A London horologist who died in 1725, Williamson was involved with equation work for clocks. Williamson worked for Daniel Quare and in 1719 claimed to have made a 400-day clock for Quare. He also claimed to have made all those clocks with equation movements sold in England, and therefore to be the true inventor of the 'contrivance'. The use of an equation kidney would appear to have been devised by Christiaan Huygens, but as Williamson made clocks with this feature to cause a rise and fall in the acting length of the pendulum it may be correct to say that Williamson *made* all those in England of his day, even though he could not claim to have invented the idea. AS

See also Equation of time (Section V).

Clockmaking in Italy

The history of horology in Italy, according to Enrico Morpurgo, the greatest expert on the subject, is one of dusty documents rather than beautiful objects. The clocks that have come down to us may be interesting, but they are certainly not of the quality one might expect from reading the codices of Giovanni Dondi or Leonardo da Vinci, or the writings of Galileo Galilei or the della Volpaia family, or from letters from kings to Italian artists ordering clocks with remarkable characteristics. All that has come down to

us from Dondi, Gianello Torriano, Pietro Giudo, Filippo Brunelleschi and many others are documents, a few drawings, and very few pictorial representations of clocks.

If the birth of the mechanical clock is set in the second half of the 13th century, Italy has one of the first, if not the very first, clear description of one. In the *Paradiso* of his *Divine Comedy*, Dante clearly describes a mechanical clock and shows it as a simple one, probably the type today known as a 'monastic alarm clock' although it was intended not merely to regulate the hours of the community in a monastery, but was probably used in noblemen's houses. At the beginning of the 14th century we hear for the first time of public clocks. Galvano Fiamma, in his chronicle of Milan, describes two clocks, one in the church of San Eustorgio, the other in the church of San Gottardo. The first appeared probably before 1309 and probably indicated the hours by the striking of a bell, without dial. The second, that of San Gottardo at Palazzo, set up in 1336, rang the hours from one to 24. This is the first account of a chime that probably involved the use of a count plate. But the outstanding figure in Italian clockmaking in the 14th century was Giovanni Dondi, the son of Jacopo Dondi, who in 1344 had made what was probably the first public non-ecclesiastical astronomical clock, set up on the tower of the Palazzo dei Signori in Padua. The clock was destroyed and rebuilt by a descendant of this same Dondi, Novello dall'Orologio, in 1430.

Giovanni Dondi deserves credit for having planned and built an extremely important clock which he called *Astrario* or *Planetario*. Unfortunately it has not survived, but we have detailed descriptions of it by Dondi himself. Copies of the clock have been made from Dondi's manuscripts in recent years.

In the 15th century there is documentary evidence of the first professional clockmakers who set up workshops, took on pupils, and began to export not merely clocks but their own talents. The history of Italian clockmaking in the 15th century is enriched by two very important sources. The first is the manuscript known as the 'Almanus manuscript', dated between 1475 and 1485 and now in the library at Augsburg, which was written in Rome by Brother Paulus Almanus. In it are described 30 clocks, obviously not all Italian, and we

2   3

1 Whitehurst, John Turret clock of chair-frame design, from Milford Mill, Derby, made by the Whitehurst firm in 1808. Derby Museum and Art Gallery.

2 Lantern clock from northern Italy with a pointed case; originally verge and balance escapement, later converted to a pendulum control; the lower dial indicates the quarter-hours, as in many Austrian clocks; Italian six-hour striking; c. 1630–40.

3 Monastic alarm clock with circular balance and 24-hour rotating dial, c. 1600. Museo della Scienza e della Tecnica, Milan.

4 Mudge, Thomas Back view of movement of Mudge's first marine chronometer. British Museum, London.

4

1

1 **Quare, Daniel** Longcase clock with year-going movement and equation dial in the trunk door; *c*.1710. British Museum, London.

2 **Vulliamy, Benjamin** Vulliamy mantel clock in the French style with a marble base, gilded metal mounts, Wedgwood jasper cameos, Derby biscuit porcelain figure; *c*.1795. Lady Lever Art Gallery, Port Sunlight.

2

1

1 **Astronomical clock** with the principal time dial in the centre and ten subsidiary astronomical and calendar dials; by Domenico Mezzanotte (1731–97), about whom little is known. Private collection.

2 **Monastic alarm clock,** early 17th century with later pendulum, and rotating dial. The 'verge' action for the alarm hammer can be seen at the rear of the movement. Museo della Scienza e della Tecnica, Milan.

3 **Automata clock** with hour and minute hands and six-hour striking sequence; early 18th century, Museo Poldi-Pezzoli, Milan.

4 **Italian night clock** by Giovan Battista Gonnon, from the Church of S. Maria della Grazia, Milan, c.1670.

5 **Italian clock** with a single-handed, six-hour dial, converted to pendulum; early 17th century.

6 **Small single-handed table alarm clock** by Giovanni Speciali, Venice, early 18th century. The gut line round the winding barrel can be seen through the glazed side of the case.

3

4

5

6

are thus given a clear idea of the kind of clock that dominated the second half of the 15th century. The clocks were either weight- or spring-driven, often had alarms and 24-hour striking with a 24-hour count plate, or in two cases with a special system of main and subsidiary count plates to produce a total of 300 strokes for 24-hour striking. Some have right-angle dial and count-plate transmission, and nearly all have a dial showing the 24 hours. There are also examples which show the calendar and the phases of the moon.

The second highly important source of information is that of intarsia panels, which show objects of everyday life, including clocks. The type shown is generally that known as the 'monastery alarm clock' [273/2]. Few examples of this type have survived; as a rule they have a train of only three wheels, which transmits the movement to a dial which turns through the 24 hours, a mechanical alarm being unlocked by a movable pin placed in a selected hole in the circumference of the dial itself.

Leonardo da Vinci mentions and describes some interesting mechanisms that made the construction of clocks easier and showed that the eclectic Leonardo was himself interested in horology, although he probably never made a clock. Contemporary with Leonardo were the della Volpaia family, in particular the head of it, Lorenzo, who made clocks and astronomical instruments. He made a clock for Pope Sixtus IV, and another on order from

Matthew Corvinus, King of Hungary. As this clock was finished only after the king's death, it remained in Italy, where for years it stayed in one of the halls in the Palazzo Vecchio in Florence. This clock has been lost, but contemporaries describe it as being constructed in two spheres (terrestrial and celestial), with the mechanism for moving all the planets in the space between them.

Halfway through the 16th century another brilliant figure appeared in the world of clockmaking, the engineer Gianello Torriano, who was born at Cremona and came to the notice of Charles V, who decided to take him to Spain. There he remained for most of his life, for after Charles V's death he served his successor, Philip II. More or less contemporary with Torriano was Giovanni Maria Barocci, who began his work at Urbino. In 1570, he made, signed and dated a clock destined for Pope Pius V. The fact that it is signed makes it particularly interesting and rare, and allows a firm attribution. Many other clocks of this period are often attributed to Italian makers, but the lack of a signature always leaves the matter in doubt.

The first half of the 17th century is dominated by Galileo, who understood the isochronometry of the pendulum and discovered its laws by having a time-measuring instrument built, controlled by a pendulum. At the end of the 17th century the Camerini family made and signed weight-driven clocks contained in cases of incised gilded brass that were simple but well proportioned. About the middle of the

17th century foreign craftsmen began to arrive in Italy, and this seems to suggest a decline in Italian clockmaking compared with that of other countries, although it also shows how much Italians favoured things which came from abroad. Giovan Battista Callin went to Genoa, Johann Philipp Treffler to Florence, Jean Baptiste Gonnon to Milan, Ludovico Lanzcron to Bologna, and Hessler to Rome – to mention only a few. Yet it was at this time that Italian clockmaking entered one of its finest phases, when the Campani brothers conceived and built night clocks [277/5]. Night clocks of the Italian kind were usually housed in wooden cases with the dial made of a thin sheet of painted copper looking like a kind of altarpiece. The hours are shown through perforated discs that move along a semicircular aperture. An essential feature of this kind of clock is the silent escapement, used in order to avoid disturbing the sleeper. Clocks of this kind were exported, and were often found in the palaces of kings and nobles, for they were expensive and undoubtedly made to order for special customers.

Another type of rare night clock which may have been made in Italy at almost the same time was the projection clock, a cross between a magic lantern and a clock. The mechanism turned a sphere drawn on a piece of glass inserted in the lens, which projected the image on to the wall beside the clock. Two such clocks are known to have been made by Giuseppe Campani, who was perhaps better known as a maker of lenses than as a clockmaker. Others were made by Hessler, Lanzcron of Bologna and Treffler.

In the 18th century Antonio Bartolomeo Bertolla and Borghesi made two remarkably complicated astronomical clocks, which were presented to Maria Theresa of Austria. Special mention should be made of Bernardo Facini of Venice for his famous planisphere clock, made *c.* 1725 for the Duchess Sophia di Parma Farnese. There are 24 kinds of information given, and two pendulums, one of them with a self-compensating mechanism. This clock is now in the Vatican Museum in Rome [278/3].

A number of good clockmakers also appeared in the 19th century, some of whom are worth recalling. One of them was Giovanni Battista Rodella, who specialised in very precise astronomical clocks, some of which can still be seen in the Specola in Padua. Giuseppe Zamboni in 1810

discovered that a dry battery could be connected to an electric clock, and another remarkable man was Pasquale Andervalt of Udine, who made a clock that worked on the variations of pressure in a barometer. This was completed in 1849 and set up in Vienna, where it worked well for many years. Another of his inventions was a hydrogen clock. He made several of these, one of which is now in the Clockmakers' Company Museum, London. It consists of a crystal vase, on which stands the actual clock. Pressure of hydrogen, formed inside the vase by the insertion of zinc balls into acid, provided power to wind the movement for the clock. Finally there was Fr Giambattista Embriaco, a monk who worked at the end of the 19th century and became famous for his hydrochronometer in which water poured into alternate containers in order to give impulse to its pendulum.

Production of clocks in Italy in the 18th and 19th centuries remained at the level of a craft. Although this was sometimes a very high level, it meant that Italian clockmaking failed to make the technical progress that was made elsewhere. However, Italian clocks were unstandardised, and their individuality made them particularly attractive.

THE ITALIAN SYSTEM OF HOURS

In Italy from the middle of the 14th century the 24 hours of the day ended at sunset. In 1600 this system was modified and the last hour was assumed to be half an hour after sunset. The practical purpose of this system lay in the fact that lighting, both public and private, was poor, so it was always useful to know how many hours were left until sunset, which generally coincided with the curfew and the closing of the city gates. With this system, however, midday and dawn continually replaced each other on the clock dial: these two moments were distinct, even from the striking of the hours of prayer.

In order to follow the changes in the time of sunset during the various seasons of the year, those in charge of public clocks had to see that the dials were adjusted two or three times a month. This meant that it was impossible to control

1

2

3

4

the clock precisely, because it could only be checked at midday by comparing the time shown on a sundial with that shown on the mechanical clock.

In almost all other parts of Europe the clock showed twelve at midday and midnight. This system did not reach Italy until the middle of the 18th century, and many Italian cities still continued to use the old system until the early years of the 19th century. In some complex clocks the indication of the time, Italian-style, took place automatically, without the dial having to be changed manually every so often. A mechanism gradually moved the hour ring through the 24 in such a way that the figure 24 moved into the position under the hour hand only 30 minutes after sunset. Such a mechanism was the masterpiece of Facini and other astronomical clockmakers. It is worth recalling the fairly common pocket-watch known in the last century, with a double dial, one for the time in the French or foreign style, the other for the time Italian-style. The hands of the two dials were set independently, but since they were synchronised it was necessary to regulate the Italian hour hand every day, or nearly every day. Tables showing the daily variation, which allowed people to unify the two, were therefore distributed. These watches were made in Switzerland. Italy's persistence in keeping to a 24-hour system unlike that of the rest of Europe hindered the development of clockmaking. AL

Almanus manuscript The Almanus manuscript was discovered in the Staats- und Stadtbibliothek at Augsburg *c.* 1947. It was written in Rome between 1475 and 1485 by Paulus Almanus, who was presumably a Franciscan or Dominican monk of German origin. We do not know exactly what his duties were in Rome, but from his manuscript it is clear that he was deeply interested in clocks and had the chance to analyse and note the characteristics of clocks in every detail. The manuscript is, therefore, an exceptional document, since it shows precisely the level clockmaking technology had reached in Rome at the end of the 15th century.

Some though not all the clocks were made in Italy, as the names of their makers show. They included Isaac Mediolani from Milan, Jacobus de Fabriano, Johannetis Virentinus from Florence and Antonius da Grassis, who was almost certainly from Milan. The manuscript is also interesting because in it there appear for the first time examples of certain noteworthy characteristics in clocks, among them the separate minute hand, the verge escapement with curved-faced pallets, the special action required in clocks for striking which have no 'warning' system and which employ what is known as 'overlift', a striking movement with double count plates, and in one clock a spring clutch action between the hour hand and the main wheel, for setting to time. The clocks described by Almanus mainly used weights, but eight of them had a spring and fusee. They were presumably made of iron, and were generally built between two flat plates connected by vertical strip bars. Often the movements have right-angled transmission, especially to the dial and the count plates. Clocks of the kind described are extremely rare today. It is very difficult, in Almanus's manuscript, to distinguish the various kinds of national and regional clocks of the time,

1 Lantern clock with alarm, six-hour striking and verge escapement; by Gandolfi, Bologna, mid 18th century.

2 Monastic clock called a 'mechanical hour', with verge escapement and simple form of *sürrerwerk* striking, using four hammers on the same bell. It was used during prayer, with a single hour dial, striking the four quarters; northern Italy, mid 18th century.

3 Mantel clock of rococo style; by Bartholomeo Ferracina, Venice, *c.* 1750.

4 Carriage clock with striking mechanism, and alarm setting dial on the left; by Luigi Gatteschi di Poppi, Tuscany. late 18th century. The hands are missing.

5 Small brass-cased carriage clock with alarm; signed 'Toscanus Mediolani, Milan'; late 18th century.

6 Almanus manuscript A page (2° cod. 209 folio 38) illustrating the going train of a spring-driven, 12-hour clock which belonged to the Cardinal of Naples. The balance, escape wheel, train wheels and fusee are clearly shown. Manuscript written in 1480. Staats- und Stadtbibliothek, Augsberg.

5

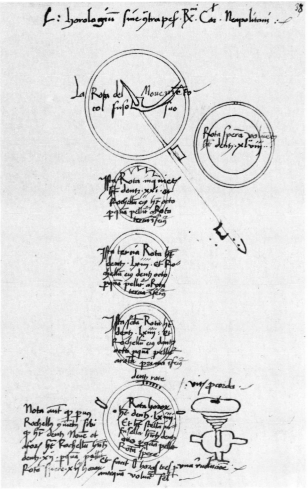

6

1 Bertolla, Antonio Bartolomeo
Mantel clock by Bertolla showing the day, date, month, and fitted with striking, chiming and alarm; *c.* 1750.

2 Dondi, Giovanni Folio from *Tractatus Astrarium*. Biblioteca Antoniana, Padua.

3 Barocci, Giovanni Maria Note the clock by Barocci in this portrait by Titian of the Duchess of Urbino in the Pitti Palace, Florence.

4 Bertolla, Antonio Bartolomeo Dial of a complex astronomical clock by Borghesi and Bertolla, 1764. Smithsonian Institution, Washington, D.C.

5 Campani, Pietro Tommaso Monumental night clock, dated 1681.

6 Campani, Pietro Tommaso Movement of 277/5 showing mainspring barrel, striking count plate (2 × 6 hours), bell and hammer. Only one barrel was used for time and strike.

1

2

3

4

particularly since none of the eight spring-drive clocks is attributed to a particular maker, and many of the others are similarly of unknown origin. AL

Barocci, Giovanni Maria Barocci had a workshop with Giovanni Battista Barocci in Pesaro in the mid 16th century, and with him made a series of splendid clocks, mostly for their patrons, the della Rovere family. One was the famous clock for Giudobaldo II della Rovere which was given to Pope Pius V. This clock is powered by a single spring and shows the movement of sun, moon and planets.

One of the few 16th-century Italian clocks to survive, it is now in the Bernard collection, Paris. Another clock made by the Barocci family is in the red hall of the chapel of St Philip Neri in Rome. This is a small oval clock with a striking movement, dated 1563 and signed 'Giovan Maria Barocci Urbino'. AL

Bertolla, Antonio Bartolomeo Born at Rumo in the Trentino, Bertolla (1702–89) was extremely hardworking and made a large number of excellent clocks, inspired by the Austrian school to which he belonged.

He is particularly famous for two astronomical clocks built in collaboration with Francesco di Mechel Borghesi (1723–1802) in 1763 and 1764 and afterwards presented to Maria Theresa of Austria. One of them has disappeared but is described in a pamphlet published by Borghesi entitled *Novissima as Perpetua Astronomica Ephemeris Automatica Theorico Pratica*. This clock showed the 'hours, the minutes and seconds, the current year, the month and the days of the week, the dominical letter, epact, and thus the day of all the feast days, both fixed and moveable, the solar cycle, the golden number, the Roman indication, the dominant planet of any year and its sign, the phases and age of the moon, and all the motions of the sun and the moon as well as longitude, latitude, eccentricity, etc.; also all solar and lunar eclipses, both visible and invisible ...'. Bertolla's second astronomical clock is today in the Smithsonian Institution in Washington.

Bertolla's workshop has been completely reconstructed, with the original tools, in the Museo della Scienza e della Tecnica in Milan. AL

Campani, Giuseppe Giuseppe (17th century) was the youngest of the three Campani brothers from San Felice in Umbria, near Spoleto, who are celebrated for the invention of the Italian silent or night clock. In 1660, in Rome, he wrote his *Discourse of Giuseppe Campani on the subject of his silent clock, the new Archimedean spheres, and other inventions*. In the same year his brother Pietro Tommaso published a letter on the 'silent clock', claiming to have invented it. In the previous year, 1659, Giuseppe Campani had obtained from the Pope the exclusive right to make silent nocturnal clocks, a right later recognised by the Grand Duke of Tuscany. All this brought Giuseppe great fame, and a great many orders for his clocks. Among those who ordered from him were the kings of Spain and Poland and the Grand Duke of Tuscany. He was also an excellent maker of lenses and other optical instruments; he invented a lathe for lenses, with which he made his famous telescopes.

As a rule, Campani's night clocks are in the traditional form of an altar, in ebonised wood; the front is taken up by an allegorical painting, and the movement has a silent escapement [281/5].

A variant of this type of night clock is an enormous clock consisting of a wooden statue of Time, six feet high, holding up a starry globe. Inside the globe a light illuminates the hours, which advance along a slit.

In his *Discourse* Campani mentions how he accidentally applied the pendulum to clocks independently of the first efforts of Galileo and Johann Philipp Treffler. He noticed that in a clock with a vertical foliot, with which he was experimenting, part of the upper arm of the foliot accidentally fell and the mechanism continued to work regularly, like a pendulum clock. AL

Campani, Matteo degli Alimeni A priest in the church of San Tommaso and a brother of Giuseppe and Pietro Tommaso, Matteo (17th century) left no clocks, but we know of him through some of his letters. Writing to Louis XIV, he says that in 1655 Pope Alexander VII asked him to apply a pendulum to clocks, according to the ideas of Galileo. Campani says he made such a clock and gave it to

Ferdinand II, Grand Duke of Tuscany. His invention was a clock with two pendulums, described in his book *Horologium solo naturae motu atque ingenio dimetiens et numeraus momenta temporis constatissime aequilia*, 1677. It was not, apparently, a total success. In another book, published in 1668, he suggested that a clock should be made to work in a vacuum in order to achieve precise chronometry and solve the problem of longitude at sea. This idea was taken over by an Englishman, Jeremy Thacker, in 1714. AL

Campani, Pietro Tommaso A brother of Giuseppe and Matteo, Pietro (17th century) was the co-creator of the Italian night clock. In a letter dated 20th January 1694, now in the archives at Spoleto, Campani said that he also built other kinds of clock without any mechanical works, but with cylinders worked by fluids such as mercury. His night clocks have altar-shaped cases with very interesting forms. AL

Comino da Pontevico Comino (15th century) is remembered for his letter, dated 1482, to Gonzago of Mantua, in which he described in detail a clock made by him. The clock had a 'spring concealed in a brass cylinder, round which is wound a cat-gut cord, so as to make it (the spring) invisible. ... The cord is tied to the cylinder ... this movement of the thread sets all the wheels of the clock in motion.' From this it can be deduced that clocks working with a spring and fusee were known all over Europe, as indeed a number of other contemporary documents confirm. AL

Dondi, Giovanni (1318–89). The father of Dondi, Jacopo Dondi dall'Orologio, brought him up to study science: astronomy, medicine and philosophy. He was a very good physician, chosen by King Charles IV of France as his personal doctor in 1349, and he treated many other famous people, among them Petrarch. His interests were wide: he taught medicine in Padua and Florence, and published treatises on a number of subjects [276/2].

The most famous of Dondi's treatises is his *Astrario*, in which he describes in detail the construction, working and characteristics of an astronomical clock, or 'sphere', as he called it. There are ten manuscripts of the work but, unfortunately, the clock itself has not survived. However, the descriptions of it in the manuscript are so detailed that it has been possible to make several copies. One of them is in

5   6

1 Embriaco, Giambattista
Clock in the Pincio Gardens, Rome, 1872.

2 Giovanni di Dondi
Reconstruction of Dondi's astronomical clock. Museo della Scienza e della Tecnica, Milan.

3 Facini, Bernardo
Astronomical or 'planisphere' clock made for the Duchess Sophia di Parma Farnese; completed *c.*1725. Biblioteca Apostolica Vaticana, Rome.

4 Facini, Bernardo Movement of 278/3, showing the compensated pendulum of steel and silver.

5 Galileo, Galilei A working model, made in 1883, from Galileo's original drawing for the application of a pendulum to a clock. It is spring-driven and shown with the winding key. Science Museum, London.

1

the Science Museum in Milan, and several others are in museums in the United States and Europe. The clock was finished in 1364 after 13 years' work and was bought by Gian Galeazzo Visconti in 1381. He put it in the library of his palace in Pavia, but it was not there long. Several times it was repaired and was finally taken to the Castello di Rosate where Charles V saw it and asked Giannello Torriano to repair it. The clock was in such poor condition that Torriano was unable to do so; instead, he offered to make a copy. This consists of seven dials on the seven sides of the structure, one for each of the five planets then known, showing their movements, and two showing the movements of the sun and moon. In order to reproduce the slightly elliptical movement of Venus, Dondi varied the gaps between teeth on the wheels, and for the movement of Mercury he used elliptical wheels.

The recent discovery of the similar description by Richard of Wallingford of his complex, enormous astronomical clock at St Albans allows us to place Dondi's clock more exactly in its historical context. AL

Embriaco, Giambattista A Dominican priest, Embriaco was born in Ceriana in 1829 and died in Rome in 1903. In 1867 he exhibited his hydrochronometer at the Paris Exhibition. The hydrochronometer is a true pendulum clock, but the movement of the pendulum is achieved through the impulses given by a pair of containers filled, in turn, with water.

One of Embriaco's clocks has been working since 1872 in the Pincio Gardens in Rome; it was restored in 1925. Embriaco made other interesting clocks, some escapements

2

3

of an unusual kind, a night clock, and a fairly cheap alarm clock which he hoped to market on a large scale, under the name of *Sveglia Italia* ('Wake up, Italy!'). AL

Facini, Bernardo Facini (18th century) was the Venetian clockmaker who completed in 1725 a 'planisphere-clock' for the Duchess Sophia di Parma Farnese. It is now in the Vatican Museum, where there is also a manuscript of 1796, by Nicola Anito, which describes the clock and illustrates it with 24 beautiful drawings. It has a single winding square which winds three springs, and two pendulums, one of which has a self-compensating mechanism. An interesting aspect is that something similar was being attempted at the same time in England by John Harrison and George Graham. The planisphere-clock is small: its dial is $13\frac{3}{4}$ in. in diameter, and the movement is 4 in. deep. There are 24 time indications, including sidereal time, Italian time, movement of the planets in the zenith, rotation of the fixed stars, times of the equinoxes, eclipses of sun and moon, and length of day. AL

Galileo Galilei When Galileo (1564–1642) was 28 he left his native Pisa because of accusations made against him by conservative supporters of traditional learning, and took refuge in Padua where he made some of his most important discoveries, among them the thermometer, the hydrostatic balance and the telescope. Other discoveries and observations of his caused him to be considered a Copernican, and he was taken before the Inquisition in Rome and condemned to exile at Arcetri, where he died, aged 78 and blind.

At the age of 19, Galileo noticed that the time taken by the oscillations of a pendulum was constant whatever the length of the arc described. He published his discovery of the isochronism of the pendulum, with the laws relating to it, in 1602. He had an idea for a time-measuring instrument with a pendulum known as a 'pulsilogium' which, with a saw-toothed wheel, registered the number of oscillations. After this he thought of applying the pendulum to clocks, or so it would seem from a letter of 1637. Vincenzo Viviani, his favourite pupil confirmed this, and so did his son Vincenzo Galilei who, helped by the engineer Dominico Balestri, made a clock with a pendulum in 1649. One of Viviani's letters, discovered only in 1856, also contains a drawing showing a movement with a pendulum and a free or semi-free escapement of the detent type which was to be perfected more than a century later. AL

Gavioli, Ludovico Clockmaker, organ builder, maker of automata and musical boxes, Gavioli (1807–75) is especially remembered for the 'Panarmonico', a musical box with several cylinders and 240 keys bought by Napoleon III. In 1844 he invented, though he did not exhibit it until 1867, a free constant-force escapement in which the escape wheel, having teeth and pins, is arrested by an arm moved by the balance. He also built the clock for the municipal tower in Modena, a remarkable clock which has two dials at least 40 yards apart. They are linked by an ingenious interacting system of levers.

Gavioli felt unappreciated in Italy and went to live in Paris, where in 1845 he started a factory making organs, with his sons Claude and Anselme. AL

4

5

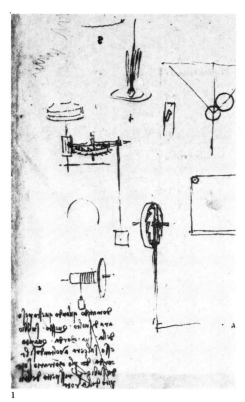

1

2

3

Kohlshitter, Giuseppe Kohlshitter (1813–85) was clockmaker to the navy and to the astronomical Observatory of Brera in Milan. He made the model of the pendulum clock envisaged by Galileo before the drawing made by Viviano had been discovered, in 1856. He was a maker of precision pendulum clocks, among them an astronomical regulator with electric transmission which, with the help of a conical pendulum, could be corrected to a margin of 0·01 second. AL

Leonardo da Vinci Although Leonardo (1452–1519) probably never made a clock himself, they were one of the

4

many interests of his wide-ranging genius. Among his notebooks are many descriptions of clocks and illustrations of clockwork mechanisms. Leonardo may have invented the articulated chain which took over from the gut line, as well as a barrel for the spring directly connected to the fusee, which avoided the need for a chain.

The question whether Leonardo applied the pendulum to clocks has been much discussed. In his notebooks he describes in detail the works of the Chiaravalle Abbey clock, and his notes suggest that he may have been more than just a careful observer or critic of the clock. AL

Miotti, Vicenzo A priest in the church of Santo Stefano at Murano, Miotti (1712–87) made a number of extremely complicated mechanical works, among them solar, astronomical and planetary clocks. He designed azimuthic clocks which indicate the azimuth angle of the points of rising and setting of fixed stars (the azimuth is the angular distance measured along the horizon between the great circle passing through a celestial body and the zenith, and either the meridian of a given place, or the cardinal point north or south). Miotti also made astronomical and other clocks. One of his clocks, now in the museum of Murano, shows hours and minutes, dates and phases of the moon, and has an alarm and chime; but the most remarkable thing about it is that it is built almost entirely of wood. AL

Rainieri, Gianpaolo and Giancarlo Gianpaolo (15th century) came from Parma in northern Italy, but before 1481 he moved to Reggio, where he worked as a maker of public clocks and astronomical clocks, helped by his son Giancarlo (d. 1529). Between 1481 and 1483 he made the public clock at Reggio which made him so famous that he was asked to make the clock for the Clock Tower of St Mark's in Venice, which he finished in 1495. Altered considerably,

1 **Leonardo da Vinci** Sketches illustrating the verge escapement and a winding barrel; from the *Codice Atlantico*. Biblioteca Ambrosiana, Milan.

2 **Miotti, Vincenzo** Clock with the movement made almost entirely of wood, fitted with a rotating moon, calendar, alarm and striking work; mid 18th century. Museo Vetrario di Murano, Venice.

3 **Miotti, Vincenzo** Movement of 280/2 showing wooden wheels, arbors and lantern pinions.

4 **Rainieri, Gianpaolo and Giancarlo** Clock Tower, St Mark's, Venice, *c*.1900.

5 **Campani, Giuseppe** Monumental night clock, 1680. Private collection.

5

1

1 Hague clock signed 'Simon Lachez à Utrecht', *c.*1715.

2 Torriano, Gianello Monumental clock made for the Emperor Charles V, attributed to Torriano, in which the Emperor moves his sceptre as the clock strikes; mid 16th century. Württembergisches Landesmuseum, Stuttgart.

2

the clock originally had a dial showing the 24 hours, and other circles which showed the movements of five planets, a dragon with a head and tail to indicate the eclipses, and the movement of the sun and moon. Two interpretative explanations of it have been made, one in the last century by Erizzo, another more recently by Colonel Antonio Simoni, who believed that before the simplification of the clock it was like that of the Lorenzo della Volpaia clock of which descriptions survive. The clock has figures which emerge in procession from the little door to the left of the statue of the Virgin; this occurs as every hour strikes, but only during Ascension Week. It is famous for its two 'blackamoors', bronze statues sculpted by Paolo Savin in 1497 and cast by Ambrogio delle Ancore which strike the hours on a big bell on top of the tower. AL

Torriano, Gianello Torriano is the most popular and also the most mysterious master clockmaker of 16th-century Italy. He came from Cremona, but his surname is not known; 'Torriano' is merely a nickname derived from the Torrazzo, the famous bell tower in Cremona. He was born in the early part of the century (d. 1585), and asked by Don Ferdinando Gonzaga, on behalf of the Emperor Charles V, to repair Dondi's *Astrario* in Milan, which had been badly neglected.

When Charles V himself met Torriano he asked him to go to Spain to rebuild an astronomical clock even more complicated than Dondi's. Here, unfortunately, legend and reality are mixed. It is not known when exactly Torriano went to Spain, but it is possible to catch a glimpse of his activity in the little court of about 50 people who surrounded the Emperor after his abdication in 1555 at the Spanish monastery of San Justo. Charles V seems to have been fascinated by Torriano's clocks, but Torriano's achievements were undoubtedly embroidered by his biographers, who wrote of mechanical birds that flew out of a window and then flew in again, or of a group of small soldiers that fought a battle. The inventory of goods belonging to Charles V includes some clocks which were probably made by Torriano: a square clock with chimes, gold decoration and figures in relief; one called '*el Portal*', another called 'the Mirror'. An armillary sphere in the Ambrosiana in Milan is credited to him, and some people have attributed to him the famous clock in the Fremersdorf collection, Lucerne, which has a small dome over a figure of Charles V, whose sceptre sways when the hours strike. AL

Volpaia, della The Volpaias were a well-known family of clockmakers in Florence working in the last quarter of the 15th and throughout the 16th century. The most famous was the head of the family, Lorenzo, who was born in 1446 and came from Arezzo. In existing manuscripts in Florence and Venice there are descriptions of a marvellous clock made by him which throughout the 16th century was kept in the Palazzo Vecchio in Florence, in the 'Clock Room'. It had a complex dial showing the movements of the planets, and was so much admired by Cosimo de' Medici that he ordered the walls of the room in which it was kept to be decorated with maps painted by Ignazio Danti.

Lorenzo's son Benvenuto is mentioned by Giorgio Vasari as an excellent clockmaker and engineer. All that is left of his work, however, is notes and descriptions. AL

Zamboni, Giuseppe Zamboni (1776–1846) was a teacher of physics in Verona and one of the first to think of the possibility of applying electricity as a source of energy in the working of clocks. In collaboration with Carl Streizig he made several clocks with two dry cell batteries, set about $1\frac{1}{4}$ in. apart, on which a pendulum swung, hitting first one then the other battery, attracted and repelled alternately by their poles. AL

Clockmaking in Japan

Mechanical clocks were introduced to Japan by Jesuit missionaries in 1549. Lantern chamber clocks of Dutch or Italian origin were used as gifts of state to the shogun from St Francis Xavier. The Jesuits remained until 1614, when the

1 **Pillar clock** showing *nama gata* graph and hour indicator in a slotted bar, with balance-controlled movement. Science Museum, London.

2 **Lantern clock** with double foliot, showing position of foliot weights for long days and short nights. British Museum, London.

3 **Bracket clock** showing pierced, diapered front plate and late characteristics; balance-controlled.

4 **Lantern clock** with a circular balance and rotating, adjustable chapter ring, in a wall bracket case. British Museum, London.

5 **Table clock** with verge escapement, controlled by a balance outside the backplate, and probably for use on barges on inland navigation; by Rinse Durks in Grouw (Friesland), second half 18th century.

1   4   2   3   5

ADAPTATIONS TO THE JAPANESE TEMPORAL SYSTEM

shogun banished all foreigners except for a tiny Dutch trading mission on the island of Deshima in Nagasaki harbour. During the sojourn of the Europeans, the Japanese admired, copied and then adapted European clockwork to the Japanese temporal system (as opposed to the equinoctial system based on a Chinese hour system used mainly by astronomers).

The Japanese temporal system, which was used until 1873, divided each day into six hours of daylight and six hours of darkness. Any mechanical timepiece required some method for varying the length of the day and night hours according to the season. The Japanese developed several methods for adapting the European movements to their own uses. The first such system was quite elementary, involving a foliot with notches and a pair of small weights hung in the notches. As the weights were moved towards or away from the verge staff, the rate of oscillation of the foliot changed as a function of the radius of gyration. In summer the weights would be close to the verge for the short night, and farther

away during the long day; in winter vice versa. On clocks with a single foliot, the weights had to be moved twice a day, at sunrise and sunset. The second method entailed the addition of a second foliot and a mechanism for changing from one to the other at the end of each six-hour period, thereby saving the labour of moving the weights twice a day [284/2]. A third system of adaptation involved simple hour characters on the dial, set on small movable plates so that they could be placed in the proper relationship to each other for a given season [284/4]. The hour plates were realigned every two weeks by the clock adjuster, who kept the clock in accordance with the proper *sekki* (fortnight) of the *setsu* (month).

Other systems were developed for use only on pillar clocks. Most pillar clocks had the simplest four-wheel weight-driven verge and balance movements, with the location of the weight indicating the time. They had adjustable hour markers, and a hand fixed in the weight indicated the time as the weight fell. Changeable scales were developed for use on the vertical dials. Sometimes they were used in conjunction with movable hour plates and sometimes alone. The scales were usually lacquer. Each was marked on both sides according to the hour durations for a specific *sekki*, and they were changed every two weeks. For instance, the scale for the first fortnight in January might be on one side, and the second fortnight on the second side. A complete set of scales consisted of seven plates with a different *sekki* scale on each side, giving 14 *sekki*, each one to be used twice a year. The same scale was used in October and March, etc. Scales were further refined into a graph, a *nama gata* scale, indicating the changing duration of the hours for a whole year [284/1]. The hand was placed on a slotted bar that allowed it to be moved back and forth across the face of the graph, and it was placed in the slotted bar according to the season of the year. When the weight descended, the hand indicated the hour by its position on the graph. The graphs were either lacquer or brass. This arrangement finally eliminated the periodic visit of the clock adjuster.

HOUR MARKS ON JAPANESE CLOCKS

The dials of Japanese clocks have two sets of characters that appear either alone or together. The first set is the Twelve Terrestrial Branches inherited from China and associated with the twelve traditional animals of oriental folklore. The characters for the Terrestrial Branches are not the same as those for the animals, but their cultural association is so close that in Japan the hours are named for the animals, e.g. midnight is the hour of the rat. The Twelve Terrestrial Branches standing alone represent the twelve hours, six of daylight and six of darkness. The characters for the animals themselves never appear on clocks.

The second set of characters, which do appear on dials, are numerals. Oriental numerals from nine to four appear in descending order, starting at six, sunset, the hour of the cock, in a repeating, broken pattern: 6-5-4-9-8-7-6-5-4-9-8-7-6. Some dials have only the numerals or only the Twelve Terrestrial Branches, and some have both.

CALENDARS

The Japanese calendrical system was imported along with most of the origins of Japanese culture, from T'ang China. It was a sexagenary cycle based on combinations of the Twelve Terrestrial Branches and the Ten Celestial Stems. Each day in a 60-day cycle was named by one such combination. The seasonal names for fortnights were based on the *chhi* of ancient China. A *chhi* and a *sekki* are the same.

Calendars in Japanese clocks consist of one or two small apertures either above or below the dial showing, in the case of the single aperture, a succession of the Twelve Terrestrial Branches which were engraved on the wheel mounted just behind the front of the clock. In the case of a double-aperture calendar, one shows one of the Twelve Terrestrial Branches and the second shows one of the Ten Celestial Stems, also engraved on a wheel behind the front of the clock. The combination of the two names the precise day in the sexagenary cycle. Sixty days made up one unit; six 60-day units made up a 'year'; and 60 'years' made up a 'century'. The sexagenary cycle was related to the sequence of *sekki*. The *sekki* and *setsu* were part of the yearly cycle of 24 *sekki*, each of which referred to seasonal change through poetic allusion. Some clocks had reference to both cycles. Two sekki made a *setsu*, and two *setsu* roughly coincided with one 60-day period. Since each day of the sexagenary cycle was named, it was convenient to know both which *sekki* (therefore season) it was as well as which precise day. The casting of horoscopes was important in Japan, and this information was very useful in discovering which days were auspicious or inauspicious.

THE POST-TRADITIONAL CLOCK INDUSTRY

In 1873 the Japanese revoked their traditional timekeeping system and adopted Western time-measurement conventions. At this time many old clocks were adapted by removing one of the foliots and verges or by setting the hour indicators for twelve equal hours. For this reason double-foliot clocks are often found missing one foliot and verge. In 1875 the first factories to manufacture clocks were established and were soon producing great quantities of clocks, many of which resemble the so-called American 'school' clocks or drop octagons. The Seikosha factory was the most successful. It was founded in 1888 and produced all kinds of clocks and watches.

The modern Japanese clock and watch industry needs no introduction; it has moved into the forefront of manufacturing and merchandising timepieces, including the production of modern digital watches and inexpensive timepieces of all types. MCR

Clockmaking in the Netherlands

The history of clockmaking in the Netherlands cannot really be separated from the economic history of the country. In the individual provinces local development of clockmaking also closely reflected local economic patterns.

A particular population group may also express, at least to some degree, some of its own special characteristics, and geographical situation will also exercise a profound influence. Similarly, proximity to international trade routes and the exchange of scientific information lead to technical developments and even changes in case style. Striking examples of this kind of exchange are the English influences on clockmaking in Zeeland and Amsterdam during the first half of the 18th century [286/1], and French influence on late 17th-century Hague clocks and Amsterdam longcase and table clocks of the second half of the 18th century.

An examination of the types of domestic clock to be found in the Netherlands will show that, by and large, the same types occur there as elsewhere; longcase clocks, table clocks, though strangely enough only a few examples of such a standard type as the lantern clock, were manufactured, and these probably only in the province of Zeeland [286/3]. Towns such as Middelburg, Goes, Den Briel and Flushing

1

2

3

1 **Table clock** in mulberry wood, showing English influence, by Adolf Witsen, Amsterdam, *c.*1720. Note the position of the calendar aperture (close to XI) and the alarm winding square (near the tip of the hour hand).

2 **Table clock** in wooden case showing French influence, signed 'J. P. Kroese en Zoon Amsterdam', *c.*1770.

3 **Large Zeeland** striking lantern clock, with calendar indicator, *c.*1780.

4 **Mantel clock,** signed 'J. van Brussel, Amsterdam'; first quarter 18th century.

5 **Backplate** of 286/4. The glazed door allows the finely engraved backplate to be seen in the mantelpiece mirror.

4

5

have very long traditions of clockmaking and, although clocks were never made in large quantities in Zeeland, those that were are characterised by their fine quality.

Relatively scarce are 18th-century Dutch hooded clocks and examples which resemble them, the hoods of which can no longer be lifted for removal as in the original examples of this kind of clock. It is probable that the makers of these clocks were influenced by English models; they were made between 1720 and 1770, originally only in Amsterdam and the surrounding region, later and eventually exclusively in the rural areas of north Brabant, the east Netherlands and west Friesland, an area to the north of Amsterdam in the province of North Holland. The oldest Amsterdam clocks were made with a verge escapement, though later Amsterdam and provincial specimens were provided with anchor escapements. The Amsterdam hood clocks with anchor escapements were eventually equipped with longer pendulums, requiring longer cases. Later Amsterdam hood clocks are known as 'Amsterdam Friesland' clocks [287/8].

Less rare, though certainly no less important, is the Hague clock, which was made between 1658 and *c.*1700, heralding two centuries of vigorous Dutch clock manufacture [289/7]. In December 1656 the Leyden physicist Christiaan Huygens considerably improved the accuracy of clocks by arranging the verge escapement vertically and adding a pendulum to regulate it. In order to make the period of swing the same for large arcs as for small ones, he added two cycloidal cheeks through which the suspension of the pendulum had to pass. An increase in the arc is thus compensated for by a corresponding diminution of its oscillation at the extremities of the swing. The significance of this innovation was not immediately recognised, and cycloidal cheeks were difficult to bend accurately and therefore only used for a short time. It is known, however,

6, 7, 8 Three Amsterdam hooded clocks from the second quarter to mid 18th century, the pendulum cases increasing in size from left to right; 287/6 and 287/7 by Jacob Kerkeloo, 287/8 by A. van Oostrom.

9 Hague clock case by Lachez (282/1), showing the hinged dial with movement fitted to it, the striking count plate, the pendulum hooked up and the inlaid star design inside the case. Note the feet on the front of the case.

10 Groningen table clock driven by weights on either side of the movement. Signed 'I. Oortwyn, Appingadam'; mid 18th century.

6   7   8

9   10

that Huygens obtained a patent for his discovery and that Salomon Coster from The Hague obtained the licence to manufacture and sell clocks built on this principle for 21 years. After Coster's death in 1659 the licence passed to Claude Pascal and Severijn Oosterwijck. It is now known, for instance, that Huygens's request to patent his method in Paris was refused, so that the Paris clockmakers, including Isaac Thuret, Nicolas Hanet, Gilles Martinot and Pierre Saudé, would not suffer competition in their production of *religieuse* clocks. It is therefore not surprising that the development of these little clocks advanced much more quickly in Paris than in the Netherlands.

When thousands of French Huguenots, including numerous clockmakers, emigrated to the Netherlands in 1685 after the revocation of the Edict of Nantes, their influence on the development of the Hague clock was deeply felt. Indeed, about the turn of the century, the

Hague clock, which for the last few years of its existence was no longer manufactured exclusively in The Hague, disappeared as a distinct type to make room for more conventional table clocks.

Table clocks showing marked English influence in both design and construction can be considered as the direct descendants of the rare Hague clock; these were originally made with square dials, later modified to break-arch dials [286/1]. The main centres of manufacture were the larger towns in the west of the country, though the slightly later and rarer products of the rural centres, strongly individual in many respects, are often considered to be visually the more interesting [284/5], [287/10]. Fine musical table clocks made with six, eight or even twelve tunes, are more frequently found in the Netherlands than in England, and the same is true of examples with lunar dials. Table clocks in cases which reflect specifically Dutch furniture styles are

1 **Longcase clock** with calendar work, phases of the moon and automata ship movement; signed 'Florens Gerard Lubert, Amsterdam', mid 18th century.

2 **Brabantine Friesland staart-klok** in wooden case with original painting, signed 'G. Van Kuick, St Antonis Me fect, 1768'.

3 **Stoelklok** with heavy twisted pillars and horizontal verge escapement; early 18th century.

4 **Large Friesland staartklok** in oak with enamel dial and movement betweeen plates. Hour striking on gong and half hour on bell; c.1840.

5 **Bakker, Carol Willem** *Stoelklok, c. 1780.*

6 **Cartel clock** in wooden case showing strong French influence, signed 'F. Pasteur, Amsterdam'; late 18th century.

7 **Ceulen de Oude, Johannes van** This Hague clock is one of Ceulen de Oude's earliest; signed 'Johannes van Ceulen – Hollandia – Haga'; third quarter 17th century.

8 **Two stoelklokken** with anchor escapements and long pendulum cases; second quarter 18th century.

1

relatively rare, and these clocks sometimes have movements imported from England. After *c.* 1750 the influence of increasing imports of cheaper French clocks was beginning to make itself felt in Holland, and strong French stylistic influence can often be seen in clocks made in Amsterdam [286/2]. It is even possible to find cartel clocks made from wood in Amsterdam, although this was not native to the Netherlands [289/6].

The longcase clock (*staande klok*) made its appearance in the Netherlands *c.* 1680, probably as an imitation of similar examples made by English craftsmen. Amsterdam was the most important centre for the making of longcase clocks, principally because it had become an important commercial centre [288/1]. The best-known clocks of the period, however, are the 18th-century Dutch bracketed clocks (*stoelklokken*) and the 19th-century Friesland clocks (*staartklokken*), types which rarely occur outside the Netherlands.

Both the *stoelklokken* and, more especially and obviously, the *staartklokken* were produced in greatest numbers in the province of Friesland. The *stoelklok* was produced during the period from *c.* 1675 to *c.* 1875 and equipped with a verge escapement, while the *staartklok* was produced

between 1775 and 1900 and equipped with an anchor escapement. Although the periods of production of the two types of clock overlap by almost a century, the Friesland *staartklok* is still considered as more or less the successor of the *stoelklok*. Although *staartklokken* were already being produced in small numbers before 1775, both in Amsterdam and in rural centres, the development of the type, unlike that of the *stoelklok*, took place almost exclusively in the province of Friesland [289/2]. The earliest Friesland *stoelklokken* date from *c.* 1730, though they had previously been made in the large towns, in the west of the country for some 50 years, with Amsterdam as the principal centre, while manufacture had also been carried on in Groningen for about 25 years. These early *stoelklokken*, sometimes also called 'forerunners', differ in many respects from the later examples. The movements of the older specimens are much stronger, while the pillars may be smooth or twisted and are very elaborately finished, with or without a square dial plate [289/3]. The back panels of the bracket or *stoel* lack the characteristic flanking mermaids, having either a flat edge or completely different embellishments. The little roof at the front of the clock bearing lead ornaments is frequently lacking, sometimes being replaced by an Atlas figure bearing a globe on the bell top. The older specimens do not have any lead ornaments on either side of the dial. There are many other small differences, and there are many transitional stages. The very rare *stoelklokken* which have an anchor escapement and a long pendulum can almost be considered as a transitional type between the *stoelklok* and the later *staartklok*, and these clocks are of exceptional interest [289/8]. The *stoelklokken* from the east Netherlands are also of interest. They display a number of very original variations. The Goor clocks have anchor escapements and long pendulums, which were hung high under the roof of the bracket, contrived by inverting the crutch. Because of its position at the crossing of north–south and east–west trade routes, this region produced clocks which show influences from Groningen, Westphalia, the Rhineland, Belgium, and north Holland.

The Friesland *staartklok* was produced in large quantities throughout the 19th century and exported to countries in and outside Europe [289/2]. In the small town of Joure alone, which was the mid 19th-century centre of Friesland clock manufacture, 4,000 clocks are supposed to have been produced in the year 1857. It is hardly surprising that this type is the most common and best-known native Dutch antique clock. Just as the Friesland clockmaking industry was beginning to expand at the start of the 19th century, clocks of a similar type were also being produced in east Friesland. These (German) clocks differ significantly in a number of ways from the Dutch models. About the end of the 19th century, however, the Friesland clockmaking industry began to lose ground in the face of competition from much cheaper and more accurate German Vienna-type regulators, which had the added advantage of not needing to be wound every day. JLS

Bakker, Carol Willem Bakker (1730–1806), clockmaker in Goor from 1755, and pupil of Antony ter Swaek, also produced bracketed clocks with anchor escapement and inverted crutch. Bakker's clocks were more carefully

2   3   4   5

6   7   8

constructed than those of his master. The projections on either side of the back panel were usually solid rather than openwork, as in most of ter Swaek's clocks. Bakker, like other clockmakers of this region, often used whalebone for the suspension of the pendulum. JLS

See also Twente and Achterhoek clocks (Section I).

Ceulen de Oude, Johannes van The 'Dutch Tompion', as he is sometimes called, Ceulen de Oude worked at The Hague in the late 17th century and died there in 1715. He

acquired his great reputation mainly between 1677 and 1684, when he was working closely with Christiaan Huygens. His craftsmanship is best seen in the clocks and instruments of this period which were commissioned in the Netherlands and abroad, and it was in 1682 that he constructed the movement with balance and spring for Huygens's planetarium.

A small number of watches and several bracket clocks of reasonable quality are known, though in his later Hague clocks he installed French movements. FK/JLS

1 **Huygens, Christiaan** Plate from Huygens *Horologium Oscillatorium* Paris, 1673.

2 **Huygens, Steven** Longcase with *stoelklok*-type month-going movement, phases of the moon, calender indication and anchor escapement; late 17th century. Private collection.

3 **Cloesen, Barent van der** Drum-shaped coach clock with striking and alarm; movement signed 'Bernard van der Cloese fecit Haga', *c.*1690.

4 **Coster, Salomon Hendrikszoon** One of the first Hague clocks, with loops for hanging and minute numbering. The clock is fitted with verge escapement and cycloidal cheeks. Signed 'Salomon Coster – Haghe – met privilege 1657'. Museum Boerhaave, Leiden.

5 **Hoogendijk, Steven** Portrait.

6 **Norris, Joseph** Elaborate engraved signature, *c.* 1680.

7 **Oosterwijk, Severijn** Signature and figure of time from the dial of a Hague clock, *c.*1680.

8 **Pascal, Claude** Signature plate from one of the earliest Hague clocks.

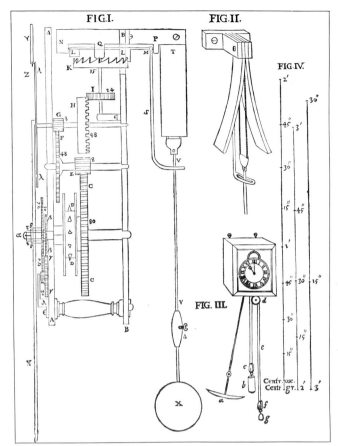

1

2

3

4

5

Cloesen, Barent van der (Clouse, Bernardus) Cloesen worked at The Hague, *c.* 1690–1715, and was responsible for improvements in the magnificent planetarium known as the *Leidse sphera* between 1710 and 1712. An early head of the clockmakers' guild (founded 1688), he also made Hague clocks, table or bracket clocks, longcase clocks and a few very beautiful watches. Van der Cloesen, who sometimes signed himself 'B. v. Cloese', also made barometers. FK/JLS

Coster, Salomon Hendrikszoon Born in Haarlem, Coster (d. 1659) became a master clockmaker in 1646. He owes his fame to the fact that he produced the first

pendulum clocks (Hague clocks), following the designs of Christiaan Huygens. He obtained the licence to make pendulum clocks, in June 1657, for a period of 21 years, but shortly after it had been granted he and Huygens were involved in numerous lawsuits to defend their privileges against the Rotterdam clockmaker Simon Douw, who also claimed the right to make them.

Coster's first pendulum clocks were, for the sake of cheapness, exceptionally simple in execution and were only meant to be used as timekeepers, in spite of the commonly held theory that these clocks represented the first stages in a long development.

Although it is known that Coster, in the two and a half

6
7
8

years remaining before his death, produced a fair number of pendulum clocks, only two examples are known. After Coster's death the licence passed to Severijn Oosterwijk and Claude Pascal. FK/JLS

Hohwü, Andreas One of the best Dutch chronometer makers of the 19th century, Hohwü (1803–85) was a pupil of his father, a clockmaker in Schleswig-Holstein, where Andreas was also born. He became a Dutch subject in 1869.

Apprenticed to Heinrich Johann Kessels (1781–1849) in Altona, he showed himself a willing pupil and in 1834 was accepted as a pupil by Abraham-Louis Breguet in Paris, where he remained until 1839. The following year he established himself as a chronometer maker on the Oude Schan ('Old Wall') in Amsterdam. He produced 28 astronomical clocks, nearly all of which were destined for use abroad; he received prizes for many of them and was awarded a gold medal at a Paris exhibition for his discovery of secondary compensation for chronometers. He received honours and decorations in many countries. FK/JLS

Hoogendijk, Steven A notable Rotterdam clockmaker, Hoogendijk (1698–1788), founder in 1769 of the Batavian Society of Empirical Philosophy, made many beautiful longcase clocks with lunar and calendar work, as was common at that period in the Netherlands. He also made table clocks and pocket watches, some of them preserved in the Historisch Museum and the Museum Boymans van Beuningen in Rotterdam. FK/JLS

Huygens, Christiaan The eminent mathematician, astronomer and physicist of The Hague, Huygens (1629–95) was the son of the statesman and poet Constantijn Huygens. In addition to other important scientific discoveries, he was responsible for two of the most important developments in the history of clockmaking. The first was the efficient application to clocks of the pendulum as a regulating mechanism. The Hague clockmaker Salomon Coster produced the first pendulum clocks according to Huygens's design, obtaining the licence for their manufacture in June 1657. The second great advance for which Huygens was responsible was the coiled balance spring. He first showed a model of a balance controlled by a spring, made by Isaac Thuret, in Paris in January 1675; the principle is still in use.

Huygens also developed an endless chain or rope form of winding for clocks c. 1664, and ten years later designed epicycloidal gearing for clock movements. FK/JLS

Huygens, Steven So far as is known, no relation to Christiaan Huygens, Steven (late 17th–early 18th centuries) was one of the first makers of longcase clocks in the Netherlands, associated with such makers as Ahasuerus Fromanteel, Jacob Hasius, Pieter Klock and Joseph Norris. A municipal clockmaker in Rotterdam, in 1704 and 1710 he was commissioned by the city authorities of Amsterdam to draw up a list of worthy men from among the best clockmakers in the city.

In 1697 Steven Huygens was advertising longcase clocks which would go for a year and strike every hour and half-hour. FK/JLS

Klock, or Clock, Pieter A famous Amsterdam maker of watches and longcase clocks, Klock (1665–1754) also dealt in paintings. Pieter Klock's workshop was situated on the Singel and later on the Osjes Sluis in the Kalverstraat, Amsterdam. His early longcase clocks sometimes had dial plates covered with velvet, usually with finely carved decoration. He also made a table clock with a seconds hand. His bracket clocks are known to have been especially fine. FK/JLS

Norris, Joseph Norris (late 17th century) learned his trade in England and came to the Netherlands c. 1675, settling in Amsterdam until he returned to England in 1693. Together with Ahasuerus Fromanteel he played an important part in extending English influence on Dutch clockmaking, particularly in the introduction of the longcase clock.

Norris's work was varied, and included bracket clocks made to English patterns, longcase and hooded clocks which look so English they might have been imported. His Hague clocks, on the other hand, are no less thoroughly Dutch in appearance. FK/JLS

Oosterwijk, Severijn A versatile 17th-century clock-maker of The Hague, Oosterwijk, together with Claude Pascal, held the licence to make pendulum clocks after the death of Salomon Coster. He worked for Christiaan Huygens and made microscopes for him. In 1664 he also did some work for the Royal Society, of which Huygens was a member. The clockmakers' company or guild was founded in 1688, thanks partly to Oosterwijk's efforts; he was its first dean. One of his surviving Hague clocks bears the inscription *met privilege* ('with privilege'). His workshop was in the Drie Vergulde Mollen ('Three Gilded Moles') along the Spui in The Hague. FK/JLS

Pascal, Claude After the death of Salomon Coster, Pascal (d. c. 1674), together with Severijn Oosterwijk, held the licence to make pendulum clocks in the Netherlands. He also worked with Christiaan Huygens. Pascal worked from c. 1650 in The Hague where he married in 1655. In 1670 he went to Paris where he died c. 1674.

There are several little Hague clocks known to have been

made by Pascal similar to French *religieuse* pendulum clocks. Several were exported to France from *c.* 1659, but none of these little Hague clocks which have so far been identified bears the inscription *met privilege* ('with privilege'). Pascal also made very beautiful watches. FK/JLS

Rikkert, Richardus Born in the west German town of Lage, Rikkert worked as an apprentice in the clockmaker's business of Hendrik Ruempol in Laren, but left in 1806 for Amsterdam. Richardus' son, Hendrik Anasias, also a clockmaker, married in 1831 and lived in Nieuw Ruempol, the house which Gosselik Ruempol had built next to the old Ruempol house when his son Hendrik took over the clockmaking business. Hendrik Anasias Rikkert had a son and a grandson who were clockmakers around Laren and Zutphen. The productive period of the Rikkert family extended from *c.* 1780 to 1880, and even today there is a clockmaker in the neighbourhood of Zutphen called Rikkert. JLS

Ruempol, Gosselik Hendriks The original family name of Koeslag was changed to Ruempol in 1715 after the acquisition of a farm called 'Den Ruempol' in Laren, Gelderland. It was there that Ruempol (*c.* 1682–1759) made clocks of exceptional quality.

Gosselik Ruempol's clocks can be recognised by their very robust movements, almost square dial plates with moulded ornamentation only at the top, and the characteristic modelling of the hands to accommodate the alarm mechanism lever. The movements are enclosed above by a plain, pointed case roof at an angle of 95°. JLS

Ruempol, Hendrik The son of Gosselik Ruempol, Hendrik (1730–96) was as famous a clockmaker as his father. The back panels of his clocks almost always have

wooden side ornamentation and much flatter tops (115°) with a curved arch or arcade at the front. Hendrik made a few clocks with repeating rack-striking work. The clocks in which signs of both Gosselik's and Hendrik's workmanship are found date from the period 1751–4, when father and son worked together. JLS

Spraekel, Jurriaan Spraekel (1615–*c.* 1690), turret-clock maker in Zutphen, was the son of Jacob Spraekel of Goor. He made and repaired turret clocks all over the Netherlands, but especially around Haarlem and Amsterdam. It is possible that he also produced domestic clocks and was the inventor of the classic east Netherlands system of alarm setting with an adjustable screw, as seen in Ruempol and Goor clocks. There are a few bracket clocks which can be tentatively ascribed to him. One of these, made in 1656, has all the characteristics of a turret clock, but reduced to the proportions of a domestic clock. JLS
See also Twente and Achterhoek clocks (Section I).

Swaek, Anthony ter Born in 1692, at work in Goor from 1735, ter Swaek died in 1772. He produced bracket clocks with anchor escapements and an inverted crutch for activating the pendulum in a *stoelklok*. There is only one known longcase clock by ter Swaek, and one hooded clock. His bracket clocks are very similar to those of Jan B. Spraekel. JLS
See also Twente and Achterhoek clocks (Section I).

Visbagh, Pieter A famous maker of Hague clocks born in Middelburg in the 17th century, Visbagh (d. *c.* 1690) was probably the most prolific maker of this type. In 1660 he took over the house and business of the widow of Salomon Coster, and obtained the licence to exercise Coster's privileges. In fact, Visbagh had occasionally worked with

1   2   3

1 **Rikkert, Richardus** *Stoelklok* attributed to Richardus Rikkert, Laren or Rotterdam, early 19th century.

2 **Ruempol, Gosselik Hendriks** *Stoelklok* with characteristic gable hood to the bracket; *c.*1735.

3 **Ruempol, Hendrik** Dial of *stoelklok* showing phases of the moon, date, month, day of the week and alarm setting disc with holes for the setting peg; painted decoration.

4 **Visbagh, Pieter** An example of a Hague clock with a square, instead of rectangular, dial, *c.*1670.

5 **Olsen, Jens** Portrait of Olsen in his workshop.

4

5

Coster from 1652. It is known that he also worked for Christiaan Huygens, and that he later became dean of the clockmakers' guild, which was founded in The Hague in 1688. FK/JLS

Clockmaking in Scandinavia

Jürgensen, Urban and Jules Urban Jürgensen (1776–1830), born in Copenhagen, was a horologist of the first magnitude. To improve himself he spent time in Paris with F. Berthoud and A. L. Breguet. He then went to London, the centre of chronometer making, more fully to perfect his skills, since the success and simplicity of English chronometers impressed him greatly. He carried on an extensive and unrivalled business in Copenhagen making a number of marine chronometers and some splendid astronomical clocks.

Urban's son, Jules Frederic, was born in 1808 in Le Locle, Switzerland, while Urban and his wife were there on a visit. Later Jules returned to Le Locle to establish the watch factory that came to be very famous. Jules was thoroughly trained by his father and demonstrated a discernment of the more subtle aspects of horological perfection as well as remarkable taste. DJB

Kessels, Heinrich Johann Kessels (1781–1849), of London, Copenhagen and Altona, was born in Maastricht, Holland. He went to Paris where he must have impressed A. L. Breguet, for he was taken in by the master and remained for some time. Going to Copenhagen in 1821, he impressed King Frederick to such a degree that the king encouraged him to settle in Altona, then a Danish city. Appointed chronometer maker to the Danish Navy, his chronometers and deck watches exhibit superb workmanship, and he was even more famous for his precision clocks. Claudius Saunier describes in his *Treatise on Modern Horology in Theory and Practice* the unusual form of Graham escapement used by Kessels with great success. Kessels died on a visit to England. DJB

Kratzenstein, Georg Kratzenstein came from Copenhagen. In 1751 he wrote about a clock driven by the variation in length of four rods, caused by temperature changes. The rods were four feet long, made of an alloy of three parts tin to one of copper, and connected by levers. The last lever ended in a sector driving a pinion which wound the clock. The mechanism was said to produce a combined movement of one-sixth of an inch for a change of five degrees. EJT

Olsen, Jens Jens Olsen (1872–1945), apprenticed to a locksmith, became a competent instrument mechanic and studied astronomy. He travelled throughout Europe, returning to Denmark in 1902 to work as a clockmaker. In 1905 he set up his business at 8 Hallinsgade in Copenhagen, staying there until his death. Olsen's lifetime ambition was to build a unique astronomical clock, and by about the age of 50 he had completed his calculations. Not until he was nearly 70 could he get the necessary finance to commence it, receiving a loan of 100,000 kroner in December 1943 in the middle of the German occupation. A workshop was placed at his disposal by the Technological Institute at Bulowsvej, construction commenced and a site in Copenhagen Town Hall was allocated for the clock. On 17th November 1945, Olsen died of a thrombosis; his clock was completed and is now acknowledged a masterpiece [323/7]. CKA

Radeloff, Niclaus Radeloff (17th century) was one of the pioneers of precision timekeeping before the introduction of the pendulum. He worked in Schleswig which at the time was in Danish territory. Jost Burgi had introduced the cross-beat escapement; this had also been used on clocks by other makers, but Radeloff, coming at the end of the pre-pendulum era, improved the cross-beat by giving it very long arms which acted as shock absorbers on account of their flexibility, and he also provided a constant-force drive by using balls which rolled down a slope and impelled a rotating cage.

A Radeloff clock with this arrangement, dated 1654, is in the National Museum at Copenhagen and another is in Rosenborg Castle in the same city [294/1], [294/2].

The cases of Radeloff clocks are of high quality with much decoration, but the clocks were obviously intended more for use than for ornament. The going mechanism is basically very simple. The rotating cage carries a large contrate wheel at the top which meshes with the escape-wheel pinion. The cage has to be delicately balanced in order to avoid unnecessary friction. When a ball has descended it falls into a drawer at the bottom and automatically releases another from the magazine at the top. Little is known of Radeloff's life. EJJ

Roemer, Olaf Roemer (1644–1710) was born in Aarhus, Denmark. Astronomical clocks by him are known and there are two planetaria in the museum at Copenhagen. He has an important place in horology because he was the first to recommend epicycloidal teeth for clock wheels and cycloidal teeth for crown wheels. He read a paper on the subject before the Académie des Sciences in Paris in 1675, and a MS of Christiaan Huygens written the year

previously calls wheels with epicycloidal teeth 'Roemer's wheels', indicating that Roemer had discussed the subject with Huygens before presenting his paper. EJJ
See Gears (Section II).

Clockmaking in Spain

The first records of mechanical clocks in Spain appear in the 13th century. Perhaps the oldest is the one listed in an inventory of the cathedral of Toledo drawn up during the second half of the century, which specifies: '45 – A broken clock'. The fact that it was out of use suggests that it was a mechanical clock rather than a solar device. In the same period, *c.* 1283, it is thought that Guillen de Bellester built the clock in the church tower of Vich (Barcelona). In the 14th century increasing numbers of church and cathedral clocks began to appear, for example at Valencia, Toledo, Burgos, Barcelona and Seville, and this growth continued during the 15th century with the making of clocks such as those of the Miguelete and Palacio Real of Valencia and the cathedrals of Huesca and Vich. During the 16th century, when Spain was united under Catholic kings as the greatest power in Europe, and the fruits of the discovery and conquest of parts of America began to arrive, clockmaking and the other arts flourished. Clocks were constructed in all the important churches and cathedrals, and earlier public clocks were replaced. At this time mention should be made of Melchior Diaz who constructed automata, and the famous Italian Giovanni Torriano, clockmaker of King Charles I (Charles V of the Holy Roman Empire). Arabs and Jews connected with clockmaking in Spain became fewer in number at this time.

Unfortunately, none of the domestic clocks which must have been made in Spain during the 17th century has survived, though there are frequent references to further turret clocks such as those of the Plaza de la Villa in Madrid (1625), the Seo de Huesca (1628), Villagarcia de Arosa (Pontevedra) (before 1657) and Mondragon (Guipuzcoa) (*c.* 1657).

During the 18th century a true renaissance in Spanish clockmaking took place [295/5]. Many Spaniards went abroad on government grants [296/7], foreign clockmakers

1 Radeloff, Niclaus Rolling-ball clock in its elaborate gilt metal case, with side door open to show ball slowly descending the spiral slope, and thus rotating a cage which drives the clock. Dated 1654. Nationalmuseet, Copenhagen.

2 Cross-beat escapement of Radeloff's rolling-ball clock; detail showing signature on the plate supporting the cross-beat arms cock. Nationalmuseet, Copenhagen.

3 Turret clock from Barcelona Cathedral, dated in the centre of the frame, 1576.

4 Turret clock Alternative view of 294/3 showing the fly on the striking train.

5 Pedestal clock by Antonio Molina of the Real Escuela Fábrica de Madrid. Signed in London, 1790. Jaén Cathedral sacristy.

6 Galician lantern clock, the oldest dated existing example, without bell or side panels, signed 'Fran Martinez', 1745. Juan E. Maurer, Barcelona.

7 Wall clock of elaborate design, with unusual striking hammers and enamelled dial; signed 'José Saldari, Mataro', late 18th century. Juan E. Maurer, Barcelona.

8 Wall clock Movement of 295/7 with dial removed, showing anchor escapement and general construction resembling the Comtoise clock.

5

6

7

8

settled in Spain, official and private schools of clockmaking were established, and royal patronage abounded. Most important were the marine chronometer makers, and the regional clockmakers of Madrid, Catalonia, Galicia and Asturias. With the great development in European clockmaking in the 18th century many Spanish clockmakers were attracted to the masters of England and France. In some instances they were sent by the Spanish government, but others went by private means. On their return it was customary for them to go into royal service or to become independent. For example, Augustin Albino studied under Ferdinand Berthoud for five years, and José Lopez de Villa, given a grant by Carlos III, studied under Berthoud and Abraham-Louis Breguet in Paris and John Arnold in London.

There has always been an interchange between Spaniards who went abroad to perfect their skills, and foreigners who came to Spain for various economic or political reasons, or by royal appointment. As early as the 16th century the Frenchman Baltasar Ruz was making clocks for the major of Compostela, while Juan Cocart, Hans de Vals and Hans de Evalo from Flanders came to construct clocks for Philip II in Seville. The Italian Francisco Filipini built the monastic clock for the Escorial in Madrid. In the 18th century the English clockmakers John Joseph Woolls, Michael Smith, William Poulton and Thomas Hatton were all engaged in the Spanish royal service, and there were also Italians, Dutchmen and Swiss. French clockmakers, in particular, came to Spain, such as the Charost family who had a clockmaking school in Madrid; Charles and Abram-Louis Guye worked in La Coruña and François-Louis Godon in the royal palace.

The most famous Spanish clockmaking school was that founded in Madrid by the Frenchmen Félipe and Pedro Charost c.1765 under the patronage of Carlos III, and called the 'Real Escuela–Fábrica de Madrid'. Clocks which

1

2

3

4

5

6

7

have survived from this school are magnificent, and its pupils included Manuel Estepar, Manuel de Frias [296/7], Francisco Rivera, Diego Rostriaga and Cayetano Sanchez. Another clockmaking school existed at Ciudad Real, south of Madrid, under the patronage of Carlos IV, apparently founded by Antonio Mathey, a native of Neuchâtel, who had been a professor at the Royal School workshop. One of his pupils was Blas Muñoz who studied with Berthoud and later became clockmaker to the king and to the Cadiz Observatory. In 1770 Manuel Gutierrez applied to establish a school in Madrid which was eventually built about 1800 and called the 'Real Fábrica de Relojería de Madrid' [301/3]. Finally, another school existed in Barcelona, founded about 1825 by the brothers José and Luis Hubert.

A group of chronometer makers was formed in 1765 when the famous sailor Jorge Juan (1713–73) announced: 'Two or three dedicated Spanish clockmakers must be sent to London. It is not enough that chronometers are sold to us; there must be qualified people to look after them and keep them in good working order afterwards.' In 1775 Berthoud had already offered his services to the Ministry of the Sea to establish a group of chronometer makers, consequently Admiral Mazarredo (1745–1812) who had founded the Marine Observatory in San Fernando (Cádiz) in 1789, sent 20-year-old Cayetano Sánchez to specialise with him. He later went to England to work with Josiah Emery, returning to Cádiz in 1793 where he died in an epidemic in 1800.

During the 18th century three well-defined regional centres of clockmaking became established in addition to the horological schools outlined above. One was a group round Madrid, including Francisco Rivera [302/4], Manuel de Rivas and Fernando Rulla, though there were many more. The second and largest group of clockmakers was centred mainly in Compostela, where Asturias meets Galicia, to the north of the province of Lugo. This group included the Miyar family, Méndez y Neira de Saavedra, José Nicolás Rouco, Ramón Antonio Iglesias and Andrés Antelo Lamas – a marine engineer in El Ferrol whose clocks were true works of art. There are many lesser-known clockmakers of the group whose work is often only known through surviving lantern clocks [295/6]. The third group, the Catalonia group, made clocks of a more rural or popular style [296/2], probably, like the Compostela group, to supply the demand for suitable clocks by those who were not wealthy enough to acquire English or French examples. Amongst this group are to be found Miguel Rosal in Manresa, José Senesteva and Francisco Crusat in Moyá and José Saldari and José Ball in Mataró.

The history of Spanish clockmaking in the 19th century was profoundly affected by the war with Napoleon in 1808 and the final loss of the colonial empire by 1898. The Napoleonic War cut off the regional groups in Galicia and Catalonia, resulting in few further important clocks or makers from these areas [296/4], and in general the clock-making industry was depressed in Spain throughout the century. The 20th century has seen the final disappearance of the great craftsmen who constructed fine clocks during previous centuries; only a few clockmakers now accept commissions to make individual clocks. The beginning of

1 **Wall hanging alarm clock** by Faliu Roca, Arenys, Barcelona, late 18th century. Claramunt collection, Barcelona.

2 **Wall hanging alarm clock** from the Catalonia region. Arenys, Barcelona, late 18th century. Eisenmenger collection.

3 **Wall hanging alarm clock** Movement of 296/2. Eisenmenger collection.

4 **Wall hanging clock** from the Catalonia region; signed 'Joan Estorch, Olot', Gerona, 18th century.

5 **Bracket clock** by Manuel de Leon, Madrid, 1716. The case is modern. Dr Botas, La Coruña.

6 **Backplate** of basket top bracket clock in the English style; signed 'Manuel de Leon, Madrid', c.1700.

7 **Table clock,** English style; by Manuel de Frias of the Royal School of Madrid, dated 1700, Museo Municipal, Madrid.

8 **Longcase clock** by José Lopez de Cruz of the Royal School of Madrid, dated 1803. Museo Municipal, Madrid.

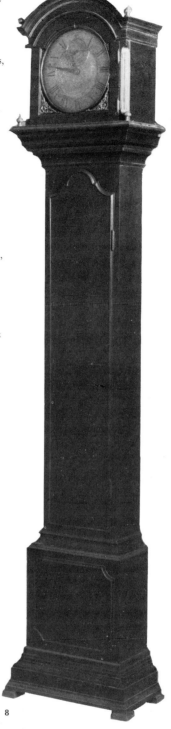

8

the century saw, however, the establishment of factories for making turret clocks and modern electric clocks. Mention must be made of Ignacio Murua who founded a turret-clock factory in Vitoria; of Mateo Bosch who designed and constructed the clock for the cathedral of Ciudadela (Mallorca); of Ignacio Tolosano who set up an electric-clock factory in Vitoria in 1920; and of José Vazquez who was awarded a prize when only 20 years old for his electric clocks. Finally, there was the nephew of Vazquez, Evangelino Taboada, who in 1945 constructed an astronomical clock in Vigo, using only manual labour, for the observatory of Compostela. JLB

297

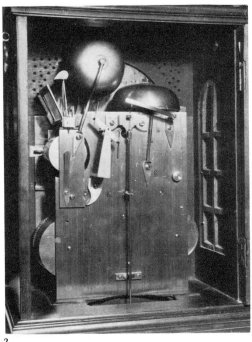

1 **Antelo Lamas, Andrés Antonio** Three-train, quarter-chiming bracket clock with side handles, calendar hand, chime/silent dial (right) and regulating dial (left) in the break arch; late 18th century.

2 **Antelo Lamas, Andrés Antonio** Movement of 298/1, showing lever to lengthen or shorten the pendulum, the quarter-chiming barrel and English-style design.

3 **Crusat, Francisco** Movement of an eight-day, three-train striking clock in a style similar to a Comtoise clock; signed 'Franco Crusat, Moya', early 19th century. Juan E. Maurer, Barcelona.

4 **Patek Philippe** Light clock; the aperture for the photo-electric cell, which provides power to wind the clock, can be seen at the top.

Antelo Lamas, Andrés Antonio A professional technician and marine engineer, Antelo Lamas (1774–1837 or 1840) was one of the best Spanish clockmakers. Besides constructing turret and domestic clocks he was responsible for sections of the shipyard in El Ferrol, and was a manager of a coin factory. He was born in El Ferrol, the son of Domingo Antelo, an iron forger in the shipyard. At the age of ten he became an apprentice locksmith, and in 1797 he rose to the position of master of steam pumps and was put in charge of locks for cannons and howitzers.

In 1817 Antelo entered into a contract for 35,000 reales to build the clock for the cathedral of Lugo, and in 1831 he was commissioned to make the clock for the cathedral of

Santiago de Compostela, a magnificent work set inside a vaulted glass niche and crowned by the statue of Santiago. It shows the time on all four sides of the tower, and is still working today. He made another clock for the marine hospital in El Ferrol, which is now in the church of San Julián. Also attributed to him are several clocks which have disappeared, including one from the monastery of Celanova. In private collections in Madrid are two domestic clocks that Antelo constructed. One is a longcase clock with eight dials and a moon-phase indicator, showing the days of the week and month, the months, hours, minutes and seconds. The other is a bracket clock with an engraved, silvered dial carrying a date hand, and a regulator hand; it also plays tunes. JLB

Crusat, Francisco Crusat (1780–after 1841) belonged to the magnificent group of clockmakers that sprang up in Catalonia at the end of the 18th century, and produced some good examples of the popular clocks of that region. Crusat was born possibly in Moyá, Barcelona, where he appears to have been the assistant of the clockmaker José Senesteva c.1805. Senesteva died in 1808 and by 1810 Crusat was married and owned his own workshop, no doubt that of his former master. In 1839, during the Carlist wars, his house was set on fire and his workshop and contents disappeared.

Several numbered clocks signed 'Moya' are known, the highest number being 502. Two that are signed respectively 'Moyá Crusat número 15' and 'Moyá Francisco Crusat' are domestic clocks in rustic style similar to Comtoise clocks. The second of these is an eight-day clock striking quarters. Both cases are missing. JLB

Estepar Alcantara, Manuel Estepar (late 18th century) is known to have been a pupil in the Escuela Real (Royal School) of the Charost brothers, where he gained the title of *maestro constructor de relojes* (master clockmaker) in 1793. Soon after, he opened a shop in Madrid making pendulum

4

1 Burnap, Daniel Tall clock with calender work and musical work comprising six tunes, with indicator in the dial arch. This was Burnap's own clock. Wadsworth Atheneum, Hartford, Connecticut

2 Lozano, Tomas Pocket watch of English design; signed in London, second half 18th century. Private collection.

3 Gutierrez, Manuel Movement of the turret clock of Toledo Cathedral, 1792.

1

clocks and pocket watches. In 1799 he sought the civic post of clockmaker of Madrid, and had to submit to tests that he had already undergone in the Escuela Real in order to become a master. These were to design a calibre for a simple eight-day pendulum clock with dead seconds, and a Graham anchor escapement, and then assemble the clock.

In a private collection in Madrid there is a longcase clock signed 'Real Escuela Manuel Estepar Ano de 1783'. It has a long pendulum, the rod of which is the blade of a sword from Toledo. JLB

Gutierrez, Manuel A native of Siguenza, Guadalajara, Gutierrez (late 18th century) was an honorary gunsmith of the King of Spain. In 1770 he attempted to found a clockmaking school in Madrid in opposition to that of the Charost brothers. In order to gain support for his project he revealed that he had constructed several notable clocks, including one for the Infante don Luis, who had presented it to Queen María Luisa Teresa. He claimed that clocks ought to be made in the English fashion, since the French method was inadequate. In 1787 he again requested royal authorisation and support to set up a complete clock-making workshop with working space for 16 craftsmen and 21 apprentices, but was again unsuccessful. Other sources indicate that in 1800 he was in charge of a workshop in the street of Fuencarral in Madrid. JLB

Iglesias Abeleira, Ramón Antonio Born in Santiago de Compostela, Iglesias (1820–77) spent his apprenticeship with his father and in Neuchâtel. He was nominated Knight of the Order of Carlos III and travelled extensively throughout Europe. In 1857 he established a clock factory in La Coruña making pocket watches and pendulum clocks, which he mainly exported to Cuba. Only one of his clocks is known, which is now in Compostela. It is a table clock in the form of a marble pavilion, with five dials to show the time in various towns. JLB

Lombardero The Lombarderos were a clockmaking family from the region of Oscos, part of Asturias close to Galicia. The head of the family was Juan Antonio Lombardero, who was born in 1705 and died in 1796. His son Francisco Antonio (1736–68) worked as an engraver for his father and helped generally in the construction of clocks. A grandson, Francisco Antonio (1769–1835) helped his grandfather in his work and himself built beautiful domestic clocks. There was also a nephew and a son-in-law.

At least a dozen clocks by this family still exist, some with serial numbers and others with inscriptions, one being dedicated to Antonio Ibanez, Marquis of Sargadelos, founder of a china factory of that name and first in Spain to use smelting furnaces. The Lombardero clocks include single-handed lantern clocks and longcase clocks with elaborate casework. Others are known from written references only.

A sundial made by Juan Antonio, signed in 1742, is in the museum of Lugo. But he also constructed turret clocks: in 1756 he built one for Ribadeo to replace a broken English clock. Juan Antonio's clock lasted until 1905, when it was scrapped. The family lived in a mountainous area, isolated from the rest of Spain by poor communications. Yet they

2   3

produced magnificent clocks, which are highly prized today. JLB

Lopez, Salvador Very little is known of Lopez's life, but he was established in Madrid in the latter half of the 18th century. Several of his works are known; one is a large clock with a long pendulum, made on special commission, dated 1796. It is to be found in the Real Oficina de Farmacia (royal pharmacy) in the royal palace of Madrid.

Lopez made a clock for the Sala de Principios in the academy of San Fernando, and a miniature table clock is also known, with alarm and striking work, signed 'En Madrid 1799, Salvador Lopez'. JLB

Lozano, Tomas For a while, Lozano was established in London; G. H. Baillie's *Watchmakers and Clockmakers of the World* refers to him there. He was also established in Cádiz, where he enjoyed a good reputation.

When several of Ferdinand Berthoud's chronometers for the navy arrived in Cádiz, No. 7 had been damaged during the journey. Lozano was chosen to repair it and the work was completed successfully. A report from the naval officers concerned in 1786, stating that Lozano was the best artisan in the town, led to his being put in charge of all future repair work. Works of his in private collections in Madrid include a mantel clock with a lacquered wooden case; a longcase clock with calendar and moon indicator, and hour and half-hour striking; a mantel clock in the style of Louis XV; and another longcase clock. All these are signed in London. JLB

Maier, Domingo Maier was apparently an early 19th-century clockmaker. A magnificent mahogany table clock with his signature is in the museum of Pontevedra in northern Spain. It seems to have been the work of three clockmakers working in collaboration, for the front is inscribed 'Lo ynbento F. Miquel Franco y construyo A. Cepada', the main dial has 'Ferrol 1811', and the backplate is signed 'Domingo Maier Offer Madrid'. The clock has six dials and a hygrometer. The main dial shows hours and minutes and has a strike/silent hand. The top dial has a regulation indicator, shows days, hours and quarters of high and low tide, and bears the letters 'RVC'. Dials at top left and right show sunrise and sunset, months, days, hours and minutes, and new moons throughout the year. Dials at bottom left and right show days and moon phases, and a calendar. All the dials are made of copper, decorated with brass inlay [302/1]. JLB

1 Maier, Domingo Mahogany table clock with six dials and a hygrometer; the movement signed 'Maier en Madrid', 1811. Museo de Pontevedra.

2 Méndez y Neira de Saavedra, Francisco Javier Dial and hood of a longcase clock with apertures for day of the week, month and date, inside the chapter ring; by the Priest of Ladrido, 1794. D. Antonio Rios Mosquera, Madrid.

1

2

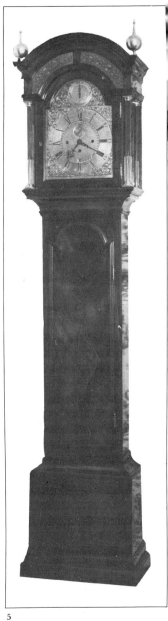

3

4

5

Méndez y Neira de Saavedra, Francisco Javier Born in Ramil, a small village in the province of Lugo, Méndez (1744–1803) studied in the seminary of Mondonedo and was nominated parish priest of Ladrino, La Coruña. In the rectory was his workshop and smelting furnace, where he cast mounts and other parts for his clocks. His pupils were his nephew, Francisco Javier Velez, and José Nicolás Rouco.

As a clockmaker, he is noteworthy for two magnificent longcase clocks, both in their original cases, and also for a lantern clock. There are twelve of his clocks, dated from 1786 to 1801, in private collections. JLB

Miyar The Miyar family constructed clocks of many types in the 19th and 20th centuries, including regulators, established in Corao, Asturias. It began with Basilio Sobrecueva Miyar (1835–90), who was born in Madrid and began clockmaking with a distinguished German clockmaker named Ganter. Towards 1860, by then established in Corao, he built a large workshop.

On his death, the workshop was inherited by his cousins Ismael and Roberto. The latter emigrated to Mexico, leaving Ismael, and later his daughter and son, in charge; the daughter looked after the painting of the dials. The factory ceased to function during the Spanish Civil War (1936–9). Afterwards, it became the workshop of a school of clockmaking and precision mechanics.

The Miyar family made clocks for railway companies, and some good regulator clocks for private individuals and business organisations. JLB

Rivas, Manuel de A Spanish clockmaker of the late 18th and early 19th centuries, Rivas (d. 1833) was appointed by the Ministry of Trade to examine applicants for the title of master clockmaker in 1794. In 1797 Prince Godoy commissioned him to produce a clock for Carlos IV and María Luisa Theresa. It had a porcelain case which was made in the porcelain factory of the Retiro, and took two years to complete. Rivas was well paid and was given responsibility for maintenance of the clock, which is now in

3 Rivera, Francisco Detail of the dial of Rivera's clock (302/4), showing the signature and the date circle.

4 Rivera, Francisco Longcase clock, with enamel dial and separate calendar hand, *c.* 1800. D. José Ignacio Llorente, Seville.

5 Rouco, José Nicolás English-style longcase clock, early 19th century. D. César Lopez Doriga, Madrid.

6 Senesteva, José Enamel and brass dial, with Dutch-style arcaded minutes, from a longcase clock by Senesteva, numbered 471, early 19th century. Manso Soler de Terrades.

7 Senesteva, José Enamel and brass dial of a longcase clock with alarm setting disc, numbered 348; inscribed 'Moya', early 19th century.

6

7

the royal palace, Madrid. It is in neoclassical style, adorned with porcelain figures.

At one time Rivas taught at the royal workshops in Madrid, where he had at least 18 pupils. From 1801 he was clockmaker to the royal household, and in 1805 became clockmaker to the king. He was again principal clockmaker to the king under Fernando VII. JLB

Rivera, Francisco Rivera (d. *c.* 1817) was the most distinguished pupil of the Royal School of the Charost brothers in Madrid, although he was accused of undertaking private studies, which was against the rules of the establishment.

Rivera was sent to Paris by Carlos IV to further his studies with François-Louis Godon, and on his return to Madrid was made clockmaker to the royal household (1799). JLB

Rodriguez Losada, José Rodriguez (d. 1875) was born in Iruela, León, at the end of the 18th century, but in 1823, political reasons compelled him to emigrate to England, where he worked in the workshop of James Moore French in London. He is supposed to have married French's widow, and took over the workshop *c.* 1840. From then on his clocks appear with the signature 'J. R. Losada, 105 Regent St, London'. He was a firm friend of the poet José Zorilla, and is referred to by Benito Pérez Galdós in his book *Episodios Nacionales*. On a journey to Spain in 1859, he considered the possibility of transferring the clock factory to his own country, but did not carry it through.

In 1856 Losada was nominated honorary clockmaker and chronometer maker to the Spanish navy, and chronometer maker and clockmaker to the royal household.

He was well known both in England and Spain for his ability and, no less, his enormous production: in 1864 the Spanish government purchased, through the Royal Observatory at Cádiz, 38 of his chronometers, following

competitive trials. It is clear that his clocks were not made by him personally but by the team in his workshop. In chronometer work Losada is remembered for his introduction of a method of winding the chronometer from the side, without having to turn it over.

On his death in 1875, his fortune and workshop were inherited by his nephews José and Miguel Rodriguez de Riego. JLB

Rouco, José Nicolás Born in Vivero, Lugo, Rouco (*c.* 1775–1852) was a pupil of Francisco Javier Neira until shortly before Neira's death, and later worked in Vivero.

Rouco's clocks are English in style. Surviving examples, both longcase and hanging clocks, are dated from 1801 to 1833. JLB

Senesteva, José Senesteva (d. 1808) was the founder of a clockmaking tradition in the town of Moyá, Barcelona, in the 18th century which was continued by his pupil Francisco Crusat. He first appears as a resident of Moyá in 1805, with his wife Teresa, and in 1807 Crusat was living with them. Senesteva died at the beginning of 1808. The turret clocks of Estany and of Mura are known to have been made by Senesteva. His domestic clocks are characteristic of those made in the area at that time – weight-driven, with a 24-hour movement, either hour and half-hour or hour and quarter striking on two bells, or only an alarm. JLB

Taboada, Evangelino Born in Lalin, Taboada (1897–1956) lived in Vigo, Pontevedra. About 1944, the restrictions and shortages of wartime Spain led Fr Ramón Aller, professor of astronomy and director of the observatory of Santiago de Compostela, to entrust the making of a sidereal clock for the observatory to the small local workshop of Evangelino Taboada.

Taboada's clock incorporates some original ideas for the escapement; in principle it is a projection of a simple Graham escapement with standard gear ratios, but in effect

1   2   3   4

is a combination of the escapements of Sigmund Riefler and of Professor Ludwig Strasser; the first has double coaxial escape wheels, one with teeth for impulsing and the other for locking, using specially shaped pin pallets, and, like the second, impulses the pendulum through the suspension spring. The difference is that the Taboada clock has double escape wheels and a double anchor with separate sets of pallets. JLB

Clockmaking in Switzerland

The visitor to Switzerland today will notice many towers with clocks in them, some quite old and elaborate. Most noteworthy are the famous tower at Berne, with its astronomical dials and automata, and Lucerne's old clock in a tower in the city wall. Winterthur is famous for the Liechti family, and one of the prized possessions of the town is the movement of a clock put up by Laurentius Liechti in a tower there in 1529. This clock has three trains and an astronomical dial with complicated gearing, and can be said to be in advance of its time. The fame of the Liechti family, however, rests on the iron Gothic clocks its members produced. Numerous examples are preserved in Winterthur as well as in other European museums. Unlike most Gothic clocks, the Liechti clocks are signed with the initials of the maker and the date [305/6].

Switzerland also had wooden clocks similar to those of the Black Forest, but they developed earlier and show a great deal of sophistication for their time. The most famous type came from Davos in the east of the country; these clocks had a tall rectangular dial, also made of wood, with a distinctive form of decoration above, fancifully resembling horns with a central finial. The wheels, pinions, frames and arbors were all of wood, and the movements were solidly made and quite well finished. The clocks were controlled by a wheel balance with a strip of metal around its edge to prevent splitting. Apart from the bell this was the only solid piece of metal in the clock, all other metal being in the form of wire, which was even used for the escape-wheel teeth. Some of the clocks sounded the quarters and most had alarm work set by a pin inserted in a selected hole in a disc which rotated with the hour hand. The timing of the alarm

was not very precise by this method but, without a balance spring, nor was the timekeeping of the clocks. Below the main dial was the small quarter-hour dial whose hand virtually performed the function of a minute hand, as in Austrian tower clocks. The dials were finished in bright colours, and the chapter rings had a white ground and black figures. Although the work was primitive, many of these clocks have given long service [304/4].

Wooden clocks were also made in other parts of Switzerland. Some of them were quite elaborate, in contrast with the wooden clocks produced in the Black Forest.

In the west of Switzerland, in the French-speaking area of the Jura, the watch industry was beginning to grow in the early 18th century and, profiting from local experience in more complicated tools and finer work, the making of clocks was carried on rather differently from that in other districts [305/5]. The early clocks in the area were weight-driven and hung on the wall. The cases were plain black wood with mouldings and sometimes a pediment, and the dials were exposed, without any glass, although the chapter ring was of metal. The term 'Louis XIII' is applied to these clocks, although they belong to about the time of the death of Louis XIV (1715) [304/1]. It is interesting to note the use of a French king's name to distinguish these clocks, for the subsequent development of the clock in Switzerland had a certain affinity with developments in France.

The basic model was modified by being driven by springs, and a glass was put in front of the dial. The clock could now stand on a table or other piece of furniture, and metal feet were added. The simple pediment was replaced by a bell or basket top and as the 18th century advanced and the rococo style became fashionable in France, so the Swiss model abandoned the rectangular shape and adopted curved sides, waisted between the dial and the base.

France soon developed enamel dials, and they were adopted in Switzerland. The Swiss dial was generally convex and easily legible, while the cases of the clocks were not so heavily decorated with bronze mounts as French clocks. Swiss decoration was limited to a restrained finish of *vernis Martin* on the case [304/3] and a gilt edge to the door covering the dial and the pendulum. The Swiss style has become known by the name 'Neuchâtel', although the clocks were made in other places in the area, such as La

Chaux-de-Fonds. The style persisted to the mid 19th century, with later examples ever more restrained in style and with separate glasses over dial and pendulum.

In addition to the Swiss model of the Neuchâtel clock, similar styles to the French were made in the Swiss Jura. The early wall clocks that gave rise to the Neuchâtel style were also developed into a longcase clock, but these are less frequently encountered.

Renaissance table clocks and various astronomical and regulator clocks are to be found in Swiss museums, but their numbers are not large. In addition to clocks Swiss clockmakers have specialised in automata such as the famous model writer, artist and musician in the museum at Neuchâtel made by Pierre Jaquet-Droz. Other museums contain model insects, animals or human figures that move, all exemplifying the Swiss genius for fine mechanisms. Another Swiss speciality is the musical box, many of which have been used as additions to clocks produced in other countries.

During the present century, the Atmos clock has been developed in Switzerland. This is a variation of the 400-day clock with a torsion pendulum. The torsion pendulum uses very little energy and slight variations in temperature are sufficient to provide the power to keep the clock going. EJT

Ditisheim, Paul One of the world's most brilliant horologists, born in Switzerland, Ditisheim (1868–1945) established a chronometer factory in La Chaux-de-Fonds, producing chronometers and precision watches that performed highly in observatory trials. Labouring constantly toward precision of the highest order, he experimented with nickel steels such as invar and elinvar to eliminate temperature problems. Among other experiments, he applied the lever escapement to the marine chronometer with considerable success. Because of financial problems after the 1921 recession, he went to Paris, where he did important research in horological lubrication, resulting in the famous Cronax oils. In the 1930s he conducted experiments in the field of quartz-crystal timekeepers and published an important paper on them in 1937. DJB

Guillaume, Charles-Édouard Guillaume (d. 1936) was the inventor of invar and elinvar, metal alloys which remain more or less of constant size at different temperatures, used for the pendulum rods and balances, and for the balance springs respectively of high-precision clocks and watches.

He was born at Fleurier, in Switzerland, and in 1883 joined the International Bureau of Weights and Measures. In 1896 invar was produced after much experiment, and Paul Perret, a clockmaker from Neuchâtel, made an experimental spring from it. Paul Ditisheim and Paul Nardin later made balances from the new metal. Researches between 1912 and 1920 produced elinvar, which assured perfect compensation. PSKM

Hipp, Matthäus Matthäus (or Matthias) Hipp (1813–93) is most famous for his contributions to electrical horology, even though he devised many ingenious mechanical improvements to clocks. Among the latter was his pendulum impulsed only when the arc dropped to a certain level [157/9].

1 **Wall hanging clock** known as 'Louis XIII', with verge escapement, single hour hand and alarm; cabinet of painted wood; by Isaac Bradt, La Chaux-de-Fonds, c. 1720. Musée International d'Horlogerie, La Chaux-de-Fonds.

2 **Table clock** known as a *religieuse*, or as 'Louis XIII'. Ebonised case with gilt-bronze mounts, verge escapement with hour and half-hour striking; by Abram and Moïse Huguenin, La Chaux-de-Fonds. Musée International d'Horlogerie, La Chaux-de-Fonds.

3 **Bracket clock** known as a *pendule Neuchâteloise*, with case decorated in *vernis Martin*, verge escapement, enamel dial, *grande sonnerie* striking; by Aimé Billon, La Chaux-de-Fonds, c. 1850. Musée International d'Horlogerie, La Chaux-de-Fonds.

4 **Wall clock from Davos,** in the east of Switzerland, with wooden painted dial and movement, the only metal component being the bell, although some wire is also used. The clock has hour striking, alarm, calendar indication, and the lower dial indicates quarter-hours; early 18th century. Uhrensammlung Kellenberger, Winterthur.

5 **Peasant wall clock,** known as a 'Toggenberg' (eastern Switzerland) clock, with single hour hand, painted wooden dial, 'cowtail' pendulum and quarter-hour dial beneath main dial; 18th century. Uhrensammlung Kellenberger, Winterthur.

6 **Liechti** Domestic iron-framed clock with painted iron dial, alarm work and moon's phases; by Ulrich and Andreas Liechti, Winterthur, Switzerland, dated 1599. British Museum, London.

5   6

While at St Gall in Switzerland during 1834, aged only 21, Hipp conceived the idea of maintaining a pendulum by electromagnetic means. He did not construct a clock on this principle until 1842, thereby losing the honour of being the first to have done so. Nevertheless, the Hipp-toggle system of contacts has stood the test of time and is still in use today. In 1890 one of Hipp's astronomical electrical clocks had a precision better than the mechanical clocks in use at Neuchâtel observatory, the first occasion that an electrical clock surpassed that of the best mechanical regulators. CKA

Jaquet-Droz, Pierre and Henri Louis Pierre Jaquet-Droz (1721–90) was born in La Chaux-de-Fonds, Switzerland, which even then was a centre for watchmaking, and gained a knowledge of the craft at an early age. He was not content to make ordinary clocks and watches but preferred to add a musical mechanism or other complications. In 1774 he began exhibiting his mechanical figures or automata throughout Europe.

Three figures are now in the museum at Neuchâtel and consist of two small boys, one of whom writes while the other makes drawings, and a somewhat older girl who plays a small musical organ. The writer was made by Pierre and the other two figures by his son Henri Louis.

Besides automata, Pierre Jaquet-Droz made clocks, including one which was wound by the difference in expansion of two metals.

His son Henri Louis (1752–91) at first worked with his father. He studied mathematics, physics, drawing and music in Nancy. In later years he worked with J. F. Leschot and established a clock and watch retailing branch in London. EJT

Liechti The Liechti family is unique in that it had at least one member working as a clockmaker during a period of over 300 years. Throughout that time the family worked in one town, Winterthur in Switzerland.

The earliest clockmaking member of the family was Laurence, who established himself before 1514, the year in which he was given the order for a clock in the Frauenkirche in Munich. An example of his turret clocks preserved at Winterthur is a three-train clock with end-to-end trains and some elaborate decoration of the frame, all executed in iron. Laurence died in 1545.

His son Laurence II carried on business as a locksmith and turret-clock maker. The brother of Laurence II, Erhard, specialised in domestic clocks, and was the pioneer of the type of Gothic wall clock always associated with the Liechti family. Laurence I had signed his work with initials and date and the custom was continued, so that the later Gothic clocks made by members of the Liechti family can be identified [305/6].

Erhard made a wide variety of clocks and was an excellent craftsman, the decoration on his clocks being very delicate for ironwork. He died in 1591, and was succeeded by his two sons Ulrich (d. 1627) and Andreas (1562–1621). Andreas made turret clocks on his own, but sometimes collaborated with his brother on domestic clocks. Joachim (1582–1638), son of Ulrich, also worked on turret and domestic clocks. Another Andreas (1582–1650) followed suit and he had three sons, Tobias (1614–73), Heinrich (1634–1704) and Jakob (1636–1707), who continued his business. Hans Ulrich (1643–1719) travelled in his early days to escape the depression that followed the Thirty Years War. In 1668 he returned to Winterthur, where he quarrelled with the local guildsmen over an unpaid fine. Hans Ulrich made watches as well as turret clocks. His sons Tobias (1670–1711) and Hans Jakob (1680–1741) were also clockmakers. Tobias made several turret clocks with pendulums in collaboration with his father. By this time the Gothic clock had died out; Hans Jakob is known for a baroque standing clock with a brass case and well-finished movement.

Another Hans Ulrich (1699–1770) was a turret-clock maker. Hans Heinrich (1733–1810) was successful in separating the functions of clockmaker and locksmith officially in 1764. The last few members of the family were mostly concerned with selling ready-made pieces and performing repairs. Jakob Ulrich was still in that business as late as 1857. EJT

Patek Philippe Count Antoine Norbert de Patek came from Poland and in 1844 formed an association with a Paris

1 **Tall clock** with walnut case and brass and pewter dial; by Jacob Graff, Lebanon County, Pennsylvania, 1765–75. Henry Francis du Pont Winterthur Museum, Winterthur, Delaware.

2 **Massachusetts shelf clock** with eight-day weight-driven movement by Aaron Willard, Boston, Massachusetts, c.1805. Metropolitan Museum of Art, New York, Sylmar Collection. Gift of George Coe Graves, 1930.

3 **O.G. shelf clock,** mahogany veneer and white pine; by Jeromes, Gilbert, Grant & Co., Bristol, Connecticut, c.1840. Yale University Art Gallery, New Haven, Connecticut.

1   2   3

watchmaker, Adrian Philippe (1815–94), for the manufacture of high-quality watches. Patek Philippe's factory was located in Geneva, and the high quality of the products encouraged another firm to set up business in the same city under the name 'Pateck & Cie'. This firm did not aim so high as Patek Philippe, but many members of the public believed they were getting a Patek Philippe watch when they were buying one marked 'Pateck & Cie'.

In recent years Patek Philippe have manufactured a clock that functions by light. The shape suggests some of the early table clocks of the tower type, and the domed top contains a photoelectric cell which can be turned towards the light source and operates a small motor for winding the clock. Four hours of exposure to light will run the clock for 24 hours [299/4]. EJT

Reutter, J. L. As an engineering graduate student at Neuchâtel, Switzerland in 1913, Reutter became interested in the problem of applying changes in atmospheric pressure and temperature to produce power for maintaining the going of a clock. His first patent, dated 28th November 1928 (no. 331,764) utilises the differential expansion of a liquid separated by a mercury column, one part maintained in constant temperature by a Dewar flask arrangement, the other part being exposed to the changing temperature of the environment. On 4th June 1930 a further patent (no. 356,216) was granted for a torsion pendulum. Both these developments were essential to the production of the successful Atmos clock [15/6]. In Great Britain these clocks appeared in 1934, and the sole distributor was D. E. Trevars Ltd, 106 Regent St, London, the movement being manufactured by Jaeger-le-Coultre of Switzerland. CKA

Clockmaking in the United States

Clockmaking in early colonial America was so closely linked with the craft in Britain that it is difficult to separate them. To determine accurately the meaning of the term 'clockmaker' in colonial America is not easy. Through printed records such as advertisements and obituaries, clockmakers are known to have existed in America in the 17th century, but it appears likely that most of them had been trained in England and imported clocks and watches from the homeland through established contacts with the trade. They were thus primarily importers and dealers, though they also did repairs.

In early America neither the materials nor the techniques vital to successful clock manufacture were readily available. Just as the London maker of those days depended on Lancashire sources for tools and materials such as pinion wire, wheels and wheel blanks, forgings, etc., so the American maker would have depended on British sources. As London makers finished or adapted Lancashire movements to their requirements, so probably did many workers in colonial America. The distances involved and the slow transportation of those days no doubt induced the more skilled, who possessed a fair range of tools, to improvise additional tooling and to utilise discarded metal to make more complete movements of their own.

Though examples exist of some very well-finished tall clocks bearing American names, to determine now if they are truly of American manufacture is almost impossible. Examination of clocks by early Connecticut makers such as John Whitear (d. 1762), Isaac Doolittle (1721–1800), John Benjamin (1730–96) or Joseph Clark (d. 1821) reveal movements that in their crude finish and rather rough materials suggest native manufacture.

Thomas Harland who, equipped with some tools, arrived in Boston from England in 1773 and settled in Norwich, appears to have made complete clocks – a conclusion borne out by the extant records of Daniel Burnap, Harland's most important apprentice, which reveal the completeness of his

shop and his capacity to make movements and dials. The existence of 18th-century clocks with American names which appear to contain finished movements from England leads to the conclusion that those calling themselves clockmakers probably included men who never made a clock but imported movements, and those who imported parts and finished and assembled them, quite apart from those who made nearly everything themselves in well-equipped shops [306/1].

To try to classify American clocks by types and periods is impractical, since various methods were used concurrently in different localities. By 1800 the famous Willards from Grafton, Massachusetts [306/2], had developed a whole school of clockmaking in the Boston area. Their influence, evident throughout Massachusetts, persisted for more than half a century and could be said still to exist in Howard clocks made today. Though tradition says that Benjamin, the eldest of the Willard clockmaking brothers, learned the craft from Benjamin Cheney of East Hartford, Connecticut, to whom he was apprenticed c. 1760, the direction of Massachusetts horological production after 1800 differed from that of neighbouring Connecticut.

The Cheneys made both brass- and wood-movement tall clocks; the Willards, however, established a tradition of good quality brass-movement clocks of various patterns. Connecticut makers leaned increasingly toward wood-movement clock production through the efforts of Eli Terry who, though he learned brass clockmaking from Daniel Burnap, saw the need for an inexpensive, popular clock in the newly independent and developing country. This required the use of cheap native materials. While Boston or Newport, with wealth coming from extensive trade, could support several makers of expensive clocks, the general populace could not hope to own such articles. Terry's natural mechanical ability, combined with exceptional business acumen, resulted in his great success in marketing relatively inexpensive shelf clocks manufactured on a kind of mass-production basis, using jigs and fixtures to process native materials to tolerances permitting simple assembly. From 1815 onwards large numbers of such clocks were produced, not only by Terry but by many other enterprising Connecticut Yankees who tried their hands at clock production with varying degrees of success.

The introduction of inexpensive rolled brass by the mills in the Waterbury, Connecticut, area eventually brought the cost of brass clocks with excellent manufacturing techniques to the point where almost anyone could afford a household clock [306/3]. Wood-movement clocks could not be exported because the long sea voyages caused swelling of the wood, but inexpensive brass clocks could be and were sold overseas in Britain and elsewhere throughout most of the 19th century. Firms like Seth Thomas, Waterbury, New Haven, Ansonia, and Ingraham turned out enormous quantities of clocks for a worldwide market. Eli Terry's annual production of 6,000 clocks early in the century had astonished those who had said it could not be done. Shortly after 1900 Connecticut factories were turning out about 8,000 wood-cased clocks daily, and nearly twice as many nickel-drum alarm clocks, many of the latter selling for less than one dollar.

The 19th century witnessed the gradual decline of the

manufacture of clocks in small family workshops in Massachusetts and elsewhere [300/1] as the Connecticut factory system increased. While the clocks produced by shops such as those of the Willards were reliable and durable, they were too expensive to compete with mass-produced timekeepers. Except for Edward Howard and David P. Davis's joint endeavour to maintain quality in combination with factory methods on a limited scale without compromising performance or durability, most Massachusetts clockmaking had died out by the end of the century. In some instances attention was turned to watch production, as at the Howard factory and the vast American Watch Co. in Waltham.

For every American factory that succeeded in horological production on a commercially profitable scale, there were numerous firms that operated for short periods and often failed with disastrous consequences for those who had invested. Behind the giants of the industry there was a combination of technical capability, a keen business sense, and a thorough understanding of the market, with the foresight to perceive changing tastes.

The coming of the cheap synchronous electric clock (not really a clock in the traditional sense) virtually destroyed the once-mighty American industry. In some instances old names may exist, but they are often applied to inexpensive imported movements from Japan, West Germany, Taiwan or Korea. Ironically, the two or three old companies still making American clocks are those which made only high-grade clocks.

When one considers that many Connecticut clocks which still give faithful service and keep time to within a minute a week were originally sold for a few dollars, the ability of their makers must be admitted. Of the finer clocks produced in the United States by past generations, many are today in almost as good a state as when they left their makers' hands. It is little wonder that these witnesses to the integrity of those whose works have outlived them are so highly regarded by their descendants [309/1]. DJB

American Clock Co. The American Clock Co. was organised *c.* 1850 to succeed the Connecticut Protective Clock Co. This had consisted of eight leading Connecticut clock manufacturers around Bristol, who had common interests in marketing. They had a large saleroom on Cortlandt St, New York, for sales of their products in the metropolitan area. Sharing the expenses of such a sales office brought it within the reach of all, and as some of the Connecticut companies failed or were reorganised, other firms were added to the combine. In the 1860s they had a sales office in Chicago and later others in Philadelphia and San Francisco. DJB

Ansonia Clock Co. About 1850 the Ansonia Brass Co. of Derby, Connecticut, organised a division to use its brass in manufacturing complete clocks. The operation was called the 'Ansonia Clock Co.'. After a fire in 1854, Anson Phelps, the founder, combined this with his mill operation under the name 'Ansonia Brass & Copper Co.', moving north of Derby to an area he called 'Ansonia'. Clocks in large numbers and great variety were made there until 1878, when the clock manufacturing was moved to Brooklyn. In October 1880 this factory, too, was burned, but manufacturing resumed there in 1881 and continued until 1929, when decline in business resulted in sale of the machinery to the Soviet Union where, for a time, with help from former Ansonia personnel, Ansonia models were made for the Russian market. DJB

Birge & Fuller John Birge, who was involved in various Bristol, Connecticut, clockmaking operations, and Thomas Fuller formed a partnership in 1844 which lasted until Fuller's death in 1848. Birge had been associated with William L. Gilbert who later founded the firm that was eventually to become the William L. Gilbert Clock Co. in Winsted, and made use of the 1825 factory of Riley Whiting until its destruction by fire in 1871, when a new plant was built. Birge & Fuller sold an extensive line of weight-driven and wagon-spring clocks, the latter with fusees of Connecticut type often fitted to steeple-on-steeple cases of which the wide lower section housed the wagon-spring assembly, a modified form of that used by Joseph Ives. These clocks are now rare. DJB

Boardman, Chauncey Chauncey Boardman (1789–1857) of Bristol, Connecticut, began to manufacture wood-movement 'hang-up' clocks with Butler Dunbar

1 2 3

1 New Hampshire mirror clock with eight-day striking movement; by James Collins, Goffstown, New Hampshire, c.1830. New Hampshire Historical Society, Concord, New Hampshire.

2 Ansonia Clock Co French style mantel clock with bronze figure of St George and the dragon, visible escapement, eight-day spring-driven movement; c.1890. American Clock & Watch Museum, Bristol, Connecticut.

3 Birge & Fuller Twin candle finial, sharp Gothic-on-frame clock, with Joseph Ives's lever-spring, or wagon-spring, eight-day brass movement, c.1845. British Museum, London.

4 Boardman, Chauncey O.G. shelf clock, with patriotic American emblems on the tablet; signed 'Boardman & Wells, Bristol, Conn.', c.1840. American Clock & Watch Museum, Bristol, Connecticut.

5 Bond, William & Son An unusual regulator with constant drive through a conical pendulum, controlled by a mercury-compensated seconds pendulum; single-arm gravity escapement, spherical double weights, on a modern stand; mid 19th century. Merseyside County Museum, Liverpool.

6 Bond regulator Detail of escapement; the large upper wheel, which is continually rotating (its speed governed by the conical pendulum) drives the lower wheel, which in turn re-sets the single gravity arm (right) at each alternate swing of the pendulum.

7 Bond regulator showing the motionwork and drive to the conical pendulum, and one of the two driving barrels.

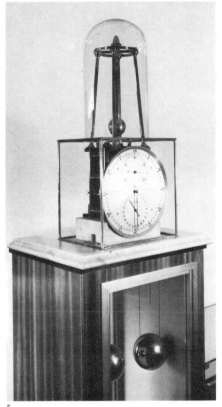

4

5

6

7

c.1810. About two years later he bought out Dunbar's interest. Boardman was a prolific maker of many kinds of Connecticut clock, which he sometimes sold under his own name and in some cases manufactured for others. He was most active during his association with his son-in-law, Joseph Wells, 1832–43, when the firm was known as Boardman & Wells. Starting out with a modified hang-up movement adapted to a shelf case, after 1837 they increasingly used rolled-brass movements. The partnership was dissolved in 1843, but Boardman continued clockmaking until his bankruptcy in 1850. DJB

Bond, William & Son One of the best-known American firms associated with chronometers was founded by William Bond of Boston in 1793. Originally finishing chronometers using English *ébauches* (unfinished movements), during the War of 1812 Bond ingeniously designed a chronometer using a weight, as the English source of supply was cut off and fine springs were not available in the United States. Richard F. Bond invented an unusual pendulum escapement releasing a conical pendulum to impart constant motion to an astronomical telescope. During the 1850s and 1860s the firm advertised as

1 Brewster & Ingrahams Sharp Gothic, four-column clock, with 30-hour movement (American Pattern); c.1845. American Clock & Watch Museum, Bristol, Connecticut.

2 Fasoldt, Charles Regulator with unique temperature compensation, causing the pendulum to rise or fall as required. Made in Rome, New York, 1855. The Wing collection.

3 Fasoldt, Charles Regulator with mercury-compensated pendulum impulsed *below* its bob, the movement and dial being at the bottom of the case; 1865. The Wing collection.

4 Forestville Manufacturing Co. Mahogany-veneered shelf clock, eight-day weight-driven movement; signed on upper tablet 'J. C. Brown, Bristol, CT' underneath a view of J. C. Brown's residence, c.1838. American Clock & Watch Museum, Bristol, Connecticut.

1   2   3   4

'chronometer maker to the U.S. Government'. In the 1870s it was agent for Victor Kullberg's 'celebrated watches', selling both Kullberg watches and marine chronometers. The last of the Bonds operated the firm until the late 1930s. DJB

Brewster & Ingrahams Consisting of the Ingraham brothers, Elias and Andrew, in partnership with Elisha C. Brewster, Brewster & Ingrahams started at Bristol, Connecticut, in 1844. Early in 1828 Elias Ingraham had gone to Bristol to work for George Mitchell, a keen businessman well known in Bristol circles, who had been seeking someone capable of producing a new and pleasing style of clock to compete with Chauncey Jerome's recently introduced and popular bronze looking-glass clock. Ingraham was successful in producing a competitively popular case and continued casemaking for Mitchell for some years. About 1844 Brewster & Ingrahams began to produce new models, of which the most popular was the sharp Gothic or steeple clock which rapidly replaced the large three-section Empire case so popular with Connecticut makers from the 1830s. DJB

Burnap, Daniel One of Connecticut's most important clockmakers, Daniel Burnap [1759–1838], spent his early life in East Windsor but moved to Coventry in 1800, remaining there until his death. He was trained by Thomas Harland and in turn trained Eli Terry, thus becoming one of the chief links in the evolution of Connecticut clock manufacture. He was an able workman producing fine tall clocks with eight-day brass movements along traditional lines, but in some instances incorporating musical trains of

his own design. His shop records have been preserved and his shop sign is at the American Clock and Watch Museum in Bristol. Examples of his work are eagerly sought today [300/1]. DJB

Clark, Heman & Sylvester Two brothers who are best known for the manufacture of a style of eight-day brass-movement striking clock generally called 'Salem Bridge', which referred to its movement. Of all the types of Connecticut shelf clock manufactured in the 19th century, this is one of the best designed and most durable. Heman Clark, who had been an apprentice of Eli Terry and probably learned both brass and wood clockmaking from him, purchased Terry's Plymouth plant in 1807 and made wood movements until 1813, when he sold this small factory to Seth Thomas. He then built facilities for making other clocks, notably a compact brass shelf-clock movement with cut-steel pinions and rack striking which would run for eight days and had a case of the pillar and scroll type, slightly refined and so proportioned as to have a deeper lower glass in the door.

Heman's younger brother Sylvester went to Salem Bridge (now Naugatuck) c.1820 to begin the manufacture of clocks there. In 1823 Heman joined him and until c.1830 they produced clocks without great financial success because of the competition of much cheaper wood clocks by Terry and others. DJB

Fasoldt, Charles A German refugee who came from the Dresden area, Charles Fasoldt (1818–98) arrived in New York in 1849, lived in Rome, New York State, for a time, and settled in Albany.

Because of his background and the influence on him of Adolf Ferdinand Lange and others involved in watchmaking in Saxony in the 1840s, Fasoldt is out of the mainstream of American horology. By employing skilled workmen in Albany and establishing high standards, he produced in limited numbers watches, precision clocks, carriage clocks and other items requiring fine workmanship – all unique in their design. The business continued, though decreasing, under his son Otto and grandson Dudley into the 1930s, at which time they were making good clock movements modelled after those of the Willards. DJB

Forestville Manufacturing Co. The Forestville Manufacturing Co. is a confusing designation since the firm involved several Bristol, Connecticut, clockmakers, apparently growing out of Elias Ingraham and William G. Bartholomew's casemaking business, c. 1831. Jonathan Clark Brown, a leading figure in Bristol clockmaking, bought Elias Ingraham's interests and with several others, including Chauncey Boardman, built a factory in Forestville, a section of Bristol, for the manufacture of complete clocks. The Forestville name was used from 1835 to 1839. J. C. Brown acquired the operation in 1842 and concurrently with his own labels used those of the Forestville Manufacturing Co. Though the firm produced a variety of clocks, they are now best remembered for an unusual form of steam-formed laminated wood case somewhat resembling an acorn in shape, a style popular in the 1840s. DJB
See also Acorn clock (Section I).

General Time Corporation A New York based corporation, earlier known as General Time Instruments Corporation, General Time Corporation acquired the assets of the Seth Thomas Clock Co. of Thomaston, Connecticut, and Western Clock Co. of La Salle, Indiana, in the 1930s. As a result of a shareholders' battle and a court contest, Talley Industries of Seattle later acquired General Time.

Seth Thomas had been one of the best-known American manufacturers of all kinds of clocks. The name continues today for imported inexpensive movements fitted to cases made outside the factory. Western Clock, a division of Talley known as 'Westclox', continues to make alarm clocks. DJB

Gilbert Clock Co., William L. William L. Gilbert, born 1806, was active in the clock business from his early 20s, both in Bristol, Connecticut, and later in Dayton, Ohio, where Bristol clocks were marketed. In the mid 1830s, on his return to Bristol, he associated himself with John Birge as Birge, Gilbert & Co. For a few years they manufactured eight-day brass movements of the strap type – strips of brass riveted together to form inexpensive plates. With Lucius Clark in 1841 Gilbert moved to Winsted, Connecticut, where they purchased the old Riley Whiting factory. In 1871 fire destroyed the factory, but new buildings were erected and the business continued successfully with a large output until recession in the 1900s created serious financial problems and, in 1932, receivership. Despite efforts to continue, lack of profit led to sale of the firm in 1964. DJB

5 Gilbert Clock Co., William L. Mantel or shelf clock in walnut, 'teardrop'-style case, spring-driven, c. 1880. American Clock & Watch Museum, Bristol, Connecticut.
6 Harland, Thomas Longcase or tall clock with arched hood surmounted by three flame finials and ornamental cresting; c.1790. Metropolitan Museum of Art, New York. Kennedy Fund, 1918.

5   6

Harland, Thomas Thomas Harland, born in England in 1735, arrived in Boston, Massachusetts, in 1773 but soon moved to Norwich, Connecticut, where he set up a shop to manufacture or finish clocks, watches, silverware and jewellery. He lived in Norwich until his death in 1807.

Harland arrived in Norwich at an ideal time, as the town had decided not to purchase goods imported from England, and he was thus able to build up a business in a relatively short time. He had brought a fairly complete set of clockmaking tools from England, and from his advertisements in the Norwich newspaper it is evident that he traded in a wide range of horological and jewellery items.

Harland's importance is partly due to the fact that he trained many apprentices who became excellent clockmakers. Among them was Daniel Burnap who, through training Eli Terry, laid the foundation for what came to be by 1850 a very large Connecticut industry. DJB

Howard, Edward Edward Howard (1813–1904) was born in Hingham, Massachusetts, and was apprenticed to Aaron Willard Jr. He set up a clockmaking business in 1842 with David P. Davis, another apprentice of Willard, and

1   2   3

with the assistance of a family friend, Luther Stephenson, a well-known Boston scale and balance manufacturer. Until *c*.1846 the firm was known as Stephenson, Howard & Davis. It was located first in Theatre Alley but shortly afterwards at 72 Water St, Boston. About 1847 Howard & Davis moved to 34 Water St where they remained until 1856 when they moved to 43 Cornhill. After the failure of their watch-making venture at Waltham in 1857, Davis withdrew, and the firm's name became E. Howard & Co., with an office at 109 Washington St. The clock factory, which was in Roxbury, produced an extensive line of banjo clocks, regulators and turret clocks. The clock operation moved to Waltham *c*.1927.

4

Though Edward Howard retired in 1881, the firm continued, known from 1934 as Howard Clock Products Co., manufacturing gears, pinions, screw machine products, etc., as well as traditional Howard Clocks. DJB
See also Howard & Davis.

Howard & Davis After completion of their apprenticeships Edward Howard and David P. Davis became partners, using the Boston office of Luther Stephenson as Stephenson, Howard & Davis. In 1847 Davis and Howard moved to their own store at 34 Water St, Boston, but operated a factory in Roxbury for the manufacture of fine-quality scales and balances where they also made fire engines. A wide range of fine clocks was manufactured including turret clocks, functionally styled banjo clocks, some with rack striking, and regulators, from simple ones to superb astronomical types with very fine trains and jewelled escapements. The finish on these clocks has rarely been equalled in the United States and never surpassed.

In 1857 Davis withdrew from the firm because of the financial problems resulting from an attempt to manufacture watches. He worked as a clock repairer in Boston for some years and was for a while associated with John Polsey. Howard continued in Roxbury until his retirement in 1881. DJB

Ingraham, E., & Co. Elias Ingraham (1805–1885) was trained in cabinetmaking by D. Dewey, a Hartford, Connecticut, cabinetmaker, and went to work for George Mitchell in Bristol, Massachusetts, in 1828. Mitchell was a shrewd businessman who sought someone with creative ability who could produce new case styles for a highly competitive market. Ingraham developed a carved-column clock with carved crest at the top. In 1830 he began to make the popular Empire cases with three sections and columns for C. & L. C. Ives. They were manufacturing eight-day brass clocks requiring a fairly long drop for the weights, and the tall Empire cases were eminently suitable.

1 Ithaca Calendar Clock Co.
Eight-day calendar clock,
'Farmer' model; c. 1875.
American Clock & Watch
Museum, Bristol, Connecticut.

2 Ives, Joseph Empire-style shelf
clock; lever-spring (or wagon-
spring) power with early, wrought
brass, eight-day movement and
roller pinions; c. 1826. American
Clock & Watch Museum, Bristol,
Connecticut.

**3 Jerome, Chauncey and
Noble** Patent movement with
solid (uncrossed) wheels;
Philadelphia label, 'William D.
Rappa', c.1838. American Clock
& Watch Museum, Bristol,
Connecticut.

4 Howard, Edward View of the
Howard display in the '1876
Centennial Exhibition',
Philadelphia.

5 Howard & Davis
Astronomical regulator with
mercury pendulum, high-
numbered wheel train, eight-day
movement; Boston, Massachusetts,
c. 1855. American Clock & Watch
Museum, Bristol, Connecticut.

5

At one time the Ithaca company produced calendars in
15 languages and shipped them to countries all over the
world. DJB

Ives, Joseph Ives (1782–1862) was one of the most
remarkable and inventive figures in Connecticut clockmaking. Ives reached maturity at a time when the wood-
movement clock was in its prime. He started making
wooden movements, but soon became interested in brass,
particularly rolled sheet brass. His work in this area had
tremendous effects on the industry. He is particularly
remembered for the rolling pinion and also used successfully
the wagon or multileaf spring to drive clocks.

A full account of his wide-ranging activities may be found
in Kenneth D. Roberts's *The Contributions of Joseph Ives to
Connecticut Clock Technology* (1970). DJB
See also Wagon-spring clock (Section I); Pinion, rolling-leaf
(Section II).

Jerome, Chauncey and Noble Chauncey Jerome
(1793–1868) was one of the most prominent men in
Connecticut clock manufacturing during the 19th century.
At 23 his ability in cabinet-work brought him into contact
with Eli Terry, for whom he briefly made cases in
Plymouth. Selling his Plymouth home to Eli Terry for 100
wooden movements, he went to Bristol and made up
movements for George Mitchell. After several other
ventures Jerome, with his brother Noble (who worked from
c. 1824–49) and Elijah Darrow, formed Jeromes, Darrow
& Co., c. 1824. In 1828 another partnership was under-
taken, and the firm became Jeromes & Darrow. The pillar
and scroll case of Eli Terry had dominated the wood-
movement clock industry, but this firm introduced the
bronze looking-glass clock with a mirror below the dial and
pilasters instead of full columns.

In the 1830s the clock business declined, and Chauncey
Jerome, looking for something to revitalise it, hit upon the
idea of a cheap 30-hour brass movement, rolled brass now
being readily available. Noble Jerome developed a suitable
movement, which led to a great revival of the industry, with
clocks being shipped overseas.

The company set up a factory in New Haven in 1844 to
be supplied with movements from the Bristol factory, but it
was destroyed by fire the next year. DJB

Juvet, Louis Paul Born in Switzerland, Juvet
(1838–1930) was trained as a watchmaker but when 26
decided to seek his fortune in the United States. After his
arrival in New York in 1864 he went to Glens Falls and
opened a jewellery shop where, besides selling the usual line
of jewellery, watches, clocks and silverware, he made a
speciality of fitting eye glasses. He operated this business in
Glens Falls until his retirement at 87, five years before his
death.

Horologically he is best known for his 'time globe', for
which he filed patent application in 1867. The globe
incorporated clockwork, so that it revolved in 24 hours,
while a clock dial on the upper axis indicated local time.
Time elsewhere on earth could then readily be seen. These
were later manufactured in Canajoharie, New York, from
1878 until fire destroyed the factory in 1886. They were

In the following years Elias Ingraham was involved in a
number of ventures. About 1845 he designed the famous
sharp Gothic four-column clock with four spires at the top,
which at once became popular. This was later modified to
the more common two-spired version, without columns. It
is probably the most popular clock case ever made in the
United States. Under various names Ingraham's company
continued as one of the world's largest clock producers. It
was sold to McGraw-Edison in 1967. DJB

Ithaca Calendar Clock Co. Several calendar mechanisms
were made in Ithaca, New York, in the 1850s but they had
some limitations. Then Henry Bishop Horton (1819–1885)
developed a mechanism indicating day, date and month
with automatic leap-year correction. A patent for this was
issued in 1865, which Horton tried to sell to several
Connecticut clock companies without success. With the
support of a number of local businessmen, he set up the
Ithaca Calendar Clock Co. on two floors in a rented
building. As the business rapidly expanded, a splendid new
building was erected, which was unfortunately destroyed
by fire in February 1876, but it was rebuilt and continued
until c. 1918. The clock movements, which had a special
cam to operate the calendar, were purchased from various
Connecticut manufacturers and cased with the calendars in
Ithaca. After 1900 the business declined and finally went
bankrupt.

made in globe sizes of 12, 18 and 30 in. diameter in both table and floor models. DJB

Marrison, Warren A. On 6th November 1947 a lecture was given to the British Horological Institute by Warren A. Marrison, an electrical engineer of the Bell Telephone Laboratories, New York, with the title 'The Evolution of the Quartz-Crystal Clock'. It was attended by the Astronomer Royal, Sir Harold Spencer Jones, and many other eminent men. Few of those present were aware that they were listening to the death knell of the mechanical timekeeper. Marrison was the pioneer of the application of the quartz-crystal oscillator to precision timekeeping, and his first ideas occurred as early as 1924. The first quartz-crystal clock was described to the International Union of Scientific Radio Telegraphy in October 1927 by J. W. Horton and Marrison. By 1937 four such quartz-crystal oscillators were used as the frequency and time standard by Bell Telephones; a clock dial controlled by these was shown in the window of 195 Broadway and was called the 'world's most accurate public clock'. Concluding his lecture, Marrison correctly forecast that atomic resonances would provide absolute standards. Marrison laid the foundation for the revolution in timekeeping methods which is taking place today. CKA

New Haven Clock Co. Hiram Camp (1811–1893), a nephew of Chauncey Jerome, was born in Plymouth, Connecticut. After working for Jerome he set up in business in New Haven, c. 1844, manufacturing movements which he sold to his uncle. When Jerome failed, Camp acquired his business and operated it for many years under the name of the 'New Haven Clock Co.'. By the 1880s the company had sales offices in Britain and Japan and was manufacturing a large range of clocks. Styles not made by the New Haven company were purchased from other manufacturers. After Camp's retirement in 1892, they continued to add models until there were so many that profits fell. Despite reorganisation the company finally ceased operations in the late 1950s. DJB

Rittenhouse, David Rittenhouse (1732–96) was born in Germantown, Pennsylvania, but moved to Norristown two years later. Though he had little formal education, like his Mennonite ancestors he was reared in a God-fearing tradition but with an interest in astronomy and other physical sciences. At twelve he inherited some books and tools from an uncle, which prompted an interest in mechanics. In 1749, he began to make clocks, and soon had a reputation for rare quality.

Later in Philadelphia, Rittenhouse displayed considerable scientific understanding. He succeeded Benjamin Franklin as President of the American Philosophical Society, and was succeeded in his turn by Thomas Jefferson. He established the first astronomical observatory in the United States, and made mathematical and astronomical instruments, including an accurate astronomical clock for observation of the transit of Venus in 1769. From 1792 to 1795 he was Director of the U.S. Mint in Philadelphia, and in 1795 was elected an honorary fellow of the Royal Society of London. One of the truly great lights

1 **Thomas & Hoadley** Pillar and scroll clock by Silas Hoadley, c. 1830. American Clock & Watch Museum, Bristol, Connecticut.

2 **Rittenhouse, David** Tall clock with case of tulip poplar, brass movement; c. 1755. Henry Francis du Pont Winterthur Museum, Winterthur, Delaware.

3 **Juvet, Louis Paul** Time globe clock, presentation model; the movement is inside the globe and is wound by means of the tail feather of the arrow. Although the globe revolves in 24 hours, the glass dial above records the time in the conventional 2 × 12 system; Canajoharie, 1879. The Wing collection.

4 **New Haven Clock Co.** 30-hour spring-driven shelf clock showing the manufacturer's label; c. 1880. Private collection.

5 **Spencer, Hotchkiss & Co.** Shelf clock, eight-day brass, rack-striking movement, by Spencer & Wooster, c. 1830–35. Private collection.

6 **Terry, Eli & Samuel** Pillar and scroll clock by Eli Terry with visible escapement, c. 1818. Greenfield Village and Henry Ford Museum, Dearborn, Michigan.

7 **Thomas, Seth, Clock Co.** Exhibition of Seth Thomas clocks at '1876 Centennial Exhibition', Philadelphia.

1

2

in American science and horology, his outstanding clocks testify to his remarkable abilities. DJB

Spencer, Hotchkiss & Co. Sylvester Clark, brother of Heman Clark, went to Salem Bridge (called Naugatuck after 1844), Connecticut, c. 1822, to negotiate for a factory to manufacture clocks and movements of a design developed by Heman. These were made of fairly heavy brass with a remarkably simple functional design employing correctly shaped cut-steel pinions and light, well-designed wheelwork of fine brass; rack striking, a half-second pendulum and 60-tooth escape wheel were used. Heman Clark joined Sylvester in 1824, and the brothers did not hesitate to warrant their clocks as superior to any others then being made in Connecticut. They acquired facilities with water power, and increased production until they could supply other clock manufacturers with their so-called 'Salem Bridge' movements.

Though the quality of the clocks was not in question, their price prevented extensive sales. The operation had to a large degree been underwritten by Salem Bridge citizens of means like the Spencer, Hotchkiss and Wooster families, and the enterprise was known as Spencer, Hotchkiss & Co. c. 1830; shortly after, it became Spencer & Wooster.

Richard Ward, who was trained in the factory, continued to manufacture a modified Salem Bridge type of movement until about 1845 in his own factory. DJB

Terry, Eli & Samuel Thomas Harland had been responsible for the training of Daniel Burnap who in turn trained Eli Terry (1772–1852). It would have been difficult to find a better candidate, for Terry combined great mechanical ability, ingenuity, foresight and business acumen. He became famous for the large-scale production of wooden-movement clocks, using jigs and fixtures to produce large numbers of interchangeable parts, so that the clocks could be rapidly assembled without fitting and modifying each piece. Tremendous ingenuity and inventiveness were involved in the accurate and speedy cutting of wheels, pinions and other clock parts.

The pillar and scroll case which is ascribed to him was a remarkably functional design for its day, providing a large clear dial in a shallow case with adequate weight run for 30 hours. He produced wooden-movement tower clocks, one of which is still in operation in Plymouth, Connecticut.

His brother Samuel (1774–1853) also made wooden-movement clocks and was for several years (1824–7) Eli's partner in the manufacture of improved pillar and scroll clocks. DJB

Thomas, Seth, Clock Co. In 1813 Seth Thomas (1774–1859) sold out his interest in Thomas & Hoadley and bought Heman Clark's factory in Plymouth Hollow (now Thomaston) near the Naugatuck River. This was the beginning of the Seth Thomas Clock Co., which in name has continued to the present day although recently as a division of General Time Corporation. Throughout most of the 19th century it was one of the largest American producers of clocks, ranging from relatively inexpensive 30-hour novelty and alarm clocks to regulators of excellent quality. Though Seth Thomas clocks were usually a little

3 4
5 6
7

more expensive than those produced by their competitors, their excellent performance and easy maintenance made them favourites in the United States and throughout the world.

Seth Thomas Jr remained as chairman of the board when General Time acquired the firm in 1931, but on his death in 1958 the operation of the company passed out of the Thomas family. Since the Second World War the firm simply uses the name 'Seth Thomas' for marketing. DJB

established in 1857 as an offshoot for the production of brass clocks and movements. By 1873 this business had grown to such proportions that a large plant was built, later expanded several times until, by 1917, it employed nearly 3,000 people.

In the 1870s the company had offices in New York and Chicago, and a little later in San Francisco, Boston, Toronto and Glasgow, where they handled an extensive British business. By 1900 the Waterbury Clock Co. was doing enormous business with mail-order houses like Sears Roebuck, which offered many styles of Waterbury clocks, some with eight-day striking movements in oak cases at two dollars each. They also manufactured the famous dollar watch for R. H. Ingersoll & Bros. A factory catalogue of 1913 illustrates over 425 styles of clocks, ranging in price from one dollar 20 cents to 210 dollars and covering, among others, alarm, carriage, French-style mantel, banjo and tall clocks. After the First World War business declined. The depression of the 1930s resulted in the sale of the company to United States Time Corporation, later Timex, in 1944. DJB

Willard The Willard brothers, Benjamin (1743–1803), Simon (1753–1848), and Aaron (1757–1844), came from Grafton, Massachusetts, but are generally associated with Roxbury, near Boston. They are perhaps the best known of all American clockmakers and were largely responsible for what has become known as the 'Roxbury' or 'Boston' school of clockmaking. It is not known just how the brothers started in clockmaking, but they produced an enormous number of high-quality clocks during their long careers. Because their clocks are of hard brass and well-cut wheelwork, they have proved durable. Their mechanical qualities, cases of fine proportion and beautiful wood, and handsome dials have made them especially popular with collectors.

It is difficult to generalise about Willard clocks, but generally speaking Benjamin's Grafton clocks have brass dials and appear rather crude compared with his later clocks, which usually look much like his brothers'. Simon's tall clocks vary in size and include monumental ones in superbly inlaid cases. Aaron's much resemble those of Simon, although he seems to have been fond of the rocking ship in the dial arch. Simon is best known for his 'improved timepiece' or banjo clock patented in 1802. Except for a few shelf clocks, nearly all American clocks were tall clocks until Simon Willard devised this remarkably functional clock, with pendulum suspended from the front, weight running behind the pendulum and separated from it, with a metal plate at the bottom allowing the pendulum to be screwed down so that the clock may be moved without injury to the suspension. With its clear seven-inch dial, fine hands, and restrained mahogany case, often crossbanded for striking effect, and generally geometric glasses with gold-leaf decoration, it was popular at once and has remained so. Aaron also made banjo clocks, but often in more elaborate forms with gilt frames to the glasses. Their weight-driven movements usually kept well within one minute's error a week. Many others pirated the design, and clocks of this type are still made in America, as the demand for them has never ceased. DJB

Thomas & Hoadley Seth Thomas (1774–1859) and Silas Hoadley (1786–1870) both started as carpenters but turned to wooden clockmaking about 1808 in association with Eli Terry. They made 30-hour wooden movements that could be cased as tall clocks. Terry sold out his interest to Thomas Hoadley in 1809, but in 1813 they separated and each pursued his own business with remarkable success. Hoadley retired with a considerable fortune in 1849.

Hoadley produced many wooden-movement clocks; some have peculiar layouts such as the so-called 'upside-down' movement in which the winding barrels are placed above the centre arbor and the escapement is below. He made a selling point of the fact that his wooden-movement clocks sometimes had ivory bushings, but time has shown that these often wore out sooner than the plain holes in the wooden plates of other clocks. DJB

Waterbury Clock Co. The Benedict and Burnham Manufacturing Co. was established in Connecticut in 1812 as a producer of brass. By the 1840s it was one of the largest brass producers in Waterbury, the centre of brass production in the United States. It produced rolled and drawn brass, German silver, copper, etc., in sheet, tubing and beadings, and made cabinet hardware, hinges, rivets, lamp burners, etc. The Waterbury Clock Co. was

1 Waterbury Clock Co. Mantel
clock showing European influence,
in black marble case with visible
escapement; *c*.1890. American
Clock & Watch Museum, Bristol,
Connecticut.

2 Willard, Simon Presentation
banjo clock, eight-day, weight-
driven brass movement; Roxbury,
Massachusetts, *c*.1810. Private
collection.

3 Willard, Benjamin Tall clock,
with painted dial; Grafton,
Massachusetts, *c*.1790. American
Clock & Watch Museum, Bristol,
Connecticut.

4 Globe, celestial, clock-driven
by Georg Roll and Johann Georg
Reinhold, Augsburg, *c*.1585.
Kunsthistorisches Museum,
Vienna.

**Overleaf: Astrolabe, plani-
spheric,** by Georg Hartmann,
Nuremberg, 1532. British
Museum, London.

4

1

SECTION V
Sundials and Astronomical Instruments

1   2   3   4

Alidade A simple sighting device in the form of a pivoted arm with a pair of sights, one at each end, found on astrolabes and other instruments for measuring altitudes. FABW

Amplitude The azimuth, or angular distance, of the sun or other heavenly body as it rises or sets, measured to the north or south of the east or west points of the horizon. FABW

Armillary sphere A skeleton form of celestial globe, consisting of a group of circles assembled and pivoted between polar bearings in an outer meridian ring; at the centre of the system is a small, fixed terrestrial globe. The circles are the most important circles of the celestial globe, i.e. the equator, the colures, the ecliptic, the tropics of Cancer and Capricorn and the Arctic and Antarctic circles.

The origin of the armillary sphere goes back to the Greeks and it was made by the Arabs and by the Chinese. One of the main functions of the great Chinese astronomical clock towers of the 10th and 11th centuries AD was to support an armillary sphere, and in the famous one of Su Sung of 1092, the sphere was clock-driven and was used for actual observations of the heavens.

European armillary spheres, made from the 15th century onwards, are usually for instruction and education. One of the earliest surviving [320/1] dates from the first half of the 15th century. A fine example [320/2] made in Louvain in 1575 by Arsenius, the nephew of Gemma Frisius, is now in Brussels, and an elaborate example by Santucci delle Pomarance, made 1588–93, is now in Florence.

Some European armillary spheres were clock-driven, and an early example is the Jagellonian globe, now in the Jagellonian University Museum in Cracow, probably made by Hans Dorn of Vienna, c. 1507. Similar spheres of the 1560s by French makers include one by Jacques de la Garde of Blois in the British Museum, London, one by Jean Naze of Lyons in the Hessisches Landesmuseum, Kassel, and one by Pierre de Fobis of Lyons, in the Kunsthistorisches Museum, Vienna; a fine example [320/3] of 1572 by Josias Habrecht is in Rosenborg Castle, Copenhagen. FABW

Astrolabe, mariner's A much simplified form of astrolabe with provision only for measuring the sun's altitude from a ship at sea [320/4]. FABW

Astrolabe, planispheric The planispheric astrolabe [318/1] is essentially an armillary sphere or skeleton celestial globe pressed flat or, more scientifically, projected upon the plane of the celestial equator or equinoctial from the south pole of the heavens. It consists of a brass disc or 'mater' with a shallow circular recess occupying almost all of one face; into this recess can be dropped thin brass discs (usually three to five), the upper surface of the topmost disc being in use at any one time. A central pivot projects through the discs and over this can be dropped a pierced disc or 'rete' and finally a rotating index. The rim of the fixed disc or mater is engraved with an hour scale I to XII, I to XII, with a scale of degrees within it [323/6].

Each thin disc represents the Earth's surface at a particular latitude and is engraved with lines representing the horizon and, above it, lines of equal altitude and of equal azimuth. The area below the horizon is marked with lines for unequal hours of the night and lines separating the astrological 'Houses of Heaven'.

The rotating rete is effectively a star map, which can be rotated around the north pole of the heavens at its centre; an eccentric circle represents the ecliptic, and a number of cusped pointers the positions of major fixed stars.

On the rear face of the mater there is an outer scale of degrees, used for measuring altitudes and, within this, various other scales and a rotating alidade, pivoted at the centre of the disc, carrying sights for determining altitude. For this last purpose, the instrument can be suspended from a ring and shackle on its upper edge.

The astrolabe can be used simply for measuring the altitude of the sun or a star, but much additional information can be obtained by transferring this reading to the front face. If the star is one of those represented on the rete, the pointer for this star can be set to the measured altitude on the scale of altitudes of the plate in use, and the sidereal time read off on the scale of hours on the rim of the mater. A second simple operation converts this to mean solar time. A similar operation enables the time of day to be found from the measured altitude of the sun. Apart from its observational use, the astrolabe is very useful as a calculator and predictor from which the times of sunrise and sunset, and the altitude and azimuth of the sun at any time and date, can be found, as can the same information for any of the fixed stars marked on its rete.

1 Armillary sphere 15th century. Museum of the History of Science, Oxford University.

2 Armillary sphere on a decorative caryatid stand; made by Arsenius in Louvain, Belgium, 1575. Musées Royaux d'Art et d'Histoire, Brussels.

3 Armillary sphere, driven by clockwork; made by Josias Habrecht, Strasbourg, 1572. De danske Kongers Kronologiske Samling på Rosenborg, Copenhagen.

4 Astrolabe, mariner's Made of brass. Found in 1845 on the island of Valencia, Co. Kerry, Ireland; probably Spanish c.1585. National Maritime Museum, London.

5 Astronomical clock showing the movement and dial. The dial arrangement illustrates an early use of epicyclic gearing; made by Laurence Liechti in 1529 for the Prison Gate, Winterthur. Museum Lindengut Winterthur.

6 Astronomical clock in Lund Cathedral, Sweden; a reconstruction made in the 1920s, the remains of the original being in Lunds Universitets Historiska Museum.

5

6

The planispheric astrolabe originated with the Greeks, but the earliest surviving specimens are from the Islamic period of the 9th century AD; the earliest known European examples occur 300 years later. FABW

Astronomical clock This term covers a wide range of mechanical devices which show the time of day on a dial and give additional astronomical information concerning the sun, moon, planets and stars. Here it is restricted to clocks which have as a main function the indication of time; those in which the astronomical aspect dominates are described under Armillary sphere, Celestial globe, Orrery and Planetarium.

The earliest astronomical clock of which we have detailed knowledge, although nothing of it now remains, was made under the direction of Richard of Wallingford, mainly between 1327 and his death in 1336, and finally completed by Laurence de Stokes with William Walsham in 1349. It survived at least until the reign of Henry VIII. From a surviving but incomplete manuscript we know that it included a dial showing the time of high water at London Bridge and an astrolabe dial showing the positions of the moon's nodes and enabling eclipses to be predicted.

Astronomical clocks with large dials mounted on public buildings were set up all over Europe from the late 14th to the 16th century. Among outstanding examples is that at

Wells in Somerset. Local records show that a clock was installed in Wells Cathedral in 1392; its movement is now in the Science Museum, London [116/2]. A fine and elaborate astronomical dial [116/1] remains in Wells Cathedral; it has an outer hour ring of 2×12 hours and a waxing and waning moon revolving once in $29\frac{1}{2}$ days around a central Earth. A jack strikes the hour with one hand and kicks the quarters, and there are two quarter-jacks outside the building. Mounted above the dial is an automata display of charging horsemen, released originally every three hours, in which one horseman is unseated at each cycle.

The tall astronomical clock [321/6] in the cathedral of Lund in Sweden has on its upper dial an outer 2×12 hour ring, an interior eccentric ring of signs of the zodiac, and indexes for the sun and moon. The clock was built originally c.1380, but its movement was taken down in 1837 and reconstructed in 1923.

The clock at Winterthur, Switzerland, is of considerable interest. Its history is fully documented, and it includes a very early example of epicyclic gearing [321/5] It was made in Winterthur in 1529 by Laurence Liechti, founder of the Liechti family of clockmakers. Laurence's turret clock is signed on one of its corner posts 'L X L 1529'. It was installed in the clock tower known as the *Käfigtor* or 'Prison Gate', demolished in 1871, but the dial, hands and movement, including the epicyclic gearing, were preserved

1

2

3

and are now on view in the local museum in the Lindengut.

With its fine and elaborate astronomical dial [322/3], the clock at Hampton Court was set up in 1540; its bells are housed in a somewhat later campanile above. All that survives of the original movement are some bars behind the dial, one of which bears the initials and date 'N. O..1540', and possibly one wheel of the astronomical gearing. The initials are almost certainly those of Nicholas Oursian. The dial has been repainted many times but retains essentially its original form. The fixed outer ring, of 9ft 8in. diameter, carries an hours scale of 2 × 12. The outermost of the three rotating dials is a ring of zodiac signs, each divided into 30 degrees, and within this a scale of dates; it rotates once per sidereal day. The middle ring, rotating once per mean solar day, carries a long sun index which reads the time of day on the fixed ring and shows the position of the sun in the zodiac; this ring also carries a scale 0–29½ for the moon's age, and an index pointing inwards. The innermost disc carries a ring 1–12, 1–12, on which the index mentioned reads off the time of high tide, and a projecting index shows the moon's age: the disc is pierced with an eccentric hole through which the moon's phase is seen pictorially.

Three great clocks in succession have been set up inside the cathedral at Strasbourg. The first, of 1354, is known to have been monumental in size – nearly 40 ft high; all that survives is the automaton cock which surmounted it, now to be seen in the museum near by. At 12 o'clock it opened its beak, thrust forth its tongue, crowed, and flapped its wings. This clock was succeeded in 1574 by a fine example by Isaac Habrecht of Strasbourg, much of which is preserved in the museum. The clock [246/3] now to be seen in the cathedral was built in 1842 by Jean-Baptiste Schwilgué with Albert and Théodore Ungerer, all of Strasbourg. In addition to conventional indications it shows the equation of time, the perturbations of the moon, the precession of the equinoxes and the movable feasts of the Church. Automata include Christ and the Apostles, Death and the Four Ages of Man, and a crowing cock. The whole is about 30ft high and 15ft wide at the base.

The clock on the tower of the City Hall in Prague was first installed in 1486; there were repairs and renewals in 1659 and 1864–5. There are now two main exterior dials, an astrolabe dial above and a calendar dial below.

A free-standing clock was set up inside the cathedral at Lyons in 1598. Its main dials were an astrolabe dial above and a calendar dial below.

An astronomical clock [323/7] of the utmost complication, made by Jens Olsen and completed by Otto Mortensen in 1955, is installed inside Copenhagen City Hall. The clock is remarkable not only for the complication of its movement, but also for the beauty of its severely technical layout.

Domestic astronomical clocks have been made in great variety. Pierre de Fobis of Lyons made typically French hexagonal vertical table clocks with hours dial on one side as usual and an astronomical dial on top in place of the usual cupola and finial; a fine example [323/4] is dated 1535.

Some south German horizontal gilt metal table clocks of the 16th century were fitted with astronomical dials. An outstanding example [322/1] is by Jost Burgi (1591), and there is another of the same date by Janus Reinhold in the Stuttgart Landesmuseum. Vertical table clocks in fine gilt-metal cases from Austria and south Germany form a group on their own, one of the earliest dated examples being by Andreas Illmer of Innsbruck, 1559 [323/5]. Two centuries later, astronomical dials were sometimes inserted in the arched portion of the dials of longcase clocks, good examples being by provincial English makers such as Edward Cockey of Warminster and William Barker of Wigan, while special free-standing astronomical clocks were made by Isaac and Josias Habrecht of Strasbourg and by Samuel Watson of Coventry and London. FABW

Astronomical compendium An elaborated form of diptych sundial, usually made of brass. There is no sharp distinction between the two, but whereas a diptych dial consists of two hinged plates, a compendium usually incorporates additional leaves and folding devices and gives additional astronomical and calendar information.

A compendium may include a nocturnal, a folding universal equinoctial sundial, a horary or sinical quadrant, a volvelle for interconverting solar and lunar times

1 Astronomical clock A gilt metal table clock; by Jost Burgi, Kassel, dated 1591. Hessisches Landesmuseum, Kassel.

2 Astronomical compendium incorporating a folding sundial and compass; by Elias Allen, London, early 17th century. British Museum, London.

3 Astronomical clock dial of the clock at Hampton Court Palace, originally set up in 1540, but repainted many times.

4 Astronomical clock A gilt metal table clock by Pierre de Fobis, Lyons, 1535. Württembergisches Landesmuseum, Stuttgart.

5 Astronomical clock A gilt metal table clock; by Andreas Illmer, Innsbruck, dated 1559. Tiroler Landesmuseum Ferdinandeum, Innsbruck.

6 The parts of an astrolabe Science Museum, London.

7 Astronomical clock designed and made by Jens Olsen; completed by Otto Mortensen in 1955. Now in the Town Hall, Copenhagen (293/5).

4

5

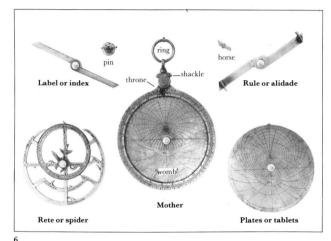

6

7

according to the moon's age, or for interconverting or relating equal and unequal hours, equal and Italian hours, date of month and day of week, length of day and of night, times of sunrise and sunset, according to the date. Other information often includes calendar material such as dominical letters and epacts, the latitudes of various towns, and in association with the compass the weather to be expected with various wind directions. FABW [322/2]

British Summer Time The idea of putting the clock forward during the summer to prolong evening daylight at the expense of early-morning daylight was first suggested by William Willett of Chelsea, London, in 1907. No action was taken then, but summer time was brought into action in the United Kingdom, for fuel-saving purposes, during the First World War when, from 21st May 1916, clocks were advanced one hour. During the Second World War a further step was taken when Double Summer Time, an advance of two hours, was applied during high summer; it ceased after 1947. Subsequent practice has been to apply British Summer Time (one hour advance) from a Sunday around mid March to a Sunday in late October.

Similar daylight-saving schemes have been introduced in other countries. FABW

Calendar, Gregorian The Julian calendar was formally adopted by the Christian Church in AD 325, but was in error

by 0.8 days per century, so that the spring equinox, set at 21st March in AD 325, had by the 16th century receded to 11th March. Pope Gregory set about correcting this error, and in 1582 proposed the modified calendar which now bears his name.

In the Julian calendar every fourth year is a leap year, but in the Gregorian the centennial years are not leap years unless they are multiples of 400. Thus 1600 was a leap year but not 1700, 1800 or 1900. This change effects the desired correction of three days every four centuries.

The Gregorian calendar was adopted immediately in most Roman Catholic countries, and to set the calendar right in the first place 5th October was renumbered the 15th in that year. In Protestant countries Pope Gregory's name was associated with the massacre of St Bartholomew's Day, (1572) and for many years his calendar was accordingly rejected. The United Kingdom did not change until September 1752, by which time an eleven-day correction was required. FABW

Calendar, Julian Adopted in Rome in 45 BC by Julius Caesar, who had consulted Sosigenes, an Egyptian astronomer. As slightly modified by Augustus, it comprised seven months of 31 days, four of 30 days and one, February, of 28 days. Every fourth year, without exception, an extra day was added to February giving it 29 days, that year being termed a leap year. An ordinary year therefore has

1 **Globe, celestial** of gilt-copper; made by Hans Dorn under the supervision of Martin Bylica, dated 1480. Museum Historyczne Uniwersytetu Jagiellonskiego, Cracow.

2 **Equation of time** The curve marked I shows the component due to the ellipticity of the earth's orbit, and curve II the component due to the inclination of its axis on the plane of its orbit. Curve III shows the net effect of the two together.

3 **Equatorium** made of brass; of unknown origin, *c.* 1500. Museum of the History of Science, Oxford University.

4 **Globe, celestial,** of painted wood; made by Johann Stöffler in 1493. Germanisches National-museum, Nuremberg.

5 **Globe, terrestrial** The earliest example known, the so-called 'apple' of papier-mâché and parchment; by Martin Behaim, 1492. Germanisches National-museum, Nuremberg.

1

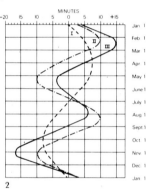

2

Divination boards, Chinese Divination boards were fairly common in China. They consisted of a round disc, of various diameters, usually of wood either lacquered or varnished. In the centre was a magnetic compass, and around it, covering the entire surface, was a circular azimuth chart. It had the characters for the cardinal points of the compass, the Twelve Terrestrial Branches, the Ten Celestial Stems, and other calendrical characters at various intersections of the radial and concentric lines on the chart. On the back of the disc were painted other similar characters in a rectangular chart.

The charts were used to measure the degrees of azimuth of certain natural phenomena that were thought to influence the course of events. In this way auspicious and inauspicious days were established, and the proper rituals were observed to celebrate fortuitous occurrences, to ward off calamities, or to appease vengeful spirits, whichever seemed to be necessary in the astrological circumstances prevailing at the time.

In a modified form, these charts appear around the compasses of Chinese sundials. Other, earlier forms of divination boards appeared on the dial surface of ancient sundials and on TLV mirrors (mirrors bearing marks resembling these letters) of the Han period (206 BC–AD 220). The specific use of the earlier boards is even less clear than that of the later models. MCR

Ecliptic The plane of the Earth's orbit around the sun, passing through the centre of the sun. Viewed from the Earth it is the apparent track of the sun throughout the year between the fixed stars. In a celestial or armillary sphere it is represented by a great circle passing through the equinoxes, and its plane is inclined at 23° 27′ to that of the equator or 'equinoctial', the Earth's rotational axis being inclined at the same angle to the perpendicular to the plane of its orbit. FABW

Epact The age of the moon on 1st January in any year; when this is known its age at any subsequent date in the year can be deduced. Since twelve lunations equal 354.36 days and a year equals 365.24 days, the epact increases by a little under eleven days from year to year, with a backward step of 29½ days each time it passes this figure. FABW

Equation table A table giving the values of the equation of time throughout the year. Equation tables were often pasted inside the doors of longcase clocks during the late 17th and early 18th centuries. FABW

Equation of time The difference between apparent solar time, i.e. the time shown at any place by a sundial, and mean time, i.e. the time shown by a clock running uniformly throughout the year. The difference arises from two factors in the Earth's orbital motion around the sun and its rotation about its own axis.

The Earth's orbit is not a circle but an ellipse, so that the sun's apparent motion is more rapid in January, when the Earth is nearer the sun, than in July, when it is farther away, the effect being enhanced by the fact that the Earth is moving more rapidly in January than in July, by Kepler's Law. The second factor in the equation of time is due to the

365 days and a leap year 366, so that the average length of a year over a long period is 365¼ days. The true length of a year, equinox to equinox, is 365.2422 days, and so the correction of 0.25 days per four years is excessive by 0.028 days in 4 years or 0.7 days per century. In ten centuries, therefore, the equinoxes would, on the Julian calendar, come seven days earlier. FABW

Calendar, perpetual A small device, usually in the form of a volvelle, enabling the day of the week to be linked with the day of the month. A revolving disc with cut-out segments is mounted above a fixed disc, the revolving disc being engraved with titles identifying the information to be seen through the cut-out portions. Times of sunrise and sunset and the lengths of the day and night according to the date were sometimes also incorporated. FABW

Colures Two great circles in the heavens, or on an armillary sphere, which pass through the poles and through the equinoxes and the solstices respectively. FABW

Declination The angular distance of the sun, moon or other heavenly body north or south of the celestial equator. Because of the inclination of the Earth's axis to the plane of its orbit, the sun's declination varies between 23° 27′ north at midsummer and 23° 27′ south at midwinter. FABW

Earth's axis being inclined by $23\frac{1}{2}°$ to a line perpendicular to its orbit.

If we take a viewpoint from the Earth itself we see that, while hour angles must necessarily be measured around the celestial equator, the sun's apparent motion is around the ecliptic, and this motion is not uniform when projected on to the equator, being greater in summer and winter when the sun is moving parallel to the equator and is nearer to the poles than at the equinoxes when its motion is at $23\frac{1}{2}°$ to the equator.

The two factors of the equation of time are roughly equal in magnitude, but the first goes through one cycle per year, the second two cycles. When plotted on a graph and added together they give a curve with two major and two minor peaks [324/2]. FABW

Equatorium A hand-operated mechanical instrument in the form of an elaborate volvelle by which the positions of the planets in the heavens can be found. FABW [325/3]

Equinoxes The dates, spring and autumn, at which day and night are of equal length, or, more precisely, the dates at which the sun's declination is zero.

On celestial or armillary spheres the equinoxes are the points at which the great circles of the ecliptic and equinoctial, or equator, intersect. On the present Gregorian calendar the spring equinox is on 20th or 21st March and the autumn on 22nd or 23rd September. FABW

Equinoxes, precession of The positions of the equinoxes are determined by the position of the Earth's axis, and if this was constant in direction the equinoxes would remain fixed in position in relation to the fixed stars. Owing to a gyroscopic effect produced by the gravitational pulls of the moon and sun on the Earth's equatorial bulge, the Earth's axis, though remaining always at the same angle to the plane of its orbit, changes its direction, making one complete revolution in approximately 26,000 years. From the Earth, therefore, the equinox points in the heavens move slowly round the equinoctial or equatorial circle. The spring equinox in the early Christian era was in the constellation of Aries and was termed the 'First Point of Aries'. It has now moved back into the constellation of Pisces, a movement of nearly 30° of Right Ascension.

Globe, celestial A representation of the starry heavens, imagined as projected on to a sphere from the centre of the Earth and viewed from outside the sphere. Some form of celestial globe must have been constructed by the Greeks, but the earliest surviving example is the Farnese globe of marble dating from the 2nd or 3rd century BC, now in the Museo Nazionale in Naples. It is almost entirely decorative and of little use for measurement.

Small Islamic bronze globes of the 11th and 12th centuries survive, but it was not until the 16th century that an interest in them developed in Europe; they were then made of gilded copper or painted wood. An outstanding example [324/1], was made in Vienna by Hans Dorn under the supervision of Martin Bylica; it is dated 1480. The magnitudes of the stars are shown by the number of rays radiating from each. A further fine example, of painted wood [325/4], is signed and dated Johann Stöffler, 1493.

One of the functions of the great water clocks of China of the 10th and 11th centuries was to drive a celestial globe, and clock-driven globes appeared in Europe during the Renaissance. The earliest surviving is mounted on the elaborate astronomical clock of 1555 by Philip Immser of Tübingen, now in the Vienna Technical Museum, and a globe which is now in the Strasbourg Clock Museum was formerly part of the second Strasbourg Cathedral clock of 1574. A group of clock-driven celestial globes of exceptional quality [317/4] was made by Georg Roll and Johann Reinhold of Augsburg in the 1580s. FABW

Globe, terrestrial A representation on a small scale of the main features of the Earth's surface, either purely geographical, showing continents, seas, islands, etc., or political, showing national boundaries also. The construction of such a globe implies an affirmation that the Earth is a sphere, or almost spherical, and although vague references to globes appear in Greek and Latin authors it was not until the Renaissance that their existence in Europe is certain. The earliest which has survived is the so-called *Erdapfel* of Martin Behaim [325/5]. It was made in 1492 of

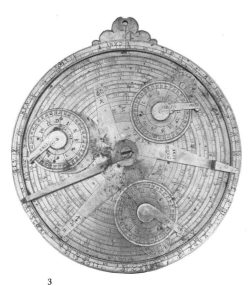

3

4

5

papier-mâché covered with parchment, with 1,100 localities marked on it. The well-known Jagellonian globe in Cracow, probably made by Hans Dorn of Vienna, consists of an armillary sphere surrounding a clock-driven brass terrestrial globe. It dates from *c.* 1507 and bears the word 'Amerika'. The great geographical discoveries of the 16th century stimulated interest in terrestrial globes. FABW

Gnomon The shadow-casting part of a sundial. The actual edge or point which casts the shadow is called the 'style', the gnomon being the whole structure. If the style is parallel to the earth's axis, the gnomon is called a 'polar' gnomon. A gnomon may be a thin piece of sheet metal, a pin, or a tautened string. FABW

Greenwich Time Greenwich Mean Time or its modified form, British Summer Time, is the legal standard time of the United Kingdom. Greenwich Royal Observatory was set up in 1675, and one of its main objectives was to establish a standard of time in connection with the determination of longitude at sea. Its famous Octagon Room [326/1], designed by Sir Christopher Wren, was equipped in 1676 with two 'great' clocks by Thomas Tompion, both with 13-ft pendulums and a year's going time. The two Tompion year clocks, fitted with dead-beat escapements of a type first proposed by Richard Towneley of Burnley, were later somewhat modified by Tompion and eventually succeeded by clocks with the Graham type of dead-beat escapement and mercury-compensated pendulums. From 1872 to 1925 the standard timekeeper was a Dent clock with G. B. Airy's modification of the spring-detent escapement, zinc-and-steel compensation pendulum and barometric compensation. This was followed in 1925 by a Shortt free-pendulum clock with its pendulum swinging almost entirely freely in a case at constant air pressure, served by a slave pendulum which impulsed the free pendulum and was afterwards synchronised by a signal from it. The error of the Dent clock was about 0.01 seconds per day, and of the Shortt clock a few thousandths of a second [266/1].

The Shortt clock was superseded in 1942 by a group of quartz-crystal clocks in which the timekeeping element is a quartz crystal vibrating at 100 kilocycles per second, electronic gearing reducing this to 50 cycles per second, the final time indication being a continuously rotating hand. Before 1955 the Greenwich timekeeper was checked against the stars by a transit instrument and since then by a photo-zenith tube.

A new precision method of measuring time, developed between 1945 and 1955, was the atomic clock, in which the timekeeping element is a molecular or atomic vibration. The caesium atomic clock [327/3], brought into practical use by Louis Essen and J. V. L. Parry at the National Physical Laboratory, Teddington, in 1955, was accurate to one part in 10^{10}, equivalent to an error of one second in 300 years. This clock is not free-running, but is used to synchronise a system of quartz-crystal clocks. Greenwich Mean Time has been based on the atomic clock since 1967.

A second National Physical Laboratory atomic clock of 1959 was seven times more accurate than the first, and was later improved still further to an accuracy of one part in 10^{12}, corresponding to an error of one second in 30,000 years. Accuracy of this order, when combined with astronomical observation, makes it possible to detect variations in the rotation of the Earth itself, revealing an annual fluctuation together with a slow drift.

By 1967 the atomic clock had been shown to be a more accurate timekeeper than the Earth itself, which led to an international decision to base the unit of time, i.e. the second, not fundamentally on the rotation of the Earth but on an atomic vibration, and the General Conference on Weights and Measures thus defined the second as the period of 9,192,631,770 vibrations of an atom of caesium 133 in zero magnetic field.

The work of Greenwich Observatory was gradually transferred to Herstmonceux, Sussex, between 1946 and 1958, but Greenwich Mean Time remains the time of the meridian of Greenwich itself. From 1st January 1972 the world time signals broadcast from many countries have

1

2

been based on atomic time and converted in steps to Universal Time to allow for the slowing down of the Earth's rotation.

Important developments in the distribution of Greenwich Mean Time took place during the 19th century. In 1833 the time ball was set up on top of the Observatory and dropped at 1 p.m. In 1852, following the invention of electric clocks and the electric telegraph, an electric clock at Greenwich released a similar time ball in the Strand, London. In 1853 a time ball was also dropped at Deal, Kent, visible from the English Channel.

At this period, different areas of England were using their own local time, but with the spread of railways this arrangement became increasingly inconvenient, and in 1880 it was enacted that Greenwich Time should be the legal time throughout Great Britain. A world conference in 1884 established a worldwide system of time zones based on and related to Greenwich Mean Time. The invention of the electric telegraph aided the distribution of Greenwich Time, and radio broadened it further. The radio time signal of six 'pips' was first broadcast by the British Broadcasting Corporation in 1924, and from 1927 precision time signals were broadcast from long-range transmitters at Rugby. The distribution of Greenwich Time by telephone began in Britain in 1936 with the first 'speaking clock', synchronised from Greenwich. FABW

Hodometer A device which can be coupled to the wheels of a carriage to record the number of revolutions made by the wheel, from which the distance traversed along the road can be inferred. FABW
See also Waywiser.

Hours, Babylonian A system of hour reckoning in which the whole day-and-night period was divided into 24 equal parts with the numbering starting at sunrise. The system was used in Bohemia and Hungary between the mid 14th and the late 16th centuries, and some pin-gnomon dials of that period indicate Babylonian hours. FABW

Hours, great and small Sets of hour lines on German sundials of the 16th and 17th centuries are sometimes entitled *Grosse Uhr* and *Kleine Uhr*. These terms refer to the Italian (1–24) and the normal 2 × 12 equal-hour systems respectively. FABW

Hours, Italian In Italy from the 14th to the 18th centuries a system of time reckoning was used in which the whole 2 × 12-hour period was numbered 1–24 in a succession of equal hours starting from zero half an hour after sunset. Thus the first eight hours are always in darkness and so do not appear on sundials; noon varies from 16 to 20 hours. Italian sundials made during this period usually show only Italian hours; many clocks and sundials made in south Germany have provision for indicating them. The odd half-hour at sunset is often ignored, but it is shown on precision instruments. FABW

Hours, Japanese The Japanese system of dividing the day, which was similar to that used in Europe in the Middle Ages, continued in use until 1873. The daylight period,

1 **Greenwich Time: The Octagon Room,** Old Royal Observatory, Greenwich, showing the two Tompion clocks on the left; detail from the etching *Prospectus intra cameram stellatam* by Francis Place, after Robert Thacker, *c.*1676.

2 **Hours, Nuremberg** An iron wall clock showing Nuremberg hours on the inner dial, and a conventional 2 × 12 outer dial; *c.*1500. Germanisches Nationalmuseum, Nuremberg.

3 **Caesium atomic clock** The original caesium resonator at the National Physical Laboratory, Teddington, Middlesex, 1955.

3

including a considerable amount of twilight, was divided into six equal parts, and the period of darkness also into six parts. These hours were numbered, from midnight to noon, 9, 8, 7, 6, 5, 4, and again in the same sequence from noon to midnight. Japanese clocks were therefore designed to indicate and strike on this system. The length of twilight included in the Japanese day may be judged from the fact that some clock dials show that (in approximately 35° latitude) 'day' and 'night' were of about equal length in winter while in summer 'day' was over twice as long as 'night'. FABW

Hours, Jewish Identical with temporal hours. FABW

Hours, Nuremberg During the late 16th and 17th centuries a special system of hour reckoning was employed in the Nuremberg area differing from that of the rest of Europe. It used equal hours, but numbered the daylight hours from 1 onwards and the night hours similarly.

Very few clocks using this principle have survived, two important examples being a 14th-century iron wall clock, formerly in St Sebaldus Church, Nuremberg [326/2], and a table clock of *c.* 1500, both now in the Germanisches Museum, Nuremberg. The dial of the latter has a set of concentric rings of hour figures and a single hour hand graduated according to the date of use. FABW

Hours, temporal or unequal In ancient Egypt and in Europe until medieval times the system of time reckoning for civil purposes was the same: to divide sunrise to sunset into twelve equal parts and sunset to sunrise also into twelve equal parts. This is demonstrated by sundials and water clocks from Egypt, Greek and Roman stone sundials, and drawings and surviving examples of portable sundials of many types, including the quadrant, and chilindre. Sundials in Anglo-Saxon England divided the day into four parts or 'tides'.

Early in the 14th century the modern 2 × 12 system of equal hours appeared in Europe, roughly coinciding with the advent of mechanical clocks. In England the first references to 'before noon' and 'after noon' occur about 1380; the earliest-known English sundial indicating equal hours is a quadrant of 1398 in Dorchester Museum. FABW

Local time The time of day at any particular place, found by astronomical instruments. The difference in local time between one place and another is proportional to the difference in longitude, 15 degrees of longitude being equivalent to one hour of time. FABW

Log, mechanical A device for measuring the distance covered by a ship at sea. It consists essentially of a propeller or fan-driven rotor suspended from a float towed behind a ship, combined with a mechanism for recording the number of its revolutions, from which the distance travelled can be calculated. FABW

Lunar cycle A cycle of 19 years after which the phases of the moon recur on very nearly the same days of the year; also known as the 'Metonic cycle', from its discoverer, in 432 BC, the Athenian astronomer Meton. The number of any given year in its current cycle is known as 'the Golden Number'. FABW

Mean time As described under Equation of time, time shown by a sundial differs from that shown by a clock of uniform rate, the difference arising from the fact that the Earth's orbit is elliptical, and the Earth's axis is not perpendicular to the plane of its orbit. The difference between true and mean solar time varies in a cycle with two maxima and two minima per year, the maximum difference amounting to somewhat less than $16\frac{1}{2}$ minutes.

The average over a whole year of a solar day is termed a 'mean solar day', and a timekeeper divides this as accurately as possible into hours, minutes and seconds of exactly equal length. FABW

Nocturnal An instrument for finding the time by night from the position of the two 'pointers' of the Great Bear or Little Bear constellations [328/1]. It consists of a wooden or metal disc with a handle, marked with an anticlockwise annual calendar scale. Superimposed on this is a smaller disc, pivoted at its centre and marked with an hour scale 2 × 12 anticlockwise, carrying an index reading on the date scale or a pair of indexes marked 'GB' or 'LB' for Great or Little Bear. Superimposed again is an index arm projecting well beyond the discs. There is a central hole through the pivot system.

To find the time, the observer faces north and sets the date index to the date of use. He then sights the Pole Star through the central hole and rotates the index until it is in line with the pointers of the Great or Little Bear, according to the index employed. The time of night is read off on the 2 × 12 hour scale. FABW

Nutation A small oscillation of the Earth's axis of rotation about its mean position, due to the moon's attraction on the Earth's equatorial bulge, superimposed on the slow rotation of the axis round the pole of the ecliptic. It was discovered by James Bradley in 1747 from observations, and amounts to 9.2 seconds of arc, with a period of $18\frac{2}{3}$ years – that of the circuit of the moon's nodes round the ecliptic. FABW

Octant To find his position at sea a navigator needs to know his longitude and latitude. For both determinations he must measure the altitude of the sun or a star above the horizon, and from the 15th to the early 18th centuries he employed simple instruments known as the 'cross-staff' and the 'backstaff'.

A much more accurate instrument, the octant [328/3], was invented by John Hadley in London and, independently, by Thomas Godfrey of Philadelphia in the 1730s. In this instrument [328/2] the horizon was sighted

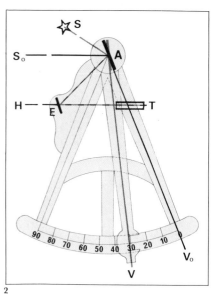

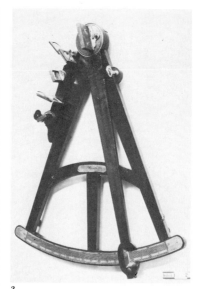

1   2   3

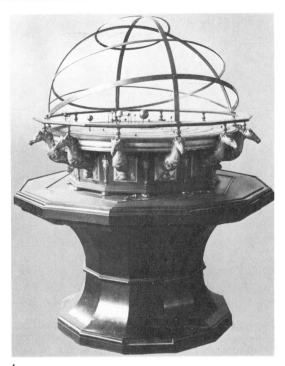

1 **Nocturnal** by Humphrey Cole, London, *c.*1676. British Museum, London.

2 **Octant** E: fixed horizon glass, half-silvered. T: observing telescope pointed at the horizon. A: rotatable plane mirror. V_0 and V: readings on the scale when observing the horizon and the sun S as reflected in A. S_0 is sunrise/sunset.

3 **Octant** An early example with a diagonal scale; maker unknown, *c.*1750. Science Museum, London.

4 **Orrery** Thomas Wright's 'Grand Orrery' made for King George II in 1733 and subsequently used for tutoring the children of King George III. Science Museum, London.

5 **Orrery** made in the Duchy of Schleswig between 1654 and 1664. Nationalhistoriske Museum på Frederiksborg Slot, Hillerød.

4

5

directly through a glass half silvered and half clear, and the image of the sun brought on to the silvered portion from the observer's side by reflection in a rotatable plane mirror. When the sun is on the horizon the two mirrors are parallel; under other conditions the angle through which the rotatable mirror must be turned to bring the two views of the sun into coincidence is half its altitude above the horizon. The sextant is a modified form of the octant. FABW

Orrery This term is usually applied to a small-scale three-dimensional representation of the movements of the heavenly bodies of the solar system, the Earth, moon, planets and their satellites, about the sun, operable by hand or clock-driven. The word is derived from a fine early example [335/4] made in or just before 1713 by John Rowley, later Master of Mechanics to George I, for Charles Boyle, fourth earl of Orrery, and named after him at the suggestion of Sir Richard Steele. The instrument shows in considerable detail the rotation of the Earth on its own axis and in orbit around the sun, also the rotation of the moon around the Earth, and the rotation of the sun about its own axis. Rowley's orrery was based on an earlier, smaller instrument invented by George Graham and made by Thomas Tompion and Graham, now in the Museum of the History of Science, Oxford. Both instruments should strictly be called 'telluria'.

The idea of the orrery was enthusiastically received, and other examples, true orreries showing planetary movements, soon followed from Rowley and other makers, prominent among them Thomas Wright, whose example of 1733 [329/4] was made for George II and became part of the George III collection of scientific instruments housed originally in Richmond Observatory. A Wright orrery of *c.* 1750 shows all the then known planets and satellites.

An instrument which antedates Rowley by 50 years is now in Frederiksborg Castle, Denmark [329/5]. It consists of a skeleton fixed celestial globe mounted on a wooden base

with driving mechanism and what is effectively a full orrery at the centre of the globe showing the rotations about the sun of the Earth and five planets, the rotation of the Earth, and the orbital motion of the moon around it. The intrument was made by a team of workers in the Schleswig area between 1654 and 1664. Many later orreries were clock-driven; there are fine examples from France by Louis Thouverez *c.* 1800, Antide Janvier *c.* 1805, and Jacques Joseph Lepaute de Bellefontaine *c.* 1810. FABW

Pedometer A device carried on the person, for counting the number of paces walked, and hence determining the distance. Counting was usually carried out by a pawl engaging with a ratchet wheel, the pawl being operated by a lever or weighted sector which rose and fell with the rise and fall of the body in walking. Occasionally an adjustment for length of pace was provided, the ratchet wheel having fine teeth and the number of teeth passed over step by step being pre-set. Otherwise the pedometer was usually set to record one mile for 1,000 double paces.

Pedometers were made in the form of watches in the late 18th century, in particular by Ralph Gout and Spencer & Perkins of London. FABW

Photozenith tube Since 1955 Greenwich Observatory near London has employed the photozenith tube (PZT) for checking its standard clock against the stars. Selected stars which transit near the zenith are automatically photographed on the same plate twice before and twice after crossing the meridian, at times dictated by the standard sidereal clock. The time of transit according to this clock can then be found by interpolation. FABW

Planetarium A mechanically operated device in which the revolutions of the Earth and the other planets around the sun are represented on a dial or dials; they may be hand-operated or clock-driven. Richard of Wallingford's astro-

329

1 **Planetarium** showing the astrolabe dial and planetary dials; by Eberhart Baldewein, 1561. Hessisches Landesmuseum, Kassel.

2 **Planetarium** clock dial, with five subsidiary dials. *Top left*: rotation of the sun and planets round the earth (ptolemaic system); *top right*: rotation of moon round the Earth and its phases; *centre*: time and day of week; *bottom left*: annual calendar and dominical letter; *bottom right*: the epact and golden number. By Samuel Watson, 1681. Royal Library, Windsor Castle.

3 **Quadrant** of 1399, one of the earliest surviving dated examples, indicating equal hours. British Museum, London.

4 **Quadrant** of the Gunter type, by Robert Gray, London, 1709. Science Museum, London.

5 **Reflecting circle** by Edward Troughton, early 19th century. Science Museum, London.

6 **Planetarium** showing the rotation of the Earth and planets round the sun, and the moon round the Earth; by Johannes van Ceulen de Oude, The Hague, 1681. Museum Boerhaave, Leiden.

7 **Planetarium** Underneath view of 331/6 showing the movement with the balance and clock train in the upper part of the illustration. Museum Boerhaave, Leiden.

1

2

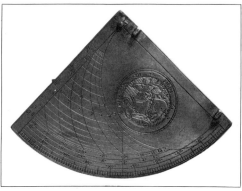

3

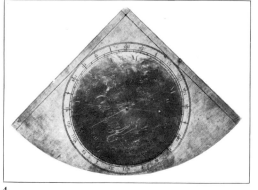

4

5

nomical clock of 1336 was also a planetarium, for although the part of his manuscript describing it is missing, John Leland, who saw the clock during the reign of Henry VIII, states that the planets were depicted.

The first planetarium of which we have full knowledge was the machine designed and made by Giovanni Dondi of Padua between 1348 and 1364. The weight-driven clock movement was contained in a seven-sided bronze vertical frame above which were mounted seven main dials on which were displayed the movements of the sun, moon and

five other known planets, moving in epicycles according to the Ptolemaic system. In 1561 Eberhart Baldewein of Kassel made to the order of Wilhelm IV of Hesse a somewhat similar planetarium mounted in a square vertical gilt-metal case, with planetary dials on all four sides, still on the geocentric principle. This fine example had a celestial globe on top [330/1]

The first English planetarium after Wallingford's was one built nearly 350 years later by Samuel Watson of Coventry [330/2]. It was ordered by Charles II in 1681 and completed by Watson six years later; this also is geocentric.

A relatively simple but effective heliocentric planetarium was made for Christiaan Huygens in 1681 by Johannes van Ceulen of the Hague [331/6]. It is spring-driven and controlled by a balance with spiral balance-spring, as invented by Christiaan Huygens in 1675. Another elaborate planetarium was made in England by Henry Bridges. It has a geocentric upper dial and a planetary heliocentric lower dial which shows the eccentricity of the planetary orbits, the latitude of each planet and the position of its perihelion and aphelion.

During the present century elaborate and effective planetaria employing optical projection have been made, mainly by the firm of Carl Zeiss, for showing to large audiences. Spectators sit below a dark dome on which images of stars, sun, moon and planets are projected from an instrument situated at the centre of the dome, with very realistic effect. FABW

Precession of the equinoxes The positions of the equinoxes are determined by the position of the Earth's axis, and if this was constant in direction the equinoxes would remain fixed in position in relation to the fixed stars. Owing to a gyroscopic effect produced by the gravitational pulls of the moon and sun on the Earth's equatorial bulge, the Earth's axis, though remaining always at the same angle to the plane of its orbit, changes its direction, making one complete revolution in approximately 26,000 years. From the Earth, therefore, the equinox points in the heavens move slowly around the equinoctial or equatorial circle. The spring equinox in the early Christian era was in the constellation of Aries and was termed the 'first point of Aries'. It has now moved back into the constellation of Pisces, a movement of nearly 30° of Right Ascension. FABW

Quadrant In its simplest form, a quarter-circle of metal, ivory or wood, with a pair of sights along its upper edge, a scale of degrees inside its curved edge, and a light plumb-bob on a string hanging from its right-angled corner. It is basically an instrument for measuring altitude, but differ-

ent models have been developed for a variety of purposes.

A quadrant intended solely or almost solely for finding the time is termed a 'horary quadrant'; it is in effect an altitude sundial. Horary quadrants have been made to indicate unequal or equal hours, and sometimes both. There are two methods of arranging for a date setting. In one, the date scale is marked vertically near one straight edge of the quadrant, and a slider on the plumb-bob line is set to this. Then a sight of the sun is taken and the string held against the quadrant face with the thumb, the slider giving the reading on the curved hour lines. In the other method, the date scale is near the curved edge of the quadrant, the line is set to the date and its slider moved to the point where it meets the 12 line, the same subsequent procedure being followed. A fine horary quadrant indicating unequal hours, dating from the early 14th century, is in Merton College, Oxford. The earliest surviving dated quadrants showing equal hours are one of 1398 in Dorchester Museum and a similar example of 1399 in the British Museum [330/3].

A development of the simple horary quadrant was the so-called 'Gunter' quadrant, invented *c.*1618 by Edmund Gunter of Christ Church, Oxford. This is engraved with two sets of lines side by side on the face of the quadrant. The set to the left forms a horary quadrant while that to the right enables the sun's azimuth to be found when its altitude is known at a given date. An unusual feature is that both sets of lines are folded over at the equinox line to permit a more open scale, but giving a complex appearance of crossed lines [330/4].

Other special forms of quadrant are the sinical quadrant, whose scales enable the sines of the measured angles to be read off directly, and gunnery quadrants, from which the angle of elevation of the target and the necessary elevation of the gun barrel can be determined. Very large fixed quadrants for accurate measurement of the altitude of stars were essential pieces of equipment in pioneer astronomical observatories. FABW

Reflecting circle An elaborated form of the sextant used for measuring the large angles required in the de-

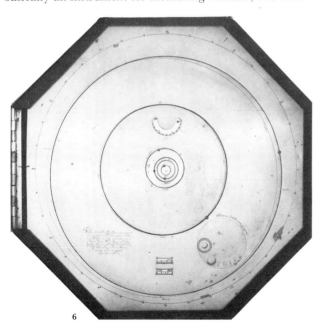

6

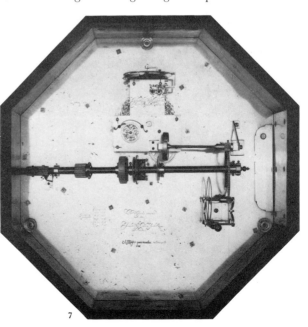

7

termination of longitude by the method of lunar distances [330/5]. FABW

Rete The rotatable circular star map of an astrolabe, in the form of a network of pierced and engraved metal. FABW

Right Ascension The angle between the plane containing any celestial body and passing through the poles, and a similar plane passing through the point of the spring equinox, measured in an easterly direction when looking south from the Earth's surface. It may be expressed in degrees, 0 to 360, or in hours, with minutes and seconds of time, 0 to 24.

The Right Ascensions of fixed stars remain constant, apart from any very small proper motion a particular star may have and the small steady drift due to the precession of the equinoxes. FABW

Scaphe A general term applied to all sundials in which the hour lines are engraved on a hollowed-out surface. Sundials of ancient Egypt had their lines marked on flat surfaces, but the Greeks and Romans constructed large, fixed stone sundials of scaphe form. The simplest is a hemispherical hollow in a horizontal slab, the gnomon consisting of a vertical spike the shadow of whose tip shows the time. In the so-called 'hemicycle' of Berosus [333/4], the useless part of the hemisphere is cut away, leaving an open front on the south side of the dial. FABW

Sextant A modification of John Hadley's octant made by Captain John Campbell *c.* 1771. Whereas the octant is in the form of a sector comprising one-eighth of a circle, the sextant occupies one-sixth of a circle. With the doubling of angle provided by the rotating mirror it enables angles up to 120° to be measured, as against 90° for the octant. FABW

Sidereal time The sidereal day is the time of one complete revolution of the Earth relative to the first point of Aries, or the spring equinox. This is not quite the same time as one revolution relative to the stars, since the first point of Aries moves very slowly around the ecliptic, owing to precession; but the difference is only 0.008 seconds. The length of the sidereal day is 23 hours 56 minutes 4.09 seconds, recorded as 24 'hours' on a sidereal clock. FABW

Solstices The dates when the sun appears to stand still in the heavens, i.e. when it reaches its greatest declination, north or south. Since these are maximum and minimum values on a smooth curve they cannot be measured precisely; on the Gregorian calendar they occur near 21st June and 22nd December. FABW

1

Sundial, adjustable This usually consists of a horizontal dial with a small number of concentric hour scales, each for use in a single latitude, with a gnomon whose inclination can be varied. Dials of this type were incorporated in some of the fine astronomical compendia made by Christopher Schissler of Augsburg between 1555 and 1565, and were popularised by Michael Butterfield. FABW
See also Sundial, Butterfield.

Sundial, altitude It is possible to measure time from the sun's altitude when the date is known. Portable altitude dials with a date setting scale take a great variety of forms, including the chalice, crescent, pillar, quadrant, ring and universal ring dials. FABW

Sundial, Butterfield A form of adjustable sundial invented by Michael Butterfield, an English instrument maker who is known to have worked in Paris between 1678 and 1680.

The Butterfield sundial [332/1] is a small, portable horizontal sundial with a baseplate, usually octagonal but sometimes oval, of brass or silver, with engraved hour lines and a small inset compass. Four or more concentric sets of hour lines are employed, each for a definite latitude, and the folding gnomon has a pivoted style edge, which slides over the main gnomon, so that the angle of inclination of the edge can be varied. The fixed portion of the gnomon carries a scale of latitudes; the pivoted portion is engraved with a bird, the tip of whose bill indicates the inclination on the latitude scale. FABW

Sundial, chalice A form of scaphe dial in which the dial is in the form of a chalice or cup, usually of metal. The hour lines are engraved on the inside of the cup, and the time is shown by the shadow of the tip of a pin-gnomon which usually rises vertically inside the chalice.

Chalice dials may be either direction or altitude dials. If a direction dial it has a built-in magnetic compass, used to set it in position; if without a compass, the interior walls of the chalice are divided into twelve equal compartments identified by the names of the months or the corresponding zodiacal signs. In use the dial of the chalice sundial is set so that the shadow of the gnomon lies within the month of use. The earliest known chalice dial [333/2] is dated 1554 and signed by Bartholomew, Abbot of Aldersbach, near Passau, Bavaria. FABW

Sundial, Chinese The Chinese have used sundials since at least the 4th century BC. Equatorial dials have been found, dating to the Han dynasty, measuring the day into 100 parts, or *K'o*, each equal to 14 minutes 24 seconds of the modern day. Portable sundials were referred to in a manuscript of the late Chou dynasty. Additional information is provided by a 14th-century Chinese manuscript, which indicates that scaphe sundials existed in the 13th century. After the arrival of Europeans in the 16th century, horizontal dials were introduced.

Post-16th-century sundials are of two main types, referred to in Joseph Needham's *Science and Civilization in China* as Type A and Type B. Type A is the Chinese descendant of the European horizontal folding sundial with

1 **Sundial, Butterfield** An adjustable pocket dial with its case; by Michael Butterfield, Paris, *c.*1680. Science Museum, London.

2 **Sundial, chalice** The earliest known example; signed by Bartholomew, Abbot of Aldersbach, dated 1554. British Museum, London.

3 **Sundial, cup,** by a member of the Volpaia family of Italian craftsmen, inscribed 'HYERONIMUS VULPARIAE FLORENTINUS FACIEBAT MDLXXX'. Science Museum, London.

4 **Scaphe** A Roman dial invented by Berosus, *c.*300 BC, found at Cività Lavinia, near Rome. British Museum, London.

5 **Sundial, diptych,** containing a compass; made of ivory. The string gnomon has five adjustments for latitudes with the main hour scale surrounding the compass. The upper dial indicates Babylonian hours and lengths of day and night (gnomon missing) and the lower cup dial indicates Italian hours; from Augsburg, signed 'Leonhard Miller, 1635'. Merseyside County Museum, Liverpool.

a compass, string gnomon, and unequal hour gradients for measuring equal-hour intervals at one or more specific latitudes. This type often has a moon dial on the reverse side of the lid. Type B is the direct descendant in Chinese lineage from earlier Chou and Sung models. It is a portable folding sundial with a compass, adjustable inclining dial, and a scale for adjusting the degree of incline of the dial according to the season. The scale has twelve different notches for inclining the dial according to the *chhi* (fortnight) of the season, going from winter solstice to summer solstice. Each notch is used twice during the year, once in the cycle of rising inclination and once in the cycle of descending inclination. In this manner the dial maintains only moderate accuracy in measuring equal fixed hours according to the season. In summer the dial can also be used for travelling if the degree of inclination for each *chhi* is known. The dial can then be used as an equatorial sundial, according to the latitude of the locality, but not in winter since the angle of the sun is below the inclined dial and there is no provision for indicating winter hours on the reverse.

The compasses on both types of sundial have the cardinal points and the characters of the Twelve Terrestrial Branches and the Ten Celestial Stems as well as seasonal references engraved in the chart of degrees of azimuth around the compass dial. They refer to the sexagenary cycle and were used for purposes of divination. MCR
See also Divination boards, Chinese.

Sundial, crescent A modified form of universal-ring dial in which the ring is divided into two equal semicircular portions placed back to back. The division is made at the '12' marks, so that the semicircles face due east and west respectively when correctly set. The pinhole is replaced by the tip of a curved gnomon, which slides on a date scale. FABW

Sundial, cup A form of scaphe dial, namely a dial with a hollowed-out surface. The term can be applied to a chalice dial [333/2], but it more often refers to dials with hour lines engraved in a shallow circular depression in a horizontal metal or ivory plate; in this type of cup sundial the gnomon is usually a short vertical pin. The cup dial often indicates Italian or Babylonian hours [333/3]; these two indications may occasionally appear on diptych dials as accessories to the main horizontal or vertical dial showing equal hours. FABW

Sundial, diptych A convenient form of pocket compass dial. It consists of a pair of rectangular metal or ivory plates, hinged along a shorter edge. When closed it is flat, but in use it is opened, with the upper plate vertical and the lower remaining horizontal. In this position the string gnomon, which passes through a hole in each plate, becomes taut. This casts a shadow on a dial marked on the horizontal plate, in which a compass is also set. The same gnomon

333

1 2 3

often serves a vertical south dial on the under-surface of the upper plate.

Diptych dials often have other 'furniture', the most common being small horizontal, vertical, or cup dials showing Italian and Babylonian hours, others being pin-gnomon dials showing unequal hours and the length of the daylight period. In some versions, a nocturnal or a volvelle for interconverting lunar and solar times may also be included. FABW

Sundial, direction Direction sundials, if portable, are oriented by a magnetic compass. They measure time by the hour angle of the sun relative to the meridian. FABW

Sundial, equinoctial, or equatorial A sundial with its hour scales on a circle parallel to the Earth's equator. Since the great circle in which this plane meets the interior of a celestial sphere was termed by medieval astronomers the 'equinoctial', this term is now generally applied to dials of the type.

A typical universal equinoctial sundial consists of a base plate embodying a magnetic compass, to the north edge of which is hinged a circular hour ring. When this is lifted it engages a latitude arc and can thus be set for latitude. A pivoted diametral bar, to the centre of which a pin-gnomon is attached at right angles, traverses the hour ring. The shadow of the gnomon gives the time on the hour ring. The pin-gnomon is turned upwards during the summer half-year and downwards during the winter; no shadow can be obtained at the equinoxes when the sun is in the plane of the ring itself.

The earliest-known equinoctial dials date from the 15th century. One example, probably by Hans Dorn of Vienna and dated 1476, is in the Stuttgart Landesmuseum; another, dated 1481 [334/1], is in the Museum of the History of Science, Oxford. FABW

Sundial, horizontal The commonest form of sundial [334/2], in which the shadow of a gnomon whose edge is parallel to the earth's axis falls on a horizontal surface. Usually this carries only the hour lines, but occasionally a ring showing the equation of time is added. Portable horizontal sundials take many forms; in the diptych form the gnomon is a tautened string; in the small accessory dials showing Italian and Babylonian hours it is a short vertical pin. FABW

Sundial, Japanese Like most astronomical and horological conventions in Japan before the advent of the Europeans, sundials were probably imported during the Asuka period (6th century AD) from T'ang China. The sundial most useful to the Japanese temporal system was used, and came to be more Japanese than Chinese. It is of an archaic design called a 'scaphe', or more accurately, a 'hemispherium', reputed to have been invented by a Chaldean priest-astronomer called Berosus in the 3rd century BC. The Japanese scaphe was a concave hemisphere with six hour divisions inscribed on the surface and a gnomon on a perpendicular axis. It measured the daylight hours equally for the given solar declination. This system was perfectly suited to the Japanese system of varying the hour duration according to the season.

Many pocket sundials are in the shape of a small 18th-century watch. In one side is the scaphe, and in the other the compass. Often around the circumference of one or both the Twelve Terrestial Branches are engraved, and sometimes the Ten Celestial Stems as well. These refer to the sexagenary calendar and to other cultural associations related to time and the celestial cycles. The characters were placed so that sunset and sunrise were in the east–west axis, and midnight and noon were in the north–south axis, respectively. The numbers corresponding to the hours were engraved either on the rim around half the circumference, or on the central axis (east–west) of the scaphe. MCR
See also Hours, Japanese.

Sundial, pillar The pillar dial is an altitude dial, sometimes called a 'column' or 'cylinder' dial; the old name was 'chilindre'. It consists of a vertical pillar, usually of constant cross-section, mounted on·a base or suspended from a shackle. The surface of the pillar is divided by vertical lines, usually six, into compartments, each for use in a given pair of months, which are indicated at the top or foot of each compartment. The cylinder is surmounted by a cap inside which is pivoted a gnomon in the form of a blade; for storage this fits in a hole in the pillar. To use the dial, the cap is removed, the gnomon swung out horizontally, and the cap with gnomon replaced on the pillar. The dial is then held with the gnomon pointed towards the sun and the pillar turned until the shadow falls straight down the side of the pillar. The time is then read from the shadow of the gnomon's tip on the hour lines, which twist helically round the pillar.

1 Sundial, equinoctial (or equatorial) An early example in gilt metal; probably by Hans Dorn of Vienna, inscribed 'Ave Maria 1481'. Museum of the History of Science, Oxford University.

2 Sundial, horizontal, made by William Deane, London, dated 1718. Science Museum, London.

3 Sundial, pillar, with the gnomon in the working position; dated 1455. Bayerisches Nationalmuseum, Munich.

4 Orrery made in 1713 by John Rowley, London, for Charles Boyle, fourth Earl of Orrery, closely copying one made by George Graham. Science Museum, London.

4

1

1 Volvelle signed 'James Kynuyn fecit, 1593'. British Museum, London.

2 Sundial, polyhedral, with 23 calibrations on its flat surfaces; gilt metal with enamelled lettering; signed 'Hans Koch, Muenchen, 1578'. Bayerisches Nationalmuseum, Munich.

3 Sundial, polyhedral, of stone, indicating the time in Peking, Port Royal (Jamaica), the Isle of Man (G.B.), Boston (U.S.A.) and Jerusalem; signed John Kewley, Ballafreer, 1774. Manx Museum, Douglas.

4 Sundial, universal ring, signed 'Hilkiah Bedford at Holborn Conduit', c.1670. Museum of the History of Science, Oxford University.

5 Sundial, ring, a simple version. The interior is divided into separate rings for use during the different seasons, intersected by the sloping hour-lines. 'S.P.F. 1736'. British Museum, London.

2

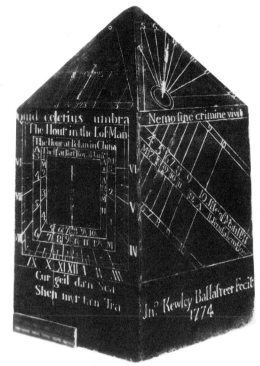

3

4

5

Pillar dials showing unequal hours are shown in manuscript drawings before 1350; the earliest surviving example, showing equal hours, is dated 1455 [334/3]. FABW

Sundial, polyhedral Providing that the style, or shadow-casting edge, of a sundial is parallel to the Earth's axis, hour lines can be drawn on any surface on which the sun shines. This allows the designer of dials to make them in a great variety of shapes, with plane or concave faces. One of the simplest forms is the cube, with dials on the top and four vertical sides [337/2]. Another is the octagon [337/1] with vertical sides, with or without corresponding sloping sides above or below the vertical ones. The whole may be capped by a horizontal dial, or by a decorative finial.

One form of the polyhedral dial is the crucifix, a cross hinged to a base with the time shown by the shadow of an edge of the cross on a neighbouring face. FABW

Sundial, ring An altitude sundial in which the time is shown by light rays passing through a small hole in a ring, giving a spot of light on a set of hour lines on the inner surface of the ring [337/5]. Such dials are sometimes called 'poke' dials: 'He drew a dial from his poke . . . and says, very wisely, "It is ten o'clock" ' (As You Like It).

Since the sun's altitude at a given hour depends on the date, being greater in summer than in winter, a fixed pinhole with a set of hour lines parallel to the axis of the ring would be correct only for one date each half-year. There are two ways of providing for the whole range of dates. The first is to make the hour lines slope and to divide them into three parallel rings, one for winter, one for summer, and one for spring and autumn [337/5]. The second is to make the pinhole in a small piece of a ring sliding within the main ring adjustable according to the season. This gives an approximately correct set of readings on hour lines parallel to the axis, though with some seasonal errors. FABW

Sundial, universal ring A ring dial is for use in a fixed latitude, but the universal ring dial [337/4] can be used over a wide range of latitudes. It consists of three rings and a strip with slider. A flat vertical brass ring, with grooved outer edge, fits within a ring of circular cross-section, and slides within it. The outer ring is suspended from a shackle or mounted on a foot. One side of the inner ring carries a scale of degrees, 0–90, for adjustment to latitude using an index on the outer ring. Pivoted within the inner ring is a further ring which can be swung out at right angles, carrying the hour scale. A diametral bar traverses the interior of this last ring; the bar has a slot in which a small piece with a pinhole slides. The slider moves along a scale of dates, or corresponding zodiacal signs. In use, the second ring is adjusted for latitude and the pinhole set to the date. The instrument is then rotated until the spot of light passing through the pinhole falls on the hour ring, where the time is read.

The invention of the universal ring dial is attributed to William Oughtred (1575–1652). Dials incorporating these principles were manufactured by the London instrument maker Elias Allen in 1652. FABW

1 **Tellurium** by Thomas Tompion and George Graham, London, *c.*1705. Museum of the History of Science, Oxford University.

2 **Transit instrument** installed at the Old Royal Observatory, Greenwich, during the directorship of John Pond, Astronomer Royal (1811–35). It is a ten-foot instrument, made by Troughton, 1816. National Maritime Museum, Greenwich.

1

2

Sundial, vertical In this type of dial the shadow of a gnomon whose edge is parallel to the Earth's axis falls on a vertical surface; if this is due south, the hour lines will be symmetrically placed. Vertical sundials are normally seen on the walls of buildings, but they also appear as the upper members of diptych portable dials and on the sides of polyhedral dials. FABW

Tellurium A mechanically operated model showing the revolution of the Earth around the sun, and of the moon around the Earth. An early example by Thomas Tompion and George Graham *c.* 1705 [338/1] immediately preceded the famous orrery by John Rowley, which was itself a tellurium, the word 'orrery' being now generally applied to later instruments showing the motions of the planets. FABW

Transit instrument A telescope mounted in horizontal bearings lying in an east–west direction, so that if the telescope is at right angles to its axle or arbor it will always lie in the meridian plane. A vertical crosswire in the centre of its eyepiece provides that when the image of a star lies exactly on this wire the star must lie exactly on the meridian, and is making its transit, the time of which can be recorded on a chronograph. FABW

Volvelle A simple calculator or reckoner, involving a rotating disc or discs, usually fitted as an accessory to a portable sundial or astronomical compendium. Each disc usually carries a projecting index, reading on a circular scale; alternatively, the disc may have perforated slots through which indications on a fixed surface below may be read. In a common form, the fixed circular scales read 1–12, 1–12 in succession, and 1–29½, and the rotating disc also has

a scale of 1–12, 1–12 at its outer edge. By setting the index to the age of the moon, the solar time corresponding to a given lunar time can be read off. The rotating disc also has an eccentric circular hole through which the phase of the moon can be seen pictorially. Volvelles are also made to relate equal and unequal hours, equal and Italian or Babylonian hours, or the lengths of the day and night and times of sunrise and sunset according to season [336/1]. FABW

Waywiser A device consisting of a wheel, usually wooden, combined with mechanical gearing to record the number of revolutions made by the wheel in rolling along a road, and in this way measuring the distance covered. Waywisers were used by surveyors in the late 18th and early 19th centuries, the wheel being mounted in bearings in a long handle with inset dial, or dials, recording miles, furlongs, poles and yards. FABW

Zodiac The zodiac is a broad band in the heavens, centred on the ecliptic, in which lie all the motions of the sun, moon and major planets. Since the orbits of these are in planes not far removed from the plane of the Earth's orbit, the zodiac extends to about 8° on either side of the ecliptic. The zodiac was divided by the early astronomers into twelve equal parts, each of 30° of Right Ascension. Each part was named after a constellation in the neighbourhood, with its name or sign represented pictorially or by a symbol. The twelve signs are Aries (Ram), Taurus (Bull), Gemini (Twins), Cancer (Crab), Leo (Lion), Virgo (Virgin), Libra (Scales), Scorpio (Scorpion), Sagittarius (Archer), Capricornus (Goat), Aquarius (Water-carrier), and Pisces (Fishes). These signs or symbols are often engraved on scientific instruments to serve as a scale of dates. FABW

Bibliography

Note on the Bibliography

Almost all the books in this bibliography are either works published during the past 25 years, or recent reprintings of older volumes. To keep the list to a reasonable length very few books have been included which deal with local geographical areas of the countries concerned, or individual clockmakers, apart from those of outstanding merit. Catalogues of important museum collections or special exhibitions have also been omitted except for a few which contain far more than itemised lists of specimens. Inevitably many of the books mentioned deal with watches as well as clocks, and although the list has been divided into groups for ease of reference some overlapping of subject matter will be found, though in only one case has a title been repeated in two groups.

General Works

Allix, Charles *Carriage Clocks* London 1974

Antiquarian Horological Society *Collectors' Pieces, Clocks and Watches* London 1964

Baillie, G. H. *Clocks and Watches: an historical bibliography* London 1951

Baillie, G. H. *Watchmakers and Clockmakers of the World* 3rd edition, London 1951 (Vol 2, *see* Loomes)

Bassermann-Jordan, Ernst von (revised by Hans von Bertele) *The Book of Old Clocks and Watches* London 1964

Berthoud, Ferdinand *Histoire de la mesure du temps par les horloges* Paris 1802, reprinted 1976

Bromley, John (compiler) *Catalogue of Books and Manuscripts in the Library of the Worshipful Company of Clockmakers – The Clockmakers' Library* London 1977

Bruton, Eric *Antique Clocks and Clock Collecting* London 1974

Bruton, Eric *Clocks and Watches* Feltham 1968

Bruton, Eric *Clocks and Watches, 1400–1900* London 1967

Bruton, Eric *The Longcase Clock* London 1977

Chapuis, Alfred and Droz, Edmund *Automata: a historical and technological study* Neuchâtel 1958

Cipolla, Carlo Maria *Clocks and Culture, 1300–1700* London 1967

Clutton, C., Baillie, G. H. and Ilbert, C. A. *Britten's Old Clocks and Watches and their Makers* 8th edition, London 1973

Collard, F. Bernard Royer- *Skeleton Clocks* London 1969

Coole, P. G. (under pseudonym Cumhaill, P. W.) *Investing in Clocks and Watches* London 1967

de Carle, Donald *Clocks and their Value* London 1968

Derham, William *The Artificial Clockmaker* London 1696, reprinted Reading 1962 (facsimile)

Edwardes, Ernest L. *The Grandfather Clock* Altrincham 1971

Edwardes, Ernest L. *The Story of the Pendulum Clock* Altrincham 1977

Edwardes, Ernest L. *Weight-driven Chamber Clocks of the Middle Ages and Renaissance* Altrincham 1965

Fleet, Simon *Clocks* London 1961

Goodrich, W. L. *The Modern Clock* U.S.A. 1905, reprinted 1967

Gordon, G. F. C. *Clockmaking Past and Present* London 1949

Guye, Samuel and Michel, Henri *Time and Space: measuring instruments from the 15th to the 19th century* London 1971

Hood, Peter *How Time is Measured* Oxford 1969

Jagger, Cedric *The World's Great Clocks and Watches* London 1977

Joy, Edward T. *The Country Life Book of Clocks* London 1967

Le Lionnais, François *Prentice-Hall Book of Time* London 1962

Lloyd, H. Alan *Chats on Old Clocks* London 1951

Lloyd, H. Alan *The Collector's Dictionary of Clocks* London 1964

Lloyd, H. Alan *Old Clocks* 4th edition, London 1970

Lloyd H. Alan *Some Outstanding Clocks over 700 Years, 1250–1950* London 1958

Loomes, Brian *Watchmakers and Clockmakers of the World* Vol. 2, London 1976 (*see* Baillie)

Nicholls, Andrew *Clocks in Colour* Dorset 1975

Ord-Hume, Arthur W. J. G. *Clockwork Music* London 1973

Priestley, John B. *Man and Time* London 1964

Robertson, J. Drummond *The Evolution of Clockwork, with a special section on the clocks of Japan and a comprehensive bibliography of horology* London 1931, reprinted Wakefield 1972

Scherer, J. Otto *Old Clocks* Berne 1964

Shenton, A. and Shenton, R. *The Price Guide to Clocks, 1840–1940* Woodbridge 1977

Smith, Alan *Clocks and Watches* London 1975

Smith, John *Horological Dialogues* London 1675, reprinted Reading 1962

Smith, John *Horological Disquisitions* London 1964, reprinted Reading 1962

Tait, Hugh *Clocks in the British Museum* London 1968

Tyler E. John *Clocks and Watches* London 1975

Tyler, E. John *European Clocks* London 1968

Ullyett, Kenneth *In Quest of Clocks* London 1950

Ward, F. A. B. *Clocks and Watches: 1 Weight-driven Clocks* Science Museum, London 1973

Ward, F. A. B. *Clocks and Watches: 2 Spring-driven Clocks* H.M.S.O., London 1972

Ward, F. A. B. *Time Measurement* H.M.S.O., London 1966

Ward, F. A. B. *Timekeepers – Clocks, Watches, Sundials, Sandglasses* H.M.S.O., London 1963

Welch, Kenneth F. *Time Measurement: an introductory history* Newton Abbott 1972

Wenham, Edward *Old Clocks for Modern Use* London 1964

Willsburger, Johann *Clocks and Watches: 600 years of the world's most beautiful timepieces* New York 1976

Wood, E. J. *Curiosities of Clocks and Watches from the Earliest Times* London 1866, reprinted Wakefield 1973

Wright, Lawrence *Clockwork Man* London 1968

Mechanical and Technical Works, Precision Clocks, Chronometers and Electrical Horology

Aked, Charles K. *A Conspectus of Electrical Timekeeping* reprinted from six articles in *Antiquarian Horology* London 1976

Antiquarian Horological Society *Pioneers of Precision Timekeeping* Monograph No. 3, London n.d.

Bain, Alexander *A Short History of the Electric Clock* edited by W. D. Hackmann (1852), reprinted London 1973

Belmont, H. *La Bulle-clock: horlogerie électrique* Besançon 1975

Berner, G. A. *Dictionnaire professionnel illustré de l'horlogerie* La Chaux-de-Fonds n.d.

Britten, F. J. *The Watch and Clockmakers' Handbook, Dictionary and Guide* 15th edition, London 1955

Britten, F. J. *Horological Hints and Helps* London 1934

Chamberlain, Paul M. *It's About Time* New York 1941, reprinted London 1964

Chance, B. *Electronic Time Measurement* New York 1946

Crom, Theodore R. *Horological Wheel-cutting Engines, 1700–1900* Gainesville, Florida 1970

de Carle, Donald *Practical Clock Repairing* London 1968

de Carle, Donald *Watch and Clock Encyclopedia* London 1959

Denison, Edmund Beckett – later Sir Edmund Beckett (*see* Grimthorpe)

Diderot and d'Alembert '*Horlogerie*' from the 18th-century *Encyclopédie ou Dictionnaire Raisonné des Sciences, des Arts et des Métiers* Paris 1765, reprinted Milan 1971

Gazeley, W. J. *Clock and Watch Escapements* London 1956, reprinted 1977

Gazeley, W. J. *Watch and Clock Making and Repairing* London 1958, reprinted 1976

Gould, Rupert T. *The Marine Chronometer: its history and development* London 1923, reprinted 1971

Gould, Rupert T. *John Harrison and his Timekeepers* London 1958, reprinted from *The Mariner's Mirror* 1935

Grimthorpe, Lord *A Rudimentary Treatise on Clocks, Watches and Bells* London 1903, reprinted Wakefield 1974

Guye, R. P. and Bossart, M. *Horlogerie Electrique* Lausanne 1948

Haswell, J. Eric *Horology: the science of time measurement and the construction of clocks, watches and chronometers* London 1928, reprinted 1975

Hill, Donald R. *On the Construction of Water Clocks* Occasional paper No. 4, Turner & Devereux, London 1976

Hoopes, Penrose R. *Shop Records of Daniel Burnap, Clockmaker* Hartford, Connecticut 1958

Hummel, Charles F. *With Hammer in Hand: the dominy craftsmen of East Hampton, New York* Charlottesville, Virginia 1968

Jones, F. Hope- *Electric Clocks and Chimes* London n.d., reprinted 1976

Jones, F. Hope- *Electric Clocks and How to Make Them* London n.d., reprinted 1977

Jones, F. Hope- *Electric Clocks* London 1931

Jones, F. Hope- *Electrical Timekeeping* London 1940, reprinted 1976

Langman, H. R. and Hall, A. *Electrical Horology* London 1923, reprinted 1946

Laycock, William *The Lost Science of John 'Longitude' Harrison* Ashford 1976

Marrison, W. A. *The First Electric Clock* New York 1940

Marrison, W. A. *The Evolution of the Quartz Crystal Clock* New York 1948

Mercer, Tony *Mercer Chronometers* Ashford 1978

Mercer, Vaudrey *The Life and Letters of Edward John Dent, Chronometer Maker, and Some Account of his Successors* London 1977

Mercer, Vaudrey *John Arnold & Son, Chronometer Makers, 1762–1843* London 1972

Mudge, Thomas *A Description with Plates, of the Timekeeper of the Late Mr Thomas Mudge; to which is prefixed a Narrative by Mr Thomas Mudge, his Son* London 1799, reprinted 1977

Nettell, D. F. *Automatic Winders for Turret Clocks* Uffington 1975

Philpott, Stuart F. *Modern Electric Clocks* London 1949

Quill, Raymond H. *John Harrison, the Man who Found Longitude* London 1966

Quill, Raymond H. *John Harrison Copley, Medallist, and the £20,000 Longitude Prize* London 1976

Rawlings, A. L. *The Science of Clocks and Watches* 2nd edition 1948, reprinted Wakefield 1974

Rees, Abraham *Clocks, Watches and Chronometers (1819–20)* from *The Cyclopaedia; or Universal Dictionary of Arts, Sciences and Literature* reprinted Newton Abbot 1970

Rossel, J. *Le mesure atomique de temps* Geneva 1954

Saunier, Claudius *Treatise on Modern Horology in Theory and Practice* 1881, reprinted London 1975

Smith, Eric P. *Clocks: their working and maintenance* Newton Abbot 1977

Smith Eric P. *Repairing Antique Clocks: a guide for amateurs* Newton Abbot 1975

Smith, H. M. *Quartz Clocks of the Greenwich Time Service* London 1953

Thiout, Antoine *Traité de l'horlogerie, méchanique et pratique* first published 1741, reprinted in one volume Paris 1972

Tyler, E. John *The Craft of the Clockmaker* London 1973

Wise, S. J. *Electric Clocks* London 1951

Wyke, John *A Catalogue of Tools for Watch and Clockmakers, c. 1758–1770*, reprinted with an introduction and commentary by Alan Smith, Charlottesville, Virginia 1978

Clocks of Various Countries

CHINA AND JAPAN

Bedini, Silvio A. 'The Scent of Time' *Trans. of the American Philosophical Society*, new series, Vol. 53, Part 5, 1963

Combridge, John H. 'The Celestial Balance: a practical reconstruction', *Horological Journal* Vol. 104, pp. 82–86, February 1962

Combridge, John H. 'The Astronomical Clock Towers of Chang Ssu-Hsun and his Successors, 976–1126 A.D.', *Antiquarian Horology* Vol. 9, No. 3, June 1975

Mody, N. H. N. *Japanese Clocks* London 1932 (later edn. n.d.)

Needham, Joseph, and others *Heavenly Clockwork: the great astronomical clocks of mediaeval China* Cambridge 1960

Needham, Joseph *Science and Civilisation in China* (7 vols. – in progress) Cambridge 1954.

Robertson, John Drummond *The Evolution of Clockwork: with a special section on the clocks of Japan* London 1931, reprinted Wakefield 1972

Yamaguchi R. *The Clocks of Japan* Tokyo 1950

FRANCE

Arts & Métiers, Conservatoire National des *Catalogue du Musée, Section JB, Horlogerie* Paris 1949

Bellaigue, Geoffrey de *The James A. Rothschild Collection at Waddesdon Manor – Furniture, Clocks and Gilt Bronzes* Vol. 1, National Trust 1974

Boller, Tom *Comtoiseklokken* (text in Dutch) Harlem 1977

Daniels, George *The Art of Breguet* London 1975

Edey, Winthrop *French Clocks* London 1967

Maitzner, Françios and Moreau, Jean *La Comtoise, la Morbier, la Morez – Histoire et Technique* Paris 1976

Tardy, H. Lengelle *La Pendule Française* Paris 1948–50 (various reprintings) *1. De l'horloge Gothique à la Pendule Louis XV; 2. Du Louis XVI à nos jours; 3. Provinces et Étrangers*

Tardy, H. Lengelle *Dictionnaire des horlogers français* Paris 1972

Watson, F. J. B. *Catalogue of Furniture in the Wallace Collection* London 1956

Wilson, Gillian *French 18th-century Clocks in the J. Paul Getty Museum* Malibu, California 1976

GERMANY, AUSTRIA AND SWITZERLAND

Abeler, Jurgen *Alt Bergische Uhren und die Uhrmacherfamilien im Bergischen Land* Wuppertal 1968

Abeler, Jurgen *Meister der Uhrmacherkunst* Wuppertal 1977

Bender, Gerd *Die Uhrenmacher des hohen Schwarzwaldes und ihre Werke* Schwarzwald 1975

Coole, P. G. and Neumann, E. *The Orpheus Clocks* London 1972

Hana, W. E. J. *Middeneuropese Klokken* Bussum 1972

Holzhey, Günther *Flötenuhren aus dem Schwarzwald* Stuttgart 1968

Jütteman, Herbert *Die Schwarzwalduhr* Braunschweig 1972

Kurz, Peter *200 Jahre Schwenninger Uhren* Schwenningen 1965

Matthey, J. P. *Le Pendulier Neuchâtelois* Lausanne 1946

Maurice, Klaus *Die Deutsche Rädenuhr* München 1977

Mühe, Richard *Uhren und Zeitmessung* Furtwangen 1972.

Mühe, R. and Vogel, H. M. *Alte Uhren* München 1976

Neher, F. L. *Ein Jahrhundert Junghans* Schramberg 1961

Schindler, Georg *Uhren* München 1975

Tyler, E. John *Black Forest Clocks* London 1977

GREAT BRITAIN

Aked, Charles K. *Complete List of English Horological Patents up to 1853* Ashford 1975

Beeson, C. F. C. *English Church Clocks, 1280–1850* London 1971

Bird, Anthony *English House Clocks, 1600–1850* Newton Abbot 1973

Bruton, Eric *The Longcase Clock* New York and Washington 1968

Cescinsky, H and Webster, M. R. *English Domestic Clocks* London 1913, reprinted 1976 (facsimile)

Ferriday, Peter *Lord Grimthorpe, 1816–1905* London 1957

Gillgrass, A. *The Book of Big Ben* London 1946

Goodison, Nicholas P. *Ormolu: the work of Matthew Boulton* London 1974

Hawkins, J. B. *Thomas Cole and Victorian Clockmaking* Sydney 1975

Jagger, Cedric *Paul Philip Barraud* London 1968

Lee, Ronald A. *The First Twelve Years of the English Pendulum Clock, 1658–1670* (exh. cat.) London 1969

Lee, Ronald A. *The Knibb Family – Clockmakers* Byfleet 1964

Loomes, Brian *The White Dial Clock* Newton Abbot 1974

Loomes, Brian *Country Clocks and their London Origin* Newton Abbot 1976

Peat, Iorwerth C. *Clock and Watch Makers in Wales* Cardiff 1945 (revised edition 1975)

Smith, John *Old Scottish Clockmakers from 1453 to 1850* Edinburgh 1921 (facsimile available)

Symonds, R. W. *A Book of English Clocks* London 1950

Symonds, R. W. *Masterpieces of English Furniture and Clocks* London 1955

Symonds, R. W. *Thomas Tompion, his Life and Work* London 1951

Ullyet, Kenneth *British Clocks and Clockmakers* London 1947

ITALY

Baillie, G. H., Lloyd, Alan H. and Ward, F. A. B. *The Planetarium of Giovanni di Dondi, Citizen of Padua* London 1974

Brusa, Guiseppe *Gli Orlog* (catalogue of the Poldi Pezzoli Museum, Milan) Milan 1974

Leopold, John H. *The Almanus Manuscript* London 1971

Morpurgo, Enrico *Dizionario degli orologiai Italiani, 1300–1880* Rome 1950

Morpurgo, Enrico *Gli orologi* Milan 1966

Pippa, Luigi *Masterpieces of Watchmaking* (contains early clocks) Milan 1966

Simoni, Antonio *Orologi dal '500 al '800* Milan 1965

Tractatus astrarii Biblica Apostolica Vaticana 1960

NETHERLANDS

Hana, W. E. J. *Klokken* Bussum 1961
Hana, W. E. J. *Klokkenkijkboek* Bussum 1968
Hana, W. E. J. *Friese klokken-Vormgeving en techniek* Bussum 1964
Morpurgo, Enrico *Nederlanse klokken-en horlogemakers vanaf 1300* Amsterdam 1970
Roo, T. de *Roentgen Atlas of Old Dutch Clocks* Alkmaar 1975
Sellink, J. L. *Dutch Antique Domestic Clocks* Leiden 1973
Spierdijk, C. *Klokken en klokkenmakers – zes eeuwen uurwerk* Amsterdam 1962
Wolters. X. F. M. G. *De Friese Stoel-n Staartklok* Holland 1973
Wolters, X. F. M. G. and Sleutjes, A. W. *Vakkundige reparaties aan Antieke Stoel en Staartklokken* Eindhoven 1978
Zeeman J. *De Nederlandse Staande Klok* Amsterdam 1977
Zeeman, J. *De Nederlandse stoelklok* Amsterdam 1969

SPAIN

Basanta, José Luis *Bibliografía relojera española* Pontevedra 1975
Basanta, José Luis *Relojeros de España* Pontevedra 1972
Fontenla, Luis Montañes *Relojes españoles* Madrid 1968
Junquera, Paulina *Relojería Palatina* Madrid 1956
Landeira, Fernando *Theatro chronometrico del Noroeste* Madrid 1957

UNITED STATES AND CANADA

Bailey, Chris H. *American Clockmaking: its early history by Henry Terry* Bristol, Connecticut 1974
Bailey, Chris H. *Two Hundred Years of American Clocks and Watches* Englewood Cliffs, New Jersey 1975
Battison, Edwin A. and Kane, Patricia E. *The American Clock, 1725–1865* Greenwich, Connecticut 1973
Burrows, G. Edmond *Canadian Clocks and Clockmakers* Ontario 1973
Distin, William H. and Bishop, Robert *The American Clock: a comprehensive pictorial survey, 1723–1900* New York 1976
Drepperd, Carl W. *American Clocks and Clockmakers* Garden City, N.Y. 1947
Drost, William E. *Clocks and Watches of New Jersey* Elizabeth, New Jersey 1966
Dworetsky, Lester and Dickstein, Robert *Horology Americana* Roslyn Hts., N.Y. 1973
Eckhardt, George H. *Pennsylvania Clocks and Clockmakers* New York 1955
Eckhardt, George H. *United States Clock and Watch Patents, 1790–1890: the record of a century of American horology and enterprise* New York 1960
Hoopes, Penrose R. *Connecticut Clockmaking of the Eighteenth Century* Hartford, Connecticut 1930, republished 1974
Langdon, J. E. *Clock and Watchmakers in Canada, 1700–1900* 1976
Maust, Don *Early American Clocks: a collection of essays on early American clocks and their makers* Uniontown, Pennsylvania 1971
Miller, Andrew H. and Miller, Dalia M. *Survey of American Clocks, Calendar Clocks* Elgin, Illinois 1972

Miller, Robert C. *Clock Guide Identification with Prices* U.S.A., latest edition 1976
Palmer, Brooks *The Book of American Clocks* New York 1950
Palmer, Brooks *A Treasury of American Clocks* New York 1967
Parsons, Charles S. *New Hampshire Clocks and Clockmakers* Exeter, New Hampshire 1976
Roberts, Kenneth D. *The Contributions of Joseph Ives to Connecticut Clock Technology* Bristol, Connecticut 1970
Roberts, Kenneth D. *Eli Terry and the Connecticut Shelf Clock* Bristol, Connecticut 1973
Schwartz, Marvin D. *Collectors' Guide to Antique American Clocks* Garden City, N.Y. 1975
Thomson, Richard *Antique American Clocks and Watches* New York 1968
Willard, John Ware *Simon Willard and his Clocks* New York 1968 (originally published Boston 1911)

OTHERS

Chenakal, Valentin L. *Watchmakers and Clockmakers in Russia* London 1972
Magnusson, Einar *Allmogeurmakeriet I Vastergotland och I Vastra Smaland* Falköping, Sweden 1967
Mortensen, Otto *Jens Olson's Clock* Copenhagen 1957

Astronomical Clocks, Other Instruments

Asprey & Co. *Clockwork of the Heavens* (exh. cat.) London 1973
Bertele, Hans von *Clockwork Globes and Orreries* London 1958
Bertele, Hans von *Globes and Spheres* Lausanne 1961
Cousins, F. W. *Sundials: a simplified approach by means of the equatorial dial* London 1969
Daumas, Maurice *Scientific Instruments of the 17th and 18th centuries* (translated by Mary Holbrook) London 1973
Environment, Department of *The Astronomical Clock, Hampton Court Palace* London 1973
Gunther, Robert T. *The Astrolabes of the World* Oxford 1932, reprinted London 1976
Herbert, Sir Alan Patrick *Sundials Old and New* London 1967
Michel, Henri *Scientific Instruments in Art and History* (translated by Francis R. and R. E. W. Maddison) London and New York 1967
National Maritime Museum *The Planispheric Astrolabe* H.M.S.O. 1976
Price, Derek de Solla *The Equatorie of the Planetis* London 1952
Price, Derek de Solla *Gears from the Greeks: the Antikythera Mechanism, a calendar computer from ca. 80 B.C.* New York 1975
Randier, Jean *Nautical Antiques for the Collector* London 1976
Rohr, R. R. J. *Sundials: history, theory and practice* Canada 1965
Waugh, A. E. *Sundials: their theory and construction* U.S.A. 1973
Wynter, Harriet and Turner, Anthony *Scientific Instruments* London 1975

Index

343

Montreal, Quebec 223, 222/4, 223/6
month clock **79**, 78/4
monumental clock *See also* planetary clock 237/7, 277/5, 281/5, 283/2
moon phases **55, 57, 159**, 51, 338, 54/1, 55/5, 57/8, 288/1. *See also* dial, lunar; globular or rotating moon; halfpenny moon or Halifax moon
Moore, George 255
Moore of Clerkenwell 118, 118/5
Moore of Dublin and Belfast 263
Moore of Leeds 38/6
mopping, mops *See* buffing, buff
Morbier clock 34. *See also* Comtoise; Morez clock
Morez clock **79**, 34
Morez-Morbier-Foncine, France 34, 79
Morphy, Paul 33
Morpurgo, Enrico 268
Morril, Benjamin 77
Mortensen, Otto 322, 323/7
motion work **160**, 94, 110, 117, 177, 178, 158/1, 160/4
lunar **159**, 51, 221, 291, 159/5. *See also* dial, lunar; globular or rotating moon; moon phases
motor **160**. *See also* barrel; spring, main-
Moulin, B. M. M. 234
movement **51, 160–3**, 18, 23, 24, 33, 44, 53, 61, 64, 73, 79–80, 221, 224, 228, 240, 266, 14/2, 21/2, 33/3, 33/4, 34/2, 46/4, 47/6, 47/7, 49/5, 50/2, 53/6, 56/5, 65/2, 98/4, 104/1, 109/2, 109/5, 109/6, 115/6, 116/3, 123/3, 126/2, 126/4, 126/6, 126/8, 127/10, 129/5, 131/4, 136/2, 136/4, 167/5, 237/5, 238/1, 238/2, 240/3, 246/2, 257/4, 258/4, 266/2, 267/5, 269/4, 277/6, 279/4, 280/3, 287/9, 289/4, 295/8, 296/3, 298/2, 310/3, 312/3, 315/3, 321/5
birdcage 118, 218, 18/3
brass 12, 22, 23, 36, 46, 47, 58, 61, 74, 84, 85, 94, 105, 109, 110, 113, 129, 160, 163, 307, 309, 310, 311, 313, 314, 316, 12/1, 160/1, 160/2, 160/3, 163/2, 163/4, 242/1, 308/3, 314/2, 315/5, 316/2
chronometer 254/5
concealed 79–80
double 47
drum 26, 49, 78, 91, 93, 96, 49/6, 86/2, 163/4
ébauche (unfinished) 235, 244, 309
eight-day **46–7, 75–6, 77**, 23, 26, 39, 45, 46, 47, 48, 54, 55–6, 58, 67, 79, 85, 87, 94, 105, 109–10, 112–13, 128–9, 136, 159, 171, 177–8, 182, 199, 263–4, 298, 301, 310, 311, 312, 316, 21/4, 27/5, 27/6, 44/2, 54/2, 55/6, 75/5, 75/6, 76/1, 77/6, 113/5, 129/4, 160/1, 160/2, 160/3, 163/6, 163/7, 168/1, 249/4, 249/6, 254/5, 258/1, 298/3, 306/2, 308/1, 308/2, 308/3, 310/4, 312/1, 312/2, 313/5, 316/2
800-day 17
fifteen-day 25, 26
400-day 18, 112, 168/7
fusee *See* fusee
iron 109, 160, 57/6, 81/3
month-going 46, 79, 112, 129, 177, 38/5, 67/5, 141/6, 155/6, 257/5, 290/2
one-day 21, 26, 51, 128, 303, 313
100-day 49–50
1000-day 17, 48
pendule de Paris 228
'Salem Bridge' 310, 315
thirty-day 54, 112, 129, 44/3
thirty-hour 23, 25, 44, 46, 55–6, 58, 74, 76–7, 83–4, 87, 94, 105, 110, 112, 129, 159, 178, 182, 218, 313, 315, 37/5, 57/7, 58/2, 84/5, 111/4, 129/4, 163/3, 163/5, 249/3, 315/4
thirty-hour fusee 61, 310/1
three-day 68/1
three-month 79, 129
tin-plate 163
T.S.M. 16/2
twelve-hour 18, 275/6
two-day 128
'upside-down' 316
visible 49/5, 60/1. *See also* skeleton clock
week-going 51
Willard's 16
wooden 24, 27, 47, 58, 74, 84, 94, 105, 110, 129, 163, 223, 307, 308, 310, 313, 315, 316, 27/5, 30/1, 58/2, 163/3, 163/5, 257/4, 280/3, 304/4
year-going **135–6**, 17, 49–50, 79, 112, 178, 258, 291, 326, 135/4, 178/1, 233/4, 270/1
Moyá, Barcelona 297, 303, 298/3, 303/7
Mudge, Thomas **263**, 34, 248, 262/3, 262/4, 269/4
'Blue' and 'Green' chronometers 263
Muller, Nicholas 63
Munich, Germany 98, 238, 239, 245, 246, 306, 337/2
university 61, 246
Muñoz, Blas 297
Mura, Spain 303
Murano, Italy 280
museum 280
Murua, Ignacio 297
Murday, James 14/1
Murday, Thomas John **263**, 249, 263/6
Museo Nazionale della Scienza e della Tecnica, Milan 247, 277, 278
Museo Nazionale, Naples 325
Museum Boymans van Beuningen, Rotterdam 291
Museum of Fine Arts, Antwerp 58
Museum of the History of Science, Oxford 262, 329, 334
Museum of Science, Milan *See* Museo Nazionale della Scienza e della Tecnica, Milan
musical clock **79**, 17, 37, 140, 142, 255, 287, 37/6, 38/7, 78/5, 180/1, 245/4
musical or organ cylinder 51, 53. *See also* musical work
musical work **164**, 73, 79, 93, 113, 141, 173, 263, 298, 37/6, 67/7, 78/5, 180/1, 300/1
'My Grandfather's Clock' 110
mystery clock **79–80**, 39, 48, 233, 79/7, 80/1

Nanking, China 227
Nantes, Edict of 287
Naples, Italy 83, 103/3
Cardinal of 275/6
Napoleon 37, 88, 98, 297
Napoleon III 279
Napoleonic wars 91, 297
Nardin, Paul 305
Nasmyth, James 106
National Maritime Museum, Greenwich *See* Greenwich
National Physical Laboratory, Teddington 96, 326, 327/3
Naugatuck, Conn. *See* Salem Bridge
Naze, Jean 320
Nederlands Goud-, Zilver-en Klokkenmuseum, Utrecht 115/4
Needham, Joseph 225, 332
Neira, Francisco Javier 303
Nelson, Samuel 200/4
neoclassical 12–13, 26, 27, 28, 88, 91, 233, 303, 221/4
Nesselwang, Germany 304–5
Netherlands **51–4, 57, 68–73, 106, 114–15, 126–7, 136, 285–93**, 17, 23, 43, 55, 61, 62, 85, 90, 92, 107, 218, 227, 236, 247, 248, 249, 283, 284, 296, 43/3, 50/2, 51/4, 51/5, 51/6, 51/7, 52/1, 52/2, 52/3, 52/4, 53/5, 53/6, 53/7, 56/2, 56/4, 56/5, 68/1, 68/2, 68/3, 73/2, 73/3, 73/4, 85/8, 86/1, 88/1, 99/5, 115/4, 126/1, 126/2, 126/3, 126/4, 126/5, 126/6, 126/7, 126/8, 127/9, 127/10, 136/1, 136/2, 136/3, 136/4, 145/4, 282/1, 284/5, 286/1–293/4, 331/6, 331/7
clockmakers' guild 293
influence 63, 114, 228, 70/1, 218/1, 303/6
netsuki 62/3
Neuchâtel, Switzerland 14, 234, 297, 301, 305, 307. *See also*: *pendule Neuchâteloise*
Neustadt, Germany 247
Neustadt, Ont. 224
Neuwied, Germany 244
Newcastle-on-Tyne 180/1
New Hamburg, Ont. 224
New Hampshire, U.S.A. 16, 46, 74, 77, 105, 110, 77/7, 163/2
mirror clock 308/1
New Haven Clock Co. **314**, 45, 307, 48/2, 315/4
New Haven, Conn. 21, 313, 314, 48/2, 86/3
New Ipswich, N.H. 77/7
New York, N.Y. 21, 56, 63, 105, 112, 308, 310, 311, 314, 316, 26/1
New York state 55, 105, 129
Newport, Maine 307
Newport Pagnell, Bucks. 261
Newton, Isaac 261
Niagara Falls, Ont. 59/4
nib *See* pallet
Nicole, Adolph 33
night clock **43, 80, 96**, 261–2, 274, 279, 43/4, 80/2
Italian **80–3**, 277, 82/1, 247/5, 273/4, 277/5, 281/5
Ningpo, China 227
nippers **207**, 206/2
Noailles, Maréchal de 236
nocturnal **328**, 322, 334, 328/1
Normande clock **83**, 89, 83/2. *See also*: *demoiselles*
Normandy 83
North, John 264
Norris, Joseph **291**, 291/6
Norristown, Penn. 314
Norton, nr. Stockton-on-Tees, Clev., 256/1
Norwich, Conn. 307, 311
Norwich, Norfolk 248, 255
notary's clock **52**, 51/7
Novello dall'Orologio 268
novelty clock 106, 166, 233
Nuremberg 15, 86, 238, 239, 244, 247, 327, 109/4, 318, 326/2
nut **164**, 138, 169, 164/1
wing **164**
nutation **328**

Oberkinche, Jacob 115
observatory clock **83**, 267, 240/2. *See also* quartz-crystal clock; regulator; Riefler clock, Shortt's free pendulum clock
Ochsenfurt, Germany 238
octant **328–9**, 332, 328/2, 328/3
'Off-She-Goes' chronometer 254
O.G. (Ogee) clock **84**, 103, 105, 84/5, 223/7, 223/9, 306/3, 309/4
ogee moulding **85**, 74, 103
Ohio, U.S.A. 58, 110, 311
oil **164**, 148, 150, 151, 172, 185, 197, 210, 211, 305, 109/5
oil lamp clock **83–4**, 25, 80, 96, 84/1, 84/2
oil sink **164**
oilstone **207**, 209, 211
Oldenburg, Henry 261
Ollivants, Manchester 160/2
Olmütz, Bohemia 218
Olsen, Jens **293**, 322, 293/5, 323/7
Oortwyn, I. 287/10
Oosterwijk, Severijn **291**, 287, 291/7
Oostrom, A. van 68/1, 287/8
organ clock **85**, 18, 79, 84/3, 84/4, 84/6, 85/7, 85/8, 86/1, 99/5
'organ grinder' 21
Orléans, France 235
Duc d' 236, 89/9, 92/3
ormolu **85–6**, 12, 17, 26, 28, 67, 12/2, 86/1
Orpheus clock **86**, 100/1
orrery **329**, 50, 225–6, 235, 338, 86/2, 329/4, 329/5, 335/4
Orrery, Charles Boyle, fourth earl of 329, 335/4
orrery clock **86**, **96–7**, 236, 86/2, 97/5, 237/4. *See also* Raingo clock
orrery system 225
Osborne's Manufactory 39/7
Oscos, Asturias 301
Osnabrück, Germany
Cathedral 239
Otis & Upson Co. 87
Ottery St Mary, Devon 263
Oughtred, William 337
Oursian, Nicholas 322
'overlift' 275
Owen, Watkin 38/4
Oxford, Oxon. 261, 262, 265, 265/5
'owl' 21
oyster shell veneer **86**, 86/4

Pace, Thomas 40/3
Padua, Italy 94, 268, 279, 330
Palazzo dei Signori 268
Specola, the 274
Paff, Jeremias 49/4
pagoda top **86**, 36, 68
Palais des Beaux Arts aux Quatre Nations, Paris 235
Palais Royal, Paris 236
Palazzo, Italy 268
Palazzo Vecchio, Florence 273, 283
pallet **164**, 108, 115, 138, 145–53, 194, 208, 213, 244, 261, 150/5, 164/4
entry and exit **164**, 165/7
gathering **164**, 114, 175, 265, 165/9
lever 164/4
pallet arbor **164**, 164/5
'pallet staff' 146, 148, 151. *See also* pallet arbor
pallet stone **164**, 148–9, 158, 164/3
'pallets complete' or 'pallets' 164
pallets, verge gut 150/5
Palmer, W. E. 61
'panarmonico.' 279
pantograph 203
paperweight clock, Japanese **86**, 87/5
papier mâché **86–7**, 63, 86/3
Papillon, Francesco 83
Paris, France 61, 93, 95, 106, 228, 233, 234, 235, 236, 240, 244, 287, 291, 293, 296, 303, 306, 332, 2/1, 80/1, 86/2, 87/7, 88/6, 90/1, 90/3, 90/4, 90/5, 90/6, 91/8, 92/1, 92/2, 92/3, 97/5, 98/1, 98/2, 102/1, 111/3, 120/1, 128/1, 200/2, 208/2, 211/7, 215/8, 228/1, 228/2, 232/1, 332/1
Exhibition, 1867 278
Exposition of 1900 106
Observatory 108
Paris, Ont. 108
Parker, George 64
Parkinson & Frodsham **263–4**, 255
Parkinson, William 263
Parma Farnese, Duchess Sophia di 274, 279, 278/3
parquetry **86**, 87/6. *See also* marquetry
Parry, J. V. L. 326
Pascal, Claude **291–2**, 287, 291/8
Pasteur, F. 289/6
'Pateck & Cie' 306
Patek, Count Antoine Norbert de 306
Patek Philippe **67, 306–7**, 299/4
'patent clock, the' 94. *See also* pillar and scroll clock
'patent elliptical springs' or 'patent accelerating lever springs'. *See* wagon-spring clock
Paulsen, Louis 33
Pavia, Italy 278
pawl **164**, 48, 123, 142, 182, 61/3, 123/4, 164/6. *See also* click
Passer, Angelo 103
Peacock, John 69/4
Pearson, Page & Jewsbury; Pearson Page **264**, 264/1
pedestal clock **87**, 90, 91, 92, 27/5, 58/2, 87/7, 295/5
pediment **87–8**
broken 88, 88/1
hollow 88, 88/3
segmental 88, 88/4
swan-neck 88, 88/2
triangular 88, 89/7
pedometer **329**
'peep-o'-day' carriage clock 26/1
pegwood **207**, 193, 211
Peking, China 337/3
Pendleton, R. 34
pendule de cheminée See mantel clock; shelf clock
pendule directoire **88**, 89/8
pendule empire **89**, 88/5
pendule longue ligne **89**, 87, 91, 228, 88/6. *See also* longcase clock, French
pendule Louis XIII **89–90**, 89/9, 304/1
pendule Louis XIV **90**, 27, 91, 228, 236, 90/1, 101/2, 111/3
pendule Louis XV **90–1**, 80, 128, 301, 2/1, 40/4, 90/2
pendule Louis XVI **91**, 90/3, 90/4, 90/5
pendule montgolfière 91
pendule Neuchâteloise 304–5, 304/3
pendule d'officier **91**, 26, 92, 91/7
pendule portative **91**, 113, 91/8, 230/1
pendule Régence **91–2**, 90/6
pendule régulateur 89, 91, 93, 228, 235/5
pendule religieuse **92**, 43, 89, 90, 228, 287, 292, 92/1, 228/1, 304/2
pendule sympathique **92**, 234, 92/3
pendule de voyage **92–3**, 25, 26, 49, 83, 91, 112, 113, 233, 234, 92/2, 234/2
pendulum **165**, 16, 21, 24, 37, 48, 52, 54, 58, 79, 83, 98, 103, 106, 108, 111, 112, 116, 123, 136, 140, 141, 145, 146, 147, 150, 151, 156, 157, 173, 177, 184, 234, 245, 265, 266, 268, 274, 278, 291, 292, 304, 305, 315, 326, 76/4, 95/4, 103/3, 107/5, 109/2, 125/6, 145/7, 171/11, 173/6, 238/2, 249/2, 250/2, 251/5, 258/4, 267/6, 268/2, 273/5, 279/5, 287/6, 287/7, 287/8, 287/9, 298/2, 310/2
bob *See* bob
compensated 83, 224, 236, 238, 254, 257–8, 261, 266, 286, 301, 326, 46/9, 86/2, 254/1, 257/5, 279/4, 309/5, 310/3
non-compensated 97
compound **165–6**, 80, 171, 165/7
conical **166**, 23, 239, 280, 309, 166/1, 181/3, 309/5, 309/6, 309/7
'cowtail' 18, 96, 110, 218, 238, 31/2, 219/2, 239/3, 305/5
double 47, 96, 243, 274, 277, 279, 159/7
Ellicott **166**, 166/2
flying 48/2
folding 34
free **166**, 35, 98, 104, 108, 238, 249, 251, 265, 326, 104/1, 266/1
gridiron **166–7**, 79, 83, 89, 97, 129, 239, 247, 86/2, 166/3, 229/3, 267/4
introduction of 55, 90, 92, 103, 117, 124, 152, 165, 218, 228, 238, 240, 247, 248, 277, 279, 286, 290, 291, 279/5
isochronometry of 149, 273, 279
long 18, 34, 44, 45, 52, 73, 87, 106, 117, 126, 127, 128, 167, 169, 218, 258, 261, 266, 286, 288, 301, 326, 289/8
mercurial **167**, 83, 97, 98, 103, 254, 257, 49/6, 119/6, 161/5, 166/4, 313/5
mock **77**, 239, 76/2
rhomboid **167**, 167/6
royal (seconds) **167**, 52, 66, 67, 97, 117, 261, 164/6, 309/5
short 26, 33, 46, 53, 56, 57, 68, 83, 117, 151, 167, 221, 22/4, 96/2
simple **167**
sympathetic 108, 264/2
torsion **169**, 14–15, 49, 50, 112, 305, 307, 15/6, 50/3, 168/7
turret-clock **169**, 168/8
U-shaped 106
pendulum aperture **88**, 51, 75, 136, 74/3
pendulum bob **165**, 51, 61, 77, 80, 126, 128–9, 166, 167, 169, 171, 208–9, 233, 144/1, 254/1, 258/4
pendulum rod 126, 129, 145, 156, 158, 165, 166, 167, 169, 305
Pennington, R. 34
Pennsylvania, U.S.A. 46, 105, 110, 314, 306/1
Péquegnat, Arthur, Clock Co. **224**, 224/1, 224/2, 224/3
Péquegnat family 224
Perkins, Spencer 329
perpetual clock 14–15, 67
Perrelet, Abraham-Louis 236, 203/4
Perret, Paul 305
Pesaro, Italy 276
Peto 252
Philip II of Spain 273, 296
Philadelphia, Penn. 88, 109, 308, 314, 328, 312/3, 312/4, 315/7
Philippe, Adrian 306
photographer's clock **93**, 93/5
photozenith tube (PZT) **329**, 326
picture clock **93**, 93/6, 221/2
Pierret, Victor-Athanase 163/4
'piezo-electric effect' 171
pigeon-racing clock **93–4**, 93/4
pillar 50/2, 223/8
pillar and scroll clock **94**, 24, 105, 109, 310, 313, 315, 95/4, 314/1, 315/6
pillar clock **94**, 86, 233, 284, 87/5, 93/7, 284/1
Japanese **94**, 94/1
pinchuck *See* pintongs
Pincio Gardens, Rome 278, 278/1
pinion **169**, 43, 124, 138, 147, 154–5, 159, 164, 169, 172, 176–8, 188, 194–5, 197, 204–5, 207–11, 213, 221, 228, 247, 254, 293, 304, 310, 312, 315, 78/3, 163/3, 168/1, 312/2
lantern **169**, 78, 114–16, 246, 138/1, 168/3, 280/3
rolling-leaf **169**
pinion-facing tool **207**
pinion leaf 216, 168/2. *See also* pinion
pinion-milling machine **207–8**, 207/4
pinion wire **208**, 197, 307, 208/1
Pinto, Manoel Fonseta 115
pintongs **208**, 186, 197, 208/4
pinvice *See* pintongs
pipe **169**, 168/4
Pisa, Italy
Cathedral 149
Pisani, Kalcidoniju 74
Pitti Palace, Florence 276/3
Pius V, Pope 273, 276
pivot **169**, 114, 124, 138, 148, 156, 166, 172–3, 184, 186, 188, 193, 208, 214, 216, 236, 168/5, 267/5
conical **169**, 168/6
pivot hole **169**, 148, 151, 158, 164, 185, 186, 187, 194, 207, 215
Plainsville, Farmington, Conn. 61/2
Plancemont, Switzerland 233
Planche, van der 108
planetary clock **94–5**, 280. *See also* orrery clock; Raingo clock
planetarium **329–31**, 294, 330/1, 330/2, 331/6, 331/7
planishing **208**, 184, 188, 209/6
planisphere clock 274, 279, 278/3, 279/4

Acknowledgements

Illustration 1 on page 32 is reproduced by gracious permission of Her Majesty the Queen.

PHOTOGRAPHS

Please note: picture references are in the form of page number/picture number.

A.C.L., Brussels 320/2; Alinari, Florence 276/3, 278/1, 280/4; Alsthom-Unelec, Beaucourt 236/1; James Arnfield 38/6, 138/1,2,3,4,5, 139/6,7,8, 140/1,2,3, 141/4,5,6, 142/1,2,3,4,5, 144/1,2,3,5,6,7, 146/1,2,3, 4, 147/5,6, 148/1,2,3, 149/4, 150/1,2,3,4,5, 151/8, 152/3,4,5, 154/1,2,3,4,5, 155/7,8,9, 156/1,2,3,4,5,6, 7,8, 157/10, 158/2,3,4, 159/5,6, 160/1,2,3,4, 161/5, 162/1, 164/1,2,3,4,5,6, 165/7,8,9, 166/1,2,3,4, 167/5, 168/1,2,3,4,5,6,7, 169/9,10, 170/2, 171/3,4,5,6,7,8,9, 10,11, 172/1, 173/4,5,6, 174/1,2,3,4, 175/5, 177/3,4, 178/1,2,3,4, 179/5, 180/1, 181/3,4,5, 182/1,2,4; Art Gallery & Temple Newsam House, Leeds 85/7; Ashmolean Museum, Oxford 21/2, 92/2; Atelier Municipal de Photographie, Mairie de Toulouse 98/1; Badisches Landesmuseum, Karlsruhe 17/4; Bath City Council 38/5, 88/4; Bayerisches Nationalmuseum, Munich 221/3,4, 243/3, 245/5,6, 334/3, 337/2; Silvio A. Bedini, Washington D.C. 62/2; Biblioteca Ambrosiana, Milan 280/1; Biblioteca Apostolica Vaticana 278/3, 279/4; Dana J. Blackwell 21/3, 33/3, 63/5, 86/3, 95/4, 96/3,4, 254/3,5, 308/2, 309/4, 310/1,4, 311/5, 312/1,2,3, 313/5, 314/1, 315/5, 316/1,2,3; Ekkehard Blender, Titisee-Neustadt 65/5; Verlag 'Die alte Zeit', Blender & Stenhart, Titisee-Neustadt 241/6, 242/1; Bo Bojesen, London 14/3; Bowes Museum, Barnard Castle 40/4, 78/5, 88/5, 89/8, 90/3,5, 98/2, 102/1, 134/1; British Museum, London 18/1, 35/5,7, 39/8, 48/3, 57/7, 62/1, 65/2, 67/5, 87/5, 100/1, 109/6, 143/6, 152/1, 233/4, 234/2, 248/1, 249/3,4, 255/6, 257/5, 261/3, 262/3,4, 269/4, 270/1, 305/6, 308/3, 317/4, 322/2, 328/1, 330/3, 333/2,4, 336/1, 337/5; J. E. Bulloz, Paris 89/9,10; Burnley Borough Council, Towneley Hall Art Gallery and Museum 264/1; Castle Museum, York 258/1; Christie, Manson & Woods, London 46/3, 254/1; City Art Gallery, Manchester 17/5, 28/1; Worshipful Company of Clockmakers, London 60/1, 234/1, 237/5, 257/4; John Combridge 225/6; Cooper-Bridgeman Library, London 231/2; Country Life Books – Sally Chappell 265/3; Country Life Books – Frank Dobinson 200/4, 210/6; Country Life Books – David Griffiths 12/2,3, 14/1, 20/1, 23/6, 25/5,6,7, 26/1,3, 33/2,4,5, 34/1,2, 36/1,2, 37/4,5,6, 38/2,3,4, 40/3, 42/1, 43/2, 44/1,2,4, 48/1, 49/6, 55/5, 58/3, 61/4, 65/6, 67/6, 72/1, 76/1, 78/4, 84/4, 85/8, 86/1, 4, 88/2,3, 93/5, 94/2, 97/5, 99/5, 103/5, 107/3,5, 119/6, 120/1, 124/1, 129/4,5, 135/4, 163/4, 184/1,2,3,4, 185/7, 186/1,2,3, 187/4,5,6, 188/1,2,3,4, 191/2, 192/1, 193/3, 194/1,2,3,4,5, 195/6,7,8,9,10, 196/2, 197/5,6, 198/1, 2,3, 199/4, 201/5, 202/1, 203/2,3,4, 204/2,3,4,5,6, 205/7,8, 206/2, 207/3, 208/1,2,3,4,5, 209/6, 210/1,2,3, 4,5, 211/8,9, 212/1,3,5, 213/6, 214/1,2,3,4,5,7, 215/8, 230/1, 249/2,6, 252/2, 253/3, 258/3, 268/1, 271/2, 309/6,7, 315/4; Country Life Books – Edward Leigh 65/7; Country Life Books – Graham Portlock 116/4, 177/2, 185/6, 196/1, 204/1, 215/9, 216/1,2,3,4, 237/6; Country Life Books – John Webb 13/4, 19/4, 22/2, 25/4, 28/2, 49/5, 56/1, 61/3, 66/2, 80/1, 90/1,2, 93/4, 98/3,4, 101/2, 105/4,7, 111/2, 220/1, 251/6,7, 254/4, 263/5; Crown copyright – reproduced with permission of the Controller of Her Majesty's Stationery Office 116/2, 322/3; De danske Kongers Kronologiske Samling på Rosenborg, Copenhagen 240/5, 320/3; F. Duchenne, Beauvais 237/7; Henry Francis du Pont Winterthur Museum, Delaware 47/7, 66/3, 109/7, 306/1, 314/2; Ernest L. Edwardes 45/6, 105/6; Ernest L. Edwardes –

the late F. K. Challen 45/7; Fratelli Fabbri Editore, Milan 70/1, 81/3, 103/3, 272/1, 281/5; Fitzwilliam Museum, Cambridge 34/3, 35/6, 122/1, 170/1, 229/3, 249/5, 259/5, 266/3; Fond du Lac Historical Society, Wisconsin 75/6; Garrard the Crown Jewellers, London 299/4; Aldo Garzanti Editore, Milan 78/2,3, 273/4; Germanisches Nationalmuseum, Nuremberg 325/4,5, 326/2; Gershom Parkington Collection, Bury St Edmunds 15/4, 49/4, 172/2; J. Paul Getty Museum, Malibu, California 87/7, 90/6, 237/2; Gillett & Johnson, Croydon 153/6,7, 158/1, 168/8, 181/2, 182/3, 256/2; Greenfield Village and Henry Ford Museum, Dearborn, Michigan 315/6; Haags Gemeente Museum, The Hague 73/2,3; Hachette, Paris 83/2; Hamlyn Group Picture Library 14/2, 29/3, 50/3, 67/4, 71/2, 84/5, 87/6, 107/6, 151/6, 152/2, 155/6, 177/5, 225/4,5, 234/3, 237/4, 244/2,3, 263/6; Heimatmuseum, Triberg 30/1, 31/2, 84/3, 240/4; Hessisches Landesmuseum, Kassel 145/4, 157/11, 240/2,3, 322/1, 330/1; D. R. Hill 130/3; Historisch-Antiquarischer Verein, Winterthur 321/5; Historisches Museum der Stadt Bamberg 15/5; Historisches Uhrenmuseum, Wuppertal 239/3; Historische Uhrensammlung, Furtwangen 18/2, 221/2, 243/2, 247/4; Horstmann Geer Company, Bath 112/1; Illustrated London News Picture Library 256/1; Jaeger-le Coultre (UK), Sutton 15/6; A. F. Kersting, London 65/3,4; Karl Kochmann, Concord, California 239/4; Kunsthistorisches Museum, Vienna 240/1, 318/1; Kunstindustrimuseet, Copenhagen 245/7; Paul Lavoie 222/4,5, 223/6,7,8,9, 10, 224/1,2,3; Leicestershire Museums, Art Galleries and Records Service, Leicester 251/5, 261/2; Edward Leigh, Cambridge 75/4, 79/7, 89/7, 105/5; Antonio Lenner 82/1, 97/6, 268/2, 273/5,6, 274/1,2,3,4, 275/5, 276/1,2, 277/5,6; Brian Loomes of the Dusty Miller Gallery, Low Laithe, Summerbridge 57/8; Lunds Universitets Historiska Museum, Lund 321/6; Mallett, London 25/2; Manchester Public Libraries 193/2, 206/1; Manx Museum, Douglas 337/3; Mas, Barcelona 294/3,4, 295/5,7,8, 296/2,3,4; S. & O. Mathews, Godstone 112/2, 233/3; Thomas Mercer, St Albans 262/1,2; Dr Vaudrey Mercer 212/2; Merseyside County Museums, Liverpool 16/1, 17/3, 26/2, 27/4, 35/4, 37/7, 40/2, 41/5, 67/7, 69/4, 84/2, 105/3, 111/4, 112/3, 167/6, 185/5, 190/1, 196/3, 197/4,7, 207/4, 212/4, 214/6, 226/1, 266/2, 309/5; Metropolitan Museum of Art, New York 306/2, 311/6; Photo Meyer, Vienna 245/4; Luis Montañés Fontenla 295/6, 296/1,5,6,7, 298/1,2,3, 301/2,3, 302/2,3,4,5, 303/6,7; Musée de Dijon 111/3; Musée des Beaux-Arts, Besançon 235/5; Musée d'Horlogerie, Le Locle 18/3; Musée du Conservatoire National des Arts et Métiers, Paris 200/2, 211/7, 237/3; Musée International d'Horlogerie, La Chaux-de-Fonds 91/7, 93/6, 304/1,2, 3; Museen der Stadt Wien 117/5, 128/2, 136/5, 219/2, 222/1,2; Museo Cuauhnahuac, Cuernavaca 115/3; Museo d'Arte Antica, Milan 13/5; Museo de Pontevedra 302/1; Museo Municipal, Madrid 297/8; Museo Nazionale della Scienza e della Tecnica, Milan 247/5, 268/3, 273/2, 278/2; Museo Poldi Pezzoli, Milan 273/3; Museo Vetrario di Murano, Venice 280/2,3; Museum Boerhaave, Leiden 43/3, 290/4, 331/6,7; Museum of Fine Arts, Boston, Massachusetts 55/3, 135/2; Museum of the History of Science, Oxford 320/1, 325/3, 334/1, 337/4, 338/1; Museum of London 40/1; Nationalhistoriske Museum på Frederiksborg, Hillerød 329/5; National Maritime Museum, London 258/2, 260/1, 264/3, 266/1, 320/4, 326/1, 338/2; Nationalmuseet, Copenhagen 294/1,2; National Museum of Antiquities of Scotland, Edinburgh 43/4; National Physical Laboratory, Teddington 327/3;

National Trust, London 115/2, 131/4; National Trust, Trerice 58/1; National Trust, Waddesdon Manor Frontispiece, 22/1, 88/6, 90/4, 228/2, 232/1; Nederlands Goud-, Zilver- en Klokkenmuseum, Utrecht 115/4; Neilson McCarthy-Aspreys 27/6, 86/2; D. F. Nettell 117/6, 118/1,3,4,5, 125/2,4,6; New Hampshire Historical Society, Concord 77/7, 108/1, 200/1, 308/1; New Jersey State Museum, Trenton 113/5; Niagara Parks Commission, Niagara Falls 59/4; Nordisk Pressefoto, Copenhagen 114/1, 132/1; Old Sturbridge Village, Sturbridge, Massachusetts 12/1, 54/2, 75/5, 77/5; Charles S. Parsons 77/6, 163/2; G. B. Pineider, Florence 149/5; Post Office Telecommunications, London 106/1; Derek de Solla Price 38/1; Rådhus, Copenhagen 323/7; Kenneth D. Roberts 22/3, 25/3, 27/5, 44/3, 47/6, 55/6, 56/3, 58/2, 61/2, 64/1, 74/2, 84/6, 103/4, 112/4, 128/3, 163/3,5,6,7; T. R. Robinson 116/1, 125/3; Mary C. Roehrich 33/6, 46/1,4, 47/5, 62/3, 94/1, 284/2,3,4; Royal Naval College, Greenwich 159/7; Royal Scottish Museum, Edinburgh 151/7, 157/9, 245/8, 250/2, 264/2; Scala, Antella 121/2; Science Museum, London 13/6, 16/2, 22/4, 23/5, 24/1, 46/2, 55/4, 66/1, 74/1, 76/3,4, 96/1, 104/1, 109/2,3,5, 116/3, 121/3, 123/3,4, 125/5, 228/1, 250/1,4, 252/1, 254/2, 258/4, 264/4, 267/4,5,6, 279/5, 284/1, 290/1, 323/6, 324/1,2, 328/2,3, 329/4, 330/2,4,5, 332/1, 333/3, 334/2, 335/4; J. L. Sellink 50/2, 51/5,6,7, 52/1,2, 53/4,7, 56/2,4,5, 68/2,3, 73/4, 88/1, 126/1,2,3, 4,5,6,7,8, 127/9,10, 136/1,2,3,4, 282/1, 290/5, 291/6, 7, 293/4; J. L. Sellink – F. Kats 290/3, 291/8; J. L. Sellink – C. Th. Ruygrok, Leiden 51/4, 52/3, 68/1, 286/3,4,5, 287/6,7,8,9,10, 289/2,6,8; Service d'Architecture de l'Oeuvre Notre Dame, Strasbourg 246/3; Sheffield City Museum 48/2; Shell, London 123/2; Alan Smith 104/2, 176/1, 257/3, 333/5; John Smith & Sons, Derby 118/2; Smith's Industries, London 63/4; Smithsonian Institution, Washington D.C 276/4, 312/4, 315/7; Society of Antiquaries of London 222/3; Sotheby Parke Bernet, Bond Street, London 111/1; Sound Stills, London 253/4,5; Staats- und Stadtbibliothek, Augsburg 275/6; Städtische Kunsammlungen, Augsberg 106/2; Documentation Stender BV, St Michielsgestel 53/5,6; Lakas Stolberg, Graz 23/7, 95/3, 218/1; Strike One, London 37/3; Teknologisk Institut, Tåstrup 293/5; Time Museum, Rockford, Illinois 50/1, 84/1, 92/3, 107/4, 133/2; Tiroler Landesmuseum, Ferdinandeum, Innsbruck 323/5; Tolsen Memorial Museum, Kirklees 200/3; E. J. Tyler 74/3, 243/4, 244/1; Uhrensammlung Kellenberger, Winterthur 44/5, 54/1, 79/6, 93/7, 96/2, 238/1,2, 304/4, 304/5; Universitetsbiblioteket, Copenhagen 130/1,2; University of Liverpool 76/2; Victoria and Albert Museum, London 78/1, 91/8, 92/1, 250/3; Wadsworth Atheneum, Hartford, Connecticut 300/1; Wallace Collection, London 128/1, 233/2, 235/4; R. H. de B. Wilmot 115/5,6; Henry C. Wing Junior 310/2,3, 315/3; Wuppertaler Uhrenmuseum 113/6; Württembergisches Landesmuseum, Stuttgart 57/6, 103/2, 109/4, 113/7, 246/1,2, 283/2, 323/4; Yale University Art Gallery, New Haven, Connecticut 39/7, 306/3; David E. Zeitlin 80/2.

Illustration 3 on page 135 is from S. Bedini 'The Compartmental Cylindrical Clepsydra', *Technology and Culture* 1962, University of Chicago.

The following illustrations are from J. L. Sellink *Dutch Antique Domestic Clocks 1670–1870*, H. E. Stenfert Kroese BV, Leiden, 1973 284/5, 286/1,2, 288/1, 289/3, 4,5,7, 290/2, 292/1,2,3.

The publishers are grateful to the many people who have given their help in obtaining illustrations, especially Dr and Mrs F. G. Alan Shenton.